Land, Kinship and Life-Cycle

Cambridge Studies in Population, Economy and
Society in Past Time 1

Series Editors:

PETER LASLETT, ROGER SCHOFIELD and
E. A. WRIGLEY
ESRC Cambridge Group for the History of Population and
Social Structure

and DANIEL SCOTT SMITH

University of Illinois at Chicago

Recent work in social, economic and demographic history has revealed much
that was previously obscure about societal stability and change in the past. It
has also suggested that crossing the conventional boundaries between these
branches of history can be very rewarding.

This series will exemplify the value of interdisciplinary work of this kind,
and will include books on topics such as family, kinship and neighbourhood;
welfare provision and social control; work and leisure; migration; urban
growth; and legal structures and procedures, as well as more familiar
matters. It will demonstrate that, for example, anthropology and economics
have become as close intellectual neighbours to history as have political
philosophy or biography.

Land, Kinship and Life-Cycle

Edited by

RICHARD M. SMITH

Fellow of All Souls College, Oxford

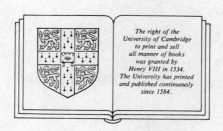

The right of the
University of Cambridge
to print and sell
all manner of books
was granted by
Henry VIII in 1534.
The University has printed
and published continuously
since 1584.

CAMBRIDGE UNIVERSITY PRESS

Cambridge

London   New York   New Rochelle

Melbourne   Sydney

Published by the Press Syndicate of the University of Cambridge
The Pitt Building, Trumpington Street, Cambridge CB2 1RP
32 East 57th Street, New York, NY 10022, USA
296 Beaconsfield Parade, Middle Park, Melbourne 3206, Australia

First published 1984

Printed in Great Britain at The Pitman Press, Bath

Library of Congress catalogue card number: 84-9475

British Library Cataloguing in Publication Data

Land, kinship and life-cycle.—(Cambridge
studies in population, economy and society in
past time)
1. Land tenure—England—History
I. Smith, Richard M.
333.3'2'0942   HD604

ISBN 0 521 26611 4

Contents

Contributors

Dr Ian Blanchard, *Lecturer in Economic History, University of Edinburgh*

Dr Bruce Campbell, *Lecturer in Geography, Queen's University of Belfast*

Dr Christopher Dyer, *Senior Lecturer in Medieval History, University of Birmingham*

Dr B. A. Holderness, *Senior Lecturer in Economic History, University of East Anglia*

Dr Alan Macfarlane, *Reader in Social Anthropology, University of Cambridge, and Fellow of King's College*

Dr Dennis Mills, *Staff Tutor in the Social Sciences, Open University*

Mr W. Newman-Brown, *Former Chief Town Planner, Livingston New Town*

Dr Jack Ravensdale, *Former Senior Lecturer in History, Homerton College, Cambridge*

Dr Zvi Razi, *Lecturer in Medieval History, Tel Aviv University*

Dr Richard Smith, *University Lecturer in Historical Demography, University of Oxford, and Fellow of All Souls College*

Mr Tim Wales, *Research Student, Queens' College, Cambridge*

Mr Richard Wall, *Senior Research Officer, SSRC Cambridge Group for the History of Population and Social Structure*

Dr Keith Wrightson, *Lecturer in Modern History, University of St Andrews*

Preface

In the era marking what some might regard as a 'rebirth' in studying the history of the family – inaugurated formally in 1972 by the publication of the essays in *Household and Family in Past Time*[1] and extended both methodologically and geographically in *Family Forms in Historic Europe*[2] – a preeminent place was reserved for the measurement of the household or the co-resident domestic group. Indeed, in the context of an emerging and increasingly 'positivistic' approach to social history, it was almost inevitable that the household with its tangible qualities should become the focus of attention of family historians with a commitment to the quantitative analysis of historical social structures. Yet a doubt has been frequently raised as to the status of 'residence' as a criterion for the analysis of the family, whether comparisons are being made over space or through time.[3] There are nonetheless perfectly sound reasons for considering that the knot of persons who sleep and frequently, if not invariably, take meals together under the same roof constitutes a unit for social analysis, and can form a basis for revealing inter-society comparisons, particularly if due attention is given to the means by which that unit has been brought together (e.g. whether initiated by marriage or

[1] P. Laslett with the assistance of R. Wall, editor, *Household and Family in Past Time* (Cambridge, 1972).
[2] R. Wall, J. Robin and P. Laslett, editors, *Family Forms in Historic Europe* (Cambridge, 1983).
[3] H. Medick, 'The Proto-Industrial Family Economy: The Structural Function of the Household during the Transition from Peasant Society to Industrial Capitalism', *Social History* 3 (1976), pp. 295–6; O. Löfgren, 'Family and Household Among Scandinavian Peasants: An Exploratory Essay', *Ethnologica Scandinavica* 74 (1974), pp. 22–3; E. A. Hammel, 'Household Structure in Fourteenth-Century Macedonia', *Journal of Family History* 5 (1980), p. 250.

through the fission of a pre-existing group).[4] But this mode of analysis, Michael Anderson might say, is still reminiscent of studying the 'family in a thermos flask', and is certainly inadequate in its interpretation of households or kin groups in the matter of the economic behaviour of their members.[5]

As we shall see in this volume of essays, many of those who study English rural families in a pre-industrial setting would insist that these can in no sense be understood without a specification of property rights and the mode of property transmission, especially if property was held and transmitted largely through kinship ties.

Yet, it has sometimes been argued by those who subscribe to the notion of the stem family, in their response to Laslett's sceptical views on its supposed prominence in the rural communities of western Europe, that this family type is most closely associated with landed peasantries, which formed only a small proportion of the population in census samples of early modern England from which Laslett drew his conclusions. As a consequence, statistics on English household structure may simply confirm that the shift from a peasant society had already occurred in England by the end of the seventeenth century, and hence that 'the emergence of the nuclear family' may represent the increase in the proportion of those social classes that at no time had been associated with a stem family organization.[6] This view has in fact been taken much further by Alan Macfarlane, in an essay which has drawn a critical response for denying the existence in England of a peasant society, at least from the thirteenth century, and by implication denying the existence in that society of a family system owing its form and function to the nature of property rights and

---

[4] For an exemplary analysis of this kind, where residence is used as a means of comparing household formation rules in two quite different societies, see J. Hajnal, 'Two Kinds of Household Formation System', *Population and Development Review* 8 (1982), pp. 449–94. For the concept of headship in relation to residential group, see R. Wall, 'Introduction' in R. Wall, editor, *Family Forms in Historic Europe* (Cambridge, 1983), and the essay by P. Czap, 'The Perennial Multiple Family Household', *Journal of Family History* 7 (1982), pp. 5–26. For a penetrating analysis of the co-residence patterns of couples and the husband's parents in relation to their reproductive behaviour, see R. Freedman, Ming-Cheng Chang and Te-Hsiung Sun, 'Household Composition, Extended Kinship and Reproduction in Taiwan: 1973–1980', *Population Studies* 36 (1982), pp. 395–412.

[5] M. Anderson, *Approaches to the History of the Western Family 1500–1914* (London, 1980), p. 37.

[6] L. Berkner, 'The Stem Family and the Development Cycle of the Peasant Household: An Eighteenth Century Austrian Example', *American Historical Review* 77 (1972), pp. 408–10.

conflicts over those rights – in as much as he argues that those rights
were not for the most part transmitted through the kin nexus.[7]

In response to many of these arguments we are, in these essays,
attempting to consider both the form and functioning of the co-
resident kin group or family organization and, in a wider sense, to
undertake an assessment of property rights: who has rights and of
what kind in the family's property, and in particular who inherits
land. We have also to consider, given significant social differentiation
in rural communities throughout the period of English history to
which our discussions relate (the mid-thirteenth to mid-nineteenth
centuries), that property gives some and not others access to resource
generating assets. For this reason we include some studies that deal
with the totally or nearly landless. Not only the presence or absence
of transmitted property in an individual's experience but the point in
his or her life-cycle at which it is transmitted will be considered, for it
is widely believed that the timing of what Jack Goody calls property
'devolution' will have profound ramifications for the structure, demography and quality of family relationships.[8]

Conscious of the view that land and its transmission through
inheritance may, as some argue, have impinged more directly on the
form and function of rural families in medieval English rural societies,
the first six essays in this collection are concerned essentially with
these very issues. These essays constitute a mixture of single manor
or community case studies and regional accounts or inter-regional
comparisons. It should be stressed, however, that they remain
selective in their socio-legal coverage, for they are based upon either
the activities of customary tenants or the transmission of customary
land by freeholders. In large measure the nature of the sources – the
records of manor courts – upon which these studies are founded
determines this preoccupation, for charters and deeds concerning the
exchange of free land have not survived in ways that make systematic
investigation so rewarding. Yet in concentrating on these groups we
should be able to give some attention to the impact of powerful
groups such as landlords on the family patterns of their tenants
holding under customary law and without access to the legal protection of the king's courts. In fact, one particularly scathing critic of
Macfarlane has drawn attention to the fact that he 'ignores the
implications of the considerable predominance in many areas of

---

[7] A. Macfarlane, *The Origins of English Individualism: The Family, Property and Social
Transition* (Oxford, 1978), and his essay in this volume.
[8] See J. R. Goody, *Death, Property and the Ancestors* (London, 1962), pp. 273–83.

customary land held in villein (i.e. servile) tenure, attempting to assimilate it to freehold as though it were equivalent to sixteenth century copyhold'.[9]

The essays in this volume located in later periods are not concerned so exclusively with land, its distribution and transmission, but consider property and resources more broadly defined. However, perhaps because they employ a wider array of evidence and in certain cases deal with individuals or families whose demographic character-istics can be identified with reasonable precision, they are able to relate changes in the total family economy to critical phases in the family life-cycle. This has, however, proved easier to accomplish in the case of those in receipt of relief, whether regular or irregular, from the local overseers of the poor. Nonetheless, these studies also go some way to providing information on the quantitative significance of kinship contacts, as compared to contacts with persons believed not to be kin, in an individual's day-to-day existence. This still remains one of the more poorly developed fields of research into family history, not least because easily operationalized and replicable methodologies have not seemed to, and may never, materialize.

Since the idea of this collection of essays was originally conceived the debate over the relationships between land, its transmission and the kin group in pre-industrial England has been pursued by histo-rians with increasing vigour. Indeed, many of the contributors to this present volume have been leading participants in these debates. In fact the unfortunately long-drawn-out process of publishing these essays has required certain of the present contributors to reflect again on their original arguments and explains, for example, the debate of a *post-scriptum* character pursued in this volume between Drs. Blanchard, Dyer and Razi on the question of the family–land bond in later medieval England. This latter debate, together with the growing interest in the family economy of the poor and the relationships between family forms and systems of welfare, seems to suggest that issues raised in this current collection of essays will serve to stimulate future investigations of these and cognate themes. It remains for me to register my gratitude to the contributors for their tolerance of the tardy appearance of this volume and to its eventual publishers, the Cambridge University Press, for their help in expediting its publica-tion. In the preparation of the manuscript of this book a special acknowledgement of the assistance of SSRC Cambridge Group sec-retarial stalwarts, Les Pepper and Amanda Tanner, should be made.

[9] R. H. Hilton, 'Individualism and the English Peasantry', *New Left Review* 120 (1980), p. 110.

Jo Bird provided valuable help in the preparation of the consolidated bibliography, and my colleagues, Peter Laslett, Roger Schofield and Tony Wrigley, have offered their critical and invariably helpful advice at various points along the book's path to completion.

July 1983 RICHARD SMITH

1

Some issues concerning families and their property in rural England 1250–1800

RICHARD M. SMITH

Property has served as a common focus in many discussions of family form. For instance, it has been seen as central in the contrast to be drawn between kinship and residence as two quite different principles of organization. One might therefore distinguish between a jurally defined corporate group linked by rights in property which its members enjoy in common and a collection of kin or indeed non-kin who share a common residence. For Peter Laslett a 'fraternal joint family' would exist only when two married brothers co-resided, but for Maurice Freedman such a family would have existed in China whenever two or more brothers were co-parceners in a family estate, regardless of whether these men were married or whether they and their respective wives and children lived in different residences.[1]

To concentrate upon rights in property that are shared by family members as a fundamental variable defining or indeed determining the form taken by the family attaches to the family the specific function of control over property, including its transmission. For it is implicit in so many studies of pre-industrial societies that the most important method of acquiring property is by the process of inheritance. Implicit, too, is the assumption that inheritance normally takes place between close kin and affines. Indeed, as Goody puts it, 'transmission *mortis causa* is not only the means by which the reproduction of the social system is carried out . . .; it is also the way in which interpersonal relationships are structured'.[2] Furthermore, David Sabean goes so far as to suggest that 'just as there is no such

---

[1] P. Laslett with the assistance of R. Wall, editor, *Household and Family in Past Time* (Cambridge, 1972), p. 3; M. Freedman, 'Introduction', in M. Freedman, editor, *Family and Kinship in Chinese Society* (Stanford, Calif., 1970), p. 9.

[2] J. R. Goody, 'Introduction', in J. R. Goody *et al.*, editors, *Family and Inheritance: Rural Society in Western Europe 1200–1800* (Cambridge, 1976), p. 1.

thing as a pure unmediated emotional attachment between individuals, so there is no system of obligations and duties which is not
mediated through a structured set of things – namely property'.[3]

Jack Goody is most notable among historically minded social
scientists in employing systems of inheritance as a key means of
differentiating the societies of Africa, south of the Sahara, on the one
hand from the societies of Europe and Asia on the other.[4] Fundamental differences in inheritance practices Goody believes justify
the ascription of sociological unity to these geographically bounded
though historically varied areas.

What Goody terms homogenous systems of inheritance have
predominated in Africa. There, inheritance has been sex-specific;
men inherited from men and women from women. Women did not
share with their brothers the property of either their father's or their
mother's brothers. In Europe and Asia, on the contrary, women
inherited from men (and vice versa), although there may have been
restrictions on the type and amount of property that could be owned
or acquired in this way. These were areas, according to Goody,
characterized by 'diverging devolution' because the effect of the
disposal of property to both sexes was to diffuse it outside the descent
group.

By focusing on different rules determining the transmission of
property in these two large geographical areas, Goody proposes to
explain the structure of domestic groups and a whole cluster of
interlinked elements such as marriage transactions, descent groups,
forms of marriage, domestic roles and even kinship terminology.
Central to this theory is the contrast he draws between African
bridewealth societies and European and Asian dowry systems, in
which two very different forms of marriage transactions generate
far-reaching consequences for domestic organization.

The *pre-mortem* acquisition of dowry as property settled on a
woman at her marriage has been, Goody believes, the major form of
female inheritance in Eurasian societies. Where marriage payments
occur in Africa, property is transferred not to the women but between
the male kin of the groom and the male kin of the bride. Dowry
systems establish a conjugal fund where the property of the husband
is added to that of the wife (thereby reproducing wealth differences)

---

[3] D. W. Sabean, 'Young Bees in an Empty Hive: Relations Between Brothers-in-law in a
Swabian Village', in H. Medick and D. W. Sabean, editors, *Interest and Emotion: Essays
in the Study of Family and Kinship* (Cambridge, 1984), p. 171.

[4] J. Goody, *Production and Reproduction: A Comparative Study of the Domestic Domain*
(Cambridge, 1976).

and considerable care may be taken to match the resources of each. In these circumstances Goody believes that marriages will be strongly controlled by the parental generation through, for example, the surveillance of courtship and especially through the promotion of ideologies of premarital virginity, intended to limit contact between the sexes and reduce uncontrolled claims on the state. Homogamy – marriage with an individual of the same status – is encouraged, and this is often achieved by endogamy within status groups. Although in dowry systems additional wives could bring additional resources, the matching of resources is hard to duplicate, and there are difficulties in setting up several conjugal funds. Thus the effect of dowry and the conjugal fund is to create widespread monogamy in Eurasia in contrast to the polygynous societies of Africa.

For Goody, where productive resources are scarce and intensively used they tend to be retained within the nuclear family, as the basic productive and reproductive unit. This leads to vertical (i.e. parents to children) rather than lateral transmission, and thus to 'diverging devolution', since in such circumstances provision is generally made for women as well as men.[5] Goody accounts for the inheritance of property by women in systems of vertical transmission through the presence of economic differentiation. Where differentiation exists parents will be concerned to maintain the status of their children and the honour of the family through the settlement of property. Economic differentiation is also partially responsible in Goody's explanation for the presence of monogamous marriage in Eurasia. However, this monogamy co-exists with in-marriage between kin and as such serves to reinforce 'family' ties and to prevent the drifting of property away from the family in the event of sons being absent. Goody identifies other strategies such as adoption, concubinage, divorce and

---

[5] Scarcity of land and maintenance of status provide the argument with its essential link between changes in the kinship sphere and differences in agricultural techno-logy. Goody argues that the plough in Europe and Asia brings a fundamental increase in agricultural productivity and generates greater economic differentiation and demographic growth. Increasing numbers of people make for land scarcity, and individuals are ranked in terms of their access to this scarce resource. In contrast, Goody sees the howe-based agriculture of sub-Saharan Africa as producing little specialization and what economic or status differentiation there was between farmers as having to do with the 'strength of one's arm or number of sons'. A common theme in studies of the relationship between agricultural intensification, increasing population density, and competition for land is a concomitant narrowing of the range of kin who have a claim to inherit property. See P. J. Greven, *Four Generations: Population, Land and Family in Colonial Andover, Massachusetts* (Ithaca, N.Y., 1970) and O. Löfgren, 'Family and Household Among Scandinavian Peasants: an Exploratory Essay', *Ethnologia Scandinavica* 74 (1974), pp. 36–40.

remarriage as means of combating the contribution of childlessness to the likelihood of property losses by the family.

In a bold thesis very recently published, Goody has developed the implications for 'diverging devolution' for what he sees as a highly distinctive evolution of the family and marriage in Europe from the fourth century.[6] In its essentials Goody's arguments are concerned with explaining how the Church came to prise property away from the domestic group that in a system of diverging devolution had practised in-marriage and other strategies to maintain the ready availability of direct vertical heirs. He suggests that the early Christian Church, faced with the need to provide for people who had left their kin to devote themselves to the life of the Church, regulated the rules of marriage so that wealth could be channelled away from the family and into the Church. The Church therefore, in Goody's view, encouraged out-marriage by forbidding marriage within strictly defined degrees of kinship, encouraged celibacy, promoted the conjugal bond as an ideal, emphasized the importance of freedom of choice by the parties in a marriage and encouraged spiritual rather than natural kinship as a basis for harmonious social relations. Through the encouragement of all of these practices Goody believes that the position of women as property holders, inheritors and dispensers was enhanced insofar as the Church by its manoeuvring was further elaborating a situation in which female property holding and inheriting rights in a system of diverging devolution were already considerable.

There can be little doubt that Goody's typological scheme both of the evolution of bridewealth systems to dowry systems (i.e. the differentiation of Eurasia from Africa) and of Europe's peculiar development through the influences of the Christian Church are both stimulating and contentious and deserve to be a focus of discussion and research on marriage and property transactions and domestic organization for some time to come. Most provocative are the questions raised about how the transmission of property – whether in the form of marriage payments, *pre-mortem* inheritance, or *post-mortem* marriage inheritances – shapes both the internal structure of domestic units and economic and political processes usually construed as external to the domestic domain. What remains to be deliberated and further researched is the empirical accuracy of Goody's typology and indeed the direction of causality in the relationship between a society's property distribution, devolution

---

[6] J. Goody, *The Development of the Family and Marriage in Europe* (Cambridge, 1983).

and kinship system. In this first chapter certain of these issues will be pursued in reference to a more restricted geographical space, with a concentration on fine historical detail.

Goody is not alone in the prime role he gives to property and the mode of its devolution in determining the fundamental structure of a society. For instance, the historian Hans Medick argues that among peasant populations the necessary connection of household formation to resources which were scarce and 'which could be acquired *only* [my emphasis] by inheritance formed the decisive structural determinant'.[7] Indeed, for certain theorists a crucial difference between workers in industry and agriculturalists is that among the latter the determinant of family forms and processes is inherited property, whereas amongst the former property recedes from centre-stage as families come into being solely as units of labour.[8]

Perhaps this juxtaposition of two hypothetical family systems deriving their forms and internal relationships from property on the one hand and their labour resources on the other is suggestive of the dangerously reductionist style of much of the work in this field. As Sabean remarks, 'Property as the dominant category for peasant society explains, however, at once too much and too little.'[9] In certain work we do encounter a willingness to admit that the study of the effects of inheritance customs and other property rights upon family life cannot take place within a vacuum. Some would argue, because of what they see as the very centrality of property inheritance along kin lines to the reproduction of social classes, that the maintenance of the dominant social relations of production will entail (as in the case of the medieval lord and peasant) direct supervision of the inheritance and family practices of their subordinates by the politically and economically superior.[10] Others would single out for emphasis such factors as the demographic conditions prevailing in a society, the possibility of alternative income generating activities such as wage labouring or access to rights in other less tangible resources such as common grazing in open moor or marsh,[11] or the presence or absence

[7] H. Medick, 'The Proto-Industrial Family Economy: The Structural Function of the Household During the Transition from Peasant Society to Industrial Capitalism', *Social History* 3 (1976), p. 303.

[8] For a widely quoted study, see D. Levine, *Family Formation in an Age of Nascent Capitalism* (London, 1977).   [9] Sabean, 'Young Bees', p. 171.

[10] For such views, see C. Creighton, 'Family, Property and Relations of Production in Western Europe', *Economy and Society* 9 (1980), pp. 129–67 and E. Searle, 'Seigneurial Control of Women's Marriage: The Antecedents and Function of Merchet in England', *Past and Present* 82 (1979), pp. 3–43.

[11] See Löfgren, 'Family and Household', pp. 35–7 and E. P. Thompson, 'The Grid of Inheritance: A Comment', in Goody et al., editors, *Family and Inheritance*, pp. 340–3.

of social constraints on personal behaviour that seem to have existed in spite of property forms or indeed may have important repercussions for the way in which property devolved (i.e. even though women can inherit they may be restricted in their range of options by a rigid sex segmentation in a broader field of economic activities).[12]

i. Family labour and family land

In varying degrees the essays in this volume attempt to locate and assess the role of these mediating factors between individuals, families and their property, whether this is held on fee-simple terms or by tenures of differing levels of uncertainty. It is in some respects ironic that the one economic model of peasant farm families which to date lacks any one rival for its comprehensiveness is based on the family enterprise not as a function of its property but as a highly distinctive unit of labour. At not infrequent intervals contributors to this volume appeal to this model of A. V. Chayanov for a theoretical justification of their evidence.[13] Those who follow Chayanov's analysis undoubtedly would be inclined to argue that the peasant economy is characterized by its social properties more than by a given degree of technological development; by social properties stemming from the importance placed upon patriarchal authority; by a preoccupation with the ratios of family land to family labour – adjustments between which were far more relevant than any concern for capital investment; by the wish to increase global income rather than the maximization of revenue per family worker; and, of supreme importance, by a family ideal which suffocated individualistic aspirations and emphasized those which worked for the good of the group.

The critical cog in this perpetually revolving but intransigently stationary wheel is the absence of a market of any sort for wage labour, leading to an inconsequential role for non-family labour in the family farm. The allocation models of classical political economy in Chayanov's view could not therefore be applied in the analysis of the peasant labour farm, for elements such as wages, profits and rents were not directly relevant in its operations. The farm could only be understood through an analysis of its internally generated needs and resources. These needs are specified as present and future family consumption requirements, and the resources are primarily family

[12] M. Cain, S. Rokeya Khanam and S. Nahar, 'Class, Patriarchy and Women's Work in Bangladesh', *Population and Development Review* 5 (1979), pp. 305–438.
[13] A. V. Chayanov, *The Theory of Peasant Economy*, edited by D. Thorner, B. Kerblay and R. E. F. Smith (Homewood, Ill., 1966).

labour supplies determined solely by the size and composition of the family. This viewpoint also assumes that complementary factors such as land and capital are in variable supply so that at the farm or holding level the factor which is dynamic is the growth and decline of the individual biological family. The addition of children to the nuclear couple will expand needs relative to resources in terms of labour power, and as a consequence the family's equilibrium will shift towards increased effort and output per worker, reduced leisure and reduced *per capita*, though increased total family, income. As the children mature, the tendency is reversed, with the family dividing into new sets of nuclear couples and the cycle repeating itself. It would be expected, therefore, that the families within a local peasant economy would manifest a degree of inequality in the utilization of labour power, productivity and income per head such as is 'demographic' or at any rate 'non-social' in origin.

One might here ask the question why did Chayanov not expect households which had reached this peak to expand their farms further by taking in more land and hiring labour? Since Chayanov offers no explanation we are left to discover one ourselves. Chayanov, furthermore, assumed that the availability of means of production was variable in the short term and fixed only in the very long term. In the short term he saw the flexible supply of non-labour units as an essential condition of the family life-cycle's determination of the farm's own life-cycle. Yet, in the long run he saw the possibilities of accumulation as limited by the 'subsistence motivation' of the peasant family. In this way ideals overrode concrete influences and gave rise to an overtly anti-materialist analysis of behaviour within the peasant milieu. The independent variables are certainly not located in property or property relations but are embedded in the socio-cultural realm; 'subsistence needs' are preeminent and are a vital factor, remaining invariant and constituting wants that are culturally limited and of modest scale, for in the true peasant economy accumulation is avoided. Social mobility consequently takes on a cyclical form, carrying the typical peasant farm family during its life-time through most of the statisticians' and historians' categories of 'rich', 'middle' and 'poor' peasants.

As is patently obvious in all that has been said above, Chayanov's views stand in marked opposition to those which see rural society divided into strata made up of the permanently rich and poor. Lenin's seminal ideas on this question were important in furthering this viewpoint for he saw every human society heading towards an increasing division of labour.

Rich peasant farms, which were larger and better equipped, had a higher capital to labour ratio, found themselves in an advantageous position as far as the optimal use of the factors of production and their further accumulation were concerned. For precisely opposite reasons, poor peasant farms were at a disadvantage in any attempt to improve their economic position. Continuing accumulation of economic advantage and disadvantage led to the polarisation of peasant into rich farmers who increasingly acquired characteristics of capitalist entrepreneurs and poor farmers who lost their farms and became landless wage labourers in the employ of rich farmers, estate owners and urban entrepreneurs.[14]

This difference – a difference between two polar opposites – created the basis for the debate that still rages on the contrasting interpretations of the state of the Russian peasantry in the late nineteenth century and the post-revolutionary pre-collectivization phase. What relevance, it may well be asked, does it have for our discussions of family–land relations in pre-industrial England? There is very ample evidence to indicate that historians have been much influenced by Russian theorists in their attempts to explain English circumstances, especially those in the period before the sixteenth century.[15] A good deal of work on late medieval English rural society sees social differentiation at work, whereby village or manorial communities became more polarized between tenants of large holdings and wage earners, foreshadowing the dichotomy between capitalist farmers and wage labourers in modern times. Indeed, it is on this question that Hilton and Postan would seem to have taken up rather different positions – the latter more inclined to stress 'social promotion' under the influence of late fourteenth- and fifteenth-century demographic decline, and Hilton the gradual emergence of yeoman farmers of no mean substance.[16]

If not easily pigeonholed in their approaches, others have certainly stressed the decline of family inheritance as a social phenomenon in the late fourteenth and throughout the fifteenth century, together with an increasing tendency for land to be transferred between rather than within families. Rosamund Faith's pioneering study of late medieval Berkshire has been followed by others: for instance, Barbara Harvey's analysis of the tenants of the estates of Westminster Abbey, Christopher Dyer's magisterial work on the west midland manors of

[14] V. I. Lenin, 'The Development of Capitalism in Russia', in *Collected Works*, vol. 3 (Moscow, 1972), p. 70.

[15] P. Gattrell, 'Historians and Peasants: Studies of Medieval English Society in a Russian Context', *Past and Present* 96 (1982), pp. 22–50.

[16] M. M. Postan, *The Medieval Economy and Society* (London, 1972), pp. 139–42; and R. H. Hilton, *The Economic Development of Some Leicestershire Estates* (Oxford, 1947), pp. 94–105 and 147–8.

the Bishops of Worcester, which are given further consideration in this volume, Andrew Jones' and Timothy Lomas' syntheses (both in the process of publication) of land exchanges respectively among the tenants of late medieval Bedfordshire and on the manors in north-east England of the Bishop and Cathedral Priory of Durham and Merton College, Oxford – all these studies, it would seem, reaffirming the late medieval loosening of family attachments to land and the existence of a very active *inter-vivos* traffic in land purchases and leases.[17] Whether this land exchange system was compatible with, or contrary to, the fundamental importance of the peasant family labour farm in the conceptual frameworks that these scholars took to this period is, except (notably) in Dyer's work, almost impossible to establish, for this particular question was never faced squarely. Yet Professor Hilton, in the review of rural society in the midlands in the late medieval period which he attempted in his Ford lectures, was certainly fairly curt in his dismissal of Chayanovian concepts, going so far as to state that the Russian economist's discovery about the relation between family size and the size of the holding were not necessarily applicable outside Russia.[18]

To date, the clearly differentiated schools of thought regarding stratification in the countryside that have developed with regard to the later middle ages are less readily apparent in writings on the thirteenth and first half of the fourteenth centuries. If a conceptual framework of any coherence has been employed it must come from Postan, who in his introduction to an edition of a Peterborough Abbey manuscript bearing the title *Carte Nativorum* undertook a wide-ranging review of the origins and functioning of a village land market.[19] The core of Postan's argument concerns the practical problems of the peasant family: how to meet these needs that varied throughout its life-cycle. The variation in needs dictated the necessity

[17] R. J. Faith, 'The Peasant Land Market in Berkshire', unpublished University of Leicester Ph.D. thesis, 1962; B. Harvey, *Westminster Abbey and its Estates in the Middle Ages* (Oxford, 1977), pp. 294–330; C. Dyer, *Lords and Peasants in a Changing Society: The Estates of the Bishopric of Worcester 680–1540* (Cambridge, 1980), Chapter 14; A. Jones, 'Land and People at Leighton Buzzard in the Later Fifteenth Century', *Economic History Review* 25 (1972), pp. 18–27; A. C. Jones, 'The Customary Land Market in Fifteenth Century Bedfordshire', unpublished University of Southampton Ph.D. thesis, 1975 and T. Lomas, 'Land and People in South-East Durham in the Later Middle Ages', unpublished CNAA Ph.D. thesis, 1976.

[18] R. H. Hilton, *The English Peasantry in the Later Middle Ages* (Oxford, 1975), pp. 6–7.

[19] M. M. Postan, 'The Charters of the Villeins', in C. N. L. Brooke and M. M. Postan, editors, *Carte Nativorum: A Peterborough Abbey Cartulary of the Fourteenth Century,* Northamptonshire Record Society xx (Oxford, 1960), also in M. M. Postan, *Essays on Medieval Agriculture and General Problems of the Medieval Economy* (Cambridge, 1973), as Chapter 7.

for resort in the absence of any effective legal ban to a land market. Postan's main and very important contribution was to draw an analytical distinction between two opposite characteristics that this market could take on: (a) it could bring about a redistribution of land, tending to level out abnormal inequalities and to preserve a given social structure, or (b) it could have the effect of increasing inequalities associated with growing commercialization in the manner of the Leninist interpretation.

Professor Postan, as already intimated, sees the major stimulus for a traffic in land as deriving from 'certain abiding features of peasant life'. The presence of a broad distribution of family types and sizes allowed, he claims, the growth of points of surplus and shortage within the local peasant society – inequalities that could in part be resolved by resort to the land market. This market could be divided into participants who were what he terms 'natural sellers' – those deficient in labour and equipment, childless couples, widows and widowers, old men and invalids, or poor or improvident husbandmen – and 'natural buyers' – smallholders with a large number of strong helpers at home, or wealthy and energetic peasants capable of providing themselves with the necessary stock. He gathered support for his main contention from examples of customary tenants surrendering their holdings to manorial lords on account of their inability to work them, and in so doing he reflected upon the frequency with which women tenants, especially widows, figure among the leasers of land. This interpretation was subsequently questioned by Paul Hyams, who regarded Postan's analysis as a 'sociological explanation' of what he considered to be an unconscious rearrangement of holdings quite distinct from another source of redistribution operating within the land exchange system.[20] He states that it is the 'buying and selling of land for money which ought to be called a land market. People are born, marry and die in all societies, and in most, these events are accompanied by some redistribution of land.'[21] Although not always easy to interpret in his presentation, Hyams goes on to suggest that given the relatively rigid spread of land resources within a peasant society and increasing demand for that land, developments are almost 'inevitably at the expense of the less protected groups'. This would appear to be quite opposite to Postan's notion and much more closely aligned with the views

[20] P. R. Hyams, 'The Origins of a Peasant Land Market in England', *Economic History Review* 23 (1970), p. 21.
[21] *Ibid.*, p. 21.

expressed by Kosminsky, who saw the wealthy getting wealthier by their land dealings with the poor.[22]

It is certainly notable (and perhaps no bad thing) that in these two approaches the names of Chayanov and Lenin are never directly employed. But their differing views can be quite easily situated within that debate. Early Populists certainly believed the inequality of farm size and wealth was primarily the product of demographic forces with different families in a randomly chosen cluster of farms being at different stages of growth and decay and as a consequence possessing differing family sizes.[23] Likewise, as families grow and decline their farms also will simultaneously grow and decline. In the Russian case the mechanism ensuring the adjustment of complementary factor supplies as family labour supplies and consumer needs expand and contract may often have been the repartition of communal land. Chayanov himself was certainly aware that in agrarian regimes less flexible than that of the repartitional commune the influence of the biological factor of family development on size of land for use would not stand out so prominently. However, he did argue that the correlation of land for use with family size and composition could be achieved 'with still greater success by short term leases of land' and that in societies with private property, sale and purchase of land could fulfil the same function.[24]

For these reasons, Macfarlane's attempt to define peasant societies as those which among other things do not participate in land markets represents a mis-specification.[25] What Chayanov was saying, however, implied that land transactions were being undertaken in order to meet family production requirements as consumption levels altered in the course of the development cycle. Furthermore, the activities of Chayanov's 'family labour farm' were not necessarily to be confined to agriculture, particularly at times when the family's consumption needs were greatest. By-employments in 'crafts and trades' were a crucial element making for flexibility in the system. Under all these various circumstances family size could still be

[22] E. A. Kosminsky, *Studies in the Agrarian History of England in the Thirteenth Century*, edited by R. H. Hilton (Oxford, 1956).

[23] On this debate, see T. Shanin, *The Awkward Class: Political Sociology of Peasantry in a Developing Society, Russia 1910–1925* (Oxford, 1972).

[24] Chayanov, *Theory of Peasant Economy*, p. 68.

[25] A number of commentators have noted that Macfarlane, *The Origins of English Individualism: The Family Property and Social Transition* (Oxford, 1978), defined a peasantry with strong similarities to the ideas of Chayanov. See Gattrell, 'Historians and Peasants' p. 45 and P. Worsley, 'Village Economies', in R. Samuel, editor, *People's History and Socialist Theory* (London, 1981), pp. 80–5.

supposed to explain the variation in farm size and total family income.[26]

It is, however, certainly a curious circumstance that by-employments in crafts and trades are energetically pursued without any attempt to sell wage labour for agricultural operations. But in this area Chayanov held firm, for he believed that in this he had solved the theoretical puzzle of peasant behaviour; the true family labour farm did not contract wage payments with its own members. Indeed, this is tantamount to claiming that in the peasant farm household labour presents itself as an overhead rather than as a variable cost. Naturally, all this stems from assuming the indivisible integrity of the family labour farm as a consumption and labour unit and can be adopted as highly plausible where either there are no competing alternative outlets for its labour or, where those alternatives exist, they are either physically or 'culturally' remote.

We have now specified three behavioural aspects of the peasant family labour farm that ought to distinguish a rural society interpretable within the framework of the Chayanov model; in the absence of something akin to periodic redistribution of land (i.e. the repartitional commune), land would be acquired by lease or purchase or perhaps grant and gift by the young but small and growing families and let, sold or given by the old and shrinking households; we might expect by-employments to be the preserve of those with smallholdings or, to sustain the Chayanovian theory in its purest form, to be practised by those with small but growing families who found their landholdings inadequate to make them self-sufficient; finally, non-family labour would be of minimal consequence, indeed almost non-existent.

On the first of these characteristics we have already referred to Postan's views, although we have not assessed the evidence upon which they were based. Cases of widows and widowers unable to cultivate their holdings because of their senility or poverty and of individuals seen to have engaged in persistent selling were taken by him from manorial court rolls. Smallholders and men of humble rank were argued to have predominated among the buyers or lessees of land, although their status was often inferred from surname evidence.[27] It was also argued that the buyers and lessees of land were rarely seen to have been substantial enough to figure among the men who served regularly on presentment juries or inquests or acted regularly in the manor courts as pledges. This essay, both wide-ranging and stimulating, was not buttressed by detailed empirical

---

[26] Chayanov, *Theory of Peasant Economy*, pp. 71–4.
[27] Postan, 'The Charters of the Villeins', pp. xxxv–xxxvi.

analysis of individual communities. It should also be noted that the charters held by villeins, an edition of which the essay in question had been written to introduce, were not specifically employed to support his argument on the 'social' characteristics of the land market.

Rosamund Faith, in her doctoral dissertation (to which we have already referred), which was being prepared when Professor Postan's essay was published, attempted to use manor court rolls to investigate the character of the land market in the Battle Abbey manor and in Brightwaltham on the Berkshire Downs. Later she went on to consider other Berkshire and Wiltshire manors in the late thirteenth and early fourteenth centuries.[28] She came to the conclusion that transfers among kin predominated over those between families, although it is not absolutely clear how to distinguish purchases and leases from inheritances in her study. Certainly, no attempt was made by Faith to ascertain whether the land market possessed the form that Postan had attributed to it.

However, in the 1960s Edmund King completed a detailed study of the land market on certain of the manorial properties of Peterborough Abbey before 1310. In fact, part of this study involved a very careful re-examination of the same material that Postan had introduced in his preface to the *Carte Nativorum*. King's conclusions were very interesting, particularly as they incorporated significant qualifications of Postan's original arguments, and in certain very important respects the two positions seem to be diametrical opposites. The most important plank in King's argument was his finding concerning the legal status of the land being transferred in these charters – all of which appeared to relate to free land and certainly not to fragments of customary tenures. Furthermore, in King's words, 'the conspicuous sellers of land were all of them freemen'.[29] There was no evidence that the Peterborough administration had gone even part of the way towards abandoning the principles that such land was both impartible and inalienable. However, it could still have been that the free land was being bought and sold for much the same purposes Postan claimed applied to the market in customary tenures. Certainly, King did argue that the land was being obtained for family purposes and more specifically so that 'younger sons should have some small independent position' and that 'daughters should have a dowry'.[30]

[28] R. J. Faith, 'Peasant Families and Inheritance Customs in Medieval England', *The Agricultural History Review* 14 (1966), pp. 88–90.

[29] E. King, *Peterborough Abbey 1086–1310: A Study in the Land Market* (Cambridge, 1973), p. 108.   [30] *Ibid.*, p. 124.

These were reasons not different in any great degree from those that Postan argued brought individuals into the market in search of land. Furthermore, King combined this reasoning with an interpretation that stressed the same argument that Homans had presented nearly forty years earlier. This pattern of purchases, King claimed, was perfectly compatible with a strong distaste for the selling off of family land or land that descended through blood, in this area of England, to the eldest son. In addition, King regarded the volume of this freeland that was entering into the market as very limited, involving small pieces that had been relatively recently brought into cultivation from the waste. So, some sort of dynamic equilibrium was proposed by which small pieces of free land were shunted from family to family via the non-inheriting children so that the principal family holding could pass from generation to generation intact.[31]

A very similar line of reasoning was presented by Cicely Howell in her investigation of the Merton College manor of Kibworth Harcourt in south-east Leicestershire.[32] In Kibworth, it was argued, no fragmentation of the virgated lands occurred; and this led to the piling up of dependent family members on the intact virgates and half virgates. No evidence relating to the way in which younger sons and daughters were established in life was presented by Dr Howell, although it was argued that the inheritance practice by which the moveables and items of farm equipment were divided equally among the younger sons and daughters ensured that they would be sustained by the family holding within a complex and certainly functionally extended domestic group. Whether all dependents married and began their own families within this economic collective is not discussed. It is assumed, furthermore, that every holding produced enough direct heirs, or if this failed that other near kin were always on hand in sufficient numbers to fill the vacancies. Clearly, there were no 'natural buyers' and 'natural sellers' in this Leicestershire manor, for in Howell's argument individuals possessed no more than usufruct in the family land and alienation away from the family was an unthinkable act. The court rolls that formed the basis of this study were certainly silent regarding any alienation, and they were accepted by Dr Howell as accurate on this matter. For Kibworth Harcourt we

---

[31] Ibid., p. 123.

[32] C. Howell, 'Peasant Inheritance Customs in the Midlands, 1280–1700', in Goody et al., editors, Family and Inheritance, pp. 112–55; see also her 'Stability and Change, 1300–1700: The Socio-Economic Context of the Self-Perpetuating Family Farm in England', Journal of Peasant Studies 2 (1975), pp. 468–82. Her arguments are developed to their fullest extent in Land, Family and Inheritance in Transition: Kibworth Harcourt (Cambridge, 1983).

would seem to have an account of behaviour that saw no social differentiation à la Lenin or demographic differentiation à la Chayanov.

King in no way denied the possibility of customary land being divided and becoming involved in an exchange system that may have had the appearances of a 'land market', and he cited the evidence that Professor Postan had presented from a survey of the Bishop of Winchester's manors in the fourteenth century, indicating the sizeable presence of sub-tenants.[33] To this point in our discussion no evidence has been considered of land transactions within customary land. Indeed, no quantitative studies have appeared in print to date. A number of estate and individual manorial case studies have pointed to instances of this practice but none have established whether this customary land formed part of standard 'virgated' tenements, or that the process had persisted to such an extent that those units were decayed beyond recognition. Dr Janet Williamson has recently investigated a number of Norfolk manors in the second half of the thirteenth century; her work includes a detailed case study of the Prior of Norwich's manor of Sedgeford in the north-western corner of the county.[34] Here, in theory, both free and villeinage land descended impartibly to a single son or closest single male heir. Between 200 and 250 tenants were shown to possess holdings that varied in size from a cottage and a quarter of an acre to units of forty to fifty acres, although the mean holding was around ten acres. Although the manorial authorities restricted individuals to the possession of only one tenement, shares within any particular tenement or tenements could be bought and sold with no upper limit on their aggregated total. In her study Williamson used the manorial court rolls, considering a series of land transactions that averaged around 20 to 25 per annum. However, she, too, viewed the active market in customary land for younger sons and daughters in much the same way as King argued had been the practice with free land among the Peterborough villeins during much the same period of the late thirteenth century. Indeed, she argues that the land market acted to reinforce the impulses of social custom rather than to oppose them.[35] This market was not therefore proceeding to further social differentiation but to ensuring that as many family members gained access to land as possible.

[33] King, *Peterborough Abbey*, p. 123 footnote 2.
[34] J. Williamson, 'Peasant Holdings in Medieval Norfolk: A Detailed Investigation of the Holdings of the Peasantry in Three Norfolk Villages in the Thirteenth Century', unpublished University of Reading Ph.D. thesis, 1976.   [35] *Ibid.*, pp. 250–1.

All these studies would certainly seem to leave Professor Postan's arguments basically unscathed and only subject to certain qualifications in rather minor respects. Both King and Williamson have identified what might in Postan's terms be deemed 'natural buyers', i.e. fathers obtaining small pieces for their sons and daughters or elder brothers for their more junior siblings – certainly constituting evidence conformable with a Chayanovian subsistence ethic, i.e. land was being purchased for use rather than for purposes of exchange. But, who were the 'natural sellers'? Neither of the studies is particularly clear on this matter; but, as mentioned earlier, King is adamant that on the Peterborough manors they were freeholders (possibly members of the lesser gentry), although they formed only a small group of the total population that might in theory have entered the land market.

The Peterborough evidence would, however, appear in King's words to be 'the archives of the more prosperous sections of the villein community, indeed a Peterborough "kulak" class enriching itself at the expense of a section of the freeholding community. Around 1300 the market for free land was certainly fluid and a wide variety of people were engaged in it. Two generations later the major families had engrossed the lot.'[36] These families were all interrelated, and land had been acquired to cement links through socially endogamous marriages. Indeed, King admits that these were the families most likely to have striven hardest in order to avoid the fragmentation of their full virgate holdings. This social bias in the evidence does raise a number of difficulties in the wider application of the findings from the *Carte Nativorum*, for as King realizes 'those with under half a virgate would probably not have had much slack of this sort'.[37] The point could be elaborated still further by suggesting that the sample of customary tenants studied by Homans came disproportionately from the upper echelons of village society where the attachment to land may have been stronger, ostensibly for dynastic purposes.[38] What the smaller tenants or the near landless cottagers did is much harder to establish; the title of Homans' study, *English Villagers of the Thirteenth Century*, is possibly a misnomer.

Zvi Razi, in his investigation of the family patterns exhibited by the

[36] King, *Peterborough Abbey*, p. 110.
[37] *Ibid.*, p. 123.
[38] Homans does in fact discuss social differences in the village, as determined by legal and land holding status, in a few brief pages in Chapter 17 of the book. In his defence it should be noted that the chronology of economic change very largely worked out by M. M. Postan, which has important implications for the economic composition of the rural populations, post-dated his pre-World War II publication.

tenants of the Abbot of Halesowen between 1270 and 1348, has inadvertently drawn attention to this problem in employing a means of explanation that derives simultaneously from both Chayanov and Lenin.[39] He found that in the three-quarters of a century before the Black Death the half and full virgaters succeeded in maintaining their presence in the community, but the quarter virgaters had only a one in three chance of maintaining a grip on their holdings. All tenants were imbued with what he terms a strong moral obligation, given that the inheritance custom was primogeniture, to provide for non-inheriting sons and daughters.[40] This strong desire to provide for all family members was one, and indeed a major, factor bringing about the economic downfall of the smallholders whose properties were 'colonized' by their more affluent full and half virgater neighbours. In other words, it might be possible to interpret Razi's findings as consistent with the notion that the demographically controlled de-volution of property among the smallholders allowed a degree of social differentiation to arise as property drifted from poor to rich. Yet Razi argues that among the wealthy echelons of the Halesowen customary tenantry land was so colonized only to provide for younger sons and daughters, presumably so that they could be established without necessitating the fragmentation of the half and full virgated patrimony.[41]

Williamson's work on the Norfolk manor of Sedgeford brings to light evidence that serves further to complicate rather than to clarify the image we have of English rural societies before the plague. In this study, as we have already seen, the inheritance custom in both free and villein land was impartible, but it is noted, in the words of the author, that the custom 'acted only upon the land of which a tenant died seised' and as such did not necessarily limit the actions of a tenant during his own life-time.[42] An active land market made it possible for those with the 'necessary capital resources to acquire land', and Williamson noted that it is necessary to know 'if any tenants were particularly prominent'.[43] Her findings apparently re-vealed that few participants in the land market both bought and sold land, and from this she concluded that the primary stimulus of the land market was not the consolidation or improvement of existing holdings, but rather the desire of the *chef de famille* to acquire

---

[39] Z. Razi, *Life, Marriage and Death in a Medieval Parish: Economy, Society and Demography in Halesowen 1270–1400* (Cambridge, 1980), pp. 77–98.
[40] Z. Razi, 'Family, Land and the Village Community in Later Medieval England', *Past and Present* 93 (1982), p. 7.   [41] *Ibid.*, p. 9.
[42] Williamson, 'Peasant Holdings in Medieval Norfolk', p. 242.   [43] *Ibid.*, p. 248.

additional land for his non-inheriting offspring. This behaviour might still, it seems, be interpretable within a Chayanovian framework; the larger the family the larger the marginal product of any additional land and hence the larger the maximum rent or price the family is willing to pay for it – a perverse process that might be seen to drive out capitalist agriculture and, indeed, prevent accumulation of any consequence. But, as Williamson notes, 'it cannot be denied that there were many with the means to acquire land simply to expand their own holdings'; she cites a number of individuals who accumulated large holdings in addition to providing for non-inheriting sons and daughters. For instance, one such individual, appropriately named Sarlo le Riche, held two messuages, a cottage and $28\frac{1}{2}$ acres, all of which he seems to have acquired personally.[44]

Williamson's remarks on the vendors of land are particularly illuminating, for they suggest that as a group these stand out less clearly than the purchasers. Many were in fact non-inheriting sons who could not take advantage of the land market to add to a small paternally derived plot that may have been intended to give them 'a start in life'. Indeed, she suggests that 'the land of such non-inheriting sons probably accounted for a large proportion of the land fed into the land market'.[45] Unfortunately, she gives no examples of this behaviour, apart from some cases of individuals inexplicably selling rather than buying land, and concludes the discussion somewhat undecidedly by noting that the motives for selling land were as varied as those for buying it.

Studies of rural social stratification in the late thirteenth and early fourteenth centuries have to date been generally confined to not particularly well substantiated hypotheses about the interaction of not particularly well defined groups. Full virgaters or half virgaters, for instance, are often considered without placing these individuals in the larger social structure (usually because the evidence does not permit). Paradoxically, in other studies the mesh of the historian's net has been too wide to catch the mass of mobility and the detailed data needed to reconstitute the progress of individual families up and down the social scale have been lacking. Professor Postan's synthesis of the evidence is of this sort; King's findings are most likely socially specific, largely owing to the evidence at his disposal; and Williamson has not attempted to assess the impact of varying social status on the larger-scale application of her arguments. What stands out from these studies is that there appears to be considerable activity in the matter

---

[44] *Ibid.*, p. 251.　　[45] *Ibid.*

of *inter-vivos* property transmission, but the consensus is that it plays a subordinate role to *post-mortem* inheritance and indeed might be seen more plausibly as helping to sustain the pattern of unfragmented virgates descending along patrilines. Indeed, we have already noted that the quantity of land being transmitted, as reflected in the *Carte Nativorum*, was quite small; the case cited of twenty acres built up by one family was completed only after two generations.[46] Howell has gone so far as to claim that a land market only had meaning when the 'units of exchange' were at least a quarter or a half virgate – not the sale of 'odd acres and rods', which she claims were not significant within the context of an agrarian subsistence economy.[47]

Rosamund Faith seems to reiterate Howell's views that 'in spite of a brisk land market in odd acres and single messuages, family inheritance and the expectation of it, dominated the transfer of holdings'.[48] By 'family' transactions Faith means those involving two tenants related by blood or marriage and, although it is not absolutely clear from the definition she adopts, persons bearing similar surnames. Her evidence is limited geographically to central southern England and is based on rather small numbers of transactions. For instance, '60 of the first 69 permanent land transfers recorded at Battle' were family transactions, as were 56 per cent of those at Brightwaltham on the Berkshire Downs. At Houghton, a manor of St Swithin's, Winchester, 64 per cent of 45 land fines recorded from 1267 to 1325 were for family land.[49]

However, small units in aggregate can accumulate into land transfers of significant total area. Williamson noted that in thirteenth-century Sedgeford the court rolls show an average of 22 transactions a year involving the sale, purchase, exchange or grant of land, although these seldom involved individual units exceeding two acres in size.[50] But she finds her evidence difficult to interpret, partly because, in the absence of a comprehensive manorial survey, it is not known what quantity of land was 'at risk' to be marketed. In this respect Campbell's findings from the Norfolk manor of Coltishall are very valuable. Acknowledging that court records which would most likely change the absolute totals derived from this study have gone astray, it appears that between 1280 and 1348 land devolving by inheritance accounted for just over 13 per cent of the transactions and

[46] King, *Peterborough Abbey*, pp. 115–17.
[47] Howell, *Peasant Inheritance Customs*, p. 135.
[48] Faith, 'Peasant Families', p. 88.   [49] *Ibid.*, p. 90.
[50] Williamson, 'Peasant Holdings in Medieval Norfolk', p. 247.

a little over 50 per cent of the area of customary land transferred.[51]
Quite evidently *inter-vivos* transfers concerned very small parcels or
slivers of land, often less than half an acre in area. Yet it is to be
expected in an area with the majority of customary holdings containing no more than two acres that transactions would involve parcels of
small sizes. Nonetheless in the quarter century before the plague
struck this community far more land was transferred by *pre-* than by
post-mortem exchanges. In this respect Campbell's findings appear to
mirror those from the nearby manor of Hindolveston, where only 10
per cent of transfers involved inheritances.[52] In the adjacent county in
the manor of Redgrave between 1295 and 1319 only 171 out of 1,979
transactions (8.7 per cent) recorded in the manor court proceedings
concerned inheritances.[53] However, as with Coltishall, the size of
properties devolved through inheritance was considerably larger
than those transferred by *inter-vivos* exchange. Between 1305 and
1319, when court roll evidence is very complete, both in the quantity
of courts surviving and as to the areal measurements of properties
recorded, it appears that 42 per cent of tenant land was redistributed
subsequent to deaths. *Pre-mortem* transfers were therefore very important, both in their absolute quantity and in the total area of land
involved, and stand in marked contrast to the levels indicated by
comparable transfers in Halesowen. Razi does not present for the
period prior to 1348 a breakdown of *post-* versus *pre-mortem* transactions. However, he estimates that 83 per cent of tenant land moved
between family members, with inheritance constituting the principal
means of exchange. Halesowen was a large manor of over 10,000
acres and for the three-quarters of a century before the plague Razi
can document, with an obvious margin for error, transfers of 8,299
acres of land (6,916 acres between kin and 1,883 outside the family).[54]
What appears interesting is that the intensity of land exchange in
Halesowen seems muted when compared with the East Anglian
manors of Coltishall and Redgrave. Coltishall was a small manor with
certainly little more than 200 acres of customary land, but over a
comparable time period to that studied by Razi, at least 787 acres of
land exchanged hands. This represents a minimum figure, for 152 of
the 782 *pre-mortem* transactions did not possess details of plot size. In
Redgrave, 2,756 *inter-vivos* transfers of customary land between 1260
and 1319 totalled 1,304¾ acres, a figure which must be seen in relation
to the total customary land of 1,317½ acres on the manor. Of course

[51] See below, p. 126.
[52] W. Hudson 'Manorial Life', *History Teachers' Miscellany* 1 (1921), p. 180.
[53] See below, p. 157.   [54] Razi, 'Family, Land and the Village Community', p. 4.

this figure also represents a minimum sum, as 652 transfers were without their dimensions in the court records.[55]

Not only in the quantity of land transferred but also in the characteristics of the parties in the transactions the East Anglian manors appear to differ from those in the midlands and southern England. In the latter areas family transactions, whether at death or *pre-mortem*, seemed in the clear ascendancy. The high proportion of *inter-vivos* transactions in Coltishall, Hindolveston and Redgrave concerning unrelated parties is most striking. Campbell estimates that only one-third of *inter-vivos* transactions concerned related persons and only 20 per cent of the transactions at Redgrave involved kin.[56] In fact in the latter manor kin dealings in land accounted for only 15 per cent of the volume transacted between living persons in the period 1305 to 1319. Even in the difficult years of dearth from 1314–19 the increased mortality brought about no noticeable rise in the proportion of land transfers passed through inheritance between the generations.[57]

The East Anglian evidence does not rest comfortably with the notion of a customary holding that grows and shrinks as free land is added in accordance with the needs of the biological families' phases of expansion and contraction. Razi's evidence points to a stratification process based upon the capacity of some groups to expand their family land resources at the expense of the economically weak. Evidence in the case study of Redgrave also points to no clear-cut life-cycle dynamic identifiable in the pattern of land transactions, although here (as against Razi's interpretation of behaviour in Halesowen) tenants appear to have acquired land not just to set up their children in marriage. Nor does the evidence from either Halesowen or Redgrave suggest a cyclical mobility of families through the socio-economic strata of the customary tenantry. There are nonetheless some indications of the existence of manors in which the integrity of the holding as a rent paying and service rendering unit was maintained, with the land market concerning itself solely with small amounts of free or assart land.[58] To what extent this pattern owes its presence to the impartibility of villein land, whereas the highly volatile land exchange system in Coltishall and Redgrave stems from the practice of partible inheritance on the customary land, is an important question that remains difficult to answer with any conviction, although I shall return later in this discussion to give it greater attention.

[55] See below, p. 153.   [56] See below, p. 183.
[57] See below, p. 157.   [58] See above, p. 14.

ii. Non-family labour and the social distribution of land

The main problem with the application of Chayanov's model to late thirteenth- and early fourteenth-century England remains not what is in the model itself but what has been excluded from it. Even allowing for the absence in England of the repartitional commune which provided in Russia a means for the re-allocation of land in line with the demands of the families' biological cycle, we still have to ask how the expansionary phase of the family labour farm in land acquisition was financed. Chaynov's model apparently assumed that finance was readily available to all on equal terms. Such a voluntaristic approach to human behaviour would not seem to be appropriate to the stratified conditions of the village land holding groups in both medieval and early modern England. Both Razi and Smith have found a social stratification that resisted the cyclical mobility that might be expected of a population of family labour farms.[59]

It is on the matter of the staffing of peasant holdings that Professor Hilton has written: 'it cannot be too strongly emphasised that at all periods during the middle ages, the bulk of the cultivated area was contained within peasant holdings and that these holdings were managed as family concerns'.[60] Of course, this should not be taken to mean that the bulk of persons derived their livelihood in family-based work groups. Yet there is enough ambiguity in Hilton's statement to indicate a supposition of the family rather than the household as the basic social and economic unit. Would it not be more useful to ask the question 'what types of primary groups fulfilled the basic functions of production, consumption, socialization, etc., in medieval and early modern English rural society and to what extent did these groups coincide with the family?'.[61] The question is especially important because the family often only partially overlapped the domestic group in north-west European societies in the pre-industrial period. For early modern England data show that many farmers augmented the family labour resources by the addition of hired hands or live-in servants.

The institution of service, or recourse to hired day labourers, is a

---

[59] Razi, *Life, Marriage and Death*, pp. 88–91; and Smith, *infra*, pp. 159–71.

[60] R. H. Hilton, 'Reasons for Inequality among Medieval Peasants', *Journal of Peasant Studies* 5 (1978), p. 274.

[61] These remarks are much influenced by Löfgren, 'Family and Household', p. 23. An instructive analysis which reveals the degree to which ethnocentric or anthropocentric biases incline scholars to give privileged status to the family as an organizational unit in their research into agrarian economies is to be found in B. Hanssen, 'Hushållens Sammansältning', *Rig* (1976), pp. 33–61.

way of adapting the domestic cycle to production that Chayanov could not reconcile with his family labour farm ideal. At the same time we should consider service from the point of view of the supply of potential servant labour from households unable to expand their own productive resources as the family grew in size and consumption: production ratios deteriorated.

Notwithstanding Professor Hilton's remarks, it is possible to marshal an impressive array of scholars who have presented evidence to suggest that, under conditions specific to the late thirteenth century, between 40 and 70 per cent of holdings were too small to absorb the labour of those families resident upon them.[62] Rather than as a familial enterprise completely isolated from the market, as envisaged in the theories of Chayanov, let us consider its work force as a potential amalgam of non-paid family and wage-paid non-family labour. In this discussion we make no assertions as to the residence of the wage-paid labour, but will assume that the relative contribution of family and wage-paid labour will depend upon the level of wages in relation to the value of a particular agricultural holding's average product of labour. In Figure 1. 1 we consider a hypothetical situation in which the social distribution of land is skewed, with a large number of small farms and a relatively low proportion of large farms. Within each size category of farms we assume that the size of holding is fixed in the short and medium term and that labour power applied to the holding is the only variable factor of production. It is furthermore assumed that no difference exists in the productivity of family or non-family labour.[63]

Let us consider the composition of the labour force upon the holding of the 'kulak' or yeoman farmer (K) in Figure 1.1. K_1 is the point where the marginal productivity of family labour curve (MPL_3), whose shape is determined by the law of diminishing returns, intersects with the surface representing the operative wage level (W), which takes the form of a horizontal line indicating an infinite supply

[62] The most up-to-date and balanced account of these patterns is to be found in E. Miller and M. J. Hatcher, *Medieval England: Rural Society and Economic Change 1086–1348* (London, 1978), pp. 141–2. For a revealing analysis see M. J. McIntosh, 'Land, Tenure and Population in the Royal Manor of Havering, Essex, 1251–1352/3', *Economic History Review* 33 (1980), pp. 17–31.

[63] This approach derives from and is closely related to models constructed by C. Nakajuma, 'Subsistence and Commercial Family Farms: Some Theoretical Models of Subjective Equilibrium', in W. R. Wharton, Jr, editor, *Subsistence Agriculture and Economic Development* (Chicago, Ill., 1969), pp. 165–84 and especially F. Mendels, 'La Composition du ménage paysan en France au XIXe siècle: une analyse économique du mode de production domestique', *Annales Économies Sociétés Civilisations* 4 (1978), pp. 780–802.

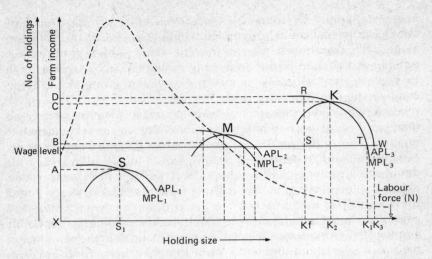

Figure 1.1. Family and non-family labour proportions in a socially differentiated farm population

of labour at that wage. Each family member receives an individual
income equivalent to the value of his or her average product (APL_3),
which is a function both of holding size and of the size of the family
labour group. For instance, at family work group size XK_2 each family
worker receives an income XC which is considerably higher than that
paid to a wage labourer (XW). At holding size K the family can
augment its income by appropriating a surplus which it can obtain by
employing wage-paid labourers. In fact, employing non-family
labour of the quantity $XKf–XK_1$ in addition to family labour XKf or as
a substitute for family labour $XKf–XK_1$ will produce for the family an
income equivalent to RST. Working with this set of assumptions it
should be clear that the relative contribution of family and wage-paid
labour will depend upon the level of wages relative to the value of the
holding's average product of labour curve. With the wage level below
the curve APL_3 it is to the household head's advantage to substitute
wage-paid labour for family labour. In fact, it can be plausibly argued
that, in a community where wages were determined in the labour
market stretching beyond the geographical limits of the village, it
could well be to household heads' advantage to exchange adult
children even if their farms were of equal size. But, in the replacement of the head's own children by the children of others, the adult
generation would be imposing a degree of social and economic
exploitation on the young and bringing about some reduction of their

living standards. Of course, it might well be that the quantity of family labour that could be supplied would at level XKf constitute the biologically determined maximum, and that in order to undertake optimal exploitation of the holding all additional labour would have to be non-family (unless members of the kin group outside the conjugal family were absorbed into the labour force). Total farm revenue would increase up to labour force size XK_1 (i.e. where the marginal productivity of labour curve cuts the line representing the regional or community wage level). Indeed it might be easier to expand the work force to this point using non-family labour, for with diminishing returns for each additional unit of labour input it will be necessary for every extra hand to work harder than the one hired previously. This might necessitate a level of work supervision on the part of the household head more easily implemented using unrelated employees whose domestic circumstances make them anxious to sell their own labour and to retain a place in the labour market. Further-more, to employ non-family labour beyond the quantity XK_3 would require, given that persons are not prepared to offer themselves for less than wage level XW, that the household head should reduce his total farm revenue by paying more than the labour is actually worth in terms of its physical output. This situation might, however, arise in the event of a serf with a large holding being required to provide labour services to a demesne farm where an abundant supply of non-family labour might make this preferable to using kin in this role. Of course, in a situation in which non-family labour was difficult to acquire and strong anti-market values were present in the society, holding K could well function through the use of a large body of kin (XK_3) each of them receiving an income equivalent to XW with the maximization of global farm income taking precedence over the maximization of *per capita* income.

At the opposite end of the spectrum of land holders we have the numerically predominant smallholders (S in Figure 1.1). Given the size of their farms, it is the case that the level of wages is far above the curve of average product of labour for the smallholding. This is a situation which, if a spirit of economic individualism were present, could only be tolerated in the short term. In the medium or longer term the peasant would be obliged to give up the holding, either abandoning it to the landlord or selling it. A tenant with a holding of size S could maximize his income (XA) from his land with the application of a family labour force equal to XS_1. This assumes too that the household head can retain family members who might well realize that they would derive higher *per capita* earnings by selling their labour to K-type households. Land might well have an equivocal value to tenants in these conditions and could be readily disposed of by those who realized that their income from wage-labouring could be greater than through the working of land. It is quite possible too that demand for such land would be restrained, with potential heirs reluctant to press their claims to inherit. However, it is equally likely in a situation of high demand for property that land could be retained and that surplus labour on these holdings would seek employment on the farms of larger landlords or the 'kulaks'.

S-type households could in the longer term, if we drop the restraint on labour as the only variable factor of production, attempt to adopt certain remedies to deal with their dilemma. The acquisition of additional land is ruled out insofar as it is difficult to see how finance would be forthcoming given the precarious economic situation of such households. More likely is the adoption of one or other of the following alternatives. Smallholders could engage in more labour-intensive cropping practices or grow higher value crops. The effect of such a development would be to raise the levels of the curves MPL and APL. Of course, this group would continue to constitute a 'harvest sensitive' element in the rural population. The activities of the smallholders studied by Campbell in Coltishall suggest that they might well have adopted this response.[64] Campbell in other research has demonstrated how remarkably productive was demesne farming in eastern Norfolk, with yields of wheat in the first half of the fourteenth century that compare very favourably with those for the late eighteenth century. Spring grain was less productive than winter-sown wheat in this area but still much higher in output than on certain contemporary demesne farms in other parts of the country. Campbell has shown how heavily dependent upon the intensive use of labour were these output figures, with labour used in the collection, transportation and spreading of animal manure and urban-derived night soil, multiple-ploughings, the digging of marl and above all frequent weeding. He believes that even more labour-intensive practices were employed on the peasant holdings (which may also have engaged in high-value row-crop production of products such as coleseed, flax, teasels, madder and hemp) to supply the large nearby urban markets of Norwich and Yarmouth.[65] Certainly

[64] See below, p. 117.
[65] Dr Campbell is in the process of making a comprehensive study of agricultural practices on demesne farms throughout the whole of Norfolk. Provisional findings are reported in 'Agricultural Progress in Medieval England: Some Evidence from Eastern Norfolk', *Economic History Review* 36 (1983), pp. 26–46.

the remarkable degree of economic and demographic resilience exhibited by the Coltishall tenantry between 1300 and 1349 would seem to imply that holdings of under five acres were anything but non-viable, especially if 'surplus' labour could be used on the farms of the larger tenants and the demesnes, which (irrespective of landlord) seem to have engaged in a very intensive system of husbandry not normally associated with traditional interpretations of medieval English agriculture.

Another remedy to the S-type household's dilemma would be for certain of its members to undertake some form of seasonal industrial work, whether on the farm, in the village or even outside, providing the income was returned into the pool of family resources. Indeed we are obliged to recall that Chayanov did argue that by-employments could act as a substitute for land so that income might be increased to a level commensurate with family size. Unfortunately, on the basis of medieval English documents we can only consider in a systematic fashion the activities of individuals in food-processing and retailing trades – the production of bread and ale for sale. However, in the case of Redgrave the pattern we unearth is interesting; an analysis of the 475 brewers who appear in the Redgrave records between 1260 and 1293, in terms of the land they were known to have held on the manor in 1289, showed only 94 to be from the property holding families (there were 425 tenants listed on the 1289 extent).[66] Only 88 out of the 475 brewers amerced for infractions of the Assize of Ale from 1260 to 1293 have left any record of themselves as landholders. Of these 88 individuals 64 held land in units of ten acres or less. In fact 88 per cent of brewing fines were paid by individuals with no land whatsoever or possessing holdings under five acres.[67] It can also be observed that with certain notable exceptions individuals with

---

[66] These findings are presented in greater detail in my 'Brewing, the Family Economy and Life-Cycle Stage' (forthcoming).

[67] The following patterns of brewing activity in relation to land holdings is found in Redgrave between 1260 and 1293.

Land holding size (ac.)	<2	2–4.9	5–9.9	10–14.9	15.0>	Total
Individuals	24	20	24	16	4	88
Brewing fines paid	510	208	297	230	27	1,272
X̄	21.3	10.4	12.4	14.4	6.8	14.5

In addition 1 cottager was finded 8 times and 4 stallholders not known to have held other land or residential property on Redgrave manor paid a total of 285 fines in the time period to which the above data relate. All references to the manorial court rolls upon which these data are based will be found in Smith, below, pp. 135ff.

smaller quantities of land brewed (or more precisely, were amerced)
more frequently than those with larger holdings. Yet before this
evidence is interpreted as indicative of a Chayanovian process of
social and economic 'levelling' at work the evidence needs to be
re-examined.

A 'pure' Chayanovian situation should display brewing frequencies increasing progressively through the early stages of the adult
life-cycle before tapering off slowly with the reduction of family
demands on land resources as the number of family members
declined. In the absence of good age data we are forced to employ a
rather crude surrogate measure of life-cycle development. Individuals
and their brewing activities have been analysed by reference to the
date of their first appearance in court proceedings – a date which
would establish them as at least in their early teens. The time elapsing
after their first appearance has been divided into five-year periods (A,
B, C, D, etc.). The largest number of fines and the largest number of
individuals are encountered in the first stage of the life-cycle of court
appearances, as it is here defined, and the number tapers off
progressively (see Table 1.1). However, the aggregated data conceal a
number of interesting variations. Clearly, the greater part of the fines
was paid by individuals who were not shown to have held land on
the 1289 extent; the majority of these individuals were, in fact,
women, young unmarried women accounting for over 60 per cent of
the fines paid by the group falling in stages A and B of the life-cycle of
court appearances. Similarly, over 75 per cent of the individuals
brewing over this whole period were shown to contravene the assize
in stages A and B. A pattern close to that predicted by the Chayanovian model is perhaps detectable among the brewers holding under
seven acres of land, but those holding seven to fourteen acres show a
distinct, if irregular pattern; they paid 60 per cent of their brewing
fines in stages E, F, G – 20 to 35 years after their first appearance in
the court record; those holding ten to twelve and twelve to fifteen
acres paid 70 and 80 per cent respectively of their fines in these
stages. Furthermore, a group of large landholders participated in ale
brewing on a very large and highly commercialized scale (reflected in
the large amercements they paid), possessing stalls and shops from
which their products were retailed, especially on the occasion of the
periodic markets held within the manor at Botulesdale.

This evidence, wholly from Suffolk, does not rest comfortably with
Chayanov's theory, for we can see young women brewing often
before rather than after marriage; full-time landless brewers who
possessed stalls in the market; full-time large-scale brewers who were

Table 1.1. *Redgrave brewers, land holding and life-cycle stage*

Holding size (rods)	Under 1		1–10		11–20		21–30		31–40		41–50		51–60		60+		Total
Life-cycle stage	No.	%	No.	%	No.	%	No.	%	No.	%	No.	%	No.	%	No.	%	
A	550	39.1	81	11.8	26	11.3	15	18.0	3	2.6	7	8.8		0.0	9	7.2	691
B	295	21.0	143	20.9	42	17.8	21	25.3	11	9.7	3	3.7	4	8.3	15	12.0	534
C	204	14.4	127	18.5	82	35.8	13	15.1	22	19.4	2	2.5		0.0	52	41.9	502
D	150	10.6	127	18.5	22	9.6	10	12.0	10	8.8	12	15.1	6	12.8	26	20.9	363
E	100	7.0	125	18.2	31	13.5	15	18.0	39	34.5	27	34.1	17	35.4	17	13.8	371
F	58	4.1	64	9.3	14	6.1	6	7.2	23	20.3	16	20.7	17	35.4	4	3.3	202
G	37	3.8	17	2.8	12	5.9	3	4.4	5	4.7	12	15.1	4	2.2	1	0.9	91
Total	1,349	50.6	684	24.8	229	8.3	83	3.0	113	4.1	79	2.9	48	1.7	124	5.1	2,754

self-sufficient in their raw materials, quite unlike any of the landless who, on the basis of the available debt evidence, clearly had to buy in their barley for brewing purposes. In addition, in the 1270s and 1280s certain middling tenants were entering into brewing for the first time; to take just one example, Philip Denewold of Redgrave is seen to have sold over twenty rods in small deals over the late 1270s and 1280s (although he had two sons to succeed him) and went on to brew on a sizeable scale, paying 37 fines from 1280 to 1293. Denewold's entry into this by-employment must be seen as a response to declining income from his eroding land reserves and not as a means by which family income would be synchronized with his family's development cycle.[68]

Of course, the middling tenants (type M in Figure 1.1) constitute the group for whom the decision as to whether use should be made of family or non-family labour would have been less clear cut. In Figure 1.1. the discrepancy between wage level (W) and the average product of labour is very narrow. Under these conditions the peasant farm unable or unwilling to hire labour because of its costs would be heavily dependent upon family labour. It might also be supposed that pooling of family resources by separate farm households would occur, especially if households were likely to have possessed rather similar material resources. This might be highly probable among middling land holders practising partible inheritance of land.[69]

We have shown in a highly theoretical fashion, although attempting to relate these theories to certain of the empirical findings in some case studies in this volume, the extent to which at various

[68] It should be noted that this pattern of brewing activity in relation to holding size or landlessness has not been documented elsewhere (although it certainly was encountered in the neighbouring manor of Rickinghall; see R. M. Smith, 'English Peasant Life-Cycles and Socio-Economic Networks', unpublished University of Cambridge Ph.D. thesis, 1974, and there are some suggestive associations mentioned in A. N. May, 'An Index of Thirteenth-Century Peasant Impoverishment? Manor Court Fines', Economic History Review 26 (1973), pp. 389–402). In fact Razi states that in Halesowen rich peasant families brewed ale on a large scale for which their members were fined more frequently than others in the community. In addition, Professor Judith M. Bennett of the Department of History, University of North Carolina is completing a comparative analysis of women in the society and economy of three English communities located in Northamptonshire, Huntingdonshire and Buckinghamshire, and finds quite different sex- and age-specific patterns of brewing from those identified in the Suffolk community of Redgrave.

[69] A strong emphasis on family relations in social and economic activities is in fact clearly evident in the Redgrave tenants holding from 4 to 12 acres in the later thirteenth century, unlike either their wealthier or their poorer neighbours (measured in terms of holding size). See R. M. Smith, 'Kin and Neighbours in a Thirteenth Century Suffolk Community', Journal of Family History 4 (1979), pp. 219–56.

points along a spectrum of land holding sizes the household economy was rarely the unit of production and consumption and was structurally linked with other economies through commodity and non-commodity relations. In all this, the most confusing, complex and, without a doubt, critical question concerns the allocation of labour between on-farm work, off-farm hired work and idleness.

It is sometimes claimed by those who derive their arguments from Chayanov's theory of peasant economy that the rent or price paid by peasants for an acre of arable land would exceed the net yield after all inputs and outputs had been valued at local market prices and wages; in other words, the return to labour on rented or purchased land was less than if the labour time required to cultivate an acre of land had been sold in the local labour market at the ruling wage. The very fact that individuals held on to or continued to pay 'inflated' prices for this land is regarded by the Chayanovian school as indicating how bourgeois accounting techniques fail to understand peasant economies, since the peasant, it is argued, would be aiming to maximize net utility in terms of universal consumption needs and annual labour supplies and not to maximize the return per day worked. These views should serve as a warning to anyone wishing to employ too formal an approach to the behaviour of agriculturalists in traditional settings, but the evidence we possess on rents and on prices both of commodities and of land in medieval England suggest that such an 'anti-economic', view of tenant behaviour would be inappropriate.

In the conditions of late thirteenth and early fourteenth centuries, particularly in the more densely populated regions where sizeable proportions of holdings comprised very small acreages, should we expect to find the family labour farm as the norm? In fact, there were relations of production developing through labour markets; for instance, the sizeable migrant labour market in agriculture as witnessed by those enormously long lists in the early fourteenth-century manor court records of 'recognitions' of young men leaving the manors of the Abbot of Glastonbury in search of employment elsewhere.[70] These developments may, when viewed in relation to the whole economy, have been shallow and marginal but they do indicate the existence of a far from minimal network of social relations between households which had important consequences for the range of options exercised by the individuals involved. A land holder such as Adam Pistor of Redgrave, referred to in Chapter 3, was

[70] See M. M. Postan, 'Medieval Agrarian Society at its Prime: England', in M. M. Postan, editor, *Cambridge Economic History of Europe*, Vol. I (Cambridge, 1966), pp. 564–5.

certainly very likely to employ labour, for we have references to his servants and indeed his shepherd.[71] The fact that none of those holding over sixteen acres in Redgrave were working their lands with family labour alone is established because each of these tenants leaves references in the court proceedings to servants and labourers whose names, where given, show them to be most likely unrelated to the tenant. Some, indeed much, of this hired labour may not have been a permanent element in the work force but seasonally employed, as is shown by the debt cases in which smallholders and landless individuals appear frequently as creditors pursuing claims to unpaid stipends and broken contracts.[72] It is interesting to note that Razi, in his detailed study of families in the Worcestershire manor of Halesowen before the Black Death, has identified a number of patterns that are certainly in close accord with the evidence from the Suffolk manors of Redgrave and Rickinghall. He points to the ability of the yardlanders to take advantage of the circumstances of the late thirteenth and early fourteenth centuries by building up their holdings. In fact, some of the interest of Razi's study lies in his detailed reconstitution of village families, which allows him to consider in detail one Henry Tinctor, who is referred to by Professor Postan in his introduction to the *Carte Nativorum* as a landless artisan in the process of upward social mobility through his land purchases, but who turns out in reality to have been a 'kulak' of no mean distinction.[73] In Halesowen, Razi notes, larger landholders set their sons up independently and 'often replaced the labour force of their children that left home with hired labour' – a pattern exemplified by Henry Tinctor after his son Richard left home.[74] There is evidence that before the Black Death at least 40 per cent of the Halesowen tenants had servants, and rich tenants had more than one servant.[75] Such findings obviously need to be viewed with some caution, for they are based on isolated case studies from rather widely scattered localities and because of their social biases may well overstate the proportion of households with servants; the Halesowen evidence most likely relates disproportionately to the agricultural tenants of this Worcestershire manor.

It is difficult to over-state the significance of servants in the family systems and social structures of north-west European societies which

[71] See below, p. 171.
[72] See, for example, Smith, 'Kin and Neighbours', pp. 244–5.
[73] Razi, *Life, Marriage and Death*, p. 89.
[74] *Ibid.*, p. 90.
[75] Razi, 'Family, Land and Village Community', p. 31.

have been investigated using reasonably accurate demographic evidence culled from village listings and early census documents. Indeed, Hajnal has recently identified the fact that 'young people circulate between households as servants' as one of three household formation rules, including also late marriage for both sexes and an association of marriage with the creation of new households, which were characteristic of this area in the past. Hajnal provides us with a succinct summary of the salient features of the institution:

(1) Servants were numerous, apparently always constituting at least 6 per cent, and usually over 10 per cent, of the total population. (2) Almost all servants were unmarried and most of them were young (usually between 10 and 30 years of age). (3) A substantial proportion of young people of *both sexes* [my emphasis] were servants at some stage in their lives. (4) Most servants were not primarily engaged in domestic tasks, but were part of the work force of their master's farm or craft enterprise. (5) Servants lived as members of their master's household. (6) Most servants were members of their master's household by contract for a limited period. (7) There was no assumption that a servant, as a result of being in service, would necessarily be socially inferior to his or her master. The great majority of servants eventually married and ceased being servants.[76]

Hajnal adduces a striking contrast in the absence of such persons unrelated to the household heads in societies following a joint household system, and believes that this category of individuals, peripatetic at a phase in their lives approximately bounded by puberty and (by wider world standards) a late age of marriage, was confined to the societies of north-western Europe.

We have already referred to the existence of servants in rural communities and stressed the extent to which the more substantial farms employed them. We have also shown theoretically why it might have been advantageous for land holders of similar social and economic status to exchange their children as servants in each other's farm households. Servant or 'servant-like' individuals appear in the medieval English documents under such nomenclature as *servus, serviens, ancilla* and *garciones* and the more ambiguous *famulus*. Their appearances in manorial records so preoccupied with land holding males may often be fleeting, but they are sufficient in quantity to indicate their significance in rural society. Yet, it is only in the taxation documents of the later fourteenth century that we can gain a clearer impression of these individuals and some indication of their overall incidence in the total adult population, and, in certain lists, of their distribution within households. For instance, a comparison of

[76] Hajnal, 'Two Kinds of Household Formation System', *Population and Development Review* 8 (1982), p. 473.

the proportion of households containing servants in the Rutland villages of 1377 with those early modern English communities for which we have age evidence gives some interesting findings: 18 per cent of the households in the early modern communities had servants over the age of fourteen and 20 per cent had had them in 1377.[77] In late seventeenth-century Kent and Wiltshire 24 per cent and 14 per cent respectively of the households contained servants.[78] These figures appear perfectly compatible with those from Rutland and those that Professor Hilton discovered in the Cotswold area of Gloucestershire for 1381.[79] They may also be minimum rather than maximum percentage values because of the strong indications of under-enumeration of females to which many scholars have referred. A major research area that yet remains to be tackled at all systematic-ally concerns among other things our need to discover whether, like those servants in the early modern communities, the medieval servants were primarily in the age group 14–25 – 'life-cycle'-stage servants as Peter Laslett has termed them.[80]

Manor court records abound in references to women who had been in service subsequently going on to marry. From the court rolls of Ramsey we find such typical entries: 'on the 18th day of June 1446 there came into the manor court of Houghton (in Huntingdonshire) Anna Gottes daughter of John Gottes cobbler, alias Belman, the son of Thomas Gottes who formerly lived in St Ives. And this Anna who was a servant of Radulphus Kerner of Ramsay and a *nativa* of the lord paid a fine to marry'; 'In the Upwood court of September 1st 1448, Agnes, daughter of the late Nicholas Albyn and *nativa* of the manor who now lives in the service of the Rector of Over paid a fine to marry whomever she wishes.'[81]

We see migration between villages and subsequent marriage in-timately related in such court entries. This same point is tantalizingly

---

[77] For a preliminary consideration of this material, see R. M. Smith, 'Hypothèses sur la Nuptialité en Angleterre aux XIII⁰–XIV⁰ siècles', *Annales, Économies Sociétés Civilisations* 38 (1983), pp. 107–36 and for more detailed consideration, L. R. Poos and R. M. Smith, 'Late Medieval English Tax Sources and English Nuptiality Patterns' (forth-coming).

[78] R. Wall, 'Regional and Temporal Variations in English Household Structure from 1650', in J. Hobcraft and P. Rees, editors, *Regional Demographic Development* (London, 1979), p. 107 and a revised version, 'The Household: Demographic and Economic Change in England, 1650–1970', in R. Wall, editor, *Family Forms*, pp. 493–512.

[79] R. H. Hilton, 'Some Social and Economic Evidence in Late Medieval English Tax Returns', in S. Herbst, editor, *Spoleczenstwo, gospordarke, kultura: studia ofiaowane M. Malowistowi w czterdzcestolencia pracy nankowej* (Warsaw, 1974), pp. 112–13, and in his *The English Peasantry in the Later Middle Ages* (Oxford, 1976), p. 28.

[80] P. Laslett, *Family Life and Illicit Love in Earlier Generations* (Cambridge, 1977), pp. 34–5.

[81] J. A. Raftis, *Tenure and Mobility* (Toronto, 1964), p. 182.

suggested in the evidence on the marriage movements of serf women of the Prior of Spalding in the Lincolnshire villages of Weston and Moulton from a 1269 serf genealogy.[82] It is intriguing to note that the distances involved in the thirteenth-century evidence are almost identical with those moved by servants in the late eighteenth century in the same area; evidence for the later period is based on the records of the Spalding servants' hiring fair.[83]

Service in husbandry and its varying incidence may well have had important implications for changes in the age and incidence of female marriage in early modern England. It may well have been an institution that helped to undermine the capacity of the English demographic regime to behave homeostatically.[84] A recent study has argued that the incidence of service in husbandry in early modern England was by no means constant.[85] Furthermore, it was not something that was linearly replaced over the centuries by wage-paid, living-out labour. Its incidence declined from a probable high point in the fifteenth century that should be of great interest to medievalists to a trough in the mid-seventeenth century, before it increased again, to die out altogether in the nineteenth century. One indicator that has been employed to measure the incidence of service is the number of October marriages in relation to that of all marriages.[86] October marriages are likely to have reflected the end of the servant year, which normally ran from Michaelmas to Michaelmas. From the early sixteenth century the decline and subsequent seventeenth-century rise in the index value of October marriages is particularly intriguing, falling as it does from a high point which may well have been located in the fifteenth century.

Assessments of the changing incidence of agrarian service needs amongst other things to take into account the changing level of real wages, the cost of living and the importance of pastoral agricultural practices relative to grain production in the rural economy. Periods of

---

[82] Smith, 'Hypothèses sur la nuptialité', pp. 128–79.

[83] A. S. Kussmaul, 'The Ambiguous Mobility of Farm Servants', *Economic History Review* 34 (1981), pp. 229–34.

[84] For a discussion of the absence of homeostasis in the demographic regime of early modern England and the role of agrarian service, see R. M. Smith, 'Fertility, Economy and Household Formation in England over Three Centuries', *Population and Development Review* 7 (1981), pp. 602–6. See also the ensuing debate involving N. Birdsall, 'Fertility and Economic Change in 18th and 19th Century Europe: An Extension of Smith's Analysis' and R. M. Smith, 'On Some Problems of Putting the Child Before the Marriage: A Response to Nancy Birdsall', both in *Population and Development Review* 9 (1983), pp. 111–36.

[85] A. S. Kussmaul, *Servants in Husbandry in Early Modern England* (Cambridge, 1981).

[86] *Ibid.*, pp. 70–93. See also her paper 'Time and Space, Hoofs and Grain: The Seasonality of Marriage in England', *Journal of Interdisciplinary History* (forthcoming).

high real wages, low living costs and a shift in the direction of greater
involvement in livestock husbandry all combined to increase the
importance of agrarian service.[87] Such was the trend in the English
rural economy from 1350 to 1470.[88]

However, historians of labour conditions in post-Black Death
England are inclined to point to the advantages enjoyed by the wage
labourer, and indeed to the attractiveness of well-paid work as a wage
labourer in a labour-deficient economy. Undeniably, there is considerable evidence in the litigation associated with the administration
of the Statute of Labourers to support this view.[89] Yet the frequent
complaints by employers who wished to hire persons as servants on
yearly terms but found men and women preferring to work as
labourers on daily or weekly terms should not necessarily be taken to
mean the wholesale flight from service into wage labouring. Indeed,
they reflect as much the hiring practice preferences of the employers,
and tend to over-emphasize the disappointments of employers in
their search for servants rather than their successes. In fact, they may
be taken to confirm the trend towards a preference for an 'immobile'
(in the sense of working on annual contracts) living-in labour force as
against the costly variant of the man or woman employed seasonally
or temporarily on a *per diem* basis. Furthermore, an increased demand
for a living-in agrarian labour force is consistent with what we know
of trends in late medieval English agriculture. The relative importance
of livestock husbandry in the mixed farming agrarian regimes of late
medieval England is a feature of this economy which marks it out in
comparison with certain other areas of late medieval Europe.[90]

What should be stressed more sharply is that 'living-in' servants
and labourers co-existed in English rural economies throughout the
period with which the essays in this volume are concerned. It is their
changing importance in relation to one another that is significant for
the discussion both of the composition of the domestic group and of
inter-household relationships. Yet their changing relative importance
within the late medieval farm economy is not a research problem
upon which great effort has been expended. For instance, Professor
Hilton has been concerned in some of his work to evaluate the per-

[87] Kussmaul, *Servants in Husbandry*, p. 98.
[88] M. M. Postan, 'Some Economic Evidence of Declining Population in the Later
    Middle Ages', *Economic History Review* 2 (1950), pp. 221–46. See also M. W.
    Beresford, 'A Review of Historical Research', in M. W. Beresford and J. G.
    Beresford, editors, *Deserted Medieval Villages* (London, 1971), pp. 3–144.
[89] N. Ritchie, 'Labour Conditions in Essex in the Reign of Richard II', *Economic History
    Review* 4 (1934), pp. 429–51.
[90] R. H. Hilton, 'A Crisis of Feudalism', *Past and Present* 80 (1978), p. 17.

centage of all 'wage earners' in the rural economy (on the basis of the late medieval tax lists) and has argued that the size groupings of 'servants' in individual households suggests that they were so little concentrated in individual enterprises that they did not alter the traditional family scale of the production unit.[91] However, in this respect late fourteenth-century England was not sharply differentiated from late seventeenth-century England, for the average size of the servant group, although variable from farming region to farming region and between town and country, seems to have been rarely greater than two persons.[92] Hilton appears to treat the wage labour force as a homogeneous rather than a heterogeneous phenomenon. On the basis of our knowledge of early modern England we may have some reasons to hypothesize that the period from the late fourteenth to the mid- to late fifteenth century experienced an increase in service-in-husbandry.

It is interesting that Zvi Razi appears to have argued for a contrary trend on the basis of his research into Halesowen before and after the Black Death.[93] Razi's assessment of the quantitative significance of service is based on the frequency with which servants are noted in manor court proceedings. The number of such references to servants is then related to the number of tenants who likewise are identified from the court records. Using this method Razi discovered that servant-keeping was halved in importance over the course of the fourteenth century. He believes this development occurred in conjunction with an increase in inter-household co-operation involving piecework and the use of 'tasking'. He comes to this conclusion because of a more than three-fold increase in the number of cases involving broken agreements between tenants over agricultural tasks in the last quarter of the fourteenth century. He equates the withdrawal from the use of hired labour on the part of the more substantial tenants, who he also believes increased the size of their holdings in these land-abundant conditions, with comparable behaviour on the part of the Abbot of Halesowen, who, like so many of his contemporaries, in the 1360s began to lease his demesne land, being unable to meet rising labour costs.

The increase in the quantity of such suits in court may reflect as much the growing concern of tenants for the non-performance of 'piece-work' in a tight and increasingly costly labour market, as the growing resort to such co-operative systems of inter-household

[91] Hilton, 'Some Social and Economic Evidence', p. 123.
[92] Wall, 'Regional and Temporal Variations', p. 107.
[93] Razi, 'Family, Land and Village Community', pp. 31–4.

relations. Indeed a growth in live-in service is not necessarily incompatible with an increase in the use of 'tasking' as a means of farming the land in a period of labour shortage. Both are expedients that indicate a wish not to use day labourers who are paid in cash, insofar as the live-in servant's remuneration is in his or her bed and board, which both decline in value as food prices stagnate or indeed fall. However, one suspects that Dr Razi's wish to provide an economic support for his view of village society flexing its corporate, political muscles against seigneurial oppression in the later fourteenth century accounts for his particular interpretation of developments in rural Worcestershire.[94]

Evidence to be seen in the attempts, explicit in late fourteenth-century Statute of Labourer's indictments, to force landless individuals into the service of others implies that medieval villagers (and not just landlords, as conventional interpretations of the background to the Ordinance (1349) and Statute (1351) of Labourers suggest) were themselves making efforts to preserve a norm of contracting servants on annual terms of employment, a norm which was becoming more difficult to maintain even with the legal support embodied in the labour legislation.[95] Of course, the labour laws themselves, insofar as they were concerned with inter-household movements of workers, might be seen as indicating, to use Razi's words, 'that the degree of economic interdependence of peasant households increased considerably after the plague'. Service is indeed a remarkably efficient means of temporarily redistributing labour for maximum productivity in a labour-deficient agrarian economy, as evidence from seventeenth- and early eighteenth-century England suggests.[96]

iii. Inheritance customs; their theory and practice

Just as demographic conditions and their implications for labour demand and supply have an important bearing upon the economics of inter-household relationships, so also they have a not insignificant effect upon the workings of inter-generational transmissions of property through inheritance. In fact the papers in this volume by Ravensdale and Dyer show how patterns of both *inter-vivos* and *post-mortem* transfers of land change quite noticeably in association with shifts in the rates of demographic growth. In general historians

[94] *Ibid.*, pp. 34–6.
[95] See the revisionist treatment of this evidence in L. R. Poos, 'The Social Context of Statute of Labourers Enforcement', *Law and History Review* (1983), pp. 27–52.
[96] Razi, 'Family, Land and Village Community', p. 32.

have been more inclined to investigate the likely demographic effects of inheritance practices rather than to consider whether demography itself can exert an influence upon the pattern of property devolution.

Much continental European scholarship working within a tradition established in the nineteenth century by Frédéric le Play has attempted to show, on the one hand, how and to what extent impartible inheritance led to the maintenance of larger holdings and also resulted in higher peasant marital fertility through fewer marriages and the permanent emigration of celibate males and spinsters, and, on the other hand, how partible inheritance led to a reduction in the size of holdings, higher levels of nuptiality, possibly lower marital fertility and an increase in non-agricultural activities as holding sizes dropped. Partible areas should therefore have had high rural population densities and growth rates, since in principle all the male offspring could remain to marry, whereas impartible areas would be expected to reveal lower population densities and nearly stationary demography as the landless or property-less either remained celibate or emigrated to other areas or the towns.[97]

It may appear platitudinous to suggest that in order to have inheritance heirs must be on hand to inherit. Yet historians of inheritance behaviour have not always been concerned to establish the demographic conditions under which heirs are likely to be present at their father's death and in what numbers. In his analysis of the impartible inheritance practices of 'champion' England, Homans, albeit subconsciously, employed the rule that in agricultural populations marriage entailed economic independence and that this economic condition was only obtainable through entry into one of a *fixed* number of positions in the land holdings available.[98] Those who were not endowed in this way, such as labourers and servants, were generally prevented from marrying. On the assumption of a steady-state subsistence environment, such niches therefore only became vacated through death, a circumstance which relates nuptiality and fertility directly to mortality through the inheritance process. The higher the mortality rate, the more economic opportunities are vacated and the higher the nuptiality. Such a responsive demographic system possesses a mechanism which produces instantaneous adjustment and will maintain a stationary state if the

---

[97] For a succinct summary of these views, see L. Berkner, 'Inheritance, Land Tenure and Peasant Family Structure: A German Regional Comparison', in Goody *et al.*, editors, *Family and Inheritance*, pp. 71–4.

[98] G. C. Homans, *English Villagers of the Thirteenth Century* (Cambridge, Mass., 1941), pp. 121–59.

marriage age of any one generation is approximately equal to the expectation of the life of the preceding generation in the middle of its productive period. In rather simpler terms, a stationary population would be maintained if the average age at marriage were equal to the expectation of life at mean age of paternity.[99]

Of course, these demographic interrelationships are not to be seen as applying to the two adjacent generations within an individual family but would be expected to persist at a higher level of social organization. Indeed, at the level of family, variations in individual fertility and mortality rates, what can be termed the effects of the 'demographic lottery', will mean that some fathers are succeeded by no heirs and some by several heirs.[100] When we consider the demographic background to areas practising partible and impartible inheritance the extent to which heirless families occur is also directly related to the proportions of men who are succeeded by groupings of two or more direct male heirs. Indeed, the chances of 'surplus' sons and daughters can be assessed more effectively if the extent of these alternative openings into *post-mortem* property acquisitions can be gauged. E. A. Wrigley has begun a tentative exploration of these matters with rather different issues in mind.[101] Wrigley compared the heirship patterns of three 'model' populations, theoretically constructed as stationary in numbers over time. Stationary demographic conditions were created by linking appropriate fertility levels to populations in which a son had either a 66 per cent, or a 50 per cent or a 33 per cent probability of surviving to his father's death. These data have been used to extend Wrigley's analysis further.[102]

[99] For a succinct consideration of these issues, see R. S. Schofield, 'The Relationship Between Demographic Structure and Environment in Pre-Industrial Western Europe', in W. Conze, editor, *Sozialgeschichte der Families in der Neuzeit Europas* (Stuttgart, 1976), pp. 147–60. For the formal demography of these relationships associated with stationary populations, see G. Ohlin, 'Mortality, Marriage and Growth in Pre-Industrial Populations', *Population Studies* 14 (1961), pp. 190–7.

[100] A point that D. Levine in '"For Their Own Reasons"; Individual Marriage Decisions and Family Life', *Journal of Family History* 7 (1982), pp. 255–64, seems not to have grasped.

[101] E. A. Wrigley, 'Fertility Strategy for the Individual and the Group', in C. Tilly, editor, *Historical Studies of Changing Fertility* (Princeton, N.J., 1978), pp. 235–54. For a similar analysis with only marginally different conclusions, see J. Goody and G. A. Harrison, 'Strategies of Heirship', *Comparative Studies in Society and History* 15 (1973), pp. 3–21, reprinted as Chapter 7 of J. Goody, *Production and Reproduction* (Cambridge, 1976).

[102] The same assumptions incorporated in Wrigley's initial analysis are repeated in this modelling: that the sex ratio at birth was 100; that the chances of any one child in a family dying are independent of the chances of each child dying before the death of his or her father and are the same without regard to the rank of the child in the family; that the chances of any given child being male or female is uninfluenced by

Looking only at populations with survivorship probabilities of 0.5 and 0.33, it is possible to indicate for differing values of completed family sizes what proportions of fathers would be succeeded by two, three or four or more male heirs (or indeed heiresses, for which the values are identical on the assumption of a sex ratio of 100 at birth). From the evidence in Figures 1.2–1.4 it should be clear that not until a

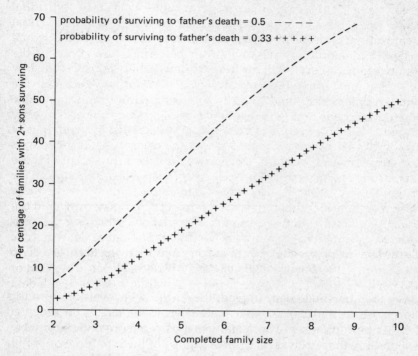

Figure 1.2. The probability of two or more sons surviving to father's death. (For assumptions, see p. 40, note 102.)

mean completed family size of 6.5 is reached in a population with a 50 per cent chance of surviving to father's death does partibility become an issue in more than one-half of the families. With the much more severe mortality conditions associated with the 33 per cent survivorship probability, mean completed family sizes of almost ten would be needed to produce a majority of inheritances that could involve

the sex of any earlier child in the family; that the life table death rates for children of both sexes are the same; and that every man marries. See Wrigley, 'Fertility Strategy', p. 138.

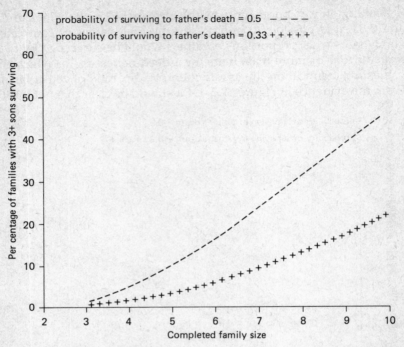

Figure 1.3. The probability of three or more sons surviving to father's death. (For assumptions, see p. 40, note 102.)

more than one male heir. Indeed, these would be levels of reproduction close to the maxima that have been identified in documented fertility performances. These features are even more noticeable when we observe the survival changes of groups of three or more or of four or more heirs surviving to their father's death. To achieve more than 5 per cent of families with four or more survivors with a 33 per cent level of survivorship would require completed family sizes of nine or more.

Wrigley fitted the 0.5 and 0.33 survivorship probabilities to appropriate family size distributions to achieve a stationary population and produced a limited but highly significant range of survivor combinations. Populations 1 and 2 in Tables 1.2 and 1.3 show the results of fitting these probability values to different fertility distributions. What is striking in these model populations is that both display roughly similar proportions of families with zero male heirs, zero male heirs but at least one female heiress, and one or more male heirs. In population 1 the above heirship patterns constitute 19.8 per

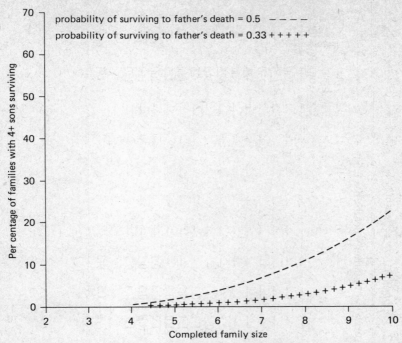

Figure 1.4. The probability of four or more sons surviving to father's death. (For assumptions, see p. 40, note 102.)

cent, 20.9 per cent and 59.3 per cent respectively of all cases and in population 2 the comparable percentages are 21.3, 18.2 and 60.5.

From such modelling it is possible to see how fertility and mortality could interact in, for instance, a community with a 'high-pressure' demographic equilibrium and practising partible inheritance and in a community experiencing a 'low- or medium-pressure' demographic regime with impartible inheritance, to produce a surface expression that to the historian with access only to its *post-mortem* inheritance practices through wills or manorial court rolls would seem almost identical. In both populations, between 25 and 30 per cent only of the families have 'surplus' sons who in theory could take up 'niches' vacated by men with no direct heirs and who could marry surviving heiresses in other such niches. For example, in a population with a survivorship probability of 0.5, completed families of five children would in 23.8 per cent of cases have no male heirs, in 7.9 per cent of these cases there would be one female, in 7.9 per cent two, in 3.9 per cent three, in 0.9 per cent four and and in 0.1 per cent of cases five

Table 1.2. Population 1

	Frequency per 1,000 families	Number of sons surviving to father's death; p = 0.50*													Total born (sons & daughters)
		0	1	2	3	4	5	6	7	8	9	10	11	12	
0	85	85.0	—	—	—	—	—	—	—	—	—	—	—	—	0
1	125	93.7	31.1	—	—	—	—	—	—	—	—	—	—	—	125
2	125	70.3	46.9	7.8	—	—	—	—	—	—	—	—	—	—	250
3	125	52.7	52.8	17.6	1.9	—	—	—	—	—	—	—	—	—	375
4	125	39.6	52.7	26.4	5.9	0.4	—	—	—	—	—	—	—	—	500
5	125	29.7	49.4	33.0	11.0	1.8	0.1	—	—	—	—	—	—	—	625
6	90	16.0	32.0	26.7	11.9	3.0	0.4	—	—	—	—	—	—	—	540
7	75	10.0	23.3	23.3	12.9	4.3	1.1	0.1	—	—	—	—	—	—	525
8	60	6.0	16.0	18.7	12.5	5.2	1.4	0.2	—	—	—	—	—	—	480
9	25	1.9	5.7	7.5	5.8	2.9	1.0	0.2	—	—	—	—	—	—	225
10	20	1.1	3.8	5.6	5.0	2.9	1.2	0.3	0.1	—	—	—	—	—	200
11	10	0.4	1.5	2.6	2.6	1.7	0.8	0.3	0.1	—	—	—	—	—	110
12	10	0.3	1.3	2.3	2.6	1.9	1.1	0.4	0.1	—	—	—	—	—	120
Total	1,000	406.7	316.5	171.5	72.1	24.1	7.1	1.5	0.3						4,075

No male heir, but at least 1 female = 208.5
No heir (male or female) = 198.2

*p = 0.50 = 50% chance of survival to father's death

44

Table 1.3. *Population 2*

Family size	Frequency per 1,000 families	Number of sons surviving to father's death; p = 0.33*													Total born (sons & daughters)
		0	1	2	3	4	5	6	7	8	9	10	11	12	
0	70	70.0	—												0
1	70	58.4	11.6	—											70
2	70	48.6	19.5	1.9	—										140
3	70	40.5	24.3	4.9	0.3	—									210
4	70	33.8	27.0	8.1	1.1	—									280
5	70	28.2	28.1	11.3	2.3	0.1	—								350
6	70	23.4	28.1	14.1	3.8	0.6	—								420
7	70	19.5	27.4	16.4	5.5	1.1	0.1	—							490
8	70	16.3	26.1	18.2	7.3	1.8	0.3	—							560
9	90	17.4	31.4	25.1	11.7	3.5	0.7	0.1	—						810
10	100	16.2	32.3	29.1	15.5	5.4	1.3	0.2	—						1,000
11	90	12.1	26.7	26.7	16.0	6.4	1.8	0.3	—						990
12	90	10.1	24.2	26.6	17.8	8.0	2.6	0.6	0.1	—					1,080
Total	1,000	394.6	306.7	182.4	81.3	26.9	6.8	1.2	0.1						6,400

No male heir, but at least 1 female = 182.1
No heir (male or female) = 212.5

*p = 0.33 = 33% chance of survival to father's death

45

heiresses. In population 1, if holdings were partible among heiresses and if the holdings without direct heirs of either sex were taken into account also, there would in theory be 544 vacancies on offer to the 426 'surplus' sons, and in population 2 there are theoretically 582 slots for the 459 'surplus' sons. However, if we create a new situation in population 3 by modelling a society with the fertility of population 2 but experiencing the mortality conditions of population 1 (see Table 1.4) the circumstances change dramatically, for now in nearly 50 per cent of the families a father will have more than one male heir alive at his death. There are consequently far fewer vacancies, since in only roughly 14 per cent of cases is there no direct heir and in a further 14 per cent of cases there are no male offspring but more than one daughter alive. If once more partibility is assumed among the heiresses we can generate 404 niches but in this case with 953 'surplus' sons seeking entry into them.

Some recent writings in thirteenth- and fourteenth-century English village social history contain references to processes that might owe a great deal to the effects of the 'demographic lottery', although their authors have sought out rather different explanations. Two examples of such work are worth consideration since they are highly critical of Homan's arguments concerning his views on the failure of men other than the designated heir in areas of impartible inheritance, to enter into matrimony because of restricted access to land. Edward Britton, in his study of the Ramsey Abbey manor of Broughton in Huntingdonshire, in which impartible inheritance was practised, finds that 23 per cent of the resident families between 1288 and 1340 had more than one son who had acquired land in the village. Britton concluded that Homans had grossly underestimated the possibilities of 'non-inheriting' sons holding land within their village and writes 'unless one is to conclude that there was an *incredible* [my emphasis] number of heiresses in Broughton during this period it would be difficult to explain the high degree of success of non-inheriting sons in acquiring land'.[103]

Zvi Razi, using manorial records of higher quality than those at Britton's disposal for his research, has been able to 'reconstitute' 788 Halesowen families living between 1270 and 1348.[104] He established that 590 had one or more sons over the age of twelve. Of these 590 families, 290 leave evidence of two or more sons over the age of

---

[103] E. Britton, 'The Peasant Family in Fourteenth Century England', *Peasant Studies* 5 (1976), p. 4, discussed again in his book, *The Community of the Vill: A Study in the History of the Family and Village Life in Fourteenth Century England* (Toronto, 1977), pp. 60–4.   [104] Razi, *Life, Marriage and Death*, pp. 50–7.

Table 1.4. Population 3

Family size	Frequency per 1,000 families	Number of sons surviving to father's death: fertility of population 2 and mortality of population 1													Total born (sons & daughters)
		0	1	2	3	4	5	6	7	8	9	10	11	12	
0	70	70.0	—	—	—	—	—	—	—	—	—	—	—	—	0
1	70	52.2	17.5	—	—	—	—	—	—	—	—	—	—	—	70
2	70	39.4	26.2	4.4	—	—	—	—	—	—	—	—	—	—	140
3	70	29.5	29.5	9.9	1.1	—	—	—	—	—	—	—	—	—	210
4	70	22.1	29.5	14.8	3.3	0.3	—	—	—	—	—	—	—	—	280
5	70	16.6	27.7	18.5	6.1	1.0	0.1	—	—	—	—	—	—	—	350
6	70	12.5	24.9	20.8	9.2	2.3	0.3	—	—	—	—	—	—	—	420
7	70	9.4	21.8	21.8	12.1	4.0	0.8	0.1	—	—	—	—	—	—	490
8	70	7.0	18.7	21.8	14.5	6.1	1.6	0.3	—	—	—	—	—	—	560
9	90	6.8	20.3	27.0	21.0	10.5	3.5	0.8	0.1	—	—	—	—	—	810
10	100	5.6	18.8	28.2	25.1	14.6	5.9	1.6	0.3	—	—	—	—	—	1,000
11	90	3.8	14.0	23.2	23.2	15.5	7.2	2.4	0.6	0.1	—	—	—	—	990
12	90	2.9	11.4	20.9	23.3	17.4	9.3	3.6	1.1	0.2	—	—	—	—	1,080
Total	1,000	277.8	260.3	211.3	138.9	71.7	28.7	8.8	2.1	0.3					6,400

No male heir but at least 1 female = 136.1
No heir (male or female) = 142.0

47

twelve, and of these families 140 present more than one son holding land at the same time. The success of the 'surplus' sons in gaining access to land led Razi to claim that 'Halesowen villagers were prepared to face economic hardships and destitution rather than to remain bachelors and spinsters. Consequently impartible inheritance did not secure as Homans had argued a stable adaptation of the village society to its economic conditions.'[105] However, we should not over-stress the numbers, or more specifically the proportions, of tenant sons who marry. Although Razi tells us that 590 families had sons of twelve years or more, we must assume therefore that 198 families at least had no sons who survived to that age. In other words, families with one or more sons over twelve years of age constituted 75 per cent of all those in Halesowen for whom a 'reconstitution' could be performed, a proportion considerably in excess of the 60 per cent that we have shown to characterize a stationary population. Yet we have to make some adjustment for deaths of those sons between the age of twelve and their father's death. If we employ the adult mortality level that Razi calculates, the 590 families with one or more sons would have been diminished to 513 with one or more sons aged twenty and above (65 per cent). Razi does argue that this population was growing before the plague, so a level of 60 per cent survivorship which we computed for the model population would most likely be too low to capture the reality of Halesowen's situation. The original 788 families leave records of 1,013 sons over twelve years, 269 (24 per cent) of whom went on to marry and to acquire land prior to their father's death.[106] Obviously, many more went on to eventual marriage.

Yet neither of these two studies appears to present evidence that is startlingly peculiar or fundamentally at odds with the findings in the model populations. Even if the populations in both Halesowen and Broughton were growing, the proportions of sons married and holding land before their father's death would be feasible given entry into vacancies left because of the 'demographic lottery'. Both these critics failed, as did Homans also, to note that it was not the death of an individual's father, nor his retirement, that really mattered in allowing this pattern so much as any death or retirement, or indeed sale or lease, by an heirless male that could make available niches to be 'colonized' by other men's surplus offspring in the community. This evidence is certainly not capable of sustaining Razi's claim that

---

[105] *Ibid.*, p. 57.
[106] *Ibid.*, Table 16, p. 84.

Table 1.5. *Heirship patterns: Redgrave, Rickinghall, Great Waltham and High Easter in the late thirteenth and early fourteenth centuries*

	Redgrave 1260–94			Redgrave 1295–1320			Rickinghall 1295–1320	
	No.	%		No.	%		No.	%
Heirs								
0	37	34.3		58	33.7		31	30.3
0M 1F	9	8.3		17	9.9		5	4.9
0M 2F	5	4.6	13.8%	6	3.5	15.7%	6	5.9	15.1%
0M 3F	—	—		3	1.7		3	2.9
0M 4F	1	0.9		1	0.6		1	1.0
1M	27	25.0		48	27.9		30	29.4
2M	16	14.9		23	13.3		15	14.7
3M	13	12.0		7	4.1		8	7.8
4M	—	—	51.9%	7	4.1	50.6%	2	1.8	54.6%
5M	—	—		1	0.6		—	—
6M	—	—		—	—		1	0.9
7M	—	—		1	0.6		—	—
Total	108			172			102	

Great Waltham and High Easter 1265–1320

	No.	%
Heirs		
0	40	31.7
0M 1F	28	22.2
1M/1 + M	58	46.1
Total	126	

it indicates the presence of a non-European marriage regime in medieval Halesowen.[107]

In considering heirship patterns from certain Essex and Suffolk manors in the pre-plague period, the value of our model populations can be further indicated. Patterns of male and female succession are presented in Table 1.5. Populations 1 and 2 appear not to predict the frequency of heirship in the Suffolk manor of Redgrave with great accuracy; between 1260 and 1294 the ratio of deaths in which a male has no direct heirs to no males but one or more females and to one or more males is 3.4:1.4:5.2 and between 1295 and 1319 that ratio is

[107] For many marriages occurring in advance of paternal death in an ostensibly west-European marriage regime, see D. Levine, '"For Their Own Reasons"'.

3.4:2.0:4.6. The neighbouring manor of Rickinghall shows a marginally better, although still relatively poor, fit, with a ratio over the whole period of 3.0:1.5:5.5.[108] What is striking in the evidence from both manors, where partibility was the inheritance custom is the relative infrequency with which more than one son actually inherited. In both manors multiple heirship took place in between 20 and 25 per cent of cases only. Population 4 (see Table 1.6), produced by combining the fertility of population 1 and the mortality of population 2, creates a model population that predicts the observed inheritances in these manors quite closely. Indeed it is very successful in its prediction of men dying heirless in the observed inheritances. There are, however, discrepancies between it and the observed numbers of instances in which only one male heir inherits. Nonetheless it does provide – quite surprisingly, given the small number of cases – a good fit with the proportions of observed cases in which more than two sons are seen to have inherited their father's holding.

In fitting a distribution producing a mean completed family size of only 3.1 to the mortality assumptions of population 1 (see Table 1.7) we produce a survivorship distribution very similar to that of population 4. An attempt to fit this distribution to the data relating to inheritances on the closely situated manors of Great Waltham and High Easter in Essex, where impartible inheritance was practised, produces fascinating and most likely fortuitous results, given the small number of heirship cases in rather broken records between 1265 and 1320.[109] On the basis of the heirship evidence from both the Essex and the Suffolk communities it would appear that the tenant populations were not growing and quite possibly declining in both areas. In fact, L. R. Poos has extended the analysis of inheritance patterns in Great Waltham and High Easter throughout the remainder of the fourteenth century and his evidence is presented in Table 1.8.[110] There are, however, certain problems in equating the frequency with which sons inherit with the frequency with which sons survive. As Ravensdale has done in his study of the Crowland Abbey manor of Cottenham in Cambridgeshire, Poos has established through an investigation of land market transactions that in certain instances the regular means of succession were circumvented by *inter-vivos*

---

[108] The evidence on Rickinghall inheritances comes from obituary entries in British Museum, MSS Add. Ch. 63394–63407.

[109] Based on *post-mortem* inheritances in Public Record Office, DL 30/62, 751–DL 30/63, 791.

[110] See L. R. Poos, 'Population and Mortality in Two Fourteenth-Century Essex Communities', unpublished Research Fellowship Dissertation, Fitzwilliam College, Cambridge, 1980, pp. 48–51.

Table 1.6. *Population 4*

Family size	Frequency per 1,000 families	Number of sons surviving to father's death: fertility of population 1 and mortality of population 2													Total born (sons & daughters)
		0	1	2	3	4	5	6	7	8	9	10	11	12	
0	85	85.0	—	—	—	—	—	—	—	—	—	—	—	—	0
1	125	104.2	20.8	—	—	—	—	—	—	—	—	—	—	—	125
2	125	86.5	34.7	3.5	—	—	—	—	—	—	—	—	—	—	250
3	125	72.3	43.4	8.7	0.6	—	—	—	—	—	—	—	—	—	375
4	125	60.3	48.3	14.5	1.9	—	—	—	—	—	—	—	—	—	500
5	125	50.2	50.2	20.1	4.1	0.4	—	—	—	—	—	—	—	—	625
6	90	30.2	36.2	18.1	4.8	0.7	0.1	—	—	—	—	—	—	—	540
7	75	20.9	29.3	17.6	5.9	1.2	0.1	—	—	—	—	—	—	—	525
8	60	13.9	22.3	15.6	6.3	1.6	0.3	—	—	—	—	—	—	—	480
9	25	4.9	8.7	7.0	3.3	0.9	0.1	0.1	—	—	—	—	—	—	225
10	20	3.2	6.5	5.8	3.1	1.1	0.2	0.1	—	—	—	—	—	—	200
11	10	1.4	2.9	2.9	1.8	0.6	0.2	0.1	0.1	—	—	—	—	—	110
12	10	1.1	2.7	2.7	2.0	0.9	0.4	0.1	0.1	—	—	—	—	—	120
Total	1,000	534.1	306.0	116.5	33.8	7.4	1.4	0.4	0.2						4,075

No male heir but at least one female = 216.6
No heir (male and female) = 317.8

Table 1.7. *Population 6*

Family size	Frequency per 1,000 families	Number of sons surviving to father's death: fertility of population 5 and mortality of population 1													Total born (sons & daughters)
		0	1	2	3	4	5	6	7	8	9	10	11	12	
0	100	100.0	—													0
1	200	150.0	50.0	—												200
2	200	112.5	75.0	12.5												400
3	150	63.3	63.3	21.1	2.3	—										450
4	110	34.8	46.4	23.2	5.2	0.2	—									440
5	85	20.2	33.6	22.4	7.5	1.2	0.2	—								425
6	60	10.7	21.4	17.8	7.9	2.0	0.4	—								360
7	35	4.7	10.9	10.9	6.1	2.0	0.5	—								245
8	20	2.0	5.3	6.2	4.2	1.7	0.6	0.1	—							160
9	15	1.1	3.4	4.5	3.5	1.8	0.9	0.1	—							135
10	15	0.8	2.8	4.2	3.8	2.2	0.9	0.2	0.1	—						150
11	5	0.2	0.8	1.3	1.3	0.9	0.4	0.1	0.1	—						55
12	5	0.2	0.6	1.2	1.3	0.9	0.5	0.2	0.1	—						60
Total	1,000	500.5	313.5	125.3	43.1	12.9	3.5	0.7	0.3							3,080

No male heir but at least one female = 220.2
No heir (male or female) = 280.3

52

transfers. Likewise, a further complicating practice stemmed from the custom of 'widow's free bench'. As this custom seems to have been observed in Waltham and Easter, a widow retained her dead husband's land for her life-time, thereby requiring a son (in the event of there being one) to wait additional time to enter his inheritance. A son would therefore find himself having to wait even longer than elsewhere, where land was not retained in the widow's possession. Because of this temporary 'lateral' movement of land it is necessary, if one wishes to establish the maximum frequency with which at least one son is alive on his father's death, to add the frequency of father-to-son inheritances to the frequency of husband-to-widow free bench succession. Although there would doubtless not be a living son in each instance of the latter occurrence, this procedure allows for the computation of an absolute maximum frequency of father-to-son 'inheritances'. In addition, in the vast majority of cases (classed as 'unresolved') when no identifiable heir came into court to enter the land, and when the tenement was subsequently re-let by the lord to an apparently unrelated individual, it can be assumed that no son survived. As Table 1.8 indicates, this results in a low survivorship estimate, never more than 45 per cent. Unless a number of surviving sons refused to take up their rightful inheritance, this suggests that the tenant population in these two manors was declining. Poos is fortunate in having access to ancillary information on population, from an annual count of males resident on these manors which shows declining numbers through the whole period apart from a short-lived phase of recovery in the decade after the Black Death.[111] It is interesting that by fitting together the arbitrarily derived fertility and mortality assumptions to produce the populations in Tables 1.6 and 1.7 we generate an annual rate of demographic decline of somewhat less than 1 per cent per annum. From the annual count in the tithing penny payments of males over twelve, population appears to have fallen through the period between 1320 and 1400, at a rate of between 0.8 and 0.9 per cent per annum. The observed and modelled survivorship frequencies show a remarkable correspondence, with more than 50 per cent of men dying after 1349 with no direct heirs of either sex.

The contrasts in the demography of two groups of tenant populations, one practising partible and the other impartible inheritance, that might be predicted by conventional theory have proved difficult to detect. Both populations were notable for exhibiting little if any

[111] *Ibid.*, pp. 22–3.

Table 1.8. *Frequencies of heirship channels; Great Waltham and High Easter 1327–89**

Deceased–heir relationship	Frequencies of relationship among successions		
	1328–48	1349	1350–89
Father–son	26.6%	15.9%	21.5%
Husband–widow	20.3%	8.9%	11.0%
Father–daughter(s)†	5.5%	9.3%	8.9%
Mother–son	13.3%	4.7%	4.9%
Mother–daughter(s)†	0.8%	3.3%	1.6%
Other familial	17.2% ⎫ 33.6%	26.6% ⎫ 57.9%	25.6% ⎫ 52%
Unresolved	16.4% ⎭	31.3% ⎭	26.4% ⎭
Total number of successions	128	214	246

*This material has been reproduced with the kind permission of Mr L. R. Poos from his research fellowship dissertation, 'Population and mortality in two fourteenth century Essex communities' (1980), p. 50.
†Includes successions by daughter and son-in-law

growth. Furthermore, it appears that the frequency with which groups of two or more sons survived to share or contest an inheritance was relatively low in the partible areas, as were the instances where younger sons were provided with land in the impartible areas. Indeed, with the absence of growth in the land holding populations there ought in theory to have been a sufficient quantity of niches for those sons to have occupied without necessarily experiencing downward social mobility. But in making such a comment we are forgetting the impact of a market in property to which we have already referred and to which we shall need to return.

It is not solely within the context of medieval villein land holders that the repercussions following from the 'demographic lottery' should be noted. That legal practices and legally engineered plans could frequently fall victim to chance effects of demography has been argued by Lloyd Bonfield in a striking criticism of a famous thesis proposed by Sir John Habakkuk concerning the process whereby strict settlement assisted in the build-up and preservation of large estates in the seventeenth and eighteenth centuries.[112] In the early seventeenth century the principal marriage settlement involved a life interest in the patrimony being secured in the groom, followed by an

[112] L. Bonfield, 'Marriage Settlements and the "Rise of Great Estates": The Demographic Aspect', *Economic History Review* 32 (1979), pp. 483–93.

entail limited to the eldest surviving son produced by the marriage. Trustees guaranteed the grandson's rights against any action by the life tenant and ensured the continuity of the arrangement for one generation until either the grandson's majority or his death. Habakkuk argued that if resettlement took place upon the son's marriage, before the death of the life tenant (i.e. a second strict settlement), and the son accepted a life estate while relinquishing his remainder, this had the potential of making entail permanent. The critical question asked by Bonfield was whether fathers actually survived to the marriage of their eldest sons, for if they did not then eldest sons came into possession of patrimonies as tenants with no such fetters.

By using the evidence contained in Hollingsworth's study of the demography of the peerage, Bonfield was able to establish what per centage of men survived to resettle at the marriage of their eldest son. In fact, Bonfield's estimate shows that between the mid-seventeenth and the mid-eighteenth century only about 48 per cent of fathers survived to this point, suggesting that in only half of the inter-generational successions was resettlement possible and in the other half eldest sons were able to take possession of the patrimony with full powers of disposition. Even the figure of 48 per cent of successions is likely to be far too high, as it actually fails to note that not all men would have had male successors. Once again the effects of the 'demographic lottery' are important, for it can be shown that if the likelihood of heiresses is taken into account the proportion of fathers who produced a surviving male child and also lived to that child's marriage hovered in the late seventeenth and early eighteenth centuries at under one-third of all cases. Bonfield consequently drew the convincing conclusion that resettlement in the manner described by Habakkuk was the exception rather than the rule.

The demographic constraints on the facility of inheritance laws or legal devices to operate as theory presupposes are therefore considerable. Reverting to the tenants of medieval English villages, the evening out of demographic anomalies would necessitate processes other than inheritance from father to son to ensure the process of social reproduction. We have discussed the role of heiresses earlier in this chapter, and Ravensdale considers the fascinating patterns that arise when widows retain life-time rights in their husbands' land, which can, under certain conditions, allow them to by-pass the offspring of the first marriage through remarriage while still in possession of their land.[113] However, in a substantial proportion of instances neither widows nor daughters will have been available to

[113] See below, pp. 197–225.

inherit in the absence of male offspring. In these cases inheritance might extend to members of a wider kin network. This constitutes an issue which the essays in this volume have in general not pursued. How far out into the wider kin network are heirs pursued in the absence of direct offspring or closely related collaterals? Keith Wrightson touches upon this issue tangentially in his contribution, when discussing testators and their beneficiaries in the Essex village of Terling between 1550 and 1699.[114] He found that fewer than one-fifth of wills extended even as far as grandchildren or nephews and nieces, and a minuscule total recognized cousins or 'kinsmen', although he does note that these latter categories of kin were more prominent in the wills of men without children and of widows and unmarried women. One change in practice that Wrightson observes, namely the decline in the recognition of godchildren after 1600, has been discovered elsewhere.[115] It should be noted that a study of will makers in the Oxfordshire market town of Banbury shows that among 'prestigious men' there was a decline in the range of 'kinsmen' recognized in wills.[116] Among the social and economic groups with which the essays in this volume are concerned no such trend is detectable from the Banbury data, and kinsmen are recognized in no greater proportions than Wrightson has established for Terling. Furthermore, a recent attempt to dispute the validity of Wrightson's findings, consisting of a larger-scale study of Terling, produces further evidence of a narrow range of recognized kin, expanded however in total by the inclusion of step-kin following on remarriage.[117]

Kin recognition in wills can, though, be a somewhat misleading source, as it tells us those kin whom an individual is prepared to single out as worthy of recognition at his or her death. Apart from failing to give information on kin (especially daughters) who may have benefited from *pre-mortem* gifts, it tells us nothing of those kin who believed they had a claim to recognition but went unacknowledged.

Indeed, it might be expected that there would be a strong awareness of legally defined rights in property in a society in which property

---

[114] See below, pp. 324–9.

[115] L. M. Munby, editor, *Life and Death in King's Langley: Wills and Inventories 1498–1659* (King's Langley, 1981), p. xv.

[116] R. Vann, 'Wills and the Family in an English Town: Banbury, 1550–1800', *Journal of Family History* 4 (1979), pp. 346–67.

[117] M. Chaytor, 'Household and Kinship: Ryton in the late 16th and early 17th centuries', *History Workshop Journal* 10 (1980), pp. 39–41. See the reactions to this paper from K. Wrightson, 'Household and Kinship in Sixteenth Century England', *History Workshop Journal* 12 (1982), p. 156 and R. Houston and R. M. Smith, 'A New Approach to Family History?', *History Workshop* 14 (1982), pp. 124–5.

transmission along kin lines was strategically highly important. It might therefore be valuable to know how frequently people failed to take up rights that in law they possessed in the matter of property. Little work has to date been done on this, in part we might suspect because any interpretation would need to take into account negative evidence which is potentially ambiguous.

For instance, in demographic conditions characterized by relatively high levels of mortality and fertility we might expect that cousins would have composed the largest group of kin within any individual's kin universe. Nephews and nieces would also have been quite prominent (in a simulation exercise this has been shown to have been the case in a population with an e_0 of 38 years and a gross reproduction rate of 3.29).[118] Cousins are only specified in inheritances in Redgrave very infrequently (0.4 per cent of occasions) between 1295 and 1319, although a further 5 per cent of inheritances in which the heir's relationship to the deceased person was not specified could have involved cousins. Nephews too, were relatively inconsequential, accounting for only 1.5 per cent of all inheritances. Nonetheless, 11 per cent of properties, in a period of evidently quite high demand for land, escheated to the manorial lord through a lack of heirs.[119] Cousins would seem, therefore, not to have been prominent recipients of property through inheritance, although presumably in those cases where holdings fell vacant they may well have been available to inherit. In this regard it is interesting to note of the 25 tenant deaths in Cottenham in 1349 that Ravensdale shows that only seven inheritances went definitively to kin.[120] In the same year on the Buckinghamshire manor of Iveagh, as Judith Bennett shows, cousins accounted for only 8 per cent of inheritances when high mortality should in theory have made available considerable inheritance opportunities for that category of kin. Yet here over 44 per cent of inheritances were not taken up because of the default of heirs.[121] We can only speculate at present on the possible effects of relatively

[118] See L. A. Goodman, N. Keyfitz and T. W. Pullman, 'Family Formation and the Frequency of Various Kinship Relations', *Theoretical Population Biology* 5 (1974), pp. 1–27. A feature confirmed by H. Le Bras in 'Evolution des liens de famille au cours de l'existence: une comparaison entre la France actuelle et la France du XVIIIe siècle', in *Les Âges de la vie*, Actes du Colloque, VIIe Colloque National de Démographie Strasbourg 5–7 Mai 1982 (Paris, 1982), pp. 27–45. It is worth noting that the pre-industrial population simulated by Le Bras had a low life expectancy, $e_0 = 30$ and a low growth rate, 0.2% per annum. Although cousins were the most numerous kin category the number surviving for any individual fell rapidly with age from 14.6 at age 20 to 6.2 at age 65 (*ibid.*, p. 35).
[119] See below, pp. 184–5.   [120] See below, pp. 199–200.
[121] Information kindly sent to me by Professor Bennett.

high levels of migration and of geographical marital exogamy on the actual pool of cousins present within the community, but that readily available and often presumed kin-aware group may well have been more limited in extent than is often supposed. Indeed it has been shown that social practices most likely leading to a restricted know-ledge of eligible heirs (i.e. families keeping track only of close cousins) helped to bring about a faster rate of extinction among the baronets elevated by James I than demographic determinants alone would predict.[122]

Much has been made of heirship patterns of customary tenants or copyholders in the two centuries after 1350, in the matter of both internal family relationships and the quality of the family's sen-timental attachment to land. Dr Faith, if not the first to notice the decline in the frequency with which inheritances went between kin, and more especially between fathers and their sons, provided a major reassessment of evidence to suggest that the family–land bond by the end of the fourteenth century had been loosened and in some places had more or less disappeared.[123] This view has been confirmed by a considerable number of studies all suggesting a major fall in the frequency with which land moved between kin either as a *pre-* or as a *post-mortem* transfer.[124] Conversely, ample evidence has been forth-coming to suggest that by the middle of the fifteenth century most land was being either transferred on an *inter-vivos* basis between unrelated persons (defined in the vast majority of cases as persons bearing different surnames) or had escheated to the lord for want of heirs who had not come to court to register their claims to inherit. In this volume Christopher Dyer provides evidence from the estates of the Bishop of Worcester to sustain this now widely held view. He, however, is cautious in drawing conclusions as to what his findings might mean for kin relations and family attitudes to land.[125]

Some historians have not always been so reticent. For instance,

---

[122] See K. W. Wachter and P. Laslett, 'Measuring Patriline Extinction for Modelling Social Mobility in the Past', in K. W. Wachter, with E. A. Hammel and P. Laslett, *Statistical Studies of Historical Social Structure* (London, 1979), pp. 113–36. See, too, Laslett's surprise in finding a better record of patriline persistence among Swiss peasants than among English seventeenth-century baronets, in his preface to R. M. Netting, *Balancing on an Alp: Ecological Change and Continuity in a Swiss Mountain Commuinity* (Cambridge, 1981), pp. viii–ix.   [123] Faith, 'Peasant Families'.

[124] Jones, 'Customary Land Market', for Bedfordshire presents evidence that at Blunham between 1415 and 1457 25 out of 115, at Willington in the second half of the fifteenth century 10% and at Leighton Buzzard, also in the second half of the fifteenth century, 33 per cent of transfers were intra-familial. Lomas, 'Land and People', shows that in the 4 Durham priory manors of Billingham, Wolveston, Cowpen and Newton between 1364 and 1500 rarely were more than 20 per cent of land transfers within the family.   [125] See below, pp. 277–94.

Barbara Harvey, on finding in her studies of land exchanges in certain of the manors of the Abbots of Westminster land transferred from A to the use of B *sibi et suis et assignatis suis,* considers that it shows a recognition on the monks' part that the incoming tenant 'would want to sell his interest in the land instead of transmitting it to his heir'.[126] Indeed Dr Faith, in her assessment of land exchanges in the pre-plague period, when the overwhelming majority of inheritances went between closely related kin, considers this period as one when 'the idea that land "ought to descend to the blood who held it of old"' was still present.

In the field of family history, perhaps more than in any other, there are great difficulties in inferring emotional attitudes or ideals from structures or actions. Indeed, Alan Macfarlane comes dangerously close to doing just this when, on finding that in Earls Colne the proportion of copyhold land transfers moving within the family rose from 23 per cent to 37 per cent of all transfers from 1405 to 1607, he writes that 'land was treated more fully as a "commodity" and intra-familial transfers were less important in the fifteenth than even the supposedly "capitalistic" later sixteenth century'.[127] What Dyer does show in his evidence is that the frequency of intra-familial transfer of property is highly sensitive to demographic pressures and to the underlying local demand for land, which varied in value in relation to other factors of production. He presents convincing evidence that the second quarter of the sixteenth century saw a sharp increase in the proportion of family transfers.[128] A concomitant of this was an increasing resort to the use of reversionary arrangements whereby a would-be tenant paid an entry fine to the lord so that the holding would pass to him in the future on the death or surrender of the sitting tenant. This development, along with a rise in fine values and increasing acquisition of copyhold land (which had previously been associated with servile status) by merchants and gentry, convinces Dyer that demand for land waxed and waned, as did the use and indeed strategic significance of inheritance as a means of gaining access to it. Given Dyer's revelation of such dynamic patterns, it is interesting that he should regard 'the relative frequency with which land remained in the family in the early sixteenth century as the *normal* [my emphasis] situation in a peasant society'.[129]

Blanchard, in a fascinating argument, takes a different approach

---

[126] B. Harvey, *Westminster Abbey*, p. 305.
[127] A. Macfarlane, *Origins of English Individualism*, p. 98.
[128] See below, p. 294. For similar evidence of an even earlier recovery of 'family inheritance' after 1470 see Lomas, 'Land and People in South-East Durham', p. 121.
[129] See below, p. 285.

and attempts to distinguish between attitudes and strategies adopted by various social and economic groups in villages in Derbyshire and Somerset with substantial non-agricultural activities. He portrays a rural society in which agriculturalists remain in the ascendancy and do so by adopting what he terms 'defensive' strategies in their land exchanges. Indeed, Blanchard opts for what will most likely be regarded as a controversial interpretation of a particular usage familiar to most who have worked extensively on land transactions in later medieval manorial court rolls. The identification of land described as now in the possession (tenure) of A but formerly held by B (*nuper . . . quondam*) is certainly a feature more evident in the court rolls of the later fourteenth and in particular the fifteenth centuries than for earlier time periods. In his interpretation Blanchard argues that these terms are in fact a means by which a 'collective memory' of the family attachment to a particular holding or plot of land was formalized, and indeed that transactions using such a terminology possessed a distinctly 'non-commercial' status.[130] This is an intriguing suggestion but will require very careful and painstaking data sifting to trace the paths taken by particular units of land between and within families. Indeed, many such units, if identified, may be found to have returned to the families or patrilines which originally discarded them through chance rather than on purpose. In a volatile situation, with land moving frequently and held for only limited time periods, this possibility cannot be discounted. Furthermore, in many manors where the *quondam* description is applied to land we find it definitely passing to the new entrant as if it were a permanent 'alienation'. For instance, in Redgrave in 1433 Robert de Mickelwode transferred one acre with a cottage of the fee of Blannchesene 'quondam Johannis Symmond' with its appurtenances to be held *sibi et heredibus et assignatis suis*.[131] Here there appears to be no suggestion that any other line had claim to the land which if not sold before the incoming tenant's death would pass on to his rightful heirs. However, more detailed analysis of the kind undertaken by Blanchard would be needed to confirm this suggestion.

What Blanchard is able to show with greater assurance is the precarious hold on land exhibited by industrial families in areas of Derbyshire, where mining activities were marginal and declining in the course of the fifteenth century, as compared with the Mendips, where a boom allowed the miners to acquire land with relative ease from the agricultural families. Such an analysis shows that the

---

[130] See below, Chapter 5.   [131] University of Chicago, MS Bacon 35.

volatility of land transfers that has been so readily identified in the court records may have possessed a social specificity that can only be unearthed when the parties' occupations and social standing are fully understood. Blanchard also draws attention to the implications of a cash flow from industrial families to agriculturalists for the character of the latter's internal family relations. The sale or lease of land by many families eased the dependence on family support of the agricultural patriarch, who in consequence lived in later life on a cash income rather than retaining land to be managed within a multi-generational family enterprise. It is interesting, too, that Blanchard should see the penetration of cash into property transfers in these terms, whereas Dyer appears to suggest that the patriarch's position was weakened as the demand for land fell and the older generation could no longer be assured of support from offspring desperate to hold land. The basis for Dyer's argument is the limited appearance of maintenance contracts in the later fourteenth- and fifteenth-century records of the west midland manors upon which his study is based.

While Blanchard in certain of his arguments has disturbed the serenity of what has come to be an orthodoxy surrounding the interpretation of the high rates of turnover of property through transactions involving unrelated persons, and of its meaning for the late medieval family–land bond, Razi provides a brief note that hits hard at the very basis of much of the work undertaken since the early 1960s and is in consequence likely to precipitate a major debate.[132] Most of the work on property transfers of customary or copyhold land in the later medieval English countryside has not been accompanied by detailed genealogical research on the parties to the land transactions. Razi suggests, as has been stressed by most who have worked on these issues, that surnames are an unreliable basis for defining kin relations, and is able to show a significant difference in the proportion of transfers regarded as intra-familial if names alone are used rather than familial linkages perceived through the reconstitution of kinship ties. Razi argues convincingly that kin, rather than coming from within the hamlets or settlements of the large manor of Halesowen, returned from outside to take land based on kin relationships primarily forged through women in a demographic era in which male offspring were in short supply. He undoubtedly forces us to rethink the use of a class of court rolls – limited on detail, lacking continuity, not extending back to the period before the Black Death

[132] See below, Chapter 7.

and deficient in information on marriages – for the purposes of
accurately investigating the family–land bond.

However, even Razi's data do show a decline in the proportions of
kin links through the male line (if surname evidence alone is used),
from 63 to 30 per cent of all inheritances. In Chapter 8 Dr Dyer returns
to present highly convincing evidence of inheritance failures in
manors where very large proportions of holdings went unclaimed on
the holder's death. We have, furthermore, to ask whether the
daughters and their husbands returning to Halesowen to take up
inheritances immigrated permanently or perhaps sublet their land
rather than working it in person. The Halesowen court records show
very few *inter-vivos* transactions, indeed fewer than two per year,
which is a very low annual figure when compared with many
manorial court series that exist from the eastern and south-eastern
counties of England, and very low given the large acreage of this
Worcestershire manor. In fact the question of geographical differences still remains to be resolved, as does the character of lord–tenant
relations in Halesowen when set alongside other communities.[133]
Perhaps the discrepancy between fines paid by kin and those paid by
non-kin on entry into land released by a death may have some
bearing on the higher demand for family land on this manor. Razi
would need, however, to provide harder evidence than he has to date
in support of his argument on the securer nature of tenure in
family-inherited land than in that granted to an incoming tenant by
the lord. In addition he would need to document more thoroughly his
claim that male immigrants who entered Halesowen society through
marriage found a readier acceptance in the offices of village government than did immigrants without kin ties.

Razi's work is characterized by a strong awareness of the presence
of lordship and of the fact that much of the land being transferred is
customary and potentially susceptible to arbitrary influences and
decisions by a landlord. Indeed he is notable in his contribution to
this volume, as well as in his other writings, in drawing attention to
the question of political power in the countryside and its implications
for the family–land relationship among villein tenants or tenants
holding villein land.

iv. Landlord–tenant relations and property devolution

In the context of certain common law views of villeinage associated
with Glanvill, Bracton and Britton, a villein would be portrayed as

[133] Razi, 'Formerly, Land and Village Community', pp. 25–7, considers these points in
greater detail.

without rights to inherit property, for his only heir was his lord.[134] In fact, Bracton's *De Legibus Angliae* expresses the view that an enfeoffment by a lord of his villein *sibi et heredibus suis* implied manumission, for it was a clear recognition that the person concerned possessed heirs.[135] With such thoughts in mind, no doubt, Edmund King has argued convincingly that charters possessed by villeins of Peterborough Abbey in their land dealings in free land with freemen and containing the term *sibi et heredibus* or *sibi et suis* were seen by the Abbey as a threat to its relationship with those villeins.[136] In confiscating these documents, King claims 'the Abbey was asserting the principle that such land lay outside the network of customary tenures, and was held in quite different conditions. It would not be allowed to descend according to the same laws.'[137]

How, then, are we to interpret the instances in the earliest of the surviving manorial court rolls that refer to customary land transferred to individual villeins to be held *sibi et heredibus*? In part, we must consider such a form of words within the context of procedures making for increasing stabilization and standardization of language in the matter of property transfers as the thirteenth century progressed.[138] This terminology was also intimately associated with the procedure of surrender and admission by which the holding was 'returned' to the lord (or more specifically his officer in court), who granted it directly to the incoming tenant. Entry was gained upon payment of a fine and the performance of fealty. It would clearly be wrong to draw the conclusion that the growing incidence of surrender and admittance procedures in the transfer of villein land, along with reference to tenure by the purchaser and his heirs, in the course of the thirteenth century coincided with any substantive change in status before the common law of either the villein or his land. It is better to view surrender and admittance in terms of their strictly economic and legal implications for villein tenure. Certainly, a statement in writing that A had, by payment of a fine, entered into land which he or she and his or her heirs could hold for rents and services 'according to the customs of the manor' was a fuller descrip-

---

[134] The classic interpretation is Sir Paul Vinogradoff, *Villeinage in England* (Oxford, 1892), p. 70. The most up-to-date survey from the vantage point of the *Curia Regis* is P. R. Hyams, *King, Lords and Peasants in Medieval England: the Common Law of Villeinage in the Twelfth and Thirteenth Centuries* (Oxford, 1980).

[135] F. W. Maitland, editor, *Bracton's Note Book* (London, 1887), fos. 24, 270, 194b.

[136] King, *Peterborough Abbey*, p. 101.

[137] *Ibid.*, pp. 101–2.

[138] I have discussed this at some length in 'Some Thoughts on "Hereditary" and "Proprietary" Rights in Land under Customary Law in Thirteenth and Early Fourteenth Century England', *Law and History Review* 1 (1983), pp. 95–128.

tion of the status of the land and the rights in it than would have been found in the majority of transactional entries in the earliest court proceedings. Indeed, the elaboration guaranteed the regulation by lords of the services owed by their tenements in villeinage. Along with receiving fines for licence to alienate or to lease villein holdings, the lords' officials would thereby both record and protect the customs and services restated in writing when land changed 'owner' or 'lessee'. Of course, it would be at this point that the lord would prevent the splintering of the villein holding by declining permission to alienate anything but a 'full land' or complete tenement.

Indeed it cannot be denied that if a lord wished to eject a villein tenant arbitrarily and was powerful enough he could do so with relative impunity.[139] But in the overwhelming majority of cases, seizure of tenements followed from judgements of the court bearing on matters such as the ejected tenant's failure to defend the law in a law suit, to surrender a charter or to secure a licence, for the alienation of customary land without licence or for persistent evasions or arrears of customs, rents and services, for removal of goods and chattels illegally or for refusal to serve on a jury.[140]

We have already referred to the potential of lords to restrain the land transactions of their tenants, for customary rights of inheritance, like other customary rights of holding land, were not absolute. But it would be unwise to treat the relationship between landlord and tenant as a constant and unchanging one, for it was subject to the pressure of people on land and to policies adopted by landlords in the matter of the management of their estates. John Hatcher has reminded us that the point of admission was a potentially profitable moment for the lord. This does have a major implication for a 'market' in unfree land.[141] As Hatcher argues, one prime requirement for the active market in unfree land during the century before the Black Death was that the land so conveyed should have a value over and above the seigneurial burden which went with it.

It was as a result of taking the elements that constituted the seigneurial burden into account in her study of the customary tenants

[139] For an analysis that promotes this view, see Searle, 'Merchet in England'. And for a view that argues that landlords increasingly in the course of the thirteenth century had the power to act without reference to a superior legal agency, see R. H. Hilton, 'Freedom and Villeinage in England', in R. H. Hilton, *Peasants, Knights and Heretics; Studies in Medieval English Social History* (Cambridge, 1976), pp. 185–90.

[140] For a balanced consideration of these reasons for the ejection of villeins from customary land, see J. S. Beckerman, 'Customary Law in Courts in the Thirteenth Century', unpublished University of London Ph.D. thesis, 1972, pp. 173–9.

[141] J. Hatcher, 'English Serfdom and Villeinage: Towards a Reassessment', *Past and Present* 90 (1981), p. 21.

of Westminster Abbey that Barbara Harvey drew the conclusion that in aggregate they created 'a very effective antidote to the fragmentation of customary holdings'.[142] She argues a complex case, exemplary in representing a particular school of thought concerning the manner in which seigneurial policy dictates peasant behaviour, by drawing attention to the hostility of the monks of Westminster towards fragmentation, because of their conception of the holding in its entirety as the necessary portion of a dependent household and their refusal to involve themselves in the time consuming process of collecting rents and administering services from divided holdings. She also asserts that the conditions of tenure on their estates ensured that the vendors in transactions would derive little profit from the deal. For, if the purchaser were not asked for a higher entry fine or licence fee than the tenant who took customary land by inheritance (an argument that we have already detected in Razi's account of the perduring strength of intra-familial property devolution in fourteenth-century Halesowen), there is certainly nothing to suggest that he paid less. These cumulative charges, Harvey considers, would have made the total yield from the land insufficient to bring anything other than very low rewards for any potential buyer or seller.[143]

Therefore, the large size of units (brought about by the unwillingness of the monks to permit fragmentation), low capital resources of potential purchasers and high costs of land in relation to yield combined to thwart an active market in customary properties. Harvey concludes her argument by stating that 'as a rule the destination of substantial holdings in the manors of Westminster Abbey was decided outside the nexus of market transactions . . . only small amounts (mainly of assarted and freeland) were transacted in ways that were not detrimental to the virgated structure of holdings that "family and feudal sentiment" both desired to uphold'.[144]

Yet Harvey's views may not possess the status of representing the modal form of landlord policy in relation to the properties of their customary tenants in medieval England. The papers in this volume by Campbell, Smith and Ravensdale provide clear evidence of very active markets in customary land on manors in estates which, as in the case of the Benedictine Abbeys of Crowland and Bury St Edmunds, exacted rents and services that compare with those paid by the Westminster villeins.[145] It has been argued more generally that under the conditions of demographic growth before the early fourteenth century the 'value' of customary land exceeded the charges

[142] Harvey, *Westminster Abbey*, p. 302.   [143] *Ibid.*, pp. 302–3.
[144] *Ibid.*, p. 317.   [145] See Smith, 'Some Thoughts', p. 118.

upon it, and in the case of Redgrave (considered in detail in Chapter 3) this discrepancy has been shown to have been very large.[146]

At Coltishall the proliferation (within the context of an active market in small pieces of land) of a large body of smallholders who would have created a valuable supply of working hands for demesne farms cropped with very high levels of labour input provided a quite different situation in the matter of landlord–tenant relations from that described by Harvey.[147] At Redgrave, where demesne farming was not practised with the intensity found in eastern Norfolk, a concern with the problems stemming from the fragmentation of rent and service rendering holdings was set aside as the income from licensing the exchange of *inter-vivos* transfers of land burgeoned to become a major element in manorial revenue when income from customary rents and services stagnated in the inflationary conditions of the thirteenth and early fourteenth centuries.[148] Here, perhaps corroborating one of Harvey's arguments, a high proportion of services was not rendered in kind but was temporarily commuted to cash surrenders.[149] Here too, contrary to some views on the reasons for limited wealth accumulation, there seems to have been no prohibition by the landlord on the acquisition by individuals of more than one holding.[150]

Of course, Coltishall and Redgrave had in common a custom of partible inheritance on villein land which may have helped to create property units of a size highly conducive to an active land market. It is nonetheless difficult to identify the causal relationships between the presence of partibility and an active land market. One effect of the

---

[146] *Ibid.*, pp. 118–19.

[147] See Campbell, 'Agricultural Progress', pp. 38–9.

[148] Smith 'Some Thoughts', pp. 116–17.

[149] When the first surviving account rolls become available for Redgrave in the 1320s they show approximately 50 per cent of services 'sold back' to the tenants. See University of Chicago, MSS Bacon 325 and 326. For example Williamson also notes that at Sedgeford the services owed by the tenants were very light in relation to the labour needs of the large, 800-acre demesne, and suggests that labour hired in the 5 weeks of harvest could include as many as 74 workers. In this context the efficient collection of services was not a vital factor in the staffing of the demesne farm labour force which may have helped to reduce the landlord's wish to thwart the fragmentation of the service rendering unit. See Williamson, 'Peasant Holdings in Medieval Norfolk', pp. 253–4. King, too, notes a greater degree of fragmentation of tenant properties on manors further from Peterborough Abbey where services were commuted. See King, *Peterborough Abbey*, p. 119.

[150] It would be unwise to exaggerate this point as Williamson shows a very active market in 'fragments' even though in Sedgeford villeins were barred from holding more than one villein 'tenement' of whatever size. For some discussion of limitations on multiple tenancies, see Postan, *Carte Nativorum*, p. xxxiii and J. A. Raftis, *Tenure and Mobility*, pp. 68–9.

market in land would be to mitigate the erosional influence of partible inheritance on the fragmentation of holdings, since 'surplus' sons (products of the 'demographic lottery') could supplement that inheritance by purchasing 'surplus' land left by men dying heirless, or by marrying into familes where there was no heir but an heiress. The simplifications encountered in this *ceteris paribus* style of argument do cause problems; for example, it would be wrong to assume that marriages were not socially specific. For wealthy heiresses might well tend to marry relatively wealthy heirs or non-heirs with other financial resources. A different assessment of the impact of partible inheritance would arise in stressing the way in which it so divided holdings to levels below which they were no longer profitable or capable of sustaining a farm family that it led to a market in property intended to reconstitute more viable units. This market could take place within the family and effectively produce an end result equivalent to *de facto* 'impartibility'.[151] If, however, the market went beyond the kin group the end results would be less predictable and might well help to bring about greater social differentiation, as was certainly evident in late thirteenth-century Redgrave.[152] In either of the situations we have considered above developments could have produced very substantial financial advantages for the seigneur. In fact, Williamson has actually documented what appears as a shift from impartible to partible inheritance in the Norfolk manor of Gressenhall at some point in the thirteenth century, the jury of trial in a land dispute reporting that the lord's seneschal *vellet habere plures tenentes*.[153]

The above instances should remind us that 'feudal and family sentiment' might not always exist in unison, and they suggest, furthermore, the probability of considerable flexibility in 'customs' of inheritance. Ravensdale's evidence concerning widowed property holders in Cottenham shows that, although it was the 'custom' that a widow forfeited her holding if she remarried, in the early fourteenth century over 51 per cent of recorded marriages in that manor involved the remarriage of widows with their land.[154] The lord without a doubt

---

[151] See Smith, below, pp. 181–2 and his references to the work of Williamson on Gressenhall and of Dodwell on East Anglia more generally.
[152] It should be stressed that it is not inevitable that a market in properties outside the kin group will lead to increasing social differentiation. Campbell's study of Coltishall suggests a particularly active market in which fragmentation led to what appears to have been a general decline in holding size as tenancies proliferated under conditions of demographic expansion.
[153] This is discussed in Smith, 'Some Thoughts', pp. 121–2.
[154] See Ravensdale, *infra*, pp. 220–1, and, for further discussion of this, Smith, 'Hypothèse sur la nuptialité', pp. 124–7.

benefited from the additional revenue brought by the high entry fines paid by grooms in these marriages, rather being concerned to derive income from the marital link itself and the access to land that it gave than deliberately inducing high fertility to sustain the ranks of a corvée labour force. Yet that would not have been the outcome if women had been unable to retain property in their own right, and cannot therefore be attributed solely to the character of rural class relations. Worthy of our attention is the fact that marital access to these widows was confined primarily to the sons of the wealthier members of the Cottenham tenantry, a factor helping to prevent the movement of land down the social scale in a resource-scarce situation.[155] The lord's freedom to act in these circumstances was strictly limited by the economic climate, for with declining property values in the second half of the fourteenth century widow remarriage diminished and, in outward appearances at least, the old 'custom' reasserted itself.

Of course, much of our discussion confirms the views of those who are critical of approaches to rural family behaviour that fail to introduce some consideration of the harsh realities of political power. But it is equally important to retain an awareness of the subtle differences that motivate the varying reactions of different groups in rural society to the changing character of the relations between landlords and tenants, which themselves are continuously mediated through the interstices of a broader socio-cultural mesh.[156]

v. Some issues in the family cycle of the propertyless or property-deficient

It was their dependence on their own labour and their lack of any other material resources that served to define the poor in England for much of the time period which the essays in this volume cover. Given this absence of property, we can in a stylized, theoretical fashion consider their family economies in terms of the surpluses and deficits that accrued as their families developed.[157] To do this we are

---

[155] Clearly, this does have implications for the 'freedom of action' of widows discussed by Chaytor, 'Household and Kinship', pp. 43–4. But see the remarks of Houston and Smith, 'A New Approach', pp. 124–5.

[156] This seems to be a dimension noticeable for its absence in R. Brenner's treatment of landlord–tenant relationships in both 'Agrarian Class Structure and Economic Development in Pre-Industrial Europe', *Past and Present* 70 (1976), pp. 30–75 and 'The Agrarian Roots of European Capitalism' *Past and Present* 97 (1982), pp. 16–113. Likewise, Creighton, 'Family, Property', prefers to ignore it.

[157] See, for example, the profiles of consumption and production in E. Mueller, 'The Economic Value of Children in Peasant Agriculture' in R. G. Ridker, editor, *Population and Development* (Baltimore, Md, 1976), pp. 98–153.

unfortunately dependent upon the use of a standard set of age schedules of production and consumption that have been computed by economists working on labour activities in agrarian economies of the present day. For this reason their status is purely illustrative as they are intended only to elucidate certain fundamental characteristics that are likely to hold true given the particular demographic regime to which they are related.[158]

In our hypothetical family in Table 1.9 any individual's production and consumption level is determined as a function of age, sex and (in the case of women) marital status. An adult male has a surplus of production to consumption equivalent to +.97 units until age 54, but not going into deficit until age 65 years. Married women are assumed never to be in surplus, consuming more than they produce (−.21 units until 55 years and thereafter worsening), insofar as their economic role is assumed to be largely 'supportive' rather than 'productive' within the family economy.[159] Children of either sex remain in deficit until age fifteen when they begin rapidly to produce more than they consume.[160] This particular exercise is intended to depict the state of the family economy at a particular point in time and additionally to consider its cumulative experience in the course of its development cycle. The stylized couple in Table 1.9 marry at 27 years when they have between them a surplus of +.76 units (husband +.97 and wife −.21). This surplus could be employed to sustain themselves and two children under five years of age. But by the time the third child has reached two years of age (assuming children come along at three-year intervals) the offspring's combined deficit reaches

---

[158] This represents only one of a number of hypothetical 'family economies' that have been modelled at the SSRC Cambridge Group for the History of Population and Social Structure using different marriage ages and ages of leaving home, by Dr R. S. Schofield with the aid of the KIDCOST computer program.

[159] Of course this may be far too restrictive, in that much of the evidence we have for the households of the poor suggests a considerable labour force participation level of women in such groups. For an interesting multivariate anlaysis of these issues see, O. Saito, 'Labour Supply Behaviour of the Poor in the English Industrial Revolution', *The Journal of European Economic History* 10 (1981), pp. 633–51, indicating that in the matter of female participation rates 'necessity outweighed opportunity' (p. 646).

[160] This remains a controversial subject even in analysis of present-day situations, where measurements in theory should be easier. A useful summary of received opinions is to be found in M. Cain, 'Perspectives on Family and Fertility in Developing Countries', *Population Studies* 36 (1982), pp. 159–76, reassuring for our model where he states: 'the slowly accumulating evidence on child labour suggests that at least as long as children are under the direct control of their parents (the period during which they are actually members of their parents' household) the product of their labour does not compensate for the cost of their cumulative consumption' (p. 164).

Table 1.9. *A hypothetical family economy based on its labour production and consumption**

| | | | Children | | | | | | | |
Age	Husband	Wife	1	2	3	4	All	Cumulation	Duration	Age
27	+.97	−.21					+.76	+.76	0	27
28	+.97	−.21	+.00				+.76	+1.52	1	28
29	+.97	−.21	−.25				+.51	+2.03	2	29
30	+.97	−.21	−.29				+.47	+2.50	3	30
31	+.97	−.21	−.32	+.00			+.43	+2.93	4	31
32	+.97	−.21	−.36	−.25			+.14	+3.07	5	32
33	+.97	−.21	−.40	−.29			+.06	+3.14	6	33
34	+.97	−.21	−.44	−.32	+.00		−.01	+3.13	7	34
35	+.97	−.21	−.48	−.36	−.25		−.34	+2.79	8	35
36	+.97	−.21	−.51	−.40	−.29		−.45	+2.34	9	36
37	+.97	−.21	−.57	−.44	−.32	+.00	−.58	+1.76	10	37
38	+.97	−.21	−.57	−.48	−.36	−.25	−.91	+.85	11	38
39	+.97	−.21	−.54	−.51	−.40	−.29	−.99	−.13	12	39
40	+.97	−.21	−.53	−.57	−.44	−.32	−1.10	−1.24	13	40
41	+.97	−.21	−.40	−.57	−.48	−.36	−1.06	−2.30	14	41
42	+.97	−.21	−.33	−.54	−.51	−.40	−.20	−3.32	15	42
43	+.97	−.21	−.07	−.53	−.57	−.44	−.85	−4.18	16	43
44	+.97	−.21	+.03	−.40	−.57	−.48	−.67	−4.85	17	44
45	+.97	−.21	+.12	−.33	−.54	−.51	+.50	−5.43	18	45
46	+.97	−.21	+.22	−.07	−.53	−.57	−.19	−5.54	19	46
47	+.97	−.21	+.32	+.03	−.40	−.57	+.13	−5.40	20	47
48	+.97	−.21		+.12	−.33	−.54	+.02	−5.38	21	48
49	+.97	−.21		+.22	−.07	−.53	+.38	−5.01	22	49
50	+.97	−.21		+.32	+.03	−.40	+.70	−4.31	23	50
51	+.97	−.21			+.12	−.33	+.55	−3.75	24	51
52	+.97	−.21			+.22	−.07	+.90	−2.85	25	52
53	+.97	−.21			+.32	+.03	+1.11	−1.74	26	53
54	+.97	−.21				+.12	+.88	−.86	27	54
55	+.88	−.23				+.22	+.86	+.01	28	55
56	+.79	−.26				+.32	+.86	+.86	29	56
57	+.70	−.28					+.42	+1.28	30	57
58	+.61	−.30					+.31	+1.60	31	58
59	+.52	−.32					+.20	+1.79	32	59
60	+.43	−.35					+.09	+1.88	33	60
61	+.35	−.37					−.02	+1.86	34	61
62	+.26	−.39					−.14	+1.72	35	62
63	+.17	−.42					−.25	+1.47	36	63
64	+.08	−.44					−.36	+1.11	37	64
65	−.01	−.46					−.47	+.64	38	65
66	−.01	−.46					−.47	+.17	39	66
67	−.01	−.46					−.47	−.31	40	67
68	−.01	−.46					−.47	−.78	41	68
69	−.01	−.46					−.47	−1.25	42	69

Assumptions
Age at marriage: 27
Children are of *combined* sex, and leave home at age 19

*For assumptions used in the allocation of age-specific levels of production and consumption, see pp. 68–9.

−1.09 units, so the family economy is now in deficit to the tune of −.34 units. By the time the fourth child reaches two years of age, the first-born child is ten and the combined children's deficit stands at −1.66 units. The creation of a deficit in the seventh year of marriage of course allows for no infant mortality. Assuming no further mortality, the deficit grows and remains serious until the eighteenth year of marriage, when the first-born begins to make a significant contribution to the family economy. The four-child family confronts its worst situation in its fourteenth year of existence, when the husband and wife are in their early forties. Of course, in aggregate across a large number of such families the situation is more favourable, as some infants and children do die. Nonetheless the basic features of this model do apply, for from seven to nine years after marriage the family economy goes into deficit with an excess of *current* consumption over production. It is noteworthy too that circumstances deteriorate again in the married couple's sixties.

Obviously, the deficits and the surpluses of individual families would vary depending upon the chance effects of the 'demographic lottery'. In addition, the loss of a father, especially if the death occurred in his forties when the children were all still largely negative in their impact on the family earnings, would have a marked effect on the household's viability, its wealth being largely dependent upon the labour input of its members. There are nonetheless some possible remedies that can be adopted in response to what outwardly seems a desperate situation. There are periods of considerable cumulative surplus in the early years of marriage and again in the couple's fifties. Of course, much would depend on whether the surpluses were consumed, saved or invested, or whether indeed they were appropriated by some extra-familial agency.

In the model in Table 1.9 it is assumed that children left home at nineteen years of age. However, on the basis of evidence collected to date, this age of departure is known to be variable and that used in the model may well over-state the age at which the children of labourers in particular departed from their natal households.[161] Indeed it would have been in the interest of household economy to ensure departure of the first child at age ten, when the fourth child had arrived to exacerbate the family income deficit further. Unques-

---

[161] See Wall below, Chapter 14, which provides some information to support a 'high' rather than 'early' age of leaving home. However, his evidence does appear to suggest that children of labourers are less likely to have been retained than other groups, especially those with substantial property. Note, too, that the age at which pauper children were apprenticed was relatively low and varied between 12 and 14 years. See Newman-Brown, below, pp. 418–19.

tionably, this model provides a ready explanation for a relatively early departure of children from the household, insofar as it might appear difficult to understand why children should be expelled from their parents' household just when their labour power was yielding a surplus in output over consumption.[162]

Bearing in mind that departing children could as individuals have had a net income surplus, it is interesting to establish whether any of that surplus was transferred back into the parental household. On this point we are currently ill-informed. Ann Kussmaul, in her comprehensive study of farm servants in early modern England, assumes that servant stipends formed a basis for savings which they would use to set up their own households on leaving service to marry.[163] Some servants might have saved enough to stock a small farm, but most would aspire to becoming nothing better than prosperous cottagers.[164] Kussmaul considers the possibility of regular remittances to parents only in the case of a Buckinghamshire servant Joseph Mayett, whose diary records the displeasure of his peers in buying his ale as he 'had no money'.[165] She knows also that in certain cases young servants were paid only small amounts which were sent home by their employers.[166] But older, better remunerated servants were much more likely to have been paid personally by their employers than through parents. Indeed, in many cases 'forced savings' seem to have been a logical possible outcome for servants, in that payment was frequently made annually and some servants collected no annual wages until they finally left their masters' service.[167] Farm service does not appear to have been an 'institution' conducive to the large-scale movement of income from children to parents but should be seen, as Kussmaul suggests, in the case of the poor rather as a means of 'getting their feet under somebody else's table'.[168]

In fact, this feature of parent–child relationships is compatible with certain other aspects of kin contacts as reflected in the evidence in Wrightson's paper in this volume, which tends to suggests that kin relations, especially of a lineal kind, were not of great functional significance.[169] In fact, he suggests they took a second place to

---

[162] Certainly this represents a more realistic explanation than does a means of 'incest avoidance'. For this view see A. Macfarlane, *The Family Life of Ralph Josselin. A Seventeenth Century Clergyman* (Cambridge, 1970), p. 205.

[163] Kussmaul, *Servants in Husbandry*, pp. 79–80.

[164] *Ibid.*, p. 82.   [165] *Ibid.*, pp. 85–93.

[166] *Ibid.*, p. 76.   [167] *Ibid.*, p. 39.   [168] *Ibid.*, pp. 75–6.

[169] See below, pp. 324–9. Also his valuable summary of evidence for the period 1580–1680 in his *English Society 1580–1680* (London, 1982), pp. 51–7.

relations of an altruistic character among neighbours. This same relationship is implied within the role played by a wider group referred to by Laslett as the 'collectivity'.[170] Indeed, Laslett argues that the kinship system and its rules of household formation gave rise to 'hardships' – brought on by the death of a spouse, unemployment, sickness or senility – such that households found it difficult to be economically self-sufficient even though their formation rules insisted that couples should be so. It is to the investigation of this problem that the papers of Wales and Newman-Brown are explicitly directed, and many of the issues raised by Holderness' study of widows have a more than tangential bearing on this matter. It is also an issue that Lesthaeghe has recognized as of central importance throughout large parts of pre-industrial western Europe, where land did not fall under lineage supervision but could be appropriated by individuals or individual nuclear families.[171] In consequence, individual wealth and inheritance predominated and also gave rise to the presence in that region of persons who were propertyless. An aspect of this 'privatization' of resources is that extended kinship solidarity and the cushioning of risk within broad kin groups were to some extent replaced by what Lesthaeghe refers to as forms of 'communal risk devolution'.[172] In other words, rather than the kin group being used a a hedge against risk, greater reliance was placed upon neighbours, and community-organized groups such as gilds or communally managed funds from charitable benefactions.[173]

Wales in his paper has indirectly identified many of the so-called family 'hardships' that are potentially present among the propertyless families of the kind modelled in Table 1.9, and has provided many insights into the means by which 'communal risk devolution' worked in seventeenth-century Norfolk. Wales draws attention to the way contemporaries were aware of these 'hardships' produced by the interaction of 'chance' and the 'high risk' phases of the life-cycle. Arthington, for instance, writing in the late sixteenth century, identified an intermediate category of persons located between 'the impotent poor' and 'such as may earn their whole maintenance'. These were those 'poore not able to live by their labour, and yett fitte

---

[170] P. Laslett, 'Family and Collectivity', *Sociology and Social Research* 63 (1979), pp. 432–42.

[171] R. Lesthaeghe, 'On the Social Control of Human Reproduction', *Population and Development Review* 6 (1980), p. 531.

[172] *Ibid.*, p. 532.

[173] Contrast systems of 'communal risk sharing' with the system in which the community fulfils none of these tasks in M. Cain, 'Risk and Fertility in India and Bangladesh', *Population and Development Review* 7 (1981), pp. 435–74.

and willing to take paines'.[174] Table 1.9 contains them all, identifiable as they are by the deficits between their production and consumption; they included (1) orphan children under seven, (2) 'such as be overcharged with children having nothing to maintain them but their hand labour', and (3) 'such as fall into decay in their works, by reasons of their years, weakness or infirmities'. These intermediate groups were, in Arthington's view, worthy of relief 'in part, as their necessity shall require'. Category 2 suggests an awareness that a large number of children brought few economic advantages to their parents, and category 3 indicates that ageing and increased poverty were to be seen as synonymous.

Historians of Tudor and Stuart poverty have frequently drawn our attention to the notion of the poor comprising two distinct groups:[175] those in need of disciplining, the 'able-bodies rogues', on the one hand; and the 'deserving poor', those unable to work, the elderly, the chronically sick and the young children in large families, on the other. But why did the kin group not deal, or at least attempt to deal, with those who had the potential of becoming part of the 'deserving poor'? We might deduce that kin were of fundamental significance as a means of support from reading the Elizabethan Poor Act, which stated that 'the children of every poor old, blind lame and impotent person . . . shall at their *own* [my emphasis] charges relieve and maintain every such poor person'.[176] We might expect in consequence a flow of resources within the family to cope with the potential hardships.

Our discussion of agrarian service provides strong suggestions that this material aid may have not been forthcoming or was of marginal assistance in reducing the costs of a household rather than adding to its income. In fact, a nuptiality regime with marriage in the middle to late twenties, certainly applying throughout most of the period relevant to this discussion, was not an optimal means of dealing with the problem of direct support of parents by their own offspring (especially if these offspring were intent upon forming neo-local and economically 'self-sufficient' households), because the married children would frequently find themselves entering their first family 'deficit' phase between approximately 35 and 45, in fact reaching their peak family deficits just as their parents were entering their own second 'deficit' period in their late sixties (see Table 1.9). Wales'

174 See Wales, below, pp. 351–404.
175 See, for instance, P. Slack, 'Poverty and Politics in Salisbury 1597–1666', in P. Clark and P. Slack, editors, *Crisis and Order in English Towns 1500–1700* (London, 1972), pp. 164–5.
176 E. M. Leonard, *The Early History of English Poor Relief* (Cambridge, 1900), pp. 133–4.

analysis shows that by the second half of the seventeenth century there were two patterns, detectable from the accounts of the Norfolk Overseers of the Poor, in the payment of those on regular relief: an 'early peak' (equivalent to the first deficit period in Table 1.9), concerning for the most part those pushed onto relief by the burden of young children, and a 'second phase' characterized by a gradual rise in payments for the ageing poor as their ability to earn their own keep by their own labour declined with the passing years. In fact, he estimates that by the late seventeenth century an ageing pauper receiving 1s per week was almost totally dependent upon the parish.[177]

We are fortunate in having some data on the social attributes of the 'poor' from certain urban settlements in the late sixteenth and early seventeenth centuries that suggest very clearly that poverty in early modern England had three main phases. The age characteristics of the poor in these populations are plotted in Figure 1.5.[178] In the first phase we find persons in childhood and adolescence, in effect those in the life-cycle phase prior to departure from the parental household for service or apprenticeship, or those who were 'parentally deprived'. In Warwick, Norwich, Ipswich and Salisbury the proportion of the poor aged from one to fifteen was consistently as high as or higher than the proportion this age group constituted in the total population of these settlements or indeed in the nation as a whole. The second phase of poverty occurred roughly from ages thirty through fifty and involved those persons who were married and had

---

[177] Poor relief to elderly widows of approximately £3 per annum in relation to annual incomes of £15 seems to have been quite common in the late seventeenth century. See the estimate of labourers' wages in K. Wrightson and D. Levine, *Poverty and Piety in an English Village: Terling, 1525–1700* (London, 1979), pp. 40–1. For a continuity in the above relationship, see the calculations for certain early nineteenth-century communities where weekly pensions to the elderly were of the order of 2s 6d to 3s when weekly labouring wages were 8s to 9s, in D. Thomson, 'Provision for the Elderly in England 1830–1908', unpublished University of Cambridge Ph.D. thesis, 1980.

[178] The sources for Figure 1.5 are: J. F. Pound, editor, *The Norwich Census of the Poor, 1570*, Norwich Record Society xl (1971), pp. 95–6; T. Kemp, editor, *The Book of John Fisher, 1580–1588* (Warwick, n.d.), pp. 165–72; J. Webb, editor, *Poor Relief in Elizabethan Ipswich*, Suffolk Record Society ix, (Ipswich, 1966) pp. 122–40; P. Slack, editor, *Poverty in Early Stuart Salisbury*, Wiltshire Record Society xxxi (Devizes, 1975), pp. 75–80. Evidence on the age structures of Ealing and Chivers Coton is from workings in the files of the SSRC Cambridge Group. National age structures for 1596 and 1686 come from E. A. Wrigley and R. S. Schofield, *The Population History of England 1541–1871: A Reconstruction* (London, 1981), Table A3.1, p. 528. It should be noted that part of this material has already been presented in an age-specific fashion in A. L. Beier, 'The Social Problems of an Elizabethan Country Town: Warwick, 1580–90', in P. Clark, editor, *Country Towns in Pre-Industrial England* (Leicester, 1981), p. 63.

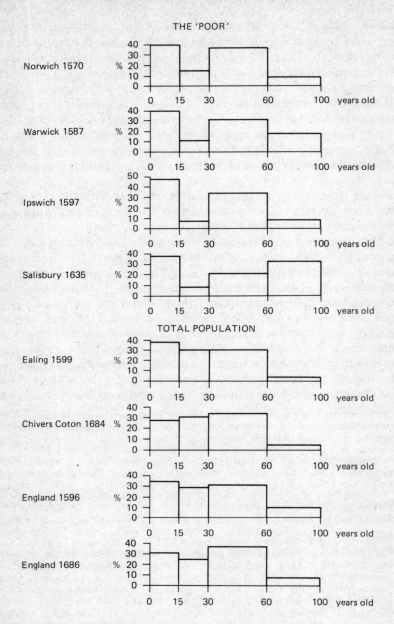

Figure 1.5. The age structures of total and 'poor' populations of sixteenth- and seventeenth-century England compared

children living at home. Also constituting a large proportion of this group were widows left with their children – a particularly vulnerable group. For instance, in Norwich almost two-thirds of the women, many of whom were widows, were engaged in spinning and only 14 per cent had no occupation. At the same time, 330 of the children aged four to twenty (50 per cent) helped to supplement, although inadequately, the earnings of their elders, with spinning and weaving appearing as their principal activities.[179] The participation of as many persons as possible as contributors to the family income pool is highly characteristic of individuals in both of these phases of the life-cycle among the poor. The third stage was old age, for the old were more numerous among the poor than in the populations of individual settlements or in the national population at large. In fact the old were far more likely to have featured among the 'poor' than any other age group of the population. Furthermore, poor women over sixty years of age outnumbered poor men by more than two to one. The only extended period of relief from 'poverty' as defined by the census takers was in late adolescence and early adulthood (i.e. age group 15 to 35), when individuals from these sections of society were most likely to be in the households of the wealthy elements of the population or as yet not burdened with costly offspring.

That these were not just urban features is confirmed by the researches of Wales on Cawston, Norfolk, and of Newman-Brown on Aldenham, Hertfordshire. Wales shows that in Cawston in 1601 the urban 'poverty' pattern is repeated with a notable preponderance in the identified pauper population of the aged and widowed with young children. Furthermore, some protection against life-cycle poverty was clearly given by the possession of a little property (in this case, a cottage and a cow). Out of 97 householders in Cawston considered too poor to pay the poor rates, nineteen were in receipt of regular relief, eight were aged (six of them widows), six were widowed with children and five were male-headed families over-burdened with children. What these findings seem to suggest is that substantial support for the aged came from the 'community'. This is another way of stating (to use the language of the sociologists) that the aged lived in a structurally dependent relationship to society at large.[180] The contribution to this volume by Wales is interesting not

---

[179] Pound, editor, *Norwich Census*, p. 17.
[180] See the use of this term with little awareness of the true historical sociology of the elderly in English society by a prominent sociologist, P. Townsend, 'The Structured Dependency of the Elderly: A Creation of Social Policy in the Twentieth Century', *Ageing and Society* 1 (1981), pp. 5–28.

only for what it says about the poor of Cawston but for its remarks about those individuals exempted from hearth tax payments on account of their poverty. Over one-quarter of the exempt poor were women. What is particularly striking is that women householders generally formed a much higher proportion of the poor than they did of tax payers. In this, the late seventeenth-century evidence is no different from that exhibited by the later sixteenth-century urban census of the poor in identifying both the most vulnerable sex and the most vulnerable marital status. For instance, P. and J. Clark in their recent discussion of the 1563 census of the outer and most definitely poorer parishes of Canterbury state that 'there can be little question who came last in the poverty stakes: the widow. More than half of those enumerated in the 1563 census were classed as poor or impotent in some way – aged or lame.'[181]

Wales' work, still in progress, of collating the exemption certificates of the Hearth Taxes, parish registers and overseers books in selected Norfolk parishes suggests ample evidence of aged parish paupers who almost certainly had adult children alive at the time either in the parish or outside but, despite these living kin, were dependent upon parish relief. In his study of Aldenham relief recipients Newman-Brown finds that, of the identifiable widows believed to be resident in the parish from 1650 to 1680, 40% were in receipt of a regular pension. Many, too, had children married and resident in the parish while relief was received. We are reminded in these patterns by behaviour, if not identical, to which Laslett drew our attention when writing of the Nottinghamshire village of Clayworth in 1676 and 1688.[182] He remarked on one Francis Bacon, a cooper, his wife Joan and their children Nicholas, Anne and Francis who together in 1676 constituted an independent household. Such a household was formed by the family of Nicholas Bacon, cooper the son, in 1688; it included Nicholas, his wife (whom he married in 1686 after his father died), and two children by her former husband. Apparently, Nicholas the son had turned out his mother Joan and his sister Anne when he became head of the household, for by 1688 they were both found in the parish institution for the poor.

Of course, in all of this discussion, particularly of the later seventeenth century, the community remains at the centre of our analysis. In the late seventeenth-century communities considered by our

---

[181] P. A. Clark and J. G. Clark, 'The Social Economy of the Canterbury Suburbs: The Evidence of the Census of 1563', A. Detsicas and N. Yates, editors, *Studies in Modern Kentish History* (Maidstone, 1983), pp. 65–86.
[182] Laslett, *Family Life and Illicit Love*, pp. 59–60.

authors there is evidence of informal and neighbourly help, but there is no doubt that many elderly people spent their years as dependents of the parish whether they had adult children or not. Neighbourly support might in reality mean the parish paying a neighbour to look after a pauper relative – hence the rather high proportion of elderly 'lodgers' in the households of the villages and small towns of early modern England. In fact, elderly persons who were either single or widowed were, from the surviving evidence in early modern censuses of Ealing, Chivers Coton, Stoke-on-Trent, Corfe Castle and Ardleigh, as likely to be living with others as lodgers as with their kin.[183] The financing of a system of social welfare to buttress households whose self-sufficiency was impaired required a local revenue gathering and redistributional system of considerable sophistication and implied transfers of wealth within the community taxation system. In fact, payment of rates for at least property holders would have been one means by which the 'surpluses' identified in our hypothetical family in Table 1.9 were 'appropriated' for the community fund. Rarely, if ever, was a majority of local inhabitants payers of the parish rate and a clear minority was responsible for providing the bulk of the funds with which the overseers undertook their work. In Aldenham between 1630 and 1680 rarely were more than 45 per cent of the householders contributing to the fund. In Warwick, when in 1582 a poor rate was levied, one in nine families was given relief. The survey identified four groups in the town's population: (1) those paying poor rates, (2) those maintaining themselves and unable to help others, (3) those ready to decay into poverty, and (4) those on relief (constituting 42 out of 373 households).[184] In 1586, after a harvest failure, a census of the poor shows for the town relief being given to 93 rather than 42 households: i.e. group three had slipped to join group four. In fact, only 26.5 per cent of households were in group one,[185] and groups three and four rose to be in excess of one-third of the total in difficult periods. Here as in Aldenham a large group existed in the 'middle ground'; and, lest it be thought that the system of support involved only the propertyless poor, it should be noted that those in the middle ground frequently did not pay into the fund. For it is frequently possible in this community to observe persons excused from rate payments while they contended with

---

[183] Laslett, *Family Life and Illicit Love*, pp. 204–5.
[184] See Kemp, editor, *Book of John Fisher*, pp. 81–94.
[185] *Ibid.*, pp. 93–4 and 165–72. Note, however, the similarity in the 'categories' used in the Warwick census to those discussed by Wales in the Cawston listing of 1601 and, indeed, to those recognized by Arthington. See Wales, below, pp. 368–75.

life-cycle-determined 'hardships'. For example, Edward Harris, who in 1651 was aged 46 and had a wife and five children of ages seventeen, fifteen, thirteen, seven and five, was given back sums equivalent to rates paid on his assessment and between 1654 and 1658 was not assessed at all. After 1658, when his youngest and oldest children were twelve and 24 respectively, he returned to the assessment roll.[186] Obviously, the affluent would have been likely to contribute to the communal fund throughout their life-cycles, while the 'middling sorts' might well have contributed early in their marriages and again in later middle age (see again Table 1.9). As a system, that in operation in Aldenham appears to have rested on the principle that those with few family dependents who were economically active gave to those with costly dependents or those who were economically inactive. In terms of the highly stylized features of Table 1.9 the system was concerned with how the community mobilized the surpluses to deal with deficits in the course of the life-cycle.

It is evident that the surpluses were not generally employed to strengthen or intensify kin links but were drawn instead into the communal fund. Indeed, the 'surpluses' were considerable in early modern English society, given its generally favourable age structure. For rarely at any point in the period 1550–1850 were there more than 800 aged under fourteen or over sixty years for every 1,000 aged between fifteen and 59. In the later seventeenth century, when those over 60 years of age made up 10 per cent of the population (and in areas of rural outmigration were a much higher proportion), the ratio of those aged between 25 and 59 to those aged sixty and over was 4:1 and was helped by the low numbers of children that stemmed from the depressed nuptiality at that time.[187] Indeed in this age structure, at periods when the elderly were a relatively large burden, children were numerically far less burdensome, and the elderly, who generally lived in their own households (Laslett's case of Nicholas Bacon's mother, notwithstanding), could be easily cared for.[188]

Yet it might appear questionable to treat the pattern in the later seventeenth century as if it were typical of the early modern English means of dealing with the life-cycle crises or hardships of the poor. For Wales appears to suggest that over the course of the sixteenth and seventeenth centuries poor relief became more structured and more

---

[186] See below, pp. 415–16.

[187] Wrigley and Schofield, *Population History*, pp. 443–50.

[188] Note Malthus' commitment to this principle, not always appreciated by those who have a distorted view of his attitude to the Old Poor Law. See William Otter, 'Memoir of Robert Malthus (1816)' (published with the posthumous second edition of Malthus' *Principles of Political Economy* (London, 1836), pp. xxi–xxii).

centred on the parish.[189] Of course this finding is not totally novel, although the evidence Wales brings to bear on the nature of parish relief – who was receiving and in what amounts, and the extent to which that relief constituted the prime, indeed the sole, form of support – represents a major step forward.[190]

Others, such as Hill and Thomas, see these changes as both symptomatic and a product of a decline in community relations.[191] Lawrence Stone takes this further and argues that the rise of parish financed and distributed relief 'effectively relieved the kin and also the conjugal family, of much of its responsibility for relief of the poor and the sick'.[192] These views do appear less convincing when placed in a broader temporal context, although with the limited research into these matters it is surprising that historians have felt able to make statements with such assurance about the extent of sixteenth- and seventeenth-century changes from what went before.

It would perhaps be easier to understand some of the developments in the second half of the sixteenth and early seventeenth centuries if we consider first the life-cycle pattern of labour affecting many individuals in the later seventeenth century. Kussmaul presents convincing evidence to suggest that agrarian servants had risen quite markedly as a proportion of the farm labour force at this period.[193] Wales' evidence appears to suggest that the parish was taking an increasing and overwhelmingly dominant role in the care of those who no longer laboured or who did so in only limited ways as they aged. In fact 'entry' into and 'exit' from the rural labour force was, for an increasing number of persons, accomplished through two regulatory 'institutions'. In certain senses both these developments owe their emergence to demographic changes; the stagnating population and indeed the presence of demographic decline after 1650 made servant labour, paid disproportionately in kind, a much sought after substitute for wage-paid, living-out day labour; a decline in fertility

---

189 See below, pp. 386–7.
190 For a useful summary of developments in towns, see P. Slack, 'Social Policies and Social Problems', in C. Phythian-Adams and P. Slack, editors, *The Traditional Community Under Stress* (Milton Keynes, 1977), pp. 92–7.
191 K. Thomas, *Religion and the Decline of Magic: Studies in Popular Beliefs in Sixteenth and Seventeenth Century England* (London, 1971), especially pp. 25–7 and 56–69 and, more generally, C. Hill, *Society and Puritanism in Pre-Revolutionary England* (London, 1964).
192 L. Stone, 'The Rise of the Nuclear Family in Early Modern England', in C. Rosenberg, editor, *The Family in History* (Philadelphia, Pa., 1975), p. 21.
193 See above, notes 88 and 89. For supportive evidence, also see K. D. Snell, 'Agricultural Seasonal Unemployment, the Standard of Living and Women's Work in the South and East: 1690–1860', *Economic History Review* 34 (1981), pp. 407–37.

also reduced the demands of what in the troubled years of the early seventeenth century had been a large component of those in need of relief – the married couple or the widow over-burdened with children.[194] Of course, in the later sixteenth and early seventeenth centuries when both parish relief and service were less deeply involved in the 'policing' of adult labour (given that service now played a relatively minor place in the agricultural work force and that parish relief perhaps coexisted in an uneasy relationship with neighbourly charity and other less formal systems of relief such as doles and benefactions from wealthy testators), there may have been potential for more tensions in the local community to erupt onto the surface.[195] But it would be wrong to assume that coping with life-cycle poverty by multiple means was a response to new problems rather than to an intensification of what had been ever-present features of the life-cycle of the poor or those whose material means of support were marginal.

Older systems of collectivist intervention into the lives of the poor, such as the manor, had been disturbed in the sixteenth century, and the Reformation had swept away the parish guilds. Neither of these institutions has yet been adequately studied with the problems of the household life-cycle in mind. The latter clearly did provide a means of insurance against risk. Cornelius Walford's now terribly dated study of gilds shows that they attempted in their provisions to deal with a wide range of personal and family disasters, and although a single gild did not provide all of these reliefs and services the following are worthy of note: poverty, sickness, old age, blindness, deafness and dumbness, leprosy and, for those in temporary financial difficulties, aid in finding work and apprenticeships and payment for burials.[196] Likewise, it is not perhaps sufficiently realized how frequently a manorial lord or his officers might intevene in the affairs of an elderly tenant. Too readily have historians been prepared to treat these cases solely as indicative of seigneurial intervention in the matter of maintaining the viability of a rent paying or service rendering

---

194 It should be noted in this context that in the later eighteenth century (also a period of relatively rapid demographic growth and in certain parts of the country quite sharp falls in real income) this category increased in importance as recipients of out-relief. Furthermore, K. Williams, *From Pauperism to Poverty* (London, 1981), Table 4.2, pp. 149–50, notes that in 1802–3 a significant number of recipients of relief were adult men of working age on account of either their low wages, or un- or under-employment.

195 Of the kind analysed by A. Macfarlane in *Witchcraft in Tudor and Stuart England: A Regional Comparative Study* (London, 1970).

196 C. Walford, *Gilds: Their Origin, Constitution, Objects and Later History* (London, 1879). See also H. F. Westlake, *The Parish Gilds of Medieval England* (London, 1919).

holding.[197] But this would be a lop-sided interpretation of the cases, many of which have been recently reported by Elaine Clark in a well-rounded treatment of a number of contracts concerning the maintenance of elderly East Anglians in the fourteenth- and fifteenth-century manorial court rolls.[198] For example, she cites a case from Hindolveston, Norfolk, in 1382, when the manorial presentment jury had said that in the village there lived a 'poor little old woman', a widow holding some eighteen acres of arable land; she was 'feeble of body and simple of mind', unable to care for herself and without the means to render service to her lord. He therefore decided to grant the land to her 'nearest heir' ordering him to support the poor woman for life, to feed and clothe her as 'befitted a widow'. In fact, Clark shows well how a dereliction of duty to the old constituted a matter of public concern and communal review. She shows, too, that this communal concern manifests itself in the fact that over three-quarters of the 114 agreements she considered for the post-Black Death period involved no explicit *filial* tie between the pensioner and his benefactor, leading Clark to reflect on the possibility that the domestic structure of rural society was 'sufficiently flexible to allow some landless peasants a way to find their place by residing with the old, by taking over their holdings in return for the promise of maintenance'.[199]

Further reasons for supposing that in these questions continuity is a better *leit motiv* than discontinuity come from the discussions by medieval canonists and decretists, which are remarkably reminiscent of the issues mulled over by writers of the sixteenth and seventeenth centuries such as Arthington and Dalton – concern, for instance, with whether relatives should be responsible for their poor kin; statements making a clear distinction between a 'deserving' and an 'undeserving' poor and a perennial preoccupation with who possessed eligibility when funds were inadequate.[200]

As Wales has argued elsewhere, to a certain extent early seventeenth-century peaks in regulatory prosecutions by village authorities, which have recently become a fashionable issue to research, may be better understood as a response to a perception of a poor who were increasingly weakly tied into social and economic relations as co-residing servants in the wealthier households, and as a concern

---

[197] See for example, Searle, 'Seigneurial Control', p. 37. But consider the discussion in Smith, 'Some Thoughts', pp. 123–6.

[198] E. Clark, 'Some Aspects of Social Security in Medieval England', *Journal of Family History* 7 (1982), pp. 307–20.

[199] *Ibid.*, pp. 310–11.

[200] See, especially, B. Tierney, 'The Decretists and the "Deserving Poor"', *Comparative Studies in Society and History* 1 (1958–9), pp. 360–76.

also with actions that made the household of the married couple precarious, such as time spent in the alehouse.[201] His work on later seventeenth-century Quarter Sessions records suggests a move away by that date from the regulation of activities outside the household, which had been so prominent in the early seventeenth century, to the regulation of relations between masters and their servants and apprentices and, in particular, the prosecution of those living outside of service. It is striking how the order of the Easter 1667 Quarter Session of the Cambridge Bench, that 'all and every single and unmarried person and persons being of able bodies and who cannot otherwise maintain themselves but by their labour to place themselves in service by Pentecost', resembles a certain section in the Ordinance of Labourers proclaimed by Edward III's council in June 1349, that 'Every man or woman, free or unfree, aged sixty years or younger must serve whoever required his labour.'[202] Of course both time periods were ones in which it is plausible to regard concern with the masterless and with employer–employee relations as a reaction to a relative shortage of labour.

They also, perhaps more directly in the seventeenth century, but indirectly in the fourteenth century, indicate a not inconsiderable level of potential governmental intervention in the life-cycle of the labouring elements in English society. It is interesting, too, that the fourteenth-century ordinance did not apply to those over the age of 60. Are we to observe similar principles concerning the rights of gleaners, as announced to reeves on some royal manors in 1282 in the following form? 'Let it be established that the young, the old and those who are decrepit and unable to work shall glean in autumn after the sheaves have been taken away, but those who are able if they wish to work for wages will not be allowed to glean.' A similar sentiment is to be found in the by-law from Brightwaltham, Berkshire, in 1340, that 'all tenants agree that none of the inhabitants may glean corn unless they be under age or over age'.[203]

---

[201] Reported in a seminar paper given in Cambridge, October 1982, the text of which Mr Wales kindly allowed me to consult. See, for examples of this concern, K. Wrightson, 'Ale-Houses, Order and Reformation in Rural England, 1599–1660', in E. Yeo and S. Yeo, editors, *Popular Culture and Class Conflict 1590–1914'*, (Brighton, 1981), pp. 1–27 and P. Clark 'The Alehouse and the Alternative Society', in D. Pennington and K. Thomas, editors, *Puritans and Revolutionaries: Essays in Seventeenth History Century presented to Christopher Hill* (Oxford, 1978), pp. 47–72.

[202] *Statutes of the Realm* (London, 1810), I, p. 307.

[203] W. O. Ault, *Open-Field Farming in Medieval England* (London, 1972), pp. 29–32, commented on by Thompson 'The Grid of Inheritance', pp. 340–1, on the matter of the 'customary rights' of the 'very young, the old, the decrepit etc. . . . .' without any reflection on why that group should have been so specified.

Obviously, it would be unwise to proceed as if there had been no change in the life-cycle crises of the landless throughout a five-century period of English history, but it is important to reflect in our future researches on the extent to which assumed changes in the character of the poor have sometimes been mistaken for alterations in the institutional means of dealing with a problem that has much to do with social rules and with the delicately balanced relationship between the kinship systems and society's collectivist agencies.[204] It may be premature to plead the case for an *histoire immobile* of 'life-cycle' poverty and society's response to it, but it is worth noting a recent study of the care of the elderly in nineteenth-century England, when for a relatively brief interlude the state, in the form of the central Poor Law authorities, attempted to order local relief agencies to desist in their payment of relief to the aged and to oblige their children to provide that support.[205] That this policy shift failed abysmally in its intentions may indicate something of the depth of a strong collectivist tradition in dealing with the problem, deriving as much from the social structure as from the relations of production. Even the economically more fortunate, such as the seventeenth- and eighteenth-century East Anglian widows described by Holderness, did not depend for their existence on the material support of a larger kin group. Their income in old age came in no small measure from interest yielding loans, as reflected in the sheaves of promissory notes or bonds of debt outstanding at their death.[206]

We have in this discussion selected certain themes in order to reflect on issues raised in the essays of this volume, themes which permit us to consider the relationships between land or property – its management and its circulation both within and between kin groups – and the family's development cycle. It should have become clear in the case of the English evidence that we have discussed an interrelationship of fundamental importance to any attempt to understand the rural family. Yet it would be difficult to conclude our discussion with any sense that this inter-relationship was for a history of rural families

[204] See the brilliant polemic of D. Thomson in his 'Historians and the Welfare State', (forthcoming), where he exposes a long-standing failure of historians to interpret practice in the matter of social welfare in the past in terms of the recurrent oscillations between collectivist and individualist doctrines.

[205] D. Thomson, 'Provision for the Elderly in England 1830–1908', exposing the grave lack of historical perspective in M. Anderson, 'The Impact on the Family Relationships of the Elderly of Changes Since Victorian Times in Governmental Income-Maintenance Provision', in E. Shanas and M. Sussman, editors, *Family, Bureaucracy and the Elderly* (Durham, N.C., 1977), pp. 36–59.

[206] See below, pp. 432–42.

the sole or indeed the most important determinant of the forms they took. Although Anderson has recently suggested, when reviewing what he termed the 'family economy of the western peasant' in the past, that the availability of agricultural resources in England through an extensive market in land may have helped to produce rather different familial practices in that country and has noted too that the early impact of the proletarianization of labour makes for difficulties in analysing change, he has singled out two variables that might also be identifiable in other European areas and were doubtlessly present in other north-western parts of that continent.[207] There is no denying that the presence of markets in both land and labour increased the decision-making options of holders of land in England as to the ways they might dispose of and manage their property resources. Yet we should be wary of too economically reductionist a position on these issues, for we would need to take equal account of certain features of the kinship system that existed independently of the economy. We would need to consider also why two quite distinct forms of non-family agrarian labour should have co-existed, without, until very late in the long-running saga of English agrarian history, one form ever apparently totally displacing the other. We would need to consider the interrelationship between legal developments to do with land that linked centre and periphery, serf and freeholder and brought a formalization to custom that most certainly allowed those 'customs' to take on a flexibility that, indeed, leads one to question the conventional meaning of the very concept. Of course, we could continue to add to our pile of elements that intrude between any simple conceptualization of the family–land bond. But to insist, as we have at various points in this introductory essay, that the relationship between two elements has been over-played in the study of the rural family, and was in fact in England blurred, is to make a statement that could well apply elsewhere if the rural family is to be adequately investigated within its total environment.

[207] M. Anderson, *Approaches to the History of the Western Family*, p. 69.

Population pressure, inheritance and the land market in a fourteenth-century peasant community*

BRUCE M. S. CAMPBELL

The first half of the fourteenth century witnessed the culmination of the first of three great waves of population growth which may be discerned during the pre-industrial period.[1] At the same time, the living standard of the mass of the population reached a nadir below which it was never again to fall, with a substantial proportion living at a level which was marginal for bare subsistence.[2] England's population of four to six millions was, in fact, at least three, and possibly even four, times greater than it had been some two-and-a-half centuries earlier.[3] The consequence of so great an increase in population, according to M. M. Postan, was that it ultimately brought about its own nemesis.[4] An over-concentration upon grain production,

---

* The research upon which this paper is based was undertaken between 1971 and 1976 and the text was originally prepared for publication in 1977. The text alone has since been extensively revised.
[1] For the chronology of pre-industrial population trends, see K. Helleiner, 'The Population of Europe from the Black Death to the Eve of the Vital Revolution', in E. E. Rich and C. H. Wilson, editors, *The Cambridge Economic History of Europe, IV: The Economy of Expanding Europe in the Sixteenth and Seventeenth Centuries* (Cambridge, 1967), pp. 1–95; J. D. Chambers, *Population, Economy, and Society in Pre-Industrial England* (Oxford, 1972); E. A. Wrigley and R. S. Schofield, *The Population History of England 1541–1871: A Reconstruction* (London, 1981).
[2] E. H. Phelps Brown and S. V. Hopkins, 'Seven Centuries of the Prices of Consumables compared with Builders' Wage-Rates', *Economica* new series 23 (1956), reprinted in E. M. Carus-Wilson, editor, *Essays in Economic History, Vol. II* (1962), pp. 179–96; D. M. Palliser, 'Tawney's Century: Brave New World or Malthusian Trap?', *Economic History Review* 2nd series 35 (1982), pp. 339–53.
[3] For the upper and lower estimates of medieval population at peak, see M. M. Postan, *The Medieval Economy and Society: An Economic History of Britain in the Middle Ages* (London, 1972), pp. 27–31 and J. C. Russell, 'The Preplague Population of England', *Journal of British Studies* 5:2 (1966), pp. 1–21. H. E. Hallam has recently postulated a maximum figure as high as 7.2 millions in 1924: *Rural England 1066–1348* (Glasgow, 1981) p. 246.
[4] This thesis is most fully elaborated in 'Medieval Agrarian Society in its Prime:

coupled with deficient agricultural technology, led to soil exhaustion and the abandonment of land and thus to a real decline in agricultural production: a decline, moreover, which was exacerbated during the late thirteenth and early fourteenth centuries by a succession of bad harvests of which the worst – the so-called Great Famine – occurred in 1315–17.[5] The latter event precipitated a major subsistence crisis from which the population never fully recovered. In Postan's view, therefore, when bubonic plague arrived in 1348–9 it struck a population which was already in decline.

Postan's neo-Malthusian explanation of events has found favour with a great many medieval economic and social historians.[6] Indeed, insofar as it has met with serious challenge this has been directed less against the circumstantial nature of so much of his evidence than against his ascription of the role of prime mover to demographic trends.[7] Thus, in two very recent and controversial articles the Marxist historian Robert Brenner has questioned whether demographic determinants *per se* are a sufficient explanation of the economic and social trends which characterized the Middle Ages.[8] He has argued instead that it was prevailing property structures and the balance of class forces that conditioned the effect of any given demographic trend upon both the development of productive forces and long-term trends in the distribution of income. For this reason he maintains that it is the establishment, evolution and transformation of class structures that should be placed at the centre of any interpretation of the long-term evolution of the pre-industrial European economy.

No matter which interpretation is favoured, however, it is plain

England', in M. M. Postan, editor, *The Cambridge Economic History of Europe, I: The Agrarian Life of the Middle Ages*, 2nd edition (Cambridge, 1966), pp. 549–632.

[5] H. S. Lucas, 'The Great European Famine of 1315, 1316, and 1317', *Speculum* 5 (1930), pp. 343–77; I. Kershaw, 'The Great Famine and Agrarian Crisis in England 1315–1322', *Past and Present* 59 (1973), pp. 3–50; M. M. Postan and J. Z. Titow, 'Heriots and Prices on Winchester Manors', *Economic History Review* 2nd series 11 (1959), pp. 392–411.

[6] J. Z. Titow, *English Rural Society 1200–1350* (London, 1969); E. Miller and J. Hatcher, *Medieval England – Rural Society and Economic Change 1086–1348* (London, 1978); J. L. Bolton, *The Medieval English Economy 1150–1500* (London, 1980).

[7] Exceptions are B. F. Harvey, 'The Population Trend in England between 1300 and 1348', *Transactions of the Royal Historical Society* 5th series 16 (1966), pp. 23–42; H. E. Hallam, 'The Postan Thesis', *Historical Studies* 15 (1972), pp. 203–22, and *Rural England*; Z. Razi, *Life, Marriage and Death in a Medieval Parish* (Cambridge, 1980).

[8] R. Brenner, 'Agrarian Class Structure and Economic Development in Pre-Industrial Europe', *Past and Present* 70 (1976), pp. 30–75, and 'The Agrarian Roots of European Capitalism', *Past and Present* 97 (1982), pp. 16–113. See *Past and Present* 78, 79, 80 and 85 (1978–9), for responses to Brenner's original paper.

that both the chronology and the processes of change were subject to significant spatial variation. As Postan acknowledged, '. . . the very nature of mediaeval trends made it impossible for them to synchronise over the country as a whole. The influences behind them were those of population, soil and settlement, and they could not possibly have combined everywhere in the same manner and at the same point of time.'[9] Likewise, Brenner has pointed out that '. . . demographic growth appears to have led to "over-population" at different population densities, at different points in time and with different socio-economic effects'.[10] What these differences were and why they occurred are clearly fundamental to any satisfactory explanation of developments during this period, and as such deserve much more explicit attention. For instance, it is at present uncertain which localities were most successful in sustaining an upward trend in population and weathering the vicissitudes which occurred with increasing frequency and severity from the late thirteenth century on. Did the old-settled areas of high population density prove least vulnerable, or were peripheral areas of more recent settlement and lower population density more resilient? Moreover, in what ways did differences in the balance of power and property between lords and peasants condition this relationship? Is there, in fact, a direct relationship between areas where feudal control was strongest and areas where demographic retreat first began? Were the respective roles of famine and plague everywhere the same, and were changes in mortality always paramount in the inauguration of a new demographic and economic era? The answers to these and other related questions will be found in the particular experience of individual communities and localities.

Accordingly this essay focuses attention upon one of the most distinctive localities in medieval England. By the fourteenth century eastern Norfolk had become the most densely settled district within the most densely populated county in the country.[11] Although less anciently settled than some other parts of England, its cultivated area had long since reached its limit. The landscape had already been virtually stripped of woodland by the time of Domesday Book, and thereafter most settlements seem to have depended upon peat and

[9] J. A. Raftis, *The Estates of Ramsey Abbey: A Study in Economic Growth and Organization* (Toronto, 1957), p. x.

[10] Brenner, 'Agrarian Roots', p. 25.

[11] See the maps in H. C. Darby, editor, *A New Historical Geography of England* (Cambridge, 1973), pp. 46, 139 and 191. Also R. R. Rainbird Clarke, *East Anglia* (London, 1960); B. M. S. Campbell, 'The Extent and Layout of Commonfields in Eastern Norfolk', *Norfolk Archaeology* 38 (1981), pp. 18–20.

turf for fuel. In this context, it has been estimated that between the tenth and the fourteenth century some 900 million cubic feet of peat were extracted from what are now the Norfolk Broads.[12] There was, however, no such simple solution to the problem of accommodating a steadily expanding population upon a finite amount of cultivable land. Instead, three basic responses may be identified. In the first place, existing fields and holdings were subdivided, a process whose endless repetition produced the landscape of intensely parcellated open fields tilled by a multitude of peasant smallholders which may be recognized at the end of the thirteenth century.[13] Second (and here direct evidence is only available for seigneurial demesnes), output per acre was raised by the adoption of extremely intensive methods of husbandry which required massive labour inputs.[14] Third, various forms of by-employment were developed – salt making, textile manufacture, fishing, and merchant shipping based upon the port of Yarmouth – to absorb the labour which was surplus to agriculture.[15]

In its economic development eastern Norfolk was therefore precocious, and in part this undoubtedly stemmed from the social institutions of the area. Thus, although open fields were extensive, their common regulations were minimal; for in all essential matters of husbandry the rights of the individual tended to prevail over those of the group. In marked contrast to more fully regulated field systems, the only regulation which seems to have been universal was that which guaranteed cultivators the right of shack feed for their livestock on the aftermath of the harvest.[16] This looseness of common regulations was matched by a manorial nexus which was both weak and fragmented. On the one hand, seigneurial authority was restricted by the fact that manor and vill were rarely coterminous, and on the other

---

[12] H. C. Darby, *The Domesday Geography of Eastern England* (Cambridge, 1952), pp. 126–9; J. M. Lambert, J. N. Jennings, C. T. Smith, C. Green and J. N. Hutchinson, 'The Making of the Broads: A Reconsideration of their Origin in the Light of New Evidence', *Royal Geographical Society Research Series* 3 (1960).

[13] B. M. S. Campbell, 'Population Change and the Genesis of Commonfields on a Norfolk Manor', *Economic History Review* 2nd series 33 (1980), pp. 174–92; and 'Commonfields in Eastern Norfolk', pp. 18–26.

[14] B. M. S. Campbell, 'Agricultural Progress in Medieval England: Some Evidence from Eastern Norfolk', *Economic History Review* 2nd series 36 (1983), pp. 26–46, and 'Arable Productivity in Medieval England: Some Evidence from Norfolk'. *The Journal of Economic History* 43 (1983), pp. 379–404.

[15] Darby, *Domesday Geography*, pp. 134–6; R. H. Hilton, *Bond Men Made Free: Medieval Peasant Movements and the English Rising of 1381* (London, 1973), pp. 171–4; A. Saul, 'Great Yarmouth in the Fourteenth century: A Study in Trade, Politics and Society', unpublished University of Oxford D.Phil. thesis, 1975.

[16] B. M. S. Campbell, 'The Regional Uniqueness of English Field Systems? Some Evidence from Eastern Norfolk', *Agricultural History Review* 29 (1981), pp. 16–28.

it was diluted by the presence of a significant proportion of freemen and sokemen within the population. The circumscribing effect which this had upon lordship may be seen from the fact that, even where attempts had been made to standardize customary holdings for the allocation of rents and services, their integrity, except as purely fiscal units, was never successfully preserved.[17] In short, eastern Norfolk is one part of medieval England where the typical 'peasant' was perhaps, as A. Macfarlane believes, a rampant individualist, market-orientated and acquisitive, and ego-centred in kinship and social life.[18]

How, then, did the inhabitants of this distinctive area fare during the difficult years of the fourteenth century? In certain respects they were comparatively advantaged. They had resolved the inherent conflict between the requirements of arable and pastoral husbandry and thereby assured themselves of a sustained high level of corn production, their economy was diversified, the burden of feudal obligations was relatively light, and individuals enjoyed considerable freedom of action. Moreover, eastern Norfolk's soils and climate are ideal for grain production (which the prevailing terms of trade between arable and pastoral farming likewise favoured), whilst its coastal location and navigable rivers meant that it was peculiarly well placed to participate in the national and international grain trade.[19] Through imports and exports the area was able to compensate for dearths and to profit from surpluses. Yet by the end of the thirteenth century these advantages had already, in large measure, been exploited to the full. Known agricultural techniques had been taken to their limit and afforded few prospects of any further rise in productivity; by-employments may have developed, but farming in one form or another remained the mainstay of the bulk of the population (indeed, the growing destitution of the population may have thrown people back upon a dependence on agriculture); and as

[17] Darby, *Domesday Geography*, pp. 114–18 and 361; B. Dodwell, 'The Free Peasantry of East Anglia in Domesday', *Norfolk Archaeology* 27 (1939), pp. 145–57; D. C. Douglas, *The Social Structure of Medieval East Anglia*, Oxford Studies in Social and Legal History ix (Oxford, 1927); B. M. S. Campbell, 'Field Systems in Eastern Norfolk during the Middle Ages: A Study with Particular Reference to the Demographic and Agrarian Changes of the Fourteenth Century', unpublished University of Cambridge Ph.D. thesis, pp. 260–2 and 275–8, and 'Population Change', pp. 176–82.

[18] A. Macfarlane, *The Origins of English Individualism: The Family, Property and Social Transition* (Oxford, 1978), p. 163.

[19] For the way in which differences in the terms of trade between pastoral and arable produce could work to the demographic disadvantage of certain areas, see A. B. Appleby, 'Disease or Famine? Mortality in Cumberland and Westmorland, 1580–1640', *Economic History Review* 2nd series 26 (1973), pp. 403–32.

holdings became progressively reduced in size even relatively modest levels of feudal rent would have become onerous and, eventually, insupportable. Eastern Norfolk therefore entered the fourteenth century with a burgeoning population, a majority of whom was dependent for support upon the produce of tiny plots of land eked out with whatever else could be earned. From this time on, with the population density of the most populous districts approaching some 500 persons per square mile and all the available economic options more or less used up, it is arguable that it was only a matter of time before the area succumbed to crisis. When and in what form the impending crisis actually materialized, however, are matters for detailed investigation based on the surviving manorial records of the area.

Of all the different classes of medieval document which are available it is manor court rolls that undoubtedly possess greatest potential value for the study of the medieval peasantry. The business which they record derives directly from the relations between peasant and peasant, and between peasant and lord, and has the very great merit of being recorded as it occurred, on a continuous basis. On the other hand, such is the bulk and diversity of the information which the rolls contain that analysis of them is far from straightforward. Indeed, there is currently considerable debate as to what is the most valid and appropriate methodology.[20] From this it is apparent that only the most complete and continuous series of court records, preferably generated by courts with extensive legal and territorial jurisdiction, will suffice for the detailed study of peasant society and demography. Ideally, they should also be supplemented by other manorial and fiscal sources. In eastern Norfolk these requirements are hard to satisfy, at least for the thirteenth and fourteenth centuries. So diligent were Geoffrey Lister's peasants in seeking out and destroying court rolls in the Rising of 1381 that virtually all the best surviving series post-date that event.[21] Within this entire locality

---

[20] Examples of different approaches to court rolls include: J. A. Raftis, *Tenure and Mobility: Studies in the Social History of the Mediaeval English Village* (Toronto, 1964); E. B. Dewindt, *Land and People in Holywell-cum-Needingworth: Structures of Tenure and Patterns of Social Organization in an East Midlands Village 1252–1457* (Toronto, 1972); R. M. Smith, 'English Peasant Life-Cycles and Socio-Economic Networks – A Quantitative Geographical Case Study', unpublished University of Cambridge Ph.D. thesis, 1974; E. Britton, *The Community of the Vill – A Study in the History of the Family and Village Life in Fourteenth-Century England* (Toronto, 1977); Razi, *Life, Marriage and Death*. See also Z. Razi, 'Family, Land and the Village Community in Later Medieval England', *Past and Present* 93 (1982), pp. 3–36.

[21] On the Peasants' Revolt in East Anglia, see C. W. C. Oman, *The Great Revolt of 1381* (Oxford, 1906), pp. 111–18; R. B. Dobson, *The Peasants' Revolt of 1381* (London, 1970),

there is only one manor with anything approaching a continuous run of rolls for the whole of the fourteenth century, and even these only narrowly escaped the conflagration of 1381.[22]

The rolls in question relate to the small lay manor of Hakeford Hall in Coltishall, a township just seven miles north of Norwich in the valley of the River Bure. A record of 335 court sessions exists for the period 1275–1405. As such the series is approximately two-thirds complete, for although there are only ten years during this entire 131-year period without any records at all, only a minority of years retain their full complement of courts. This compares with the 1,667 court sessions used by Z. Razi in his study of the Worcestershire manor of Halesowen during the almost equivalent 130-year period, 1270–1400.[23] Moreover, in contrast to the Abbots of Halesown, who exercised jurisdiction over a contiguous block of some 10,000 acres and no fewer than twelve separate rural settlements, the lords of Hakeford Hall exercised an extremely limited jurisdiction. One reason was that Coltishall, as was characteristic of this area, contained a number of different manors. Another and related reason was that the manor of Hakeford Hall was territorially both small and fragmented. Its demesne amounted to less than 100 acres and it is

---

pp. 256–61; and Hilton, *Bond Men Made Free*. On the Bishop of Norwich's manor at Hevingham the August court for 1381 records that 'rotulus curie, custumarium, rentale, et rotulus secte curie et alia monumenta dicti manerii cremata fuerunt per tenentes domini et alios comunes quando comunes Comitatus Norffociensis et aliorum comitatus surexerunt contra pacem domini Regem et magnum dampnum fecerunt etc.'. 22 tenants were prosecuted for destroying these documents and they were ordered to return any damaged rolls which they still held in their custody upon pain of a £5 fine. The tenants of the Bishop's 3 manors of Ripton, Parkhall and Crictots were then each ordered to make fresh custumals, rentals, extents, terriers and nominative listings of tenants owing suit of court, also upon pain of a £5 fine. Norfolk Record Office (hereafter NRO), NRS 19558 42 D2. Other manors in this locality whose court rolls only survive from 1381 are Felbrigg, Gimingham, Metton, Neatishead, Tunstead and Westwick.

[22] King's College, Cambridge (hereafter KCC), E 29–38. The fate which nearly befell these rolls in 1381 is revealed by a court entry of that year: 'viginti et unus de tenentibus domini quorum nomina patent in una billa huic rotulo annexa offerunt domino pro contemptu sibi facto; videlicet pro eo quod die Jovis proxima ante festum natale Sancti Johannis sexdecim eorundem tenentium quorum nomina prenotant in dicta billa de concesu aliorum equitaverunt usque Saxthorp ad domum Ed(ward)i Kempe Seneschall curie domini et graviter manu forti contra voluntatem domini et voluntatem dicte [sic] Ed(ward)i, nisi pro timore, ceperunt baggam cum rotulis curie domini et aliis memorandis in eadem bagga existentibus et illa asportaverunt et penes se retinuerant usque nunc diem. Ideo dant domini etc.' (KCC E 37). It was probably as a result of this that a number of rolls got out of sequence, at least 32 being wrongly attributed to the reign of Edward I instead of Edward II (a fact which only came to light in the course of this analysis).

[23] Razi, *Life, Marriage and Death*, pp. 5–10.

unlikely that there were more than 200 acres of land in the hands of the customary tenants; the latter straddled the boundary with the adjacent township of Belaugh and does not seem to have formed a single discrete unit but to have lain inter-mixed with the land held from other lords.[24] To compound matters there are virtually no ancillary documents.

No detailed reconstitution of Coltishall's demographic and social structure (along the lines of R. M. Smith's of Redgrave's and Razi's study of Halesown's) is therefore possible.[25] Instead, rather more modest aims must suffice. In this study attention is therefore focused upon the very large number of *inter-vivos* and *post-mortem* land transactions which the court rolls document. Since land holding lay at the very foundation of the peasant economy much can be revealed by the frequency with which land was bought and sold and the circumstances under which this took place. In particular, the ease or difficulty with which peasants bought land, and the readiness or reluctance with which they sold it, can be used as indicators of the level of peasant well-being. Fortunately the court rolls also provide just sufficient information to reconstruct the demographic context within which these transactions occurred. All this assumes considerable interest when it relates to a diminutive lay manor where the majority of tenants were smallholders, where holding size and layout were in a constant state of flux and where pasture resources were extremely scarce: a manor, in fact, of a class which is under-represented by surviving sources and which has hitherto received but limited attention from historians.[26]

---

[24] In 1293 and 1315 the sown area of the demesne amounted to 71.75 and 87.75 acres respectively: KCC, E 29–30. In the late fifteenth century, when the manor was acquired by King's College, Cambridge, it comprised the advowson of the church, 20 messuages, 6 tofts, 200 acres of land, 30 acres of meadow, 100 acres of marsh, and £10 annually in rent: KCC E 23. In 1348 it supported a population of at least 168 male tenants, 35% of whom were of free status: KCC E 34.

[25] Smith, 'English Peasant Life-Cycles', and below, 'Families and their Land in an Area of Partible Inheritance: Redgrave, Suffolk 1260–1320', pp. 133–95; Razi, *Life, Marriage and Death.*

[26] The manors studied by Raftis, Dewindt, Britton, Smith and Razi (note 20) all belonged to ecclesiastical magnates (the Abbots of Ramsey, St Edmundsbury, and Halesowen). For studies of lay manors, see R. H. Britnell, 'Production for the Market on a Small Fourteenth-Century Estate', *Economic History Review* 2nd series 19 (1966), pp. 380–7 (Langenhoe, Essex), and J. Williamson, 'Peasant Holdings in Medieval Norfolk: A Detailed Investigation of the Holdings of the Peasantry in Three Norfolk Villages in the Thirteenth Century', unpublished University of Reading Ph.D. thesis, 1976 (Gressenhall, Norfolk).

i. Population trends at Coltishall

Unequivocal evidence of changes in the total size of medieval populations is elusive, and opportunities for the direct measurement of fertility, mortality and migration still more so. Even Razi's painstaking work on Halesowen, which has come close to providing information on these crucial variables, is not entirely free from ambiguity.[27] Where evidence of a quasi-demographic nature does exist it generally relates to the landholding group within society (non-land holders rarely being consistently mentioned) and is usually of unverifiable accuracy. Information on population trends at Coltishall is no exception. Nominative listings of tenants are available for the years 1314, 1349, 1359, 1370 and 1406, whilst the obituaries of deceased tenants, of which 350 are recorded between 1280 and 1400, give details of the name and filiation of the heir or heirs.[28] Apart from these data, merchet payments are recorded too infrequently to provide any reliable indication of trends in nuptiality, although the court rolls do furnish some incidental evidence of migration from this manor. A tentative reconstruction of population trends during the crucial period from the end of the thirteenth to the opening of the fifteenth century is therefore possible, but the associated changes in the underlying vital rates must remain largely conjectural.

The numbers enumerated in the five successive nominative listings are summarized in Table 2.1. With the exception of the 1349 listing, which was drawn up shortly after the outbreak of plague, each of these listings dates from the incumbency of a new manorial lord and comprises the names of those tenants who swore fealty in the manor court. Unfortunately, since this procedure was often spread over several court sessions whose records have not always survived, these listings are not always exhaustive. Differences in the numbers of tenants listed at successive dates may therefore be partially a function of differences in the comprehensiveness of the respective listings. The listings of 1314 and 1349 are a case in point. The former is spread over several court sessions and, as is clear from an injunction recorded in one of them, does not provide a complete record; whereas the latter was specially commissioned, appears in the proceedings of a single court session and from subsequent additions and annotations bears every sign of a full and accurate listing. On the other hand, the

[27] *Life, Marrriage and Death in a Medieval Parish: Economy, Society and Demography in Halesowen 1270–1400*, reviewed by R. M. Smith in *Journal of Historical Geography* 8 (1982), pp. 305–6.

[28] KCC, E 32, 34–6 and 38.

Table 2.1. *Coltishall, Norfolk: tenant numbers according to nominative listings recorded in the court rolls*

	Total no. male tenants	% change	Total no. female tenants	% change	Total no. tenants	% change
Date						
1314	119		22		141	
		+41.2		+36.4		+40.4
1349	168		30		198	
		−56.0		−83.3		−60.1
1359	74		5		79	
		−55.4		−40.0		−54.4
1370	33		3		36	
		−36.0		+100.0		−25.0
1406	21		6		27	

difference in the numbers enumerated at these two dates is so large that it is unlikely to be entirely attributable to this case.

These listings, though of variable accuracy, may therefore be used to infer the general chronology of population change. As Table 2.1 shows, a clear distinction emerges between the first and second halves of the fourteenth century, the former being characterized by expanding and the latter by contracting population. Between the eve of the Great Famine and the eve of the Black Death the population increased: the listings of 1314 and 1340 may misrepresent the scale of this increase, but it is unlikely that they mislead as to its reality. By December 1350, however, over half of the 198 tenants named in the 1349 listings were dead, their obituaries recorded in the court rolls bearing witness to the terrible toll exacted by bubonic plague. Since the deaths of dependents (among whom the young, old and infirm would have been disproportionately represented) are not recorded, total plague mortality on this manor may have been as high as 60 per cent.[29] This is the only plague outbreak of which the documents provide direct testimony, but a further decline in tenant numbers of approximately 55 per cent between 1359 and 1370 suggests that Coltishall did not escape unscathed from the national epidemics of 1361–2 and 1368–9.[30] In the space of just two decades this manor's

[29] For an account of the Black Death in East Anglia, see J. F. D. Shrewsbury, *A History of Bubonic Plague in the British Isles* (Cambridge, 1970), pp. 94–9.

[30] At Halesowen approximately 40% of male tenants died in the initial plague outbreak of 1349, 14% in the outbreak of 1361, 16% in 1369, and 12% in 1375: Razi, *Life, Marriage and Death*, pp. 109 and 128. Nevertheless, the overall decline in the number of adult males on the manor between 1351–5 and 1391–5 was only 6.7%: *ibid.*, p. 117.

population appears to have been reduced by 80 per cent. Thereafter the downward trend in numbers seems to have slackened but not to have halted.

Whether the population trends interpolated from the nominative listings were quite so continuous, however, can only be confirmed from evidence which was itself recorded on a continuous basis. This requirement is fulfilled by the information on heirship given by the obituaries of deceased tenants recorded in the court rolls. The obituary evidence permits the derivation of two different indices of population change. On the one hand, the ratio of inheriting sons to deceased fathers may be used to calculate the replacement rate of the tenant population (see Table 2.2), and, on the other, the proportions of tenants with or without filial heirs may be used to yield an alternative measure of population change (see Table 2.3). In the case of the replacement rate, a ratio in excess of unity was necessary if the population was to reproduce itself, the exact level depending upon the fertility and mortality of both the parental and the child generations. As E. A. Wrigley and R. M. Smith have demonstrated, replacement would also have been ensured when the ratio of sons, to daughters, to non-filial heirs was 6:2:2.[31] As will be appreciated, these two measures of replacement make rather different demands of the same data and both are more reliable as a guide to relative than to absolute change. Their calculation from the Coltishall court rolls is greatly facilitated by the fact that inheritance by sons and daughters was in both cases partible. The results which they yield are closely comparable and largely confirm the chronology of population change established from the nominative listings.

Between 1280 and 1314, a period before any nominative listings are available, both the replacement rate and the pattern of heirship exceeded the minimum conditions notionally required for Coltishall's population to have reproduced itself. Moreover, the same rate and a similar pattern continued to prevail between 1315 and 1348, a period for which the nominative listings indicate a substantial increase in tenant numbers. In other words, all three measures accord in showing a consistent upward trend in tenant numbers during the crucial and controversial interval between the Great Famine and the

---

[31] E. A. Wrigley, 'Fertility Strategy for the Individual and the Group', in C. Tilly, editor, *Historical Studies of Changing Fertility* (Princeton, NJ, 1978), pp. 235–54; Smith, *supra*, 'Some Issues Concerning Families and their Property in Rural England 1250–1800', pp. 40–54. For an early attempt at the calculation of replacement rates from obituaries recorded in court rolls, see S. L. Thrupp, 'The Problem of Replacement Rates in Late Medieval English Population', *Economic History Review* 2nd series 18 (1965), pp. 101–19.

Table 2.2. *Coltishall, Norfolk: replacement rates (calculated from obituaries recorded in the court rolls)*

	No. of deceased tenants	No. of surviving sons	Replacement rate
Years			
1280–1314	81	97	1.20
1315–48	82	98	1.20
1349–50	99	49	0.49
1351–75	34	19	0.56
1376–1400	54	37	0.69

Table 2.3. *Coltishall, Norfolk: incidence of filial and non-filial heirs (calculated from obituaries recorded in the court rolls)*

	Filial heirs				Non-filial heirs		Total
	Sons		Daughters but no sons				
	No.	%	No.	%	No.	%	
Years							
1280–99	26	68.4	4	10.5	8	21.1	38
1300–14	32	74.4	6	14.0	5	11.6	43
1315–22	15	62.5	1	4.2	8	33.3	24
1323–48	39	67.2	7	12.1	12	20.7	58
1349–50	42	42.4	12	12.1	45	45.5	99
1351–75	16	47.1	7	20.6	11	32.3	34
1376–1400	25	46.3	6	11.1	23	42.6	54

Black Death, a trend which represents a continuation of what had gone before. Taking the entire period 1280–1348, there was a mean replacement rate of 1.2 (comparable to the rate of 1.22 calculated by Razi for Halesowen, where an upward trend in population likewise seems to have prevailed),[32] and 68.7 per cent of tenants were succeeded by sons.

Of course, it is doubtful if the rate of population growth remained absolutely constant throughout this seventy-year period: on the other hand there appear to have been no major mortality crises – certainly nothing on the scale of the plague mortality of 1349 or, for that

[32] Razi, *Life, Marriage and Death*, p. 33. In contrast, the heirship evidence for Redgrave and Rickinghall in Suffolk, and Great Waltham and High Easter in Essex, suggests that tenant populations were declining in both areas: Smith, above, p. 54.

matter, of the 15 per cent reduction in population which occurred at Halesowen during the famine years 1316 and 1317.[33] An increase in the proportion of non-filial heirs to 33.3 per cent of the total during the years 1315–22 probably indicates some excess mortality at this time; and the unusually large number of instances of inheritance by minors between 1312 and 1323 (twelve of the fifteen cases recorded between 1280 and 1348 date from these years) invites the same interpretation. Nevertheless, there was no marked increase in the number of obituaries recorded in the court rolls, the proportion of tenants succeeded by sons remained in excess of 60 per cent, and it is by no means certain that instances of inheritance by minors were always recorded on a consistent basis. There were, for instance, suspiciously few cases of inheritance by minors in 1349, despite the disruption to normal inheritance patterns caused by the massive plague mortality. Overall, the impression of demographic trends during the period 1280–1348 is therefore a largely favourable one.

After 1348 conditions were very different. The obituaries provide ample evidence of the decimation wrought by the Black Death and thereafter, as will be seen from Tables 2.2 and 2.3, confirm the impression conveyed by the nominative listings that there was no recovery of population in the immediate aftermath of the plague. The replacement rate fell to 0.49 in 1349–50 and remained at virtually the same low level for the rest of the century. The pattern of heirship reflects the same negative trend: a persistent shortage of filial heirs, and of sons in particular, becomes a permanent feature of heirship at Coltishall after 1348. This pattern is paralleled on at least one other manor in this locality. Thus on the Prior of Norwich's manor at Martham, eleven miles further east, where the pre-plague density of population had been even greater than at Coltishall, of 96 tenants whose deaths are recorded between 1351 and 1375 only 44 per cent were succeeded by sons.[34] The reasons for this persistent downward trend in population invite speculation. A continuing high level of mortality is one possible explanation,[35] but so too is a temporal shift in fertility or a net outflow of population by migration. Certainly the increase (to almost one-fifth of the total) in the proportion of heirs who were below the age of majority when they inherited, along with the reduced numbers of sons and daughters who succeeded their parents (see Table 2.4), are as consonant with a concept of fertility

[33] Razi, *Life, Marriage and Death*, p. 40.
[34] Campbell, 'Field Systems', pp. 120–2.
[35] J. Hatcher, *Plague, Population and the English Economy 1348–1530*, Studies in Economic History (London, 1977).

Table 2.4. *Coltishall, Norfolk: the survival rate of sons (calculated from the obituaries of deceased tenants recorded in the court rolls)*

	1280–1348		1349–50		1351–1400	
	No.	%	No.	%	No.	%
Total no. of tenants	163	100.0	99	100.0	88	100.0
No. with at least 1 son	112	68.7	42	42.4	41	46.6
No. with at least 2 sons	50	30.7	6	6.1	7	8.0
No. with at least 3 sons	24	14.7	1	1.0	5	5.7
No. with at least 4 sons	6	3.7	0	0.0	2	2.3
No. with at least 5 sons	2	1.2	0	0.0	1	1.1

decline as with one of mortality increase. Indeed, the possibility of a significant lowering of fertility through later and less frequent marriage, and even of a reduction in marital fertility, is well attested from later historical experience.[36]

Yet it is for migration rather than for fertility that a modicum of direct evidence is available. This relates in the main to those migrants whose whereabouts were known and especially to those who paid chevage for permission to leave the manor. By contrast, villeins who fled the manor, particularly those of little property, are probably under-represented in the court record. Nevertheless, although this evidence points to an increase in mobility during the second half of the fourteenth century (the reduced post-plague population producing migrants at the rate of one every sixteen months as compared with the previous rate of one every 28 months), it does not indicate migration on any considerable scale until, perhaps, the 1370s. This may represent nothing more than a heightened seigneurial concern with migration at a time of labour and, particularly, of tenant shortages, although of the 42 individuals recorded as having left the manor between 1350 and 1405 no fewer than 28 departed during the brief period 1371–81.[37] This was a time of acute social and economic

---

[36] Wrigley and Schofield, *Population History*.

[37] Much the same phenomenon may be observed on the Prior of Norwich's manor at Martham. Here, out of a total of 40 out-migrants recorded between 1350 and 1405, 19 men and 2 women left between 1377 and 1388; of these, 13 went to Yarmouth, 2 to Lynn, 1 to Norwich, 1 to London and the remainder to various local villages. Men and women had left Martham before and they would leave the village again, but neither before nor since would they leave in such large numbers and show such a marked preference for an urban destination. Similarly, on the Bishop of Norwich's manor at Hevingham 12 of the 53 individuals recorded as having left the manor between 1381 and 1451 did so in the 1380s: Campbell, 'Field Systems', pp. 139–40 and 292.

dislocation which culminated in the Peasants' Revolt of 1381, a movement which received widespread popular support in eastern Norfolk.[38] Insofar as migration contributed to the post-plague decline in Coltishall's population it therefore had little appreciable impact until some time after the downward trend in numbers had become firmly established.

ii. Changes in holding size at Coltishall

In the Coltishall economy, where the working of land was the principal basis of wealth, such pronounced changes in the size of the population would have had important implications for the number and size of holdings, the methods of cultivating them and consequently the material well-being of the population.[39] That the number of holdings increased until the Black Death and decreased thereafter is, of course, obvious from the trends in tenant numbers which have just been discussed. What is less obvious is what changes in holding size derived from these changes in holding numbers. Did the pre-plague proliferation of land holdings take place at the cost of a soundly ubiquitous decline in holding size or did it promote a relative polarization of land ownership? As Smith has shown in the introduction to this volume, either outcome was possible, depending upon familial and social attitudes towards land and its ownership, the structure of peasant society, the nature of prevailing economic conditions, the type of inheritance custom in force and, above all, the relative importance of *inter-vivos* and *post-mortem* land transfers.[40] In fact, given that *inter-vivos* predominated over post-mortem transfers at Coltishall, the answer to this question has a direct bearing upon the debate concerning the genesis of social differentiation within medieval English rural society.[41]

At Coltishall evidence of holding size can only be obtained from the obituaries contained in the court rolls, the majority of which record the amount of land held by the deceased. This evidence has the great

---

[38] Socio-economic conditions in the 1370s are discussed in A. R. Bridbury, 'The Black Death', *Economic History Review* 2nd series 26 (1973), pp. 584–92. See above, note 21 for the Peasants' Revolt in Norfolk.

[39] Some tenants may have supplemented farm incomes with employment in crafts and trades but the evidence for this is slight. The single clear instance is the case of Richard Collys, who died in 1384. The inventory of his goods which is recorded in the court rolls suggests that he combined weaving with smallholding for, in addition to a messuage, 7 acres, three cows, a heifer, a sow, and two stots, he also possessed 30 ells of cloth 'de Wordeston super le stodeles': KCC, E 37.

[40] See above, pp. 19–21.

[41] *Ibid.*, p. 21.

merit that it allows an analysis of change over time, although it is also subject to certain limitations. In the first place, the occasion for recording the size of a holding was the death of a tenant, and yet mortality was neither random nor, with the notable exception of the 1349 plague mortality, indiscriminate. As a result the obituaries will tend to be biased towards individuals nearing the end of their life-cycle and will thus tend to convey a somewhat conservative picture of change. To compound matters, many individuals reduced the size of their holding as they neared the end of their life-cycle, settling land upon their heirs or disposing of it on the land market.[42] In some cases tenants retired altogether by trading their holdings for a pension, so that the amount of land which they held at death bore little relation to that which they had held during life.[43] Finally, most of these obituaries only list customary land held directly of the manor of Hakeford Hall. Yet so complex was land tenure in this locality that few holdings comprised land held entirely either of one tenure or of one lord.[44] It is inevitable that holding size will therefore be understated by evidence drawn from a single manor, and it is impossible to tell by how much. This does not invalidate the obituaries as a source for analysing changes in holding size, but means that they are more reliable as a relative than as an absolute guide.

Table 2.5 and Figure 2.1 present the data on holding size for successive 25-year periods from 1275 to 1400, taking 1349–50 separately on account of the exceptional number of obituaries recorded in those years. Mean and median holding size, together with the coefficient of variation, are given for each of these same periods in

[42] For example, in 1306 Andrew Leggard settled a messuage and 6 acres of arable upon his son Bartholemew, who then regranted them to his father for the remainder of the latter's life: KCC, E 31. The previous year John Welleman had died leaving 3¼ rods of arable and a little over 1 rod of marsh to his three married daughters, yet a dozen years earlier his holding had amounted to over 4 acres, for between 1292 and 1295 he disposed of 3 acres 1 rod 10 perches on the land market: *ibid*. Some indication of the scale of this life-cycle effect is provided by the fact that between 1280 and 1349 almost one-third of all conveyances took place between kin, many of them (as in the case of Andrew and Bartholemew Leggard) representing direct transfers from one generation to the next.

[43] In 1373, for instance, William Lyf granted a messuage and a little over 12 acres to his son Nicholas in return for an annual livery of barley to be paid twice yearly and the free use of a dwelling house in the messuage for the rest of his life: KCC, E 36. For the significance of such peasant maintenance contracts, see E. Clark, 'Some Aspects of Social Security in Medieval England', *Journal of Family History* 7 (1982), pp. 307–20.

[44] Thus the obituary of the substantial tenant Andrew Gritlof records that he held 17 acres of customary land of the manor of Hakeford Hall together with *xiiij terre quas perquisunt per cartas de diversis dominis*: KCC, E 29. Hudson cites the case of a tenant of the manor of Wykes in the township of Bardwell who held 14¾ acres of 8 different lords in the late thirteenth century: W. Hudson, 'Three Manorial Extents in the Thirteenth Century', *Norfolk Archaeology* 14 (1901), pp. 1–56.

Table 6. These demonstrate that there was a fairly simple inverse relationship between holding size and population trends. During the period of population growth between 1275 and 1348 mean and median holding size were both halved and there was a general tendency for small holdings to proliferate at the expense of large. As will be seen from the coefficient of variation, the size differential between large and small holdings was considerably narrower by the middle than it had been at the beginning of the fourteenth century, as the tenants of this manor were steadily compressed into a single class of impoverished smallholders. Figure 2.1A-D indicate the stages by which this process progressed, with the large number of obituaries recorded in 1349–50 affording a view of a particularly clear cross-section of the size distribution of holdings when tenant numbers were at a maximum. By this date no holding was larger than twelve-and-a-half acres and most were smaller than two acres. During the next half-century there was some increase in holding size as the population contracted, but for the first generation after the plague recovery seems to have taken place but slowly. In a period during which the population may have declined by 80 per cent, mean holding size barely doubled and holdings of under three acres continued to predominate. Even in the aftermath of the plague there was evidently no shortage of tenants on this manor. And although conditions were beginning to change by the end of the fourteenth century, as the proportion of very small holdings began to dwindle and the proportion of more substantial holdings began to grow, it is perhaps surprising that there are not clearer signs of emergent social polarization among the land holders on this manor. The proportion of holdings in excess of eight acres, the mean holding size, and the coefficient of variation, all remained no greater at the end of the fourteenth century than they had a century earlier (see Figure 2.6). To judge from the experience of other manors elsewhere in this area, it was not until the fifteenth century that particular individuals began to accumulate land on a hitherto unprecedented scale, so that by the end of that century an incipient yeomanry was firmly established. This process was both reflected in, and made possible by, a steady increase in *inter-vivos* at the expense of *post-mortem* land transfers.[45]

In the context of the fourteenth century, however, it is the absolute smallness of even the largest holdings that most attracts attention. Taking the period 1275–1400 as a whole, no tenant held more than thirty acres, 85 per cent held less than five acres, and the mean and median quantities held were two-and-a-half and one acre respect-

[45] Campbell, 'Commonfields in Eastern Norfolk', pp. 26–9.

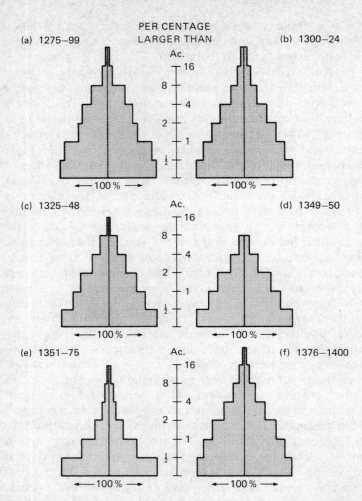

Figure 2.1. Coltishall, Norfolk: size distribution of holdings 1275–1400

ively. Even allowing for a substantial under-statement of holding size, it is difficult to resist the conclusion that a majority of holdings at Coltishall were well below the ten acres usually considered to represent the minimum required to ensure bare subsistence.[46] Furthermore, contemporary extents and surveys show that equally small

[46] Titow, *English Rural Society*, pp. 78–93. For a review of estimates of peasant budgets, see E. A. Kosminsky, *Studies in the Agrarian History of England in the Thirteenth Century* (Oxford, 1956), pp. 230–42. For a re-evaluation of the food sources available to smallholders, see Britton, *Community of the Vill*, pp. 156–63.

Table 2.5. Coltishall, Norfolk: size distribution of holdings 1275–1400 (according to the obituaries recorded in the court rolls)

Size of holding	1275–99		1300–24		1325–48		1349–50		1351–75		1376–1400	
	No.	%	No.	%	No.	%	No.	%	No.	%	No.	%
at least 16 ac.	1	2.9	3	5.2	0	0.0	0	0.0	0	0.0	1	2.0
,, 8 ac.	4	11.8	7	12.1	1	1.9	0	0.0	1	3.1	5	10.2
,, 4 ac.	12	35.3	15	25.9	9	17.3	10	11.6	3	9.4	12	24.5
,, 2 ac.	18	52.9	28	48.3	19	36.5	25	29.1	4	12.5	21	42.9
,, 1 ac.	21	61.8	39	67.2	30	57.7	48	55.8	9	28.1	32	65.3
,, ½ ac.	31	91.2	49	84.5	39	75.0	64	74.4	18	56.3	42	85.7
,, 0 ac.	34	100.0	58	100.0	52	100.0	86	100.0	32	100.0	49	100.0

105

Table 2.6. *Coltishall, Norfolk: Mean and median holding size 1275–1400 (according to the obituaries recorded in the court rolls)*

	No.	Median (rods)	Mean (rods)	Coefficient of variation
Years				
1275–99	34	8.0	12.0	116.74%
1300–24	58	6.75	15.3	144.11%
1325–48	52	4.0	8.0	107.94%
1349–50	86	4.0	6.4	99.48%
1351–75	32	2.0	4.5	169.69%
1376–1400	49	5.0	11.2	120.16%

holdings were characteristic of other manors in this locality: mean holding size was 4.8 acres at Worstead *circa* 1270, 5.5 acres at Hevingham *circa* 1284, 2.9 acres at Martham in 1292, 3.8 acres at Hautbois *circa* 1300, and 2.2 acres at Burgh in 1328.[47] Hence, even had the tenants of Hakeford Hall held land from three or four different manors, the chances are that their holdings would still have been below the ten-acre minimum. Moreover, this shortfall would have widened as holding size steadily dwindled during the first half of the fourteenth century. There can be little doubt, therefore, that holdings at Coltishall were small, not perhaps as small as the obituaries on their own suggest, but certainly too small to accord with conventional notions about the peasant family farm economy.

Anywhere else such small holdings might have been of dubious economic viability, but in eastern Norfolk physical, economic and social circumstances evidently combined in such a way as to permit holdings to remain viable at a far smaller size than was possible in much of the rest of the country. Nevertheless, even allowing for the possibility that peasant holdings were intensively cultivated, highly productive and subject to low 'rents', and that wage labouring may have yielded an important supplementary income, there is no escaping the fact that the conditions of life on these holdings would have been hard.[48] They would have become still harder as successive

---

[47] NRO Dean and Chapter Register V, ff. 132–5; British Library, MS Stowe 936; Public Record Office (hereafter PRO), SC 11 Roll 475; PRO, SC 11/22/10. An extent of the manor of Guton in Brandiston for 1334 records 156 tenants and 709 statute acres of land, giving a mean of 4.5 acres per tenant. But since only 121 of these tenants actually held land, and of these landholders only 76 were also householders in Brandiston, the mean holding size of tenants actually domiciled in Brandiston was 9.4 acres: Magdalen College, Oxford, Estate Papers 130/16.

[48] In this context see Smith's remarks, above pp. 25–7.

generations added to the population to be supported on the land. Yet, even though the relentless increase in numbers may have driven the population perilously close to the brink of the Malthusian precipice, no major subsistence crisis ever materialized. Throughout the difficult half-century 1300–48 the peasantry of the manor of Hakeford Hall evinced a quite remarkable degree of economic and demographic resilience. Some insight into this, and some indication of the response elicited by the dramatic release of pressure occasioned by the Black Death, are provided by an analysis of the land market and the propensity of individuals to buy and sell land.

iii. The land market at Coltishall

Under the demographic conditions which prevailed at Coltishall access to land was plainly critical to an individual's survival; hence *inter-vivos* and *post-mortem* land transfers can be assumed to have held a particular significance for the parties concerned. It was also in the lord's interest to ensure that all such transfers were registered in the manor court, for not only did customary land carry with it certain obligations, but the lord was also entitled to charge a fine whenever it changed hands. For these reasons transfers of land represent one of the most prominent items of business in the Coltishall court rolls. Between 1275 and 1405 the 335 court sessions whose proceedings survive record no less than 1,500 different *inter-vivos* land transfers, which, allowing for the incompleteness of the record, indicates a total turnover on this one small manor of perhaps 2,250 transactions and some 1,150 acres of land.[49] Since each of these transfers generally states the nature and extent of the properties transacted and the names of the vendor and the vendee, and is datable from the manor court in which it was registered, a very substantial body of potentially interesting data is available for analysis. That the manor court succeeded in netting and recording so many transactions itself

[49] In the thirteenth century these land transactions assume several guises – licences to sell, licences to buy and surrenders *ad opus* – but by the beginning of the fourteenth century surrenders *ad opus* had become the established format for all conveyances recorded in the court rolls (leases excepted). See Smith, below, p. 150, for the situation in Redgrave, Suffolk. On the peasant land market in general, see M. M. Postan and C. N. L. Brooke, editors, *Carte Nativorum: A Peterborough Abbey Cartulary of the Fourteenth Century*, Northamptonshire Record Society xx (Oxford, 1960); R. J. Faith, 'The Peasant Land Market in Berkshire during the Later Middle Ages', unpublished University of Leicester Ph.D. thesis, 1962; P. R. Hyams, 'The Origins of a Peasant Land Market in England', *Economic History Review* 2nd series 23 (1970), pp. 18–31; E. King, *Peterborough Abbey 1086–1310: A Study in the Land Market* (Cambridge, 1973); Smith above, pp. 12–20.

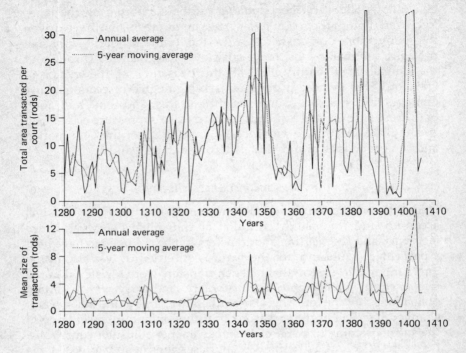

Figure 2.2.

implies that an illicit traffic in land cannot have amounted to very much; but the vigilance of these courts is also testified by the regularity with which individuals were prosecuted for buying and selling land illegally. In fact, the written title which the court rolls provided was an incentive for peasants to register their land transfers with the manor court, for this provided the means by which any subsequent dispute of ownership might be resolved. The entry of title in the court rolls was to a customary tenant as a charter was to a freeman. There are consequently compelling reasons for accepting as full and reliable the record of the land market which these court rolls provide.

The land market may be analysed in two main ways: according to the volume of transactions, and according to the individuals making the transactions. Calculations of the aggregate number of transactions and the total area transacted are, however, complicated by the incomplete survival of court rolls. This problem can be overcome in part by calculating turnover in terms of the rate per court per year and

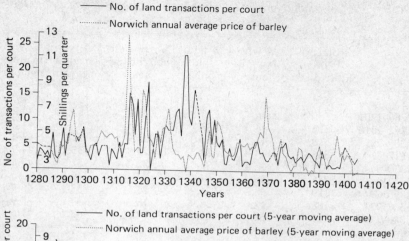

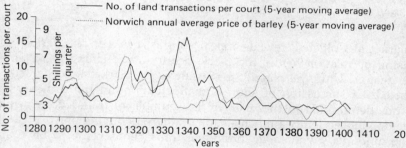

Figure 2.3.

in part by the use of moving averages (see Table 2.11 and Figures 2.2 and 2.3). Such an exercise remains valid as long as the loss of court rolls is more or less random and provided there was no temporal change in the frequency with which courts were held (special allowance can always be made for individual years with abnormally large numbers of court sessions). Much the same problem and solution apply to the biographical analysis of those buying and selling the land, although in this case the need to transpose the data from their original format represents another and rather different difficulty. The answer here lies in mechanical methods of data sorting, and it is by these means that the information contained in Table 2.7 and Figures 2.4 and 2.5 has been derived.[50]

As might be expected, an analysis of the dynamics of the land

[50] In this context I wish to acknowledge the assistance of Dr R. S. Schofield (Cambridge Group for the History of Population and Social Structure) and Mr P. Clarkson (Department of Engineering, University of Cambridge).

Table 2.7. *Coltishall, Norfolk: total numbers of individuals engaged in the land market 1280–1404*

	Total no. of individuals	% who bought only	% who sold only	% who both bought and sold	% who made a net gain	% who made a net loss
Years						
1280–1304	185	46.7	33.3	20.0	57.8	42.2
1292–1316	312	44.5	33.1	22.4	55.8	44.2
1305–29	318	42.1	34.0	23.9	52.2	47.8
1317–41	356	43.8	33.2	23.0	55.1	44.9
1330–54	333	42.4	35.5	22.2	52.3	47.8
1342–66	264	38.3	44.4	17.4	45.5	54.6
1355–79	179	38.0	36.9	25.1	53.1	46.9
1367–91	188	42.6	38.9	18.6	52.1	47.9
1380–1404	161	52.3	29.1	18.6	58.4	41.6

market at Coltishall reveals a clear contrast between the periods of rising population before the Black Death and of falling population thereafter. Until the plague, for instance, the market was character- ized by a succession of short-term fluctuations in the turnover of land, determined in the main by the number of transactions being made. Subsequently a much steadier pattern of buying prevailed and the amounts involved in individual transactions came to have an increasing influence upon overall turnover. Also, until 1348 the market was crowded, with large numbers of different individuals participating in it, but from 1350 numbers were substantially reduced and they continued to fall as the fourteenth century drew to a close (see Table 2.7): a trend which provides further incidental support for the chronology of population change which has already been out- lined. Nevertheless, perhaps the most striking difference between these two periods is that until the middle of the fourteenth century there was a strong correlation (mostly positive but at times negative) between the number of land transactions and the price of grain (and by implication, therefore, the quality of the harvest), yet throughout the second half of the century there was little or no correlation between these two variables (see Table 2.8). In other words, before the Black Death the land market was harvest-sensitive; thereafter it was not.

Between 1280 and 1350 grain prices underwent first a period of steady inflation (until about 1320) and then one of mild deflation associated with monetary changes and a long run of good harvests. Superim-

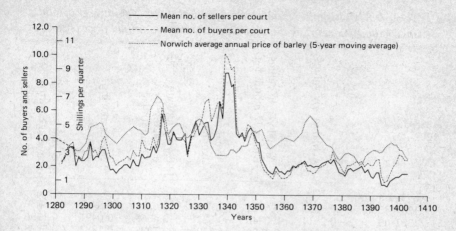

Figure 2.4.

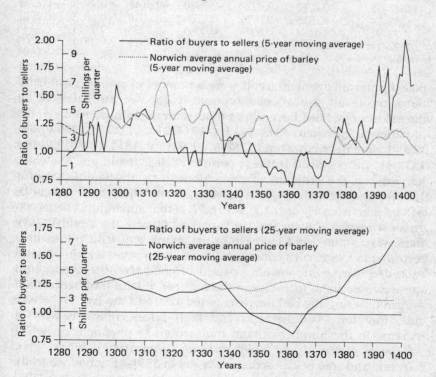

Figure 2.5.

Table 2.8. *Coltishall, Norfolk: correlation coefficients of number of land transactions per court against the Norwich average annual price of barley*

Years	Actual yearly values	Actual yearly values with a 12-month lag	3-year moving average	3-year moving average with a 12-month lag	5-year moving average	5-year moving average with a 12-month lag
1287–1300	0.5653	0.6014	0.7563	0.6221	0.8969	0.8039
1301–12	−0.2514	0.0940	−0.5211	−0.4569	−0.0491	−0.1396
1313–32	0.0365	0.5908	0.3298	0.7278	0.1282	0.5708
1333–42	−0.6108	−0.1277	−0.6258	−0.2545	−0.8133	−0.5633
1343–52	0.0763	−0.4227	−0.2980	−0.5646	−0.4999	−0.6716
1353–74	−0.0165	−0.0751	−0.2769	−0.2016	0.0893	−0.1721
1375–91	0.1894	0.3969	0.0063	0.5238	0.2745	0.4148
1392–1403	−0.1180	−0.0615	0.7489	0.7329	−0.3515	0.1603

posed upon this general trend were a number of short-term fluctuations, the result of years of exceptionally good or bad harvests. On the evidence of Lord Beveridge's figures for the annual average price of barley at Norwich, 1293–4, 1314–17, 1321–2, 1330–1, 1346–7, and 1350–1 were dear years, and 1287–8, 1299–1300, 1312, 1318, 1326, and 1334–41 cheap ones.[51] In these periods of dearth and glut the worst harvests on the criterion of price alone were the famine years of 1314–17 and the best those of 1334–41. It was these two periods (as will be seen from Figures 2.2, 2.3 and 2.4) that apparently elicited the greatest response from the land market. During the Great Famine there was a three-fold increase in the number of land transactions recorded in Coltishall's court rolls, a rate of turnover which was only exceeded during the ensuing period of good harvests. Apart from these two periods, increases in the number of land transactions also occurred during the bad harvests of the 1290 and the late 1340s. As a rule, therefore, bad harvests and high prices coincided with an increase in the number of land transactions (a phenomenon which has been observed on other manors at this time), whilst good harvests and low prices occasionally, as in 1334–41, gave rise to the

[51] London School of Economics, Beveridge Price Data, Box G9.

same. The inference to be drawn from this would appear to be that
consecutive years of harvest failure reduced the peasantry to such a
state that they were obliged to sell land in order to buy food, and that
only a fortuitous run of good harvests put them in a position to
recoup their losses.

The relationship between grain prices and land transactions is most
clearly manifest during the closing decades of the thirteenth century:
abundant harvests and low prices in 1287–8 and 1299–1300 framed a
period of high prices and mounting rural crisis during which harvest
failure thrice (in 1293 and 1294 and then again in 1297) narrowly
approached famine proportions. Throughout this period, as Table 2.8
shows, there was a consistently high positive correlation, higher than
at any other period, between the price of grain and the number of
land transactions. In contrast to those of later periods, the low prices
of 1287–8 and 1299–1300 failed to promote any appreciable increase in
the activity of the land market. In fact, on both occasions the activity
of the market was at a relatively low ebb, which is perhaps to be
attributed to the reluctance of individuals to sell land rather than to
any shortage of demand. It would seem that, whereas the propensity
of individuals to sell land was increased by bad, it was reduced by
good, harvests. Furthermore, the effect of successive bad harvests
appears to have been cumulative, the number of transactions recorded in the court rolls steadily mounting during the 1290s (in which
context it is especially unfortunate that none of the court rolls for 1297
have survived).[52] As already noted, however, a return to more normal
harvests at the close of the decade soon halted this spate of transactions and marked a return to a more sluggish level of turnover. The
immediacy with which the supply of land contracted as soon as bad
harvests had passed is shown by the sudden improvement in the
ratio of buyers to sellers at the turn of the century (see Figure 2.5).
The same phenomenon may also be accounted for by the high
demand for land which undoubtedly prevailed in the aftermath of
such harvests, as individuals endeavoured both to make good their
losses and to protect themselves from renewed harvest failure.

After 1300 a continued inelasticity of supply ensured that the land

---

[52] A similar peaking of land transfers during the 1290s has been observed by Smith at
Redgrave and Rickinghall in north-west Suffolk and by D. G. Watts on the Titchfield
Abbey estate in southern Hampshire. It is also just discernible on the Bishop of
Norwich's manor at Hevingham. In the two Suffolk townships the land market was
also characterized by a marked surplus of sellers over buyers during this period:
Smith, 'English Peasant Life-Cycles'; D. G. Watts, 'A Model for the Early Fourteenth
Century', *Economic History Review* 2nd series 20 (1967), p. 543–7; Campbell, 'Arable
Productivity', p. 380.

market remained relatively inactive, for the opening decade of the fourteenth century was punctuated by neither dearth nor glut. Nevertheless, such a crisis-free period could not last indefinitely, particularly in the face of a continued rise in tenant numbers and fall in holding size. Sooner or later harvest failure was bound to unbalance this precarious equilibrium. When harvest failure assumed the scale of the Famine of 1314–17 the effect was therefore traumatic. In 1314 there was a partial, and then in 1315 and again in 1316, a total, failure of the grain harvest (in 1316 grain prices soared to two-and-a-half times their average); the harvest of 1317 was also deficient; and after an interlude of three years harvests again failed in 1321 and 1322. Dearth had occurred in no fewer than six out of nine years.

The response of the land market to these harvest failures was immediate and dramatic and on an altogether different scale from the near-famine of some twenty years earlier. The response was also more complex. By 1316 the number of transactions recorded in the court rolls had trebled, and by 1317 the number of individuals participating in the market had doubled.[53] Since many of the plots which were changing hands were extremely small, it seems likely that in most cases peasants were selling land to buy food but at the same time were endeavouring to keep their losses to a minimum. Also, so widespread was the economic distress at this time that difficulty may have been encountered in marketing larger plots of land; the ratio of buyers to sellers certainly indicates an excess of the latter over the former (see Figure 2.5). With the improved harvests of 1318–20 there was some amelioration of conditions: the number of transactions fell and the ratio of buyers to sellers improved. But this recovery was abruptly curtailed by the bad harvests of 1321 and 1322, which precipitated a further rush of land sales.[54] On this occasion, however, there was a short lag between the period of maximum dearth and the peak of land sales (which occurred in 1323), reflecting either an upsurge in the demand for land in the aftermath of acute harvest failure (as was to occur in 1326 and again in the 1330s) or, more probably, the growing difficulty which sellers were experiencing in

[53] Much the same response has been identified on many other manors at this time: W. Hudson, 'The Prior of Norwich's Manor of Hindolveston: Its Early Organization and Rights of the Customary Tenants to Alienate their Strips of Land', Norfolk Archaeology 20 (1921), pp. 179–214; Watts, 'A Model'; Kershaw, 'Great Famine', p. 38; Smith, 'English Peasant Life-Cycles', pp. 23–4; Razi, Life, Marriage and Death, p. 37.

[54] The same occurred at Hindolveston (Hudson, 'The Prior of Norwich's Manor'), where a correlation of the number of land transactions per court against the price of barley, with a 12-month lag, yields a correlation coefficient for the period 1309–26 of 0.8905. This compares with an equivalent correlation coefficient at Coltishall of 0.5908 for the period 1313–32.

finding ready buyers at times of dearth. Nevertheless, the flood of sales which followed the dearth of 1321–2 was proportionately far greater than that which had followed the more spectacular harvest failure of 1314–17, or for that matter the bad harvests of 1293–4 and 1297. It is significant that the ratio of buyers to sellers sank below unity for the first time in over a generation in 1321.[55] The resilience of rural society was clearly deteriorating. Economic conditions were conspiring to depress the ability to buy land at the very time that more and more land holders were left with no other alternative than to sell it.

From 1323 the activity of the land market again began to subside, and with a return to more normal conditions the respite was more substantial. Harvests steadily improved and prices fell until in 1326 a near-record harvest enabled the peasantry to recoup some of their earlier losses. There was a slight improvement in the ratio of buyers to sellers, an increase in the numbers transacting land, and a moderate increase in the turnover of land on the market. Significantly, this is the first occasion on which good harvests acted as a positive stimulus to the activity of the land market. But recovery did not long proceed unchecked and two consecutive bad harvests, in 1330 and 1331, triggered off yet another sharp rise in prices and a further spate of land sales. Once again the peasantry were reduced to a very distressed state. These, however, were the last in this extraordinary run of adverse years, and from 1334, with the advent of a succession of unusually good harvests, the activity of the land market was transformed.

During the 18-year period 1314–31 there had been no fewer than eight years of dearth; during the ensuing nineteen years there was but one. In two other years harvests were deficient, but of the remaining sixteen harvests over half were of above average quality. Coming in the aftermath of such a lean period, these favourable harvests therefore served to render more universal the process of reconstruction whose modest beginnings may first be detected in the late 1320s. For the first time in at least half a century a strong inverse relationship existed between the price of grain and the number of land transactions (see Table 2.8). Prices began to fall in 1332, were well below average in 1334, and by 1338 had fallen to a record low,

[55] This is in marked contrast to developments on the two Suffolk manors of Redgrave and Rickinghall, where, although the chronology of the land market was superficially the same, sellers had been surplus to buyers since the penultimate decade of the thirteenth century. As a result Smith has concluded that, unlike Coltishall, land was tending to become concentrated into fewer hands: Smith, 'English Peasant Life-Cycles', pp. 64–79.

lower even than in 1287–8. As prices fell so the number of land transfers rose. The increase was slow at first but gained momentum following the bumper harvest of 1334, and by 1337 the turnover of the market had surpassed even that of the famine years 1316 and 1317. At the same time there was a marked improvement in the ratio of buyers to sellers, so that by the mid-1330s the margin between the numbers buying land and those selling it was wider than at any time since the beginning of the century.

There can be little doubt that an upsurge in demand lay behind all this activity. Bountiful harvests had at long last presented the peasantry with an opportunity to make good some of the losses they had sustained during the preceding decades. At the same time, land purchase was probably viewed as the best possible insurance against renewed harvest failure. Although few peasants could finance the purchase of more than the meagrest amounts of land, few seem to have hesitated now that economic circumstances were finally in their favour. Indeed, an upturn in the activity of the land market followed much more closely upon these good harvests than had ever been the case after bad ones. Ironically, however, the more the lot of the peasantry improved and their ability and desire to acquire land increased, the smaller became the number of those prepared to sell it. The natural indisposition of peasant cultivators to part with land ensured that its supply was fundamentally inelastic, with the result that high levels of turnover could only be sustained when the peasantry were squeezed by adverse economic circumstances. Following the record harvests of 1337–8 and 1341 the activity of the land market at Coltishall therefore began to subside, a trend which was perhaps hastened by the poor harvest of 1343 and a mounting financial crisis in the country at large.[56] By the early 1340s the process of reconstruction appears to have run its course, and by 1345 the number of land transactions had fallen to the lowest recorded level since the Famine. A revival in the activity of the market the following year therefore represents a reversion to the earlier pattern of crisis-generated land sales, first as a result of the renewed food shortages of

[56] The same peaking of land transactions in the early 1330s and falling away in the early 1340s occurred on the Titchfield Abbey estate. According to Watts the 1330s were 'fortunate years of favourable weather and good harvests. The population was recovering after a temporary check in the Great Famine, and the peasants were actively exploiting their opportunities. . . A run of bad weather and poor harvests would have brought another period of dearth, and perhaps a Malthusian situation; but it does not seem to me that a Malthusian situation already existed in 1340'. On the financial situation at this time, see J. R. Maddicott, 'The English Peasantry and the Demands of the Crown, 1294–1341', *Past and Present* supplement 1 (1975), pp. 45–67.

1346–7 and then as a result of the combined plague and dearth of 1349–50.

That deficient harvests such as those of 1346–7 were still capable of taking their toll even after more than a decade of fat years is a reminder of the precarious equilibrium in which Coltishall's population continued to exist. Indeed, the generous harvests of the 1330s may have promoted a false sense of security, whereas all the while the relentless increase in population was tipping the balance ever more adversely for the peasants. The immediate spate of land sales triggered by the poor harvests of 1346–7 is an obvious manifestation of this. What the long-term consequences were of this final instance of dearth is, however, impossible to ascertain, for within two years they were overshadowed by the massive upheaval in the established pattern of land holding precipitated by the outbreak of plague. At one stroke the mounting pressure of population upon the land was released and the old crisis-determined pattern of land transactions was terminated. Thenceforth the behaviour of the market would be very different.

What is most impressive about the behaviour of the market up to this point, though, is the sheer frequency with which these subsistence cultivators bought and sold land. For a community which was so heavily dependent upon farming for a living and where land was in such short supply, the peasants were remarkably ready to part with it and demonstrated surprisingly little difficulty in buying it. Moreover, their propensity to transact land appears to have increased rather than decreased as the population grew and holdings diminished in size. Rather than being a healthy sign, however, this increased involvement in the land market is symptomatic of a mounting rural crisis. Such an interpretation is borne out by the harvest-related pattern of land transfers which can be identified from at least the last quarter of the thirteenth century. In this context, the significance of the harvest undoubtedly lay in its influence upon subsistence levels rather than profit margins; for, had the latter been the operative factor, the effective demand for land would not have been strongest when grain prices were most depressed, as was in fact the case in the 1330s. That a majority of peasants was only able to redeploy some resources for the purchase of land when harvests were exceptionally bountiful, even though the price which they received for their meagre surpluses was a comparatively poor one, emphasizes their role as subsistence cultivators. Market forces, in fact, served to penalize the peasantry, for when harvests failed many of them were obliged to sell land in a buyer's, and purchase food in a seller's, market. To exacerbate matters, on those rare occasions when these same individuals were in a position to buy back land its supply was generally highly inelastic. The behaviour of the land market at Coltishall between 1280 and 1348 is therefore characteristic of a situation in which land holders were becoming increasingly impoverished and ever more vulnerable to harvest failure. In this context, a comparison of the relative impact upon the land market of the successive dearths of 1293–4, 1297, 1314–17, 1321–2, 1330–1, and 1345–7 is illuminating (see Table 2.9).

Any attempt to compare the relative severity of the recurrent harvest failures of the late thirteenth and first half of the fourteenth centuries suffers from the limitation that the scale of these failures can only be measured in monetary terms. Moreover, the value of money did not remain constant throughout this period: up to about 1320 was a period of general inflation, whilst the next two decades witnessed a mild deflation.[57] With this qualification, changes in the activity of the land market (the number of transactions, area transacted and numbers selling land) have been related to unit changes in the price of barley. The mean of each variable during the period 1280–9 has been taken as base and the results are summarized in Table 2.9. From this it will be seen that there was a clear tendency for successive periods of dearth to elicit a progressively greater proportional response from the land market. This was especially the case when bad harvests occurred in close succession, as in 1293–4 and 1297, and again in 1314–17 and 1321–2, but it was also true of the period as a whole. Thus, the hardship inflicted by the dearths of 1321–2, 1330–1, and 1346–7 was in proportional terms more severe than that suffered during the famines of either 1293–4 or 1314–17. Patently, the population was losing its ability to weather the periodic food shortages which were the inevitable lot of all pre-industrial societies. A further symptom of this process of marginalization was the increasingly exaggerated response to periods of glut. As a growing proportion of the population faced the prospect of having to sell land if harvests failed, so increasing numbers seized the opportunity to buy it whenever circumstances permitted. By the second quarter of the fourteenth century this panic buying of land had become so great that in years of good harvests the turnover of land on the market exceeded even that of the worst famine years.

---

[57] Phelps Brown and Hopkins, 'Seven Centuries of Prices'; M. Prestwich, 'Edward I's Monetary Policies and their Consequences', *Economic History Review* 2nd series 22 (1969), pp. 406–16; M. Mate, 'High Prices in Early Fourteenth Century England', *Economic History Review* 2nd series 28 (1975), pp. 1–16.

Table 2.9. Coltishall, Norfolk: a comparison of the response of the land market to successive periods of dearth 1280–1350*

Period of dearth	Max. unit rise in price	Max. unit rise in no. of transactions	Unit rise in no. of transactions per unit rise in price	Rank score	Max. unit rise in area transacted	Unit rise in area transacted per unit rise in price	Rank score	Max. unit rise in no. of sellers	Unit rise in no. of sellers per unit rise price	Rank score	Total rank score	Rank of total score
1293–4	203	205	1.01	6	243	1.20	4	95	0.47	6	16	6
1297	163	263	1.61	3	139	0.85	5	118	0.72	3	11	4
1314–17	388	483	1.24	5	268	0.69	6	214	0.55	5	16	6
1321–2	229	552	2.41	1	360	1.57	2	157	0.69	4	7	2
1330–1	211	284	1.35	4	268	1.27	3	173	0.82	2	9	3
1346–7	162	356	2.20	2	507	3.13	1	170	1.05	1	4	1

*Mean of period 1280–9 = base 100 in each case.

119

Yet, although the possibility of a Malthusian crisis seems to have become ever more real, even the worst subsistence crises made remarkably little impression upon the prevailing demographic trend. Famines occurred and caused great distress, but in no single instance did they lead to any permanent departure from the demographic *status quo*. This is true even of the Great Famine of 1314–17, for which so much has sometimes been claimed. In fact, the very readiness with which the peasantry was able to liquidize its assets, selling off land to buy food, may have been one of the factors which gave this community so much resilience. When times were hard few peasants took the dramatic step of disposing of all their land; instead most no doubt hoped and intended to recoup the bulk or all of their losses when the immediate crisis had passed and good harvests returned. It is only surprising that under these circumstances greater resort was not had to short-term leases, unless, of course, sales yielded a greater immediate cash income.[58] Viewed in this way, the land market is seen as one of the means by which peasant society maintained itself in a state of dynamic equilibrium. As a result, although the progressive build-up of population may have pressed hard upon resources, and although that population's ability to withstand dearth and famine may have been tested to the full, the threatened crisis never material-ized. The mortality crisis when it occurred, as it did in 1349, was a result not of economic but of biological factors. Coltishall's population may have been able to endure the scourge of famine but it was incapable of withstanding the ravages of plague. On this manor therefore the Black Death marks the end of an era, at least insofar as the close relationship between harvest quality and the activity of the land market is concerned.

The immediate effect of the Black Death and of the dearth which accompanied it was to precipitate a flurry of *inter-vivos* land transfers, with the result that in 1349 the amount of land changing hands reached an unprecedented level. As the death toll steadily mounted, however, this sudden spate of activity began to subside. For the next few years a downward trend persisted, and by 1354 the number of land transfers had been reduced to its lowest level for thirty years. In fact, fewer land transfers are recorded for the decade immediately succeeding the plague than for any previous period of equivalent length. Furthermore, this is the only decade on record when sellers consistently outnumbered buyers. There had been other occasions on

---

[58] Only 88 leases are recorded in the court rolls in the period 1275–1349; the mean area leased was 1.8 rods and the mean length of lease was 6 years.

which the ratio of buyers to sellers had fallen below unity – the early 1280s, the late 1320s and the late 1340s – but, as has been shown, this had always been associated with a deterioration in subsistence levels and was generally very short-lived. The circumstances in the 1350s were rather different: prices were low and plague had reduced the pressure of population. The explanation on this occasion would therefore seem to lie with the massive *post-mortem* transfer of land ownership which had recently occurred and to which the population was now adjusting. In other words, land was being redistributed in the aftermath of plague. Distinctive features of the market at this time are the reduced proportion of individuals who entered it as both buyers and sellers, and a relative decline in the number of transfers between kin (although the latter can partly be accounted for by the recent sudden reduction in population). There was also an increase in the number of transactions involving residential property, of which there was now presumably an excess, and an increase in the number of leases registered in the court rolls.[59] The frenetic buying and selling of the land-hungry years before the plague was plainly over and the path was now open, in the absence of any recovery in population, for an entirely new pattern of buying and selling to emerge.

The quiescence of the land market in the early 1350s gave way to some revival of activity in the late 1350s, but this was abruptly curtailed in 1361–2 by a further sharp fall in the number of land transfers. The turnover of land on the market was reduced to a level lower even than that plumbed in the opening years of the fourteenth century, and at the same time the ratio of buyers to sellers sank to an all-time low. On the face of it the events of twelve years earlier were repeating themselves, and this depression in the activity of the land market is perhaps to be accounted for by a recurrence of plague. There is certainly nothing to suggest that abnormal harvests had anything to do with it. Yet although 1361–2 was a national plague year, direct evidence that Coltishall was again affected is lacking. The nominative listings indicate that a substantial reduction in tenant numbers occurred between 1359 and 1370, and the obituaries show that there was a continued shortage of direct heirs and of sons in particular, but in both cases this evidence is entirely circumstantial.[60]

---

[59] Comparing 1325–49 with 1350–74, conveyances between kin fell from 37% to 20.4%, conveyances involving residential property rose from 13.3% to 30.1% and the mean area leased per court rose from 1.65 rods to 2.04 rods. At Martham the area being leased actually exceeded that being sold, a situation which persisted until the very end of the fourteenth century: Campbell, 'Population Change', p. 189.

[60] A nominative listing of uncertain accuracy lists 62 tenants in 1361, indicating a decline of at least 19.5% in male tenant numbers since June 1359: KCC, E 25 no. 6.

By the same token, the unremarkable number of obituaries recorded during these years has to be set against the incompleteness of the court record. Whatever the cause of this recession in the land market, its effect was transitory; for within two years the amount of land changing hands began once more to rise.

From 1363 the number of individuals participating in the land market began to increase, the ratio of buyers to sellers improved, there were more land transfers and on average they dealt with more land. By 1365 the turnover of land had at last regained the level of the immediate pre-plague years. Again, however, the recovery proved short-lived. From 1367 harvests seem to have deteriorated, for prices began to rise and as they rose so the number of land transfers fell. 1367 was the dearest year since 1351, prices were still high in 1368, and in 1369 they reached famine level. In fact, 1369 was the dearest year since 1321 and the fourth dearest in the entire period 1280–1405. Prices were still well above average in 1370 and 1371, and 1373 was the first really cheap year for seven years. In the congested conditions prevailing before the plague such a period of sustained high prices would undoubtedly have precipitated a flood of land transfers. That precisely the opposite response actually occurred is therefore a measure of the demographic and economic transformation which had come about. From 1367 the number of individuals participating in the land market contracted so sharply that by 1370 it had been reduced to the same very low level of ten years earlier. Moreover, since the number of buyers contracted more rapidly than the number of sellers, there was an abrupt deterioration in the ratio of buyers to sellers. In 1370 the number of land transactions and the amount of land changing hands were back on a par with those of 1360–4. This similarity between the state and behaviour of the land market at these two dates is significant, for 1369–70 witnessed another major outbreak of plague. Indeed, although direct evidence of plague mortality at Coltishall is lacking, the abrupt decline in *inter-vivos* transfers and the relative predominance of sellers over buyers together suggest that this depression in the activity of the land market had as much to do with the plague as with dearth.

Whether or not Coltishall was again visited by plague in 1360–1 and 1369–70, there is no reason to doubt that its population was smaller in 1370 than it had been in 1350. All the available evidence points to this conclusion. Such a reduction in population, coming on top of the reduction which had already occurred as a result of the Black Death, had a liberating effect upon the land market. From the mid-1370s the contrast with the pre-plague pattern of buying and selling begins to become pronounced.[61] In particular, although the number of land transfers remained at a low level the amounts of land being trans- ferred became increasingly large. More and more transactions were dealing with not just one plot of land but several, and the result was an expansion in the amount of land changing hands and a greater annual variation in the volume of turnover. Troughs in turnover occurred in 1374, 1378–9 and 1384, and peaks in 1368, 1372, 1377, 1382 and, above all, 1386. The last year saw grain prices fall to their lowest level for 100 years and the amount of land changing hands reach a record for the fourteenth century in a market in which buyers increasingly predominated over sellers. Since at the same time there was a steady downward drift in the number of individuals entering the market either as buyers or sellers, or, to some extent, as both, there was a strong upward trend in the *per capita* transfer of land. Comparing the years 1380–1404 with the equivalent 25-year period 1280–1304 (see Table 2.10), the mean *per capita* amounts bought and sold increased by 306 and 361 per cent respectively. The tendency for certain individuals to buy or sell much greater amounts of land than others also became more marked, and this is reflected in a rise in the variance of the *per capita* amounts bought and sold of 550 and 911 per cent respectively. The net result was a greater differentiation of holding size, as is borne out by the evidence of the obituaries (see Table 2.5). That being said, on the evidence of these same obituaries land ownership would appear to have been no more polarized at the end of the fourteenth century than it had been some 100 years earlier. Class differentiation may have been latent in the action of the land market, but it still had a long way to go.

The 1390s witnessed a major lull in the activity of the land market at Coltishall: between 1393 and 1398 less land changed hands than during any other equivalent period on record. The number of individuals participating in the market was greatly reduced, especi- ally in 1394–6, there were very few land transfers, and those that there were transferred comparatively small amounts of land. Why the land market should have been so depressed at this time is unclear (unless it was a delayed reaction to the plague outbreak of 1391), but whatever the reason its influence was not confined to Coltishall, for the land market was similarly depressed at Hevingham (five miles to the west) and at Martham (eleven miles to the east).[62] At Coltishall and Martham the late 1390s brought some recovery, and then at

---

[61] Bridbury, 'The Black Death'.
[62] Campbell, 'Field Systems', pp. 377 and 380; Shrewsbury, *History of Bubonic Plague*, pp. 137–8. 8 obituaries are recorded in 1391, more than in any other year since 1349.

Table 2.10. *Coltishall, Norfolk: comparison of the gross areas bought and sold by individuals 1280–1304 and 1380–1404*

	1280–1304	1380–1404	1380–1404 as % of 1280–1304
No. who bought land	124	114	91.9
% who bought at least 1 ac.	16.1	41.2	255.9
% who bought at least 2 ac.	5.6	21.9	391.1
% who bought at least 3 ac.	2.4	18.4	766.7
Variance of area bought	1.02	5.6	549.0
Mean area bought (ac.)	0.55	1.68	305.5
Max. area bought (ac.)	7.75	10.0	129.0
No. who sold land	98	77	78.6
% who sold at least 1 ac.	23.5	61.0	259.6
% who sold at least 2 ac.	8.2	41.6	507.3
% who sold at least 3 ac.	5.1	23.4	458.8
Variance of area sold	1.17	10.66	911.1
Mean area sold (ac.)	0.69	2.49	360.9
Max. area sold (ac.)	7.9	14.5	183.5
Ratio of buyers to sellers	1.27	1.48	116.6

Coltishall between 1400 and 1403 the turnover of land rose to new heights. The number of *inter-vivos* transfers was still small, but the average amount of land being transferred was now larger than ever before, as was the relative excess of buyers over sellers. The latter phenomenon does not, however, indicate a return to fragmentation. Rather, it reflects the fact that tenants who disposed of their holdings were outnumbered by those endeavouring to enlarge them. In most cases choice rather than force of circumstance now decided whether individuals remained as land holders or sought alternative sources of livelihood. Since a majority of tenants seems to have chosen to remain on the land, there were more individuals buying land than selling it and such land as came onto the market rapidly found a purchaser. Under these competitive conditions engrossing was bound to make only slow progress.

Unfortunately, the court record ends in 1405 and does not resume again until 1471, by which date the turnover of land on the market had expanded still further. In the period 1471–6 the mean annual turnover of land at Coltishall was approximately two-and-a-quarter times greater than it had been during the years 1399–1405,[63] and three

---

[63] KCC, E 39.

times greater than it had been during the years 1380–1405. Since the number of transactions declined by more than half, this increase was entirely due to an expansion in the amounts of land being transacted. The latter grew from a mean of slightly less than one acre in the period 1380–1405, to 1.4 acres in 1399–1405 and no less than 6.8 acres in 1471–5: an almost five-fold increase in the space of 70 years. Such a transformation in the amounts of land being transacted presupposes a concomitant growth in the financial resources of the individuals buying the land, which implies a substantial increase in the size of holdings. It also implies a greater disposition on the part of certain individuals to sell land. What determined who retained their land during this period and who did not is an intriguing question which cannot as yet be answered. Ultimately, of course, those families who held onto their land made it through to the ranks of the prosperous yeoman class of the sixteenth and seventeenth centuries, whereas the majority of those who gave up their land went to swell the number of landless wage labourers.[64]

In eastern Norfolk the crucial years for the advance of this process of differentiation seem to have lain less in the fourteenth then in the fifteenth century. This was certainly the case at Martham and Hevingham, where the survival of relatively complete series of fifteenth-century court rolls means that its course can be charted fairly closely.[65] On these two manors it was in the middle years of the fifteenth century that certain tenants first began to accumulate land on a hitherto unprecedented scale: once under way the process gathered momentum, and by the last quarter of the century proto-yeoman farms of relatively substantial size had emerged at both Martham and Hevingham.[66] The land market was the basic instrument by which this redistribution of property came about, but its operation was greatly facilitated by the demise of customary inheritance as an institution. Signs that customary inheritance was falling into abeyance are already apparent in the closing years of the fourteenth century, and during the following century it was increasingly superseded by both land transfers made immediately prior to

[64] By 1584, when a detailed survey was made of the parish, mean holding size at Coltishall had risen to 26.1 acres and 8 of the 48 farmers in the parish held at least 40 acres of arable: KCC, E 28.

[65] Campbell, 'Field Systems', pp. 97–102, 117–35 and 293–300.

[66] At Martham holdings of at least 18 acres accounted for 42.8% of the arable area in 1497: NRO, Dean and Chapter MS 2765. The first holding of at least 30 acres was recorded in 1434: NRO, NNAS 5940 20 D4. At Hevingham holdings of at least 18 acres accounted for three-quarters of the arable area *circa* 1500: NRO, NRS 13714 28 D6.

death and testamentary bequests. At Martham by the second half of the fifteenth century *inter-vivos* transfers accounted for two-and-a-half to three times more land than *post-mortem* transfers, and there is no reason to suppose that the situation at Coltishall was any different.[67] Underlying this development, in the absence of any renewed growth of population, was a continued shortage of direct heirs. Its behaviour thereafter was patently very different from that of the land market before 1349. Gone are the symptoms of mounting rural distress in the form of an extreme sensitivity to harvests. Bad harvests no longer provoked a spate of selling, nor did good harvests necessarily promote a surge of buying. Coltishall may have remained populated by smallholders but the worst pangs of land hunger had been assuaged. After 1349 the land market became less and less a market in individual plots, many of them pathetically small, and more and more a market first in substantial portions and then in entire holdings. As a result an increased proportion of transfers involved residential property and a decreased proportion took place between kin. Most important of all, however, consolidation had displaced fragmentation as the principal net outcome of the land market. That being said, it is not until some considerable time after 1349 that a strong trend towards the polarization of land ownership becomes apparent. The greater part of the second half of the fourteenth century represents a transitional period during which the population readjusted to repeated onslaughts of plague and holding size was returned to the level of the late thirteenth century. At this stage, had population growth been resumed it is probable that the peasantry would eventually have been returned to the same distressed state that it had experienced in the first half of the fourteenth century. Significantly, and for whatever reason, such a regrowth of population did not occur and the way was left open for land ownership to regroup itself in a new and novel way. The land market was the principal instrument by which this change was effected, although it was undoubtedly assisted by the demise of customary inheritance. But above all it was the postponement of any recovery in population for the greater part of the fifteenth century that encouraged the decay of such customary institutions, ensured that wage labouring remained an attractive economic alternative to land ownership and

---

[67] At Martham the ratio of the area sold to the area inherited was as follows: 1276–1300 1.2; 1351–75 1.1; 1376–1400 1.5; 1401–25 1.9; 1426–50 1.7; 1451–75 3.2; 1497–1509 2.6. Over the same period sales made *in extremis* accounted for the following proportions of the total area sold: 1351–75 6.4%; 1376–1400 17.6%; 1401–25 26.4%; 1426–50 20.4% 1451–75 30.1%; 1497–1509 44.6%. Campbell, 'Field Systems', pp. 123 and 135.

maintained a sufficiently flexible supply of land to permit the build-up of substantial holdings by piecemeal acquisition.[68] Not until the middle years of that century is a category of incipient yeoman farms clearly recognizable, and as they subsequently grew in size so the process of class differentiation among the peasantry became irreversible.

Conclusion

Coltishall between 1280 and 1348 manifests all the symptoms of a society trapped in the Malthusian deadlock between population and resources. All the classic features of land hunger were present, notably farm fragmentation, morcellation, immiseration and a mounting vulnerability to harvest failure. Yet the conventional Malthusian expectation that a ceiling to population growth must eventually be reached does not appear to have been fulfilled. Despite the ineluctable growth of population, no Malthusian positive check ever materialized. Great as was the distress which it caused, the Great Famine, whose effects are discernible over the years 1315–18, does not represent a demographic or economic watershed on this manor. Indeed, if the economic breaking point was ever reached at Coltishall it was in 1346–7, although the aftermath of this crisis is for ever buried beneath that of the more devastating catastrophe of plague which followed it just two years later. Plague accomplished within twelve months what the recurrent famine had signally failed to achieve during the preceding seventy years: the population was drastically reduced and a new downward trend in numbers was inaugurated. There were probably at least another two and possibly even three, plague outbreaks at Coltishall during the remainder of the fourteenth century, although like the Black Death none of them had anything whatever to do with prevailing economic conditions. Plague is an exogenous variable and as such it is neither easily nor happily accommodated within an exclusively Malthusian or Marxist inter-

---

[68] At Coltishall 30 male customary tenants are enumerated in a listing given in the court rolls in 1475: KCC, E 39. At Martham 69 male customary tenants are enumerated in 1454, 80 in 1480, and 74 in 1505 (there were 271 male tenants on the manor in 1292): NRO, NNAS 5948 20 D4, NNAS 5951 20 D5, NNAS 5952 20 D5, British Library MS Stowe 936. On the same manor deceased tenants were succeeded by sons in the following proportions: 1401–25 57.7% (No. = 52); 1426–63 76.0% (No. = 25); 1497–1509 69.0% (No. = 29): Campbell, 'Field Systems', p. 121. At Hevingham the number of customary tenants declined from 57 in 1407 to 46 in 1499: NRO, NRS 14772 29 D4, NRS 19566 42 D2. During the fifteenth century deceased tenants were succeeded by sons in proportions as follows: 1425–60 57.1% (No. = 21); 1483–1509 66.7% (No. = 21): Campbell, 'Field Systems', p. 299.

pretation of events. Yet there is no doubting the profound influence which it exerted upon demographic and economic developments at Coltishall.

That is not to say that demographic trends were uninfluenced by economic factors, but rather that if they were it was possibly in a way other than that generally envisaged. The extraordinarily prolonged demographic recession which followed the advent of plague at Coltishall, as elsewhere in the country, defies simple Malthusian or even Ricardian logic. In its earliest stages much of this recession can undoubtedly be attributed to plague, the experience of Coltishall thus paralleling quite closely that documented in more detail by Razi for Halesowen; but it is difficult to account for the stagnation of a further hundred years in terms of plague, or even of mortality, alone.[69] In this context the analogy of seventeenth- and eighteenth-century Colyton is instructive.[70] Colyton, like Coltishall, experienced a major mortality crisis at a time of considerable population pressure (in this case as a result of the plague of 1646), and thereafter, for the next hundred years or so, as at Coltishall, the population exhibited a marked disinclination to grow. As E. A. Wrigley has convincingly shown, this was partly due to a continuing high level of mortality, but more particularly to a significant reduction of fertility, through later and less frequent marriage and the reduction of fertility within marriage, reinforced by out-migration. Such a pattern of behaviour – the adoption of preventive measures after the immediate need for them had passed – has been termed by Wrigley a demographic lurch and can be recognized in other pre-industrial communities where the build-up of Malthusian-type forced conditions was suddenly defused by a mortality crisis of the proportions usually only associated, either directly or indirectly, with some kind of biological agency.[71] Clearly, the possibility that such a demographic lurch occurred in the late fourteenth- and fifteenth-century England merits serious consideration. Certainly, the demographic evidence available for Coltishall,

[69] Nevertheless, see J. Saltmarsh, 'Plague and Economic Decline in England in the Later Middle Ages', *Cambridge Historical Journal* 7 (1941–3), pp. 23–41; J. M. W. Bean, 'Plague, Population and Economic Decline in England in the Later Middle Ages', *Economic History Review* 2nd series 15 (1962–3), pp. 423–37; Hatcher, *Plague, Population and Economy*, pp. 55–62.

[70] E. A. Wrigley, 'Family Limitation in Pre-Industrial England', *Economic History Review* 2nd series 19 (1966), pp. 82–109; E. A. Wrigley, 'Mortality in Pre-Industrial England: The Example of Colyton, Devon, over Three Centuries', *Daedalus* 97 (1968), pp. 546–80.

[71] For example, K. H. Connell, 'Peasant Marriage in Ireland: Its Structure and Development Since the Famine', *Economic History Review* 2nd series 24 (1961–2), pp. 502–23.

although tantalizing in its ambiguity, is fully compatible with such an interpretation. Nevertheless, much less equivocal data will be required before it can be verified.[72]

More amenable to explanation is why, if Coltishall's increasingly hard-pressed population continued to grow right up to the outbreak of plague in 1349, communities in other less populous localities evidently fared so much worse and succumbed to the successive subsistence crises of the late thirteenth and early fourteenth centuries so much more readily.[73] The answer would appear to lie partly with the peculiar geographical and economic advantages enjoyed by eastern Norfolk – climate and soils well-suited to intensive grain production, a favourable position for local, national and international trade, access to major urban centres, a diversified economy and the employment of advanced agricultural methods – and partly with the nature of social-property systems and the balance of class forces within the area. Apart from the unique opportunities for wage earning afforded by the intensively cultivated and market-orientated demesnes of eastern Norfolk, the rural population benefited from relatively low levels of feudal rent and the absence of an all-powerful feudal authority. Of special importance is the fact that lords did not enforce a particular social distribution of land but were prepared to countenance and profit from an active market in customary land. Hence, as well as experiencing almost no communal interference in the management of their land, tenants were also free to buy and sell land as opportunity or occasion required. Indeed, the rate at which customary land changed hands is one of the most remarkable features of East Anglian manors compared with those located in other parts of England, and is an interesting commentary on the attitudes of land holders to both their families and their land. At Coltishall this market provided a kind of security against risk, enabling peasants to raise cash or credit at little notice and thereby weather periods of often acute economic hardship. In the decades before the Black Death these peasants emerge from the court rolls as a hard-bargaining and resilient lot, emotionally unattached to their land, and inured to crisis. That they survived the manifold vicissitudes of the periods was because they lived in an area whose social-property system was conducive to their survival. In this respect Coltishall's experience

[72] R. M. Smith, 'Hypothèses sur la nuptialité en Angleterre aux XIIIe–XIVe siècles', *Annales Économies, Sociétés, Civilisations* 1 (1983), pp. 107–36.

[73] J. Z. Titow, 'Some Evidence of the Thirteenth-Century Population Increase', *Economic History Review* 2nd series 14 (1961), pp. 218–23; above, pp. 95–101 and Table 2.5, p. 105.

bears out Brenner's observation that the potential for peasant-based economic and demographic development was noticeably greater in areas of weak lordship.[74]

Nevertheless, it is hard from the Coltishall evidence to relegate demographic change to a secondary role in favour of a class-based explanation of economic and social development. The balance of class forces and the nature of the social distribution of property within the area may have conditioned the response to population change, but in the final analysis it was population change that was the catalyst. This is manifest in the behaviour of the two processes most affecting land ownership. Under the conditions of high and rising population which prevailed before the Black Death customary inheritance and the land market both served to promote the trend towards morcellation. Thereafter, with a downward trend in population firmly established, the former gradually fell into abeyance and the latter was transformed in its effect. Not only was there a relative and absolute increase in the sale of land but, instead of perpetuating and accentuating the *status quo*, the land market became the single most powerful solvent of the established pattern of peasant land holding. It took some time, of course, to redress the extremely fragmented state to which land holding had been reduced by the eve of the Black Death, and hence it is not until well into the fifteenth century that a strong trend towards a more polarized social distribution of land becomes clearly recognizable. Eventually it was this trend that led to the evolution of a capitalist farmer/landless wage labourer division within rural society, a development which was to prove fundamental to the economic breakthrough in agriculture of the seventeenth and eighteenth centuries. In this context it is particularly significant for Brenner's line of reasoning that this new class structure arose through processes which were essentially internal to the peasantry. Thus it was the initiative of successive peasant proprietors, not landlords, that lay behind that progressive accumulation of land of which the substantial yeoman farm was the most important end-product. But whilst the demographic circumstances under which this process occurred were crucial, as a development it represents more than demographically determined social promotion. The business by which certain individuals set about systematically enlarging their holdings whilst other equally systematically disposed of them was a complex and protracted process and as such merits much closer investigation.

Just as in the thirteenth and fourteenth centuries the agricultural

[74] Brenner, 'Agrarian Roots', p. 61.

Table 2.11. *Coltishall, Norfolk: land transactions recorded in the Court Rolls 1275–1476*

Year	No. of courts	No. of transactions	No. of transactions with area	Area transacted (rods)	Mean size of transaction (rods)		Mean no. of transactions per court		Mean area transacted per court (rods)	
					Mean	5-year mean	Mean	5-year mean	Mean	5-year mean
1275	3	9	9	12.5	1.4		3.0		4.2	
1280	2	3	3	4.75	1.6		1.5		2.4	
1281	2	8	8	24.0	3.0		4.0		12.0	
1282	2	7	6	9.3	1.55	2.0	3.5	3.0	4.65	6.3
1283	2	5	5	8.75	1.75	3.1	2.5	3.1	4.4	8.6
1284	2	7	7	16.25	2.3	2.7	3.5	3.7	8.1	7.2
1285	2	4	4	27.3	6.8	2.5	2.0	3.5	13.65	6.5
1286	1	7	5	5.0	1.0	2.45	7.0	3.4	5.0	6.1
1287	3	8	6	3.9	0.65	2.4	2.7	3.3	1.3	5.6
1288	3	6	5	7.5	1.5	1.25	2.0	4.5	2.5	4.2
1289	1	3	3	5.75	1.9	1.2	3.0	3.6	5.75	3.75
1290	1	8	6	7.1	1.2	1.4	8.0	4.5	7.1	5.4
1291	2	5	5	4.25	0.85	1.4	2.5	5.1	2.1	6.1
1292	2	14	11	18.9	1.7	1.5	7.0	6.0	9.45	8.3
1293	1	0	0	0.0	0.0	1.5	0.0	5.6	0.0	8.2
1294	2	13	13	29.0	2.2	1.55	6.5	6.4	14.5	9.2
1295	4	26	25	27.0	1.1	1.5	6.5	6.2	6.75	9.1
1296	2	11	10	12.0	1.2	1.6	5.5	6.7	6.0	8.9
1297	0	0	0	0	0.0	1.6	0.0	6.1	0.0	7.3
1298	3	25	13	25.0	1.95	1.5	8.33	5.1	8.33	6.0
1299	2	8	7	16.0	2.3	1.4	4.0	4.2	8.0	4.9
1300	4	11	11	7.0	0.65	1.5	2.75	4.2	1.75	5.1
1301	3	5	5	4.0	0.8	1.4	1.66	3.6	1.33	4.1
1302	2	9	6	12.0	2.0	1.1	4.5	3.3	6.0	3.2
1303	7	18	12	12.6	1.1	1.1	5.1	3.7	3.6	3.3
1304	4	10	10	13.0	1.05	1.2	2.5	4.2	3.25	3.8
1305	4	19	13	10.0	0.75	1.65	4.75	4.3	2.5	5.4
1306	1	0	0	0.0	0.0	1.8	0.0	3.2	0.0	6.0
1307	3	14	10	37.0	3.7	2.15	4.7	3.7	12.33	7.3
1308	1	1	0	0.0	0.0	3.9	1.0	3.3	0.0	12.6
1309	4	17	14	28.5	2.0	3.35	4.25	3.05	7.1	10.2
1310	3	10	9	55.0	6.1	3.0	3.3	3.2	18.3	9.6
1311	2	4	4	6.5	1.6	2.6	2.0	3.4	3.25	8.1
1312	7	38	32	69.1	2.15	2.6	5.4	3.6	9.9	8.1
1313	4	9	6	7.1	1.2	1.6	2.25	4.7	1.8	5.5
1314	4	21	16	29.0	1.8	1.5	5.25	6.7	7.25	7.8
1315	6	15	14	16.2	1.2	1.4	5.0	8.1	5.4	9.05
1316	3	46	35	44.5	1.3	1.4	15.3	9.0	14.8	10.7
1317	2	25	22	32.0	1.45	1.3	12.5	10.8	16.0	12.1
1318	2	14	14	20.0	1.45	1.4	7.0	10.4	10.0	11.9
1319	2	28	22	29.0	1.34	1.3	14.0	8.0	14.5	10.6
1320	4	13	12	16.0	1.33	1.4	3.25	7.2	4.0	9.9
1321	3	25	22	25.0	1.15	1.4	3.33	9.3	8.3	12.2
1322	4	33	30	51.75	1.7	1.4	8.25	8.1	12.9	11.7
1323	2	35	29	43.0	1.5	1.5	17.5	8.2	21.5	12.05
1324	2	0	0	0.0	0.0	1.7	0.0	9.2	0.0	12.9
1325	4	15	12	22.0	1.8	1.8	3.75	8.9	5.5	11.7
1326	3	22	21	34.9	1.7	2.3	7.3	5.1	11.6	8.1
1327	1	7	4	8.25	2.1	2.1	7.0	5.3	8.25	8.4
1328	2	5	4	14	3.5	2.1	2.5	6.4	7.0	9.7
1329	2	12	12	19.0	1.6	2.2	6.0	6.5	9.5	9.95
1330	1	9	7	12.0	1.7	2.25	9.0	6.7	12.0	11.5
1331	1	8	6	13	2.15	2.0	8.0	8.0	13.0	13.05
1332	2	16	14	32	2.3	1.9	8.0	8.9	16.0	13.3
1333	4	32	26	59	2.27	1.9	8.0	9.6	14.75	14.3
1334	3	35	29	32	1.1	1.7	11.7	9.4	10.7	13.4

(Cont.)

Table 12.1 (*Cont.*)

	No. of courts	No. of transactions	No. of transactions with area	Area transacted (rods)	Mean size of transaction (rods) Mean	5-year mean	Mean no. of transactions per court Mean	5-year mean	Mean area transacted per court (rods) Mean	5-year mean
Year										
1335	2	25	23	34.0	1.5	1.4	12.5	12.4	17.0	13.8
1336	3	21	20	26.0	1.3	1.2	7.0	15.4	8.7	15.9
1337	1	23	20	18.0	0.9	1.1	23.0	15.3	18.0	15.3
1338	1	23	23	25.0	1.1	1.1	23.0	14.6	25.0	13.8
1339	1	11	9	8	0.9	1.0	11.0	16.4	8.0	15.5
1340	2	18	17	19.0	1.1	1.05	9.0	14.75	9.5	14.9
1341	1	16	16	17.0	1.1	1.0	16.0	12.0	17.0	11.5
1342	0	0	0	0.0	0.0	1.4	0.0	10.7	0.0	14.8
1343	0	0	0	0.0	0.0	3.8	0.0	8.3	0.0	15.8
1344	1	7	9	18.0	2.0	4.4	7.0	6.6	18.0	20.2
1345	2	4	3	25.0	8.33	4.1	2.0	7.8	12.5	22.7
1346	5	27	27	75.0	2.8	3.7	10.8	7.3	30.0	19.9
1347	6	34	27	91.0	3.35	3.9	11.3	7.9	30.3	22.7
1348	3	16	15	27.0	1.8	2.6	5.33	8.7	8.9	21.9
1349	4	41	38	128.0	3.35	3.2	10.25	7.5	32.0	20.9
1350	3	17	14	25.0	1.7	3.05	5.7	6.5	8.3	17.8
1351	3	14	13	75.0	5.75	3.6	4.7	5.7	25.0	17.3
1352	5	16	14	37.0	2.65	3.4	6.4	3.9	14.8	11.6
1353	2	3	3	13.0	4.33	3.4	1.5	3.7	6.5	11.1
1354	4	5	5	14.0	2.8	2.7	1.25	3.3	3.5	7.25
1355	3	14	13	17.0	1.5	2.6	4.7	2.45	5.7	5.15
1356	4	10	10	23.0	2.3	2.1	2.5	2.95	5.75	4.85
1357	3	7	7	13.0	1.85	1.9	2.3	4.1	4.3	6.3
1358	3	12	8	15.0	1.9	2.0	4.0	3.3	5.0	5.5
1359	5	17	14	26.5	1.85	1.9	6.8	3.2	10.6	5.1
1360	1	1	1	2.0	2.0	1.7	1.0	3.2	2.0	4.6
1361	1	2	2	3.5	1.75	1.55	2.0	2.6	3.5	3.9
1362	2	4	4	4.0	1.0	1.75	2.0	2.1	2.0	4.3
1363	3	4	4	4.5	1.15	2.2	1.3	3.1	1.5	8.0
1364	5	11	11	31.0	2.85	2.6	4.4	3.9	12.4	10.9
1365	6	18	15	62.0	4.15	2.7	6.0	4.2	20.6	11.65
1366	5	15	12	45.0	3.75	3.8	6.0	4.7	18.0	16.15
1367	4	14	13	23.0	1.8	3.9	3.5	4.3	5.75	14.8
1368	3	11	11	72.0	6.5	3.3	3.7	3.5	24.0	11.1
1369	4	9	7	23.0	3.3	3.15	2.25	2.9	5.75	9.4
1370	1	2	2	2.0	1.0	4.4	2.0	3.0	2.0	14.7
1371	0	0	0	0.0	0.0	4.0	0.0	3.0	0.0	13.3
1372	1	4	4	27.0	6.75	3.6	4.0	2.8	27.0	12.5
1373	4	15	15	74.5	5.0	3.8	3.75	3.5	18.6	14.1
1374	3	4	4	7.0	1.75	3.6	1.3	3.8	2.3	14.3
1375	2	10	10	17.0	1.7	3.2	5.0	4.2	8.5	14.6
1376	1	5	5	15.0	3.0	2.7	5.0	4.2	15.0	12.2
1377	3	18	18	86.0	4.75	2.7	6.0	4.4	28.7	12.7
1378	4	14	11	26.0	2.4	2.9	3.5	4.1	6.5	12.75
1379	3	8	8	14.5	1.75	3.2	2.7	3.5	4.8	11.5
1380	4	13	13	35.0	2.7	4.3	3.25	2.8	8.75	11.2
1381	4	8	8	34.5	4.25	4.7	2.0	2.8	8.6	12.8
1382	3	8	8	81.5	10.2	4.7	2.7	2.65	27.2	12.7
1383	3	10	10	44.0	4.4	5.6	3.3	2.6	14.7	15.15
1384	2	4	4	8.5	2.1	6.8	2.0	3.0	4.25	21.9
1385	1	3	3	21.0	7.0	5.2	3.0	3.2	21.0	17.85
1386	5	10	10	105.5	10.5	4.9	4.0	3.0	42.2	16.05
1387	4	14	14	28.5	2.0	4.8	3.5	3.0	7.1	15.8
1388	3	7	6	17.0	2.8	3.6	2.3	2.6	5.7	11.7
1389	1	2	2	3.0	1.5	2.5	2.0	2.7	3.0	8.1
1390	3	3	2	2.0	1.0	3.0	1.0	2.5	0.7	8.7
1391	4	18	18	96.0	5.35	2.6	4.5	2.2	24.1	7.8
1392	3	8	7	30.0	4.3	2.6	2.7	2.2	10.0	7.7

(*Cont.*)

Table 12.1 (*Cont.*)

	No. of courts	No. of transactions	No. of transactions with area	Area transacted (rods)	Mean size of transaction (rods)		Mean no. of transactions per court		Mean area transacted per court (rods)	
					Mean	5-year mean	Mean	5-year mean	Mean	5-year mean
Year										
1393	1	1	1	1.0	1.0	2.6	1.0	2.2	1.0	7.7
1394	3	5	5	7.5	1.5	1.9	1.7	1.5	2.5	3.2
1395	2	2	2	2.0	1.0	1.1	1.0	1.2	1.0	1.3
1396	2	2	2	3.0	1.5	1.0	1.0	1.2	1.5	1.2
1397	3	4	3	1.5	0.5	1.2	1.3	1.6	0.5	2.55
1398	1	1	1	0.5	0.5	2.3	1.0	2.4	0.5	9.0
1399	2	7	7	18.5	2.7	2.5	3.5	2.75	9.25	10.9
1400	5	13	13	83.5	6.4	3.2	5.2	3.2	33.4	14.4
1401	0	0	0.0	0.0	0.0	7.9	3.8	3.8	0.0	25.61
1402	0	0	0	0.0	0.0	7.9	0.0	3.3	0.0	24.2
1403	3	8	7	103.0	14.7	6.6	2.7	2.6	34.3	15.6
1404	1	2	2	5.0	2.5		2.0		5.0	
1405	1	3	3	7.5	2.5		3.0		7.5	
1471	1	6	5	137.0	27.4		6.0		137.0	
1472	2	8	8	254.5	31.8		4.0		127.25	
1473	1	3	3	124.0	41.33		3.0		124.00	
1474	1	5	5	74.0	14.8		5.0		74.0	
1475	1	3	3	62.0	20.66		3.0		62.0	
1476	1	3	3	82.0	27.33		3.0		82.0	

methods employed on demesnes in eastern Norfolk bore a close resemblance to those found in the Low Countries, so too in the fifteenth and sixteenth centuries agrarian developments in these two areas had much in common.[75] In both cases the transformation of agrarian class structure which came to fruition in the early modern period derived directly from the peasant-based agricultural economy of the medieval period. Rising population in the sixteenth century confirmed and accelerated the trend firmly established during the period of stagnant population in the fifteenth century, towards the supersession of smallholders and the build-up of large farms. Instead of parcellation and subdivision, competition for land promoted consolidation and engrossing, and these in their turn paved the way for capital investment, technical change and a wider adoption of wage labour. Brenner, in fact, acknowledged that the Flemish pattern of agricultural development is an exception to his model of European economic development, demonstrating as it does that a peasant-dominated agricultural economy could provide the foundation for agricultural breakthrough.[76] If the pattern of agricultural develop-

[75] Campbell, 'Agricultural Progress'; Brenner, 'Agrarian Roots', pp. 107–10.
[76] Brenner, 'Agrarian Roots'.

ment identified in eastern Norfolk holds valid for much of the rest of East Anglia, then the latter region, which was to lie in the van of English agrarian advance, may also prove to be an exception. Too many exceptions tend not to prove a rule.

3

Families and their land in an area of partible inheritance: Redgrave, Suffolk 1260–1320

RICHARD M. SMITH

In his classic discussion of inheritance customs and practices in the thirteenth century, published over forty years ago, G. C. Homans gave much attention to the relationship between the rural family and its land in the areas of impartibility that coincided with 'champion' England.[1] His reflections on the areas where partible inheritance prevailed were, by contrast, brief and confined mainly to evidence of Kentish gavelkind.[2] He did, nonetheless, use the Kentish findings as a basis for more general remarks about multigeniture that were, he believed, applicable to medieval East Anglian society, where he noted there was considerable evidence for partible inheritance on both socage and customary land.[3]

Homans, considering Kentish gavelkind, assessed the likely differences in social organization stemming from practices on the one hand which allowed or encouraged co-heirs to subdivide their inheritances and to hold their shares individually and from those on the other which led to the co-heirs living together in common. He believed that Kentish families of the thirteenth and early fourteenth centuries 'must have resembled those that still existed in Auvergne, the Nivernais, and other parts of France in the nineteenth century: descendants of a common ancestor living in one large house or in a small group of adjoining houses and holding a domain in common and undivided'.[4] In fact, Homans preferred to stress the prevalence of

[1] G. C. Homans, *English Villagers of the Thirteenth Century* (Cambridge, Mass., 1941), pp. 109–219.
[2] *Ibid.*, pp. 109–20.
[3] Repeated in his 'The Rural Sociology of Medieval England', *Past and Present* 4 (1953), pp. 32–43, and 'The Explanation of English Regional Differences', *Past and Present* 42 (1969), pp. 18–34.
[4] Homans, *English Villagers*, p. 112. For recent studies of this area in the nineteenth century, see L. K. Berkner and J. W. Shaffer, 'The Joint Family in the Nivernais',

what he termed 'joint-family organisation' in these areas. Land he saw, in most instances, as descending to a man's sons jointly; only where the population of such joint families passed beyond some critical threshold did fission occur in the form of a partition of the holding so that new family enterprises could be initiated. Homans' research method perhaps gave undue emphasis either to the moment of property transmission at death, when the co-heirs were most clearly evident as a group in the manorial court rolls, or to survey evidence which provided information on tenure by co-heirs at one particular moment in time.

Since Homans wrote, relatively little detailed research has been undertaken on family forms in the areas of partibility in medieval England. Historians have been mainly concerned with identifying and indeed extending the areas over which partible inheritance practices were to be found rather than with investigating their detailed operation.[5] Agricultural historians and historical geographers to date have provided the most detailed work, mainly concerned with the likely effects of partibility on holding sizes and field fragmentation and with its possible role in the creation of strip-field systems in periods of demographic growth.[6] In fact this work, in the case of Kent, has gone some way to qualifying Homans' conclusions as to inheritance practices in that county. Alan Baker has drawn attention to the relative rarity with which fragmentation would have proceeded in an unobstructed fashion through time, with heirs waiving their claims to their parts of the holding for some cash compensation from a sibling under whose control it eventually fell.[7] Baker, too, noted that joint tenure seems to have been restricted to

---

Journal of Family History 3 (1978), pp. 150–62; and J. W. Shaffer, *Family and Farm: Agrarian Change and Household Organisation in the Loire Valley 1500–1900* (Albany, N.Y., 1982), the latter written within a clear materialist interpretative framework.

[5] R. J. Faith, 'Peasant Families and Inheritance Customs in Medieval England', *Agricultural History Review* 14 (1966) pp. 77–95.

[6] See H. L. Gray, *English Field Systems* (Cambridge, Mass., 1915), pp. 199–202; J. Thirsk, 'The Common Fields', *Past and Present* 29 (1964), pp. 11–14; R. A. Dodgshon, *The Origin of British Field Systems: An Interpretation* (London, 1980), pp. 41–3, and 'The Interpretation of Sub-Divided Fields: A Study in Private or Common Interests', in T. Rowley, editor, *The Origins of Open Field Agriculture* (London, 1981), pp. 134–5; H. E. Hallam, 'Some Thirteenth Century Censuses', *Economic History Review* 2nd series 10 (1958), pp. 349–55; F. R. H. Du Boulay, *The Lordship of Canterbury* (London, 1966), pp. 52–67; A. R. H. Baker, 'Open Fields and Partible Inheritance on a Kent Manor', *Economic History Review*, 2nd series 17 (1964–5), pp. 1–22; and especially B. M. S. Campbell, 'Population Change and the Genesis of Common Fields on a Norfolk Manor', *Economic History Review*, 2nd series 33 (1980), pp. 174–92.

[7] A. R. H. Baker, 'Some Fields and Farms in Medieval Kent', *Archeologia Cantiana* 80 (1965), pp. 152–74.

'that short period after a man's death when his estate was awaiting its disposal among his heirs', although it must be admitted that he provided relatively little evidence to support this view.[8]

Barbara Dodwell, in a general survey of the East Anglian evidence of the thirteenth and early fourteenth centuries, extended our know-ledge of behaviour in this area beyond Homans' remarks most considerably.[9] Adopting, however, a style of analysis highly reminiscent of that of her predecessor, she presented examples indicative of both partition and joint ownership of land. She does, however, appear to have moved away from one position implicit in Homans' earlier work concerning the role of the joint family or minimal lineage, noting that inheriting sibling groups seem not to have inherited land with cousins or uncles as one might expect from a clan-based land holding system.[10] She also drew attention most forcefully to the potential effects of property alienation, for she suggested that there was nothing to prevent one of the heirs from selling his share to another.[11] She presented, however, a somewhat discouraging view of the possibilities of further investigation of these problems, as she stressed that manorial court rolls are not as helpful as they might be in the matter of *post-mortem* relations between co-heirs, for the clerks of the courts 'were not interested in what the sons did with the land' after they had inherited.[12]

In certain important respects Dr Dodwell is correct. But, it should be emphasized that the sons themselves may have been interested in their rights singly or as groups of individuals and may have made considerable use of the court as a means of confirming their legal claims to land. Lords, too, may have possessed some interest in the activities of these sons that placed in doubt specific personal responsibilities for the payment of rents or the rendering of services. Further-more, lords might wish to use the court machinery in 'taxing' the moment of any intra-familial readjustment of rights in land. In theory, a full run of court rolls should make it possible to consider the activities of siblings concerning their land both before and after their father's death. If, in addition, a detailed survey or extent of tenant holdings is available it is reasonable to expect that it would prove possible to investigate the process leading to the disposition of land

---

[8] A. R. H. Baker, 'Field Systems of South-East England', in A. R. H. Baker and R. A. Butlin, editors. *Studies of Field Systems in the British Isles* (Cambridge, 1973), p. 409, citing Du Boulay, *Lordship of Canterbury*, pp. 147–8.

[9] B. Dodwell, 'Holdings and Inheritance in Medieval East Anglia', *Economic History Review* 2nd series 20 (1967), pp. 53–66.

[10] *Ibid.*, p. 60.   [11] *Ibid.*, pp. 61–4.   [12] *Ibid.*, p. 60.

both prior and subsequent to the tenurial patterns exhibited in the cross-sectional 'snap-shot'.

We are fortunate in having both a detailed survey of tenant lands and a reasonably complete series of manorial court rolls preceding and succeeding it for the Abbot of Bury St Edmunds' manor of Redgrave in north Suffolk. Redgrave possesses one of the earliest series of court rolls in East Anglia, indeed the whole country, beginning in 1260 and running with few breaks into the eighteenth century. A particularly full survey of the manor was produced in 1289.[13]

The aims of the present paper are relatively simple: first, to consider the extent to which group or conjoint tenure of property by siblings is detectable on the survey; secondly, to assess the degree to which death was the critical event in property transmission; thirdly, to consider the evidence in the manorial court rolls bearing on the economic relationships between family members, especially siblings, both before and after inheritance of the patrimonial estate. Limitations on space preclude any detailed discussion of the local topography and economy, although consideration of certain features of Redgrave's setting and economy is essential for a full understanding of the relationships between families and their lands in the period under review.[14] The manor, located on the border of Suffolk and Norfolk, was crossed on its northern flank by the valley of the river Waveney. Although the demesne farm was situated in Redgrave, the manor court had jurisdiction over its tenants holding land in seven other nearby settlements.[15] The manor comprised a set of hamlets and farms; there was no large tightly knit nucleated village dominant, and although arable farming was the principal source of livelihood significant pasture resources formed an integral part of the local economy. There were commons at Botulesdale and Wortham, a fen in

---

[13] The court rolls covering the period 1260–1320 are currently deposited in the Dept of Special Collections of the University of Chicago Library and constitute University of Chicago Bacon Manuscripts, nos. 1–11. The 1289 extent of Redgrave exists in two copies: MS Bacon 805 and British Library, MS Add. 14850, fos. 65–84ᵛ. See R. M. Thomson, editor, *The Archives of Bury St Edmunds Abbey*, Suffolk Record Society xx (Woodbridge, 1980), pp. 98, 102 and 161.

[14] A fuller account can be found in R. M. Smith, *English Peasant Life-Cycles and Socio-Economic Networks*, unpublished University of Cambridge Ph.D. thesis, 1974, Chapter 1.

[15] These were Redgrave *marescum*, Botulesdale, Mickelwode, Estgate, Burgate, Musehalle, Wortham and Gislingham, all of which today have a topographical distinctiveness. Burgate, Wortham and Gislingham are separate parishes. Wortham had its own court leet, the records of which have been used in this study. For a map of the area over which the Redgrave court had jurisdiction, see R. M. Smith, 'Kin and Neighbours in a Thirteenth Century Suffolk Community', *Journal of Family History* 4 (1979), p. 221.

the Waveney valley on the manor's northern edge and a significant area of woodland in the area appropriately named Mickelwode. Of considerable importance, too, was the periodic market in Botulesdale that helped to encourage a large range of small-scale by-employments and tertiary trades.[16] The area of land in demesne was large, 704 acres relative to 1,317.5 acres of customary land and 730.5 acres of land held freely. Almost 50 per cent of the customary land (648 acres) was located in Redgrave, where free tenants were few in number.

i. Individual and group tenure of land in 1289

The Redgrave survey of 1289, when concerning itself with tenant lands, was for the most part drawn up on the basis of the *tenementum*. Rents and services were generally affixed to these units rather than to individual holdings and in this respect the Redgrave evidence displays close similarities to that analysed from tenant surveys in Kent and Norfolk.[17] For each *tenementum*, usually named after a current or previous holder, total area and the size of the units comprising it are listed. The collective rents and services of the *tenementum* are listed, although the specific responsibility for their payment and performance is not stated. The great variation in the size of the *tenementa* within the lowest levels of 1½ acres and an upper level of 40 acres is apparent when Table 3.1 is considered. However, the units present a pattern comparable to that suggested by Dodwell to be the norm for Suffolk where five-, ten-, fifteen-, twenty- and 30-acre units seem to have predominated.[18] Of the 106 tenemental units, 44 were of those sizes. Although the earliest structures from which the situation in 1289 evolved are not an issue for present discussion, the picture presented by the survey is one in which we can observe the original units in a state of 'decay'. There is no strong reason to suppose, as some have done,[19] that the *tenementa* were really large fields consisting of the strip-holdings of a number of villagers, over which two- or three-course rotations were practised independently of other similar units. Their composition strongly resembles the yokes described in the medieval surveys of Gillingham in Kent and analysed by Baker.[20]

---

[16] *Calender of Charter Rolls, Vol. I*, p. 30: market grant to Bury for Redgrave, 5.4.1227 (11 Henry III). For a detailed discussion of the property holders and their trading activities in Botulesdale market, see R. M. Smith, 'Social Groupings and Their Relationships in a Suffolk Market Settlement 1260–1320' (forthcoming).

[17] Baker, 'Open Fields', p. 6; and Campbell, 'Population Change', p. 178.

[18] Dodwell, 'Holdings and Inheritance', p. 68.

[19] J. Z. Titow, *English Rural Society 1200–1350* (London, 1969), p. 23.

[20] Baker, 'Open Fields', p. 12.

Table 3.1. *Tenemental sizes: Redgrave 1289*

Size (ac.)	1½	2	3	4	5	6	7	8	10	12	13	14	15	16	17	18	20	21	23	24	30	36	40
No.	3	4	4	2	9	7	6	2	20	6	5	4	3	4	1	2	8	1	1	3	4	1	1

The *tenementa* are unlikely in themselves to have been fields, but were made up of arable, pasture, meadow and wood (21 of the 106 units are shown to have a mixture of land-use types), along with messuages of varying degrees of complexity. This evidence suggests that the tenemental network had been superimposed upon a field system, although some of the smaller *tenementa* may possibly have been fields in their own right.

In the 1,440 acres comprising the 106 tenemental units (70 per cent of the tenant land), there were 725 separate parcels. Some tenemental units included a large number of tenants; there were, for instance, 34 tenants in a 26-acre *tenementum* held by Augustus Cristemesse and his co-parceners, nineteen tenants in the thirty-acre *tenementum* held formerly by Warin and Thomas Gossyng and seventeen tenants in the ten-acre *tenementum* held formerly by Odonis le Gardener. To a certain extent the examples cited above distort the level of the fragmentation, as frequently between one-half and one-third of the *tenementum* was held by one individual and the remainder was distributed among the others.

The majority of tenants (marginally under 60 per cent) held all of their land within one *tenementum*. 34 per cent of the tenants held their parcels in two to five *tenementa* and 6 per cent had their land in six or more units. Only 1.3 per cent held land in more than eleven *tenementa*. These distributions are remarkably similar to those presented recently by Campbell for the manor of Martham in the neighbouring county of Norfolk.[21] However, given that the sizes of the tenemental units in the two manors differed, the similarities should not be over-stressed.

72 of the 403 tenants (18 per cent) had land in more than one of the hamlets or sub-regions of Redgrave manor, suggesting strongly that an individual's holding tended to be confined to one area of the manor rather than being scattered randomly over it. There is little reason to suppose that the parcels were contiguous, although the survey provides no evidence permitting us to position either parcels within a *tenementum* or *tenementa* in relation to one another. Table 3.2 lists those six individuals who held land in eleven or more *tenementa*

[21] Campbell, 'Population Change', p. 187.

Table 3.2. *Leading landholders and 'tenementa' in Redgrave 1289**

	Thomas Docke	Adam Jop	Rad. Mercator	Walt. Mercator	Adam Pistor	John Wodecock
Redgrave village		158½	32	32	5½	59½
Mickelwode	96				32	
Botulesdale Market	2, 6 stalls, 1 shop	1 shop			40, 4 stalls	
Marescum		12	5	5		3
Wortham		4				
Estgate						
Gislingham						
Musehalle		6	6½	6½		
Number of *tenementa* within which land held	16	19	16	16	14	11
Percentage land held in 1 sub-region	97	83	74	74	52	95

*Amounts held are expressed in rods.

and also confirms the tendency for land to be heavily concentrated in one geographical location. For example, Adam Jop, holding the largest quantity of customary land on the manor, whilst possessing property in five of the eight sub-regions, had 83 per cent of his land and his principal messuage in Redgrave.

From the point of view of the Abbot's bureaucracy the most important function of the *tenementum* was in the assessment of rents and services. Although the tenemental areas and the tenant numbers within them varied, the rents and services owed by each showed an identifiable consistency. For example, George del Wro and his four co-parceners performed services and paid rents on a twenty-acre *tenementum* and all subsequent 20-acre *tenementa* listed in the survey were assessed as 'predictus Georgius et sui parcenarii'. The 1289 survey suggested in theory the co-parceners had a joint responsibility to see that all services were performed and rents paid. For example, the service obligations of George del Wro and *parcenarii sui* are listed and frequently the plural form of the verb is used when extended fully, i.e. 'item debent arrare' and 'si non mesurerunt istorum bladorum debent metere . . . item debent quaelibet septimam in autumpno'. Furthermore, after the listing for George del Wro and his co-parceners, the services due from other *tenementa* are not listed in full but summed up in the statement 'et faciunt omnes consuetudines

in omnibus quas predictus Georgius et sui parcenarii faciunt'.[22]
Although George del Wro as principal land holder in the *tenementum*
may have been the individual who organized the service tasks, the
co-parceners as a group did have certain collective responsibilities.
The failure of these groups to fulfil their obligations is reflected in
amercements in the court rolls of groups of co-parceners to pay rents
or perform labour services attached to particular holdings.[23] The legal
liability to pay rents or perform services may have been collective,
although the actual practice may have devolved upon an individual.
This is in fact suggested by inter-personal agreements or contracts
registered in the manorial courts concerning individual responsibility
to meet the obligations of a whole *tenementum*.[24] Individual failure to
fulfil such agreements was a not infrequent cause of litigation
between co-parceners.[25]

For most individuals personal responsibilities to the collective
obligations would have been quite minimal as average holding sizes
were particularly small. Mean and median acreages are not particularly revealing measurements given the distribution of holding size
presented in Table 3.3. The cumulative distribution shows that a little
under half of the holdings were below two acres in size and only
marginally more than 10 per cent exceeded ten acres in area – the
holding size proclaimed by J. Z. Titow as the minimum sufficient to
sustain a thirteenth-century peasant family.[26] Undoubtedly, the smallholding class predominated on this manor, with almost 30 per cent of
holdings less than one acre in size. Campbell's careful reconstruction
of holding size on the Norfolk manor of Martham reveals a similar

---

[22] BL, MS Add. 14850 f. 76ʳ.
[23] For instance, at the court of Saturday, 18.11.1274, Walter Thede and his 7
co-parceners were amerced for failure to perform carrying services for which they
were summoned. Each co-parcener was fined individually and they pledged each
other: MS Bacon 2.
[24] The 8 co-parceners of Alan Long paid 2s so that he could do suit of court on their
behalf (court of 15.3.1262, MS Bacon 1). Similarly, Richard le Tannur paid a fine of 2s
6d so that he could do suit for his co-parceners (court of 10.10.1264, MS Bacon 1).
[25] In 1265 there was a dispute between Richard le Tannur and certain of his
co-parceners over rents they owed him. Richard had his plaint against Thomas le
Router upheld but was amerced for slandering 3 of his co-parceners in this dispute
(court of Wednesday, 22.1.1265, MS Bacon 1). Sometimes the co-parceners would
pay others to perform their services for them: for instance, Simon Skyl was fined for
not coming with 2 carts at the sowing of the lord's wheat as had been agreed by
Adam Seward and Alex del Wro and their respective co-parceners (court of
3.12.1269, MS Bacon 1). For a discussion of steps taken by co-parceners to apportion
responsibilities for the payment of rents and performance of services on the Norfolk
manor of Gressenhall, see J. Williamson, 'Peasant Holdings in Medieval Norfolk',
unpublished University of Reading Ph.D. thesis, 1976, pp. 68–71.
[26] Titow, *English Rural Society*, pp. 79–81.

Table 3.3. The distribution of holding sizes: Redgrave 1289

Sizes (ac.)	<2	%	2–6	%	6½–10	%	10½–14	%	14½–18	%	18>	%	Total
Customary tenants (land in 1 sub-region only)	133		87		17		7		4		2		250
Customary tenants (land in more than 1 sub-region)	6		18		17		7		1		1		50
Customary tenants (with minority of free land)	4		9		8		1		1		3		26
Sub-total	143		114		42		15		6		6		326
Free tenants (with minority of customary land)	4		7		3		3		–		4		21
Free tenants	30		13		3		2		2		4		54
Sub-total	34		20		6		5		2		8		75
Grand total	177	44.1	134	33.4	48	11.9	20	5.0	8	2.0	14	3.6	401

preponderance of small holdings, providing further evidence to support the views of East Anglican tenancies as smaller than those encountered in central–southern and midland England.[27] Of course, some allowance would have to be made for land held by individual tenants in addition to that held from the Abbot in Redgrave. However, very few Redgrave tenants, among the smallholders at least, appear in the records of the adjacent manors of Hinderclay and Rickinghall as property holders, and given the geographically concentrated pattern of property holding revealed in the Redgrave survey it would be highly unlikely that mean holding size could have, at its maximum, exceeded five acres.[28]

Of course the meaning to be attached to this high degree of fragmentation so clearly observable in the tenurial record would become a matter for considerable debate if it were found that the holdings of individuals were in practice combined to form larger areas of land held and indeed worked by laterally extended kin groups, as suggested by Homans. Although at no point does the survey specify the inheritance custom, evidence from the manorial court rolls indicates that customary land was partible among male and indeed female children of the deceased.[29] Furthermore, in the event of an individual dying childless the land passed laterally to his brothers or sisters.[30] Free land on this manor was, however, inherited

---

[27] Campbell, 'Population Change', p. 177; and E. A. Kosminsky, *Studies in the Agrarian History of England in the Thirteenth Century*, edited by R. H. Hilton (Oxford, 1956), pp. 217–18.

[28] Based on MSS Bacon 114–20 and BL, MSS Add. Ch. 63394–407.

[29] Inquests concerning the rights of individuals on property provide the most frequently encountered evidence confirming the practice of partibility. For instance, in 1280 (court of Wednesday, 24.7.1280, MS Bacon 4) John Beneyt and his brother paid for an inquest jury to investigate whether all of their father's land in Wortham was partible or not. Likewise, statements about past practices by inquest juries provide useful evidence on holding division. For example, the jury reported in 1298 (court of 9.7.1298, MS Bacon 8) that one Roger of Botulesdale, who once had a messuage and 16 acres of villein land, had 5 sons, Ralph, Robert, Warin, William and Adam, among whom the property was partitioned on his death. Afterwards, Ralph, Robert and Warin surrendered their shares to Adam. Adam had 1 heir, Nicholas, who now holds his father's 4 shares, and William had 2 sons, Adam Pistor, who still lives (see below, pp. 170–1) and Richard de Dale whose sons, Richard and Miles, now hold his share. Nicholas, son of Adam, now holds the 4 shares of the original holding.

[30] For detailed evidence of this, see the evidence discussed below, pp. 185–6. This gave rise to interesting disputes, such as that from the neighbouring manor of Rickinghall (where inheritance customs were identical with those in Redgrave) when Hugh Fuller died in 1284 and his brother William questioned the right of his niece Matilda to inherit, on the grounds that she was born outside of wedlock. Hugh won his case, as bastards, although able to hold land, were not able to inherit or themselves have heirs: BL, MS Add. Ch. 63400. For further discussion of this case and others like it, see R. M. Smith, 'Some Thoughts on "Hereditary" and "Proprie-

by the eldest son although it was partible among heiresses.[31]

The 1289 extent provides us with some means of considering the ways in which brothers, and to a certain extent sisters, held land subsequent to inheriting patrimonial holdings. Providing siblings can be identified, it can be ascertained whether or not they held land as individuals in different *tenementa* or in the same *tenementum*, whether they held equal or unequal amounts and whether they were co-tenants of individual units or of whole *tenementa*. We are able in this document to identify fifty male sibling sets, either through stated relationships or from further evidence provided in the contemporary manorial court proceedings, containing in all 116 individuals who constituted approximately one-third of the 345 male tenants (56 female tenants appear on the survey). This proportional estimate must be interpreted as a minimum since some kin relationships will have left no traces in the record and a certain instability in surnames is still present at this date. Of the 50 male sibling sets 33, accounting for 77 individuals, held land jointly in the same *tenementum*, amounting to 253.6 acres or approximately 20 per cent of the total area of customary land on the manor. The proportion of freeland so held was much less, at a little over 4 per cent. The term used to describe such tenure, *pro equalibus porcionibus*, is ambiguous in translation but most

tary'' Rights in Land under Customary Law in Thirteenth and Early Fourteenth Century England', *Law and History Review* 1 (1983), pp. 113–14.

[31] Litigational evidence provides interesting insights into relationships between brothers when both free and customary land was held by the father on his death. For instance, immediately after their father's death in 1261 the 3 sons of Geoffrey Reeve were in dispute over a portion of their father's property. An inquest established that free land by which their grandfather Robert had been enfeoffed by charter of Abbot Samson did not descend partibly but went to Thomas, Geoffrey's eldest son (court of 8.8.1261, MS Bacon 1). However, this dispute festered for a long time, as in 1282 Thomas' younger brothers, John and Henry, initiated a plaint claiming that the original inquisition had been held by the seneschal without their permission and that they had been fined unjustly (court of 26.4.1282, MS Bacon 2). The records of the court providing the result of this dispute have unfortunately gone astray. The difference between inheritance practice on free and villein land is more readily apparent after 1295, when information provided in obituary entries in the court record grows. For example, in 1318 John Lord died holding freely 1 messuage and 1½ acres, which went to his older son Gilbert, and in villeinage 1½ acres, which were to be shared by his 7 sons, Gilbert, Adam, Walter, Edmund, Ralph, Robert and Benedict, who, significantly perhaps, did not come to take their inheritance (court of 16.5.1318, MS Bacon 13). A further distinction existed between land held freely or in socage tenure; an interesting case suggesting an attempt to make use of this distinction by a younger son is to be found in the court of 17.4.1304 (MS Bacon 1): John le Messager, a free tenant, died holding in total 1 messuage and 21¼ acres of land. His eldest son Walter came as his rightful heir, but the younger son, John, claimed that his father's holding was socage and consequently was to be divided. The inquest jury, however, ruled in favour of Walter.

likely indicates a joint tenure, since other examples occur of brothers holding similar amounts of land within the same *tenementum* without any such qualifying clause, suggesting that partition had occurred.

This attempt to establish the proportion of the tenant area in the joint tenure of sibling groups represents an underestimate, as we would most likely need to include in our total a further fifty acres of land held by fifteen indeterminate groups appearing in the survey solely as 'the heirs of X or Y'.[32] To this area of land probably under joint tenure we might add a further 215 acres which siblings held individually but in 'common' *tenementa*. This, however, would produce a total that might best be interpreted as an absolute maximum proportion of customary land held by the laterally extended family as detected through sibling relationships. We might, therefore, conclude that the minimum proportion of customary land so held was 24 per cent and the maximum 40 per cent. Some intermediate value might be a not unreasonable estimate of the land area among the villein population of Redgrave in some kind of 'joint tenure' involving brothers.

Forty of the fifty sibling sets held land, as a group, in more than one *tenementum*, although only five displayed absolute equality of amount in each *tenementum*; for example, the sons of Richard Mercator appear as joint holders of their father's land scattered over Redgrave village, Redgrave *marescum* and Musehalle in thirteen *tenementa* (see Table 3.4). Much more frequently encountered, however, were the cases in which sibling sets possessed equal or approximately equal amounts of land in one or two, but unequal quantities in other, *tenementa*. In many cases one brother would appear to hold land in *tenementa* in which his other siblings had no share whatsoever. Robert, Adam and Walter Wulstan are one of the nine sibling trios holding land in more than one *tenementum* and are a particularly good example of such a pattern (see Table 3.5).

39 of the sibling groups had shares in two or more *tenementa*; the 29 sibling pairs would potentially have held land in 137 *tenementa* of which 68 (49.6 per cent) were actually occupied by both members of the pair; sibling trios, of which there were nine, could have held land in sixty *tenementa*, although in only thirteen (21.7 per cent) did all three brothers possess some land. A different method of measuring

---

[32] For instance, 'heredes Ade Bigot . . . tenent ix acras terre et partem messuagii' in the messuage and 16 acres 'quondam Rogeri de Herdewyk' along with 8 named co-parceners and the 'heredes Henrici le Carpenter' who had a solitary rod of land: BL MS Add. 14850 fo. 70^v. Adam Bigot died in 1287 and his wife Margaret had custody of his son's holding as he was under age (court of 14.3.1287, MS Bacon 5).

Table 3.4. *The holdings (in rods) of Radulphus and Walter Mercator in the manor of Redgrave 1289*

Tenementum (name of former co-holder)	Radulphus Mercator	Walter Mercator
Hubert son of Hugh	5½	5½
Walter of Smalebusc	2½	2½
Robert Goldwyne	1	1
Wydon Skyl	½	½
Peter Kypping	2½	2½
Simon Pikerel	2	2
John Wodecock	½	½
Folcard de Stigulo	1	1
Robert son of Agnes	4	4
Sickle Olon	1	1
Eustace Blome	½	½
William Sket	4½	4½
Matilda Spore	3½	3½
Total	29 rods = 7 ac. 1 rod	29 rods = 7 ac 1 rod

the extent to which the location of the patrimonial holding had an effect upon the placement of the male offsprings' land can be undertaken as follows: among the 39 sibling sets the 29 pairs held in total 340 acres of land. Of this total 249 acres (73 per cent) were located in *tenementa* in which all the brothers within an individual set had a share. For the nine sets involving three brothers, 64 per cent of their land (122 acres) was held in *tenementa* in which all had some land, if not in equal amounts.

Given that approximately one-third of all tenants were male siblings and that a roughly similar proportion of the customary land was held in what appears to have been a form of joint tenure, there can be no denying that the sibling bond was a kin relationship that had left a notable impression on the tenurial patterns of the tenants, especially the Abbot of Bury St Edmunds' villeins in late thirteenth-century Redgrave. In the absence of comparable statistics from other communities, it is at present unclear what conclusions to draw from these findings in the matter of sibling group tenure in an area of partible inheritance.[33] That the lateral kin links between brothers

[33] Some interesting statistics are presented by Williamson, 'Peasant Holdings' p. 46, concerning an extent of Gressenhall for 1282, where of 107 holdings 18 were held jointly by 2 or more brothers or sisters.

Table 3.5. *The holdings (in rods) of Walter Wulstan, Robert Wulstan and Adam Wulstan in the manor of Redgrave 1289*

	Walter Wulstan	Robert Wulstan	Adam Wulstan
Tenementum (name of former co-holder)			
Sickle Olon	2	—	—
Eustace Blome	2	—	—
Hubert son of Wulstan	16	16	16
Beatrix Burs	—	11	1
Warin Gossyng	—	4	4
William Sket	4	—	2
Alfrich Buntyng	6	—	—
William Ketel	3	—	—
Matilda Spore	1	—	—
Total	34 rods = 8 ac. 2 rods	31 rods = 7 ac. 3 rods	23 rods = 5 ac. 3 rods

impinged more deeply upon the lives of customary tenants than did vertical links between fathers and sons is partially borne out by the paucity of instances in which fathers and their sons or daughters simultaneously held land or did so jointly or in close geographical proximity one to another.[34] Of fourteen such cases involving lineal relations, six concerned fathers and sons and a further two fathers and daughters of freeholders. This kin link is clearly disproportionately (although not overwhelmingly) encountered among freeholders, given their relatively small number within the overall tenant population, and it can be no coincidence that land devolved impartibly among this section of the community's landholders.

However, we should not disregard the findings indicating that only five of the sibling groups who held land in more than one *tenementum* displayed absolute equality in the area of their holdings as well as in the size of their individual shares in the *tenementa*. It is significant that in four of these five cases the inheritances had all taken place in the five years prior to the survey's construction in 1289.[35] This fact may help to explain why such symmetry was maintained undisturbed, during this short interval, by disruptive forces. We should note, too,

[34] See below, pp. 182–4, where evidence indicating the low incidence of *pre-mortem* transfers from father to son relative to transactions between parents and daughters and among siblings is noted.

[35] For instance, the father of Walter and Ralph Mercator (see below, p. 171) died in 1284 (court of 18.10.1284, MS Bacon 4) and Adam and John de Ponte's father had died in the year before the extent's construction (court of 7.4.1288, MS Bacon 5).

Table 3.6. *Holding sizes of individuals in male sibling groups: Redgrave 1289*

Acres	2	2–6	6¼–10	10¼–14	14¼–18	18
No.	15	70	17	10	2	2
%	13.0	60.3	14.7	0.6	1.7	1.7

that as a whole the holdings of the 116 members of the fifty identifiable sibling groups possessed a size distribution that differed significantly from that among the remainder of the tenant population. Only 13 per cent of the siblings had individual shares that were under two acres in size, compared with 44 per cent in such a category for the total population (see Table 3.6). Does this pattern suggest that joint tenure may have been a means by which individuals were able to resist the processes that had led or were leading to the fragmentation of properties in the remaining population? Or is it that the sibling groups whose individual holdings were for the most part between four and six acres in size were at a particular phase in their life-cycle immediately subsequent to their father's death, after which many, indeed the majority, would lose land as they slid into the ranks of the smallholders and near-landless?

ii. The relative importance of 'pre-' and 'post-mortem' transfers of land

To answer these questions with conviction requires an analysis of both *pre-* and *post-mortem* transfers of land in Redgrave before and after the 1289 extent. Given Redgrave's location in eastern England, we might expect there to have been an active pattern of *inter-vivos* land transfers, for it has long been noticed that a traffic in land was particularly prominent in that region when compared, for instance, with the midlands.[36] Homans was perhaps the earliest to note this, although he thought it only 'an impression' and suggested that 'it would be useful but difficult to get quantitative information on this from the court rolls'.[37] The difficulty Homans noted should not be under-estimated, as manorial court rolls might be expected to record

[36] See M. M. Postan, 'The Charters of the Villeins', in C. N. L. Brooke and M. M. Postan, editors, *Carte Nativorum*, Northamptonshire Record Society xx (Oxford, 1960), pp. l–li. However, Postan made some interesting and cautious remarks about the differences that may be exaggerated, insofar as evidence from eastern England might well reflect the *pays réel*, whereas that from other areas could be distorted by recording the unreal world of the *pays légal*: ibid., p. lx.

[37] Homans, *English Villages*, p. 204.

only those peasant activities which the lord wished or was able to record. However, this problem might be expected to have been greater in the matter of short-term leases than in fully fledged 'alienations'. For, on the one hand, in the matter of 'alienations' lords would wish to have a clear record of those upon whom obligations to meet rent or service charges fell and, on the other, tenants would desire the existence of a means of proving their claim to property in the event of later dispute.

In fact it can be shown that the legal instruments relating to the tenure and transmission of customary land developed considerably in the course of the second half of the thirteenth century.[38] In the manor courts of Redgrave and indeed of other East Anglian communities we can observe a growing resort to procedures making for increasing stabilization and standardization of language concerning property transfers as the thirteenth century progressed.[39] In the courts of Redgrave in the early 1260s a bewildering array of forms was employed to record both *inter-vivos* and *post-mortem* transfers; the majority of transfers of customary land was licence payments for permission to buy (*pro licentia emendi*), or to sell (*pro licentia vendendi*), or (less often encountered) to lease (*pro licentia allocandi*), or to give (*pro licentia donandi*). In none of these forms were references ever made to the heirs of the recipient. Yet, by the 1270s, in a small number of cases, most often but by no means invariably, involving *inter-vivos* transfers of land between kin, we encounter land surrendered to the use of another (*reddere sursum ad opus*) to be held *sibi et heredibus suis*.[40] This usage grew gradually, so that by the 1280s it had become the predominant form specifying the return of the property to the lord for its regrant to another, whether the latter was purchaser, grantee or lessee. In such transfers 'A reddit sursum in manu domini x acras

---

[38] For a consideration of this issue, see Smith, 'Some Thoughts', pp. 98–107.

[39] Williamson, 'Peasant Holdings', p. 248, notes on the Prior of Norwich's manor of Sedgeford in the extreme north-west of Norfolk in the early rolls (which are suspiciously similar in vintage to those from the Abbot of Bury St Edmunds' manors), that from 1259 to 1265 'licences for land transactions were purchased by either the seller or the purchaser of the land involved . . . by 1273 the licence fee is invariably paid by the purchaser rather then the seller, until approximately 1282 after which date all land is surrendered into the Prior's hands for the use of the purchaser or grantee.' Williamson also notes that similar changes appear to have taken place at much the same time on the Prior's manors of Newton and Hindringham and on the lay manor or Gressenhall, all in Norfolk: *ibid.*, p. 113.

[40] For instance, in a Redgrave court of 8.11.1264 (MS Bacon 1) we find the following adjacent entries in the court proceedings: 'Ricardus le Markant dat ijs jd. pro licentia emendi j acram terre de Simon' Jop plegius Thomas Servient.' 'Eodem die venit Johannes Sket et sursum reddit dimidiam acram terre et dimidiam rodam terre ad opus Walteri fratri sui et finem condonatur per Thomam senescallum.'

terre ad opus Y tenendum sibi et heredibus suis.'[41] Occasionally, as in 1275, the 'old' and the 'new' forms co-existed in a single transfer.[42] The increasingly standardized format may well have occurred in association with a more rigorously maintained record, although it did have the effect of making gifts, sales and exchanges appear alike in our sources. Obviously our ability to distinguish between gifts and sales becomes of great significance in any consideration of transfers between relatives.

The proceedings of Redgrave manor court survive from 1260, and we have chosen to investigate the record of land transactions registered in those courts during the thirty years before and after the 1289 extent. However, as for two years, 1278 and 1306, no court proceedings have survived and as certain courts of other years have occasionally gone astray, we possess (given the additional problem of lapses in the registration of all transactions) a far from complete account of land transfers. However, the sheer quantity of evidence is such that some fundamental behavioural patterns are readily identifiable. Furthermore, assuming that there is no evidence to indicate a better recording of *post-mortem* than of *inter-vivos* transfers or vice versa we can proceed to consider the degree to which inheritance was the principal means by which the redistribution of land was achieved in this community.

Campbell, in his contribution to this volume, has adopted an analysis of land transactions registered per court session per annum as a means of avoiding the difficulties that confront any attempt to estimate annual totals from incomplete series of court proceedings.[43] This technique is to be encouraged when courts have apparently gone astray in a random fashion and there is no reason to believe that the annual frequency of court sessions was changing over time. However, the Redgrave evidence suggests that neither of these two

[41] The first instance in the surviving Redgrave court proceedings of the use of the term *heredes suis* comes in 1268 in the decision of a trial jury in a land plea between Adam Mandrake and Alice, his wife, and one Alice Kebbel. The jury reported that Adam Mandrake 'et Alicia uxor eius et heres suis habuerunt maius jus in dimidiam messuagii iij acras et iij rodas terre cum pertinenciis suis': MS Bacon 2. In 1284 a clear effort seems to have been made to employ a standard form for *inter-vivos* transfers. In the court of June 1284 there were 13 such transfers, all identical in form with the following, in which 'Walterus Oky et Matilda uxor eius reddunt in manu domini j rodam terre ad opus Walteri Bunting et heredibus suis et dat domino pro seisina habenda vjd faciendo inde etc. plegius Adam Jop': MS Bacon 4.

[42] 'Walterus But dat domino dimidiam marcam pro licentia emendi totam partem tenementi Galfridi fratri sui sic idem Galfridus venit in plena curia et sursum reddit ad opus dicti Walteri et heredibus suis faciendo inde servicia et consuetudines etc. plegii Walterus Medicus et Edwardus Cat': MS Bacon 2.

[43] *Infra*, pp. 108–9.

conditions strictly applied in the period between 1260 and 1319. There are indications that the annual frequency of court sessions fell somewhat in the early fourteenth century; the years 1278–9, 1293–4 and 1305–7 seem to have suffered particularly severe documentary losses. Tables 3.7 and 3.8 present the evidence on *inter-vivos* land transactions arranged both annually and decennially. It would appear that the quantity of land transferred between living persons was markedly under-stated in the decades 1270–9, 1290–9 and 1300–9. Nonetheless, the small number of courts surviving for individual years makes their representativeness somewhat questionable. It is particularly unfortunate that records have survived so partially for 1278 and 1279, coming as they do after the harvest failure in 1277 and given that the years 1293, 1294 and 1296 are situated in a decade with at least three years of near-famine conditions.[44] Nonetheless, there are grounds for supposing that inadequate harvests were associated with considerable surges in both the quantities of land sold and the number of sales. The years including and immediately following the harvest difficulties of 1272 seem to have witnessed considerable increases in the quantity of transactions, as did the year 1277 and the year following the poor harvest of 1283. The 1290s as a whole reflect the almost ever-present economic difficulties, with 54 courts recording 571 transactions, compared with the 455 transactions registered in the 78 courts of the 1280s when no years display strikingly inadequate documentary coverage. A burst of activity is also to be found in the early years of the second decade of the fourteenth century, after the poor harvest of 1311, and the infamously bad spell of years stretching from 1314 to 1317 saw a two- to three-fold increase in land transactions.[45] However, the growth in these latter years is, most likely, less extreme than the data suggest, given the problems already discussed concerning the quality of documentary coverage for the 1290s and the very early years of the fourteenth century.

[44] This assessment of harvest qualities is based upon grain price data in D. L. Farmer, 'Some Grain Price Movements in Thirteenth Century England', *Economic History Review* 2nd series 10, (1957), p. 212; M. M. Postan and J. Z. Titow, 'Heriots and Prices on Winchester Manors', in M. M. Postan, editor, *Essays on Medieval Agriculture and General Problems in the Medieval Economy* (Cambridge, 1972), pp. 175–8; and Titow, *English Rural Society*, pp. 97–9; and the decennial means presented in E. Miller and M. J. Hatcher, *Medieval England: Rural Society and Economic Change 1086–1348* (London, 1978), p. 66. See also Campbell, above, pp. 109–10.

[45] For similar patterns on the Titchfield Abbey estates, see D. G. Watts, 'A Model for the Early Fourteenth Century', *Economic History Review* 2nd series 20 (1967), p. 544; and, on the Abbot of St Albans' manors of Park, Codicote and Barnet in Hertfordshire and the Prior of Barnwell's manor of Chesterton in Cambridgeshire, see I. Kershaw, 'The Great Famine and Agrarian Crisis in England', *Past and Present* 59

Although these data do create obvious difficulties in highly precise time series analysis they allow us to obtain an estimate of the minimum quantity of customary land changing hands in the form of *inter-vivos* transfers. Out of the 2,756 transactions, the exact dimensions are not given for 690, many in fact concerned with residential property, farm buildings or shops and stores in the local periodic market. However, the total customary land exchanged in 2,756 transactions amounted to 1,305 acres, and, constituting as it does a minimum, it suggests a strong possibility that in the course of this sixty-year period an amount of land larger than the 1,317 acres in customary tenure on the manor was exchanged by means other than inheritance. This potential rate of turnover is remarkably similar to that proposed by Campbell for the two Norfolk manors of Coltishall and Martham.[46]

Of course, tenancies were also being reallocated in association with inheritances, and these latter transfers constitute an even more difficult set of evidence to assess. The greatest shortcoming afflicting these data concerns the perfunctory amount of information associated with each obituary entry before the early 1290s. Until that date we frequently find a reference to 'the heriot paid by A' or 'the heriot paid by the heirs of A' with no mention of the quantity of land involved or identification of heirs by name. Although after 1295 heirs are always named, it is only for the final years of the period of this analysis that we can derive a reasonably accurate estimate of the size of the inheritance.[47] Nonetheless, these final years are revealing, yielding as they did rather larger yearly numbers of inheritances than the annual totals for the period as a whole. In Table 3.9 we can observe that, between 1295 and 1319, 172 inheritances are recorded

---

(1973), p. 38. In the court rolls of the Norwich Cathedral Priory manor of Hindolveston the number of transactions during the years 1315–17 was almost 3 times greater than in other years in the early fourteenth century: H. W. Saunders, *An Introduction to the Obedientiary and Manor Rolls of Norwich Cathedral Priory* (Norwich, 1930), p. 40.

[46] Campbell, 'Population Change', pp. 186–7. Evidence presented by Williamson for the Norfolk manor of Gressenhall also suggests a rapid turnover of land. However, in this study only the number of transactions for 12 Edward I (1283–4) is given and, possibly containing as it does a deficient harvest year, represents an annual total of above average quantity: Williamson, 'Peasant Holdings', p. 54.

[47] Compare the entry 'De herietta Alexi Loveday dimidiam marcam plegius Ricardus Jop' from the court of Friday, 19.2.1261 MS Bacon 1) with the obituary entry relating to Simon Brunger in the court proceedings of Wednesday, 2.3.1317 'Simon Brunger obiit post ultimam curiam qui tenuit de domina in villenagio unum cotagium et iij rodas terre. Et dicunt quod Adam, Willimus et Phillipus sunt filii et heredes dicti Simon' Et petunt admitti et admittuntur. Et dominus habet unum equum pro herietto' (MS Bacon 13).

Table 3.7. 'Inter-vivos' land transactions: Redgrave 1260–1319 (annual totals)

Year	Total transactions	Total intra-familial	No. of courts	Total transactions per court	Total family transactions per court	Mean size of transactions (rods)	Variance	Standard deviation
1260	17	1	9	1.9	0.1	1.766	1.762	1.327
1261	11	2	11	1.0	0.2	1.875	1.109	1.053
1262	19	3	10	1.9	0.3	2.857	2.265	1.505
1263	17	1	5	3.4	0.2	7.045	57.929	7.611
1264	12	3	8	1.5	0.4	2.916	1.701	1.304
1265	7	1	5	1.4	0.2	4.666	14.888	3.858
1266	19	1	5	3.8	0.2	3.375	9.421	3.069
1267	20	4	4	5.0	1.0	1.583	2.618	1.618
1268	18	1	5	3.6	0.2	1.357	0.872	0.934
1269	24	4	10	2.4	0.25	2.178	1.914	1.384
1270	31	11	5	6.2	2.2	2.265	6.003	2.450
1271	36	2	7	5.1	0.3	2.138	1.383	1.176
1272	47	6	4	11.8	1.5	2.462	4.146	2.036
1273	59	12	10	5.9	1.2	1.903	1.216	1.102
1274	59	15	8	7.4	1.9	1.807	2.309	1.519
1275	32	5	11	2.9	0.5	2.892	3.399	1.843
1276	27	12	11	2.5	1.1	5.055	41.747	4.461
1277	52	11	10	5.2	1.1	2.075	3.006	1.734
1278	—	—	—	—	—	—	—	—
1279	5	1	2	2.5	1.5	2.250	1.562	1.250
1280	33	3	7	4.7	0.4	1.625	1.771	1.331
1281	49	11	12	4.1	0.9	1.563	0.637	0.798
1282	52	5	9	5.8	0.6	3.879	26.404	5.138
1283	42	4	8	5.3	0.5	1.962	1.017	1.009
1284	89	13	9	9.9	1.4	2.793	12.483	3.533
1285	51	7	10	5.1	0.7	1.905	2.338	1.529

1286	37	7	5	7.4	1.4	3.400	5.565	2.359
1287	57	13	7	8.2	1.9	2.153	3.095	1.759
1288	16	4	5	3.2	0.8	2.687	9.558	3.092
1289	31	17	7	4.4	2.4	2.318	2.785	1.669
1290	43	10	7	6.1	1.4	2.400	3.306	1.818
1291	50	13	8	6.8	1.6	3.725	11.223	3.350
1292	55	15	6	9.2	2.5	2.437	8.234	2.869
1293	36	7	2	18.0	3.5	2.900	15.005	3.874
1294	23	5	1	23.0	5.0	2.115	1.582	1.258
1295	100	9	7	14.2	1.3	2.899	7.681	2.771
1296	28	3	2	14.0	1.5	2.456	3.563	1.887
1297	82	18	6	13.7	3.0	2.779	4.022	2.005
1298	65	9	5	13.0	1.8	2.206	2.731	1.653
1299	89	24	10	8.9	2.4	3.526	37.014	6.084
1300	52	10	10	5.2	1.0	2.203	1.732	1.316
1301	11	4	5	2.2	0.8	1.500	0.125	0.354
1302	15	7	4	3.8	1.75	2.250	0.646	0.804
1303	40	10	5	8.0	2.0	2.886	10.839	3.292
1304	61	21	8	7.6	2.6	3.721	61.250	7.826
1305	37	3	3	12.3	1.0	2.945	7.761	2.785
1306	—	—	—	—	—	—	—	—
1307	29	1	3	9.7	0.3	1.936	1.663	1.289
1308	65	11	6	10.8	1.8	1.922	1.881	1.371
1309	58	19	8	7.3	2.4	4.428	57.305	7.570
1310	51	16	5	10.2	3.2	3.667	40.662	6.377
1311	98	25	9	10.9	2.8	2.208	6.935	2.633
1312	83	7	5	16.6	1.4	2.106	12.547	3.542
1313	46	7	5	9.2	1.4	2.145	2.767	1.663
1314	64	22	5	12.8	4.4	3.199	10.279	3.206
1315	87	4	4	21.8	1.0	3.090	21.761	4.665
1316	188	39	7	26.9	5.6	2.438	9.840	3.079
1317	135	30	5	27.0	6.0	2.286	8.674	2.945
1318	67	11	4	16.8	2.75	2.372	6.495	2.548
1319	31	7	4	10.3	1.75	1.944	3.767	1.941

Table 3.8. 'Inter-vivos' land transactions: Redgrave 1260–1319 (decennial totals)

	A	B	C	D	E	F	G	H	I	J	K	L	$\frac{I}{A}$ (Total) (Family) %
	Total transactions	Total no. (area given)	Total no. (area not given)	Total courts	Mean no. per court	Mean size (rods)	Variance	Standard deviation	Total no. intra-familial	Total no. intra-familial (area given)	Total no. intra-familial (area not given)	Mean no. intra-familial per court	
Years													
1260–9	164	111	53	72	2.3	2.760	11.597	3.405	21	10	11	0.3	12.8
1270–9	348	199	149	68	5.1	2.326	5.547	2.355	75	42	33	1.1	21.6
1280–9	455	330	125	78	5.8	2.418	7.661	2.767	84	68	16	1.1	18.5
1290–9	571	445	126	54	10.6	2.726	10.480	3.237	113	82	31	2.1	19.7
1300–9	368	294	74	54	6.8	2.597	14.212	3.769	86	69	17	1.6	23.4
1310–19	850	687	163	53	16.0	3.137	256.395	16.012	168	141	27	3.2	19.8
1260–1319	2,756	2,066	690	379	7.3	—	—	—	547	412	135	1.4	19.8

Table 3.9. 'Post-mortem' and 'inter-vivos' property transfers: Redgrave 1295–1319

Years	Total no. inter-vivos	Total no. (area not given)	Quantity* transacted (ac.)	Intra-familial inter-vivos total number	Intra-famial inter-vivos (area not given)	Intra-familial† quantity transacted (ac.)	Post-mortem‡ number	Port-mortem§ area (ac.)	Total area intra-familial, inter-vivos and post-mortem (ac.)
1295-9	364			63			26(2)		
1300-4	179			52			21(1)		
1305-9	189	38	88.7 (151)	34	5	26.3 (29)	23(1)	67.6	93.9
1310-14	342	68	148.8 (274)	77	17	28.3 (60)	33(2)	115.7	144.0
1315-19	508	95	239.9 (413)	91	10	25.8 (81)	52(11)	219.7	245.5
1305-19	1,039	201	477.4	202	32	80.4	108(14)	403.0	483.4

*Figures in parentheses = number of transactions with area given.
†Figures in parentheses = number of transactions with area given.
‡Figures in parentheses = properties escheating to lord and re-granted.
§Acreages do not include properties escheating to lord.

157

compared with 1,582 *inter-vivos* transactions. Between 1305 and 1319, 1,039 *inter-vivos* transfers, of which 201 give no precise areal measurements, accounted for a turnover of at least 477.4 acres representing a minimum figure, although considerably in excess of the 403 acres transferred in the 108 intra-familial inheritances over the same fifteen years.

Whether the ratio of *inter-vivos* to *post-mortem* redistribution of land identified in the last fifteen years of this sixty-year period is representative of the earlier years is difficult to assess given the lack of accurate obituary evidence for the last third of the thirteenth century. Table 3.10 presents a breakdown of curial income in surviving courts deriving from *post-mortem* and *inter-vivos* transfers. In the second half of the period we find that 'death duties' often generated less than 30 per cent of the revenue from the taxing of land transfers. The values of death duties have been derived from the amounts paid for entry fines, from cash heriots and the valuation attached to animal heriots and from reliefs paid on free land. It is impossible in the absence of reliable information on holding size to see whether seigneurial charges on these duties were increasing over time. It is possible that the apparent growth of *inter-vivos* relative to *post-mortem* transactions may reflect a rise in the licence fees charged on the latter category of transactions. There is some indication that this occurred, as the sixty 'death duties' recorded between 1280 and 1289 yielded £14 2s 6d, and the eighty paid between 1310 and 1319 £20 3s 5d, in seigneurial revenue, whereas the 850 *inter-vivos* transactions between 1309 and 1319 yielded £77 7s 2d, and 455 similar such transactions yielded £23 16s 3d in the 1280s. Although the average size of *inter-vivos* transactions appears to have increased marginally in the latter of the two periods (see Table 3.8) it would seem that licence fees per unit area of land transacted approximately doubled in the thirty years prior to 1320. Apart from the possibility of a different pattern in the decade 1260–9, there are no strong grounds for supposing that *post-mortem* transfers were the principal means by which land was redistributed throughout the period centring upon the 1289 extent. Nonetheless, we should note that the seigneurial income from the sale of licence fees for *inter-vivos* transactions grew significantly after 1290, when it came to account for over one-half of curial revenue.[48] In fact, in the second decade of the fourteenth century the yield from licence fees was annually close to 40 per cent of the total value of fixed customary

---

[48] For further discussion of the respective gains and losses of lord and tenants during these years, see Smith 'Some Thoughts', pp. 115–22.

Table 3.10. *Curial income from transfers of customary land: Redgrave, Suffolk 1260–1319*

	A	B	
	Post-mortem transfers	*Inter-vivos* transfers	A:B
Years			
1260–9	£14 12s 0d	£11 3s 10d	1.304
1270–9	£12 13s 4d	£20 6s 4d	0.623
1280–9	£14 2s 5d	£23 16s 3d	0.593
1290–9	£8 0s 11d	£30 17s 3d	0.261
1300–9	£6 19s 0d	£23 2s 6d	0.301
1310–19	£20 3s 5d	£77 7s 2d	0.261

rents, and in 1317, at the height of the economic distress associated with harvest failure, these fines actually exceeded the rental value of all customary lands. In sum, our evidence points to an active system of *inter-vivos* land transfers that grew in scale over the period 1260–1319, although much of the growth was irregular, being concentrated in years associated with harvest difficulties.

We have now to consider the implications of this volume of *inter-vivos* transfers of land for the operation of inheritance practices. On the one hand such an active exchange system could itself be a function of holding fragmentation brought about by partible inheritance, yet on the other it could increase the quantity of land disposed of by *pre-mortem* means, which would help in the longer term to reduce the overall significance of the inter-generational transfers of property *mortis causa*. Since the exchange of such large quantities of land could have been working to further either the engrossing of holdings or their fragmentation, it is important to identify the net and gross effects of the land market. At this point it is instructive to recall Campbell's findings from Coltishall, particularly as in the matter of the scale and the chronology of *inter-vivos* land transactions the Suffolk and Norfolk evidence appears remarkably similar. Accepting that the ratio of buyers to sellers provides a crude measure of the state of demand for land and the extent to which fragmentation or consolidation was proceeding, we can compare conditions in Redgrave with those in Coltishall over part of the period from 1260 to 1319. The manor court rolls of Coltishall provide evidence from 1280 onwards allowing the calculation of the ratio of buyers to sellers, and, although the pattern is quite volatile prior to the early 1320s, there was in most years an excess of buyers over sellers. Indeed, for much of the period prior to 1315 there were approximately 1.2 buyers for every one seller of property, although the difficult years in the period 1315–1322 witnessed a sharp increase in the number of sellers relative to buyers. Campbell rightly, given ancillary evidence, suggests that this most likely indicates increasing fragmentation of properties in association with demographic growth.[49]

We can see from the data presented in Tables 3.11 and 3.12 that the character and impact of the land market in Redgrave differed from that in Campbell's Norfolk community. In 22 of the 58 years for which the calculation can be made buyers exceeded sellers, and in only five of those years was the ratio greater than 1.2. In 28 years the ratio fell below unity, leaving just eight years when the numbers of buyers equalled those of sellers. In only eleven of the 28 years before the 1289 extent were sellers in excess of buyers, although in seventeen of the years following sellers exceeded buyers. Furthermore, this excess of sellers over buyers was particularly marked in the 1290s and in the period prior to the good harvest of 1312. What is noteworthy is the sharp recovery in the number of buyers in the years of severe harvest failure between 1316 and 1318, a pattern quite the opposite of that found in Coltishall.

It should be noted that when buyers and sellers are considered solely in relation to their non-family transactions the ratio of sellers to buyers increases markedly. In fact, in no five-year period after 1289 do buyers exceed sellers, and only in the five-year period 1270–4 are there as many as 110 buyers for every 100 sellers. The pattern of intra-familial transactions simply represents, in part, *pre-mortem* gifts of land by parents to children, especially daughters, who may well become 'lost' in our statistics if this land is sold by their husbands subsequent to their marriage. In the analysis of these data, transactions involving husbands and wives as joint either buyers or sellers have been classed as if they were undertaken by the husband alone. As will be seen from Table 3.19, husbands and wives were more than twice as likely to sell than buy land together; most likely, indeed, to sell land brought to the marriage as dower by the bride, in the receipt of which she most probably appears as a 'buyer' in our statistics. In other words, the data are biased in favour of buyers, suggesting that, overall, sellers were more numerous than our evidence superficially indicates. We should note, too, that the apparent growth in the number of buyers relative to sellers in the period 1315–19 can in large

[49] See Campbell, above, pp. 111–13.

part be attributed to an expansion of intra-familial transactions concerning parental gifts to daughters among wealthy tenant families.

In the course of the period 1260–1319 it is possible to identify 1,426 individuals who appear as parties in *inter-vivos* land transactions. In Table 3.13 an attempt has been made to categorize these individuals on the basis of whether they were observed to buy or to sell only or whether they both bought and sold land. The pattern, when presented *in toto*, appears to resemble that calculated by Campbell for overlapping 25-year periods extending from 1280 to 1329 in Coltishall, although marginally fewer participants in Redgrave displayed a net surplus in their *inter-vivos* dealings.[50] However, before the similarities are over-stressed, we should, as we have in our discussion of the ratio of buyers to sellers, consider the effect of distinguishing between the patterns exhibited by male and female participants. When men alone are considered the majority can be observed to have been in deficit in their dealings in land. Among the women who accounted for 28 per cent of the participants almost 65 per cent appear in surplus compared with only 45 per cent of the men.[51] Furthermore, over 42 per cent of the females derived their 'surpluses' through transactions with their family, suggesting that a high proportion of their acquisitions most likely represented gifts that preceded their eventual marriage. Of the men who displayed a surplus in their market dealings only 11 per cent were so classified because of land dealings solely with kin (see Table 3.13b). By including women, especially those who were unmarried and who undoubtedly constituted the vast majority of the 398 female participants, we have biased our findings in favour of persons who would appear to have been in net

[50] *Ibid.*, p. 110.

[51] Published studies relating to the relative roles of men and women in the markets for customary land in medieval rural communities are at present non-existent, although a recently completed Ph.D. thesis by Judith M. Bennett provides some valuable data, in particular, for the Northamptonshire manor of Brigstock. Her analysis was not of participants but of individual appearances in *inter-vivos* transfers. Of the 2,933 appearances in the Brigstock court for *inter-vivos* land deals women were responsible for 540 (18.4%), although women accounted for 28% of the participants in the market in Redgrave (see below, p. 167). The recording of transactions suggests a less active market in *inter-vivos* transfers at Brigstock, totalling as they did 2,933 in 549 courts over the period 1287–1348, compared with 6,115 appearances in 379 courts in 58 years in the period 1260–1319 in Redgrave. The degree of female participation in the land market also appears to have been greater at Redgrave, although the discrepancy may not be very significant given the different methods in the 2 studies of presenting the data. See J. M. Bennett, 'Gender, Family and Community: a Comparative Study of the English Peasantry', unpublished Toronto Ph.D. thesis, 1981, p. 234 note 52.

Table 3.11. *The ratio of property buyers to sellers: Redgrave 1260–1319 (annual totals)*

Date	Inter-familial transactions			Intra-familial transactions*		All transactions		
	Buyers	Sellers	Buyers:Sellers	Buyers	Sellers	Buyers	Sellers	Buyers:Sellers
1260	13	12	1.08	3(–)	3(1)	15	14	1.07
1261	12	10	1.20	2(–)	2(–)	14	12	1.17
1262	12	13	0.92	4(–)	5(1)	16	17	0.94
1263	12	13	0.92	1(1)	1(1)	12	13	0.92
1264	9	8	1.13	4(–)	4(–)	13	12	1.08
1265	7	7	1.00	1(–)	1(–)	8	8	1.00
1266	10	10	1.00	2(–)	2(–)	12	12	1.00
1267	12	9	1.33	5(–)	4(–)	17	13	1.31
1268	10	15	0.67	2(–)	2(1)	12	16	0.75
1269	18	15	1.20	3(–)	3(–)	21	18	1.16
1270	17	19	0.89	9(1)	9(1)	25	27	0.93
1271	19	18	1.06	4(–)	4(–)	23	22	1.05
1272	27	25	1.08	4(–)	4(1)	31	28	1.11
1273	41	30	1.37	11(1)	11(2)	51	39	1.31
1274	30	23	1.30	22(2)	21(1)	50	43	1.16
1275	32	29	1.10	13(3)	8(2)	42	35	1.20
1276	17	19	0.89	13(1)	12(1)	29	30	0.97
1277	30	29	1.03	12(2)	13(–)	40	42	0.95
1278				(missing)				
1279	2	2	1.00	1(–)	1(–)	3	3	1.00
1280	32	15	2.13	6(1)	7(3)	37	19	1.95
1281	35	32	1.09	15(1)	12(1)	49	43	1.14
1282	33	39	0.84	9(1)	9(1)	41	47	0.87
1283	27	30	0.90	10(2)	8(2)	35	36	0.97
1284	50	54	0.93	11(5)	11(3)	56	62	0.91
1285	27	31	0.87	6(1)	7(–)	32	38	0.84
1286	22	19	1.16	6(–)	7(–)	28	25	1.12

1287	38	38	1.00	9(2)	8(1)	45	45	1.00
1288	9	13	0.69	3(–)	3(1)	12	15	0.80
1289	16	14	1.14	16(3)	18(–)	29	32	0.91
1290	34	35	0.97	10(1)	11(1)	43	45	0.96
1291	26	33	0.79	8(1)	7(3)	33	37	0.89
1292	39	38	1.03	19(–)	16(2)	57	52	1.09
1293	26	26	1.00	7(–)	10(–)	33	36	0.92
1294	12	13	0.92	4(–)	4(–)	16	17	0.94
1295	43	56	0.77	16(–)	17(2)	59	71	0.83
1296	16	17	0.94	9(1)	7(1)	24	23	1.04
1297	44	48	1.00	17(1)	18(4)	60	62	0.97
1298	38	46	0.83	10(2)	11(2)	46	55	0.83
1299	41	50	0.82	19(5)	18(–)	55	68	0.81
1300	35	35	1.00	12(1)	14(1)	46	48	0.96
1301	4	4	1.00	3(–)	4(–)	7	8	0.88
1302	8	10	0.80	4(–)	3(–)	12	13	0.92
1303	23	24	0.96	9(1)	8(1)	31	31	1.00
1304	29	39	0.74	21(2)	15(5)	48	49	0.98
1305	22	28	0.79	9(–)	9(1)	31	36	0.86
1306				(missing)				
1307	18	21	0.86	6(–)	6(–)	24	27	0.89
1308	37	44	0.84	11(1)	8(3)	47	49	0.96
1309	31	31	1.00	17(1)	14(3)	47	42	1.12
1310	28	33	0.85	7(3)	7(–)	32	40	0.80
1311	46	61	0.75	22(4)	21(6)	64	75	0.85
1312	54	48	1.13	9(1)	8(4)	62	52	1.19
1313	27	28	0.96	9(–)	9(2)	36	35	1.03
1314	36	34	1.06	13(3)	15(2)	46	47	0.98
1315	42	46	0.91	16(2)	14(4)	56	56	1.00
1316	83	85	0.98	37(9)	31(16)	111	100	1.11
1317	61	62	0.98	25(2)	22(9)	94	75	1.25
1318	46	38	1.21	7(2)	5(1)	51	42	1.21
1319	18	15	1.20	8(1)	7(–)	25	22	1.14

*Figures in parentheses = intra-familial buyers and sellers who also buy or sell with non-kin.

Table 3.12. *The ratio of property buyers to sellers: Redgrave 1260–1319 (decennial totals)*

Years	Inter-familial transactions			Intra-familial transactions*		All transactions		
	Buyers	Sellers	Buyers:Sellers	Buyers	Sellers	Buyers	Sellers	Buyers:Sellers
1260–4	57	53	1.08	14(4)	13(5)	67	61	1.09
1265–9	46	47	0.98	11(–)	11(1)	57	57	1.00
1270–4	95	86	1.11	46(4)	47(13)	137	120	1.14
1275–9	71	69	1.03	38(8)	34(8)	101	95	1.06
1280–4	142	130	1.09	47(14)	40(16)	176	154	1.14
1285–9	92	91	1.01	41(6)	50(12)	126	119	1.05
1290–4	105	117	0.89	43(8)	44(18)	140	143	0.98
1295–9	126	158	0.79	65(22)	63(19)	169	202	0.84
1300–4	79	96	0.82	48(10)	40(14)	117	122	0.96
1305–9	91	98	0.93	39(6)	33(14)	124	117	1.05
1310–14	142	154	0.92	50(17)	46(21)	175	179	0.98
1315–19	172	176	0.98	79(29)	64(36)	222	204	1.08

*Figures in parentheses = intra-familial buyers and sellers who also buy or sell with non-kin.

surplus in their dealings. For that reason a less ambiguous interpretation of the redistributive effects of *inter-vivos* land transactions on the social distribution of land would need to exclude women unless they could be analysed comprehensively both as married and as unmarried participants in the system of exchanges.

In Table 3.14 we present data that indicate the distribution of 'surpluses' and 'deficits' in *inter-vivos* dealings by males. The initial impression gained from this distribution is that the surpluses are almost exactly counterbalanced by the deficits. There were marginally more persons, both proportionally and absolutely, displaying deficits in excess of two acres than there were individuals in surplus in comparable amounts, although the difference is not significant. However, it is when we consider those individuals who produced surpluses or deficits in excess of eight acres that we observe some marked contrasts between those in surplus and those in deficit. For instance, the purchases of the seventeen individuals in surplus by eight or more acres amounted to 273 acres from non-family members and a further 43.2 acres obtained from kin. In contrast, those eleven individuals in deficit in excess of eight acres had sold 134.5 acres to unrelated persons and 25.5 acres to related participants in the exchange system. But eight of the seventeen individuals exhibiting the largest surpluses were interrelated: a father and a son, a father and three sons, and two siblings.[52] There is no evidence to suggest that any of those who were in substantial deficit were so interrelated. These discrepancies in the pattern suggest that a small number of individuals in a small number of families were amassing a disproportionately large share of the customary land, for many of the accumulators are to be seen amongst the largest land holders at the time of the 1289 extent and proceeded subsequently to increase their holdings or to add to holdings they had inherited of well above average size.

The most striking pattern of acquisitive behaviour was that of Adam Jop and his sons Richard, John and John junior. Adam Jop was, by the standards of his community, a wealthy tenant, holding 39 acres of customary land in 1289, along with two full messuages and part of another under customary terms. In addition, he held freely a messuage and nine acres. Of the 39 acres of customary land held in 1289, Adam had acquired a little over sixteen acres through 27 *inter-vivos* dealings. Before his death he secured a further eight acres

---

[52] The father and son were Adam Pistor senior and junior, the father and 3 sons were Adam Jop and his sons, John senior and junior and Richard, and the 2 brothers were Robert and Augustus Jop.

(a)

Table 3.13. Net effects of 'inter-vivos' land transfers: Redgrave 1260–1319

	Participants in surplus		Participants in deficit		Participants in balance		Total
	No.	%	No.	%	No.	%	
All							
Buy only	565	78.3					
Buy < sell	157	21.7					
Buy = sell					70		
Sell only			452	71.3			
Sell < buy			182	28.7			
Total	722	50.6	634	44.5	70	4.9	1,426
Males							
Buy only	317	68.2					
Buy < sell	148	31.8					
Buy = sell					63		
Sell only			332	66.4			
Sell < buy			168	33.6			
Total	465	45.2	500	48.6	63	6.2	1,028
Females							
Buy only	239	93.0					
Buy < sell	18	7.0					
Buy = sell					7		
Sell only			120	89.6			
Sell < buy			14	10.4			
Total	257	64.6	134	33.7	7	1.7	398

166

(b)

	Males	Females
Type		
Buy only (non-family)	234	101
Family buy only	54	116
Buy only (family and non-family)	29	22
Buy < sell (family sell only)	29	
Buy < sell (family buy < family sell)	23	
Buy < sell (family sell < family buy)	7	18
Buy < sell (family buy only)	41	
Buy < sell (non-family only)	58	
Total	465	257
Sell only (non-family)	220	80
Family sell only	60	80
Sell only (family and non-family)	52	15
Sell < buy (family sell only)	60	
Sell < buy (family buy < family sell)	8	
Sell < buy (family sell < family buy)	24	14
Sell < buy (family buy only)	29	
Sell < buy (non-family only)	47	
Total	500	134

167

Table 3.14. *The distribution of surpluses and deficits (in rods): male participants in Redgrave land market 1260–1319*

	Residential property	1	1–1.9	2–2.9	3–3.9	4–7.9	8–11.9	12–15.9	16–19.9	20–23.9	24–27.9	28–31.9	32+	Total
Surplus	99	53	58	43	27	69	39	24	15	7	10	4	17	465
Deficit	86	58	60	46	32	90	47	26	24	8	7	5	11	500

of customary land.[53] In contrast to his purchasing activities, he sold outside his family very infrequently, with only five instances in the surviving court rolls amounting to a little under three acres.[54] He did, however, pass on land before his death to his sons in varying amounts. Certainly no less than ten acres had been granted to John Jop and John Jop junior.[55] Richard had accumulated a few acres in the 1280s and did not begin to acquire further land until after his father's death, in the period of great activity in the community's land market between 1315 and 1317.[56] In addition to their father's gifts, John senior and John junior had acquired a further fifteen acres between them, and on sharing the patrimonial estate in 1314 they proceeded to add to their holdings so that by 1320 the three brothers had over ninety acres of customary land.[57] Their involvement in the land market had not been continuous but was disproportionately concentrated in the 1280s and 1290s and again between 1315 and 1317. The Jop family's hold upon Redgrave's customary land was indeed considerable because Adam Jop's nephews, Robert, Augustus and Benedict, had, by 1320, at least a further sixty acres, approximately two-thirds the result of their *inter-vivos* dealings.[58] Indeed, by 1320 the

---

[53] After 1289, Adam Jop appears in the proceedings of the following courts acquiring property: 6.2.1291, 18.10.1291, 24.11.1291 (2), 21.7.1292 (MS Bacon 6); 8.6.1295, 6.12.1295 (MS Bacon 7); 24.7.1297 (3), 9.7.1298, 1.10.1298, 29.6.1300 (MS Bacon 8); 11.11.1312 (MS Bacon 9).

[54] Transactions on 7.11.1282, 4.11.1283 (MS Bacon 4); 9.4.1288 (MS Bacon 5); 21.7.1292 (MS Bacon 6); 26.5.1298 (MS Bacon 8).

[55] In 1295 he granted his son, John senior, 1 messuage and 8 acres, 8.6.1295 (MS Bacon 7), ad 2 years later, 9.10.1297 (MS Bacon 8) John senior received the holding that was once held by Adam Loce. John junior received 2 acres at the court of 20.10. 1307 (MS Bacon 11).

[56] John Jop senior purchased land in the following courts: 2.5.1291, 28.12.1293, ?.5.1293 (2) (MS Bacon 6); 3.11.1294, 1.6.1295, 6.12.1295 (2) (MS Bacon 7); 15.6.1296, 24.7.1297, 27.5.1299 (MS Bacon 8); 1.12.1304 (MS Bacon 10); 7.10.1311 (MS Bacon 11); 17.2.1313 (MS Bacon 12); 31.7.1316, 22.4.1316, 30.9.1316, 20.12.1316 (4), 2.3.1317, 4.6.1317, 16.12.1317, 7.4.1318 (MS Bacon 13). As a seller John Jop senior appeared in the following courts: 24.7.1297, 3.9.1299 (MS Bacon 8); 30.11.1308 (MS Bacon 11); 7.4.1318 (MS Bacon 13). John Jop junior is identifiable in the following courts acquiring land: 2.9.1295 (MS Bacon 7); 20.10.1307, 6.6.1310 (MS Bacon 11); 7.4.1310 (MS Bacon 12); 4.4.1315, 4.3.1316 (MS Bacon 13). His sales are recorded in courts of 8.6.1314, 4.3.1316 and 22.4.1316 (MS Bacon 13). Richard, the eldest of Adam Jop's sons bought land on: 12.7.1283, 15.4.1284 (2), 5.10.1285 (MS Bacon 4); 4.3.1316, 22.4.1316, 20.12.1316 (4), 4.6.1317, 20.8.1317, 16.12.1317 (2), 7.4.1318 (4), 16.5.1318 and 15.1.1320 (MS Bacon 13). One reference to a sale of land by Richard survives in the court of 4.6.1317 (MS Bacon 13).

[57] 29 of their 51 purchases took place after their father's death, primarily in 1316 and 1317.

[58] Augustus Jop appears in the court records acquiring land in the following courts: 14.3.1281 (MS Bacon 4); ?.5.1287 (MS Bacon 5); 11.2.1295, 8.6.1295 (4) (MS Bacon 7); 15.6.1299 (2), 13.12.1299, 24.12.1299, 24.2.1300, 6.7.1300, 30.12.1300 (MS Bacon 8);

five cousins held at least 11 per cent of the total customary land in Redgrave, although they constituted only marginally over 1 per cent of the tenantry.

Similar, if less extreme, examples can be found in the actions of Adam Pistor and his two sons, of William Crane and his two sons, of Simon Ogood and indeed of Simon Palmer senior and junior. Adam Pistor senior and junior were two others among the seventeen individuals displaying the largest surplus in their dealings. Adam Pistor senior's economic activities were highly diversified, for in 1289 he had in Redgrave a little over nineteen acres of land, two messuages, two cottages, two stalls and a shop in the local market. Before his death in 1320 he amassed a further twenty acres of land in Redgrave and four acres in the adjacent manor of Rickinghall.[59] As in the case of all those individuals and families who seemed to be accumulating property, Adam Pistor's individual purchases were rarely other than small, only infrequently exceeding an acre in size and usually comprising a rod or indeed a fraction of a rod in area. Adam's sons, Adam junior, Robert and Thomas were all active in the market as individuals, accumulating collectively a further eight acres and two shops in the market, to supplement *pre-mortem* gifts from

---

26.7.1303, 7.2.1309, 9.4.1309, 30.4.1310, 6.5.1311, 15.6.1311, 7.10.1311, 6.11.1311, 30.5.1312 (MS Bacon 11); 22.10.1315 (2), 4.3.1316, 8.6.1316 (2), 2.3.1317, 6.9.1318 (MS Bacon 13). His only appearances as a seller of land were: ?.?.1301 (badly damaged MS Bacon 9); 6.5.1311, 7.10.1311 (MS Bacon 11). Benedict Jop bought land in the following courts: 14.3.1281 (MS Bacon 4); 15.6.1296 (2), 20.4.1297, 9.10.1297, 19.5.1298 (MS Bacon 8); 24.10.1303 (MS Bacon 10); 17.2.1313 (2) (MS Bacon 12); 25.1.1314, 8.6.1314, 4.6.1317 (2), 16.12.1317, 3.4.1318, 1.1.1320, 15.1.1320 (2). On no occasion prior to 1320 did Benedict Jop sell land. Robert Jop, like his brother Benedict, appears in the following court proceedings as a buyer only: 14.3.1281, 7.11.1282 (MS Bacon 4); ?.7.1293 (MS Bacon 6); 8.1.1295, 11.2.1295 (MS Bacon 7); 26.2.1296, 20.4.1297, 9.10.1297, 3.2.1298 (2), 1.10.1298 (2), 3.2.1300, 6.7.1300 (MS Bacon 8); 13.9.1307 (2), 20.10.1307, 18.9.1310, 25.1.1311, 7.10.1311, 7.4.1312 (MS Bacon 11); 27.10.1315, 22.4.1316, 16.12.1317 (MS Bacon 13).

59 Adam Pistor senior acquired land in the following court sessions after 1289: 3.8.1290, 6.11.1290, 26.5.1292 (2), 10.11.1292 (MS Bacon 6); 5.11.1294, 7.2.1295, 8.6.1295 (2), 6.12.1295 (MS Bacon 7); 15.6.1296, 17.7.1297 (2), 24.7.1297 (2), 9.11.1297, 14.11.1297, 17.1.1299 (MS Bacon 8); 30.6.1305 (MS Bacon 11); in this period he never sold land outside his family, but transferred it to his sons and daughters on: 18.6.1308 (MS Bacon 11); 1.4.1314, 31.5.1315 and 1.1.1320 (MS Bacon 13). His land acquisitions in the neighbouring manor of Rickinghall can be traced in BL MS Add. Ch. 63394–407. It is evident that Adam Pistor was not the head of a subsistence enterprise employing solely family labour, for we have reference to his servants amerced for petty offences in the following courts: 22.1.1282 (BL, MS Add. Ch. 63398), 9.7.1288 (MS Bacon 6); 26.4.1291 (MS Bacon 6); 1.6.1295 (MS Bacon 7); 13.6.1296, 2.6.1298 (MS Bacon 8); and 20.6.1301 (MS Bacon 8). For further discussion, see Smith, 'Kin and Neighbours', p. 246, and 'Some Thoughts'.

their father, and some small slivers of land provided by their uncle.[60]
On their father's death Adam and Robert Pistor shared over sixty
acres of customary land that they and their father had accumulated
over the preceding fifty years and had sizeable business interests as
stall and shop holders in the Botulesdale market and a scattering of
odd cottages and messuages.

Although the evidence suggests that there were individuals who
both accumulated large quantities of land through *inter-vivos* dealings
and engrossed quantities that were not matched in area by those in
overall deficit, it would be incorrect to assume that there were
inconsiderable numbers of individuals feeding, through a sequence
or series of deals, rather large amounts of property into the system of
land exchanges. One striking case was that of Walter Mercator or
Chapman whose own father in the course of our period of study had
accumulated over twenty acres of land in small purchases and had
died just prior to the extent's construction in 1289. In that extent his
sons Walter and Ralph were described as possessing absolutely
identical amounts of land (see Table 3.4).[61] However, in the course of
the 1290s this symmetry was destroyed, as in 1297 Ralph sold out his
share in the family holdings to Walter.[62] Before his death, however,
Walter sold over twenty acres, so that the holding he passed on to his
sons was a good deal smaller at fourteen acres than that which he had
inherited from his brother and father sixteen years earlier.[63]

[60] Adam Pistor junior acquired land from persons not known to have been his kin on:
7.4.1313, 1.4.1314, 8.6.1316 (2), 13.9.1316, 2.3.1317, 13.4.1317, 4.6.1317 and 15.1.1320
(MS Bacon 13); and from his father and uncle: 1.4.1314, 31.5.1315 and 1.1.1320 (MS
Bacon 13). His brother Robert bought from persons to whom he was unrelated on:
22.12.1295 (MS Bacon 7); 21.1.1305 (MS Bacon 11); 17.2.1313, 1.4.1314 and 2.3.1317
(MS Bacon 13); and obtained land from his father and uncle on: 18.6.1308, 30.9.1308
(MS Bacon 11); 1.4.1314 and 31.5.1315 (MS Bacon 13). On 22.4.1316 he sold a piece, $\frac{1}{2}$
rod in size, to his brother-in-law (MS Bacon 13).

[61] Richard Mercator sold land between 1260 and his death in 1285 on only one
occasion, 8.2.1263 (MS Bacon 1). His purchases were recorded in the following
courts: 3.5.1260 (2), 7.8.1260, 29.6.1262, 8.2.1263, 30.6.1263 (2), 8.11.1264 (MS Bacon
1); 14.1.1270, 1.7.1270, 17.3.1271, 25.5.1271 (2), 6.6.1271, 18.2.1273 (2), 6.2.1275,
22.12.1276 (MS Bacon 2); 25.2.1280, 4.12.1280, 4.10.1283 (MS Bacon 4).

[62] Ralph, son of Richard Mercator, appears to have purchased once jointly with his
brother Walter in 1293 (court of ?.7.1293, MS Bacon 6); he sold land outside his
family in 1290 and 1293 (courts of 26.4.1290 and 8.6.1295, MSS Bacon 6 and 7); in 2
transactions he transferred his share in the inheritance to Walter: 9.10.1297 and
27.5.1299 (MS Bacon 8).

[63] Walter Mercator purchased land once jointly with Ralph, ?.7.1293 (MS Bacon 6) and
received his brother's share in their father's land (see above, note 62). His sales
before his death in 1304 (17.4.1304, MS Bacon 10) are recorded in the following
courts: 26.4.1290 (MS Bacon 6); 5.11.1294, 8.6.1295, 5.11.1295, 6.12.1295 (2) (MS
Bacon 7); 26.2.1296, 15.6.1296 (2), 9.2.1297 (2), 17.7.1297, 20. 5. 1298 (2), 9.7.1298,

A similar pattern is observable in the dealings of Walter Beneyt who held in 1289 nine-and-a-half acres but saw his holding increased in 1290 when his brother John sold out to him his share in their father's estate. Yet in the following decade we have a record of Walter selling at least sixteen acres, so that on his death his two sons inherited a minuscule property of only three-quarters of an acre of customary land. In some cases, too, the selling appears not to have been distributed widely among the many purchasers our analysis has identified. For instance, William Wluard, who sold over thirteen acres outside his family in many sales of small plots extending through the second decade of the fourteenth century, provided the basis of almost half of the purchases that helped to place Thomas Knot among those with the largest surpluses produced through their market dealings.[64] Given these examples, it should be stressed that there were certain opportunities in such a volatile system of exchanges for a small number of individuals to piece together holdings of above average size, as well as cases of family fortunes literally dissolving overnight. Nonetheless, these developments co-existed with another pattern; at one end of the spectrum of land holders a small number of families proceeded to strengthen their grip on the community's land and resources, while at the other end the vast majority made only one or two brief sorties into the market, either to sell the rod or two that constituted their sole landed wealth or to buy similar such amounts that would, if they could be retained (which they frequently could not), provide a small and inadequate inheritance in the event of surviving offspring having been produced.

In a strongly patriarchal social and economic system it might be expected that the decision of the father to retire from active involve-

---

1.10.1298 (2), 17.1.1299, 27.5.1299 (2), 15.6.1299, 28.10.1299, 6.7.1300 (3), 13.12.1300 (MS Bacon 8); 8.6.1303 (MS Bacon 9).

[64] Walter Beneyt's sales of land were recorded in the following courts: 26.7.1280, 31.7.1284, 11.12.1285 (MS Bacon 4); 14.3.1287 (2), 25.11.1289 (MS Bacon 5); 26.4.1290, 22.12.1292 (MS Bacon 6); 8.1.1295 (2), 6.12.1295 (3) (MS Bacon 7); 19.2.1296, 20.4.1297 (2), 16.7.1297, 20.5.1298, 1.11.1298 (2), 5.2.1299, 3.9.1299, 6.6.1300, 6.7.1300 (MS Bacon 8). Sales continued regularly until Walter's death, the record of which was entered in the court held on 20.6.1301, (MS Bacon 9). Thomas Knot appears in the court records between 1303 and 1319 on 24 occasions as a buyer. 17 of these purchases were from William Wluard, and are recorded in courts of 21.3.1308, 30.11.1308 (2), 11.6.1309, 24.11.1309, 18.3.1310, 18.9.1310, 11.1.1312, 17.4.1312, 14.9.1312 (MS Bacon 11); 17.2.1313, 25.1.1314, 1.4.1314,15.11.1314, 4.4.1315, 27.10.1315, 4.3.1316 (MS Bacon 13). In addition, Thomas Knot purchased on 3 additional occasions from Thomas, brother of William Wluard: 7.4.1313, 22.4.1316, 2.3.1317 (MS Bacon 13). There is no evidence whatsoever that Thomas Knot was related by blood or marriage to the Wluards.

ment in farming, or his death, would be a prime determinant of whether sons gained access to land which they themselves could control and upon which they might establish their own families. Indeed, such a pattern of inter-generational relations might act to limit the extent of any active market in land. From the proceedings of Redgrave's courts between 1260 and 1293, it is possible to extract information on 116 'two-generational families' in which sons survived to or beyond the age of majority and were alive on their father's death; these data include either the holding size of the parent or his role as a pledge in the manorial court or both, numbers of recorded sons (assumed to be at least twelve years of age), numbers of recorded daughters, numbers of purchases and sales by father, numbers of gifts by father to sons and daughters and numbers of pledgings done by fathers for sons and daughters in their own land purchases.[65]

At Redgrave, fifty of the 116 families show no signs of land being acquired through *inter-vivos* transactions, although 23 of these families were freeholders whose acquisitions of freehold land would have been most likely recorded by charter and in consequence not, or only rarely, a matter of concern for the manorial court. In the absence of comparable data, it is difficult to assess the significance of the fact that 70 per cent of 93 two-generational families among the customary tenants of Redgrave had sons engaging in the market in the acquisition of land. We know from the demographic models discussed earlier in Chapter 1 that in a stationary population up to 40 per cent of men would have had no surviving male offspring at their death.[66] Of course, that figure could have been somewhat higher in the years prior to their death if we make some allowance for deaths during the years between the legal age of majority and the mean age of paternal death. However, such calculations help to place the 93 'two-generational' families of the customary tenants within wider context. A question of still greater importance concerns the meaning that should be attached to the fact that of the transactions undertaken by sons in these families over 50 per cent were completed prior to their father's death.

[65] It is impossible to establish the representativeness of the 116 'two-generational' families, although it should be stressed that in this and in all matters dealt with in this paper, the data relate almost entirely to the customary tenants of Redgrave whose proportional contribution to the community's total population cannot be estimated.

[66] See above, pp. 41–55. It should be noted that, in Table 1.5 (p. 49), of the 108 inheritances recorded in the courts between 1260 and 1294 for which heirs are specified, almost half show men dying without direct male heirs.

Table 3.15. *Redgrave: land marketing activities of sons*

	Nos. of pledgings by father					
	0–5	6–10	11–15	16–20	21–5	26+
Sons						
Not partaking in land market	12	7	7	1	2	4
Buying land before father dies	5	4	11	2	2	8
Buying after father dies only	18	2	4	2	1	1
Total	35	13	22	5	5	13

Table 3.15 shows that of the 48 families in which the father pledged on ten or fewer occasions only nine (19 per cent) had sons who bought land before their father died, whereas of those families whose father was relatively frequently encountered in the court proceedings as a pledge almost 50 per cent had sons active in the land market before the point of paternal death. Such behaviour was especially characteristic of the offspring of important pledges. An active pledge and a powerful figure in both village and manorial society, such as Adam Jop, exemplifies this pattern of behaviour: Adam, who died in 1314, had at least seven children who survived to become young adults. Four daughters appear in the record, of who at least three were married between 1284 and 1293, and three sons, the oldest of whom began to acquire property in 1284.[67] We have already discovered aspects of these activities in our earlier discussion. Two of the daughters received gifts of land as dowries in the year of their marriage and a third bought a small piece of land with her father as pledge to the transaction and the licence fee that secured her legitimate tenure of it.[68] Adam Jop's eldest son, Richard, seems to have received no parental gift of land, and apparently no pledging support from his father, although both of his younger brothers, John senior and John junior, obtained from their father the gift of holdings

[67] The marriages of the daughters are recorded in the following courts: Adam Jop paid a merchet of 2s for Alice to marry on 23.1.1284 (MS Bacon 4); Isabel's merchet of 1s was paid by her father in 1289, giving her permission to marry *infra homagium*, 26.1.1289 (MS Bacon 5); Cristina paid 2s at the court of 22.12.1292 (MS Bacon 6) for permission to marry John Reynold.

[68] Alice received, at the same court that her merchet was paid, a gift of 1 acre from her father on condition that if she died without offspring, the land would revert to him. Basilia, a daughter whose marital status is unknown, purchased 1 rod from Richard Stanmere with pledging support from her father; court of 23.6.1295 (MS Bacon 6). Isabel, like her sister Alice, received, in the same court as her merchet payment, a gift of 1 acre of land from her father.

that were very large by local standards.[69] In addition, in their earliest ventures into the land market these two sons secured their father's pledging support which may indicate that he was acting as their financial guarantor. However, the sons acquired their properties independently and did not undertake joint purchases, nor do they appear, at least prior to their father's death, to have engaged in transactions with a common set of individuals. Many of those who sold to them did, however, have one characteristic which they shared, in that they were frequently co-heirs from less exalted families in the ranks of the tenantry who were selling off shares they had recently inherited in a patrimony. Of the twenty purchases made between 1284 and 1314 by the three brothers fifteen were clearly made from persons who appeared in the extent of 1289 as co-heirs.

We have in our discussion drawn attention to certain individuals noteworthy for the sizeable amounts they sold even though they had heirs on hand to inherit. In addition, we have pointed, at least in the more affluent layers of the tenantry, to instances of very significant *pre-mortem* acquisitions by sons that pre-dated their inheritance or complemented small paternal gifts. This evidence, when assessed in conjunction with the aggregate patterns of land turnover (which suggested a subsidiary role for inheritance as a mechanism for the redistribution of property), requires us to consider the relationship between the inheritance practices and *inter-vivos* transfers in more detail. It will force us at the same time to reflect on the evidence bearing upon the degree to which the siblings prior to, at and after inheritance displayed strong signs of acting together in jointly owned and operated economic enterprises.

Of the fifty sibling groups identified on the 1289 extent and traced in the subsequent thirty years only thirteen showed an overall gain in their land and resources, whereas 27 saw their holding shrink. Indeed, even among five of those groups that gained one or more of the siblings suffered a personal deficit in his transactions. This pattern appears to mirror that presented in a different set of evidence on the fortunes of 41 sets of sons who are shown in the court rolls between 1260 and 1289 to have inherited partible holdings. Of these 41 sets of sons 33 are known to have included at least one sibling who transacted land with persons outside his immediate family. 25 of these sets were in absolute deficit with respect to their dealings, seven in surplus and one with no gains or losses. These 33 sets contained 104 individuals, 52 of whom were individually in net deficit

[69] See above, note 55.

in their extra-familial dealings, nineteen in surplus and 33 showing no evidence whatsoever of entering the land market.

Clearly, on the basis of this evidence it would seem that there were more sons subsequent to inheriting partibly who went on to sell land to persons outside their families than there were sons who proceeded to acquire land. This inevitably led to fragmentation of family holdings and must have been a major influence accounting for the reduction over time in the holding sizes of co-heirs; it also helps to explain the discrepancy we noted earlier between the holding sizes of sibling groups as identified on the 1289 extent and those of the remainder of the customary tenants.[70] On the basis of the modal holding sizes displayed in Tables 3.3 and 3.6, it would seem that a significant group of co-heirs was selling a high proportion, if not all, of their inheritance outside the family.

It would, however, constitute a gross over-simplification and distortion of the evidence to view land exchange patterns in Redgrave solely in terms of a small group of 'kulaks' preying upon the misfortunes of co-heirs who found themselves forced to divide and alienate their inadequate inheritances. Data in Table 3.15 suggest a notable involvement of sons in the acquisition of property while their fathers still lived. The likelihood of receiving a relatively small share in one's father's holding, if partible, could have drawn sons into the market in an attempt to expand the area they would farm after his death. Partible inheritance might therefore be viewed as an indirect stimulus in such action. The Cristemesses were most likely typical of many among the comfortably situated middling tenants of Redgrave. In 1289, two years before his death, Reginald Cristemesse, father of Augustus, Nicholas, Robert and Margaret, held twelve acres distributed in Redgrave, Redgrave *marescum* and (the largest portion) in *Musehalle*. At this stage his eldest son, Augustus, already held eight-and-a-half acres distributed in the same areas of the manors but with the majority in Redgrave. Nicholas, the second son, also had land in all three areas but held most in Redgrave *Musehalle*. The youngest brother, Robert, held his quarter of an acre in Redgrave *marescum*. By 1289 both Augustus and Nicholas were married. In fact, Augustus had appeared first in the record in 1262, the same year that he married Mabilia, daughter of John Em, thereby entering into land long before his father's probable retirement which came in 1277, or his death in 1292. Part of Augustus' marriage agreement entailed an arrangement whereby John Em would be supported by his daughter

[70] See above, p. 149.

and son-in-law, while he acquired seisin of the messuage and two-and-a-half acres of land, with John agreeing to pay their heriot for entry and the marriage fine for which the Abbot allowed his daughter to marry. In return, although the exact terms are not entered onto the court roll, Augustus and Mabilia agreed to sustain John in food and clothing in accordance with the size of the holding to the end of his life and to perform services owed by the land. That agreement was pledged for Augustus by his father Reginald and his father's co-parcener, William Irelande.[71]

John Em appears to have had no male offspring surviving as heirs, which may account for the sizeable gift that Augustus received on marrying Mabilia and the payment by John of the heriot accompanying that transfer. John had provided another daughter in 1261 with half an acre of land as a gift but had sold another four-and-a-half acres outside the family prior to Mabilia's marriage in 1262.[72] Augustus had acquired land on marriage and was apparently residing in Redgrave, although not a near neighbour of his father, for in 1264 he was indicted for stealing 24 sheaves of corn at night from his father's land and furtively threshing them in his own land.[73] In 1267 Augustus paid 3s to enter one acre of land which had been his father's, and the court roll entry stating this added that Reginald was to have the remainder of this land to the end of his life, neither selling nor leasing any of it and ensuring that the house was adequately maintained.[74] A clue to what had happened comes from an entry in that same court from

---

[71] Augustus Cristemesse first appears in the surviving Redgrave court rolls in 1262, when he received his father's pledging support when amerced for trespass (court of 21.7.1262, MS Bacon 1). Reference to Reginald Cristemesse's retirement can be found in the court of 5.2.1277 (MS Bacon 3) and to his death in the court of 13.3.1292 (MS Bacon 6). The marriage contract between John Em and Augustus Cristemesse appears in the court of 6.12.1262 (MS Bacon 1): 'Mabilia Em inveniet plegius videlicet Reginaldus Cristemesse et Walterus Irelande de dimidiam mercam pro seisina habendo d j messuaio et ij acras et dimidiam terre que Johannus Em pater ipsimus Matilde sursum reddit in plena curia etherietta eius de terre et pro licentia habendo se maritandi Augustini Cristemesse et Mabilia inveniet simul dicto Augustino predicto Johanne Em victu et vestitu eiusdem ronabiliter secundum extensione dicti tenementi ad totam vitam ipsuis Johannis et predicti Augustinus et Mabilia facient servicia et consuetudines que dictum tenementum debuit ad Aulam.'

[72] Courts of 3.5.1260, 2.7.1260, 7.8.1260, 30.5.1263 (MS Bacon 1) and 1.7.1270 (MS Bacon 2).

[73] 'Item quod Augustinus Cristemesse in autumpno ullero in pars noctante carcessit xxij garbas frumenti de frumento Reginaldi Cristemesse et illad duxit ad domum suam et noctante illas trituravit et illas garbas demandata sunt in ecclesia dictus Augustinus noluit conf' sec postea pacem fecit cum dicto Reginaldo plegii Petrus Wluard et Robertus Pedelat iijs. Idem Reginaldus in misericordia pro dicte transgressione plegii Augustinus Fox, Eustacius Cutting et Simonus Skyl' (court of 28.6.1264, MS Bacon 1).

[74] Court of 4.2.1267, (MS Bacon 2).

which we discover that Reginald had remarried; it is highly likely that the land, the subject of the memorandum, had been his first wife's, to which Augustus had a claim, particularly if it had been taken into the marriage with a specific statement of its proceeding to her offspring.[75] Between 1270 and 1277, Augustus bought land in eight transactions in pieces never exceeding half an acre in size, so that by the fourteenth year of his marriage he appears to have been holding approximately five-and-a-half acres of land, a little over half of which had been acquired from his father and father-in-law.[76] In that year (1277) Reginald had made a sizeable gift of almost three acres to his second son Nicholas and three-quarters of an acre to his youngest son, Robert.[77] Furthermore, at a later court in that year all the land that Reginald had sold after his first wife's death, except the land he had 'acquired', was temporarily taken into the possession of the court.[78] This act most definitely relates to the breaking of the agreement that he had made with Augustus in 1267.[79] A further concordance ensued, by which Reginald agreed not to alienate any of his first wife's land, which should revert to Augustus on his death.[80] It is noteworthy, too, that in the gifts made to his sons, Nicholas and Robert, the land is described *de terre sue propre adquisitione*. However, this terminology should not be confused with comparable usages sometimes found in areas where the villein tenement remained inviolate and where 'acquired' land was the only property entering into *inter-vivos* transfers. At Redgrave, quite clearly, the evidence is overwhelming that there was no prohibition on the alienation of villein tenements and that the term was used to refer to land acquired after a specific point in time and should not be interpreted as indicating a principle enshrined in customary law prohibiting the alienation of 'family' land.[81] Indeed, in the example of the Cristemesse family we see clear evidence of the internal family tensions

---

[75] A contingency clause sometimes found in gifts to daughters by fathers specified that land would revert to them or their heirs if the daughter had no direct heirs of her own. This presumably was a device to ensure that land did not pass into the control of the husband. See, for example, the gift of Adam Jop to his daughter Isabella, 26.1.1289 (MS Bacon 5).

[76] Purchases appearing in the courts of 24.9.1270, 29.2.1272, 25.11.1272, 24.11.1273, 31.12.1273, 1.2.1274, 16.1.1275, 16.6.1277 (MSS Bacon 2 and 3).

[77] Court of 26.2.1277 (MS Bacon 3).   [78] Court of 27.4.1277 (MS Bacon 3).

[79] Court of 16.6.1277 (MS Bacon 3).   [80] See above, note 74.

[81] In the case of Reginald Cristemesse's gift to Nicholas and Robert, the land so described had been acquired since his marriage and had to be distinguished from that forming his wife's dower. The term was used in only 3 other instances in the court rolls between 1260 and 1319 to describe land given by fathers to daughters as marriage gifts: see courts of 24.11.1273 (MS Bacon 2); 3.9.1276 (MS Bacon 3); and

that stemmed from a presumed freedom of the father to exercise considerable choice in the manner in which he disposed of his property. Reginald Cristemesse's *pre-mortem* gifts to his sons were certainly variable but, when combined with the sons' own activities in the land market, can account for the fact that, at the time of the extent in 1289 and Reginald's death in 1291, their individual possessions varied from the nine acres held by Augustus to Robert's one-and-a-half acres. Even though the residue of the patrimony would have been divided equally among the three brothers, sufficient time had elapsed to ensure that land purchases, marriages to heiresses and variable quantities of *pre-mortem* parental gifts would, prior to that event, have already created considerable economic differentiation within the sibling group.

Patterns such as those exhibited by the sons of Reginald Cristemesse, where intra-familial transfers of property were of considerable importance to the individuals as a means of acquiring property, should nonetheless suggest that any notion of the sanctity of the family holding must be viewed with a good deal of scepticism. Evidently, fathers with sons and daughters as potential heirs or heiresses, especially amongst the precariously situated tenants, frequently sold land outside the confines of their immediate family, sometimes while making no *pre-mortem* provision for their offspring or doing so inadequately in combination with, or as a consequence of, their extra-familial sales. For instance, Thomas Odeline had marginally less than five acres of land in 1289 and in 1302 passed two of these acres to his son William with a reversionary arrangement to the end of his life.[82] In 1304 he made a small gift of a curtilage, 40 feet by 25 feet, in Redgrave *marescum* to his daughters Mabilia and Cristina.[83] Mabilia, a year earlier, had been amerced for giving birth outside wedlock, and Cristina went on three years later to marry. Two other daughters, Alice and Margaret, had married, with Thomas paying their merchets, in 1292 and 1300.[84] Although a further son, Henry, inherited the holding jointly with William in 1312, no provision had been made for him, although in three further extra-familial sales

---

27.11.1291 (MS Bacon 6). For discussion of 'acquisition' land in a context of undivided and (it is argued) indivisible villein holdings that never or only rarely entered a 'land market', see B. Harvey, *Westminster Abbey and its Estates in the Middle Ages* (Oxford, 1977), p. 296; and E. King, *Peterborough Abbey, 1086–1310* (Cambridge, 1973), p. 123.

[82] Court of 24.10.1302 (MS Bacon 10).
[83] Court of 17.4.1304 (MS Bacon 10).
[84] Courts of 19.5.1292 and 30.12.1300 (MSS Bacon 6 and 8). Matilda's *childwyte* payment was made in the court of 2.5.1301 (MS Bacon 9).

Thomas had reduced that inheritance by almost two acres.[85] The two brothers John and Walter Moyse appear in 1289 sharing a holding of six acres. They apparently proceeded to divide most of their inheritance, selling off approximately half of it to persons outside their family.[86] For when John died in 1318 his son, Eustace, received marginally over half an acre as his inheritance.[87] Walter, although marrying in 1276, may have been widowed without surviving offspring, for in the years before his brother's death he passed the residue of his holding (which had also been eroded after 1289 by sales) to Matilda, daughter of Simon Hicche, with reversion to him for the remainder of his life.[88]

These patterns were relatively common amongst those individuals who engaged in inter-vivos transactions. Among the 273 individuals who, by that means, transferred land to kin 210 sold additional land to individuals outside the kin group (see Table 3.13b). Peculiarities of family structure, as when daughters were superabundant, or as in the case of Walter Moyse, who had no surviving direct offspring, may have influenced the propensity of parents to enter the land market. For instance, Robert Godfrey, who in Table 14 would be found among those exhibiting a large deficit in their land dealings, sold over ten acres and unspecified pieces of property in seventeen transactions between 1270 and 1280.[89] His only son had died in 1274 and his smallholding of one acre had been inherited by Robert's only daughter, Alice.[90] What is notable in Robert Godfrey's case, as in the experience of others, is the limited involvement in either pre- or post-mortem transfers of land of the wider kin group – indeed, even of uncles, aunts and cousins.

Although much of the evidence we have considered so far in this

---

[85] Court of 7.4.1312 (MS Bacon 11). Thomas Odeline's extra-familial sales are recorded in courts of 17.4.1302, 8.5.1302 (MS Bacon 10); and 15.6.1311 (MS Bacon 11).

[86] Sales to persons outside his kin group were made by John Moyse on 6.11.1311, 7.10.1311 (MS Bacon 11); 4.3.1316, 9.6.1316, 20.12.1316, 2.3.1317, 4.6.1317 (MS Bacon 13). Walter Moyse likewise sold to unrelated persons at courts on 27.6.1290 (MS Bacon 6); 11.11.1312 (MS Bacon 11); 25.1.1314, 4.3.1316, 22.4.1316 (MS Bacon 13).

[87] John's death is recorded in the court of 5.12.1318 (MS Bacon 13). His son Eustace, who succeeded him, outlived his father by only a few months and was succeeded by an under-age heir on 20.7.1319 (MS Bacon 13). Eustace had also sold land, which had most likely been brought into the marriage by his wife on 8.6.1303, 7.11.1304 (MS Bacon 10); 7.10.1311 (MS Bacon 11); and 4.3.1316 (MS Bacon 13).

[88] Court of 8.6.1316 (MS Bacon 13).

[89] Sales recorded in the following courts: 14.1.1270 (2), 29.2.1272 (2), 29.3.1272, 28.6.1272, 9.2.1273 (2), 20.4.1273, 24.11.1273, 15.5.1274, 11.7.1275, 24.7.1275, 27.9.1275, 26.11.1275, 7.7.1276 (MS Bacon 2); and 14.3.1281 (2) (MS Bacon 4).

[90] An inheritance recorded in the court of 18.11.1274 (MS Bacon 2). Alice married some years later in 1280 (court of 26.7.1280, MS Bacon 4).

discussion indicates a net outward drift of land from the inheritance of the co-heir – or, indeed, an erosion of the patrimony by similar actions prior to paternal death – especially among the lower echelons of Redgrave's customary tenants, internal adjustments of property within the sibling group have left another distinctive pattern of behaviour in the manor court proceedings, which may have co-existed with or preceded that in which the sibling group as a whole showed itself unable to retain a hold on the inherited patrimony. In fact, among 29 of the 50 sibling groups identifiable on the extent of 1289, there is clear evidence of these adjustments taking place in one or a combination of two ways: by an *inter-vivos* sale of his or their portion of the holding by one or more brothers to another brother (sometimes uncles or nephews, and very infrequently cousins might have been involved in these processes); by a *post-mortem* transfer involving a brother dying without direct heirs and his holding consequently reverting to his remaining brother or brothers.[91]

For instance, Thomas and Walter, the two sons of William Walays, who died in 1274, appear on the 1289 extent sharing a messuage and holding of seven and nine acres respectively. Being under age on their father's death, their mother took custody of their land until their majority.[92] Walter died in 1311,[93] holding three acres which his son William inherited to add to the one acre his father had passed to him after 1305.[94] There is, however, evidence that Walter had sold three-and-a-half rods in two transactions to persons outside his family, but that the remaining sixteen-and-a-half rods had been sold or granted to his brother Thomas in a series of transactions extending over the years 1289–99.[95] In this case, Thomas was able, in addition to acquiring over half of his brother's inheritance, to accumulate a small surplus of one-and-a-quarter acres in a large number of transactions with persons to whom he appears to have been unrelated.[96] The net effect of these dealings was to ensure that the total land area in the possession of two siblings did not in their life-time diminish.

---

[91] For a discussion of similar processes on the Norfolk manor of Gressenhall, see Williamson, 'Peasant Holdings', pp. 62–6.

[92] Court of 20.2.1274 (MS Bacon 2).   [93] Court of 16.11.1311 (MS Bacon 11).

[94] Transactions recorded in courts of 5.5.1305 and 6.12.1307 (MS Bacon 11).

[95] Sales were recorded to persons outside his family in courts of 11.2.1295 (MS Bacon 7), 9.4.1309 (MS Bacon 11). Walter's sales to Thomas are recorded on 18.11.1289 (2) (MS Bacon 5), 18.10.1292 (MS Bacon 6), 1.11.1298, 15.6.1299 (MS Bacon 8).

[96] Thomas' extra-familial sales were recorded in the courts of 15.6.1296, 30.12.1300 (MS Bacon 8); 5.5.1305 (MS Bacon 11); 1.4.1314, 4.6.1317 (2), 6.3.1319, 15.1.1320 (MS Bacon 13); and his purchases on 19.5.1292, ?.7.1293 (MS Bacon 6); 7.11.1294, 7.1.1295 (MS Bacon 7); 15.6.1296 (MS Bacon 8); 28.2.1308 (MS Bacon 11); 12.7.1318 (2) (MS Bacon 13).

In 1297 William Walter, who in 1289 held part of a messuage and seven-and-three-quarter acres, died and his land was inherited by his sons, William, John and Eustace.[97] Eustace appears to have been the oldest of the siblings, holding himself in 1289 one-and-a-half acres which had evidently been obtained with his father's assistance, judging from the pledging support he gave his son. Although he sold three-quarters of an acre in the course of the second decade of the fourteenth century, he managed to increase his holding size overall.[98] Likewise, his brother John, apart from the sale or gift of half an acre to his sister Matilda, acquired almost one-and-a-half acres from extra-familial purchases.[99] However, John also purchased an acre of land from his brother William, who died in 1317 holding only one cottage and three rods, having sold a quarter of an acre to persons outside his family.[100] Since William had no heirs, apparently dying a bachelor, his property was shared by his brothers, Eustace and John.

That the two examples we have considered above are only partially representative of patterns exhibited by others in late thirteenth- and early fourteenth-century Redgrave is evident from data presented in Table 16. In describing the adjustments among the Walays and Walter families we have considered a particular form of lateral transfer of property within the sibling group. Of course, any form of intra-familial property exchange was of limited importance when considered within the great mass of transactions. In fact, a little under 20 per cent of the 2,756 transactions recorded in the extant court proceedings were between relatives, although this must be seen as representing a minimum value because of our inability to identify with great accuracy possible affines who may have been related through marriages, parties to which our record may have failed to disclose (see Table 3.8 also).[101] Yet that record is striking in identifying

---

[97] Court of 11.1.1297 (MS Bacon 8).

[98] Before 1289 Eustace bought land, with his father's pledging support on each occasion, in the following courts: 16.1.1284, 31.3.1285 (MS Bacon 4); 28.11.1286, 7.5.1287 (MS Bacon 5). Eustace, between 1289 and 1291, purchased 2¼ acres of land in transactions registered in courts of 2.5.1291, 14.9.1293 (MS Bacon 6); 26.2.1296, 11.3.1297 (MS Bacon 8). He sold land in the following courts: 18.9.1311 (MS Bacon 11); 4.3.1316 and 2.3.1317, before sharing with John Walter the cottage and 3 rods they inherited from his brother William on 16.12.1317 (MS Bacon 13).

[99] John Walter's extra-familial acquisition of almost 1½ acres was made in 5 purchases in courts of 13.1.1299 (MS Bacon 8); 30.9.1308 (MS Bacon 11); 13.4.1317, 16.5.1318, 20.7.1319 (MS Bacon 13). He granted or sold land to Matilda Walter on 3.11.1309 (MS Bacon 11).

[100] Transactions registered in courts of 4.4.1315, 4.3.1316, 2.3.1317 (MS Bacon 13).

[101] A somewhat lower level of intra-familial transfer of property than indicated by Campbell's analysis of *inter-vivos* transactions in Coltishall: see below, p. 121. Note, too, a level of intra-familial exchanges in the years 1315–16 to 1324–5 (approximately

Table 3.16. Types of intra-familial dealings in property: Redgrave 1260–1319

	1260–9		1270–9		1280–9		1290–9		1300–9		1310–19		Total	
	No.	%	No.	%	No.	%	No.	%	No.	%	No.	%	No.	%
Intra-familial land transfers														
Vertical														
Parent to child	15	71.4	36	48.0	30	35.7	38	33.6	42	48.8	23	13.7	184	33.6
Vertical														
Child to parent			1	1.3			2	1.8	2	2.3	2	1.2	7	1.3
Lateral														
Brother to brother	2	9.5	16	21.3	19	22.6	37	32.7	16	18.6	78	46.4	168	30.7
Sister to sister	1	4.8	6	7.8	13	15.5	6	5.3	5	5.8	5	2.9	36	6.6
Lateral														
Husband to wife														
Wife to husband			3	3.9			7	6.2	1	1.2	1	0.6	12	2.2
Vertical*/Lateral (old to young)			1	1.3	2	2.4	5	4.5	4	4.7	16	9.5	28	5.1
Vertical/Lateral (young to old)			1	1.3							1	0.6	2	0.4
?Relation	3	14.3	11	15.1	20	23.8	18	15.9	16	18.6	42	25.1	110	20.1
Total (A)	21		75		84		113		86		168		547	
All land transfers total (B)	164		348		455		571		368		850		2,756	
A/B%	12.8		21.6		18.5		19.8		23.4		19.8		19.8	

*Aunt or uncle to nephew or niece.

183

the predominance of lateral transfers between siblings over any other kin relationship in the matter of *inter-vivos* transactions between kin. In fact, if we include transfers between aunts, uncles, nephews and nieces, the lateral component accounts for almost 43 per cent and parent to child transfers for only 34 per cent of intra-familial exchanges. Furthermore, with only 11.7 per cent (64) of the intra-familial transactions concerning the *pre-mortem* transfer of land from father to son, we see clear indications of the ascendancy of lateral over vertical exchanges of property among males. If we concentrate solely on transactions involving sisters, their proportion of the total drops, but only marginally. However, the transactions between brothers grow sharply in importance in the economically difficult years of the 1290s, and especially in the 1310s (when the father–son transactions almost disappear from the records), and represent two trends which may well be closely inter-related.[102]

In Tables 3.17 and 3.18 we can compare the directional biases in both *post-mortem* and *inter-vivos* family transfers over the period 1295–1319. These years have been selected only because of the fuller evidence contained in the obituary records after 1295, in which heirs are listed by name in relation to the deceased person. Although there was clearly a greater degree of inter-, rather than intra-, generational inheritance, almost 10 per cent of deaths resulted in land escheating to the lord in the absence of heirs either available or wishing to take up their inheritance; if included in our consideration of all deaths involving persons holding customary land, this would mean that fewer than half of all inheritances involved land descending from father to son. Approximately one in four deaths involved inheritances by brothers, placing into perspective the experience considered above of individuals such as William Walter, whose property upon his death was shared by his brothers.

We began our consideration of the relationship between the practices of partible inheritance and the *inter-vivos* transfer of land with the observation that the holdings of the individuals within the groups of co-heirs identifiable on the 1289 extent appeared larger than those of the remainder of the tenantry. We noted, too, that equality of holding size characterized certain sibling groups whose father had

---

25% of 192 transactions) for the St Albans Abbey manor of Codicote in Hertford-shire, similar to that for Redgrave cited by Kershaw, 'Great Famine', p. 39.

102 In the decade 1310–19 almost one-half of intra-familial transfers involved brothers as both parties, and between 1295 and 1297, when the land market was especially active, over 40% of *inter-vivos* transfers between family members concerned male siblings only.

Table 3.17. *'Post-mortem' family transfers: Redgrave 1295–1319*

	Father–son(s)		Lateral (siblings)		Other familial		Total	
	No.	%	No.	%	No.	%	No.	%
Years								
1295–9	14	50.0	7	25.0	5	17.9	26	(2)
1300–4	9	40.9	5	22.7	7	31.8	21	(1)
1305–9	14	58.3	8	33.3	1	4.2	23	(1)
1310–14	17	48.5	11	31.4	5	14.3	33	(2)
1315–19	31	49.2	11	17.5	10	15.9	52	(11)
1295–1319	85	49.4	42	24.4	28	16.3	155	(17)

Table 3.18. *'Inter-vivos' family transfers: Redgrave 1295–1319*

	Father–son(s)		Lateral (siblings)		Other familial		Total
	No.	%	No.	%	No.	%	
Years							
1295–9	14	22.2	30	47.6	19	30.2	63
1300–4	10	19.2	16	30.8	26	50.0	52
1305–9	7	20.5	5	14.7	22	64.8	34
1310–14	3	3.9	34	44.2	40	51.9	77
1315–19	1	1.1	49	53.8	41	45.1	91
1295–1319	35	11.0	134	42.3	148	46.7	317

recently died. We should now add that of the five such sibling groups none had engaged in the land market in advance of inheriting the patrimony.[103] All the evidence we have considered so far suggests that the net effect of the inheritance system in conjunction with an intensive *inter-vivos* system of land exchanges was to ensure the fragmentation of holdings in ways that produced considerable economic differentiation within sibling groups and aided the progressive, if not extreme, differentiation of the customary tenantry as a whole. It would seem, furthermore, that property devolution through inheritance in the aggregated mass of property exchanges was subordinate to an intensive system of *inter-vivos* sales and purchases that was itself subjected to periodic surges of quite frantic activity in the years coinciding with, or immediately following, harvest-induced economic difficulties.

[103] See above, pp. 148–9.

iii. The sibling group: its internal and external relations

What are the implications of these exchange patterns for the views of
Homans concerning the likely existence of a 'joint-family organization' among the customary tenants of communities such as Redgrave?
We should recall that processes of economic fission – with which, in
fact, most of our discussion to this point has been concerned – were
an integral part of the joint-family system but would, as argued by
Homans, become evident only when the joint-family had passed
beyond some critical size and would certainly be delayed well past
the moment of paternal death.[104] In fact, one would expect to detect
evidence of the joint-family in action in the land market, perhaps as it
added to the collectively managed patrimonial estate. The 2,756
inter-vivos transactions of which the record has survived in the court
rolls involved 6,115 'parties'. Of these parties 618 involved 'groups',
the composition of which is set out in Table 19. It is clearly evident
from these data that group-participants were much more likely to
have been selling or disposing of land than accumulating it. Furthermore, the group-type most frequently found, whether as buyer or
seller, was the conjugal pair (which accounts for one half of the
recorded instances) and not the group founded upon the sibling
bond. Notable also is the fact that the conjugal pair was marginally
more likely, when participating in the land market, to have been
purchasing property than were sibling groups. In fact, fewer than 1
per cent of the instances in which parties to land transactions are
identifiable involved sibling groups as buyers and almost 2 per cent
involved them as sellers. It is significant that the conjugal bond shows
through so clearly, as in many 'classic' joint-family systems the
husband–wife relationship most certainly takes a subordinate position relative to those kin relationships that link males related by
blood.[105]

---

[104] Homans, *English Villagers*, p. 119. For general discussions of processes likely to have
fostered or hindered fission, see E. Wolf, *Peasants* (Englewood Cliffs, N.J., 1966),
pp. 67–71; J. Goody, 'The Evolution of the Family', in P. Laslett and R. Wall,
editors, *Household and Family in Past Time* (Cambridge, 1972), pp. 118–22. For a
fascinating discussion of a joint-family system among Russian serfs, in which
fission did not proceed according to the idealized developmental cycle, see P. Czap,
Jr, 'The Perennial Multiple Family Household, Mishino, Russia 1782–1858', *Journal
of Family History* 7 (1982), pp. 14–23. For an argument proposing a vital role for
share-cropping tenancy terms in maintaining the joint-family and thwarting its
natural tendency towards dissolution in the Nivernais, see Shaffer, *Family and Farm*,
pp. 20–36.

[105] See, for instance, the discussion on Indian joint-families in W. Goode, *World*

Table 3.19. *Group participants in Redgrave land market: 1260–1319*

Group type	Buyers						Sellers						Total	
	All	Column %	Row %	Intra-familial	Column %	Row %	All	Column %	Row %	Intra-familial	Column %	Row %	No.	%
Siblings (male)	47	17.1	29.0	13	25.0	34.2	115	28.4	71.0	25	43.9	65.8	162	23.8
Siblings (female)	40	14.5	59.7	21	40.3	63.6	27	6.7	40.3	11	19.3	36.4	67	9.9
Siblings (mixed)	4	1.5	66.7	—	—	—	2	0.4	33.3	—	—	—	6	0.8
Father and child(ren)	23	8.4	71.9	5	9.6	100.0	9	2.2	28.1	—	—	—	32	4.7
Mother and child(ren)	31	11.2	72.1	3	5.8	74.0	12	2.4	27.9	1	1.8	25.0	43	6.3
Parents and child(ren)	4	1.5	100.0	—	—	—	—	—	—	—	—	—	4	0.7
Husband and wife	105	38.2	31.4	10	19.3	33.3	229	57.7	68.6	20	35.0	66.7	334	49.1
Other kin	17	6.1	63.0	—	—	—	10	2.0	37.0	—	—	—	27	4.0
Others unrelated	4	1.5	80.0	—	—	—	1	0.2	20.0	—	—	—	5	0.7
Total	275	100.0	40.4	52	100.0	47.7	405	100.0	59.6	57	100.0	52.3	680	100.0

In our discussion of property transmission and its effect upon likely patterns of co-tenancy our evidence has been inevitably drawn from data on land transactions. Of course, it could be argued that we have adopted too narrow a definition of the joint-family in assessing the extent to which siblings in the curial records and surveys appeared as co-inheritors, co-holders or co-purchasers of property. We have certainly not given sufficient attention to matters of residential propinquity or to the broader question of social and economic relations connecting kin in relation to those links these same persons had, either as individuals or collectively, with non-kin. We cannot, unfortunately, in this discussion, concerned as it primarily is with land and its transmission, pursue these questions in detail.

However, an important statistic that emerges from the evidence in the 1289 extent concerns the geographical concentration of property held by the 116 individuals in the fifty sibling sets among the Redgrave tenants. Those 116 individuals held 538 acres, of which 518 (96 per cent) were located within a single sub-region of the manor. The comparable total for the tenants as a whole was somewhat lower, at 83.7 per cent. Evidently, partible inheritance had the effect of increasing the residential and tenurial propinquity of male heirs, at least for a particular phase in their life-cycle. The residential propinquity of heirs may have been sustained by the fragmentation of the patrimonial farmstead and the reallocation of buildings within it. The court rolls of Redgrave suggest an active market in pieces of residential property, although this has been analysed only for the years 1260–93. Imprecision in the descriptive terminology of residential property makes for difficulties in a definitive consideration of the structure of that market: a messuage might have had more than one house (*domus*) upon it, and a cottage (*cottagium*) was not necessarily a term reserved for just the residential structure;[106] 'toft' (*tofta*), the term used for houses in areas influenced by the Scandinavian language, existed alongside *domus*, and the exact difference between *cottagium* and *costedil'* remains unclear. The records of 165 *inter-vivos* transac-

---

Revolution and Family Patterns (New York, 1963), pp. 238–47, or sub-Saharan Africa in M. Gluckman, *Custom and Conflict in Africa* (Oxford, 1955), pp. 54–80, and on southern European societies, such as the Sarakatsani of Greece, in J. K. Campbell, *Honour, Family and Patronage: A Study of Institutions and Moral Values in a Greek Mountain Community* (Oxford, 1964), especially pp. 65–9.

106 For instance, 'Rogerus Cutting reddit sursum in manu domini j messuagium cum edificiis et aliis pertinenciis super Botulesdalehel ad opus Johannis de Ramesey . . .' (court of 16.10.1290, MS Bacon 6); and 'Edmundus Prest et Alicia mater eius dant domino vjd. pro licentia emendi j cottagium cum domibus et edificiis sic mete et bunde testantur de Waltero Sket . . .' (court of 28.10.1286, MS Bacon 5).

tions concerning residential property have survived in the court proceedings for the period 1260–93, of which 62 (38 per cent) involved kin as both partners, this representing a much greater degree of intra-familial exchange than characterized dealings in agricultural land. It is likely, therefore, that because of relatively close residential proximity brothers might be expected to interact frequently and to conduct their social and economic relations with a common set of neighbours. It was possible in the proceedings of the manorial court between 1260 and 1293 to consider 65 sibling groups who had a total of 1,359 recorded contacts with others outside their kin group. In constructing a measure of the degree to which members of the sibling group involved themselves with the same persons the following method was employed consistently: all persons with whom the individual members of the sibling group had contact in the course of the period 1260–93 were identified; making no allowance for frequency or type of relationship, the persons with whom more than one member of the group had contact were expressed as a proportion of the total. Obviously this exaggerates the degree of overlap in small, in relation to large, sibling groups, particularly as over two-thirds of the sibling groups considered were no larger than pairs. The distribution of sibling group affinity patterns is shown in Figure 3.1 and suggests a very high degree of overlap in the extra-familial contacts of sibling groups. For fifty of the 65 sets it was possible to secure data on the holding size they had inherited or were to inherit from their father, and these were a basis for an economic ranking of the brothers. The brothers were also classified as to whether as individuals they were positioned above or below the mean value for all brothers of 72 per cent of sibling group affinity in extra-familial relations. It would seem that there were significant differences within the rankings of sibling sets, with the siblings amongst the larger landholders evidently far more individualistic in their social and economic relations.

For instance, Edmund and Simon Hicche jointly held a thirty-acre portion of a *tenementum* in Redgrave Musehalle in which nine other persons held shares. In addition, Edmund had a parcel of land in the Redgrave *tenementum* on which Simon also possessed a small share. Simon, however, had another six acres in Redgrave in four other *tenementa*. Simon's more widely scattered land holdings increased the number of persons with whom he became involved in other areas of the manor. The degree of overlap between the personal-contact fields of the two siblings was limited. Only six of the 32 persons with whom the two brothers had contacts in the court were linked with both of

RICHARD M. SMITH

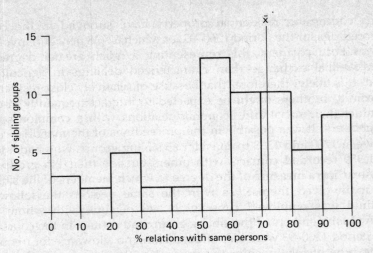

Figure 3.1. Overlap in the social and economic relations of male siblings: Redgrave, Suffolk 1260–93

them. Furthermore, in no instances did Simon and Edmund act together.[107]

The three brothers Simon, Henry and Hugh Seward in 1289 held land in three *tenementa* in Estgate. Of their 99 recorded relationships in court proceedings, 53 were with fellow co-parceners. In fact, at least two of the three brothers were involved with sixteen (47 per cent) of the 36 persons with whom they came into contact as a group. Most of their reciprocal pledgings were done with the families of Walter Thede, Geoffrey Goding, Ademyn Sutor and the Redings, who were also their co-parceners. Furthermore, the brothers were far less individualistic in their litigational involvements, and less autonomous, than the Hicche brothers. For example, Simon and Henry were jointly involved in selling a *costedil'* to John de Bosco in 1275 and together pledged their brother Hugh. In the same year Simon and Hugh settled a land dispute with Ademyn Sutor out of court, in exchange for a rod of land, although there is no other instance of them buying land as a group. Being jointly amerced was not a rare experience for members of this sibling group: in 1275 Simon and Henry were fined for failing to fulfil their pledging responsibilities to Robert de Bosco and, with their co-parcener, Walter Thede, were fined for damage to part of the *tenementum* formerly under the charge

---

[107] 2 of the 6 persons with whom Edmund Hicche had relations in common with his brother Simon between 1281 (the date of his first apperance in the court) and 1293 were their co-parceners.

of Ademyn Sutor; in 1271 Henry and Hugh had been jointly amerced for illegally raising the hue and cry against Geoffrey Goding, whose wife Henry later assaulted, as did Hugh's son in 1276, the same year his father had trespassed in Geoffrey Goding's corn.[108] It should be stressed, however, that patterns of close inter-sibling contact, such as is reflected in the curial evidence relating to the Sewards, was more generally characteristic of the period following the inheriting of the patrimony. In most cases we observe the sibling group, in union with a widowed mother pressing claims for, or defending claims against them, to disputed property, frequently following their father's death, or fined for failing to perform services owed to the manorial demesne. Of the 65 sibling groups 27 were fined jointly and of these 21 received their amercements within ten years of their inheritance.

We may, indeed, in these actions be observing patterns highly specific to a particular phase of the sibling group's life-cycle, for these years were as likely to display inter-sibling strife as support or joint action. Between 1260 and 1293 we have evidence of 141 individuals from 52 families appearing in court as litigants in disputes with other family members. These individuals constituted 41 per cent of all those known to have some form of curial contact with kin over these same years. Highly significant is the evidence bearing upon the principal

[108] Court of 27.9.1275 (MS Bacon 2): 'Johannes de Bosco dat xijd. pro licentia emendi j costedil' de Simone et Henrico Seward fratres faciendum inde dicto Henrico per annum ijd. et idem Henricus acquietabit per annum ad aulam omnes consuetudines etc. . . . pro dicto Johanne plegius Hugonis Seward.' The registration of an agreement concerning individual responsibilities in the performance of services to the lord following the transaction is noteworthy: see above, note 25. When Hugh passed land to his son in 1283 his brothers Simon and Henry pledged the transaction (court of 25.1.1283 MS Bacon 4); court of 16.1.1275 (MS Bacon 2): 'Simonus Seward et Henricus Seward petens versus Ademyn Sutor defendens per licentiam concordati sunt ita quod predicti Simonus et Henricus sursum reddiderunt in plena curia pro se et heredibus suis totus jus et clamores suos de omnibus demandis de placito terre versus dictum Ademyn ad opus dicti Ademyn et heredibus suis imperpetuum. Et idem Adam per dictam quietclamationem dat dicto Simone et Henrico j rodam jacentem super Heythe reddendo dicto Ademyn et heredibus suis per annum jd. et pro dicta concordia etiam dant domino xijd'; court of 3.9.1275, MS Bacon 2: Simonus Seward et Henricus Seward primiplegii Roberti de Bosco in misericordia ut ponitur pro melioribus ad respondendum Thomae de Bosco plegius prosequendi alteri Thede; court of 13.7.1281 (MS Bacon 4): 'Walterus Thede et Simonus Seward et Henricus Seward in misericordia quia distruxiverunt tenementum quondam Hodemyn' plegius adinvitem; court of 7.8.1271 (MS Bacon 2): 'Item quod Henricus et Hugonis Seward inuiste levaverunt huthesium super Galfridum Goding plegios Simonus Seward et Ademyn Sutor; court of 12.6.1276 (MS Bacon 3): 'Item quod Simonus Seward traxit sanguinem de Alice Goding'; court of 8.7.1277 (MS Bacon 3): 'Item quod Semanus filius Hugone Seward traxit sanguinem Alicie Goding plegius Hugonis Seward'; court of 28.7.1277 (MS Bacon 3): 'Hugonis Seward in misericordia pro transgressione facto Galfrido Goding in blado suo plegios Simonis Seward et Willelmus Messor.'

Table 3.20. *The kin relationship of litigants in intra-familial disputes:*
Redgrave 1260–93

	No.	%
Kin relationship		
Brother/brother	80	57.2
Father/son	15	10.7
Mother/son	11	7.9
Brother/sister	8	5.8
Brother/sister-in-law	8	5.7
Sister/sister	3	2.1
Father/son-in-law	5	3.6
Brother/brother-in-law	3	2.1
Cousin/cousin	3	2.1
Uncle/nephew	2	1.4
Father/daughter	1	0.7
Husband/wife	1	0.7
Total	140	100.0

category of kin relationship that gave rise to intra-familial discord
displayed in Table 3.20. Over 57 per cent of recorded disputes were
between brothers, these being followed a long way behind in
importance by disputes between parents and children (18 per cent).
36 of the 65 sibling groups to which we have already referred showed
signs of conflict on at least one occasion, although (as in the case of
siblings acting as joint plaintiffs or defendants) these were, in 32
cases, confined to the decade following entry into their inheritance.

Following their father's death in 1292, Nicholas and Augustus
Cristemesse (to whom we have already referred) were accused by
their stepmother of unjustly withholding her dower and by their full
brother, Robert, of not permitting him entry to his rightful
inheritance.[109] Augustus' relations with Robert remained uneasy, as
in 1295 an entry in the court rolls states that Augustus' youngest
brother had broken a joint agreement by selling three rods of land in
his part in a messuage; for this he was forced to give Augustus, who
had also been unjustly slandered in the course of this case,
compensation.[110] For these brothers, the individual shares in their
inheritance were resolved finally in 1296 by a court-registered
agreement.[111] Likewise, Walter Oligrant appeared in court in 1269 to

[109] Courts of 22.7.1292 and 8.10.1292 (MS Bacon 6).
[110] Court of 6.12.1295 (MS Bacon 7).
[111] Court of 19.2.1296 (MS Bacon 8).

inform the jury by what authority he had entered into the holding of his brother Ralph (an action perhaps induced by Ralph's failure to fulfil services owed by the holding over the previous two years).[112] In a later court that same year Ralph charged that on two occasions Walter had entered his house, beaten him with a stave and in so doing drawn blood. The jury found Walter guilty, fining him heavily and forcing him to pay Ralph damages of forty shillings.[113] However, as was so characteristic of these events involving siblings, subsequent to their father's death Ralph sold out his share in the original holding to Walter and may have left the community, for we find no further reference to him in the records.[114]

There can be no denying the existence of economic processes and social pressures leading to fragmentation of property – processes that in aggregate overwhelmed in quantity those that our source materials have left us concerning the continuity of the sibling group as a functioning joint-family-organized economic enterprise. We should note, however, that in his theory of the peasant economy A. V. Chayanov argued that holding division was an integral and indeed fundamental trait of a 'peasant' society.[115] That tendency we should expect to increase with the size of the holding, so that family partition would explain a high proportion of the downward social mobility that the larger holdings would undergo to ensure that social differentiation did not become intensified. In Chayanov's view, a specifically peasant culture attached social status only to the male heads of households, and consequently disintegration was brought about by intra-familial conflict; frequent reference is therefore made by scholars to the role of family quarrels as a proximate inducement to partition, because of the peculiar forces that were internal to the peasantry itself.[116] In Redgrave, as we have seen, divisive influences were most apparent in their effects upon the middling tenants, very rarely, if at all, operating among the offspring of the tenants in the higher echelons of land holders. Inter-sibling conflict was particularly concentrated among the middling and indeed smallholding tenants, as also were excessive holding fragmentation and sizeable extra-

---

[112] Court of 17.9.1269 (MS Bacon 2).
[113] Court of 4.5.1269 (MS Bacon 2).   [114] Court of 30.10.1270 (MS Bacon 2).
[115] A. V. Chayanov, *The Theory of Peasant Economy* (Homewood, Ill., 1966), pp. 60–9.
[116] See, for example, T. Shanin, *The Awkward Class: Political Sociology of Peasantry in a Developing Society: Russia 1910–1925* (Oxford, 1966), pp. 28–32 and 85–8; and the discussion in M. Harrison, 'Resource Allocation and Agrarian Class Formation: The Problem of Social Mobility among Russian Peasant Households, 1880–1930', *Journal of Peasant Studies* 4 (1978), pp. 135–7.

familial sales of land.[117] It would, indeed, be hard to argue that the division and readjustments that took place in the internal disposition of land were necessarily associated with the acquisition of full adult status on the part of each of the siblings. The acts of division, or more precisely of re-adjustment, through extra-familial alienations of property were linked with the movement of the majority of the siblings more often than not to the ranks of the landless or near-landless labourers rather than to a position heading a freshly created family labour farm. Indeed, for an important minority (58 out of 178 inheritances) there were possible important demographic consequences, for when no direct heirs were available to inherit a brother or brothers inherited, this suggesting that marriage may have been forgone.[118] Because the court roll series of Redgrave begins only in 1260, we cannot be certain whether we are observing the shifting and erosion of 'traditional' forms of patriarchal domination or fraternal solidarity as 'market' influences became more apparent and holding sizes diminished. Nonetheless, we do know that there is certainly no indication of the manorial lord or his officials intervening to arrest the land grabbing activities of the village 'kulaks' like Adam Jop and Adam Pistor and their children in Redgrave in the 1270s, 1280s and 1290s and between 1315 and 1317. In fact, the marked lack of concern on the part of the manorial authorities with holding fragmentation and its implications for the collection of rents and the performance of services on a large demesne may have been a factor which, if not

---

[117] I have in 'Kin and Neighbours', pp. 240–9, considered the pattern of relations an individual had with his kin and his unrelated neighbours in Redgrave between 1283 and 1292 and draw the conclusion that 'middling' tenants, i.e. those holding 4–10 acres of land, concentrated their social and economic contacts on kin and closely residing neighbours, unlike the smallholders and land-abundant inhabitants of the community. An exchange theoretical framework was employed to explain these patterns. The findings in this paper would require these earlier conclusions to be modified somewhat. The high contact frequency both with kin and neighbours may well reflect a particular life-cycle phase through which individuals, especially those co-heirs whose inheritances had yet to be eroded by land sales, progressed.

[118] It is unlikely, given the proportion of inheritances not proceeding from father to son between 1295 and 1319, and less certainly between 1260 and 1294, that the population of customary tenants was expanding. Some attempts to relate heirship patterns to population growth rates are made in Chapter 1, pp. 43–53. It would seem, therefore, that the property devolution patterns observed in Redgrave cannot be attributed to demographic growth except in the very long term. It is worth noting that Campbell, in his discussion of land transactions in Coltishall, gives great stress to the demographic background and finds a far higher proportion of men succeeded by at least one male heir than characterized the Redgrave tenantry. A similar demographic buoyancy appears to have prevailed on the Norfolk manor of Gressenhall in the late thirteenth century, although the sample of deaths considered by Williamson does not appear large enough to be acceptable without some qualification. See Williamson, 'Peasant Holdings', pp. 47–8 and 107–8.

actively promoting the patterns we have described, certainly in no way hindered them.[119] Unfortunately, we do not have space to consider the question of the association of peasant behaviour with seigneurial attitudes, but we should not necessarily accept conventional views of the direction of any supposed causal relationships between them.

---

[119] The active encouragement by landlords of an intensive exchange of land among their tenants in an era of inflationary land values, as a means of increasing seigneurial revenues, is considered at some length in Smith 'Some Thoughts', pp. 114–19.

4

Population changes and the transfer of customary land on a Cambridgeshire manor in the fourteenth century

JACK RAVENSDALE

In their pessimistic accounts of the economic conditions of the English peasantry in the late thirteenth and early fourteenth centuries Professor Postan and Dr Titow not only used evidence on entry fines, rents, shrinking holding sizes, limited livestock resources and the coincidence of harvest failures and surges of tenant deaths, but also gave considerable attention to the position of the widow in the network of village land exchanges.[1] They showed that marriage to widows who had succeeded to their husband's land was a prominent means of access to property by males, on manors without sizeable reserves of colonizable land. Dr Titow's analysis of these matters was static over space rather than dynamic over time.[2] In this discussion we wish, with the aid of a detailed manorial case study, to consider the position of widows in the context of the inheritance and land transaction practices exhibited by the customary tenants on the Abbot of Crowland's Cambridgeshire manor of Cottenham. Our focus will be on the first eight decades of the fourteenth century, when demographic changes substantially shifted the ratio of labour to land in favour of the customary tenants.

Cottenham was one of the three Cambridgeshire manors of the Abbot of Crowland for which Miss Page estimated the intensity of mortality from plague in 1349.[3] Her calculations showed 33 out of 58 tenants (57 per cent) dying in the plague. There are many difficulties presented by the methods she adopted to calculate the tenant

---

[1] J. Z. Titow, 'Some Differences Between Manors and Their Effects on the Conditions of the Peasantry', *Agricultural History Review* 10 (1962), and his *English Rural Society, 1200* (London, 1969), p. 87; M. Postan, editor, *Cambridge Economic History of Europe, Vol. I* (Cambridge, 1966), p. 564.
[2] Titow, 'Some Differences'.
[3] F. M. Page, *The Estates of Crowland Abbey: A Study in Manorial Organisation* (Cambridge, 1934), pp. 120–1; hereafter *ECA*.

population 'at risk' of dying before plague struck and it has proved
necessary to attempt a new estimate of mortality. The details of this
estimate can be found elsewhere,[4] but some of its features are worthy
of comment in our present discussion.

We are lucky in having for Cottenham a homage list which was
ordered to be drawn up by a jury in 1346.[5] The list has fifty names,
but not all of these were at risk at the outset of the plague. Four had
died. Thus the base population was 44 of whom 21 are recorded as
dying in the rolls of 1349. We know also that Thomas Kille, a
Cottenham villein, who died in 1349, had received a cottage and a
half-acre in 1345 on the death of William Turvel, who appears on the
homage list. Thomas Kille should be added to the list, to make a
population at risk of 45 persons. This gives us 22 deaths out of 45 or
49 per cent.

There can be no doubt that the short-term demographic impact of
plague was very severe, comparable with mortality levels calculated
recently from other manorial case studies.[6] Furthermore, it seems that
there was little difference in the fatality rates of tenants of varying
economic status. A list of offenders for over-digging turf in the fen
survives for 1348, and as digging rights varied with the size of
holding we find most of the customers listed in groups according to
the acreage held.[7] If those holding five acres or less are considered
together they experience nine deaths and thirteen survivors. We
consequently cannot attach great significance to the distribution of
deaths by size of holding (see Table 4.1). In fact this pattern may have
had more to do with accidental contacts or even with the topographical lay-out of the houses. Plague, then, seems to have drawn
few distinctions in the manner of its impact upon the customary
tenants of Cottenham.

The pattern of succession to holdings of which over half were
vacated by plague deaths in 1349 shows that there is little evidence
here to suggest a 'normal' succession of family holdings descending
through kin (see Table 4.2). The villein custom at Cottenham, which
differed from freehold, was for the widow to take the whole holding,

[4] See J. Ravensdale, 'Re-Estimating Plague Mortality on the Abbot of Crowland's
Manor of Cottenham in 1349' (forthcoming).
[5] This homage list is found in the manor court rolls, documents which form the basis of
this study. The court rolls are deposited in Cambridge University Library. All
references from them in this article are to be found under Queens' College, 3 and 4.
[6] Z. Razi, Life, Marriage and Death in a Medieval Parish (Cambridge, 1980), pp. 99–107; C.
Dyer, Lords and Peasants in a Changing Society (Cambridge, 1980), pp. 237–9; and L. R.
Poos, unpublished research for University of Cambridge Ph.D. on the Essex manors
of Great Waltham and High Easter.
[7] ECA, p. 87.

Table 4.1. *The fates of holders of land in 1349*

| | Size of holding | | | | |
	10 ac.	5 ac.	3 ac.	less than 3 ac.	unknown
Deaths	13	0	5	3	1
Survivors	10	9	1	0	3

if she wished, *dum casta* or *dum sola*. In the absence of or in succession to a widow, the inheritance custom was 'Borough English', which involved impartible inheritance by the younger son, with customary maintenance for brothers and sisters until they married. In the case of defect of heirs the holding was taken into the lord's hand to be granted out again or retained if no acceptable candidate offered himself. When the heir was a minor, guardianship arrangements for both holding and chattels might be registered.[8]

Table 4.2 suggests that neither widows nor children figured with much prominence among the successors to holdings in 1349. Caution should be exercised in that some of the first listed category in Table 4.2 were almost certainly relatives. But Miss Page's comment on the operation of the law of inheritance is of the utmost importance: 'It was, however, a rule more honoured in the breach than the observance.'[9] This was quite literally true. Land transfers *inter-vivos*, or the purchase of the reversion, could break the hereditary line. The idea of a 'family holding', due to pass on from generation to generation, has some relatively small and undefined place in practice, most clearly seen in proper names (such as Tancreds) attached to some holdings, although even such instances are not common.[10]

It seemed possible that to understand the reasons for the patterns associated with the mortality of 1349 there was something to be gained by carrying the investigation of death rates forwards through the Second Pestilence of 1361 and its aftermath, and backwards through the Great Famine of 1316–19. Table 4.3, among other things, presents information on deaths, marriages and retirement contracts of, and surrenders of complete holdings by, Crowland customary tenants at Cottenham between 1303 and 1379. The evidence in Table 4.3 is at first glance astonishing. On the basis of the information we considered above and the data in Table 4.3, illustrating so dramatically the appalling scale of the catastrophe of 1349, both the other most

[8] *ECA*, pp. 108–9.
[9] *ECA*, p. 109.
[10] *ECA*, p. 281: 'terre vocate Tancreds in Cottenham nuper in tenura Willelmi Bonde'.

Table 4.2. *Successors to holdings*

Persons of different surnames but familiar locally	16
Children	4
Wives	0
Persons of the same surname	3
Unknown	2
Plots in the lord's hand	0

notorious periods of crisis appear extremely healthy. Yet, we know from a casual reference in the account rolls that the Second Pestilence visited nearby Dry Drayton. A unique case of burglary of malt and loaves by night appears in the court rolls for Cottenham during the famine period of the second decade of the fourteenth century. Furthermore, Dry Drayton's sufferings caused special concessions by the lord to all the peasantry 'on account of the hardness of the years and their want' in 1322.

It appears therefore that the evidence for 'normal' mortality is problematic. Using evidence from the formal notification of deaths and of the transfers arising from them, the totals are far too low to accept. The 35 years from 1303 to 1338 produce only eleven deaths, and the 25 years from 1355 to 1380 produce only twelve, and yet each period contains a major crisis. From what we know of the death rates in the area in the early modern period we would expect something much nearer to two per year in normal times for the age group constituting the tenant population. There is obviously a need to examine the process of recording in the court rolls: the completeness of the record of deaths in 1349 is clearly atypical.

Yet we must accept that the purpose of the rolls was not to collect vital statistics for the benefit of posterity, but primarily to keep track of all the dues and services to which the lord was entitled. These arose particularly, though not exclusively, from land holding and land transfers. For our purposes transfers may be considered in six main classes:

1. Death followed by inheritance according to the custom of the manor.[11]

---

[11] SS Simon and Jude, 7 Abbot Henry. 'Walterus Katelyne qui tenuit de domino unum messuagium et decem acras terre custumarie in Cotenham *obiit* Et super hoc venit filius euis *et heres* et capit illa de domino tenenda ad voluntatem domini faciendo consuetudines et servicia secundum consuetudinem manerii per fine xvj s. plegii Simon Warlock, Willelmus Pepiz.'

2. Marriage to widows with land.[12]
3. The surrender which was for another named person, usually signified by the phrase *ad opus*.[13]
4. A special version of the above, occasionally made by a holder on his death-bed before witnesses, usually including the bailiff. This is very similar in form to other nuncupative surrenders, but needs to be distinguished carefully because it indicates the holder's death. It is extremely rare.
5. Simple surrender of the holding into the lord's hand with no indication of the eventual destination of the property.[14]
6. Purchase of the reversion to land, becoming effective on the death of the holder.[15]

[12] Vigil of the Nativity of the BVM, 15 Simon Abbot. 'Henricus Makeheyt dat domino quattuor marcas pro se maritando Florencie que fuit uxor Willelmi schayl et pro gersumma terre ipsius Florencie. Tenende sibi et heredibus suis secundum consuetudinem manerii post mortem dicte Florencie.' (ECA, p. 346).

[13] Easter, 10 Hen. IV.
'Ad istam curiam Thomas Pepiz sursum reddit in manum domini in plena curia unum messuagium cum una virgata terre nuper Johannis Pepis ac tertiam partem unius messuagii cum tertia parte unuis virgate terre quondam Johannis Warlock atte Cherche *ad opus* Thomas Pepiz filii predicti Thome tenenda et sequelis suis per virgam ad voluntatem domini per servicia et consuetudines secundum consuetudinem manerii Et liberata est eidem inde seissina Et nichil dat de fine quia condonatur per senescallum eo quod pauper Et fecit fidelitatem Et insuper invenit plegios Thomam Pepis seniorem Johannem Warlock ballivum et Willelmum Lovell ad dicta tenementa reparanda necnon servicia et consuetudines domino soluendum ad terminos usuales.' (ECA, p. 434, 1409)
(Note: this form here survives into the age of disintegration of the old forms of villein land holding.)
Retirements usually take this form also:
St Luke, Evangelist, 11 Abbot Henry.
'Alicia que fuit uxor Hugonis Wymer reddit in manum domini i messuagium et decem acras terre custumarie in Cottenham *ad opus* Johannis filii Thome Tankret Et super hoc venit predictus Johannis et capit illa tenenda ad voluntatem domini faciendo consuetudines et servicia secundem consuetudinem manerii pro fine c.s. per plegium ballivi dictus vero Johannis per licenciam curie concessit eadem Alicie dicta messuagium et decem acras terre tenenda sibi a festivale sancti Michelis ultimo preterito usque ad finem duorum annorum proximo sequente plene completorum dictus quis Johannis durante termino duorum annorum proximo sequente predictorum fideliter deserviet predictam Aliciam et post terminum ille dote sue in messuagio predicto duas acras terre in campis et unum sellionem in crofto iuxta curtilagiam quod huiusmodi viduis reddi debet tenendo sibi ad terminum vite eiusdem Alicie et post eius decessum dicto Johanne plene reversit per finem supradictum dictus vero Johannis debit etiam predicte Alicie annuatim duos trussos fene pro bestiis suis sustinendo.'

[14] St Hilary, 2 Abbot Henry and 19 Ed. 11.
'Johannes Hoseborn reddit in manum domini propter impotencie sue x acras terre custumarie Et super hoc venit Thomas Erneys et capit dictam terram per licenciam curie tenendo ad voluntatem domini per servicia et consuetudines etcetera secundum consuetudinem manerii Et date domino pro fine pro dicta terra gersumando iijs. i iijd. per plegium ballivi.'   [15] Trinity, 21 Abbot Henry.

The first form usually gives rise to a note in the roll, naming the holder and giving some detail of the nature and extent of his tenement on his last day, or directly reporting the fact of death and of the acceptance by the heir or successor, together with the terms on which he is to hold. Heriot (if any) and entry fine are noted.

Through purchase of permission to marry a widow with land a man could certainly obtain a holding without waiting (with or without hope) for an inheritance. In the records such marriages are usually clearly distinguished from others, and the woman's status as widow is nearly always given. In the rare cases where less information is given, and widowhood not specifically mentioned, nearly all are in fact widows.[16] An unmarried girl heiress was not subject to the normal widow's disability of forfeiting her holding through marriage. She would therefore not have to buy a licence at such a high price. In ordinary marriages the bride, her parents and relatives usually paid the fine for the licence, but where the bride was a widow with land the groom normally sought the licence and paid what, by our local standards, was an enormous fine. Although in Cottenham these never reached the astronomical heights found elsewhere by Postan and Titow, it is the difference between the fines paid by widows and those paid by younger women without land that matters. This can easily be demonstrated from, for example, the rolls for 1310.[17] There John, son of Reginald Attepond, paid five marks (66s 8d) for Agnes, widow of John son of Nicholas, with her land. At the same court Henry Waveneys paid a mere 2s for licence to have his daughter Custancia married.

Sometimes the enrolment spells out the fact that land acquired by marrying a widow passed to the new husband's heirs after his death. In 1318 Henry Makehate paid four marks to marry Florence Schayl and for *gressum* into her land.[18] It was specifically stated that it was to be held by him and his heirs according to the custom of the manor after the death of the said Florence. What was normal custom probably needed definition in this case. Four years previously Simon, son of Agnes Porter, had taken her for 100s. The deterioration of her person may not have been considerable over the years, for when Simon married her the executors of her previous husband still owed her three quarters of barley worth 4s a quarter. Hidden assets in the form of chattels held by some widows may account for some of the unexplained variations in their value and for the willingness of

---

[16] Titow, *English Rural Society*, p. 87, and 'Some Differences'.
[17] Ascension, 7 Abbot Simon.
[18] Nativity of the BVM, 5 Abbot Simon.

hopeful grooms to submit to such exactions.[19] But it does seem to have been possible to get a widow and her land at a reduced rate by taking her and her land for her life only. In 1376, for instance, John Aleyn paid only 20s for a widow with a full bondland, but it was specified that he was to hold by right of his wife Margaret.[20]

It was clearly the right of the lord to seize and re-grant a widow's land on her remarriage or fornication, this right being the source of his power to exploit the land hunger of the early fourteenth century by levying high fines. Wherever a transfer involved a breach of custom such as required a licence, with forfeiture as the alternative, he could charge what the market would bear. Thus in the business of licensing the remarriage of widows, the lord seems to have been operating in a surprisingly open market. It might perhaps be better, with earlier royal precedents in higher social realms in mind, to term the process the sale of widows with land. But we can find no direct evidence of widows being forced to marry against their wills. Agnes Tancred, for instance, remained a widow with a full land for some years until she was carried off by the pestilence rather than by a husband.[21] There is, however, an example of the lord interfering with a widow marriage at a very late stage. When in 1342 Matilda, widow of Walter Buck, surrendered a cottage and three rods of customary land in Cottenham for Walter's son Robert, immediately after Robert took the land the jury presented that Matilda had entered into an agreement to marry (presumably a troth-plighting) Robert the Hayward of Swavesey, and that this agreement could not take effect since she was 'a widow of the lord' and as such not permitted to marry without licence. Order was made to seize all her goods on the lord's bond tenement, valued at 26s 8d, to be held as security that she would not marry without the lord's assent.[22] In this case the marriage itself was not an issue, only the failure to have it licensed in the court brought about a seigneurial intervention.

No detailed evidence has been found for routine seigneurial pressure on widows to marry, except the size of widows' land

---

[19] Pentecost, 11 Abbot Simon. There is a doubly interesting series of transactions beginning in 1311. Margaret, widow of William son of Hugo was presented because her *serviens* had encroached on the demesnes with the plough. John Syger of Dryton then paid 7 marks fine to marry her with land. She may well have been a lady of substance in Oakington, and the shift from one village to the next may also account for the extraordinarily high fine. Within 2 years he paid another mark's fine to exchange his lands with those of John Cosyn in Cottenham, thus transferring to the third of the Crowland manors in Cambridgeshire (Ascension, 7 Abbot Simon; St Luke, 9 Abbot Simon).

[20] St George Martyr, 16 Abbot Thomas and 50 Ed. III.

[21] St James, 25 Abbot Henry.   [22] St Margaret, 18 Abbot Henry.

because of their incapacity, and this must have been a threat in the long run to any widow who held out against marriage or retirement into old age. Yet the overall picture perhaps suggests that the pressure was very real in times of land hunger.

Surrender could take several forms, but very commonly a man or woman surrendered for the use of a specific named person. The usual form employs the phrase *ad opus*, but this does not seem to be strictly necessary. In 1307, when Alice Attehill surrenders her holding and Henry Attehill takes it, the phrase does not occur in the original entry. But later in the court an inquisition is set up as to whether a heriot is owed, and the surrender is described as *ad opus* Henry Attehill.[23] In 1311 Alice Martyn, widow, surrendered a cottage and two rods which were taken by Ralph Attehill. He immediately paid for a licence to marry her daughter Margaret. It is difficult to believe that the surrender was not by agreement with Ralph, as much as if this had been specifically indicated.[24] It is probable that many of the apparent simple surrenders where there was an immediate re-grant were made for the new tenant and no one else.

We have little evidence, except in special cases, of any consideration passing between the peasants for surrenders, but we should certainly expect them between peasants who bear no relationship to each other. Where there is often a very clear bargain between the two parties in the same family is in the frequent retirement provisions. Very specific responsibilities are taken on by the receiver for the provision of house-room, and for maintenance of the old person or couple. This is not necessarily between parent and heir. In many cases where no specific arrangement is written in the context makes it probable that we are seeing such a retirement agreement. In spite of legal advice, many families still today take such things upon trust. Wherever surrender for retirement has taken place we are not likely to find a record of the death of the original holder, and in theory successive retirements could prevent deaths of holders from coming to light in the rolls *ad infinitum*.

Surrenders *ad opus*, in words or in effect, may well amount to sales or settlements of debts between peasants, rather like foreclosure of mortgages. This is a subject worthy of detailed investigation outside the scope of this study. On the other hand there are surrenders in the late fourteenth century which are quite clearly the abandonment of holdings which the peasant no longer wished to cultivate into the hands of the lord. Any form of surrender except that made on a

[23] St Guthlac, 4 Abbot Simon.   [24] Annunciation, 8 Abbot Simon.

death-bed before witnesses hides the death of the holder from us. When surrenders abound, death rates become unobtainable.

The alternatives to allowing the natural course of death and inheritance within the kin by customary form are in effect means of speeding up the circulation of land. Some may permanently frustrate inheritance custom. The purchase of reversion to a property may or may not influence the property's ultimate destination, but it neither speeds up the transfer nor conceals the death of the land holder.

When the son and heir wished to make sure of his inheritance in face of the temptation to his parents to break the custom and sell his rights, he appears to have been able to secure the reversion by paying a heriot before his father's death. The very fact that an heir might find it worth his while to buy the reversion shows how restricted the right of inheritance was. This 'right' could not operate if any other arrangement had been made.

There may have been some bargaining with the lord over what we today might call the actuarial position of the father. In 1310 William Caunt paid a heriot of only 3s before his father's death. His father must have been in uncommonly good shape since the heriot was normally from 9 to 12s and could go higher.[25] Where it was someone other than the heir securing the reversion that person paid the *gressum*. In 1345 Thomas Kille received William Turtel's cottage having paid and then waited six years.[26]

The type of land transfer that causes most difficulty in following the lives and deaths of the land holders is the lease in all its various forms. The early leases of bondlands, which were intended to be temporary, began in the early 1350s and could be extremely complex. In 1353 a formal lease was made by the steward of ten acres of customary land (formerly John Makehate's) in Cottenham to John Pepys senior, and to his sons John and William for twelve years. The rent was to be paid half in works and half in cash. They were to rebuild a complete house forty by eighteen feet. They paid half a mark for the lease, and at the same time were licensed to sublet two three-acre parcels of it for the twelve years, the Pepys family being responsible to the lord for the whole.[27] The slow conversion of villein tenements on such terms as these would be likely, since many tenants would outlive the lease, again to reduce the number of deaths recorded. Syndication to groups of peasants could only make for more difficulties in tracing the fate of individuals.

[25] Annunciation, 7 Abbot Simon.
[26] Trinity, 21 Abbot Henry.
[27] St Peter in Cathedra, 29 Abbot Henry.

Some of the figures extracted from the court rolls are displayed in Table 4.3 to illustrate the links between economic and social changes. The first column includes deaths specifically mentioned either direct-ly (*obiit, interfectus*), or indirectly in the form of death-bed surrenders or reports of what a man was seised of on the day of his death. The second column notes the marriage licences for widows with land. The third notes other marriage licences, the two together giving some general indication of social and economic health. These are all for what appear to be daughters of known Cottenham villeins. Retire-ments and other surrenders have been distinguished but not noted in the same column, because some of the surrenders where no retire-ments are given are almost certainly retirements also. The distinct symbols are intended to reveal any clusters of known retirements.

At first glance the outstanding feature is how the disastrous mortality of 1349 stands out in comparison with the rest. The information summed up in the second column, marriage of widows with land, reveals a situation very like that found by Postan and Titow on some west country manors in the Bishop of Winchester's estate.[28] In the early years of the fourteenth century this seems to have been overwhelmingly the dominant form of property transfer among the Cottenham villeinage. In the first twenty years of the table, six transfers on the death of the holder and eleven surrenders, including two retirements, are matched by 31 marriages of widows with land. This form is thus not merely almost twice as common as all the others put together, but is even more dominant if the size of the holdings transferred is taken into account. Nearly all the full lands that are transferred are conveyed by this means.

Since, as we have seen, retirement, surrender or marriage with land are all likely to leave deaths unrecorded, it is easy to see why more of the deaths in 1349 are to be found in the rolls. The disaster of that year was relatively short, much shorter than Miss Page im-agined. For the victims there can have been little time for amendment of life, and less for disposition of property for the future. For a few months men died: the peasant's land passed into the lord's hand, as he left no widow to take it and had felt no need because of infirmity to dispose of it ahead of his inevitable fate. On the other hand, the Great Famine lasted, and the agony was slow but perhaps not ineluctable. The picture of these years in Cottenham, with its extensive pastoral interests, makes Kershaw's delineation of a longer agrarian crisis, rather than simply three successive years of bad harvests, particularly

---

[28] Titow, 'Some Differences'.

apt.[29] The account rolls for 1322–3 show the struggle still going on against the weather and disease on the demesnes. Cows yoked in the plough-teams were a symbol of the disasters that lasted in this area. We learn of the difficulties of the lord from the rolls, and can only speculate as to what happened to the peasants. The living-in workers at the manor were on short rations from Easter until July: not many of the villeins are likely to have been better off.[30]

Apart from the vast resources of Cottenham fens in wildfowl, fish and eels, which could have been exploited to enable human life to carry on, borrowing and leasing or sale of land always seemed to be possible in that village. As Miss Page says, 'Leases between tenants were very frequent, especially in the period 1320–1340.'[31] Illicit subletting may well have been much more frequent than that entered in the rolls, because the temptation to avoid the fine for registration at court must have been particularly strong in times of desperation. An open example of the sort of expedient that was possible comes from the St Mark's court of 1316, where John Gerard let eight selions for two crops. At the St Luke court in the same year, in what appears to be a unique example in the rolls, Isolda Turboyt let Nicholas Schayl an ox worth 9s for one year for 2s 6d.[32] Such temporary expedients could stave off the permanent sale of land, and perhaps keep starvation at bay. In Cottenham survival may have been possible because, with all the various alternative land uses on the edge of the fens, in the end something would turn up. It is remarkable that in the crisis years on this manor few complete surrenders of a kind which would have meant total defeat appear. Nor do we find any sign of high mortality among the peasants in the form of heriots. Those without land, who would have been the most likely to have starved, are not recorded in the court rolls. But things were never quite the same again.

In neighbouring Dry Drayton, with its wet sticky clays and no fens, matters seem to have been worse, and the agony to have been particularly prolonged. In 1322 the lord as a matter of grace, to help the tenants in their poverty, temporarily conceded to the tenants half of his fold-right. In 1325 John Roger's land fell into the hands of the lord because of his insufficiency, and there was no one within the homage capable of paying the entry fine. It was therefore handed over to four men for four years.[33] There can be little doubt that the years of agrarian crisis left a heritage of impoverishment.

---

[29] I. Kershaw, 'The Great Famine and Agrarian Crisis in England, 1315–22', *Past and Present* 59 (1973), pp. 3–50.
[30] *ECA*, p. 238. [31] *ECA*, p. 112. [32] 13 Abbot Simon. [33] *ECA*, p. 352.

It is obvious that transfers *inter-vivos* do not give rise to a record of the death of a land holder, since by definition the person making the transfer is alive at the time and will die without record after he ceases to become a holder. The only exception to this is the rare case of death-bed surrender. Of the types of transfer listed above only the first and fourth automatically produce a record of death. The sixth form produces a few further notices of deaths, but only where succession may be in doubt.

If the contrast between the appalling roll of deaths recorded in 1349 and the absence of such a record for the earlier agrarian crisis can thus be easily explained, it is much more difficult to give a satis-factory account for the lack of evidence for the impact of the Second Pestilence in 1361. Apart from damage to the membranes, the records of some of the courts are so cursory that it is hard to detect any sign that the homage from Cottenham actually came over to Oakington to attend. This was the time for which Miss Page detected signs that the administration was losing its grip, but in our present state of knowledge we cannot dismiss the possibility that the Second Pesti-lence was better contained and less severe in its impact. Any hope of finding direct evidence for this in Cottenham is diminished by the paucity of information in the critical rolls.

It seems clear that except for 1349, when villein deaths outstripped the possibility of other alternative forms of land transfer, and when supplementary material enables the totals derived from the court rolls to be checked, the death rates, even those simply for villein holders of land, are likely to elude us. But any of the forms of land transfer discussed above could be, and were, used at any time during the period studied. Thus the shifts in relative importance between the various forms must be explained by force of circumstances or by deliberate choice. Changes in such relative frequencies may be a richer source for understanding social change in Cottenham in the period than any crude death rates of land holders might have been.

The fall in the number of marriages after the Black Death as compared with preceding periods may seem strange, since many scholars think that pestilence was followed by a rise in the marriage rate. The fall seems to have begun with the famines, but if we consider the eight marriages in 1349 as anticipation of events that, but for the deaths and the consequent availability of land, would have come in the following two decades, this second fall is much less than meets the eye at first sight. If we also allow for the probable smaller size of the population, then it turns into a slight rise. However, since the number of holdings is still approximately the same, the rate compared with the number of holdings is lower than before the onset of the pestilence. This might be accounted for by the falling off of widow remarriages. The proportion of the population that were married, as with the proportion holding land, was almost certainly higher: the average age for all marriages had probably fallen, although the trend in ages at first marriage is difficult to predict.

On the other hand, the total number of transfers, when we take similar twenty-year periods and omit the inflated year 1349 (Table 4.4, column 6), does not seem very significantly below that of the earlier decades of the century.

We examined the possibility of constructing a table of fines for land transfer. Unfortunately, attempts to generalize about the changing level of medieval fines, as with rents, are fraught with difficulty. The picture, when our sources first begin to make it at all clear, is a conglomeration of survivals from a long and varied history. Occasional declarations of custom suggest that some at least are fixed and certain, but in practice it is difficult for us to see rhyme or reason in the variations from one holding to another. This is especially true of the smaller holdings. It is hardly possible to arrive at an average fine per acre, since acreages are not always given, and when they are they are usually for arable alone, though a house, perhaps with other buildings, an undefined area of croftland, and valuable appurtenances in the rich Cottenham fens may also have been included. The court would know about these, but we do not. There is another terminological problem: the rolls from time to time use the expressions 'full land', 'bondland', 'bondage', or 'virgate' as apparent synonyms, but one cannot always be quite sure that a ten-acre arable holding is intended.

The marriage of widows with land was normally subject to fines of a much higher order than were other marriages. This differential might be interpreted as the 'price' the lord might ask to waive the right to confiscate a widow's holding of her previous husband's land for remarriage or fornication. Such fines were arbitrary, and the lord appeared to be taking what the market would bear. At times it appears that something like a standard rate may be emerging, but this disappears again almost as rapidly. Such instances would probably be an indication of the current 'going rate' of the land market.

There are two other cases in which transactions can produce similar high fines: in some of the retirements and in some of the surrenders, usually among those specifically *ad opus*. These would also appear to be cases in which the lord is licensing a transfer out of the line of customary inheritance. If we cannot derive as precise a measure as we would wish of changing land values from tabulating all fines, we can at least get some general indication from observing how the ceiling of the high group of fines varies over the period.

There is just one time when our sources appear to indicate something more complete. It is again the year 1349. The fines for full lands in the records of the courts during the period in which the pestilence was raging tumble rather like a Dutch auction. At the July court we start off with fines of 21s, 1 mark, 21s and 1 mark again. The November court ends with fines of ½ mark and 10s for similar lands.[34]

In the first ten years of our survey the level of the high fines suggests that business is brisk and rising. A number of landed widows fetch from 50s to 66s 8d. Two surrenders bring in 66s 8d apiece. The most costly retirements run to 40s and 60s. By 1311 the most expensive widow costs £4.

In 1313 we have a clear case of inheritance by an elder son in agreement with the younger, and this involves a 60s *gressum* for entering the land. 1315 sees a peak of £5, and even in 1318, after the famine, 5 marks (66s 8d), is still obtainable. During the prolonged agrarian crisis the best widows can reach 4 marks (54s 4d), and a retirement in 1322 fetches 5 marks. In 1335 we find a new peak for retirement at 100s, but the widows seem slightly cheaper, the highest in these years going at 44s 8d in 1337.

After the great collapse of land value in the Black Death, fines for transfers make little recovery. A full land surrendered in 1350 is charged 26s 8d, and a retirement in the next year pays a 40s fine, but there is on the whole a downward drift. As well as becoming lower, the high fines become fewer. After the Second Pestilence a surrender of a full land in 1362 is fined only 40d and although a widow with a bondland in the same year costs 20s, this figure is only reached twice again until an odd surrender in 1377 is assessed at 26s 8d. The only further high fine in the period studied is in 1379, when a holding passes to both father and son and so pays double, 40s.

One type of fine has a pattern of change very much its own: 'leyrwite', the fine to which a female villein was subject if she committed fornication. The usual explanation is that it was to compensate the lord for possible loss of a marriage fine and carried no punitive connotations. In our records there are very few cases indeed of widows incurring this fine: in such a case the widow was subject to a much fiercer additional penalty, forfeiture of the holding she had acquired from her former husband. Seizure of lands is usually a

---

[34] St James, 25 Abbot Henry; St Edmund King, 26 Abbot Henry.

means of compelling the offending party to come to court and make fine, but for a widow with land the threat was real enough: 'Clemencia has now fornicated and committed leyrwite, on account of which the lord may enter into the aforesaid land and tenements according to the custom of the manor and let them to whomsoever he wishes.'[35]

This was certainly not a fine where the lord charged what the traffic would bear, except perhaps in the rare case of a widow who had a possible husband waiting. In the thirteen cases of leyrwite where we know the size of the fine between 1305 and 1322, one is 6d, one is half a mark, and all the rest are 12d. Thereafter, until 1340, the fines virtually all seem to be for 3d or 6d. The few in this period that reach 12d appear to be the result of a combined leyrwite and marriage fine, which amounted to excusing the leyrwite. It is fairly clear that during the years of agricultural crisis, the reduction of leyrwite was one of the ways in which the lord showed consideration for distress. The lord not infrequently reduced or excused fines on account of poverty. It may be of interest and indicative of the degree to which the personal feelings of the lord were involved to notice that Richard Smith found the childwyte fine in the Suffolk manors of Redgrave and Rickinghall at its highest during the period of the Famine.[36] This difference could possibly be due in part to leyrwite not necessarily involving pregnancy.

In 1349 we find our first example of the new, higher, fine. Agnes daughter of John Not is charged 5s, but 3s is excused on account of her poverty.[37] As the number of cases of leyrwite decreases, according to the rolls, so the fine comes to be virtually standardized at 5s 4d. By 1359 this figure is given *ex consuetudine*, as of custom.[38] The price of fornication has been rising even more than other fines have been falling, and it is difficult not to interpret its height after the Black Death as punitive. Indeed, there may have been a change of attitude a few years before, when the Archdeacon seems to have been cleaning up Cottenham.[39] In 1344 at the Easter court Henry Waveneys was fined for wasting the lord's substance in the court Christian, having been fined there for adultery with one woman in Dry Drayton and another in Cambridge. In 1339 had been the notorious Warlok case, written up by Miss Page, where Simon Warlok had thrown out his wife and installed her niece as his mistress. He refused to obey both courts in spite of increasing fines. Certainly the number of cases

---

[35] *ECA*, p. 109 note.   [36] Personal communication.
[37] *ECA*, p. 388.   [38] *ECA*, p. 133.   [39] 20 Abbot Henry.

recorded fell, but no one can tell for sure whether fornication decreased or discretion increased.[40]

At Cottenham we did not find the same story that Razi tells of Halesowen.[41] In the latter community, as the marriage of widows with land lost its importance after the Black Death, fornication increased among widows while it decreased among unmarried girls. There the fall of the landed widow from social dominance at the beginning of the century ended in the depths of degradation. To judge from Table 4.3, in Cottenham marriage and fornication flourished in the same hedgerow, and in a number of cases were patently connected, probably in more ways than we have yet discovered. But there, as it became easier and cheaper for anxious couples to get land in order to marry, the lesser and now more expensive substitute for marriage may well have been more cautiously avoided.

The fornication rate was too low, if the figures bear any relation to the reality, to have any significant effect on the population of the Cottenham villeinage. But there were certainly other social forces besides mortality affecting population growth. When our sources for estimating mortality deteriorate after the Great Black Death, there still remain other items suggesting changes that would affect marriage and fertility. Some of those elements which we have examined as symptoms of changing population pressure, once established, would generate further changes to accelerate or retard population growth. Central to the whole complex are patterns of land holding.

As long as there was some stability in the pattern of unitary peasant holdings, so that the number of holdings remained roughly the same and most holdings supported one family and one family only, certain consequences must follow from the changes we have already detected. Unless the plague reduced fertility to an incredibly low level, the crop of marriages in 1349 must have been followed by a baby boom among the villeinage. This would have increased population but would not have been reflected in the pressure of couples queueing for holdings and waiting to get married until the mid-1360s at the earliest.

Since the rush to the altar (or should it be the church door) in 1349 represented marriages that would have been postponed even longer but for the plague, the average age at marriage would have been depressed, thus bringing increased fertility within marriage. Insofar as the pestilence had lowered the population, without altering the

---

[40] *ECA*, p. 59.
[41] Z. Razi, *Life, Marriage and Death*, p. 139.

number of holdings that were available as bases for families, a higher proportion of the villeins would have been married.

This again should have been reflected in a relatively high birthrate, but one which would have increased pressure for land holdings at a phase later in time. But this renewed population pressure on land may never have arrived: the Second Pestilence, if it struck Cottenham at all severely, would have fallen on the babies of the bulge when they were aged eleven or twelve, a few years too early for them to be serious contenders for land and brides.

The effect on demographic trends of changing habits as to re-marriage of widows is quite complex. With the move away from remarriage, insofar as widows kept their land this would depress the birthrate in comparison with the earlier period when remarriage flourished, but insofar as they got rid of their land and it passed to young couples the opposite might have occurred.

The court rolls seem unlikely to yield us much more satisfactory evidence of mortality directly, but there may well be more to be gained by an exhaustive attempt to follow the fortunes of individual holdings over a much longer period than has yet been possible. Unless the plague drastically reduced fertility generally among villein wives, we would expect the increase in marriages to have resulted in sufficient births to distort the age structure of the population, and to start an oscillation in the rates which we are attempting to glimpse. Where direct evidence of mortality fails us, there is perhaps something to be discerned by looking at its reflection in other rates. Such a study may also be of some help in illuminating the rise in the standard of living of the peasantry which is thought to have followed the easing of population pressure on land as a result of the pestilences and famines. The break-up of the pattern of unitary holdings, and the possible shift towards a nuclear type of family both by residence and work group is of considerable importance in this question.

The appearance of multiple holdings, and even more their increase, together with the increase of leases and subleases of fragmentary holdings towards the end of the century, is crucial for family formation. Here we can see two opposite tendencies at work, engrossment and fragmentation. These would respectively decrease or increase the chances of the formation of new families and so retard or accelerate population growth. The rolls may well yield information as to the balance between these, and in so doing indicate what proportion of the villeinage became better off, and what worse off. Even the apparently dramatic fall in the condition of widows may not turn out to be quite what we feared. If the late fourteenth-century widow who surrendered her land instead of marrying again was in fact selling it, then she may not have fallen into such dire poverty as might be imagined at first sight.

We have been examining information dealing with only one small group of peasants on a single manor, the villeinage of the Crowlands manor in Cottenham. Few of the social forces determining their fates would necessarily be paralleled exactly elsewhere. But we have found little to suggest that any force could rival the effects, in changing their lot, of the famine and pestilence. We seem to be witnessing a customary pattern of succession under strain and disintegrating through the pressure of economic and demographic forces. One of the easiest points for such a change to start was retirement. Here the 'customary poor law', so neatly anatomized by Miss Page, could be replaced by *ad hoc* individual arrangements. The two systems could operate side by side as alternatives, the customary arrangements being still operational if the holder did not make what would be to him a more satisfactory agreement.

The villein holding seems to have been in theory an impartible family unit to be handed down the customary line of descent. In practice this could be varied temporarily or permanently; temporarily by such means as inter-peasant subletting for so many crops or so many years; permanently when the line of succession was extinguished through death or through alienation by widow remarriage or surrender. The Warlok case shows that a customary impartible holding could in fact be divided and pass down divided through the generations. The theory of impartibility was maintained by the responsibility to the lord for rent and services remaining with one branch. Impartibility here seems to have reflected liabilities for rent, payments rather than cultivation practices.

The 'family holding' could be supplemented by either the holder himself or his sons renting fragments of freehold, demesne or customary land either from his own lord or from other tenants in the community. New lines of descent could be established by marriage to widows with land, or by grant from out of the lord's hand. If there were an inadequate supply of such supplements, the heir to an impartible holding might be forced to defer marriage. That there was an element of this pattern among the Cottenham villeinage is suggested by the way in which the record number of deaths noted in the rolls for any one year is matched by the record number of marriage licences. Something of such a tradition, in a loose form at least, can be found lingering on in the village in the nineteenth century, where the restless and bitter heir found waiting almost intolerable.[42] Where deferment of marriage took place until land was acquired, we have an inbuilt sociological system restraining population growth. Insofar as a group was shut up within a system whereby the unitary family holding descended by impartible inheritance, this would tend to place a ceiling on population increase, and the relation of this to subsistence level would depend on the productivity of the holdings. Insofar as it was possible for anxious young bachelors to find easements rather than waiting for their inheritance (an inheritance which for many of them might never come), the population ceiling would be somewhat lifted. But the less the situation was alleviated by opportunities created through fragmentation of holdings or by the availability of free land outside the system the more readily should population have recovered from extraneous natural disasters which brought an abnormal number of deaths. There would have been a reserve of young men champing for a wife and land.

In Cottenham such a reserve was particularly likely to be high. The fen which barred the colonizing plough from further advance was almost without limit as a source for subsistence for the landless and poor. If the villein holdings were in practice so often moving back and forth between families, the unitary nature of the holdings was regularly reinforced on transfer, and there was a further reserve of landless men in subsidiary occupations and of others who had acquired temporary scraps in other manors from which they would return when land became available to them. Titow found a predominance of marriage to widows with land associated with manors where there was no chance of increasing the amount of available land.[43] It is under such conditions of extreme population pressure that the Cottenham villeinage appears to be operating at the beginning of the fourteenth century. There seems to have been some slight slackening in demand for land and a partial return to inheritance on death as a way of acquiring land from the time of the Great Famine, and a settling of such practices at a 'normal' low level, possibly about the time of the Second Pestilence.

In the earliest years the lord seems to have been taking advantage of the population pressure to extract the maximum economic return from selling his widows dearly, yet enough men seem to have been willing and able to pay, and to pay such sums as never seem to have passed through their hands on other occasions. Some of the widows may in fact have advanced the money themselves. Keen grooms may have borrowed within the village from other peasants, or even from

---

[42] J. R. Ravensdale, *Liable to Floods* (Cambridge, 1974), p. 169.
[43] Titow, 'Some Differences'.

neighbouring villages. One wonders how many surrenders *ad opus* are foreclosures on mortgages in such a desperate market for holdings. Many debts between peasants that actually came to the notice of the courts had inbuilt arrangements for payment by instalment, but we do not know whether the lord offered easy terms on his widows. The unique case where it is insisted that a leyrwite fine should be paid 'in one lot' suggests that instalments may have been normal.

If the famine checked the population pressure, it would appear to have been rising again on the eve of the Great Pestilence, to judge by the way retirement arrangements built up. There would be no point in an heir entering into such an arrangement if additional land could easily be obtained.

Why do not marriages to widows with land increase likewise? It is certainly not because the supply of such widows has dried up: there is unfortunately an infinitely renewable supply. Widowers remarried quickly. Of the ten reported deaths between 1345 and 1348 five are widows. In the homage list of 1346, of the six single persons listed the four women were all widows. The last person to retire during the Black Death was Agnes Edmond, widow.[44] Marriage to widows with land was an expensive business. Possibly greater in its effect on population in Cottenham than any of the famines was the drying up of the village capital market. This, as well as population pressure, could affect the height to which fines could rise. In other words, in Cottenham, with all the varied wealth of its resources, the famine may have brought poverty rather than death.

Whatever the cause, the peasants seem to have been taking the initiative from the lord in matters of land transfer by the time of the pestilence, which collapsed the land market completely. In times of acute land-hunger the lord's power to license marriage to widows had given him a powerful tool to extract a maximum economic value from land transfer. After 1349 conditions in the land market seem to have been such that the peasants were increasingly concerned to get rid of land rather than to take it at the old customary terms. As land was handed back to the lord by surrenders, he in his turn was forced to get what he could by leases, with terms reduced to what any acceptable tenant was willing to pay. The increasing use of a clause compelling the prospective tenant to find pledges that he would inhabit and maintain the tenement shows the way that things had gone. After the Black Death land was undoubtedly available in a buyer's market.

---

[44] St Edmund King, 26 Abbot Henry.

In the early part of the century, the lord's anxiety to maintain his income in the face of rising prices led him to exploit his power to license marriage to widows. In doing so, although he was able to maintain the unity of peasant holdings, these became less and less *family* holdings that would pass down an unbroken line of inheritance through the kin. When falling population tipped the balance completely against him in favour of the peasants, they have already grasped the initiative. At the worst, their prospects after flight were no longer unattractive: between 1348 and 1368 there were seven cases of illegal flight by Cottenham villeins. In the meantime more and more peasant land was being priced by market forces. When the manorial administration had earlier asserted its authority, it had kept the unity of the villein holding but had weakened the traditional tie between particular families and particular tenements. When land was plentiful and the peasants were able to resist taking it at the old high terms a steady erosion of the unity of the holding itself began.

All these were slow processes, which worked through individual transactions, and examples of the old forms still appeared much later, even as odd survivals into the Tudor period. Nevertheless, although the landed widow might still be desirable, her land was devalued, and she was no longer the main agent by which the social units reproduced themselves.

Before the fifteenth century land had become a drag on the market. By 1394 tenants were entering holdings that were imposed upon them, without having to pay entry fines. In that year Agnes Warlock wished to take the holding of her husband who had died, but the homage declared her incapable of maintaining it.[45] It went with a right of inheritance to three men of old families, but they avoided entry fines on the grounds that it had been 'imposed' upon them. Robert Schaill's tenement and ten-acre holding was empty, because his wife had refused it and gone away. Again the homage chose some of their senior members, five in this case, who took the holding, having declared that there was no single tenant sufficient to take it on. Again they escaped an entry fine because it was 'imposed' on them. The same court shows a widow from Oakington likewise refusing her husband's land. What had been a very scarce and very valuable asset early in the century had become an embarrassing liability for a woman without a husband, or without access to non-kin who were prepared to take it in return for supporting her 'til death'.

The land-hunger of the late thirteenth and early fourteenth cen-

[45] *ECA*, pp. 418–19.

turies put the lord in a very strong position to exploit his power by way of fines for marriage to widows with land. The process reached the point where it became one of his substantial sources of income. This does not seem to have prevented such widows, in their turn, from exploiting the scarcity value which their share of the then most desirable commodity in the village, land, gave them. In 1326 we find Maria Buk binding her son to take on all the responsibilities of maintaining and working her holding, in exchange for a half share in all the crops and the reversion of her land after her death. In the very first roll that survives in this series (1290) there is a case which suggests an even harder bargain by a widow. A young courting couple appear to have slipped from grace and to have anticipated their marriage. Cecilia Saleman is in mercy for leyrwite. Her mother, Matilda, enters into a covenant whereby Henry Cosyn, presumably a father-to-be, takes Cecilia, and the young couple undertake to serve Matilda well and faithfully for the rest of her life. As long as they do this Matilda will provide them with food and clothing and let them have an unsown acre each year which they will sow and crop at their own expense. Henry's father, Robert Cosyn, will provide within the year, in cash or kind, 40s as dowry. The bride and groom are to make and enjoy the comfort from the acre and the 40s. Matilda seems set up for life, with any luck, and she does not even appear to have secured the reversion of her land to the fortunate (or unfortunate) groom. Nor does she appear to have closed the door against possible remarriage taking her land with her.[46] Such marriage arrangements involving property can rarely be glimpsed in the court rolls. As with so many payments between peasants, manorial records, containing only disputes, show only the tip of the iceberg, while the mass, not giving rise to payments to the lord, leaves no trace. Licences to peasants to sublet land rarely indicate what rent the peasant will receive, but only the fine to the lord.

In the early fourteenth century the landed widow could lean very heavily on bargains outside the immediate family circle. In 1345, Alice, a full-landed woman, and widow of Hugh Wymer, surrendered house and land for John son of Thomas Tankret. John was to serve her faithfully while she retained the whole holding for two years, and after this she would have two acres in the fields and a selion in the croft for life, and John would supply her with two trusses of hay each year for her beasts. After her death he would have the reversion to the whole holding. The lord took the very substantial fine of five marks.

[46] *ECA*, p. 333.

This case shows a consideration (the two years' services and the provision for Alice's retirement) passing between peasants in a surrender *ad opus*. It is part of a retirement arrangement, and as such has many parallels, but we scarcely ever hear in the rolls of *cash* passing between peasants, except where an unpaid debt is claimed. However, there is a case in 1290 where the father-in-law is claiming six bushels of barley as owing from the husband and wife from twenty years back, but the jury say that it was paid at the time of the wedding.[47]

Looking at all the conveyances of land among the Crowlands villeinage in Cottenham in the first generation of the fourteenth century, it appears that the widow, thanks to her automatic inheritance of her husband's holding, calls the tune socially. The men may look after the business of the manor courts, but at the height of the land-hunger the widow with land is the keystone in the social structure.

But for the possibility of charging such high fines for widows with land, their automatic right of inheritance to all their husbands' property would have made widows a wasting asset for the lord in a time of rising prices. For instance, in 1329 a widow who paid 12d per annum for a cottage containing one rod died without heirs. Thomas Attewell took it but paid 4s rent instead. The inheritance custom and economic change had combined to turn a widow into something much more desirable. A widow who got through several husbands in a few years would, as long as the land market was buoyant, have been a great source of profit to the lord.

If fines for marriages to widows with land brought in substantial income to the lord, he got something not always dissimilar in the way of fines from retirement arrangements; but for an old peasant a modest security with much less work might have seemed a more attractive proposition than the search for a new marriage partner and increased work. The shift away from marriage to widows with land as the dominant form of peasant land transfer probably marks the first phase of the change from landlord to peasant initiative which characterizes social change in rural society in the fourteenth century. Poverty may have drained the village capital market, and when land values revived there were new and cheaper opportunities for acquisitiveness. The temporary innovations after 1349 drifted into permanence. When the lord had difficulty in finding adequate tenants for an empty holding, the more substantial tithingmen frequently shared it

---

[47] *ECA*, p. 331.

Table 4.3. *Crowland, Cottenham: holders of servile lands*

Abbot	Year	Deaths	Marriages of widows + land	Marriages without land	Retirements and surrenders	Flight	Leyrwite
Simon	1303		MM		ss		
	1304		MMM				
	1305		MMMM	mmm	sss		1
	1306		M	m	R		1
	1307		MM	mm	R		111
	1308						
	1309						
	1310	†		m	s		11
	1311		MMM	m	s		11
	1312	†	MM	mmmm			
	1313	†	MM	mmmmmm			1
	1314		MM	mmmm			1
	1315		M	m			11
	1316	†			s		
	1317		MMM	mmm	s		
	1318		MMM	m			
	1319						
	1320	†	M	m			1
	1321		M	mm			11
	1322	†(murder)	M				1
	1323	†		mm			
	1324			mmm			
Henry	1325		M				
	1326		M		R		1
	1327		MM	mmm			1
	1328		M	m	R		11

220

	+	M	m	R/s	f	1
1329	+	M	mmmm			111
1330	+					111
1331			mm			
1332			mmmm			1
1333	+	M	mm	Rs		11
1334			mm	R		111
1335						
1336				s		
1337	+	M	m	Rs		
1338			mm			
1339						
1340	++	M	mm	ss		
1341	+	M	mmmm			
1342	+		m		f	1
1343		M			ffff	
1344						
1345	+++		m	R	f	1
1346	+++		mmm	RRRs	f	111
1347	++		mm	RRRs		
1348	++		mm	RR		111
1349	+++++++++++++++++++++++++		m mmmmmmmm			
1350	+		m	s		1
1351	++++		m	s		1
1352	+		mmm	s		
1353	+			s	f	1
1354	++					
1355	+	M	m	R	f	1
1356						
1357			m			1
1358						

(Cont.)

221

Table 4.3. (Cont.)

Abbot	Year	Deaths	Marriages of widows + land	Marriages without land	Retirements and surrenders	Flight	Leyrwite
Thomas	1359						
	1360					ff	1
	1361						
	1362				s		1
	1363	++					
	1364	+	M				
	1365	+			ss		
	1366			mmm			
	1367	+	M	mm	s		
	1368	+	M	m	sss	f	
	1369						1
	1370			m	s		
	1371				s		
	1372	++		m	s		
	1373			mm			
	1374			m	ss		
	1375			m			
	1376		M		s		
	1377				Rs		
John	1378	+		m	R		
	1379						

222

Table 4.4. *Summary of Table 4.3 by 20-year periods*

	1 †	2 M	3 m	4 Rs	5 1	6 †MRs	7 Mm	8 MRs
Years								
1309–28	7	24	33	6	17	37	57	30
1329–48	18	7	34	17	17	42	41	24
1350–69	17	4	13	13	6	34	17	17

Table 4.5. *Summary of Table 4.3 by social and economic phases*

	1 †	2 M	3 m	4 Rs	5 1	6 †MRs	7 Mm	8 MRs
Years								
1303–19	4	28	27	11	13	43	55	39
1320–48	21	15	46	19	27	55	61	34
1349–60	36	1	15	8	7	45	16	9
1361–80	11	4	14	17	3	32	18	21

and willy-nilly learned the ways of engrossment of land by the time market conditions made it desirable again.

At the time that our records open there is little sign on the Crowlands manor of Cottenham that the normal way for a villein holding to change hands was by the death of the holder followed by inheritance, so that it passed down the line of family succession from generation to generation. This could and did happen in a minority of cases throughout the period of study and long after, and it is tempting to think that this may have been the 'normal' form of succession at some time in a stable past. For the fourteenth century we have been tracing only transfers made under extreme conditions in the land market. In the early decades there is every sign of high population pressure: the extension of ploughland has come to a halt against the waters of the fen. Colonization has ceased. In the later decades of the century, after the famines and Black Death, population has been savagely reduced. Both extremes, through the reaction of the lord and peasant in taking advantage of changed conditions, serve to undermine the tradition of the unitary family holding. On the manor of Crowlands in Cottenham the main source for what we know of relations between lord and villein is the court rolls. What we can see is certainly not a simple case of naked exploitation. The power of the lord was limited by custom, and that custom was enshrined in the memories of villein jurors, supplemented by the written records of the courts. In practice also the powers of the lord could be tempered by humanity or beneficence to those in distress. The cynical view that this was merely care for the goose that laid the golden egg (the villein who cultivated the lord's land and contributed to his income) could only be proved by evidence that we do not have. Whatever the legal theory of the time that the villein, his family, his land and his goods were the lord's chattels, the lord could (and did) only seize a holding in the case of serious failure on the part of the peasant to perform his duties, and then seizure was usually only temporary as a means to secure obedience or surety for a fine. This, of course, only applies where there was a living peasant in possession. Even seizure where the holding reverted to the lord because of defect of heirs was usually followed by re-grant as soon as possible.

But customary law could be converted into a source of income through the sale of licences to break it, as well as through fines for unlicensed breaches. The high land prices in the earlier period of our study could tempt the administration to develop this source of profit, and thereby in some measure to redress the drift of real income from lord to peasant. Within and outside custom there was room for bargaining, especially over transfers of land. Licensed exemptions might increase to a degree where custom was almost superseded in practice by bargains, although never quite. Through sale of licences the exception could become the rule and the rule the exception. While population pressure kept the value of land high, the lord was in a bargaining position which allowed him to take the full economic value, or something approaching it, from many transfers of land *inter-vivos* between villeins. When pressure of population was drastically removed and the land market collapsed, the villein was sometimes in a position to call the tune, refuse the old customary terms, and make a bargain favourable to himself. If the lord with his power did not wish this, in the last resort he could do little in face of surrender of unwanted land, and less in face of flight.

In the dread months of 1349, when customary inheritance appears to have been re-emerging as the dominant form of transfer, the way in which the fines tumble show that the villein was already beginning to feel his new bargaining power.

The erosion and replacement of unchanging custom by the bargain operates whenever conditions in the land market are extreme. Perhaps this should not surprise us. A good deal of custom seems at the very least to have grown out of old bargains that have become standardized by repetition. It would be very hard to understand the variations in such rents and fines as have been fixed in the past for similar holdings except by some such process. It is surely logical to expect times of relative economic and social stability to favour standardization through repetition of bargains, promoting thereby the slow growth of custom, while times of rapid or violent economic change would open new opportunities for bargaining that would erode custom. The fourteenth century had its fill of such social turbulence.

5

Industrial employment and the rural land market 1380–1520

IAN BLANCHARD

Studies of the medieval village land market have revealed a kaleido-scopic pattern of change in the methods of land transference, as first one and then another of the means, encapsulated in the nineteenth-century adage concerning rustic advancement, 'patrimony, matri-mony and parsimony', came to the fore, in changing economic and social circumstances, as the principal modes of property transference.[1] Gradually the chronology and form of these changes are being charted, and although the indicators are fewer and more widely dispersed for the later middle ages than for the century and a half before the catastrophic collapse of population in the 1380s, the broad outlines of change seem to be slowly emerging.[2] Irresistibly,

---

[1] By property is meant those rights of usufruct embodied in what Professor Thompson has called the 'corporate inheritance-grid' of the period; the term embraces not only the rights of use of land and moveables but also those embodied in contemporary usage. Transference also includes not only those methods embodied in *post-mortem* settlements but also those encapsulated in *pre-mortem* arrangements. See the stimu-lating commentary of E. P. Thompson, 'The grid of inheritance', in J. R. Goody, J. Thirsk and E. P. Thompson, editors, *Family and Inheritance: Rural Society in Western Europe, 1200–1800* (Cambridge, 1976).

[2] Since Professor Homans' classic *English Villagers of the Thirteenth Century* (Cambridge Mass., 1941; repr. New York, 1960) most work on rural society has concentrated on the period 1280–1380. Only recently, however, thanks to the work of Professors Postan, Hilton and Raftis and Drs Titow, Hyams, Smith and Razi amongst others, have the peasantry rather than their social superiors become the focus of attention. With regard to demographic change, whilst the process of secular decline may have begun in the 1310s, as suggested by Professor M. M. Postan, 'Some Economic Evidence of Declining Population in the Later Middle Ages', *Economic History Review* 2nd series 2:3 (1950), p. 245, it is increasingly clear from the indirect evidence, presented by A. R. Bridbury, 'The Black Death', *Economic History Review* 2nd series 26:4 (1973) and in the works listed in *Social History* 5 (1977), p. 663 note 8, that the 1380s witnessed a catastrophic collapse of population. Moreover, the picture outlined in these works of demographic recovery after the Black Death, a recurrence of over-population in the 1370s and a subsequent collapse of population in the 1380s is

the increasing importance of the cash nexus seems to be revealed as
the dominant theme pervading the rustic land market during the
years 1380–1520.[3] Yet, whilst the changing pattern of land transfer –
the shift from a non-monetary system, dominated by marital–inheritance transactions, to a commercial one – is slowly revealed, less
attention has been paid to the mechanisms utilized by the peasant in
his market operations. We know little of how the unendowed son or
landless man courted the young heiress or ageing widow and how he
overcame the stigma associated with his position, in order to make
the contacts necessary to establish himself on the path to that tryst
which would be consummated over the scrivener's table. Nor, in
spite of the *dicta* of lawyers from Glanvill to Blackstone, do we as yet
know much about the realities behind the legal formulas of inheritance or how social and demographic circumstances combined to
thwart the ambitions of one sibling whilst favouring another.[4] Similarly, whilst the brief, enigmatic court roll entries concerning land
dealings have provided a basis for analysis of the changing incidence
of familial and non-familial transfers, they reveal little of the travail
and heartbreak involved in raising the cash which was a necessary
prerequisite for such dealings – the struggles to secure freedom from
subservience to an unfeeling master; the long years of loneliness
spent in exile, far from the home hearth, by the unendowed son
striving to secure a niche in the village land market. Accordingly, in
this essay it is hoped to examine two of the ways followed by men in
search of land – the paths of familial patronage and of parsimonial
accumulation – and to explore the relationships which existed between them.

If the nature of the mechanisms utilized by the peasantry in their
village land market operations remains clouded in the mists of
obscurity it is no more clear to us how men utilized these mechanisms

confirmed by a demographic analysis of the Derbyshire villages considered here,
undertaken by the present author and by studies of two groups of Essex villages,
made by Dr Richard Smith, Dr L. R. Poos and by Mrs Elspeth Moodie. I should like to
thank Dr Smith and Mrs Moodie for placing the preliminary findings of their
researches at my disposal.

[3] This phenomenon, although alluded to earlier by others, was first systematically
investigated by Dr R. J. Faith in her 'The Peasant Land Market in Berkshire during the
Later Middle Ages', unpublished University of Leicester Ph.D. thesis, 1962, briefly
summarized in 'Peasant Families and Inheritance Customs in Medieval England',
Agricultural History Review 14 (1966), pp. 88–92. Her findings are certainly confirmed
by Christopher Dyer's study 'Changes in the Size of Peasant Holdings in Some West
Midland Villages, 1400–1540', in this volume.

[4] A classic example of the 'flexibility' of inheritance 'custom' is provided by C. C. Dyer,
'Changes in the Size of Peasant Holdings', p. 280.

to deploy land, once obtained, amongst family members in order to create household units. The study of the household remains dominated by stereotypes. A classic 'medieval' household is juxtaposed against an 'early modern' household. The former, extended in structure, is seen as enjoying an existence, maintained by tradition and custom, independent of changing economic, demographic and social circumstances.[5] The latter, nuclear in form, established at some stage in the sixteenth century, has been analysed much more fully in its social context.[6] It is thus one of the further objectives of this essay to explore the household arrangements of the late medieval villager and to see how they relate to the mechanisms utilized by him in the land market.

i

In order to examine the ways in which villagers utilized both the marital – inheritance mechanism, rooted in the exigencies of a rustic society lacking cash, and the commercial mechanism, available to those who took advantage of industrial and commercial employment opportunities, to participate in the late medieval land market, attention has been focused on two groups of villages.[7] The first encompasses the Derbyshire townships of Rowsley, Nether Haddon and Alport, situated between the rivers Derwent, Wye and Lathkill along with Stanton to the south and to the east, beyond the Derwent, Baslow, at the foot of the great gritstone edge towering over the river (Figure 5.1). The history of these communities was dominated during the years 1355–80 by the emergence of an important cloth making complex.[8] Employment in the production of coarse local weaves had

[5] R. H. Hilton, *The English Peasantry in the Later Middle Ages* (Oxford, 1975), pp. 28–30, 40, 50–1, 101, 106–9.

[6] On the late sixteenth-century household's size, see P. Laslett, 'Mean Household Size in England Since the Sixteenth Century', and R. Wall, 'Mean Household Size in England from Printed Sources', both in P. Laslett and R. Wall, editors, *Household and Family in Past Time* (Cambridge, 1972). On some aspects of household deployment strategies in late sixteenth-century rural society, see M. Spufford, *Contrasting Communities: English Villagers in the Sixteenth and Seventeenth Centuries* (Cambridge, 1974), Chapters 3–5, and 'Peasant Inheritance Customs and Land Distribution in Cambridgeshire from the Sixteenth to the Eighteenth Centuries', in Goody *et al.*, editors, *Family and Inheritance*, as well as C. Howell's study, 'Peasant Inheritance Customs in the Midlands, 1280–1700', in the same volume.

[7] On the sources utilized in the 'reconstitution' of these communities, see below, pp. 269–75.

[8] Because of the nature of its output the industry does not figure in the (reliable) aulnage accounts of Richard II's reign (PRO, E 101/346/9). The great weaving enterprises of Haddon, Baslow and Rowsley, like those at neighbouring Wirksworth,

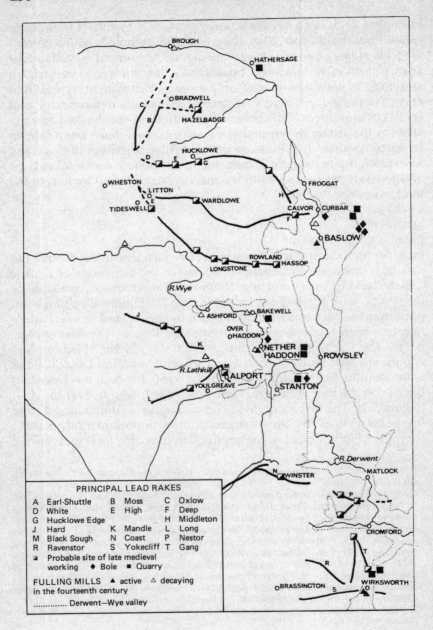

Figure 5.1. Derbyshire principal lead rakes

expanded rapidly in the manors of Baslow and Nether Haddon, providing the newly built or renovated fulling mills with a constant flow of work, until in the 1370s the industry, dominated by three large concerns with their attendant constellation of small enterprises and one-man businesses, provided wages for about a quarter of the village populations.[9] Nor were the other villages immune from this burgeoning growth. At Rowsley the immigrant enterpreneur Bartholomew the Tailor established during the years 1379–81 an enterprise which provided direct employment for almost one-third of the villagers.[10] Meteoric in its rise, the rumbustious, not to say on occasion tempestuous, community of cloth workers collapsed almost as rapidly as it had emerged.[11] From about 1380 numbers employed dwindled and the fulling mills, which had seemed such promising investments, fell into decay.[12] The village economies, with the passing of this burgeoning but ephemeral growth, were not, however, denuded of industrial activity; rather the more permanent

worked to the direct order of the customer, weaving the wollen and linen thread that was delivered to them and returning the finished product direct to the customer, who subsequently put out the woven clothe to a fuller and finally had the finished wares made up by a tailor (see, e.g., PRO, DL 30/45/522, court of 7.12.1372 and manuscripts of his Grace the Duke of Rutland, Belvoir (henceforth Rutland MSS), court at Haddon of 27.3.1359). A later document (Bodleian, MSS D.D. Weld C19/4/2.4) illustrates the whole system at work. By this date, however, the position of the 'contract weaver' had been seriously eroded by competition, as cloth from Yorkshire and from the locally important urban industries of Nottingham, Derby and Chesterfield flooded the markets of north Derbyshire.

[9] In the early fourteenth century fulling mills, operating on the basis of seigneurial monopolies, were situated on all of the major rivers of north Derbyshire – on the Dove at Hartington, the Wye at Tideswell, Ashford, Bakewell and Haddon, on the Lathkill at Conkesbury and on the Derwent at Brough and Bubnall; all declined steadily during the 150 years after 1300 (see I. Blanchard, 'Economic Change in Derbyshire in the Late Middle Ages, 1272–1540', unpublished University of London Ph.D. thesis, 1967, pp. 372–81, where the question of the 'contract weaving system' described above is not dealt with) and a number, including that at Haddon, had already been extinguished by 1340. The 1350s, however, witnessed the foundation of new mills (which were let at enormously higher rentals than the previous 'seigneurial' ones and provided the facilities required by the 'contract weaving system') at Haddon and Baslow (Rutland MSS courts at Baslow of 7.5.1354 and 30.11.1364 and court at Haddon of 20.10.1372). On the structure of the 3 great weaving enterprises employing more than 4 full-time 'servants', see PRO, E 179/242/10. Of these enterprises, 2 were headed by women – Agnes Webster and Agnes de Sheldon – whilst the largest was the preserve of one Richard de Darley.

[10] The story of Bartholomew the Tailor's career is derived from the reconstitutions referred to above, and the structure of his enterprise may be discerned in PRO, E 179/242/10.

[11] Those engaged in the cloth industry attracted a higher proportion of presentments in the manorial courts than other inhabitants of the villages.

[12] On the fortunes of the Haddon mill see Rutland MSS, account nos. 1091, 1103, 1012–25, 1092, 1027, 1032–4.

though diverse structural elements, previously overlain by the emergent cloth industry, were revealed.

Paramount amongst these were the elements which made up the mining and metallurgical complex, of which lead mining is perhaps the best known. This once important Derbyshire industry was, however, during the fourteenth and early fifteenth centuries, in the final stages of decay. Successive production cycles had left output at progressively lower and lower levels until, at the peak of the post-plague boom in the 1380s, it was but a fraction of that attained during the industry's hey-day two hundred years before.[13] Yet paradoxically, amidst this general decay, those miners who worked in the extra-forest jurisdictions of the High Peak at this time enjoyed a relative importance within the Derbyshire industry to which they had never previously aspired.[14] As the foci of production shifted away from the old fourteenth-century centres of Hucklowe and Winster, new centres emerged, and the mines north of the Wye, within the Peak jurisdiction of the Dean and Chapter of Lichfield, became, in spite of a somewhat chequered history, the premier producers in the county, engrossing in excess of 50 per cent of output.[15] A major industrial metamorphosis was taking place in the High Peak, and, whilst production within the Duchy of Lancaster mines on the High Rake declined in spite of the progressive extension of working into the Deep Rake, activity further south, within the lordships of Longstone, Rowland, Hassop and Ashford, was intense, albeit the path followed was one of recovery rather than of growth.[16] During the 1430s and 1440s, when production was about 200–300 tons of ore annually, the workings were packed with the local tenantry, some 450–600 of whom passed each summer working in the shallow pits or 'meres'.[17] Whilst the inhabitants of the plateau were thus held in the

---

[13] I. Blanchard, 'Derbyshire Lead Production, 1195–1505', *Derbyshire Archaeological Journal* 91 (1971), pp. 125–7, 129.

[14] *Ibid*. Table 2, p. 127.   [15] *Ibid*., pp. 127–8.

[16] In the course of the fourteenth century the focus of production within the Peak Forest had shifted from the northern branch of the High Rake about Hucklowe to the southern member of the same vein, thereby establishing the supremacy of Tideswell and Wardlowe in the 'King's Field'. From Richard II's reign, however, production declined, and even the extension of working to the extra-forestial jurisdiction of Calvor, on the Deep Rake, where ore production of about 20 tons per annum in the 1430s was not sufficient to prevent overall decline. Production had shifted southwards, where the post-plague recovery carried the Ashford mines to supremacy. In the 1430s they engrossed about 80% of total production and only ceded their dominant position in the 1440s to the workings of 'Cheprak' in Hassop (I. Blanchard, 'Derbyshire Lead Production', pp. 132–4).

[17] On production, see I. Blanchard, 'Stannator Fabulosus', *Agricultural History Review* 22:1 (1974), p. 64 note 1; and, on productivity, I. Blanchard, 'Labour Productivity

grip of mining fever, however, those who lived within the fork of Derwent and Wye were not. Few if any of the villagers of Alport or Rowsley, Haddon or Baslow sought to make their fortunes in the speculative activity which pervaded the northern mines.[18] Insofar as they were connected with lead mining at all, families like the Fichelers or Hublyns obtained their cash by excavating the ores of the Long and Mandel Rakes or the Black Sough, in mines where production, in spite of short-term upswings in the 1370s and 1420s, was set on the path of long-term decline.[19] Yet, if the inhabitants of the Vernon and Basset fees did not participate directly in the mining boom of the early fifteenth century, they did benefit indirectly from it, as smelting establishments were founded on the gritstone edges at Haddon, Baslow and Darley to reduce the ores from both the new mining area and the older declining centres to north and south.[20] Each autumn a flurry of activity heralded the arrival of the ore, as carts trundled back and forth and men cut and carted the brushwood required to fuel the 'boles', but employment opportunities afforded by such work were slight and the real rewards went elsewhere, as the highly paid 'bolers' and their assistants were recruited from outside the lordship.[21] Lead mining, which thus figured importantly in the economy of the region as a whole, was of but scant significance to the inhabitants of the villages with which we are concerned. Employment in smelting was small. It was, however, more stable than that deriving from mining. During the late fourteenth century, whilst the Duchy mines on the High Rake still retained some importance in the

and Work Psychology in the English Mining Industry 1400–1600', *Economic History Review*, 2nd series 31:1 (1978), pp. 1–24.

[18] The Vernons engrossed about one-third of the output of the northerly rakes, yet amongst their mining accounts there is no mention of their tenants supplying lead ore from thence.

[19] The only inhabitants engaged in lead mining, the Fichelers, Baystowes, Hublyns and Bargons, lived in or adjacent to Alport, where the Black Sough provided a focus for their work. With the collapse of mining activity therein they emigrated from the village, settling during the late 1420s in nearby Rowsley. Henceforth the area was devoid of lead mining activity until the 1490s when workmen, prospecting the Mandel Rake, ventured into Over Haddon. On this latter episode, see the evidence of John Weyne printed in I. Blanchard, *The Duchy of Lancaster's Estates in Derbyshire, 1485–1540*, Derbyshire Archeological Society, Record Series iii (Derby 1967), Doc. A5, p. 34.

[20] See Figure 5.1.

[21] Two men were normally sufficient to carry the ore to five 'boles' and to undertake the necessary carting work at the smelt. The necessary wood could be cut by one, whilst another could undertake the carting of the brushwood. It is accordingly unlikely that the establishment of smelting at Haddon and Darley created more than 3 or 4 jobs or that the incremental gains within the lordship were, in the years after 1380, of any importance, the gains at Haddon being offset by decline at Baslow.

lead mining economy of the High Peak, Baslow smelters, operating on the basis of a six-mile exploitative circle, held a dominant position in the area. The ten 'boles' being worked within the manor during the 1390s probably processed about 90 per cent of total output.[22] The subsequent shift in production southward, however, undermined the hegemony of the Baslow men. By 1430 competition became intense as the new production centre was brought within the ambit of smelting establishments founded on the southerly edges of the area, at Haddon and Darley.[23] Yet, whilst a rationalization was enforced on industrial capacity at Baslow, total employment opportunities from smelting were maintained within the lordship through new growth at Haddon – at least until 1450 when the collapse of the Ashford–Hassop workings seemed to threaten the whole edifice.[24] It was not to be. The ability of smelters to extend their supply networks from a six- to an eight-mile radius, due to a fall in unit transport costs, allowed them to re-orientate their networks to engross the ores of the newly emergent production centres of the late fifteenth and early sixteenth centuries.[25] Thus from the 1460s the 'bolers' of Baslow and Holmesfield increasingly drew upon the ores of the Earl and Shuttle rakes about Hazelbadge, whilst their counterparts at Haddon utilized ores excavated at Brassington and Matlock, important centres on the newly exploited Nestor and Ravenstor veins.[26] Lead mining accordingly did little, either directly or indirectly, to fill the void created by the collapse of cloth manufacturing after 1380; its contribution was

[22] Rutland MSS, court at Baslow, 29.9.1393; and, on the capacity of 'boles', I. Blanchard, 'Derbyshire Lead Production', p. 130 note 25.

[23] Rutland MSS, account nos. 1012–13, 1015–16; Sheffield City Library, MS Bagshawe 339, court of Darley of 20.10.1434.

[24] On the decay of capacity at Baslow and new growth at Haddon, see Rutland MSS, account nos. 1012–16, 1034.

[25] The question of transport improvements and their effects on fifteenth-century mining and smelting is briefly dealt with in I. Blanchard, 'Resource Depletion in Historical Perspective: The European Mining and Metallurgical Industries, 1400–1800', paper presented at the conference on 'Resources in Economic History', held at Bellagio 12–18 April 1977.

[26] On the renovation of four 'boles' at Baslow in the early 1460s, see Rutland MSS, account no. 1034. From 1467 until 1484 there were in addition to the seigneurial 'boles' two private ones operating in the lordship (ibid., nos. 1045–52). In the 1480s, however, these private establishments at Lambartlowe were abandoned, and new works, comprising two boles and adjacent 'blackwork ovens', were founded at Hewood Hill within the Lovell manor of Holmesfield (ibid., no. 1052 passim, and court at Holmesfield 28.5.1505). From 1467 these establishments drew their ore predominantly from Hazelbadge (ibid., no 1035). At Haddon reorientation towards southern supplies from Matlock began in the 1430s and was subsequently extended to Brassington, thereby establishing the broader supply network which persisted into the next century (ibid., nos. 1012–18, 1025, 1035).

rather in providing a small but permanent number of job opportunities for the villagers.

Such was also the major characteristic of the other extractive industry of the area, quarrying – if such a conglomeration of diverse activities and products may be called an industry. Plaster and lime burning; alabaster manufacture; the production of building stones including slates, free stone, cob-stone and crest-stones; millstone and grindstone production: all were engrossed under the one generic term, describing an industry which displayed marked characteristics of regional specialization. In the south of the county the working of limestones predominated. In the north the gritstones were excavated, either on the moorland wastes or from the great cavities opened up on the edges bordering the Derwent.[27] Within the villages with which we are concerned it was this latter class of quarrying that was of importance. Apart from the production of slates at Catton, quarrying activity may be divided into two groups.[28] The first, encompassing the production of grind- or 'grindle' stones, was located on the moorlands above Rowsley, Stanton and Baslow, where production, as further south in the Longridge quarries at Wirksworth, expanded rapidly from 1380 to 1470, before declining thereafter.[29] The second, located on the gritstone edges, involved the manufacture of millstones. Subject to a slow process of decline during the fifteenth century, this sector of the industry was, north of the Wye, dominated by the great workings at Baslow, whence, in the 1420s, stones were exported to three counties as well as supplying a major part of the Derbyshire market north of the Trent.[30] Indeed, the supremacy of the Baslow quarrymen was such that, even when their own workings were subject to major dislocations during the years 1430–65, they continued to dominate the economies of the new quarries which were opened up in that period, like the Ernecliff quarry at Hathersage, which supplied 90 per cent of its output to Baslow quarrymen in the

[27] I. Blanchard, *Economic Change*, pp. 368–76.

[28] On the Catton slate quarry, see Rutland MSS, court at Bakewell of 28.10.1466.

[29] The production of grindstones at Rowsley and Stanton was largely in the hands of 3 families – the Ashbournes (1420–80), Websters (1420–70) and Halleys (1430–80) – with others like the Lindrops and Aspinalls engaging in the industry in the 1460s and 1470s, when working was also extended to Baslow. Rutland MSS, account nos. 1091, 1021, courts of Haddon 1468–80, court at Baslow of 29.5.1472; Sheffield City Library, MS Bagshawe 339; John Rylands Library, Manchester, MS Crutchley 86. On the fortunes of the Longridge quarry see I. Blanchard, *Economic Change*, Figure 15, p. 370.

[30] On the fortunes of the Baslow quarries, see Rutland MSS, courts at Baslow of 26.10.1356, 26.4.1385, 10.4.1485 and accounts nos. 1095, 1012–13, 1015–18, 1032, 1034–79. Of particular interest is the improver's account of 1427–8.

early 1460s.[31] Yet once again, even in this sector of the industry which was of some importance in intra-regional trade, employment opportunities were few.[32] Taken as a whole, quarrying, even at the height of the boom in grindstone production, probably provided work for no more than fifteen, or about the same number as found employment at Bubnall, manufacturing ironwares.[33] The incremental gains to employment provided by the mining and metallurgical complex were smaller still, in no way compensating for the collapse of cloth manufacturing.

Less spectacular, perhaps, but more important, were those activities related to the agrarian base of society. Opportunities for wage labouring in agriculture were plentiful, and references to the agrarian trades are legion, but few of these activities seem to have expanded after 1380.[34] Only the exploitation of the rivers, which abounded with trout and other species of fish including the mysterious 'keper', stands out as a growth sector in the traditional economy.[35] Initially, during the 1370s, fishing had been of but small import, providing a cash income for only two families, the Fishers of Rowsley and Alport, who deployed their nets in the Wye, Derwent and Lathkill, and the Ruyleys, who worked the stretch of the Derwent within the manor of Baslow.[36] Numbers employed, however, gradually increased over the years 1380–1520. By the late 1460s there were three families at

---

[31] During the struggles between the Vernons and Talbots production at Baslow was brought to a halt as outsiders occupied and plundered the workings. On the operations of the Hathersage quarry, see Bodleian, MSS D. D. Weld C19/4/1 fos. 1–4ᵛ, c19/4/2, fos. 12ᵛ, 16ᵛ, c19/4/3, fo. 6ᵛ; John Rylands Library, Manchester, MS Crutchley 234.

[32] After the 'times of the troubles' production was organized on the basis of hereditary familial exploitation rights, whereby 5 families paid 10s 8d (from 1467 to 1468 13s 4d) and a millstone for a hereditary right, known as a 'pick', to work in the quarry. Rutland MSS, account nos. 1034–5 and court at Baslow of 10.4.1485.

[33] Apart from the 5 workmen at Baslow in the 1470s there were the Ashbournes (4 persons), Halleys (3 persons), Webster (1) and 2 others working at Rowsley and Stanton.

[34] In most years of the fifteenth century the great Vernon sheep run provided employment for about a dozen men, fencing, shearing, hay making and cutting holly for winter feed, as well as working about the buildings. It is debatable, however, if this compensated for the decline in employment amongst the peasantry with the demise of grain marketing by that group. On the servants employed by the greater peasantry in the 1370s, numbering about 20 in all, see PRO, E 179/242/10; and, on the decline of the local grain trade after 1380, BL, MS Harley 4799, fo. 73ᵛ; Rutland MSS, account nos. 1047, 1067, 1069–70, 1073, 1076–7, 1079, 1082. There are also indications of decay in such activities as milling and tanning: Rutland MSS, account nos. 1035–6 and court at Baslow of 19.11.1467.

[35] On the species of fish, Rutland MSS, courts at Haddon of 23.12.1449 and 15.12.1461.

[36] Rutland MSS, courts at Haddon of 7.10.1396 and at Baslow of 13.4.1356, 29.11.1374, 2.5.1397: account no. 1091.

Haddon and a similar number at Baslow using 'angilyards' and lances in the local waters, and with the systematic deployment of fish traps in every river and stream at the end of the century, fishing provided work for about twelve families.[37] The story thus repeats itself once again with growth, but of modest proportions. Thus, within the first group of villages with which we are concerned, the collapse of cloth production in the 1380s heralded, in spite of some growth in the traditional sector, the beginning of a process of de-industrialization.

The second group of villages lay far to the south, on the Mendip hills in Somerset, where the inhabitants garnered a cash income predominantly from animal husbandry and mining. The basis for this latter activity was the lodes and veins of galena ore, coursing in two main rakes east–west through the carboniferous limestone of 'the Hill' (Figure 5.2). These rakes were highly fragmented, due to major structural displacements, and this characteristic endowed the lead industry with a high degree of geographical mobility and ensure a spacial discontinuity in mining activity.[38] Thus, as production cycles followed each other, at about the same periodicity as in Derbyshire, the industry was subject to a constant process of relocation.[39] This process, in the late fourteenth century, established production on the southerly branch of the main rake, where new workings were opened up within the Hospitallers' lands at Temple Hydon and in the adjacent property of Richard Cheddar at Ubley.[40] Here output expanded rapidly in the years to the late 1380s, when production reached about 140 tons a year. Thereafter decline set in, alleviated only by ephemeral growth elsewhere.[41] During the 1410s the old 'forester's mine', a relic of the late twelfth-century workings on Mendip, passed into the Crown's hands during the minority of Edmund Mortimer, and on 3 February 1418 letters patent were issued empowering John Bays and William Milward junior to re-open the

---

[37] By 1500 there were fish traps with associated weirs and leaps in the Derwent at Froggat, Curbar, Wollshaw, Bubnall, Baslow and below Hellcarre; in the Wye at Stanton and in Baslow, Bere and Umberley brooks. Rutland MSS, courts at Baslow of 14.10.1483, and of 1499–1500 and at Haddon on 5.5.1501.

[38] H. Dewey, *Lead, Silver Lead and Zinc Ores of Cornwall, Devon and Somerset*, Memoirs of the Geological Survey of England and Wales (1921).

[39] Production on Mendip followed the same course of 'A' cycles found in Derbyshire (No. 1 peak 1190–trough 1245–peak 1290. No. 2 trough 1345–peak 1390). On production patterns and nomenclature see *Derbyshire Archaeological Journal* 91 (1971), pp. 125–9.

[40] Winchester College, Longload 12864 (5); Somerset County Record Office, Taunton (hereafter SRO), DD/S/HY B2 and A1 mm. 1–2, 6–8; L. B. Larking, editor, *The Knights Hospitallers in England*, Camden Society, old series lxv (London, 1857).

[41] SRO, DD/S/HY B4–5, 6 mm. 1–8, B7–8, A2.

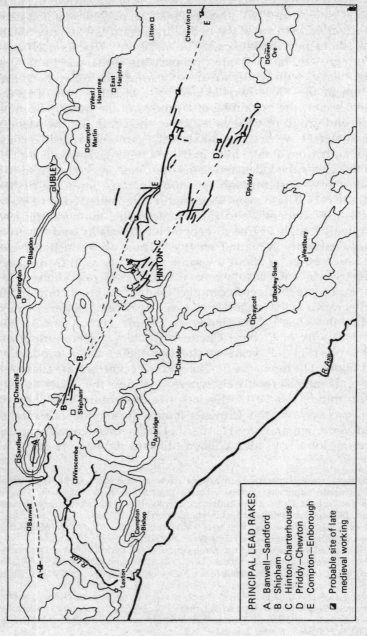

Figure 5.2. Mendip principal lead rakes

PRINCIPAL LEAD RAKES

A   Banwell–Sandford
B   Shipham
C   Hinton Charterhouse
D   Priddy–Chewton
E   Compton–Enborough

▨   Probable site of late
    medieval working

derelict workings. However, political good fortune was not enough when confronted with unfavourable economic circumstances and a mineralogy of low-grade galenas in highly fragmented veins. Having extracted during the summer only enough ore to produce some nineteen hundredweights of lead, the lessees decided to abandon the unfruitful work.[42] Equally ephemeral were the workings which grew up on the basis of a rich find far to the west, within Banwell parish, during the 1430s.[43] Banwell was included in the Bishop of Bath and Wells' north-western manorial complex, separated from the main mining area by the Lox Yeo valley, where the river flowed from above Winscombe to join the Axe.[44] Here miners working Banwell Hill at Dalby, near 'the Caves', discovered the rick pocket of ore which provided the basis for the industrial complex which grew up here in the 1430s but which soon disappeared. All that remained, therefore, in 1445 from the industrial relocations which had accompanied the production cycle of the previous century were the shattered remnants of the late fourteenth-century growth centres – Hinton alias Hydon and Ubley.[45]

From about 1445, when the upswing of the next production cycle ushered in a period of recovery within the industry, relocation pushed the focus of mining further and further eastwards, thereby integrating the industry into a whole string of villages stretching from Hinton Charterhouse in an arc to Priddy above Wells. During the years 1445–61, as Ubley's production returned to the level of the 1430s, workmen started to exploit the deposits at Priddy and Compton.[46] Thereafter, following a brief lull, production expanded in all three centres to the turn of the century. By 1500, however, those centres, Ubley and Hinton, which had been in the vanguard of the

---

[42] J. W. Gough, *The Mines of Mendip* (Oxford, 1930) pp. 58–9. On the properties comprising the forestership, see PRO, SC 6/972/28; and, for its early history, E. T. MacDermott, *History of the Forest of Exmoor* (Taunton, 1911) pp. 107–74, 441–2. The descent of the property from the de Wrothams until it finally came into Mortimer hands during 1359 is traced by R. Krauss, 'Chaucerain Problems: Especially the Petherton Forestership and the question of Thomas Chaucer', in *Three Chaucer Studies* (New York, 1932) pp. 60–9. It is perhaps worthy of note that the phrase used in the letters patent of 1418 is the same as the heading in the Mortimer accounts: PRO, SC 6/1113/1, 11: 972/28.

[43] Lambeth Palace ED 1187–9, 222–3; Bodleian, Somerset Rolls 4–5.

[44] On the administrative structure of the episcopal estates, see R. W. Dunning, 'The Administration of the Diocese of Bath and Wells 1401–1491', unpublished University of Bristol Ph.D. thesis, 1963; and P. M. Hembry, *The Bishops of Bath and Wells 1540–1640*, University of London Historical Studies xx (London, 1967).

[45] When production amounted to about 10 tons of ore each year (SRO, DD/S/HY B7).

[46] When production started at Priddy we cannot be sure but the earliest reference dates from 1457–8 and it seems probable that mining had commenced within the preceding decade: Dean and Chapter of Wells, unnumbered account of 1457–8.

advance a century earlier, were long past their peak. Priddy now reigned supreme.[47] It was not long, however, before even this centre was eclipsed. When records again begin in 1525 the industry was depressed, but with the subsequent expansionary phase from 1531 to 1535 a whole series of new centres was integrated into the arc of mining villages. During the years 1525–31 the Chewton rakes were discovered, and from 1532–5 workings were established within Enborough, Litton and Harptree parishes.[48] By 1536, therefore, the workings had assumed the form made familiar by Elizabethan mining maps, stretching fan-like along the northern edge of Mendip, with particular concentrations about four geological complexes forming the natural foci for the administrative division which evolved during the years 1540–57.[49] In the west lay the late fourteenth-century workings at Ubley and Temple Hydon alias Hinton which, when coupled with the mid-fifteenth-century growth centre at Compton Martin, formed the administrative unit, the West Minery. Moving east-ward along the northerly rake, one comes to the second concentra-tion – East Harptree, Litton and Enborough – which formed the East or Harptree Minery. If one swings south, the two largest groups within the sixteenth-century workings follow next in sequence. First one comes to Chewton Minery, founded in the second quarter of the sixteenth century, and then, passing eastward along the southern rake, one comes to that minery established in the mid-fifteenth century within Chewton and Wells lordships – Priddy. Such was the form that the Mendip field had assumed by 1540, the product of a gradual locational migration which only assumed a stable morpho-logy at that date. That same migration, however, whilst promoting growth in the eastern mineries, had doomed the western workings, with which we are concerned in this study, to decay. Yet, paradox-ically, the growth of lead production in centres like Chewton also provided the solution to the problems which beset the West Minery after the 1380s, encouraging secondary growth in the ancillary timber industry and trades.[50] Accordingly the two groups of villages with which we are concerned afford a striking contrast to each other. Both

---

[47] SRO, DD/S/HY B8–9, B10 mm. 1–2, 6–7, 9, 11, 13; A3 mm. 1–4, A4–9; Dean and Chapter of Wells, unnumbered accounts 1457–8, *passim*; SRO, DD/SAS BA3; Gough, *Mines of Mendip*, pp. 59–60.

[48] On mining activity within each of these localities in 1536, see SRO, C924/DD/WG 16/3; and, on the economies of these manors during the first quarter of the sixteenth century, see PRO, E 315/385, and Bodleian, Somerset Rolls 7.

[49] Gough, *Mines of Mendip*, frontispiece.

[50] On the development of the timber trades from the 1440s, see, for instance, SRO, DD/S/HY B8 court at Ubley of 24.4.1448, B9 court of 19.10.1452, B10 courts of 6.4.1456 and 6.4.1463, B12 court of 28.5.1492. B14 court of 24.8.1524.

were heavily industrialized in the 1370s; but, whilst in Derbyshire the communities were subsequently subject to a process of de-industrialization, on Mendip the story is one of stabilization and growth in industrial employment. The dynamics of cash flow were thus quite different in the two communities over the period 1380–1520. We may now turn to see how this affected the mechanisms utilized by the villagers in their land market operations.

ii

Throughout the period under consideration a basic dualism characterized the mechanisms utilized by the Somerset and Derbyshire villagers in their land market operations. Amongst those families who obtained a livelihood solely from agricultural pursuits the mechanism assumed what may be described as a 'defensive' character. In family after family throughout the period 1380–1520, as cross-sectional analyses reveal, the dominant mechanism and associated market strategy was a 'defensive' one, which evolved at two levels.[51] The first, displayed in familial land transactions recorded on the court rolls, represents the primary stage of defensive action, which, whilst allowing the release of land to family members in *pre-* or *post-mortem* arrangements based on marriage or inheritance, was aimed at the preservation of the integrity of the family holding. A cohesive family living on an inviolable holding was the *leit motiv* pervading all such transactions.[52] Thus, whilst land might be deployed within the kin network, the mechanism incorporated safeguards to prevent permanent alienation, for example through second marriages of wives or daughters-in-law. Whilst such methods preserved the integrity of the family holding, however, they provided little flexibility for short-term adjustments in line with the constantly changing land–labour balance within the family unit.[53] It is at this point that the second level of

[51] See Appendix, Tables 5.1–5.4. The data embodied therein, which provide the basis for the following analysis, are derived from the 'reconstitution' of each and every family within the village communities, whose history forms the basis of a biography which includes information on land market operations such as that illustrated in Figures 5.3–5.4. On the method of 'reconstitution', see below, pp. 269–71. Rather than cite the source of each piece of information contained in the biographies, throughout the remainder of this essay the reader is referred to the above descriptions of methodology.

[52] 'Cohesive' is used here to refer to the close kin links existing in those families utilizing the 'defensive' mechanism.

[53] On the concept of the familial land–labour balance, see A. V. Chayanov, *Organizatriya krest'yankogo khozyaistva*, translated by R. E. F. Smith, in D. Thorner *et al.*, editors, *A. V. Chayanov on the Theory of Peasant Economy* (Homewood, Ill., 1966) pp. 53–69; and the critique of M. Harrison, 'Chayanov and the Economics of the Russian Peasantry', *Journal of Peasant Studies* 2:4 (1975), pp. 392–412.

'defensive' action, revealed not in formalized written agreements but in the behavioural patterns of those sharing a common 'group affinity', becomes important.[54] Its objective was the externalization of the tensions inherent in familial evolution: the elimination of super-fluities of land during phases in the family's history when the young enjoyed a numerically dominant position, and the relief of tensions when land was required to provide a livelihood for an important group of adolescents. Its form was embodied not in written arrange-ments but in a complex of 'reversionary rights' retained in the 'collective memory' of the villagers. Alienations which superficially appear as 'non-family' transactions, antithetical to the preservation of the family holding, when viewed in the context of 'group behaviour', operating on the basis of the second level of 'defensive action', often assume a different character; for, in spite of the passage of such land through as many as three or four non-family hands, there was a marked tendency for it ultimately to revert into the possession of either the original family who had alienated it or their 'successor' in the land market.[55] The second level of 'defensive action', revealed in the land dealings of the agricultural families, thus reinforced the first, allowing these families to shed superfluous land by 'temporary alienations' and then to resume it when required through the exercise of their 'reversionary rights', without at any stage having to resort to the commercial land market. For those families without access to the cash flows generated by industrial activity, therefore, a mechanism existed which permitted them both to dissipate short-term familial tensions caused by ephemeral land–labour disequilibria and to pre-serve the long-term integrity of their holding. Indeed, the all-pervasive influence of the 'defensive' mechanism was such that, in spite of an intermittent process of restructuring in the land market, particularly concentrated in the years 1383–5, 1427–32, 1459–62 and 1514–18,[56] many holdings survived the demise of one family and the

---

[54] A preliminary report on the nature of 'group affinity' was presented at St Andrews in the spring of 1977. I should like to thank Dr Keith Wrightson for his invitation to participate in the seminar and all those present for their helpful comments.

[55] I hope to discuss the process of 'structural change' in the land market on a future occasion.

[56] Restructuring, occasioned by periods of demographic upheaval, is also revealed in the studies of C. Howell of Kibworth Harcourt. See her 'Peasant Inheritance Customs in the Midlands, 1280–1700', in Goody et al., editors, Family and Inheritance, pp. 123–5, revealing intense activity in the land market during the years 1412–40 and 1500–27. Unfortunately, because Figure 1 (ibid, p. 124, also reproduced as Figure 4 on p. 481 of her 'Stability and Change 1300–1700: The Socio-Economic Context of the Self Perpetuating Family Farm in England', Journal of Peasant Studies 2:4 (1975), pp. 468–82) is based upon rental evidence, it is impossible to be more specific about timing.

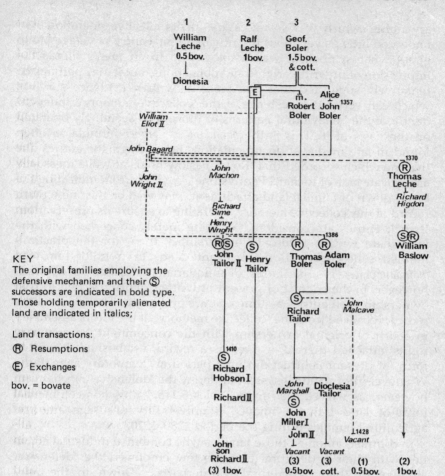

Figure 5.3. Defensive strategy: the Boler–Leches of Baslow

emergence of a successor to enjoy a continuity of existence which might go beyond the period of this study.[57]

Whilst the 'defensive' mechanism may be observed, however, it is more difficult to see how the families involved maintained, in the absence of written agreements, the 'collective memory' of 'reversion-

[57] In spite of such periods of restructuring, many holdings enjoyed an incredible continuity of existence. At Baslow, for instance, of 22 holdings in existence in 1520, 13 had retained their form throughout the previous 165 years, another 5 had existed for 120–150 years, whilst the remaining 4 may be traced back 75–95 years. For an example of one such holding, illustrating both the process of 'temporary alienation' and the long-term continuity of its existence, see Figure 5.3.

ary rights' which was so necessary for its effective operation. We know too little as yet about the ritual and pageantry of village life to guess what symbolism was employed to fix in men's minds the impression of unwritten rights and obligations, but it may perhaps be tentatively suggested that one piece of written evidence survives which can verify the existence of the 'collective memory', independently of the behavioural patterns of those who seemingly operated on the basis of it. This is the *quondam . . . nuper* formula so often found in late medieval documentation. Brief, enigmatic entries like the one which recorded that 'Roger Baslow holds at will a messuage and bovate *once* of Richard Pennystone . . .',[58] far from indicating the break-down of familial land attachment, may well be the one written record of the 'collective memory' operating to ensure its preservation. If such entries are considered as being merely concerned with the immediate written record of ownership,[59] then, for the practical-minded seneschal with the relevant deeds in front of him, the *quondam* clause is superfluous, of antiquarian interest only.[60] Viewed, however, in the context of present unwritten rights attached to past ownership such entries assume a new significance. They became the record, retrieved from the 'collective memory' of the jurors assembled in court, of original ownership with the concomitant 'reversionary rights' attached thereto, as well as a record, established in written form, of present usufruct during a period of 'temporary alienation'. Whatever informational system underlay the 'defensive' mechanism, however, as will be seen from Tables 5.1–5.4, this non-commercial form of land transfer enjoyed a universality of usage amongst agricultural families during the period 1380–1520.[61]

In contrast, amongst those families who combined industrial activities with their agricultural pursuits few employed the 'defensive' strategy of their agricultural counterparts.[62] Down to the mid-

[58] Rutland MSS., court at Baslow of 25.7.1460.
[59] As suggested by Dr R. J. Faith, 'Peasant Families and Inheritance Customs' *Agricultural History Review* 14:2 (1966), p. 89, and by C. Dyer, 'Changes in the Size of Peasant Holdings', in this volume, p. 286. Both authors provide examples of the *quondam . . . nuper* formula.
[60] On the procedures involved in making the rental, see E. Kerridge, *Some Agrarian Problems of the Sixteenth Century and After* (London, 1969).
[61] Amongst agricultural families the numbers employing the 'defensive mechanism' varied slightly: 1363 79–91%, 1381 71–82%, 1445 95–100%, 1520 60–85%. Of the residual families employing an 'aggressive strategy', in almost all cases in the fourteenth century sons buying land had obtained the necessary cash from employment in the holdings of the greater tenantry who probably market grain. In 1520 the source of cash for families like the Shepherds of Ubley, who pursued an 'aggressive' policy, seems to have been employment on large pastoral 'farms'.
[62] On the nature of industrial activity, see I. Blanchard. 'The Miner and the Agri-

fifteenth century less than one in five families could, via the process of restructuring, establish itself with sufficient permanency in the agriculturally dominated land market to operate on the basis of a 'defensive' mechanism or a 'hybrid' variant of it.[63] Thereafter, in the villages of Baslow and Ubley, 'group' realignment allowed the proportion to increase, but as late as 1520 less than half of the industrial families were utilizing any variant of the 'defensive' mechanism.[64] Accordingly, throughout the period under consideration, the great majority of 'industrials' had to acquire land to satisfy their familial requirements as it was made available to them by the temporary alienations of the 'agriculturalists', utilizing the cash generated by their industrial work to make predatory forays into the market in order to seize opportunities whenever and wherever they occurred. A quite distinctive life-style thus emerged amongst 'industrials', affording a marked contrast to that of their 'agricultural' counterparts. Amongst these families, until their assimilation into the pre-existing market structure, attachment to land was slight. With the cash available from their industrial activity those involved developed an 'aggressive' or predatory strategy, taking up land by purchase when required and equally rapidly alienating it when it was superfluous to their needs.[65] Moreover, amongst 'industrials' expectations of land acquisition were slight and ephemeral. Their children lacked that assurance of obtaining a holding which was the birth right of the *pueri rustici*. Only if they could acquire cash had they any hope of such an acquisition. Thus from an early age such children may be discerned working on the looms, fishing the rivers or excavating ore in the mines of their father or his associates, either in the village of

---

cultural Community in Late Medieval England' *Agricultural History Review*, 20:2 (1972), pp. 93–106, and 'Stannator Fabulosus', pp. 62–74.

[63] For the 'industrial' the process of restructuring involved abandonment of a land market strategy based upon the acquisition of land held on the basis of temporary alienation and assimilation into the pre-existing system of 'defensive' mechanisms, as a 'successor' to one of the established families. As indicated in note 55 above I hope to discuss in a later study the process by which 'successor' status might be achieved and the effects that changes in the personnel, operating the 'defensive' mechanisms, might have on the networks based upon 'group affinity'.

[64] See Appendix, Tables 5.1–5.4 below. In 1363 22% of industrial families employed a market strategy involving some 'defensive elements'. Thereafter the proportions were: 1381 11%, 1445 22% and 1520 48%.

[65] Amongst transactions involving 'industrial' families by far the largest number took place between members of the same group. Indeed, it was not uncommon for a piece of land, temporarily alienated from an agricultural patrimony, to pass through the hands of 3 or 4 industrial families before being resumed. The occasions of such inter-industrial family transfers seem to be related to the exigencies of their respective family cycles.

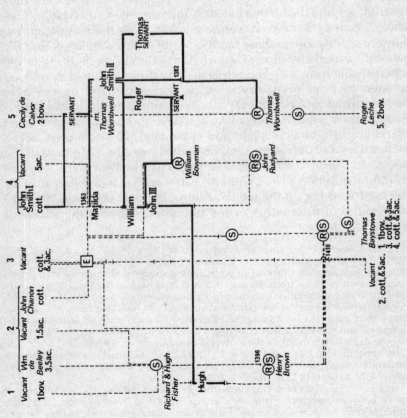

KEY

The families employing the
defensive mechanism in
relation to holdings at Haddon
(1–4) and Baslow (5) are
indicated in italics

Symbols are as for Figure 5.3

The pattern of land and work
acquisition of the Smiths is
indicated by a heavy line

Figure 5.4. Aggressive strategy: the Smiths of Haddon

their birth or in alien settlements where work opportunities existed, gradually amassing that wealth which would allow them to pursue an 'aggressive' policy in the land market in order to buy those rights of usufruct in land which would ensure them a stable livelihood.[66] Aggressiveness and insecurity thus characterized the life of the 'industrial' members of these communities in contrast to the 'agricultural' members, whose destiny was mapped out from birth. Yet, though so different in character, the two groups and the mechanisms they deployed in the land market existed in a symbiotic relationship, for the industrial family perforce had to operate in a market where supply was determined by the availability of land temporarily alienated by the 'defensive' mechanisms of the 'agriculturalists'.[67]

The structure of the village land market thus evolved during the years 1380–1520, and perhaps beyond, within the framework of a series of mechanisms deriving their probity from a bi-partite 'system of law' encompassed within the manorial court. The first element in that system, which gave birth to the basic mechanisms, emanated from the guardians of village custom – the jurors – whose utterances in court provided the basic legal framework of 'customary law'. The second element, administered by a steward and recorded by his clerks, merely interpreted in the context of common law precedent and detailed in terms of contemporary legal formulas those aspect of the court's deliberations which were, usually for fiscal reasons, of concern to the lord. Together these elements, discernible both in the written records of the court and in the behavioural patterns of those who participated in its processes, shaped the mechanisms utilized by the peasantry in the land market, amongst which the 'defensive' mechanism of the 'agriculturalists' enjoyed a position of primacy. This mechanism evolved to ensure the integrity of the agricultural family's holding, whilst at the same time providing a flexibility, through temporary alienations, which allowed short-term adjustments to be made in accord with the exigencies of that family's life-cycle. Village land, which was the sole preserve of the 'agriculturalists', was thus either maintained in hand by them or was temporarily alienated, thereby becoming the object of the 'aggressive' strategies of the 'industrials'. The extent of such alienations, however, was solely determined by the decisions of the 'agriculturalists', who attempted, within the context of the prevailing agrarian technology,

---

[66] An examination of the 'cycles' of the 86 industrial families recorded in Tables 5.1–5.4 reveals that most children were engaged in industrial work *before* taking up land.

[67] For an example of an industrial family employing an 'aggressive strategy' in the context of the agricultural 'defensive mechanism', see Figure 5.4.

to ensure the optimal deployment of family labour within the
confines of the holding and the optimal level of consumption for that
closely related group of kin who were resident therein.

iii

In conditions of high population pressure such as had existed before
the Black Death questions of land alienation were of but little
importance to the patriarch of the agricultural family. His primary
concern was to ensure an adequacy of land supply for the members of
the closely related kin group, comprising as many as five adults and
an indeterminate number of children, for whom he was responsible;
accordingly, there was, to this end, a tendency to concentrate 'family
land' in the family's own hands. Property which had been previously
temporarily alienated was resumed to accommodate the growing
number of his dependents. The numerous medium- and small-size
holdings held by 'clients' of the dominant agricultural families earlier
in the century began one by one to disappear, being gradually
reincorporated into their original patrimonial holdings. New alienations from those patrimonies, moreover, became increasingly rare. By
the 1340s temporarily alienated land was virtually non-existent and
the great bulk of village land was held in virgate holdings worked by
family labour.

In the aftermath of the great pandemics of 1348–9 and 1362,
however, this situation was transformed. The amount of land
temporarily alienated from the agricultural patrimonies was enormous, amounting to 24–6 per cent of the total tenant land area.[68] The
once important extended families in the agricultural sector had been
decimated, and the children born to the survivors in the post-plague
'baby boom' had not yet attained adulthood.[69] Accordingly, extended
families were few and the average number of adults per agricultural
family rarely numbered more than three, far below pre-Black Death
levels.[70] Within the framework of the existing 'defensive' mechan-

[68] See Table 5.5 for the situation in 1365. Land superfluous to the needs of the
agricultural families is listed therein as either being (B) temporarily alienated or (C)
vacant.
[69] The statements concerning demographic trends here and in subsequent pages are
based upon the preliminary findings of the study referred to in note 2 above.
[70] See Table 5.1 for the situation in 1363, when the proportion of extended families was
38% at Baslow, 40% at Haddon and 30% at Rowsley/Alport, and the average
number of adults per agricultural family was 3.47, 2.6 and 2.6 respectively. Data on
pre-plague family size is scant, but an examination of early fourteenth-century
Baslow rentals suggests a figure of about 5, comparable with the figure for Kibworth
Harcourt quoted by C. Howell, 'Stability and Change', p. 480.

isms, therefore, land was plentiful and even its deployment to optimal usages amongst family members could not eliminate superfluities.[71] The 'industrials' thus faced a market with an abundant supply of land for temporary alienation which could be acquired subject only to to the availability of cash from employment in industrial activity. Within the group of Derbyshire villages under consideration here, however, only at Baslow did such employment opportunities exist during the years 1350–65. Quarrying, iron working and cloth manufacturing all flourished in the village and its associated hamlets on the east bank of the Derwent, providing both indigenes and immigrants with the means of earning a cash income. Nor were men slow to seize the opportunities provided. The 1350s and early 1360s witnessed a flurry of activity within both the industrial community and the village land market. The major beneficiaries were the established industrial families, like the Tailors or Darleys, who used the wealth amassed in textile production to move from the ranks of cottagers to positions as major land owners; but immigrants such as the Milners, Cudys, Chapmans, Saddlers and Smiths each found a niche in the market with the cash they obtained from their industrial work.[72] A buoyant industrial sector at Baslow presaged an active land market, so that by 1365 all the land superfluous to the needs of the agricultural families had been temporarily alienated to industrials.[73]

Such was not the case at Haddon, Rowsley and Alport. Land unwanted by the agricultural families was available in abundance, but the cash to buy it was not.[74] Industrial work during the years 1350–65 was virtually non-existent within these villages and the only way that indigenes could obtain cash from this source was by migrating. Between 1350 and 1365 one family in six pursued this course, sons departing from the home hearth to find work in neighbouring Baslow or such distant centres as Youlgreave, Wirksworth and Brassington, where mining production was rapidly recovering on the Long and Gang Rakes.[75] When they returned they could buy land, and at Haddon and Rowsley it was returned migrants

---

[71] On optimality of land usage within the framework of the prevailing technology, see I. Blanchard, 'Labour Productivity and Work Psychology', *Economic History Review* 2nd series 31:1 (1978), Appendix A, pp. 17–24.

[72] The Tailors, Darleys, Cudys and Milners were engaged in textile production and the Chapmans in the sale of quarry products, whilst the Smiths and Saddlers pursued the crafts indicated by their surnames.

[73] See pp. 231 and 233 and Table 5.5.   [74] See pp. 236–7 and Table 5.5

[75] On mining activity, see I. Blanchard, 'Derbyshire Lead Production', pp. 127–8; and for employment opportunities at Baslow, see above, pp. 232 and 234.

like Hugh Somers or Matilda Smith who played the major role in taking up land temporarily alienated by the agricultural families. The part played by returnees, however, in the village land markets was slight, for of those who migrated in search of cash only 20 per cent returned. Most of the cash generated by the industrial work of migrants was dissipated in alien land markets, causing an acute shortage of funds in their home villages. Accordingly, at Haddon, Alport and Rowsley, of the land available for temporary alienation only a small proportion was taken up, the remaining lands being left vacant.[76]

Such conditions did not last long, however, for the rapid spread of industrial employment through the Derbyshire villages during the years 1365–80 and burgeoning demographic growth in the industrial communities created the desire amongst members of industrial families to acquire more land and also provided them with the means to fulfil their aspirations.[77] Between 1363 and 1381 the number of industrial families pursuing an 'aggressive' land policy increased from fourteen to seventeen, or by 20 per cent, whilst the number of individuals involved in these policies increased by much more.[78] Unfortunately, the possibilities of their translating the cash obtained into land purchases were diminishing, for over the same period the agricultural families, subject also to the same demographic experience, were rapidly resuming into their own hands the land that they had previously temporarily alienated.[79] By the 1380s the numbers of people wanting 'reversionary' land and possessing the means to acquire it had increased markedly. The supply of such land, however, had diminished. The drama of the industrial families' 'aggressive' policies was thus increasingly enacted outside the land market. Many children took up industrial employment, in order to secure the cash that was necessary to buy 'reversionary' land, but few succeeded in realizing their dreams. During the 1370s, out of 36 children engaged in industrial employment only six secured rights of usufruct in temporarily alienated land, and of that six half acquired no more than a cottage. As the price of land rocketed upwards, whilst wages did not, the long years of service extended into life-times.[80] If in the 1350s

---

[76] Table 5.5.

[77] On the spread of cloth production to Haddon in the early 1370s and Rowsley in the latter part of the decade, see above, pp. 229–32, whilst the post-plague recovery and upswing in lead ore production on the Black Sough in the 1370s is dealt with on pp. 232–3.

[78] Tables 5.1–5.2.

[79] Table 5.5.

[80] The movement of rents and wages in the Derbyshire villages, considered here,

two or three years' full-time service in industrial employment would have provided the young aspirant with enough money to acquire a holding, in the early 1370s the time-span had extended to at least five years. By 1380 the gap between entering service and acquiring a holding was often fifteen years – and, at contemporary levels of life expectation, this simply meant that many never survived to see their dreams fulfilled.[81] Full-time industrial employment, which once had been the preserve of the young, thus increasingly became an activity which was age-undifferentiated from other pursuits.[82] During the opening years of Richard II's reign those in pursuit of an 'aggressive' land policy rarely if ever were afforded the opportunity of entering the market. Paradoxically, then, when the amount of money available to buy land was probably at its greatest, the impact of the cash nexus on the village land markets was probably at its slightest, with between 73 and 95 per cent of all tenant land engrossed in the hands of agricultural families employing non-commercial 'defensive' mechanisms.[83]

The decline in population from 1380 to 1460 and from 1490 to 1520, however, served to redress the balance between the two mechanisms. As the extended families who had comprised half of all the agricultural families in the 1380s disintegrated, and the average number of adults per family fell from 3.65 in 1381 to 2.5–2.7 in 1445

conforms to the picture of late fourteenth-century conditions described by A. R. Bridbury, 'The Black Death' *Economic History Review* 2nd series 26:4 (1973). In considering the land dealings of the peasantry, the seigneurial bias of the documentation must be taken into account. In transactions on the court rolls whereby a peasant surrenders usufruct in land to another in exchange for a monetary payment it is only of interest to the lord to record who is responsible for the payment of 'rent' and to collect that share of the monetary transfer which is due to him as fine. The inter-peasant aspect of the transaction is not of direct concern to him. If this involves the creation of a debt relationship it may be recorded on the court roll as a 'private' transaction. In such circumstances the nature of the debt is occasionally recorded, but the importance of inter-peasant land dealings is only revealed by a total analysis of village debt networks.

[81] At Baslow, for instance, the length of service preceding the acquisition of land was at the minimum 1 year in the 1350s and early 1360s, lengthening to 5 years in the early 'seventies and 10 in the latter part of the decade. The average was much longer: 1.5, 6, 10, 12 years respectively. Moreover, whilst before 1370 no one died in service, the proportion thereafter steadily increased. 25% of those entering service in the 1360s died (3 in 1370, 1 in 1382) before acquiring land; 50% suffered the same fate as the 1370s entrants, and all of the 1380s entrants succumbed. Average life expectancy amongst 'industrials' reaching adulthood was in the 1350s 31.5 years, in the 1360s 26 years, in the 1370s 25 years and in the 1380s 23 years.

[82] The average age of full-time industrial workers at Baslow rose steadily from 14 in the 1350s to 19 in 1370 and 21 in 1380. At the latter date the average age of peasantry who engaged solely in agricultural pursuits was 27.

[83] Table 5.5.

and 2.5 in 1520, the need for the elaborate arrangements which had characterized the 'defensive' mechanisms of the 1370s and 1380s disappeared.[84] With the numbers to be provided for diminishing, the arrangements became simpler and the amount of land retained in familial hands within the 'defensive' mechanisms declined.[85] Only where industrial families managed to secure a niche within the 'defensive' networks during periods of market restructuring, and utilized the wealth amassed in their industrial pursuits to extend the land holding capacity of individual family members, was the pattern delayed.[86] Yet such influences were ephemeral, and over the period 1380–1520, in all the villages encompassed by this study, there was a distinctive long-term trend towards diminution in the amount of land retained in hand by families employing the 'defensive' mechanism. Accordingly, the amount of land available for those who wished to pursue predatory activities with cash earned in industrial employment increased.[87]

Where employment opportunities were maintained or grew, as on Mendip, the industrial community once more reverted to conditions not dissimilar to those which had prevailed at Baslow in the 1360s.[88] Numbers were maintained, as immigrants filled the gaps rent in the fabric of the community by the violent process of demographic change and each individual, indigene and immigrant, sought to re-establish that harmonious balance between industrial and agricultural activities which had been distorted during the period of over-population in the 1370s.[89] By 1450, aspirations, for most, had been fulfilled. Cross-sectional analyses of the industrial sectors at that date reveal only two groups at work. First, there were those whose dreams had been realized – the land holders, who engaged in industrial work in order

---

[84] Tables 5.1–5.4. It is perhaps worthy of note in the context of the discussion on p. 248 that the average size of family was already smaller in Derbyshire than on Mendip in 1445 and that both declined at about the same rate thereafter.

[85] Table 5.5.

[86] As at Rowsley and Haddon from 1380 until 1415, Baslow from 1485 until 1520 and on Mendip in the 1430s and 1460s, where families like the Billings (in the 1460s) and Hassoks (in the 1430s) of Ubley, or the Baystowes of Rowsley/Alport, utilized the wealth amassed in industrial pursuits to establish large pastoral holdings. The instability inherent in this latter activity, however, made these accretions of land, retained in hand within the 'defensive' mechanism of the family, an ephemeral phenomenon.

[87] Table 5.5.

[88] See above, pp. 237–41.

[89] On the relationship between the industrial and agricultural activities of the peasantry in a situation of plentiful land availability, see the works referred to in note 62 and on how the balance was affected by the emergence of conditions of overpopulation, I. Blanchard, 'Labour Productivity and Work Psychology'.

to earn enough cash to pay their rent and to buy that basket of consumables commensurate with their status in landed society.[90] Second, there were those aspiring to a dream – the young, who were willing to spend one or two years in full-time industrial service in order to acquire a holding.[91] For such men industrial work provided the path to land holding and in such communities, where opportunities for employment in industry were maintained, the amount of land encompassed within the 'defensive'/'aggressive' mechanisms remained stable, whilst the amount of 'temporarily alienated' land held by those pursuing 'aggressive' policies increased.[92] As has been discerned elsewhere, the cash nexus was spreading within the confines of a stable land market.[93]

On the other hand, where industrial employment opportunities declined conditions emerged analogous to those prevailing at Haddon, Rowsley and Alport in the 1360s. Only two options were open to the inhabitants of such communities. Sons could either remain and, lacking cash to buy land, await their father's death to enter their inheritance, or they could migrate, seeking work in the hope of returning to buy land. In many villages they chose the latter course, and during the years 1380–1460 a trickle of emigration turned into a flood.[94] Of their fortunes we know little, but few seem to have returned, and the villages from which they departed dwindled and declined. In the Derbyshire villages with which we are concerned, however, few chose to emigrate, and, although land was released by the agricultural families for the purposes of temporary alienation, fewer and fewer of the 'industrials' who remained had the cash to take it up.[95] At Baslow the collapse of the cloth industry and the

---

[90] By the 1430s the number of landless full-time workers in the Mendip mining camps, for instance, had been reduced to 15% of the labour force. In the 1450s they had disappeared totally leaving only farmers working optimal size holdings, who spent their summers mining to meet current expenditures: I. Blanchard, 'Labour Productivity and Work Psychology', pp. 7–8.

[91] If in the declining Mendip lead industry of the 1450s the young aspirants had deserted the camp they may be found in the contemporary timber trades. Of the 14 individuals working in the timber trades in 1452, 12 were adult tenant farmers (8 working optimal holdings and 4 cottagers) and 2 were young men spending an average 2 years in the industry before acquiring a holding.

[92] Table 5.5.   [93] See the works referred to in note 3 above.

[94] For an analysis of the patterns of emigration from agricultural communities, indicating numbers of emigrants, social composition and destination, see J. A. Raftis, *Tenure and Mobility* (Toronto, 1964) pp. 153–82; E. B. De Windt, *Land and People in Holywell-cum-Needingworth* (Toronto, 1972), pp. 176–81.

[95] Annual emigration rates per thousand of population: Haddon 1380–4 8.9, 1385–94 0, 1395–1464 0; Alport 1380–4 18.0, 1385–94 0,1395–1404 0, 1405–14 0, 1415–24 0, 1425–34 60; Rowsley 1380–1514 0; Baslow 1380–1424 0, 1425–34 9.0, 1435–44 5.1, 1445–54 5.3, 1455–64 4.4, 1465–74 0, 1475–84 9.8, 1485–1514 0.

steady decline of quarrying precipitated a cash flow crisis amongst
industrial families and ensured that a dwindling amount of land
would be taken up by them. Similarly, after a brief recovery of mining
at Rowsley and Alport in the 1420s, the market there for temporarily
alienated land collapsed in the 1430s, to recover only in the former
centre during the grindstone quarry boom of 1445–75.[96] Yet, in spite
of ephemeral openings up of job opportunities, the long-term prospects of industrial employment in the Derbyshire villages were slight,
and as fewer and fewer families possessed the cash to acquire the
land released by the agricultural families so the amount of land held
within the 'defensive'/'aggressive' mechanisms of the tenantry at
Haddon, Rowsley, Alport and Baslow declined. By 1520 the amount
of vacant land in the Derbyshire villages was enormous, ranging from
a third or a half of the tenant land at Rowsley and Baslow to all of it at
Haddon and Alport.[97] Superfluous to the needs of the agricultural
families and inaccessible to those without cash earned in industrial
employment, the land lay in the lord's hands and was incorporated
into the Vernons' great park, which survives to this day.

If, therefore, the phenomenon of a spreading cash nexus in a stable
land market, discerned on Mendip and elsewhere in the later middle
ages, was the product of abundant industrial or commercial work
opportunities, so the lack of such opportunities to earn cash may go a
long way to explaining that other familiar phenomenon of the later
middle ages, exemplified in the fate of the Derbyshire townships –
the deserted village. Whether the changes in the land market resulted
in the healthy agricultural community on Mendip or the deserted site
set amidst the grassy parkland of Derbyshire, however, the dealings
of those who operated in that market amply illustrate the interdependent relationship which existed between agricultural and industrial
families in the late medieval village.

iv

As the agricultural families, operating within the relationship described above, could retrieve land which had been either temporarily
alienated or abandoned, subject only to the tenurial arrangements
involved in its original release, their dependency upon that relationship seems to have been slight.[98] Such was not the case for the

---

[96] On industrial conditions, see above, pp. 234–5, and, on the state of the land
    market, Table 5.5.   [97] Table 5.5.
[98] Retrieval of 'temporarily alienated' land in either the late fourteenth or the early
    sixteenth century seems not to have been particularly difficult. Of 25 'resumptions'

industrial families. The supply of land for their operations, involving the 'aggressive' strategy, was entirely conditional upon the 'defensive' postures of the agriculturalists. Yet the seemingly one-way dependency situation is perhaps more apparent than real, for the cash handed over in return for the temporary alienations played a major role in shaping the lives of the agricultural families who received it. Without this money the family patriarch had only one resource – land – to deploy in the formulation of those domestic arrangements which were designed to provide an adequate sustenance for family members through each phase of their life-cycles. With it he was allowed an extended range of action.[99] In organizing how familial resources were to be used to provide a livelihood for members he had both money and land at his disposal in making his household arrangements. The land market operations of the agricultural families thus became inextricably intertwined with their household deployment strategies and in the latter may be sought the power base of the familial structure.[100]

Where cash flows were slight in village society the power of the familial head was rooted in his control over a single resource – land – and he retained throughout his life a vested interest in maintaining his grip on that resource. During his prime he could exercise a petty tyranny over sons resident at the domestic hearth who, unable to secure land elsewhere, would toil long and arduously to secure ultimately their patrimony. Nor, as long as he retained control of the family land, would this power over his dependents slacken as he grew older. In old age, by exercising this authority, he could ensure either that other members of the family would work for him when, through sickness or infirmity, he could no longer work for himself, or that they would enter into maintenance contracts to provide him with food and board in return for his surrendering of control.[101] In such

amongst Derbyshire families employing the 'defensive' mechanism during the late fourteenth century, 20 were achieved by the incumbent surrendering the land during his life-time. Only where land was abandoned and subsequently incorporated into seigneurial pastoral holdings does there seem to have been difficulty in securing its release back into the tenant land market.

[99] In the absence of cash flows the head of the family had to utilize his land both to produce for family subsistence and to provide a market surplus.

[100] The reasons for shifts in the power base of the familial structure may be sought in changes in the advantages and disadvantages that the actors therein obtained from the existing arrangements: see M. Anderson, *Family Structure in Nineteenth Century Lancashire* (Cambridge, 1971), Chapter 2.

[101] For reasons given above, such arrangements tended to predominate in periods of overpopulation, see C. Dyer, 'Changes in the Size of Peasant Holdings' in this volume, p. 289. In such circumstances the reasons why some familial heads chose

circumstances household arrangements would reflect the concentration of power in the hands of the family patriarch – household, family and holding structures would be synonymous.[102] Throughout the father's life-time family members, linked by close kin relationships, would group themselves in a unitary extended household to work an undivided holding which remained, both nominally and actually, under the control and tyrannical direction of the patriarch. On his death the promises which had been used to maintain his rigid discipline were realized in a series of *post-mortem* transfers of land.

Such was not the case, however, where cash availability allowed the familial head to utilize monetary resources to secure his old age independently of land. In deploying land amongst familial members he could surrender control and allow independence, secure in the knowledge that his own future was not dependent upon the act. Where the cash nexus existed, therefore, sons in agricultural families could enjoy an existence independent of their father's control, acquiring a holding within the 'defensive' mechanism of the agricultural family, providing for their own sustenance and establishing their own household. Fathers, on the other hand, had sufficient cash, obtained from their temporary alienations to industrial families, to accommodate all the vagaries of their own individual life-cycle. During the minority of their children they could use such money to provide supplementary food supplies. In old age they were not reliant upon their kin and could live independently either in a cottage or in the household of another, endowing their children and still retaining enough money to buy their sustenance, either with a lump sum cash payment or with instalments yielded by an annuity.[103] In such circumstances the internally interdependent, mutually cohesive and hierarchically ordered family which characterized the purely rustic community, and within which the father maintained his authority through the control of land, disappeared, shattered into atomistic elements. Each member of the family, in his economic activities, pursued his own destiny. His household assumed a nuclear form reflecting his independence. His share in the land of the family patrimony mirrored his individual labour capabilities: large for

to surrender control in return for a contractual obligation, entered into by the grantee, to provide maintenance remain obscure. On such maintenance contracts in the early fourteenth century, see the work referred to in note 22 of Dr Dyer's study; and, for examples from the latter part of the century, R. H. Hilton, *English Peasantry*, pp. 29–30.

102 Table 5.20

103 The above description is of a composite nature, drawing upon information derived from the 'reconstitutions' of individual family histories.

the young, virile and able bodied; small for the old, feeble and infirm. Within a stable production unit, encompassed in its own 'defensive' mechanism, power, which resided in the control of land and the ability to establish independent personal relationships, was being diffused.

Yet in the ordering of family affairs this liberty was not associated with licence. Amongst individual family members there was no quest after that chimaerical freedom which, as contemporaries were only too aware, brought anarchy to social, political and economic relationships. In both the rustic community and that permeated by the cash nexus, the proper working of the family land required its own discipline. The differences between the two resided rather in how this was secured. In the former, familial arrangements were ordered on the basis of ties of kinship and inheritance, manipulated in an atmosphere of tyrannical paternalism. In the latter, such arrangements were a product of transactions made by individuals exercising freedom of choice. The patrimonial holding thus comprised a series of independent households, inhabited by family members retaining land in hand and outsiders holding land temporarily alienated to them, the two groups being conjoined in a desire to ensure the holding's proper working and ordering their affairs in a complex series of *pre-* and *post-mortem* arrangements involving transfers of cash and land.

Once again, therefore, the importance of the symbiotic relationship between agricultural and industrial families is revealed, but, in this instance, it was the agricultural family that was dependent upon its operation, for only with the cash made available to it by the industrial family could the agricultural family enjoy freedom in making its household arrangements.[104] These arrangements, moreover, rooted in part at least in this relationship, conformed to no stereotype but constantly responded to changing economic, demographic and social circumstances.

v

Prior to the Black Death demographic factors were of primary concern to the heads of agricultural families in the ordering of their household arrangements. Dominant in their minds were the problems of providing sustenance for a growing number of dependents, which necessit-

[104] The freedom was ensured both by giving the family a greater control over the disposal of the produce of its land and by extending the range of resources at its disposal.

ated the concentration of patrimonial land in familial hands. The resultant resumption of previously temporarily alienated land, however, reduced their cash balances and, leaving land as the sole familial resource, yielded power to the patriarch, which he wielded in ways sanctified by contemporary moralists. During his prime his control over familial land ensured that subordination of the children to his authority, which found such popular approval, reflected the hierarchical norms of society in the context of family relationships. In old age it entitled him to that 'loving' care and respect which the dutiful child was expected to afford its elderly parents. Thus emerged the internally interdependent, mutually cohesive and hierarchically ordered family household which characterized the agrarian sector of the village community in the early fourteenth century, with up to three generations of closely related kin living together at the family hearth under patriarchal direction and authority. Yet this structure was not rooted in any traditional value system based upon the Christian virtues of obedience and charity, as contemporary moralists would have us believe. These were ideals more sought in hope than realized. It grew rather out of short-term circumstances which, by endowing the patriarch with power, allowed him to impose this pattern of family relationships in a spirit of tyrannical paternalism. Both the power and the structure, however, were as ephemeral as the circumstances which gave them birth.

In the aftermath of the Black Death (1350–65) demographic conditions threatened to undermine the whole edifice, but in the event, in the villages under consideration, the dissolution of the prevailing order was, owing to economic circumstances, only partial and ephemeral. The increase in the amount of land available for temporary alienation posed a threat to paternal authority, but the low level of industrial activity in all the Derbyshire villages save Baslow prevented its materialization. Unable to dispose of the superfluous land, agricultural families maintained only low cash balances and stem or extended families continued to assume a synonymous household form. Only at Baslow, where the cash nexus began to permeate village society, may signs of nuclearization be discerned; and, whilst hybridization (that is, the assumption of 'aggressive' strategies by families employing 'defensive' mechanisms to create independent households) affected almost half of the agricultural families, its extent in terms of land holding was slight.[105]

Nor, in spite of increasing cash availability due to the extension of

---

[105] See Table 5.1, where of the 5 extended families organizing their households in hybrid forms only 17% of the land had been acquired by 'aggressive' activities.

industrial activities through the village communities during the years 1363–80, was there any increase in household fragmentation amongst agricultural families.[106] The tendency towards land resumption in conditions of resurgent population growth, by reducing the cash flow to agricultural families, deprived familial heads of their monetary reserves and forced them to sacrifice familial sustenance to meet recurrent monetary outlays.[107] Patriarchal authority, eroded slightly during the post-pandemic years in centres like Baslow, thus once more, in conditions of resource scarcity, reasserted itself during the 1370s and early 1380s, causing a reduction in the number of agricultural families deploying households in nuclear or hybrid forms. In Baslow, that bastion of familial freedom, where half of all extended families in the agricultural sector of 1363 had displayed some tendency towards nuclearization, the proportion was reduced, accounting for no more than one-third in 1381.[108] Elsewhere, where the proportion had been much lower in 1363, the tendency towards nuclear household formation amongst stem or extended families was all but extinguished. During the opening years of Richard II's reign household organization and familial structure once more coincided. The internally interdependent, cohesive and hierarchically ordered family, in which the father maintained his authority through the control of land, and the extended family household went hand in hand, provided the dominant family-household form in 1381. High population pressure prior to the Black Death and in the years 1365–80 had brought with it a distinctive form of household organization.

Demographic decline, from 1380 to 1460 and from 1490 to 1520 saw the demise of the stem or extended family in conditions reminiscent of the post-pandemic era. Where there was a long-term tendency for employment opportunities in industry to be maintained or even to grow, as on Mendip, and for the amount of land held in temporary alienation to increase, there was a parallel trend in the size of the cash balances held by agricultural families. In such circumstances sons possessed the means to seek their independence and fathers were not inclined to impede them, preferring rather to slacken their grip over

---

[106] On industrial activities, see above, section 1.

[107] Table 5.5. Enforced grain sales to meet rent charges and other recurrent cash outlays, obtained by the reduction of familial consumption, may well have contributed to the buoyant local grain trade of the 1370s (on which see *supra*, note 34).

[108] Tables 5.1–5.2.

[109] Extended families comprised 50% of all families in the agricultural sector of 1381 and encompassed almost three-quarters of all individuals therein, and more than two-thirds of these families were organized in a synonymous household form. For the importance of this group elsewhere, see Hilton, *English Peasantry*, pp. 29–31.

both family and land holding – with dramatic effect. The years
1380–1445 in such localities witnessed a rush for freedom.[110] By the
latter date the cohesive family unit had disappeared. Each member of
the extended family now pursued his own destiny. In one case,
perhaps because of a conservative recalcitrant father, a son was
forced to assume an 'aggressive' posture, engaging himself in industrial activity in order to establish an independent household. In the
great majority of instances, however, such independent action was
unnecessary. Sons, on coming of age, established their own household within the 'defensive' mechanism of the family, with moral and
perhaps pecuniary help from their fathers. Fathers equally enjoyed
their independence, shedding land in temporary alienation as they
grew older, in return for cash to secure their retirement. Household
forms thus assumed a ubiquitous nuclearity, reflecting each individual's independence. Such households' contributions to the working of the patrimonial holding and shares in its produce equally
reflected their individual labour capacities: large for the young, virile
and able-bodied; small for the old, feeble and infirm.[111] The extended
holding of the 1370s, utilizing the corporate labour of the family
under the direction of the patriarchal head, was gone. Its internal
ordering, moreover, no longer conformed to the dictates of paternal
authoritarianism but reflected the desires of individuals formulated in
conditions of free choice.[112]

Only where industrial employment declined, as in Derbyshire, was
the process stayed and patriarchal authority maintained. Yet, paradoxically, in the demographic conditions of the fifteenth century this

[110] On Mendip the process had already been completed by 1430. In Derbyshire the
trend was already apparent in the 1420s, during the mining 'boom' and before the
'troubles' of the 1430s caused a general collapse of industrial activity.

[111] On Mendip, as the numbers of able-bodied 'cottars' declined because of the
assimilation of that group into the ranks of peasants possessing 'optimal' holdings,
the proportion of cottages, in a stable stock, held by the elderly increased from
20% in 1430 to 58% in 1460 and 63% in 1520. Moreover, whilst in the late
fourteenth century cottages formed a component element of larger familial
holdings/households, in the fifteenth century they formed the basis of independent
households.

[112] Within the framework of the 'defensive' mechanism, 'ownership' was vested in
individual members, familial and non-familial, whose land reflected their individual labour capabilities. There was thus a tendency towards 'polarization',
which reflected age differentials rather than 'capitalistic' relationships. On the
phenomenon of 'polarization' and the hypothesis of its 'capitalistic' origin, see
R. H. Hilton, *The Economic Development of Some Leicestershire Estates in the Fourteenth
and Fifteenth Centuries* (Oxford, 1949), pp. 94–105 and 147–8, and *English Peasantry*,
pp. 51–3, where the view is modified somewhat. In the fifteenth century cottagers,
far from being young, able-bodied wage labourers, were elderly members of
established village families.

very process destroyed the household structure it was supposed to protect, hastening such economically depressed communities rapidly along the path towards total extinction. Lacking cash from temporary alienations, ageing fathers in these villages attempted to keep their sons at home during their dotage, to till the land and provide them with sustenance. Lacking the means to establish their independence, children were forced to submit.[113] Accordingly the siblings in such families only acquired land late in life, on the death of their parents, and by delaying marriage reduced their own chances of having offspring.[114] In a society where, even under optimal conditions of early marriage, replacement rates rarely exceeded 0.4–0.6, the effect was disastrous.[115] Generation by generation the family diminished in size, and, whilst the patriarch maintained his authority, it was exercised over a rapidly declining number of dependents.[116] Household and family maintained a unity of form, but in such Derbyshire villages as Alport and Haddon the extended family gave way to the nuclear one much more rapidly than on Mendip, and even before 1520 most nuclear families had been totally extinguished.[117] Only where industrial activity was maintained did the community survive, and amongst the agricultural families in such localities the nuclear household reigned supreme in 1520.

Such had always been the case amongst the industrial families, although in periods of industrial restructuring there might be a tendency, in declining sectors, for some families to assume an extended household structure.[118] Fathers and sons alike pursued their

[113] It is apparent that from the 1430s there was a distinct tendency for sons to acquire a holding only on the death of the father. In the 1410s only half of sons acquiring land had worked on their father's holding until his death and this proportion fell to 40% in the 1420s. Thereafter, there is not one instance amongst agricultural families of sons establishing *new* independent households during their father's life-time. As will be seen from Table 5.3, however, some of the arrangements established before 1430 continued to exist as late as 1445.

[114] On the assumption that sons were born shortly after their father had acquired a holding, the average age at which they took up land increased from 18 in the 1410s and 1420s to 25 in the 1440s, 35 in the 1460s and 1470s, 42 in the 1480s and 50 in the 1500s.

[115] From a replacement rate – encompassing *all* sons, not just those inheriting their father's land (as in S. L. Thrupp, 'The Problem of Replacement Rates in Late Medieval Population', *Economic History Review* 2nd series xviii, 1 (1965), pp. 102–3), whether in *pre-* or *post-mortem* arrangements – of 0.7 in the 1410s there was thereafter a steady decline to 0.4 in the 1440s and 0.3 in the 1470s. On Mendip, where sons had the opportunity of establishing an independent household on reaching adulthood, replacement rates remained at 0.6–0.7 to the 1440s before falling to 0.4 in the 1470s.

[116] See above, note 84.   [117] Table 5.4.

[118] As at Ubley in 1445, where the 4 extended industrial families assuming a synonymous household form were involved in withdrawal from mining.

own independent destinies, though prior to the Black Death their formulation of household strategies took place largely outside the land market. Only with demographic decline after 1348–9, and an abundant availability of land to be taken up on temporary alienation, could industrial workers, in centres like Baslow, regard land as a component element of their strategies. Their quest after the resource, moreover, was frenzied, for only through the acquisition of land could they obtain that stability of food supply which the grain market could not ensure. By 1363 at Baslow all of the land made available for temporary alienation had been taken up by 'industrials' whose holdings, each with its own independent nuclear household, tended to approximate optimal size – at least during the individual's working life.[119] In old age, however, for reasons as yet unexplained, the familial head seems to have shunned residence in a cottage and to have bought himself a place at the hearth of one of his peers.[120] During the years *circa* 1350–65 the process of household formation in centres like Baslow took place, therefore, within the land market, each individual 'industrial' creating his own independent nuclear structure.

Nor did household forms change during the years 1365–80. They continued to assume a nuclear format, but as the agriculturalists, in conditions of resurgent population pressure, once more resumed the land previously let out on temporary alienation, holdings held by members of industrial families became smaller and smaller, until during the opening years of Richard II's reign most industrial families were forced to make their household arrangements *outside* the land market. Accordingly, at that time a 'community of servants' began to emerge, consisting of two groups. Numerically most important were the sons, lacking obligations to their fathers because of the abundant cash availability within the community, who became servants in order to seek, more in hope than expectation, a livelihood based on land. Second, there were the fathers who in old age, as already noted, found a place in the household of another. Each enjoyed an independent existence, but outside the land market.[121]

With the transformation of the demographic situation and the

---

[119] On the 'optimal' size of holding in the context of the prevailing technology, see I. Blanchard, 'Labour Productivity', Appendix A.

[120] With an average life expectancy of less than 35 years, the industrial population was not markedly affected by the problem of providing for old age. In the one instance in which this did arise, the case of John Machon of Baslow, he seems to have chosen residence in the household of another.

[121] In 1381 the average land holding per adult member of Derbyshire industrial families was 1 acre.

onset of a protracted phase of population decline from 1380 to 1460 and from 1490 to 1520, however, their situation underwent a considerable amelioration. The dreams and expectations of the 1370s were turned into reality. The landless industrial family of the 1370s had by the mid-fifteenth century become a thing of the past.[122] In those villages where industrial employment opportunities were maintained the increasing supply of land available for temporary alienation was rapidly taken up by 'industrials', whose household structures and shares in patrimonial land were indistinguishable from those of the 'agriculturalists'.[123]

Viewed in its totality, encompassing both industrial and agricultural families, the landed sector of the village community therefore underwent a major metamorphosis during the years 1380–1520. Dominated during the early years of Richard II's reign by agricultural families, lacking cash reserves, the characteristic household unit of those operating within the land market was the extended family household in which an internally interdependent, cohesive and hierarchically ordered group of closely related kin worked together, under the direction of the patriarchal head, to till the patrimonial land, which was retained in hand.[124] Within half a century, however, this structure was well on the way to disappearing and by 1520 the process of disintegration was all but complete. In those villages where industry declined, so too did the rustic community, resulting in the appearance of that familiar late medieval phenomenon – the deserted village. On the other hand, where industrial employment opportunities were maintained the community survived. The industrial families re-established their place in the land market, the landless full-time worker of the 1370s becoming the peasant worker of the fifteenth century.[125] Moreover, both agricultural and industrial families, bound together in a symbiotic relationship, basically altered their household structures. Patriarchal power was dispersed and each familial member, whether industrial or agricultural, was left free to order his own destiny. Accordingly, within the framework of the patrimonial holding encompassed in its own 'defensive' mechanism, each individual,

---

[122] On Mendip the average land holding per adult member of industrial families in 1455 was 14 acres, in Derbyshire it was 12 acres.

[123] On Mendip the average land holding per adult member of agricultural families in 1455 was 13 acres, in Derbyshire it was 12 acres.

[124] See also R. H. Hilton, *English Peasantry*, pp. 29–31.

[125] On the general phenomenon of labourers taking up land, see M. M. Postan, 'Medieval Agrarian Society in its Prime: England', *Cambridge Economic History of Europe, Vol. I*, 2nd edition (Cambridge, 1966) pp. 631–2, and *The Medieval Economy and Society* (London, 1972), where the process is related to a general trend towards 'social promotion' of agricultural families.

whether a family member retaining land in hand or an outsider who had secured by his industrial work land in temporary alienation, formed his own household. By 1520 the nuclear household thus reigned supreme.

vi

Lest we fall into the danger of creating another stereotype, however, seeking in the nuclear household of 1520 a predecessor of the structures of the late sixteenth century, it should be stressed that the early sixteenth century household was an ephemeral structure born of short-term circumstances, a conjunctural creature whose existence could not transcend the conditions which had given it birth. Indeed, it is only necessary to move a few years forward in time – to 1526 – to see that there were no linear trends linking the households of 1520 and 1580. Already by that date resurgent population growth was creating conditions which were more reminiscent of the early fourteenth century than prophetic of the late Elizabethan era.

Within the surviving Mendip communities, 1526 saw the inhabitants in a process of transition.[126] For most families existing arrangements did not alter significantly during the second and third decades of the sixteenth century, in spite of resurgent population growth. As long as most tenants' children had not attained their majority there remained land available for temporary alienation, and the long-established pattern of deployment continued. Yet even before more fundamental changes were wrought, by demographic factors, in the fabric of the familial strategy, it was becoming clear that circumstances were changing. As inflation became an endemic feature of everyday life, from the 1510s, so the future value of cash payments began to be eroded. Arrangements which had looked attractive in an age of stable prices began to lose their appeal. In response, from the second decade of the new century, family heads, in arranging the temporary alienation of land, would no longer take payment in cash. By 1526 one may discern, in all such arrangements made during the previous fifteen years, a new pattern emerging. Recipients of land in temporary alienation seem to have made their payments in labour rather than money. The arable sectors of their shares in the patrimonial holding were uniformly 'sub-optimal', leaving them with time to expend on the lands of the granting family, who now cultivated an area in tillage which was correspondingly larger than the amount that

---

[126] The following analysis of families on Mendip in 1526 is based on the 'reconstitutions' (referred to in note 51 above), relating to the villages of Ubley and Chewton.

family members were either willing or able to cultivate.[127] Instead of receiving money, the head of the granting family thus obtained the product of his 'client''s labour and thereby secured a hedge against inflation. The pattern of temporary alienation within the framework of the family's 'defensive' mechanism thus, for the moment, continued. Only the form of payment had been changed. For most families the legacy of the past thus continued to weigh heavily on their present arrangements. In maintaining constant levels of family sustenance through the various phases of its life-cycle, they utilized, within the framework of their 'defensive' mechanism, a basic strategy of land deployment by temporary alienation.

Whilst most families in 1526 thus looked to the past in ordering their affairs, in a few cases arrangements were being made which heralded grave portents for the future. In families where children born in the vanguard of the 'baby boom' of the 1490s had already attained adulthood and their parents had already commenced on the path towards their dotage, a new strategy in the ordering of family affairs was emerging. The previously important pattern of transactions, enacted in an impersonal atmosphere between individuals exercising free choice, was in this instance not modified but totally abandoned for a non-commercial strategy dominated by transfers of property at marriage. In order to make provision for their children's future families could no longer temporarily alienate land, and they thus denied themselves the payments, whether in money or labour, which derived from that act. The family's links with the system of commercial transactions, which had dominated the village land market for almost a century and a half, were severed. Henceforth family land would not enter the market. Instead, it would be used by fathers attempting to manipulate their children with promises of inheritance. Their objectives remained the same – to ensure the maintenance of their sustenance through the phases of their life-cycle – only now the arrangements to achieve this were internalized within the family rather than externalized through the market. Household arrangements thus reflected the concentration of power in the hands of the family patriarch, who, with promises of inheritance, could ensure that deployment of family labour which was necessary to maintain the stability of sustenance he so desired. Sons were in no position to resist. As population growth within the village community increasingly limited their scope for independent action they were forced to assume the role of providers during their parents' declining

[127] On 'optimality' of land holding, see I. Blanchard, 'Labour Productivity', Appendix A.

years. A pattern of familial arrangements reminiscent of the early
fourteenth century was thus beginning to reappear amongst those
families with an adult child to provide for in 1526.

Nor was the situation different in the case of the one family in the
villages at that time where the father had to make provision for more
than one adult son, although in this instance the arrangements
extended beyond the confines of the paternal household. The eldest
son remained at home, deploying his labour under patriarchal
direction, in the manner described above. To accommodate the
second son, however, the father exercised his rights, within the
framework of the arrangements encompassed by the family's 'defensive' mechanism, to resume land which had previously been temporarily alienated. Such an act required, though, the compensation of the
existing holder of the land. In an earlier age this would have been
achieved by running down the family's cash reserves, but in these
inflationary times the holder did not want, any more than any other
villager, payment in money. Accordingly, the second son temporarily
assumed the position of a servant in the household of the sitting
tenant in order to secure his rightful patrimony. In spite of the tag –
servant – however, the life of the younger son was indistinguishable
from that of his elder brother, as each worked in a subordinate
position within his respective household in order to secure his
rightful patrimony, a fact which was freely recognized by contemporaries. Indeed, the interchangeability of the two categories, servant
and child, was a commonplace in English rural society through time.
Just as the tax assessors in 1381 had labelled children resident in the
parental household as *servientes*, so also, in similar conditions,
sixteenth-century authors of books of etiquette, in addressing advice
to heads of households about the ordering of their affairs, regarded
the positions of children and servants as indistinguishable.[128]

The portents for the future were clear. As agricultural families
began to resume land which had previously been temporarily alienated, in order to make provision for their children, the commercial
land market gradually disappeared. Land transfer would henceforth
increasingly take place through a mechanism within which transactions based on ties of kinship and inheritance were dominant. The
days were passing, moreover, when familial arrangements were

---

[128] PRO, E 179/242/10; H. Rhodes, *The Boke of Nurture, for Men, Servauntes and Chyldren*
(*c. 1554*) edited by F. J. Furnivall, Roxburghe Club (London, 1867), pp. 7 and 17;
J. Christopherson, *An Exhortation to All Menne to Take Hede and Beware of Rebellion*
(1554).

made in an impersonal atmosphere through the free consent of the participating parties. Soon an age would arrive when parents would impose a pattern of family relationships conforming to the hierarchical norms of society, on their children, exercising a petty tyranny over sons resident at the domestic hearth, who toiled long and arduously to secure their patrimony ultimately, or displaying that 'want of affection' which foreigners felt they 'strongly manifested towards their children', and which caused them, 'having kept them at home till they arrive at the age of seven or nine at the utmost', to 'put them out, both males and females, to hard service in the houses of other people, binding them generally for another seven or nine years . . . during which time they perform all the most menial offices' until they secured for the family the land which was patrimonial in origin.[129]

In 1526 past and future mingled together, but it was already clear that the nuclear household, which had characterized the village community during the opening years of the century, was doomed. In conditions of resurgent population growth household arrangements were emerging reminiscent of those of the early fourteenth century. Family members, linked by close kin relationships, would increasingly group themselves in unitary extended households to work an undivided holding which would remain under the control and authority of the family patriarch. Yet the similarities were not absolute. Inflationary pressures in the sixteenth century ensured that those participating in the formation of such a structure would eschew the use of money in their transactions, thereby endowing the edifice with a distinctive character.

There was thus no evolutionary progression which linked the households of 1500 and 1580. The nuclear household of the former date was replaced by the extended household of the 1520s and 1530s. Both were the product of *conjunctural* forces working with a *structural* framework. The late Elizabethan household owed its existence to another structure. In this essay we have been concerned with phenomena associated with conjunctural fluctuations; questions of structural change must await another occasion. Within such limitations, however, it is clear that the years 1380–1520 witnessed momentous changes within village society.

---

[129] *A Relation or Rather a True Account of the Island of England about 1500*, edited by C. A. Sneyd, Camden Society, old series xxxvii (London, 1847).

vii

The present study has concentrated on two groups of industrial villages, one on Mendip, where industrial employment opportunities were maintained throughout the period 1380–1520, the other in Derbyshire, which was subject to de-industrialization over the same period. In both the land market was subject to momentous, if different, changes, which were rooted in the symbiotic relationship which existed between the agricultural and industrial families. The phenomena observable in their land markets, however, have a significance transcending their particular bounds. The Mendip villages were not the only ones to experience a spreading cash nexus in a stable land market. The Derbyshire villages were not the only ones to experience the process of decay and decline, leading to desertion. Whether a common experience was rooted in a common causation we cannot be sure, but perhaps it is permissible to close this essay with the speculation that perhaps the mechanisms described above also transcended the confines of the villages investigated – that industrial activity, far from being an alien accretion to village society, was in fact an integral part of it.

Appendix

The present paper is based upon materials collected for a wider study concerning the effect of industrial activity upon the process of social change in fifteenth- and sixteenth-century rural communities. This project involved the reconstitution of two groups of industrial villages, utilizing their manorial documentation. The records of the first group of villages, situated on Mendip, fall into two categories, although both are engrossed on documents of manorial provenance. First there are the records of the minery courts. These documents, which are preserved in two collections at the Somerset Record Office – the Chapel MSS (DD/S/HY) and the Waldgrave MSS (C924/DD/WG) – record not only the deliberations of the minery court but detail the lead which was due to the lord of each field as 'lot' from each individual workman who worked within the mining jurisdictions. In order to extend the analysis to encompass other industrial activities as well as the villagers' agricultural pursuits and to explore the interaction between the industrial and agrarian activities of the inhabitants, it proved necessary to utilize the second group of records – manorial records of a more conventional character. By analysing the ministers' accounts, rentals and, above all, court rolls in the above-mentioned collections, together with documentation of a similar character from the episcopal manuscripts at Lambeth Palace and Wells, the Somerset Rolls at the Bodleian, the Seymour Papers at Longleat, the Ashton Court MSS at Bristol and records from the central government archives, it proved possible to investigate the fortunes of each and every family within certain of the mining communities over specified periods of time. The oldest late medieval mining complex – Ubley and Hinton (comprising *circa* 25 families) – was studied for the whole period 1403–1553, whilst within the newer mining centres, Wells and Chewton (*circa* fifty families each), the

269

Table 5.1. *Family structure and land management strategy: Derbyshire 1363*

| | | | | Family/household structure | | | | |
| | | | | Family | | Household | | |
		No. of families	Inhabitants	Stem or extended	Nuclear	Stem or extended	Nuclear	Hybrid
Baslow	Agric.	19	66	8	11	4	12	3
	Indust.	13	35	4	9	1	12	0
Haddon	Agric.	5	13	2	3	1	3	1
	Indust.	3	11	2	1	0	2	1
Alport	Agric.	6	14	1	5	1	5	0
	Indust.	0	0	0	0	0	0	0
Rowsley	Agric.	4	12	2	2	1	2	1
	Indust.	2	10	2	0	1	1	0
Total	Agric.	34	105	13	21	7	22	5
	Indust.	18	56	8	10	2	15	1

| | | | | Land management strategy | | |
		No. of families	Inhabitants	Defensive	Aggressive	Hybrid
Baslow	Agric.	19	66	14	2	3
	Indust.	13	35	2	10	1
Haddon	Agric.	5	13	3	1	1
	Indust.	3	11	0	2	1
Alport	Agric.	6	14	6	0	0
	Indust.	0	0	0	0	0
Rowsley	Agric.	4	12	4	0	0
	Indust.	2	10	0	2	0
Total	Agric.	34	105	27	3	4
	Indust.	18	56	2	14	2

investigation was restricted to the years 1523–53 and 1523–1603 respectively. For other centres such as Compton Martin and Harptree the documents permitted only brief glimpses of social structure. By juxtaposing these two reconstitutions – of mining camp and village – it proved possible to examine the interplay between mining, other industrial, and agricultural activities.

A similar process of 'village reconstitution' was undertaken for a second group of townships in Derbyshire – Haddon, Baslow, Rowsley and Alport – which fell within the lordships of the Vernons and Bassets from 1355 until 1425 and then passed solely into the former's hands at the latter date. Once again this involved the utilization of the manorial documentation of the lordships during the years 1355–1605,

Table 5.2. *Family structure and land management strategy: Derbyshire 1381*

		No. of families	Inhabit-ants	Family		Household		
				Stem or extended	Nuclear	Stem or extended	Nuclear	Hybrid
Baslow	Agric.	15	58	10	5	7	6	2
	Indust.	15	54	5	10	0	14	1
Haddon	Agric.	6	22	4	2	3	3	0
	Indust.	4	27	3	1	0	3	1
Alport	Agric.	7	20	1	6	0	6	1
	Indust.	0	0	0	0	0	0	0
Rowsley	Agric.	6	24	2	4	1	4	1
	Indust.	1	2	0	1	0	1	0
Total	Agric.	34	124	17	17	11	19	4
	Indust.	20	83	8	12	0	18	2

		No. of families	Inhabit-ants	Land management strategy		
				Defensive	Aggressive	Hybrid
Baslow	Agric.	15	58	11	2	2
	Indust.	15	54	0	14	1
Haddon	Agric.	6	22	6	0	0
	Indust.	4	27	1	2	1
Alport	Agric.	7	20	3	2	2
	Indust.	0	0	0	0	0
Rowsley	Agric.	6	24	4	2	0
	Indust.	1	2	0	1	0
Total	Agric.	34	124	24	6	4
	Indust.	20	83	1	17	2

preserved amongst the muniments of his Grace the Duke of Rutland at Belvoir Castle, for the purpose of investigating the fortunes of each and every family in the villages under consideration and of examining the interrelationship between their industrial and agricultural activities. On the basis of these 'reconstitutions' it proved possible to undertake an analysis of the demographic, economic, social, religious and political behaviour of the villagers and to explore, amongst many other questions, their dealings in the land market. To this end data have been collected, which are incorporated in Tables 5.1–5.5 and which provide the basis for the discussion on pages 241–57 above, concerning (1) the land market mechanisms and (2) the family-household arrangements of the villagers.

Table 5.3. *Family structure and land management strategy: Derbyshire and Mendip 1445*

		No. of families	Inhabit-ants	Family/household structure				
				Family		Household		
				Stem or extended	Nuclear	Stem or extended	Nuclear	Hybrid
Derbyshire								
Baslow	Agric.	12	34	4	8	0	12	0
	Indust.	6	14	1	5	0	6	0
Haddon	Agric.	2	4	0	2	0	2	0
	Indust.	3	6*	0	3	0	3	0
Alport	Agric.			0	0	0	0	0
	Indust. DESERTED			0	0	0	0	0
Rowsley	Agric.	7	14	0	7	0	7	0
	Indust.	6	12	0	6	0	6	0
Mendip								
Ubley	Agric.	8	22	2	6	0	7	1
	Indust.	12	42	8	4	4	8	0

		No. of families	Inhabit-ants	Land management strategy		
				Defensive	Aggressive	Hybrid
Derbyshire						
Baslow	Agric.	12	34	11	1	0
	Indust.	6	14	1	5	0
Haddon	Agric.	2	4	2	0	0
	Indust.	3	6	0	3	0
Alport	Agric.			0	0	0
	Indust. DESERTED			0	0	0
Rowsley	Agric.	7	14	7	0	0
	Indust.	6	12	2	4	0
Mendip						
Ubley	Agric.	8	22	8	0	0
	Indust.	12	42	2	9	1

*Estate servants.

As regards the market mechanisms deployed, descriptions are given on pages 241–7 above, whilst familial types are characterized in accord with Dr Laslett's classification.[130] In order to facilitate identification and to distinguish familial and household forms in the data derived from the reconstitutions, however, it has proved necessary to extend Dr Laslett's definitions. In the case of the *nuclear family* or *solitary*, the problem of distinguishing household and family form

[130] For definitions of family forms, see P. Laslett and R. Wall, editors, *Household and Family in Past Time*, pp. 28–32.

Table 5.4. *Family structure and land management strategy: Derbyshire and Mendip 1520*

				Family/household structure				
				Family		Household		
		No. of families	Inhabit-ants	Stem or extended	Nuclear	Stem or extended	Nuclear	Hybrid
Derbyshire								
Baslow	Agric.	10	26	1	9	0	10	0
	Indust.	6	16	2	4	0	6	0
Haddon	Agric.			0	0	0	0	0
and		DESERTED						
Alport	Indust.			0	0	0	0	0
Rowsley	Agric.	3	6	0	3	0	3	0
	Indust.	2	4	0	2	0	2	0
Mendip								
Ubley	Agric.	7	18	2	5	1	6	0
	Indust.	13	38	4	9	0	13	0

				Land management strategy		
		No. of families	Inhabit ants	Defensive	Aggressive	Hybrid
Derbyshire						
Baslow	Agric.	10	26	8	2	0
	Indust.	6	16	3	2	1
Haddon	Agric.			0	0	0
and		DESERTED				
Alport	Indust.			0	0	0
Rowsley	Agric.	3	6	3	0	0
	Indust.	2	4	0	2	0
Mendip						
Ubley	Agric.	7	18	4	2	1
	Indust.	13	38	6	7	0

within the context of the broad categorization used in Tables 5.1–5.4 is not great. The family consisting 'of a married couple, or a married couple with offspring or a widowed person with offspring' will always, whatever its form of household organization, deploy its family members in *solitary* or *nuclear units* of a single or multiple character. Such an identity of family and household need not exist, however, in the case of stem or extended families. An *extended family* thus consists of 'a conjugal family unit with the addition of one or more relatives other than offspring . . .', who provide the basis for vertical or lateral extension, and who, if subsequently forming their own conjugal units, effect a transformation into a *stem family*; these

Table 5.5. *Deployment of property within the village land market:*
*Derbyshire and Mendip**

	Derbyshire									Mendip					
	Baslow			Haddon			Alport			Rowsley			Ubley		
	A	B	C	A	B	C	A	B	C	A	B	C	A	B	C
Date															
1365	69	31	0	70	8	16	73	0	27	64	11	25			
1375	73	27	0	94	6	0	80	20	0	68	21	11			
1385	76	24	0	85	15	0	73	27	0	95	2	0			
1395	82	15	3	85	15	0	73	27	0	100	0	0	Not		
1405	81	12	7	99	1	0	73	27	0	100	0	0	available		
1415	80	12	8	89	11	0	73	27	0	100	0	0			
1425	73	18	9	89	11	0	63	37	0	88	12	0			
1435	64	6	30	61	15	24	0	0	100	76	6	18	66	33	1
1445	59	11	30	61	15	24	0	0	100	61	21	18	61	38	1
1455	56	14	30	56	20	24	0	0	100	61	21	18	58	37	5
1465	56	12	32	0	0	100	0	0	100	37	45	18	68	24	8
1475	56	12	32	0	0	100	0	0	100	33	36	31	61	34	5
1485	58	10	32	0	0	100	0	0	100	54	15	31	61	34	5
1495	58	10	32	0	0	100	0	0	100	48	15	37	52	39	9
1505	62	6	32	0	0	100	0	0	100	51	12	37	52	39	9
1520	62	6	32	0	0	100	0	0	100	48	6	46	51	36	13

*All figures are expressed as percentages.
Key
A = Land retained in hand by families employing the 'defensive' mechanism.
B = Land temporarily alienated by families employing the 'defensive'
    mechanism.
C = Vacant land, in lord's hands.

household forms provide the basis for categorization in cols 5–6 of
Tables 5.1–5.4. For this familial form to become synonymous with the
household cohabitation is unnecessary, but the constituent elements
must be conjoined by ties other than those of kinship. For the
purposes of this paper the ties have been regarded as economic – the
members being united in the working of a unitary holding, dependent for its operation upon the manpower of all the household/family
members. For example, if the family consists of a married couple and
the elderly father of either husband or wife, it is said to be extended in
form and is so categorized in cols. 5–6 of Tables 5.1–5.4. If the father
has a messuage and bovate and a separate cottage in which the
couple lives, then the form may be described as an extended family
household (and will be so categorized in cols. 7–9 of Tables 5.1–5.4),

for the working of the bovate is inconceivable without the joint labour of both male members of the family. If, on the other hand, the familial holding comprises a bovate organized so that the couple possesses a cottage and half a bovate, whilst the other half bovate and messuage are held by the father, then the extended family (in cols. 5–6 of Tables 5.1–5.4) is said in its household arrangements to have assumed a nuclear and solitary form (in cols. 7–9 of Tables 5.1–5.4).

6

Changes in the size of peasant holdings in some west midland villages 1400–1540

CHRISTOPHER DYER

In examining the developments in the size of peasant holdings in the later middle ages historians have tended to concentrate on long-term structural changes in the social distribution of land. One school of thought argues that as a result of the drastic loss of population from the mid-fourteenth century 'economic promotion' took place, which meant that all groups within the peasantry increased the size of their holdings. Others see differentiation at work, by which peasant society became more polarized between tenants of large holdings and wage earners, and which foreshadows the dichotomy between capitalist farmers and labourers in modern times.[1]

Neither explanation is fully satisfactory. The promotion theory is perhaps too simplistic, and fails to explain some very large holdings that developed, while the stagnant market for agricultural produce in much of the period would not have made an ideal environment for differentiation.

It is also necessary to take into account the small-scale and short-term changes in the size of peasant holdings, dependent on the circumstances of individual families. This factor has attracted more attention recently because of the translation into English of the writings of the Russian agricultural economist, A. V. Chayanov, who developed the concept of the peasant holding as a 'family farm', in which the consumption needs and labour contribution of the family

---

[1] M. M. Postan, *The Medieval Economy and Society* (London, 1972), pp. 139–42, for 'promotion'. The classic statement of the differentiation idea is V. I. Lenin, *The Development of Capitalism in Russia*, in *Collected Works*, Vol. 3 (Moscow, 1964). It is applied to late medieval England in R. H. Tawney, *The Agrarian Problem in the Sixteenth Century* (London, 1912), pp. 96–7, and R. H. Hilton, *The Economic Development of some Leicestershire Estates in the Fourteenth and Fifteenth Centuries* (Oxford, 1947), pp. 94–105, 147–8, but the latter author's views are modified in *The English Peasantry in the Later Middle Ages* (Oxford, 1975), pp. 51–3.

helped to determine the size of the holding. The development of the family farm was seen as a cycle, in which a young peasant began with a smallholding which increased in size as his children grew older and consumed more, reaching a peak when the children were old enough to help with working the land, and then declining as children left home and the parents became less active in their old age.[2]

Of course, it is unlikely that ideas based on nineteenth-century Russia will be directly applicable to medieval England. So many circumstances – forms of tenure, agricultural techniques and the state of the market – were very different. However, some aspects of both societies are analogous, and an explanation is needed of how English tenants of, say, a yardland (about 30 acres) managed to work their land at both the beginning and end of their land holding careers. Although the first attempt to apply Chayanov's theory to the English peasants, in the case of the serfs of the Peterborough Abbey estate in the late thirteenth century, has met with some very effective critic- isms, we ought not to ignore it in examining our evidence.[3]

The purpose of this essay is to look at both short-term and long-term movements in the size of holdings, and to see how both types of change relate to one another.

The field of enquiry is a number of west midland villages from the late fourteenth century until 1540. The information comes from the archives, principally the court rolls, of the estates of the bishopric of Worcester, supplemented with wills of the early sixteenth century relating to the same villages. The starting date of the study is determined by the survival of the records. The end-date of 1540 has been chosen to include the reorientation of the economy in the early sixteenth century.

There are of course many problems in the use of manorial court rolls. Although the collection involved is bulky – records of about 1,300 court sessions have been consulted, in which at least 1,600 land transfers are recorded – the series are often not sufficiently con- tinuous. The best run of documents is for the manor of Kempsey,

[2] A. V. Chayanov, *The Theory of Peasant Economy*, edited by D. Thorner, B. Kerblay and R. E. F. Smith (Homewood, Ill., 1966), pp. 53–61.

[3] M. M. Postan, 'The Charters of the Villeins', reprinted in *Essays on Medieval Agriculture and General Problems of the Medieval Economy* (Cambridge, 1973), especially pp. 114–17. Critical comments are P. R. Hyams, 'The Origins of a Peasant Land Market in England', *Economic History Review* 23 (1970), pp. 18–31; and E. King, *Peterborough Abbey, 1086–1310* (Cambridge, 1973), pp. 99–125. Although the data are not related to Chayanov's theories, some adjustment of the size of holdings of a Chayanov type is apparently shown in E. B. Dewindt, *Land and People in Holywell- cum-Needingworth* (Toronto, 1972) pp. 117–21 and 129–33, and in J. A. Raftis, *Warboys: Two Hundred Years in the Life of an English Medieval Village* (Toronto, 1974), pp. 179–92.

with the years 1435–1520 covered almost completely, the only major gap being the years 1489–95. In using such a series to trace individuals, identification presents many difficulties. Surnames sometimes change, but the main problem lies in the presence at any one time of two or even three individuals with the same name. For this reason some families have simply been left out of the analysis because individuals could not be disentangled from their namesakes. In examining inheritance it is often not possible to identify remote relatives who bear different surnames. I have had to assume that individuals with different surnames were not related, and that individuals with the same surname were related. This is clearly unsatisfactory, as it may lead to under-estimation of the extent of inheritance by relatives outside the nuclear family and through the female line. Finally there is the problem of subletting, which can be assumed to be under-recorded in the documents. My general impression is that concealed subletting was not so widespread that conclusions based on records of 'official' tenants are invalid.[4]

The manors whose records are mainly used in this study are Kempsey, Whitstones and Wick Episcopi, which lay in the Severn valley near to the city of Worcester, Hartlebury, also in the Severn valley some miles to the north of the city, Hanbury in the woodlands of north Worcestershire, Bredon and Pladbury in the valley of the Avon in Worcestershire, and the Gloucestershire manors of Blockley and Bishop's Cleeve, both on the edge of the Cotswolds.[5]

The settlements included in these manors varied from large nucleated villages in the Avon valley and Cotswold edge, to small villages (often of about a dozen households, with up to ten in each manor) in the Severn valley, to dispersed settlements in the wooded landscape

---

[4] One reason for thinking this is the close correlation between tax payments recorded in the 1524 Subsidy, and the land holding recording in court rolls.

[5] Rather than cite the source of each piece of information deriving from the court rolls throughout the essay the references for the main series used are given in full here:
Kempsey, 1394–1520 and 1537:. Worcestershire County Records Office (hereafter WRO) ref. 705:4, BA 54.
Hanbury, 1375–1504: WRO ref. 009:1, BA 2636/165 92229, 2636/166 92231–4, 92236–9, 92241–5, 92247–50, 92253, 92255, 92258–9, 922967, 2636/169 92359, 2636/167 92270, 2636/166 92269, 2636/167 92271–5, 92277, 92279–81, 2636/192 92626$\frac{6}{12}$, 2636/167 92286–91, 92293–300, 92302, 92304, 92307–12, 2636/168 92314–5, 92318–20, 92323–4, 92327–8, 92331, 902334, 92338, 92345–6, 92349, 2636/169 92253–4, /165 92226$\frac{3}{3}$, 2636/169 92358, 92356, 92361, 92363, 92366–7; ref. 705:192,BA 5589/82; ref. 705: 7, BA 7335/64, 7336/65.
Whitstones and Wick Episcopi, 1377–1505: WRO ref. 009:1, BA 2636/173 92447–8, 2636/175 92474, 92476, 92482, 2636/176 92491, 2636/192 92626$\frac{5}{12}$, 2636/176 92492. For these manors, and the others on the estate, in the period 1520–39, WRO ref. 009:1, BA 2636/177 92504, 92508–9, 2636/178 92510–11, 92515, 2636/18 43762–5.

of Hanbury. The economy, especially in the river valleys, was based on arable cultivation, though pastoral farming developed in importance in the later middle ages. The density of population before 1350 in the west midlands was less than in south-eastern England, but the surveys of 1299 show that at Kempsey, Whistones and Wick Episcopi holdings of less than a half yardland, many of them quarter yardlands or less, formed between 68 per cent and 91 per cent of holdings. Elsewhere on the estate half yardlands or yardlands were more numerous, representing about 65 per cent of the total.[6]

A common feature of all of the manors was that they had experienced centuries under the lordship of powerful ecclesiastics. So there was a preponderance of customary tenure, and serfdom continued on the estate into the mid-sixteenth century. Labour services were still demanded in the 1390s, but by the fifteenth century tenants were paying rents and dues entirely in cash. The tenants secured some significant reductions in rent and the abolition of some seigneurial dues, particularly in the early fifteenth century.[7] Heritable copyhold tenures evolved in the fifteenth century. Forfeitures and other seigneurial interference in customary tenures declined after 1480, so that the tenants enjoyed considerable security of tenure. The prevailing inheritance custom was primogeniture, sometimes admitting daughters as well as male heirs, with widows having rights to free bench in all or part of their husband's holding.

The economic environment at the end of the fourteenth century and in the fifteenth century can be characterized as one of low demand for both agricultural produce and land. Prices of wheat – a major cash crop – in the west midlands fell below 5s per quarter in the late 1370s and rarely rose much above that level for well over a century.[8] Wool prices declined in the fifteenth century, reaching their low point in the 1450s.[9] These trends did not favour large-scale agriculture for the market, so that seigneurial demesnes were leased at the end of the fourteenth century, and the rents paid by the demesne farmers tended to decline or stagnate after 1400.

The numbers of tenants on the manors of the bishopric were

[6] *Red Book of Worcester*, edited by M. Hollings, Worcestershire Historical Society (Worcester, 1934–50).

[7] C. Dyer, 'A Redistribution of Incomes in Fifteenth Century England?', *Past and Present* 39 (1968), pp. 11–33.

[8] C. Dyer, 'The Estates of the Bishopric of Worcester, 680–1450', unpublished University of Birmingham Ph.D. thesis, 1977, pp. 144 and 401.

[9] T. H. Lloyd, *The Movement of Wool Prices in Medieval England*, Economic History Review Supplement vi (1973), pp. 40–4.

drastically reduced in the epidemic of 1348–9 by about 42 per cent.[10] There was a subsequent recovery on some manors, but on most the numbers of tenants in the fifteenth century were between one-third and two-thirds of those recorded at the end of the thirteenth century.[11]

The population as a whole was at a low level. Small family sizes are indicated by a census of serfs made on four manors in 1476. The mean was 1.92 children per family, closely comparable with figures available for other parts of the country in the post-plague period. Twelve of the 38 families recorded had no children at all.[12]

A high rate of migration is suggested by comparison of surnames mentioned in rentals and court records, which show that about three-quarters of all families disappeared every 40 to 60 years in the fifteenth century, to be replaced, but not always fully, by new immigrants. Details of migration are given in the presentments to the lord's courts that serfs had left the manor. These were frequent up to the 1450s, and were then given up because the authorities realized the futility of attempting to secure their return. Most moved to places less than ten miles from their native villages, though longer journeys to such places as London, Salisbury and Sussex are recorded.

An indirect indication of the reduced demand for land is the level of entry fines. These were negotiated every time a new tenant took up a customary holding, and seem to have been sensitive to market conditions. Fines at a rate of £1 or £2 per yardland are recorded in the last quarter of the fourteenth century, but by the 1430s on most manors they had sunk to less than £1. Nominal fines of a few poultry, or the waiving of the fine altogether, were not uncommon in the fifteenth century.

A lowered demand for land did not usually lead to large numbers of holdings falling vacant for long periods of time. A few villages on the estate were deserted in the late fourteenth and early fifteenth centuries, but these were exceptions. The largest numbers of vacant holdings at any one time were reported in the 1370s and 1380s; 25 at Hanbury in 1376 were 'lying in the lord's hand', but this was unusually high, and most were taken up soon afterwards. The peak

---

[10] *Red Book of Worcester*; PRO, E368/124 and 126.

[11] Rentals: Bishop's Cleeve: WRO ref. 009:1, BA 2636/161 92113⅔; Hanbury: 2636/9 43696 fols. 28–30, and 263669168 92332; Hartlebury: 2636/37(iii) fols. 78–83; Henbury: 2636/185 925746, 2636/165 92226¾.

[12] For comparable family sizes, see C. Howell, 'Peasant Inheritance Customs in the Midlands, 1280–700', in J. R. Goody, J. Thirsk, and E. P. Thompson, editors, *Family and Inheritance: Rural Society in Western Europe, 1200–1800* (Cambridge, 1976), p. 125. The figure quoted here is that recorded in the census, without corrections.

of vacancies at Whitstones was four, at Wick Episcopi eight, with five at Bredon. A possible explanation for their appearance at this time is the reluctance of tenants to pay the high rents demanded. A holding at Whitstones, for example, had been rented for 18s 10d per annum up to 1393. A rent of 26s 8d was demanded when the holding came into the hands of the lord, and no one was willing to take it until 1398. In the fifteenth century the number of vacant holdings recorded in any one year was rarely more than one or two.

So the great majority of holdings were tenanted, but the number of tenants being low, many had more than one holding. Rentals show that the numbers of tenants with holdings of a yardland or more represented 43 per cent of tenants in the fifteenth century, as compared with 25 per cent according to the late thirteenth-century surveys. Another symptom of the 'multiple' holdings of many tenants was the high proportion – between 17 and 46 per cent – of holdings associated with 'tofts', that is plots from which the buildings had decayed. When a tenant held more than one tenement, he allowed some of the buildings to collapse as they were surplus to his requirements.

There are signs of important changes in the last quarter of the fifteenth century and in the early sixteenth century. The prices of agricultural produce picked up a little in the 1480s, but a clear upward movement began in the 1510s.[13] The population was increasing by the second decade of the sixteenth century. The numbers of children recorded in serf families was between 2.31 and 2.65 children per family in 1515–20 and 1536–9.[14]

The demand for land seems to have been increasing on the more economically active manors in the 1470s, judging from the level of entry fines, which more than doubled between the 1460s and 1480s at Hanbury, Kempsey and Wick Episcopi. Fines fell in the first twenty years of the sixteenth century, though remaining higher than in the early to mid-fifteenth century, and then revived.[15] A further indication of a growing demand from the 1460s, but especially marked after 1500, is the increased number of arrangements for reversion, whereby a would-be tenant paid an entry fine to the lord so that the holding would pass to him in the future on the death or surrender of the

[13] J. Thirsk, editor, *Agrarian History of England and Wales*, Vol. IV (Cambridge, 1967), pp. 815–18.

[14] For similar increasing family size in the early sixteenth century among an urban poulation, see A. D. Dyer, *The City of Worcester in the Sixteenth Century* (Leicester, 1973), p. 35.

[15] I. S. W. Blanchard, 'Population Change, Enclosure, and the Early Tudor Economy', *Economic History Review* 23 (1970), pp. 427–45.

sitting tenant. Such speculative deals suggest considerable anxiety to secure a claim to land. Land was so attractive – even copyhold land, which had so recently been associated with servile status – that merchants and gentry acquired a number of customary holdings.

The number of tenants in the late fifteenth and early sixteenth centuries tended to remain stable or even to decline slightly. The engrossing of holdings is recorded in the presentments to the Enclosure Commission in 1517.[16]

How did these social and economic trends affect the peasant family and its relationship with the land? An overall indication of some trends is provided by an analysis of the types of land transfer recorded in the court rolls (see Table 6.1).

The first column shows holdings passing from a tenant to the lord (that is, after death, surrender or withdrawal by the tenant the land was not taken up immediately by a new tenant but lay 'in the lord's hands') and also holdings being taken from the lord by a new tenant. Both types of transfer indicate gaps between tenancies. These were not very long, often no more than a few months between court sessions, but are still indicative of a lack of eagerness on the part of tenants to acquire land at the moment that it became available. The figures appearing in the first column seem to confirm the other evidence already discussed of an increasing demand for land from the late fifteenth century, as transfers involving the lord represent between 21 and 60 per cent of all land transactions up to the 1460s or 1470s, and then decline, with an occasional revival.

Column 2 indicates the number of land transfers in the category most likely to reflect a land market – those in which holdings passed from one tenant to another (who was not a relative) while the sitting tenant was still alive. The forms of words used include simple statements that a holding has been surrendered and taken by another tenant, or surrenders *ad opus* or *ad usum*. At Kempsey and Whitstones there is a clear rising trend in these *inter-vivos* transfers in the course of the fifteenth century, but they tend to decline in some decades in the early sixteenth century. Similar developments are apparent at Hanbury, but these types of transfer were not very numerous there at any time.

On manors like Kempsey the transfer of holdings was very rapid, so that as many as 10 per cent of holdings could change hands in a

---

[16] *The Domesday of Inclosures*, edited by I. S. Leadam, Royal Historical Society (London 1897), Vol. II, pp. 427–9 records engrossing of holdings paralleled in the court rolls of the same manor, Hampton Lucy.

Table 6.1. *Analysis of land transactions 1376–1540*

Years	1 Transfers involving the lord		2 Inter-vivos (non-family)		3 Transfers within family		Others		Total	
	No.	%	No.	%	No.	%	No.	%	No.	%
Hanbury										
1376–94	13	36	0	0	9	25	14	39	36	100
1420–39	21	60	0	0	6	17	8	23	35	100
1440–9	6	21	4	14	10	36	8	29	28	100
1450–9	14	40	1	3	11	31	9	26	35	100
1460–9	4	16	4	16	10	40	7	28	25	100
1470–9	3	14	4	19	6	29	8	38	21	100
1480–99	3	10	7	22	4	13	17	55	31	100
1500–19	4	13	1	3	11	37	14	47	30	100
1520–40	1	5	0	0	17	77	4	18	22	100
Kempsey										
1394–1421	6	35	4	24	4	24	3	18	17	100
1430–9	10	43	6	26	2	9	5	22	23	100
1440–9	25	37	15	23	8	12	19	28	67	100
1450–9	17	23	19	26	8	11	29	40	73	100
1460–9	9	15	26	43	4	6	22	36	61	100
1470–9	6	10	23	37	11	18	22	35	62	100
1480–9	0	0	12	40	4	13	14	47	30	100
1490–9	5	23	9	41	2	9	6	27	22	100
1500–9	10	27	10	27	6	16	11	30	37	100
1510–20	0	0	14	40	9	26	12	34	35	100
1521–40	4	8	12	24	13	26	21	42	50	100
Whitstones										
1377–89	17	31	14	26	9	16	15	27	55	100
1390–9	11	27	8	19	6	15	16	39	41	100
1430–9	10	45	1	5	3	14	8	36	22	100
1440–9	6	21	13	45	5	17	5	17	29	100
1450–9	7	54	1	8	2	15	3	23	13	100
1460–9	14	40	7	20	5	14	9	26	35	100
1470–9	1	3	11	38	6	21	11	38	29	100
1480–99	0	0	14	56	2	8	9	36	25	100
1500–10	6	19	9	29	4	13	12	39	31	100
1520–40	0	0	2	10	7	35	11	55	20	100

year, and some holdings went from tenant to tenant with bewildering rapidity. A cottage at Stonehale in Kempsey, for example, had no less than thirteen tenants in the 45 years between 1441 and 1486, the longest recorded tenancy being seven years.

To some extent there was an inverse relationship between transfers *inter-vivos* and transfers of land within the family. Column 3 includes all such transfers, both *inter-vivos* and *post-mortem*, excluding widows acquiring free bench. They tend to represent a relatively small proportion of land transactions on those manors with large numbers of *inter-vivos* transactions – sometimes sinking below 10 per cent at Kempsey and Whitstones, but consistently higher at Hanbury. The explanation for this difference lies with the much higher proportion on this manor of free tenants, who practised inheritance more frequently than customary tenants. On most manors there was a marked increase in the number of transfers within the family, both before and after death, in the early sixteenth century. In addition to those included in the tables, the proportion of family transfers increased at Bishop's Cleeve from 13 per cent in the fifteenth century to 32 per cent after 1500, and at Hartlebury the comparable figures were 20 per cent and 33 per cent.

The general conclusion that can be drawn from the tables seems to be that in the late fourteenth century and much of the fifteenth century land holding was very fluid. Tenants frequently surrendered land, either to the lord or to other tenants, and often at death their land passed outside the family. For example, between 1377 and 1499 at Whitstones the disposal of property at death is recorded in 88 cases. Thirty-seven of the holdings went to the widow; of the remaining 51 cases in which the land could have passed to a new generation in only 23 (45 per cent) was it inherited by relatives. In the remainder the land either passed to another family or went to the lord's hands. In the smaller sample of sixteenth-century *post-mortem* transfers 67 per cent (eight out of twelve) stayed within the family.

The relative frequency with which land remained in the family in the early sixteenth century should perhaps be regarded as representing the normal situation in a peasant society. Although there are no surviving court records for our manors in the period before 1349, those of the nearby manors of Worcester Cathedral Priory show that 32 per cent of land transfers in the early fourteenth century took place between relatives.[17] Before 1349 and after 1500 sons helped parents to work the land and took over the holding on their death or retirement. Under these circumstances close links would be built up between the family and its land, such as are common in other peasant societies.[18]

---

[17] J. West, 'The Administration and Economy of the Forest of Feckenham during the Early Middle Ages', unpublished University of Birmingham M.A. thesis, 1964, p. 229.

[18] E. R. Wolf, *Peasants* (Englewood Cliffs, NJ, 1966), p. 67; *Peasants and Peasant Societies*, edited by T. Shanin (Harmondsworth, 1971), pp. 30–5.

By contrast, in the fifteenth century the traditional ties were broken. It is not unusual to read in a rental such entries as: 'Thomas Yardyngton holds a messuage and six acres of land formerly held by Thomas Wever and before that by John Smythe.'[19] Increasingly the tenant of a holding did not bear the name of the family traditionally associated with it – Smythesplace was often not held by anyone called Smythe.[20]

Was the low level of inheritance in the late fourteenth and early fifteenth centuries simply a result of the decline in the size of families? This provides only part of the explanation. Even when sons survived to maturity they tended to migrate. A possible incentive to do so was provided by the higher rents and entry fines owed for customary tenures, and some customary tenants were still burdened with the ignominious status of serfdom, so that they would have very good reasons to move. The Rok family of Kempsey is a case in point. Richard Rok held a half yardland by customary tenure in the second quarter of the fifteenth century, and he was a serf. His two sons, Thomas and Richard Rok junior, were reported, because of their servile status, which in theory prohibited unlicensed migration, to be living in London and Worcester in the period 1435–58. When Richard senior died in 1449 his widow, Alice, succeeded him in his holding, but within a year she remarried and went to live at nearby Wyre Piddle. The holding passed into the hands of a Walter Rogers. The sons remained away from Kempsey, and the last Rok mentioned in the records was another Richard, who was living at Wyre Piddle in the years 1455–61. Sons were able to leave home because land was relatively plentiful, or they could obtain employment as apprentices or as servants – like John Smyth of Whitstones, whose father, Henry, complained in 1387 that a chaplain of Claines had employed him for three years, and so deprived the father of his son's services.

The land holdings of individuals can be investigated by drawing up biographies from continuous series of court rolls. From the Kempsey records 109 biographies of tenants who took part in more than one transfer of property can be compiled. At first sight tenants with a relatively simple career of acquiring a holding and then dying or surrendering it, seem to predominate. Fifty-six of those for whom we have biographies are of this type. However, seventeen of these were

[19] WRO ref. 009:1, BA 2636/161 92113$\frac{2}{6}$.
[20] R. Faith, 'Peasant Families and Inheritance Customs in Medieval England', *Agricultural History Review* 14 (1966), pp. 77–95; C. Howell, in Goody *et al.*, editors, *Family and Inheritance*, pp. 130–1; Dewindt, *Land and People*, p. 134.

widows, who acquired land as their free bench after the death of their husbands and were a rather special category of tenants. A further nine were cottagers with three acres or less, who doubtless worked primarily as wage earners or artisans and not as peasant cultivators. So of the 83 biographies of male tenants with land holdings in excess of three acres, 30 were of the simple type, and the remaining 53 involved transfers of more than one property. Some could be very complex, involving as many as nine transfers in a single life-time, and defy rational explanation. It should be remembered that the Kempsey customary yardlands (apparently of 24 acres) had been fragmented in the twelfth and thirteenth centuries, so that land was being held and passed between tenants in units of three, six and twelve acres. A coherent pattern is discernible in many cases: fifteen tended to increase the size of their holdings, nine seemed to experience decline and fifteen accumulated land and then lost it.

Some examples will show that the changes in land holding can be related to the life-cycle of the tenant and his family.

Walter Rushmere acquired his first holding, totalling nine acres, from his widowed mother in 1456. In 1478 he next appears acquiring a half yardland as a sub-tenant. At the time, as revealed by a census of 1476, he had a family of six children and would need the extra land to feed them, and he may well have received assistance from his older children. It is likely that the subletting arrangement had ended by 1488; Rushmere died in 1506 holding his original nine acres. We do not know Rushmere's date of birth, but if he acquired his first holding when he was in his twenties, as was common in the fifteenth century, he expanded his holding in his forties, reduced it in his fifties and died in his seventies. It seems likely that as he grew older his children either died or left home. Certainly none of his three sons succeeded him; the holding was taken by a Perceval Rawlins.

Thomas Pensham seems to have begun his land holding career by acquiring a parcel of the Kempsey demesne on lease in 1471. In 1472 he married a widow, Alice Sylvester, and so gained her nine-acre holding. In 1488 he acquired a share in a substantial holding of meadowland for which he paid a rent of 20s. Expansion continued in 1497 and 1503, when his holding reached a peak of at least thirty acres. In 1511–12 he began to make arrangements for the disposal of his property, as other tenants acquired the reversion of his holdings. As with Rushmere, the pattern would fit a first holding's being gained in Pensham's twenties, expansion in his late thirties and forties and decline in his late fifties. Like Rushmere, no son succeeded him.

Sometimes the pattern of expansion and contraction can be followed for more than one generation. Thomas Bate's early career belongs to the period before the court roll series begins. We find him in the 1450s with a multiple holding of more than eighteen acres, but in decline, for in 1456 twelve acres were declared forfeit because he did not live on that part of his lands. He died in 1464 holding only six acres. Thomas' son Walter Bate was sworn into assize at the age of twelve in 1450, so he was eighteen years old when he took over the twelve acres lost by his father in 1456. In 1470 he paid a fine to secure the reversion of his father's other six-acre holding, then in the hands of his widowed mother. He also acquired a parcel of demesne on lease in 1471, and by 1477 held the farm of the rectory glebe. Walter seems to have reached his peak between the ages of 32 and 39, which seems young, but he acquired his first holding, and perhaps married, in his teens, so that his family would have reached its maximum size in the 1470s. No children stayed to take over his holding. He evidently shed much of his land, like his father, for when he died in 1500 at the age of 62 he held only a six-acre holding on customary tenure; he was succeeded by John Leverok.

The absence of sons has been suggested as an explanation of a declining pattern in a tenant's later years. It would obviously be difficult for an aged tenant to keep a large holding intact. For example, John Walker had acquired in the 1460s and 1470s a half yardland, a six-acre holding, a messuage and appurtenances, and a parcel of demesne on lease. The total was probably in excess of a yardland. Between 1477 and 1500 he surrendered his customary holdings to three different apparently unrelated tenants, John Byrte, Richard Buk and Thomas Pensham, all of whom were accumulating land at the time of Walker's decline. Walker had a son in 1476, but he was already established at the Kempsey hamlet of Stonehale away from his father's home at Draycote, and he inherited none of his father's land.

The examples given so far are of holdings diminished in size in the old age of the tenant. How do we explain those that expanded but did not decline? In some cases it is clear that the cycle of expansion and decline was interrupted by early death. John Beke began his land holding with twelve acres in 1453, and he added another six acres in 1459 but then died, holding eighteen acres, in 1466, after a career of only thirteen years. John Waren, also in a brief thirteen-year period, assembled a composite holding of more than a yardland and a half, and a parcel of demesne on lease but died in 1474. Both Beke and Waren were succeeded by apparent non-relatives; Waren's large holding was split up on his death, one holding going to his widow, the others to William Sharpe and Walter Rogers. Presumably any children that such tenants had were too young to inherit. If they observed the normal peasant practice of marrying at the time that they took their first holding, the eldest would have been less than thirteen years old.

The cyclical nature of land holding, with tenants gaining and shedding land to suit their needs and the labour resources of their families, helps to explain the large number of land transfers between families and the small proportion of inheritances and transfers within the family. The failure of sons to survive and their tendency to move away when they reached maturity created problems for old people. It has been plausibly argued that before the fifteenth century a normal part of the life-cycle of a peasant family was a three-generational phase in which retired peasants or widows continued to live on their holdings, which were worked by a young successor, often a son, who would have his own wife and children.[21] Such arrangements seem to be recorded less often in the fifteenth century. Only nine agreements for the maintenance of retired tenants have been found in the 1,300 court records used for this study. They are much more frequent in comparable series of the late thirteenth and early fourteenth centuries.[22] It is understandable that young would-be tenants should avoid taking on holdings encumbered with the expensive and inconvenient obligation to maintain an old couple. The result can be seen in references to aged tenants struggling to keep their lands going and eventually giving up in destitution. John Baty of Kempsey, for example, surrendered his holding of a half yardland in 1452 because he was *senex et decrepitus*. He had nothing that could be taken as a heriot 'because he is poor'. His successor in the land was the unrelated Richard Pers; if Baty had sons, they were evidently not interested in his holding. Such withdrawals, often by elderly tenants, were not uncommon in the period 1370–1470 – nine are recorded at Whistones for example. The phenomenon of the tenant unable to obtain assistance in his old age helps account for the references in court records to poverty (in explaining non-payment of heriots and other dues) among tenants of quite substantial holdings, even yardlands.

[21] Hilton, *English Peasantry*, pp. 29–31.
[22] An examination of the Worcester Cathedral Priory court rolls for the pre-1350 period suggests a much larger number of maintenance agreements than appear in the post-1375 series under examination here. A published series for the early fourteenth century with a considerable number is *Chertsey Abbey Court Roll Abstracts*, edited by E. Toms, Surrey Record Society xxxviii (1937) and xlviii (Guildford, 1954).

All of this may create the impression that the peasant family had disintegrated in the fifteenth century, but this would be a great exaggeration. Some families retained their continuity for a number of generations. In 1440 Richard Hervey of Kempsey retired and handed over his half yardland to his son Roger. Roger died in 1465 and was succeeded by his son John. He died in 1485, and it was only then that the holding passed into the hands of another family.

Although land was relatively plentiful in the fifteenth century, it was not available to all. As has been noted already, cottagers often acquired no extra land in the course of their lives. Young men who began building up their holdings with a small parcel of land often came from tenant families who may well have provided them with assistance. Parents might acquire holdings on behalf of their sons. For example, in 1463 Walter Rogers, already the tenant of an eighteen-acre holding, acquired a further six acres, which was stated to be for his son when he reached the age of 21. Others may have helped their sons with cash which would have been needed to pay entry fines and to obtain equipment and stock, but this is not recorded until the early sixteenth century, when wills of our tenants are available.

A variety of arrangements existed by which land could be transmitted from one generation to another. We have already seen how Walter Bate gradually took over his father's holding. The Byrtes' arrangements ensured continuity over a longer period. In 1445 Thomas Byrte acquired a half yardland from Walter Western, and in 1446 inherited another half yardland from his widowed mother. His earlier career is obscure, but he evidently already had a mature family, for in 1448 he made over a half yardland to his son John, and replaced it by taking a half yardland surrendered by John Wattes, who was 'impotent'. So in 1448 the already middle-aged Thomas Byrte held a yardland, and the young John Byrte had a half yardland. In 1456 John added another six acres to his tenement (from John Kerewode), and his holding finally outstripped that of his father in 1464, when Thomas surrendered six acres to his son. Presumably John now had a growing family to keep, and Thomas' capacity to work his holding was declining. Thomas died late in 1464, still holding a half yardland, which went to his widow. She remarried in 1466, and left the village, and the holding passed out of the family.

John Byrte had no need of his father's last holding, as he had already accumulated a yardland, three-quarters of it from his father during his life-time. Unlike Thomas, he was able to keep the yardland intact for twenty years, presumably with the help of his son, William. In 1488 John formally surrendered the holding in court, and took it back as a joint tenancy with his son. John probably died between 1489 and 1495 (when the court roll series is interrupted), and the holding passed intact to William Byrte, who still held it in 1529.

A branch of the Herdman family was able to use joint tenancies to keep an eighteen-acre holding intact for more than 60 years. In 1454 John Herdman made a joint tenancy with his son Richard. Richard made a similar agreement with his son Robert in 1476, and Robert was still alive in 1514, with his son living with him, ready to take over the holding into the next generation.

Joint tenancies, which helped to bind the generations together and ensure inheritance, were more frequent towards the end of the fifteenth century. Of fifteen recorded in the court records studied, eleven belong to the period after 1470. By the early sixteenth century they were superseded by reversionary agreements within the family. At Kempsey between 1510 and 1540, of 83 land transfers 32 involved reversions, of which a half were between relatives, usually between tenants or widows and their sons.

Both joint tenancies and reversionary agreements were used to advantage younger sons. For example, Robert Herdman, who became the heir of an eighteen-acre holding in 1476 (as mentioned above) was the second son of Richard Herdman. The eldest son, William, was living independently of his father in 1476 and had two children of his own. In another branch of the Herdman family, in 1504, Richard Herdman, fourth son of John, took reversion of his father's half yardland. Richard Pantynge junior, second son of Richard Pantynge, obtained the reversion of his father's six-acre holding in 1517. Elder sons were still able to obtain a living away from their parents' holdings, so their younger brothers benefited and presumably stayed at home to assist on the land. The link between inheritance and continued coresidence with the parents is suggested by the will of Thomas Wilkys or Wyllys of Blockley, who left his extensive leasehold lands to William Wyllys 'now dwelling with me'.[23] The manipulation of inheritance customs in favour of the younger children still living in the family home is reminiscent of the systems of inheritance prevailing in parts of medieval France.[24]

Inheritance disputes were rare in the fifteenth century. The problem was to find an heir, not to settle quarrels between rival claimants. In the 1530s peasants again began to argue about successions, notably over the rights of daughters. In 1538 the customary tenants of

[23] WRO ref. 008:7, BA 3950/1, Vol. ii, fol. 46.
[24] E. le Roy Ladurie, 'Family Structures and Inheritance Customs in Sixteenth Century France', in Goody *et al.*, editors, *Family and Inheritance*, pp. 37–70.

Whitstones stated in the context of such a dispute that 'they never knew any man's daughter was adjudged to any customary tenement . . . and that ever (i.e. never) they had any such custom there used', in flat contradiction of the court rolls, which show daughters inheriting as late as 1462.[25]

As the number of surviving children increased, peasants must have been tempted to practise some form of partible inheritance. William Gibbes of Blockley did this in 1529, splitting up his lands in Blockley and Stretton-on-Fosse between his nephew and three sons. Normally early sixteenth-century wills show the lands passed intact to one heir, the other children being bequeathed goods or cash. On two occasions the heir was enjoined to provide for siblings; William Courte of Tredington even specified quantities of grain to be given annually to his younger son and son-in-law. The prevailing aim was that expressed by a Fladbury testator: 'my son shall have all my meses and lands to himself whole and to his heirs'.[26]

The desire to keep holdings intact is reflected in the court rolls. As we have seen in the Kempsey cases, holdings in the fifteenth century tended to be split up in the later life of the tenant, or accumulations of land broken up on his death. Both of these trends diminished in the late fifteenth and early sixteenth centuries. This can be demonstrated at Whitstones by examining the proportion of tenants who still held multiple holdings when they died. Between 1377 and 1479 only 23 per cent of tenants had more than one holding at the time of their death. The comparable figure for the period 1480–1540 was 47 per cent. In the early part of our period multiple holdings tended to be broken up after death, but by the early sixteenth century fourteen out of fifteen passed intact to the next tenant, who was often an heir.

So larger holdings became more stable in the late fifteenth and early sixteenth centuries. This trend should be regarded as contributing to a structural change in the distribution of land among the villagers. The instability and fluidity of land holding in the late fourteenth and fifteenth centuries was tending to diminish after 1500, as a small number of families established their control over multiple holdings that were transmitted as a unit from generation to generation. At Kempsey some holdings reached the equivalent of a yardland and a half or more in the mid-fifteenth century, but these were temporary

[25] WRO ref. 009:1, BA 2636/18 43763.
[26] WRO ref. 008:7, BA 3590/1, Vol. II, fol. 104; Worcester Wills 1540/32, 1537/80; M. Spufford, 'Peasant Inheritance Customs and Land Distribution in Cambridgeshire from the Sixteenth and Eighteenth Centuries', in Goody et al., editors, Family and Inheritance, pp. 157–63.

accumulations. It was not until the early sixteenth century that holdings of one-and-a-half or two yardlands passed intact from one tenant to another. This happened seven times between 1509 and 1530. There was a similar development at Bredon, with again seven comparably large holdings recorded as being transferred intact between 1520 and 1538. There must be more uncertainty about this phenomenon at Hanbury and Whitstones, because the size of holdings was not always assessed in terms of yardlands. At Whitstones few holdings exceeded a half yardland, and of the four cases of holdings of three-quarters of a yardland or more moving from tenant to tenant without fragmentation, the first was in 1474 and the other three after 1500.

Two imponderables must be considered in discussing the relationship between the family and land holding. The first is subletting. This practice is mentioned quite often in court records, either in licences to allow tenants to sublet, or, more rarely, in action by the courts to deal with illicit subletting. There are not enough examples for them to be related to the life-cycle, except in the case of such licences granted when a new tenant took up a holding. This could be taken to imply that he was an absentee, but it could be related to difficulties in cultivating a holding in the early stages of a family's life-cycle.

The second ill-documented factor is wage labour. The family has been regarded as the major source of labour available to the peasantry, but both full-time employees and casual labour are mentioned occasionally in the court rolls, though we can assume that wage earners were relatively scarce and expensive. Full-time 'servants' could have been employed as substitutes for sons when the latter were absent, as has been shown in the case of eighteenth-century Austrian peasants.[27] For example, John Pantynge of Kempsey, who had a servant in 1442 (mentioned because he was involved in an assault), held a half yardland. He was clearly near to the end of his active life, and lacked the help of a son, for he surrendered his half yardland in 1443 and obtained a small holding, a messuage and appurtenances; he died in 1445, and his smallholding was not inherited. Other elderly tenants also employed servants and were thus able to keep their holdings going. William Churchyard of Whitstones died in 1513, and his widow Joan succeeded him as tenant of a double holding of a nook (quarter yardland) and an

[27] L. R. Berkner, 'The Stem Family and Developmental Cycle of the Peasant Household: An Eighteenth-Century Austrian Example', *American History Review* 77 (1972), pp. 413–16.

arkeland (probably of comparable size); she maintained the holding for eleven years. Their wills mention no children, but Joan employed at least two servants. John Nurton of the same place, who maintained two nooks until his death, had three servants.[28]

Most of our evidence relates to manors with relatively small holdings – quarter yardlands in the late thirteenth century, rarely exceeding one-and-a-half yardlands between the 1370s and 1540. On the manors where yardlands predominated in the earlier period, holdings commonly grew to two or three yardlands in the fifteenth century. Tenants of such holdings would have needed to employ wage workers even if family labour was also available. For example, yardlanders were numerous at Hartlebury in 1299, and by *circa* 1480 twenty tenants (a third of the total) were recorded as holding two yardlands or more. A contemporary ecclesiastical court book shows that there was also a large body of servants in the parish.[29] As larger holdings on this and other manors tended to increase in numbers, and to enjoy a more continuous existence, the need for wage labour must have grown. The supply of wage earners presumably expanded with the rise in population apparent by the 1510s, as there was no growth in the opportunity to acquire land.

To conclude, in the late fourteenth and fifteenth centuries the relative abundance of land made possible the accumulation of multiple holdings. The economic and social climate did not favour the stability of the accumulations of land, and in particular the bonds of the peasant family were weakened. It is possible to relate the rise and fall of holding size to family circumstances.

Changes can be observed from the last quarter of the fifteenth century: a tendency towards greater stability and continuity of larger holdings, followed by an increase in the frequency of inheritance and transfers within the family after 1500. The underlying causes are uncertain. There was an increased demand for land from the 1470s, but an upward trend in the prices of agricultural produce and population is not apparent until the 1510s. Evidently a combination of circumstances favoured the viability of larger agricultural units, which by 1540 enjoyed both market opportunities and increased supplies of both family and wage labour. This could represent a significant stage in the development of commercial agriculture.

[28] WRO ref. 008:7, BA 3590/I, Vol. II, fols. 110–11; Worcester Wills 1534/146.
[29] WRO ref. 009:1, BA 2636/1143700.

7

The erosion of the family–land bond in the late fourteenth and fifteenth centuries: a methodological note

ZVI RAZI

It has been argued forcefully by many students of the village land market, including contributors to this volume, that the conditions of supply were significantly different in the late middle ages from what they had been earlier. The family sense of inseparable association with a particular holding, which had been so marked a feature of rural society in the early middle ages, weakened; indeed, in some cases it more or less disappeared. The change is usually interpreted as reflecting the growing abundance of land in this period, and the declining importance of inheritance as the mode of acquiring it. Heirs are assumed to have had no need to wait for long periods for the succession to the family holding, as other land became available in the meantime and proved attractive.

Rosamond Faith, a pioneer in the documentation of an active land market in the fifteenth century, noted that this trend began in the fourteenth century. She stated that while the

idea that land 'ought to descend in the blood of the men who had held it of old' is of course common in many peasant societies . . . there does seem to have been a period in English history – roughly that of the fourteenth and fifteenth centuries – when in many rural communities this fundamental idea was in practice abandoned. Family claims to land were disregarded or seldom pressed, and in place of the strict and elaborate arrangements which had previously governed the descent of land, there came to be no laws but those of supply and demand.[1]

In this short note I shall attempt to test the above mentioned arguments with data derived from the Halesowen court rolls. The manor of Halesowen is located west of Birmingham. The parish of Halesowen was coterminous with the manor, which was eight miles

---

[1] R. J. Faith, 'Peasant Families and Inheritance Customs in Medieval England', *Agricultural History Review* 14 (1966), pp. 86–7.

long and about two-and-a-half at its greatest width. The manor was therefore very large, covering some 10 000 acres. In addition to the small market town of Halesowen there were twelve rural settlements or townships in the manor: Oldbury in the north and Romsly in the south with the largest settlements in the parish; each had about thirty to 35 families in *circa* 1300. The other hamlets had only between ten and twenty families each, and Illey no more than six.[2]

All transfers of land (*post mortem* as well as *inter-vivos*) and grants from the lord recorded in the Halesowen court rolls between 1351 and 1430 were examined to see how many remained in the family and how many went to non-family members. Transfers from husband to wife were regarded as non-kin transfers. The results are presented in Table 7.1. We can see that 57 per cent of all the transactions were between family members. This is clearly an under-estimate of intra-familial transfers, because the genealogical information available in the court rolls is incomplete. Moreover, the mere number of land transfers does not give us an accurate indication of the areal quantity of land transferred within the family, because while family members usually bequeathed or transferred whole or half holdings, some 40 per cent of the land sold by the peasants and granted by the lord consisted of parts of holdings. Taking into consideration the area of land transferred in each transaction it was found that, although only 57 per cent of all the land transactions were intra-familial, the land transmitted within the family amounted to 71.3 per cent of the total. There is a decline of some 10 per cent in the amount of land transferred to kin in the 80 years after the plague when compared with the period 1270–1348. But the difference is neither great nor anything like that found by other historians who have studied the problem. Dr Faith, for example, has found that on many south-eastern manors family transactions dropped from 56 per cent of the total in 1300 to around 35 per cent throughout most of the fourteenth century and fell sharply to 13 per cent after 1400.[3] Other historians have also found that intra-familial transactions in the late fourteenth and the beginning of the fifteenth century were much lower than in Halesowen. Such transactions constituted 26 per cent of all those recorded in the Holywell court rolls between 1397 and 1457. In the midland manors of the Bishop of Worcester, Dr Dyer has estimated that transfers within the family constituted only between 18 per cent

---

[2] For a more extensive discussion of Halesowen, see Z. Razi, *Life, Marriage and Death in a Medieval Parish: Economy, Society and Demography in Halesowen 1270–1400* (Cambridge, 1980).
[3] Faith, 'Peasant Families', pp. 89–91.

Table 7.1. Land transactions recorded in Halesowen court rolls 1351–1400*

Years	Post-mortem		Inter-vivos		Grants by the lord		Total transactions	Total kin		Total non-kin
	Kin	Non-kin	Kin	Non-kin	Kin	Non-kin		No.	%	
1351–60	14	1	3	10		11	39	17	43.6	22
1361–70	35	2	4	18		10	69	39	56.5	30
1371–80	11	1	10	13	1	9	50	27	54.0	23
1381–90	15		5	6	1	9	36	21	58.3	15
1391–1400	24	2	9	12		10	58	34	58.6	24
1401–10	27	1	14	15		17	74	41	55.4	33
1411–20	28	1	7	8		3	47	35	74.4	12
1421–30	14	1	9	6		13	44	24	54.5	20
Total	174	9	61	88	2	82	417	238	57.0	179

*Grants husband to wife or wife to husband were regarded as non-kin transactions.

and 39 per cent of all transfers. On the Westminster Abbey manor of Launton 82 per cent of *inter-vivos* transfers were between family members before the Black Death, but in the following century over half of such transactions went to non-family members.[4]

It is possible, of course, that the difference between Halesowen and other places for which figures are available was perhaps a result of a more stable family structure in the former parish. But it is more probable that the difference is due both to the methods used in this study and to the quality of the records. All the historians who have attempted to measure the extent of kin land transfers in the post-plague period have grossly under-estimated such transactions because they have used surnames as their sole guide and have not undertaken comprehensive family reconstitution. It is a commonplace that in the field of nominative linkage persons with different surnames can nevertheless be related. However, historical research on the land transfers of customary tenants in the late middle ages seems to have disregarded or downplayed this matter. This may lead to considerable under-estimation of the intensity and the extent of familial relationships. For example in January 1403 Roger Webb came to the court and took a customary holding in Cakemor which was previously held by Richard Jurdan.[5] Given the different surnames it might be supposed that we have here an extra-familial land transfer. However, on checking the file of Richard Jurdan we find that 21 years earlier in 1382 he transferred this half yardland holding in Cakemor to a newcomer to the manor, a fellow by the name of William Scot.[6] Again we might assume that this is also an extra-familial transfer and that the holding changed hands three times in 21 years between villagers who were not related. However, comprehensive genealogical linkage indicates that Richard Jurdan, William Scot and Roger Webb were related, as Richard was the father-in-law of William and Roger. We know of these relationships because in the record of the land transfer of 1382 it is stipulated that if William Scot and his wife die childless the half virgate holding in Cakemor will revert to Roger Webb.[7] In 1401, when the wife of William Scott died, a court enquiry

---

[4] E. B. Dewindt, *Land and People in Holywell-cum-Needingworth* (Toronto, 1972), p. 134; C. Dyer, *Lords and Peasants in a Changing Society: The Estates of the Bishopric of Worcester, 680–1540* (Cambridge, 1980), p. 302; Barbara Harvey, *Westminster Abbey and its Estates in the Middle Ages* (Oxford, 1977), pp. 324–7. Dr C. Howell also finds 'a sharp decline in hereditary continuity between 1350 and 1412' in Kibworth Harcourt: C. Howell, 'Peasant Inheritance Customs in the Midlands 1280–1700', in J. R. Goody, J. Thirsk and E. P. Thompson, editors, *Family and Inheritance: Rural Society in Western Europe, 1200–1800* (Cambridge, 1976), p. 127.

[5] Birmingham Reference Library (hereafter BRL), 346380, 17.1.1403.

[6] BRL, 346359, 13.1.1382.   [7] *Ibid.*

decided that Roger Webb had a right to share her chattels with her surviving husband, William.[8] In June 1403, when Roger Webb sold the holding he took from the lord six months earlier, it is stated that he was holding the half yardland in Cakemor in his wife Agnes' right, and she declared in the court that she voluntarily agreed to the transaction.[9]

A half yardland holding in Romsley was held between 1357 and 1402 by five villagers with different surnames who were nevertheless related. In 1357 Roger Sprig took the holding which was the dowry of his wife, Alice atte Lych. Since they had no children they transferred the holding in 1377 to her brother John atte Lych, and got it back from him for life. In 1380 Roger Sprig died and his brother-in-law, John, took a part of the holding. However, John atte Lych organized a rebellion against the Abbot for which he was put in the Shropshire gaol, where he died in 1386. Thus the land reverted to Roger atte Lowe, who was the second husband of Alice atte Lych. In 1392 they transferred the half yardland holding to John Sadler, who was married to Agnes atte Lych, Alice's niece. In 1402 Agnes and John Salder transferred the same half yardland holding to Richard Squier, the cousin of Agnes.[10] Stephan de Baresfen, who lived in the township of Langley in the parish of Halesowen in the beginning of the fifteenth century, had a brother, Edmund Stevens, who lived in Stanton (either in Worcestershire or Staffordshire), and both of them had another relative in Halesowen by the name of Thomas Turhill.[11] It is possible to gain a much more realistic estimate of intra-familial land transactions in Halesowen in the post-plague period, not only because a comprehensive family reconstitution from 1270 to 1430 is available, but also because for these 162 years the records of only fourteen years are missing, eleven of them between 1282 and 1292. Moreover the court records survived *in extenso* without any editing so that it was possible to reconstruct an almost complete and very detailed land register for the parish.

If only surnames are used, 132 of the 417 land transfers (31 per cent) recorded between 331 and 1430 are identified as intra-familial. This suggests that by using surnames only we under-estimate intra-familial transfers by at least 80 per cent. Moreover, the use of surnames as the sole criterion to estimate the role of kinship in the transmission of land is bound to lead to the current view that, unlike

---

[8] BRL, 346375, 10.12.1401.
[9] BRL, 346379, 25.7.1403.
[10] BRL., 346340, 346357, 346359, 346822, 346823.
[11] BRL, 3467377–97.

the pre-plague period, in the post-plague years kinship became less important, even if such a change never occurred, simply because the population was rising in the first period and declining in the second. Professor Wrigley has found that theoretically in a *stationary* population 20 per cent of the married men will have no children to succeed them when they die, 20 per cent will have only daughters, and 60 per cent will have at least one daughter and one son. When the poulation is rising the percentage of married men who die childless or only with daughters is falling, while the percentage who have sons to succeed them is rising. On the other hand when the population is declining the proportion of married men who have no children or only daughters to succeed them is rising, while the proportion who have sons to succeed them is falling.[12] Consequently, even if kin relationships were as important in the transmission of land in a period of population decline as they were in a period of population growth, by using only surnames as a criterion one is bound to find that kinship becomes much less significant in a period of decline. This is because in such a population the proportion of land holders who are succeeded by people with the same surname is likely to be much lower than it would be in a period of growth. The distorted results obtained by the use of surnames as the only criterion to estimate the role of kinship in the transmission of land becomes even greater if the extent of migration intensifies during the period of population decline, because often peasants changed their surnames when they emigrated, particularly in the case of out-marrying females. Since the population of England was rising through most of the hundred years which preceded the 'Black Death', and was declining during the hundred years which followed it, and since it is very probable that the rural population became more mobile, the usual evidence brought by historians to substantiate the hypothesis that kinship became less important in the transmission of land in later medieval England is ambiguous in the meaning that can be attached to it. Because familial relationships are more difficult to detect in the post-plague sources, in order to find out what really happened it is necessary to use only those records which enable us to study a locality over a long period and to do complete family reconstitutions. Moreover, even if an excellent series of fifteenth-century court rolls is available it is impossible to find out the true extent of kin relationships in that locality if at the very least the records of the period from 1350 to 1400 are missing.

[12] E. A. Wrigley, 'Fertility Strategy for the Individual and the Group', in C. Tilly, editor, *Historical Studies of Changing Fertility* (Princeton, NJ, 1978), pp. 135–54.

We have found that in Halesowen during the period 1350 to 1430 kinship was almost as important in the transmission of land as it had been during the period 1270 to 1349. This becomes even clearer when one reads the exceptionally detailed and informative court roll entries which deal with land. For example, in November 1385 the death was recorded of Agnes, the wife of Philip Hypkys, who held from the lord a toft and certain lands and a holding in Lapal. After death duties of two oxen valued at 16s had been taken there

came John le Warde the closest heir to the above mentioned Agnes, namely the son of her sister by blood, and claimed to succeed to the above mentioned holding with all its appurtenances which Philip Hypkis held in his wife Agnes' right in the manor of Hales, to be held by the above mentioned John and his descendants for services and customs.[13]

In 1404 Thomas Adams succeeded by hereditary right to half of the half yardland holding of Roger Ketel in Illey, after the death of his niece, Alice. It is stated that if Thomas died childless, his younger brother William was to inherit the land.[14] The court rolls for 1382 show that Thomas' father, William, arranged a marriage between his sister, Felicity, and one Roger Ketel.[15] In 1420 Felicity gave the rest of the Ketel place to her nephew Thomas Adams, but nine years later, as if by chance, a certain Henry Putter came to Halesowen manorial court and claimed to have rights in the Ketel holding. After an enquiry conducted by twelve villagers it was decided that he had a claim to the holding since he was the closest blood relative to Roger Ketel.[16] In 1404 John Baker and his wife Margaret transferred to their son John the customary tenements which were previously held by Robert Sweyn and John Watterhurst, both of whom were cousins of Margaret. The rolls state that if John died childless his brother Thomas would inherit from him, and if Thomas died childless his brother William would inherit the land, but if William also died childless he would be succeeded by one of the descendants of Robert Sweyn.[17] These and many other examples in the Halesowen court rolls, not less than the overall proportion of intra-familial land transactions, cast serious doubts upon the validity of the view that the importance of inheritance as a mode of transmitting land was fading, and that familial claims to land were disregarded or seldom pressed in the post-plague period. Not only inheritance by near and more distant relatives, but also marriage, played a very important role in the transmission of land in Halesowen. It would seem that many 'kulaks' accumulated more or as much land by good marriages as

[13] BRL, 346365, 28.12.1385.   [14] BRL, 346381, 30.4.1404.
[15] BRL, 346359, 10.12.1382.   [16] BRL, 346399, 5.10.1429.   [17] BRL, 346382, 26.11.1404.

they acquired via the land market. For example, Thomas Collin, the son of John Collin of Oldbury, was amerced 2s for seducing young Isabel Lovecok.[18] Isabel, however, was not only attractive, but also well endowed with land, as she had inherited her uncle John Lovecok's half yardland holding in Hasbury in 1382, and therefore Thomas subsequently married her. Sixteen years later Thomas obtained another half yardland in Oldbury, which his wife inherited after the death of her mother Agnes.[19] Richard Moulowe of Hill, by far the wealthiest villager in Halesowen, came from an affluent background, but his family did not rank among the most prominent in the village during the first half of the century. Richard's meteoric rise was due to a successful marriage and to the 'Black Death'. Just before the outbreak of plague Richard married one of the daughters of Philip Hill. Philip, who had four daughters and four sons, was one of the five richest peasants in the manor. Philip himself, and many others of his family, fell victim to the plague, and only three of his daughters survived to share the vast fortune he left. Richard Moulowe acquired a third of the Hill lands through his wife Juliana, and another through his wife's elder widowed sister, Agnes, whom he took into his household. The third part of Philip Hill's lands and property went to his daughter, Milicentia, and her husband, Robert Cutler.[20] Thus, through his marriage, young Richard acquired within four years some 60 acres of land and probably a lot of cash, much livestock and other property, which enabled him to build a huge fortune in the second half of the fourteenth century. A tough, cunning and ruthless peasant who made a good marriage and fared well in the 'demographic lottery' had an excellent chance of becoming a veritable village millionaire.

The main difference between the post- and pre-plague periods, as far as the relationship between family and land is concerned, was that before 1349 the majority of the holdings in Halesowen were transferred to local villagers who were closely related, usually through the male line. After the Black Death, as a result of the demographic crisis and recession, a higher proportion of the holdings were transferred to villagers, many of them immigrants, who were more distantly related to the deceased tenants and often through the female line. Therefore one often finds in the pre-plague period court rolls that a certain holding is associated with the same surname over a long period of time, whereas in the post-plague court rolls it becomes much rarer.

---

[18] BRL, 346363, 9.10.1383.
[19] BRL, 346360, 26.11.1382; 346376, 19.3.1399.
[20] BRL, 346317–57.

It is reasonable to assume that the shortage of tenants, the scarcity of labour and the opportunity to regain freedom from serfdom, encouraged migration in the post-plague period. However, there is some evidence which suggests that the peasants during this period did not wander all over the place to snatch the first opportunity which came their way, as Silvia Thrupp and some other historians have implied. It would seem from the evidence, at least for one west midland manor, that a villager usually left his native village either because he had inherited land or to marry a bride with land in another village. In the court rolls between 1349 and 1430 there are 137 cases (30 per cent of all the recorded land transfers) in which outsiders came to Halesowen either to claim hereditary rights in land or to quitclaim such rights. For example, in 1424 the three daughters of John Bate came to Halesowen to surrender their rights in their father's holding in the township of Warley to Thomas Haket, of the same vill and probably the husband of the fourth daughter. One daughter came with her husband from Cradely, the second came with her husband from Northfield and the third, who was a widow, came from Thickbroom in Staffordshire.[21] In 1414 Alice and Juliana, the daughters of Joanna Sweyn, succeeded to the family half yard-land in Oldbury. A year later Alice, who was married to William de Feleford, who lived in Yardeley, quitclaimed her rights in the holding to her sister Juliana and her husband Gerald Wower.[22] In 1423 John Perkys of Frankeley and Lucy his wife surrendered her rights in the Hameford half yardland in Romsley to her nephew, Roger Stampis.[23] In 1409 John Stevens, who lived in Harborn, succeeded his brother Nicholas in the Palmer holding, which he transferred to John Kembersley and his wife Juliana in 1413.[24] There are also many cases of outsiders who settled in Halesowen when their titles were recognized by the court. In 1414, for example, William, son of the late Henry Atkys of Ludlow, took the yardland holding of Philip Whyteley from Hasbury, and since he was under age he paid the lord a mark for his ward and marriage.[25] In 1407 John Taylor left Stourbridge and took the holding of his father, John Smyth of Oldbury.[26] Several members of the large Turnhill family of Rowley Regis moved to Halesowen in the second half of the fourteenth century and the beginning of the fifteenth century because they inherited land there.[27] The majority of the outsiders who had relatives in Halesowen or who married local

[21] BRL, 351345–7.   [22] BRL, 346390, 4.7.1414; 346391, 31.7.1415.
[23] BRL, 346826, 6.10.1423.
[24] BRL, 346386, 22.5.1409; 346389, 22.6.1412.
[25] BRL, 346391, 10.10.1414.   [26] BRL, 346384, 20.7.1407.   [27] BRL, 346331–77.

girls came from the neighbouring parishes around Halesowen, but others immigrated from more distant parishes in Warwickshire, Shropshire, Worcestershire and Staffordshire, and even from Herefordshire and Derbyshire.

The evidence from Halesowen suggests that in the eighty years which followed the Black Death the bond between family and land was not severed; it simply became less visible in the records. The major change that occurred after 1350 was the increasing involvement of more distant relatives in the network of family land transfers. In fact, the extension of effective family ties beyond the nuclear group after the plague coincided with a spatial extension of the family group at least for the purposes of land transfers *post-mortem* and *inter-vivos*. Whether this widening of the geographical range of kin ties based on land altered the nature of the affective ties between individual members of the kin group is a question that manor court rolls are poorly equipped to answer.

8

Changes in the link between families and land in the west midlands in the fourteenth and fifteenth centuries

CHRISTOPHER DYER

Dr Razi has done us a great service by applying his detailed researches into the manorial court rolls of Halesowen to the problem of inheritance in the late fourteenth and early fifteenth centuries. He has shown that the use of surnames alone to indicate the existence of blood relationships provides an inadequate guide to the transfer of land within the family, and that the use of sensitive research methods shows that remote relatives, many of them living at some distance from Halesowen, claimed holdings when they became available. However, it is important to recognize Halesowen's special characteristics, and if we examine the records of a wider range of manors in the west midlands we can see that the generalizations of Faith, Harvey or Hilton about the changes in the link between peasant families and land still have some validity.

At the centre of Halesowen lay a small urban community which must have exercised a considerable influence over the surrounding countryside.[1] Halesowen borough lay in the centre of a knot of boroughs, eight of them within a radius of ten miles.[2] Through this relatively urbanized district ran long-distance trade routes, notably the droving roads that brought large numbers of Welsh cattle into the midlands and ultimately to London; here also were short-distance routes for the local trade in foodstuffs and iron and leather goods. Rural and small-town industries had developed in the district by the thirteenth century, and seem to have flourished in the later middle ages. The agricultural economy was less dependent on cereal cultivation than that of the older-settled or more densely populated champion districts of the midlands. The field systems of Halesowen and its

---

[1] R. H. Hilton, 'Lords, Burgesses and Hucksters', *Past and Present* 97 (1982), pp. 3–15.
[2] M. W. Beresford and H. P. R. Finberg, *Medieval English Boroughs* (Newton Abbot, 1973), *passim*; and the addenda in *Urban History Year Book*.

neighbours were complex, with areas of open field with intermixed strips adjoining land divided into numerous small enclosed fields. Agrarian economies such as those of Halesowen and its district adapted to the changes in the later middle ages more readily than the more specialized champion villages, as they were able to expand their pastoral activities with relative ease.[3]

The tenants of Halesowen fought bitter struggles in the thirteenth century against increases in their rents and services imposed by the Abbey; because of the manor's ancient demesne status, and no doubt also because of the vigour of their resistance to new impositions, the Halesowen peasants' burdens were relatively low, with annual rents of 6s 8d per yardland in the late thirteenth century and a maximum of eighteen days' labour service from a yardland.[4] Rents in the region at this time could commonly exceed 13s 4d per yardland and many tenants owed fifty or a hundred days' labour service or more.[5] It is hardly surprising that land in Halesowen should be especially attractive to heirs, as it was capable of giving good returns, while rents and services were not particularly high. One of the chief disadvantages for a peasant of the manor – the aggressive posture of the Abbey – became less of a problem in the later middle ages. One special feature of Halesowen's customs gave heirs an incentive to claim lands, namely the two-tier system of entry fines, by which heirs paid much less than non-relatives on taking up a new holding.[6]

Halesowen was not unique in the attractiveness of its lands. Thornbury in Gloucestershire shares some of Halesowen's characteristics, and its court rolls are informative because the practice developed of customary holdings vacated by death or surrender being formally proclaimed at three successive courts, and of the proclamations being noted in the court rolls.[7] The courts met every three weeks, so any heirs were given six weeks to make a claim. On the third occasion the land was granted, and the relationship between the old and new tenants, if any, was recorded. Taking a sample of 27 holdings proclaimed in the years 1438–44 we find that five were taken

---

[3] For an elaboration of this argument in relation to the nearby Warwickshire Arden, see C. Dyer, *Warwickshire Farming, 1349–c. 1520: Presentation for Agricultural Revolution*, Dugdale Society Occasional Paper xxvii (London, 1981).

[4] Z. Razi, 'The Struggles between the Abbots of Halesowen and Their Tenants in the Thirteenth and Fourteenth Centuries', in T. H. Aston *et al.*, editors, *Social Relations and Ideas* (Cambridge, 1983), pp. 151–67.

[5] R. H. Hilton, *A Medieval Society*, 2nd edition (Cambridge, 1983), pp. 122–3, and 131–47.

[6] Z. Razi, 'Family, Land and the Village Community in Later Medieval England', *Past and Present* 93 (1981), pp. 25–6.

[7] Staffordshire Record Office, D641/1/4c/7.

by tenants' widows, ten by non-relatives, and twelve by relatives, eight of them having the same surname as the former tenant, and four having different surnames. So almost a half of the holdings passed to relatives (if we treat widows as non-kin as Dr Razi does); if the court rolls had been less informative, so that surnames alone would have been used as evidence of kinship, we would have identified 30 per cent of transfers as passing between relatives. The Halesowen figures, 57 per cent for transfer between kin, and 31 per cent for transfer between people with the same surname, are very comparable. This is not surprising, because Thornbury also lay within the sphere of influence of urban markets: a borough lay within the manor, and the great town of Bristol was only twelve miles distant. The local agrarian landscape can be categorized as belonging to the wood/pasture type, with some emphasis on animal husbandry, and much land lying in enclosed fields. Thornbury's rents were very much higher than those at Halesowen, but some of the land was superior in its fertility. Thornbury's holdings can thus be regarded as desirable assets and worth claiming by heirs.

When we turn away from well-documented places like Halesowen and Thornbury we have necessarily to use surnames as crude indicators of the relationship betwen the new tenant and his or her predecessor. Judging from the Halesowen and Thornbury examples, it appears that between a half and two-thirds of the transfers between kin will be indicated by surname evidence, so if we bear this factor of under-recording in mind, the proportion of new tenants with the same surname as the former tenants will give some guide to the relative importance of inter-familial transfers in different manors and also at different times. Such variations are apparent in the figures that can be calculated from the records of the estates of the bishopric of Worcester, where the range of transactions between kin with the same surname lay, according to Dr Razi between 18 and 39 per cent of all transfers. The actual minimum in any one decade was 0 per cent, and the maximum 77 per cent.[8] The nil figure came from Hampton Lucy, a champion manor in south Warwickshire, very different from Halesowen and dedicated to cereal production in a fully developed two-field system. This is the type of rural economy that is often found to be suffering a malaise in the later middle ages. Of a total of 132 land transfers recorded at Hampton between 1450 and 1530 only five involved successive tenants with the same surname, 4 per cent of the total. Now of course this can be no more than a minimum figure for

[8] C. Dyer, *Lords and Peasants in a Changing Society: The Estates of the Bishopric of Worcester, 680–1540* (Cambridge, 1980), p. 302.

the transfer between kin, and we should make some allowance for the more remote relationships concealed by the different surnames of the old and new tenants. Even so, if parties to transfers with the same surnames occur six times less frequently than at Halesowen, it would be dangerous to assume that cousins, nephews and so on were more enthusiastic in their claims to land at Hampton than at Halesowen. It is not unreasonable, therefore, to estimate that 90 per cent of Hampton land transactions were between unrelated parties. It would be difficult indeed to regard inheritance as a major factor in the social and economic life of Hampton Lucy. Yet Hampton was in a more fortunate position than some of its champion neighbours. So unattractive were holdings at such places as Hatton-on-Avon, Thornton, Chapel Ascote and at least another hundred west midland villages that land fell vacant and either lay in the lord's hands or was taken up by an engrossing neighbour until eventually there were no peasants left.[9] In such villages no refinement of method, no painstaking reconstruction of family trees, can undermine the reality of the crumbling houses and untilled land that resulted from a collapse in the inheritance system. Heirs of all kinds, from both close and remote kin, had migrated and showed no desire to return to their ancestral holdings.

Most medieval peasants lived in villages whose circumstances lay somewhere between those of Hatton-on-Avon at one extreme and Halesowen at the other. There are many examples that could be used to indicate the sharpness of the break that severed the link between a family and its land. It would be tedious to recount the numerous occasions on which customary tenants 'withdrew from the lordship without licence' or 'left the holding vacant', taking the goods, chattels and animals which in theory belonged to the lord, and which in reality would in the event of inheritance have been passed on to the heir. Often holdings so abandoned were left in the hands of the lord for some time before a new tenant could be found. Such was the interest of some heirs that they refused to take the lands that were offered to them, like Richard Aleyn of Grafton (Worcs.), who surrendered the yardland that he inherited in 1455.[10] Landlords had an interest in maintaining holdings as viable units in the hands of rent paying tenants, and in the late fourteenth and early fifteenth centuries sometimes nominated men to take over lands that were either vacant or were being worked incompetently. We may suppose that

[9] C. Dyer, 'Deserted Medieval Villages in the West Midlands', Economic History Review 2nd series 35 (1982), pp. 19–34.
[10] Worcestershire County Record Office, ref. 705:100, BA 1120/12.

such tenants were chosen because of their capacity to be effective peasant cultivators, not by virtue of any hereditary right.

The point that is being stressed is that inheritance varied in quantity, depending on the general demand for land in a manor or district. Relatives would be anxious to claim attractive holdings and to frustrate non-relatives willing to pay for entry. When debilitated holdings in decaying villages were on offer, the heirs stayed away. One indication of the demand for land is provided by the rate of entry fines, which stayed relatively high at Halesowen, and could exceed £1 per yardland at Thornbury in the early fifteenth century, while they normally fell elsewhere in the west midlands to a few shillings per yardland, or a few capons, or nothing at all in the early and mid-fifteenth century.

The demand for land varied from place to place, and fluctuated over time. Dr Razi has studied the earlier part of the post-plague period, 1350–1430, while many of the studies criticized by him draw their evidence from the whole of the fifteenth century. We would expect to find that inheritance reached its low point in the middle of the fifteenth century, when the general demand for land in many manors reached a nadir. Another variable may lie in the form of tenure. Although manorial court rolls are a poor source for the transfer of freeholdings, these tenements do make an intermittent appearance because landlords had an interest in the levying of heriots and reliefs. We gain the impression that transfers between kin were more common than those involving customary holdings, because a free tenement, burdened with light rents and few restrictions, would have been a desirable asset for a would-be heir. There is scope here for research in those neglected sources, deed collections, which survive in large numbers for some places. We also need to know more about the effects of changes in the forms of customary tenure on inheritance. Did the adoption of copyhold for lives, or leasehold for years, lead to a lower level of transfer among kin than in those manors retaining the traditional pattern of tenures? It would be surprising if within the stipulated terms for lives lands were claimed by heirs as frequently as when the holdings were not subject to any time limit.

In examining this complex but important subject we are investigating two related developments – changes in the reality of the transfers of holdings, and changes in the mentality of the peasant community. We might expect attitudes towards inheritance to fluctuate with social and economic trends, no doubt with a lag between reality and sentiment, but with *perceived* interests often coinciding with *real* interests. Certainly there were declarations of the rights of heirs when manorial customs were codified, but these seem to have been strongest at places, and in times, of high demand for land. For example, the Thornbury customs of 1486 stated that if a claimant was 'lawfully begotten' 'he should inherit to the ninth degree', which if put into effect would have allowed rights to kin beyond the scope of even the most thorough modern research to recognize.[11] Village opinion does not always seem to have regarded the claims of remote heirs as paramount. At Sambourne (Warks.) in 1476 a holding was disputed between two claimants on the death of Thomas Mekulton. One was the nephew of the first husband of Mekulton's widow, the other the son of the niece of a previous tenant. The homage decided to disallow both claims, and the lord granted the holding to a non-relative who was prepared to pay a fine of £10.[12]

In searching for evidence of the inheritance of land by cousins and nephews we are in danger of losing sight of a vitally important change in both reality and sentiment. When a holding was inherited within a nuclear family, it was passing to someone who had at some point actually helped to cultivate that land. A son of a tenant would already be a participant in the co-operation and conflicts of the village community. We can all agree that inheritance by sons did become less frequent after 1350, even at Halesowen, if only because sons were less likely to survive to adulthood, even among the better-off peasants.

The new tenants of the period after 1350 often came from outside the nuclear family, and from outside the village. Frequently they were relatives by marriage, sons-in-law notably; when we are told that daughters inherited, we may suspect that the effective heir was again a son-in-law. Dr Razi includes such heirs among the kin, although he rather inconsistently treats transfers between husband and wife as lying outside blood relationships. Often these more remote relatives, as strangers to their new villages, without neces-sarily having a direct interest in agriculture, did not settle at all. For example, the Coventry shearman who acquired a holding at Stoneleigh before 1374 would have substituted a sub-tenant to work the land.[13] Inheritance served as a further agency by which the peasant family and the village community were thrown open to outside influences. The relationship between the *nuclear* family and the land changed in the later middle ages, and this was a real social

[11] Gloucester City Library, RQ 303.2.
[12] Shakespeare's Birthplace Trust Record Office, DR5/2357.
[13] *The Stoneleigh Leger Book*, edited by R. H. Hilton, Dugdale Society Occasional Papers xxiv (London, 1960), pp. 186–7.

change, bringing in its wake movements in the settlement pattern and the character of the village community. This was not just a decline in the *visibility* of the bond between the peasant family and the land.

9

Kinship in an English village: Terling, Essex 1500–1700

KEITH WRIGHTSON

The intention of this paper is simple: to provide information which may help to answer the question 'How important was kinship in the social structure of an English village community and in the lives of English villagers in the early modern period?' An investigation of this kind is timely, perhaps even overdue, when one considers the current stage of research in both history and the social sciences. It is now some twenty years since Professor Williams argued that 'it does seem as if the general structure of English kinship is now clearly established'. He pointed to the general predominance of the nuclear family in household structure; the bilateral tracing of descent which gives a unique set of kin to each individual; a recognition of kin which is both shallow in depth and narrow in range. He emphasized that English kinship is 'a flexible permissive system' having few strong obligations or rules of behaviour between kin; that kin sentiments are rarely sufficiently strong to overcome geographical or social distance; that kinship is in general functionally unimportant as compared with neighbourliness, being merely one of several networks of connection from which individuals might select one another for various purposes.[1]

Historians probing the very distant past might perhaps expect to discover a very different situation. Those concerned with the early modern period have long been aware of the preoccupation with lineage and of the effective importance of kinship ties among the ruling class of the time.[2] Of realities lower in the social scale,

[1] W. M. Williams, *A West Country Village: Ashworthy. Family, Kinship and Land* (London, 1963), pp. 183–4 and Chapter 6 *passim*.

[2] See, for example, L. Stone, *The Crisis of the Aristocracy, 1558–1641*, abridged edition (Oxford, 1965), pp. 269–71, and *The Family, Sex and Marriage in England, 1500–1800* (London, 1977), pp. 4–7 and Chapters 3 and 4 *passim*; J. T. Cliffe, *The Yorkshire Gentry from the Reformation to the Civil War* (London, 1969), p. 10; A. M. Everitt, *Change in the*

however, little is known, and recent work suggests that expectations based upon practice among aristocrats and gentry may be unjustified. The last decade has seen two major advances in the discussion of English kinship. Peter Laslett's work on census-type listings has transformed our knowledge of kinship links *within* households, revealing an overwhelming predominance of nuclear family households as early as the sixteenth century and demonstrating that the complexity of households diminished sharply as the social scale was descended.[3] Secondly, Alan Macfarlane's careful and inventive analysis of the diary of the Reverend Ralph Josselin for the mid- and later seventeenth century has displayed Josselin's lack of interest in lineage and very restricted recognition of kin. While stressing the closeness of ties within the nuclear family and the probable early importance to Josselin of relationships with uncles, Macfarlane shows firmly that 'apart from the nuclear family, there was no effective kin "group" in Josselin's world'. Josselin's key relationships outside his own nuclear family were with personal friends and neighbours.[4]

These findings prompt further research into issues which the nature of their documentation has not permitted these scholars to explore. Laslett, for example, is less able to examine kin links between households from listings alone. Nor is he able to explore the nature of kinship relations either within or between households, though ultimately these issues may prove of more significance for social change than the preliminary problem of household structure.[5] Macfarlane's analysis faces problems of typicality. Josselin was a clergyman, geographically isolated from kinsmen and so forth; was his experience therefore unusual?

These are the issues which will be examined in this paper. An attempt will be made to examine the network of kinship links between households in the Essex parish of Terling in 1671. This

Provinces: the Seventeenth Century Occasional Papers of the Department of Local History, second series: (Leicester, 1970), pp. 26–9; M. E. James, *Family, Lineage and Civil Society: A Study of Society, Politics and Mentality in the Durham Region, 1500–1640* (Oxford, 1974), pp. 25–7.

[3] P. Laslett, 'Mean Household Size in England Since the Sixteenth Century' in P. Laslett and R. Wall, editors, *Household and Family in Past Time* (Cambridge, 1972), pp. 125–58.

[4] A. Macfarlane, *The Family Life of Ralph Josselin, a Seventeenth Century Clergyman: An Essay in Historical Anthropology* (Cambridge, 1970), pp. 82 and 149 and Chapters 7–10 *passim*.

[5] See, for example, the stimulating essay by David Sabean, 'Aspects of Kinship Behaviour and Property in Rural Western Europe before 1800', in J. R. Goody, J. Thirsk and E. P. Thompson, editors, *Family and Inheritance: Rural Society in Western Europe, 1200–1800* (Cambridge, 1976), pp. 96–111.

accomplished, wills will be analysed to provide information on kinship recognition and on relations between close kin over the period 1550 to 1700. Finally a variety of sources will be used to examine the relative importance of kin and neighbours for a range of practical purposes. Throughout, the analysis will be as comprehensive as possible, dealing with the whole community. Most importantly, the results reported will be comparable to results which may be provided in the future for any other village for which the same basic sources are available.

The parish of Terling lies in east-central Essex. The settlement in the sixteenth and seventeenth centuries was nucleated, most of the households living within easy walking distance of one another, with a few dwellings outside the main settlement on outlying farms. The economy of the parish was entirely agricultural but characterized as early as the late sixteenth century by large-scale commercial farming. A sector of relatively small peasant holdings remained, but most of the land was farmed in large units worked by landless or near-landless labourers and living-in servants in husbandry. Between 1520 and 1670 the population of the parish almost doubled, rising from perhaps three hundred to some six hundred inhabitants. The same period saw a substantial increase in the proportion of labourers in the population. The population of Terling was also highly mobile. The great majority of men and women marrying and subsequently baptizing children in Terling were not born in the parish. Geographical mobility and geographically exogamous marriage may have been important influences on both the kinship network and kin relations in Terling and should be borne in mind in considering the findings which will be presented in the remainder of this essay.[6]

i. The network of kin in Terling

As a preliminary to the discussion of kinship relations an attempt must be made to establish the extent to which households in Terling were linked by kinship and also the density of their linkage. Subordinate questions concern the nature of these links and the extent to which they varied with social position, age and sex.

---

[6] A full study of society and social change in Terling, 1525–1700, written in collaboration with Dr D. C. Levine, was published in 1979 (K. Wrightson and D. C. Levine, *Poverty and Piety in an English Village – Terling 1525–1700* (London, 1979)). The principal sources used for both the broader study and the present essay include parish registers, parish account books, wills, manorial records, deeds, taxation records and the records of the secular and ecclesiastical courts. A full list of records used can be found in the bibliography of *Poverty and Piety*.

Terling, like most English villages, has no census-type listing. It does have, again like many other villages, a series of Hearth Tax assessments of the 1660s and 1670s. These vary in quality, but that of 1671 is a complete listing of household heads assessed for the tax, including even those exempted from payment on grounds of severe poverty. The completeness of the list has been checked against Overseers of the Poor accounts contemporary with the listing. All householders receiving relief are represented on the Hearth Tax list.

The kin of each householder on this list have been traced as far as possible using the Family Reconstitution Forms prepared by Dr D. C. Levine, together with a name index based upon the major categories of records for the village over the period 1524–1700. All evidence of connection between individual villagers is recorded in this name index. Where possible, the kin of each householder were traced back for two generations and forward to the date of the listing. Uncles, aunts, cousins and second cousins, siblings, nephews and nieces were included where possible. If the householder was or had been married, affines were also traced in the same fashion, thus allowing for the fact that listed householders were predominantly men. In effect, then, the kin of each married couple were traced. Despite the effort to be thorough, it is clear that the data used were often incomplete. For this reason the kin links established will be regarded as a minimum estimate. Alongside this, a maximum estimate of kin links has been arrived at which includes suspected or simply possible links, based on, for example, identical surnames. Some of these additional links are strongly suspected to have existed, others are 'long shots' based on slight evidence. Nevertheless, the maximum estimate provides a range of error. The truth doubtless lies between the minimum and maximum estimates. The results of this analysis are given below.

To say that some 50 to 60 per cent of householders were unrelated even distantly to other householders is not, of course, to say that they had no kin in Terling. Most of these persons were married and had children. It is to say rather that their _households_ (which in the English context we can confidently expect to have been predominantly nuclear family households) were isolated within the village in terms of kinship, unlinked to other households by either blood or marriage. Many, of course, would have kin in other villages, an issue to which I shall return.

Figures of this kind, whatever their intrinsic interest, are of little value unless placed in some sort of context. Do they indicate a high or low degree of kin linkage? Comparative material is unfortunately

Table 9.1

	Min.		Max.	
	No.	%	No.	%
Total householders	122	100	122	100
Related to other householders	48	39.3	64	52.5
Unrelated to other householders	74	60.7	58	47.5

hard to come by. Compared to Professor Williams' study of Gosforth in the 1950s, however, the extent of kin linkage in Terling was low, whichever estimate is used. Williams found that 80 per cent of occupiers and their wives in Gosforth were 'closely related' to at least one other household.[7] This comparison, while a useful warning to those who might expect a greater degree of kin linkage in the past than in the twentieth century, is of limited usefulness because of the great disparity between the economies of the two villages, let alone the different historical contexts. However a better comparison can be made with the three eighteenth-century French villages examined in an important recent thesis by Emmanuel Todd, each of which had an economy based on commercial farming.[8] This comparison necessitates the use of first-order kin links only (i.e. those links between households established through parents and children or through siblings).[9] Reworking the Terling figures in this way means using only proven links and dropping more distant links. For the sake of comparability Todd's minimum estimates of linkage are used. The results of the comparison are presented in Table 9.2, together with the comparable figures for Gosforth.

As will be evident from Table 9.2, a lower proportion of Terling households was linked to other households by first-order links than

[7] W. M. Williams, *The Sociology of an English Village: Gosforth* (London, 1956), pp. 69–85.

[8] E. Todd, 'Seven Peasant Communities in Pre-Industrial Europe: A Comparative Study of French, Italian and Swedish Rural Parishes in the Eighteenth and Early Nineteenth Centuries', unpublished University of Cambridge Ph.D. thesis, 1976. I must express my gratitude to Dr Todd for permission to quote findings from his dissertation.

[9] It should be noted that the links traced by Dr Todd were between Conjugal Family Units (CFUs) rather than between householders. His results, however, are very nearly comparable to those for Terling since the overwhelming majority of households in the French villages were in fact simple nuclear family households, while in the case of Terling the kin of householders' spouses have been traced. Absolute comparability is unfortunately precluded by the different nature of the documents available for use in the two studies.

Table 9.2. *First-order kinship links between households/conjugal family units**

	Terling	Gosforth	Wisques	Longuenesse	Hallines
Total no. of	1671	1950–3	1778	1778	1776
HHs/CFUs	122		23	42	50
Unrelated to others	67%	50%	43%	26%	18%
Related to 1	26%		39%	36%	30%
Related to 2	7%		14%	19%	22%
Related to 3+	0%		4%	19%	30%
Total % related	33%	50%	57%	74%	82%

*Householders in the case of Terling; Conjugal Family Units in the case of the French villages. See note 9.

in any of the French villages. Terling's experience is closer to that of modern Gosforth, though even here the difference is considerable. Two other comparative measurements can be made. The first of these, *Absolute Kinship Density*, is a measure of the absolute number of kin links of the average householder or conjugal family unit in the respective villages. It has the advantage of going beyond the simple categories of 'unrelated' or 'related' and allowing for the fact that some households have links to several others. The second, *Relative Kinship Density*, represents the proportion of kin links of the total number of possible kin links in the respective villages.[10] The results are presented in Table 9.3.

Again we find that in comparison with the French villages, the kinship network in Terling was very loose indeed. Furthermore this would continue to be the case even were the Terling figures corrected up substantially.

This comparison, while useful in setting the Terling findings in context, has necessarily been based upon only the closest kin links. Returning to Terling alone, consideration can be given to all kin links, and maximum and minimum estimates can again be introduced in Table 9.3.

These results once more indicate the relative looseness of the network of kinship in the parish. Whichever estimate is used it is clear that most of the householders with kin among other households had only one such link. Extensive kinship networks were very few and no householder was linked to more than four others.

[10] An extremely clear exposition of the method of calculation used is to be found in Todd, 'Seven Peasant Communities', pp. 218–20 and 232–4.

Table 9.3. *The density of kinship networks: first-order links*

	Terling 1671	Wisques 1778	Longuenesse 1778	Hallines 1776
Total no. of HHs/CFUs	122	23	42	50
Absolute kinship density	0.39	0.77	1.36	1.73
Relative kinship density	0.3%	3.5%	3.3%	3.5%

Whether these findings are characteristic of all English parishes or of *certain* types of community – for example lowland parishes pre- cociously involved in a tenant farming system – or are the result of circumstances peculiar to Terling it is as yet impossible to say. One would expect to find considerable variation in England, as in France. What is of ultimate significance is the question of the range of variation and the factors influencing it – economic system, social structure, age structure, demographic rates.

While comparison between parishes with different economies and demographic rates must await further research, some progress can be made in investigating the influence of age and social position upon the network of kin in Terling.

Analysis by age carries us onto rather dangerous ground. The Family Reconstitution Forms yield the exact baptismal dates of only 41 householders. In other cases age could be estimated to within five years on the basis of marriage dates, but in fifteen cases no reasonable estimate could be attempted. The resultant figures need not be repeated here. Suffice it to say that the distribution of householders with at least one kin link by age was, on both maximum and minimum estimates, very close indeed to the distribution of house- holders by age in the whole population. The calculation of kinship densities for age groups showed little variation save that the kinship density of the groups 60–9 and 70+ was somewhat lower than that of younger groups. Most householders with kinship links, single or multiple, were aged between thirty and fifty, as were most house- holders in the population. Presumably this is a simple reflection of the fact that persons of this age were most likely to have adult brothers, affines and perhaps parents and parents-in-law still alive and heading households.

Turning to the question of wealth and social position, we step onto firmer ground. The number of hearths on which householders were assessed in 1671 provides an indication of their housing standards and a roughly accurate measure of their relative wealth. Comparison

Table 9.4. *Kinship links in Terling: all links*

	Minimum		Maximum	
	No.	%	No.	%
Total no. of householders	122	100%	122	100%
Unrelated to others	74	60.7	58	47.5
Related to 1	32	26.2	39	32.0
Related to 2	10	8.2	16	13.1
Related to 3	4	3.3	6	4.9
Related to 4	2	1.6	3	2.5
Total related	48	39.3	64	52.5
Absolute kinship density	0.59		0.83	
Relative kinship density	0.5%		0.7%	

between these assessments and other independent evidence of social status, wealth and poverty provides a few exceptions to the rule among the middling ranks of village society, but satisfactorily proves its general validity. On the basis of assessment and other evidence, householders have been divided into four categories (see Table 9.5). These categories will be used as the basis of all further socially specific comparisons.

It can be said immediately that relative social position and wealth seem to have had very little influence on the likelihood of a householder having kin among other householders. On both minimum and maximum estimates, the distribution by social category of householders with at least one kin link was very close to the distribution by social category of householders in the whole population. To this extent the experience of householders was homogeneous. This general statement, however, must be slightly modified when consideration is given to multiple links, the density of linkage and the types of links concerned.

Householders with multiple kin links to other householders were, as we have seen, rather few. These householders were, however, concentrated in social categories IV and II. As a result variations in kinship density emerge between social categories, as can be seen in Table 9.6.

The significance, if any, of these variations is difficult to assess. What is more clear is that the kinship network was very loose for all social ranks.

In examining the types of links involved the analysis must once

Table 9.5

Category	No. of hearths	Social position	Households	
			No.	%
I	6–20	Gentry and very large farmers	10	8.2
II	3–5	Yeomen; wealthy tradesmen; parish officers	29	23.8%
III	2	Husbandmen; craftsmen	21	17.2
IV	1 and excused*	labourers; poor craftsmen; poor widows	62	50.8

*40 of 62 excused on grounds of chronic poverty, i.e. in receipt of poor relief.

more be restricted to proven links. There were 74 such links, connecting 48 householders.[11] Of these 68 per cent were first-order links viewed as links to householder and spouse. More precisely, and from the point of view of the householder alone, 30 per cent were between householder and closest affines (i.e. parents and siblings of spouse); 24 per cent were parent–child links between householders; 16 per cent were distant affinal links (e.g. wife's second cousin); 14 per cent were between brothers, 11 per cent between second cousins and 5 per cent between aunt and nephew/niece or between first cousins. Most links, then were close links by blood or marriage. Reassembling the material in order to determine whether links were between or within generations, it emerged that 60 per cent of links were between generations and 40 per cent within generations. This difference, like the very low kinship density of the parish, probably relates to the geographical mobility of children leaving the parish to enter service and/or marrying and settling elsewhere.

The kinship network in Terling, then, was relatively loose. Variations by age in the likelihood of having kin among other householders were as might be expected given the age structure of the householders. Social position had little effect upon the chances of

[11] Using the convention of counting a connection between two householders as two links. This is a matter of convenience only. The alternative convention of counting each such connection as one link could be adopted. The results of the analysis remain the same.

Table 9.6. *Kinship density of social categories*

	I		II		III		IV	
	Min.	Max.	Min.	Max.	Min.	Max.	Min.	Max.
Absolute kinship density	0.02	0.04	0.16	0.20	0.08	0.13	0.34	0.46
Relative kinship density	0.02%	0.03%	0.13%	0.16%	0.07%	0.11%	0.28%	0.38%

having kin available. Such kin links as existed were generally close and were rather more likely to be between than within generations. One final question can be asked before leaving the network of kin. Did kinship links cross the social scale or were they contained within particular social categories?

Some 54 per cent of proven kinship links in Terling were in fact between individuals in different social categories.[12] Having said so much, however, one must go on to ask the nature of these links and to determine which sections of village society were linked by them.

Close analysis of interlinking rapidly becomes exceedingly complex and somewhat opaque. However, a number of general points stand out clearly. First, although an overall majority of kin links were vertical socially, the proportion of vertical as against horizontal links varied between social categories. All the links of householders in category I were vertical, as were over 80 per cent of those of householders in categories II and III. Only 31 per cent of the links of householders in category IV were vertical. Category IV, then, was the only social category closely internally linked by kinship. Secondly, the examination of links by social category reveals certain patterns of linkage. Householders in category I were linked only to category II save for a single link to category IV. Two-thirds of householders with links in category II were linked upwards to category I, downwards to category III or internally, rather than down to category IV. Nevertheless linkage between categories II and IV was actually more frequent than linkage between categories III and IV. The links of householders in category III were predominantly upward or internal. Links

---

[12] The fact that kinship links quite frequently crossed the social scale has been noted in a number of village studies, though not subjected to further analysis. See W. G. Hoskins, *The Midland Peasant: The Economic and Social History of a Leicestershire Village* (London, 1957), p. 199; M. Spufford, *Contrasting Communities: English Villagers in the Sixteenth and Seventeenth Centuries* (Cambridge, 1974), p. 111; D. G. Hey, *An English Rural Community: Myddle under the Tudors and Stuarts* (Leicester, 1974), p. 204.

between more substantial householders and those at the bottom of the social scale, then, were evident, but were the exception rather than the rule, despite the fact that category IV contained 50 per cent of all householders.

What circumstances lay behind those links which crossed the social scale? There is a little evidence of upward social mobility. One householder in category I had a mother in category IV, while one in category II had a father in category IV. Otherwise such evidence is absent. Upward social mobility must commonly have required geo- graphical mobility. A further two links between householders and sons in lower social categories suggest an element of life-cycle social mobility, though again such evidence is sparse. There is some evidence of differentiation between brothers, perhaps resulting from differing inheritances. The great majority of close links which crossed the social scale, however, were produced by marriages between the daughters and sisters of men in category II and men drawn from categories III and IV. Some of these brides might expect to rise again in the social scale in the course of their lives; others were undoubtedly downwardly socially mobile. Of the more distant links which crossed the social scale less can be said save that they were produced by the same variety of circumstances operating in earlier generations. The network of kinship in Terling, then, extended across the social scale of a community highly differentiated in terms of wealth and social position. Such extension, however, was largely among the middling ranks of village society and was very limited in form. The labouring poor participated little in this; unlike those of their wealthier neigh- bours, most of their kinship links were to one another.

ii. The recognition of kin

The analysis of the network of kin reveals much about the place of kinship in the social structure, but it is no more than a prologomenon to the question of relationships between kin, about which it tells us nothing. Without further evidence and, in particular, evidence of a more subjective cast, it is impossible to assess the significance of kinship in the lives of these villagers. A valuable form of evidence is that provided by references to kin in the wills of the villagers. Such references yield evidence of the range of kinsmen recognized by testators. It must be said immediately, however, that such references are not good evidence of the full range of kin of whom testators were aware. Those mentioned in wills can be assumed to have been only those to whom the testator felt strong ties of sentiment or obligation.

Presumably they were aware of others. For this reason the evidence to be presented here cannot be regarded as fully comparable to that derived by Macfarlane from the diary of Ralph Josselin.[13] Nevertheless wills alone can provide evidence of the kin held closest at a critical point in the lives of individual testators.

192 wills have been examined for the period 1550–1699.[14] All references to kin have been included, and not simply references to beneficiaries of the will. The nature of the relationship involved is usually clear from the internal evidence of the will. Where necessary, relationships have been clarified from the family reconstitution forms and other evidence. Finally, concern here is not with the actual number of kin mentioned by testators but only with the range and depth of recognition of kin.

Over the whole period mention of kin beyond children (140 wills) and spouse (116 wills) is rare. Next in order beyond the testator's nuclear family come grandchildren, brothers, nephews and nieces, sons-in-law and sisters of the testator (all mentioned in between twenty and 35 wills). Brothers-in-law (seventeen wills) followed a little behind. Cousins, 'kinsmen' and a scattering of other relatives follow very far behind in order.[15] The concentration of testators was clearly very heavily upon their individual nuclear families, those of their married children, and their own and their spouses' nuclear families of origin. The frequency with which brothers and brothers-in-law are mentioned, commonly as supervisors or executors of the will, suggests that from the point of view of the testator's children relationships to uncles may have been of some significance. Overall, the range of kin mentioned is both narrow and shallow.

Looking at the evidence by fifty-year periods, very little change is observable over time. Only two chronological changes are worthy of note. First, godchildren are not infrequently mentioned in the very early wills. Such references disappear in the seventeenth century. Secondly, illegitimate children or grandchildren are occasionally mentioned at the end of the sixteenth century (a time when the illegitimacy ratio was peculiarly high in Terling). Such references are absent after 1600.

[13] Comparison of the range of kin mentioned in Josselin's diary with those mentioned in his will provides excellent illustration of this point. See Macfarlane, *Family Life of Ralph Josselin*, p. 158 and Appendix C.

[14] For the 50-year sub-periods used to investigate the possibilities of change over time the numbers of wills were as follows: 1550–99 63 wills; 1600–49 65 wills; 1650–99 64 wills.

[15] It can be noted in passing that the kinship terminology used by testators was very simple.

These results are fully compatible with the interpretation of Josselin's kinship recognition offered by Macfarlane, even to the likely significance of uncles, especially paternal uncles. They also tally with the near-comparable study by Johnston of eighteenth-century wills from Powick, Worcestershire.[16]

Did the range of kin mentioned by Terling testators vary with social position, sex and stage in the life-cycle? Taking the question of social position first, testators have been placed in four categories approximating as closely as possible to the categories used in the analysis for 1671. Most testators fell into groups I to III.[17] Between these categories no variations of any significance can be reported. The sample of wills from category IV (seven in all) is small but consistent in showing that testators in this category had the narrowest recognition of all – a single testator mentioned one kinsman beyond wife and children. The search for variations by sex of testator was equally fruitless; women did not vary from men on the grounds of sex alone in their recognition of kin.

In examining the issue of life-cycle variations, testators were separated, on the basis of internal evidence and of evidence from Family Reconstitution Forms, into four groups: those whose children were all married; those whose children were part married and part unmarried; those whose children were all unmarried; those with no children. Some obvious variations emerged. Testators whose children were all unmarried or who had no children clearly had no grand-children or sons- or daughters-in-law to mention. Otherwise, the same concentration on very close kin, in particular the testator's nuclear family, was evident throughout, with two exceptions. First, mention of the testator's or testator's spouse's brothers and sisters was most common among testators who either had no children of their own or whose children were all young and unmarried. This was for two reasons. On the one hand testators without direct heirs turned to their nearest kin. On the other hand testators with young

---

[16] Macfarlane, *Family Life of Ralph Josselin*, pp. 157ff.; J. A. Johnston, 'The Probate Inventories and Wills of a Worcestershire Parish, 1676–1775', *Midland History* 1 (1971), p. 32. Johnston's study is unfortunately not fully comparable since his analysis is confined to legatees. M. E. James' discussion of wills from the Durham lowlands further supports the conclusions indicated by the Powick and Terling studies, though his comments on upland wills offer the intriguing possibility of a different situation in the Durham hills: James, *Family, Lineage and Civil Society*, pp. 23–4.

[17] In this Terling testators differed from those of the fenland parish of Willingham analysed by M. Spufford, 'Peasant Inheritance Customs and Land Distribution in Cambridgeshire from the Sixteenth to the Eighteenth Centuries', in Goody, Thirsk and Thompson, editors, *Family and Inheritance*, pp. 169–71.

children sometimes brought in their brothers or brothers-in-law as executors and overseers of their wills who could be trusted to look to the children's interests. The second exception is that more distant kin, from nephews and nieces to 'kinsmen' and also godchildren, were most often mentioned by men without children or by widows and unmarried women. The reasons for this are sufficiently obvious to require no further comment.

Kinship recognition as evidenced in wills, then, shows a heavy concentration on very close kin. It varied little with social position or sex and only in ways that might be expected when consideration is given to the family life-cycle stage of the testator. One final issue can be dealt with before moving on to other evidence of kin relations – the geographical spread of kin.

It is evident from the wills that many of the kin mentioned were not inhabitants of Terling. Unfortunately testators did not always deem it necessary to specify the whereabouts of particular kin. However, there are 62 specific references to kin living in 33 other villages and towns in Essex in addition to kin in London, Kent, Suffolk, Hertfordshire and overseas (one in New England!). Of these kin, 24 per cent lived under five miles from Terling, and 68 per cent under ten miles from the village. Nevertheless, this leaves 32 per cent living more than ten miles and 24 per cent more than fifteen miles from their kin in Terling. Recognized kin bound to Terling testators by strong ties of sentiment or obligation were scattered over a considerable area.

iii. Relations within the nuclear family: inheritance

Wills provide evidence not only of kinship recognition but of inheritance customs, which allow some insight into relationships between parents and children and between husband and wife.

The first point to be made is that there was no rigidity in the inheritance customs of Terling villagers. On first examination the wills give the impression of a bewildering variety of inheritance strategies which might be adopted by the individual testator. On closer analysis it emerges that there were certain regularities within a range of options which appears to have been governed by the types and amount of property to be disposed, the family life-cycle stage of the testator and the demographic fortunes of the testator's primary family. In the absence of inventories, the exact wealth of testators cannot be given. Nevertheless the types of property involved could be significant. Over the whole period 38 per cent bequeathed land, 39 per cent houses, 11 per cent stock, 78 per cent cash sums and 83 per cent household goods. Turning to the issue of the family cycle, 22 per cent of testators had no children, 25 per cent had all their children already married, 22 per cent had some children married and some unmarried and 31 per cent had only unmarried children. Testators were fairly evenly divided between those who were wholly or partly responsible for providing for their children and those who had no such responsibility. Clearly the marriage of sons was *not* dependent upon inheritance, and family property could be passed on to the rising generation over a considerable period of time.[18] Demographic fortunes varied very widely indeed. Only 11 per cent of male testators were faced with an unproblematic inheritance in that they had only a single son or daughter. A further 24 per cent had no children. For the test a distribution of property among their children was necessary, and this could sometimes be a very difficult matter indeed. All these factors must be taken into consideration in examining the actual decisions made by testators and recorded in their wills. No single variable is in itself sufficient to explain their behaviour. Analysis by social position alone, for example, does nothing to clarify the situation, and wealth seems to have been of less overall significance than the family cycle and demography. Where wealth *was* of significance was in broadening the options open to the testator, by providing more and more varied types of wealth for transmission. It did not influence aspirations. These can now be examined.

Male testators clearly felt a strong desire and sense of obligation to provide as far as possible an independent home and living for their widows. The possibility of the remarriage of widows does not seem to have been something which disturbed them, and there are very few examples of remarriage conditions being placed on bequests. Where there were no children of the marriage, widows most commonly received the entire inheritance if it was in personal property alone or a life interest where house and lands were involved, these being bequeathed ultimately to more distant kin. Where all children were married, widows usually received a life interest in a house and/or land where these were involved, or at least a share of personal property to secure their future. In a handful of cases precise maintenance or annuity arrangements for widows were laid down. A few of these suggest that the widow might dwell with a married child, but such arrangements were clearly viewed with suspicion since alterna-

---

[18] Terling's experience in these respects was similar to that of other English villages in the period: see, for example, Hey, *English Rural Community*, pp. 204–5; C. Howell, 'Peasant Inheritance Customs in the Midlands, 1200–1700', in J. R. Goody *et al.* editors, *Family and Inheritance*, p. 145; Spufford, *Contrasting Communities*, pp. 173–4.

tives were provided for in the event of such cohabitation proving
fragile or disagreeable. In cases where only some children were
married, widows received an interest in house and lands either for
life or until their children's majority, or alternatively portions of cash
and goods. It is clear in such wills that, while married children were
to receive their part of the inheritance promptly, the portions allo-
cated to unmarried children were to be managed by the widow until
their majority or marriage. Where all children were unmarried
widows were clearly left in control of house, lands and personal
property. Allocations of property were made but were intended to
take effect only at a future date, the widow's ultimate share being laid
down along with those of the children. Clearly, the principal duty of
the widow was that of completing the upbringing and 'putting out' of
children. Testators laid down the guidelines for the task and provided
the wherewithal to see it through, together with provision for the
widow's future thereafter. No change over time is observable in
either aspiration or practice.

Turning to provision for children, it should be clear from the above
discussion that in a very substantial number of cases (about half)
bequests to children were not expected to be of immediate effect, but
were mediated through the widow. Frequently the ultimate outcome
would be different from that laid down by the testator, as a result of
the deaths of children. This point deserves stress since it was
something of which testators were very much aware – provision
being commonly made for the redistribution of portions in the event
of a child's death, a point to which we shall return.

Where a testator had only a single child, inheritance was unproblematic. The child – or, if this was a married daughter, sometimes the
son-in-law – usually received all save the portion left for the widow.
Where there was only one son, but also a daughter or daughters, land
and house usually went to the son. An additional house or houses
might go to the daughters. Cash and goods were divided among
children in a manner which does not appear to have been grossly
unequal, though the valuation of goods is clearly difficult to obtain in
the absence of inventories. Where there were two or more sons, with
or without sisters, several arrangements were possible. If house and
land were involved these usually went to the eldest son, the other
child or children receiving cash or goods, sometimes in fairly equal
division, sometimes not. If the eldest son was already married and
independently established, however, house and land might go to a
younger child. In wealthier families it was sometimes possible for
several or even all children to be provided with houses and some-

times land too. It is clear, however, that this did not involve the subdivision of a family's main holding – rather extra accumulations of land, commonly geographically distant, were hived off. In cases where all children were already married, real property was rarely involved. This finding may be fortuitous, but may also indicate an earlier setting up of children. Where some children were married and some not, the eldest son receiving land was often required to pay out cash legacies to his younger siblings, a practice which could have the effect of ultimately equalizing apparently unequal inheritances.[19] In those wills where no real property was involved at all, there was usually either a fairly equal division of cash and goods among entirely married or entirely unmarried children or else tokens were left to married children and larger sums given to the unmarried. Finally, where a testator had no sons, but two or more daughters, house and land usually went to the eldest, cash and goods to the others, or else where cash and goods only were involved there was an equal division among entirely married or entirely unmarried daughters.

Clearly these practices show a bias in the direction of primogeni-ture, but to classify them as constituting a 'primogeniture system' would be crude and erroneous. If there was a single concern running through the varieties of behaviour observed, it was that of maximizing the opportunity of as many children as possible to set up their own family units in due course. The primogeniture bias might indeed be interpreted as a preparing of the way for the child who would first face the world independently. As we have seen, testators were very aware of mortality and must often have realized that the ultimate portions received by younger children might be larger and more equal than those specified, as some children died and their portions were reallocated among survivors. Again, land left to the eldest might be the most prestigious inheritance, but it was burdened with the need to provide for siblings. Ultimately the system may have operated in such a way as to set children forth fairly equally provided in a world where they would be expected to stand on their own feet. The extent to which they stood alone or could expect aid from kin or others is the concern of the final section of this paper.

iv. Kinsmen and neighbours

Several classes of document permit the examination of the extent to which individuals drew upon kin for services of various kinds; these will now be considered. This evidence will enable some estimate to be

---

[19] Cf. Howell, 'Peasant Inheritance Customs', p. 145; M. Spufford, *Contrasting Communities*, p. 157.

made of the relative importance of kin and neighbours in the lives of the villagers of Terling.

The first relationship to be considered is that between testators and the chosen executors of their wills. Over the whole period, 192 testators chose 222 executors. Of these 87 per cent were kin and only 13 per cent non-kin. Of the kin selected, 95 per cent were first-order kin, 78 per cent being the wives, sons and daughters of testators. The non-kin selected were often designated as friends or neighbours. No change took place over time. Clearly there was an overwhelming bias towards the closest kin in the handling of family property.

Over the whole period 71 overseers or supervisors of wills were named – a custom which was dying in the seventeenth century. Of these, 45 per cent were kin, the rest non-kin. The kin selected were most commonly drawn from the nuclear family of origin of the testator or his wife – brothers and brothers-in-law predominating. Otherwise more distant kin were drawn upon, especially cousins. Non-kin were sometimes named as particular friends or were neighbours within Terling. Again, then, there was a quite strong tendency to draw upon kin, many of them non-resident in Terling, in matters involving family property.

In contrast, the witnesses of wills were overwhelmingly neighbours – only some 5 per cent being known to have been kin. For the simple, but potentially important, task of witnessing wills testators drew upon their neighbours within Terling. Some of these neighbours were a very personal choice and were referred to elsewhere in wills or were designated as friends. Others appear to have been particularly prestigious neighbours and recur in many wills. This evidence suggests that, given the looseness of the kinship network within the village, the tendency was to draw upon the neighbourhood for more immediate aid. Other evidence would support this suggestion.

References to debts are frequent in wills. These are for the most part unspecific, but it has proved possible to collect information on seventy specific debt and credit relationships. Of these 17 per cent were between kinsmen, 67 per cent were between neighbours and 16 per cent were between Terling villagers and unrelated outsiders. It is clear that financial aid of this kind was most commonly sought and found among neighbours.

Two other forms of support for which evidence survives are those of acting as compurgator for a man in the church courts (i.e. swearing to his innocence) and acting as surety for a person in a recognizance issued by the Justices of the Peace.

Seven Terling men were required to find compurgators in the church courts within the period. Of these, five brought neighbours only, one brought kin only and one brought a single kinsman and five neighbours. This might suggest that the compurgators were recruited from a pool of contacts which included kin only if they had a close personal relationship to the individual concerned. The more extensive evidence of recognizance sureties strengthens this impression.

84 recognizances have been examined for the period 1578–1693, most of these falling in the period 1600–30. In most cases the principal in the recognizance provided two sureties. In 6 per cent of recognizances the principal found kin only to act for him; in 18 per cent one kinsman and one other acted; in 76 per cent only non-kin acted as sureties. Where kin acted, they were most commonly the fathers, brothers or brothers-in-law of the principal. Of the non-kin involved, some were outsiders from other villages. Regarding those who were neighbours from Terling something can be said of the factors which appear to have influenced their recruitment. Occupational solidarity was influential. Craftsmen drew on fellow craftsmen while husbandmen and yeomen who held land of the same manors tended to stand by one another. Personal friendship is also evident, being indicated by the fact that individuals concerned were also linked in other contexts, for example in wills. There was a certain group solidarity among the elite of parish notables who acted as churchwardens, sessions jurymen and so forth. Being party to the dispute which had resulted in court proceedings could also lead men to give support of this kind. Finally there is evidence of the influence of patronage and clientage within the village community. Village notables, husbandmen and craftsmen showed much solidarity in standing surety for one another, and their recognizance links are almost wholly horizontal. Labourers, however, were almost completely dependent on recruiting support from above, where they found patrons to assist them.

The examination of the recognizances of men who were bound in this way shows on several occasions that some of the connections revealed to kin or neighbours were enduring and recur. Other supporters were recruited on an *ad hoc* basis. Overall it is clear that the assistance of kin or neighbour was not simply a function of the relative availability of kin and neighbours in the village. Of the recognizances where no kin were used, almost half were cases where the principal involved can be shown to have had adult kinsmen available in the village. They either chose not to use them or were unable to gain their support.

The various strands of this essay can now be drawn together. Evidence has been presented of a kinship network which was relatively loose in Terling. Households were relatively isolated in the parish in kin terms. It has been suggested that this phenomenon was a product of the high degree of geographical mobility and the geographically exogamous marriage patterns which characterized the villagers. The recognition of kin appears, on the evidence of wills, to have been very restricted. Inheritance customs were flexible and varied with the particular circumstances of the testator. They reveal strong internal ties within the relatively isolated nuclear families of the villagers and a general desire to set children into the world independently. Experience and behaviour in these respects varied little with social position but was influenced by the developmental cycle of the nuclear family and by demographic fortune. No change of any significance could be observed over the period of the study.

In practical matters, the assistance of kin was clearly preferred in all matters concerning family property. Even here, however, kin beyond the nuclear family and the nuclear families of origin of married couples were of little functional importance. In other forms of aid and assistance, will witnessing, financial aid, support as compurgators and sureties, kin of any kind were of little importance compared to neighbours. In part this was because they were simply not available locally, but even where adult kin were available they were called upon selectively.

In sum, the historical evidence suggests a flexible and permissive system strikingly similar to that described by modern sociologists. The nuclear family was very important indeed. Beyond it, kinship was not in itself an important independent element in the structuring of social relations. In Terling, neighbours and particular personal friends selected from amongst them seem to have played the supporting role which in other societies might be played by the wider kin group. The evidence provides a glimpse of neighbourly interaction structured by occupational solidarity, shared roles in the institutions of village government, personal friendship, patronage and clientage. Neighbourliness was of strong practical importance to Terling villagers, and good neighbourliness was a critically important social virtue. It is perhaps to changes affecting the quality of neighbourly relations, rather than to the enduring structures of family and kinship, that we must look for the key to social change in this period.

10

The myth of the peasantry; family and economy in a northern parish

ALAN MACFARLANE

Historians and sociologists agree that England between the thirteenth and eighteenth centuries was a 'peasant' nation.[1] By this they often mean no more than that it fitted within the definition proposed by Firth when he wrote that by a peasant community 'one means a system of small-scale producers, with a simple technology and equipment, often relying primarily for their subsistence on what they themselves produce. The primary means of livelihood of the peasant is cultivation of the soil.'[2] England would also appear to have been a peasant nation in the more precise sense that it was, to follow Kroeber and Redfield, a society where those living in the countryside constituted a 'part-culture' dependent on towns, markets and a state.[3] One consequence of this interpretation is that the basic contrast is held to be between industrial nations on the one hand and 'peasant' nations on the other. Thus England is lumped with continental Europe, Ireland and Scotland up to the nineteenth century, with pre-revolutionary Russia and China and with contemporary

[1] There is a more detailed discussion of the stereotype and of the definitional problem in a paper, which complements this essay, entitled 'The Peasantry in England before the Industrial Revolution. A mythical model?', in D. Green, C. Haselgrove and M. Spriggs, editors, *Social Organization and Settlement* (Oxford, 1978), pp. 325–41, cited hereafter as Macfarlane, 'Peasantry'. Two examples of similar studies are R. H. Hilton, *The English Peasantry in the Later Middle Ages* (Oxford, 1975), and J. Thirsk, *English Peasant Farming* (London, 1957). The research on the parish of Kirkby Lonsdale upon which this article is based has been funded by the Social Science Research Council and King's College Research Centre, Cambridge, to whom I am most grateful. Much of the work has been carried out by Sarah Harrison. I should also like to thank Cherry Bryant, Charles Jardine, Iris Macfarlane and Jessica Styles for their help. I also acknowledge the help of the County Archives offices at Kendal, Carlisle and Preston.
[2] Quoted in G. Dalton, 'Peasantries in Anthropology and History', *Current Anthropology* 13: 3–4 (1972), p. 386.
[3] R. Redfield, *Peasant Society and Culture* (Chicago, Ill., 1960), p. 40.

India and Mexico. It is assumed that useful lessons can be learnt by comparing basically similar social and economic structures. There has been a growing interest recently in refining such a crude dichotomy in order to make it possible to distinguish between different agrarian systems. Following the lead of Chayanov it has been suggested that one extra feature is needed in order to make the label 'peasant' appropriate for an agricultural 'part-society'. This final criterion is described by Thorner as follows.[4]

Our fifth and final criterion, the most fundamental, is that of the unit of production. In our concept of peasant economy the typical and most representative units of production are the peasant family households. We define a peasant family household as a socio-economic unit which grows crops primarily by the physical efforts of the members of the family . . . In a peasant economy half or more of all crops grown will be produced by such peasant households, relying mainly on their own family labour . . .

As Shanin states, the basic feature is that 'the family farm is the basic unit of peasant ownership, production, consumption and social life. The individual, the family and the farm, appear as an indivisible whole . . .'[5] Among the consequences of this situation is the fact that the head of the family appears as 'the manager rather than proprietor of family land', that the fertility of children is encouraged in order to increase the labour force of the productive unit, that peasant villages or communities are usually more or less self-sufficient.[6] As Chayanov had stated much earlier, 'The first fundamental characteristic of the farm economy of the peasant is that it is a family economy. Its whole organization is determined by the size and composition of the peasant family and by the co-ordination of its consumptive demands with the number of its working hands.'[7] Thus, when we speak of peasantry we are trying to describe not merely a particular technology, but also the basic organization of ownership, production and consumption.

In the article cited above I have argued at some length that certain central features of English society in the sixteenth and seventeenth centuries lead us to suspect that the situation was very far removed from that of an ideal-type peasant society. For example, the property rights of women and children were totally contrary to those in other peasant societies. Furthermore, a detailed analysis of the Essex parish of Earls Colne in the period 1500–1750 showed that in every respect it

---

[4] In T. Shanin, editor, *Peasants and Peasant Societies* (Harmondsworth, 1971), p. 205.
[5] Shanin, *Peasants*, p. 241.
[6] Shanin, *Peasants*, pp. 242–4.
[7] Quoted in E. Wolf, *Peasants* (Englewood Cliffs, NJ, 1966), p. 14.

was 'non-peasant'.[8] A brief survey of some other villages studied by Hoskins and Spufford confirmed that Essex was not exceptional in this respect. Yet all these studies are based on the lowland area of England where the market was well developed. It is well known that there was great regional variation in England during the sixteenth to eighteenth centuries. If we are attempting to establish an *English* pattern, it is necessary to produce evidence from an upland area. Furthermore, if we are to find a pre-industrial peasantry anywhere in the country it seems likely that it will be in the higher, supposedly more remote and backward, upland region. It is generally agreed by those familiar with such regions that kinship and the family were more important in the upland region. There, if anywhere, we will be dealing with a domestic economy, based on extended kinship and family labour. Groups of kin are the basic unit of production in a peasant society. In association with low geographical mobility this will lead us to expect a high degree of kin co-residence in an area with 'peasants'. It is therefore relevant that a number of local historians have spoken of the 'kindreds' and 'clans' of these upland areas, in contrast to the dispersed kin of the lowlands. Describing Troutbeck in Cumbria, Scott noted the frequent occurrence of identical surnames and wrote: 'These families – we might rather call them clans – inter-married so frequently that their descendants are inevitably related many times over . . .'[9] Cowper, describing Hawkshead in north Lancashire, wrote: 'what we venture to term, in default of a better word, the clan system – the cohabitation of hamlets and areas by many folks owning the same surname and a common origin'.[10] More recently James has suggested that 'upland' areas in the Durham region were more familistic,[11] and Thirsk has noted that while the 'clan' was only strong in Northumbria, in many upland areas 'the family often exerted a stronger authority than the manorial lord'.[12]

---

[8] The nature of the sources and methods used in the study of Earls Colne, a project funded by the Social Science Research Council, is described in A. Macfarlane, *Reconstructing Historical Communities* (Cambridge, 1977).

[9] S. H. Scott, *A Westmorland Village* (London, 1904), p. 261.

[10] H. S. Cowper, *Hawkshead* (London, 1899), p. 199. See also, on 'kindreds' in the area, C. M. L. Bouch and G. P. Jones, *A Short Economic and Social History of the Lake Counties 1500–1830* (Manchester, 1961), p. 90. Cowper's observation is confirmed in one respect by the recent discovery that in the Hawkshead parish register for 1560–1800, twelve out of 506 name sets account for 36% of the total baptisms. I owe this fact to Dr Richard Smith and the SSRC Cambridge Group for the History of Population and Social Structure.

[11] M. E. James, *Family, Lineage and Civil Society: A Study of Society, Politics and Mentality in the Durham Region, 1500–1640* (Oxford, 1974), p. 24.

[12] J. Thirsk, editor, *The Agrarian History of England and Wales, Vol. IV* (Cambridge, 1967), pp. 9, 23.

Speaking of the northern fells, and in particular the areas of partible inheritance, Thirsk writes that 'the family was and is the working unit, all joining in the running of the farm, all accepting without question the fact that the family holding would provide for them all . . .'.[13] Of all the upland areas of England, the area most likely to be inhabited by peasants was southern Cumbria, that is parts of the Lake District, west Yorkshire and north Lancashire. It is known that a special form of social structure, based on small family 'estates', existed there. A peculiar form of land tenure had given rise to the 'statesman' in an area of weak manorial control and difficult communications. As Scott wrote of Troutbeck, 'Under this system of customary tenure there has grown up a race of men singularly sturdy, independent, and tenacious of their rights . . . Instead of the land being occupied by two or three squires, and a subservient tenantry, this single township has contained some fifty statesmen families, which have held the same land from generation to generation with the pride of a territorial aristocracy.'[14] The security, the immobility, the equality, all seem to indicate a peasant society.

In this region lies the parish of Kirkby Lonsdale, where the stone walls and substantial farmhouses remain very much as they were in the seventeenth century. The parish produced grain, wool and cattle in an area stretching from rich riverside meadows in the south up to high fells of nearly two thousand feet on the east. The approximately 2,500 inhabitants in the late seventeenth century were distributed in nine townships. The tenurial situation varied from township to township, and consequently each had a different social structure. According to Machell, who travelled through the parish in 1692 and whose findings are corroborated and expanded by Nicholson and Burn,[15] the tenurial situation in the various townships at the end of the seventeenth century was as follows:

Kirkby Lonsdale: some tenants free (about one third), some customary, some customary at fine arbitrary, some arbitrary (copyhold), some heriotable.
Casterton: tenants about half free and half customary, paying a fine certain for three years rent.
Barbon: six or seven freeholds; all tenants are finable and arbitrary (i.e. copyhold), they were sold to freehold in 1716.

---

[13] 'Industries in the Countryside', in F. J. Fisher, editor, *Essays in the Economic and Social History of Tudor and Stuart England* (Cambridge, 1961), p. 83.
[14] Scott, *Westmorland Village*, pp. 20–1.
[15] J. M. Ewbank, editor, *Antiquary on Horseback* (Kendal, 1963), pp. 18, 26, 29, 36, 39; J. Nicholson and R. Burn, *The History and Antiquities of the Counties of Westmorland and Cumberland* (London, 1777), Vol. II, pp. 243–65.

Middleton: the tenants purchased their estates to freehold in the time of
Elizabeth and James I.

Firbank: all freeholders, having purchased their customary tenures in 1586.

Killington: all freeholders, having purchased their customary tenures in 1585.

Lupton: only about two freehold tenements, all the rest customary.

Hutton Roof: some divided customary estates, but generally bought themselves free.[16]

This illustrates the variability even within a parish, supporting
Gilpin's contemporary observation that 'Customs especially in the
Northern Parts of this Nation are so varied and differing in themselves as that a man might almost say that there are as many severall
Customes as mannors . . . yea and almost as many as there are
Townshipps or Hamletts in a mannor.'[17] We may examine in more
detail two townships which were adjacent, but which contrast strikingly in their tenurial situation, namely Lupton and Killington. In
Lupton there was an absentee lord of the manor, but he owned very
little of the township land directly, there was no 'demesne'. Almost
all the land was held by customary tenants with holdings of between
fifteen and forty acres apiece and some rights in the common grazing.
In Killington the form of tenure had originally been the same as that
in Lupton, but in 1585 the customary holdings had been converted to
freehold. One consequence was that there were two persons styled
'gentlemen' living in Killington according to the listing of inhabitants
of 1695,[18] whereas there were none in Lupton. But even these were
minor gentry. The largest land holder's holding in Killington before
the Civil War consisted of a capital messuage, Killington Hall, forty
acres of arable, twenty acres of meadow, one hundred acres of
pasture and one hundred acres of moss and furze called 'Killington
Demesne', another messuage with sixteen acres of land and a water
mill.[19] This was roughly five times the size of the average holding in
Killington, but, since there were about forty estates in the township,
it only constituted about one-eighth of the total land area.

It is clear that English 'freehold' tenure, which gave an individual
complete and total rights over his land, is diametrically opposed to
the form of land holding that is characteristic of peasant societies,

---

[16] W. Farrer and J. F. Curwen, *Records Relating to the Barony of Kendale* (Kendal, 1924),
Vol. II, p. 416.

[17] A. Bagot, 'Mr Gilpin and Manorial Customs', *Transactions of the Cumberland and
Westmorland Antiquarian and Archaeological Society* new series 62 (1961), p. 228.

[18] The listing, which covers the whole of Kirkby Lonsdale parish, is in the Record Office
at Kendal among the Fleming papers (WD/RY).

[19] An inquisition of 1639, reprinted in Farrer and Curwen, *Records of Kendale*, Vol. II,
p. 437.

where there is a form of joint family ownership.[20] It thus seems very likely that, whatever may superficially appear to be the case, Killington after 1585, Firbank after 1586, Barbon after 1716, Middleton since the early seventeenth century and parts of Kirkby Lonsdale and Hutton Roof had a form of land tenure system incompatible with peasantry. Yet in the areas with 'customary' tenure, particularly Lupton, where nearly all was held in this way, some form of family estate might have existed, surviving longer there than in the other townships. We therefore need to examine this northern customary tenure, known as 'border tenure' or 'tenant right' in more detail.

The parish of Kirkby Lonsdale lay within the barony of Kendal, and consequently all the manors, except the rectory manor, were held of that barony.[21] 'Customary' tenure was thus part of that general border tenure which has been particularly well documented since it was a peculiarity of the area and the subject of considerable litigation in the seventeenth century. An excellent contemporary description is given by Gilpin,[22] and there have been a number of more recent descriptions.[23] Supposedly in exchange for armed service on the border, the tenant held by a form of tenure which lay somewhere between ordinary copyhold as known in the south of England and freehold. As with copyhold, the tenant paid certain fines and rents to the lord, though these were usually fixed and small, and performed certain services or 'boons'. But unlike copyhold, the holding of land was not 'at the will of the lord' but by the custom of the manor. The land holdings were known as 'customary estates of inheritance' and could be transferred from one 'owner' to the next without the permission of the lord, only being registered, and a fine being paid, in the manorial court. The estates were 'descendible from ancestor to heir under certain yearly rents'. Furthermore, 'the copyholder had no property in the timber on the land; the customary tenant owns everything, as if it were freehold, except the minerals beneath the soil'.[24] Customary tenants could devise their land by will, and it descended automatically to their children or other legal heirs if no will was made. This situation has been described as 'tantamount to

---

[20] For a more detailed discussion of this opposition, see Macfarlane, 'Peasantry'.
[21] Farrer and Curwen, Records of Kendale, Vol II, p. 305.
[22] Bagot, 'Mr Gilpin and Manorial Customs'.
[23] Bouch and Jones, Economic . . . History of the Lake Counties, pp. 65ff; J. R. Ford, 'The Customary Tenant-Right of the Manors of Yealand', Transactions of the Cumberland and Westmorland Antiquarian and Archaeological Society new series (1909), pp. 147–60; W. Butler, 'The Customs and Tenant Right Tenures of the Northern Counties . . .', Transactions of the Cumberland and Westmorland Antiquarian and Archaeological Society new series 26 (1926), pp. 318–36.   [24] Scott, Westmorland Village, p. 16.

freehold',[25] and in regard to security of tenure this was the case, though the fines, rents and services made it akin to copyhold in other respects. The estates could be bought and sold by ordinary deeds of bargain and sale, though they would also be registered as admittances in the court roll.[26] This was a form of transfer exactly similar to freehold.[27] The major restriction on the tenant was that the inherited estate should not be subdivided. In order that the land holding should be large enough to provide a warrior for the border defences, the customs stated that all of the holding should go to one person, the widow, then to a son, and in default of a son to only one daughter. As we shall see, this was a very strict form of impartibility.

One supposed result of such a system was that wealth was evenly distributed between equal 'family farms'. This equality was noted by those who had witnessed the collapse of the old tenurial system in the second half of the eighteenth century. Looking back to the first half of that century, a writer in 1812 described how 'excepting the estates of a few noblemen and baronets, the land was divided into small freeholds and customary tenements, in the occupation of owners . . .'.[28] Another supposed result was that a certain family would be identified with an estate, and that it would pass for many generations down the same family.

Yet, if we look a little more closely at the precise nature of ownership, the pattern is not so simple. We have noted that farm and family are merged in peasant societies; it is the family or household as a group that owns the farm holding, the head of the family merely being the *de facto* manager. Individual ownership is alien. This is absolutely the opposite of the case in both Lupton and Killington, where it would be difficult to envisage a more individualistic form of land holding, either by freehold or by customary tenure. There is no evidence in any of the multitudinous court records or customs of the area that the property was jointly owned by the family. In fact, all the indications are in the opposite direction. First, it is clear that in both townships the landed property was transferred to one person, who was not merely the nominal title holder but the owner in an exclusive sense. This owner might as easily be a woman as a man. If anything, the individualism of ownership was even more extreme than in most copyhold tenures in the south, for whereas in Essex, for example, all

[25] Butler, 'Tenant Right Tenures', p. 320.
[26] *Ibid.*, p. 319.
[27] Ford, 'Customary Tenant-Right', p. 157.
[28] J. Gough, *Manners and Customs of Westmorland . . .* (Kendal, 1847; first printed in 1812), p. 25.

daughters received shares in the estate as co-parceners if there was no male heir, in Lupton the principle of individual property prevented this division. By the custom of that manor, and generally under tenant-right tenure, in the event of no sons surviving the holding went to only one daughter. As Machell put it, quoting from a Chancery decree of the early seventeenth century,[29] there was a general custom in the barony of Kendal 'that the eldest daughter/sister/cousin inherits without copartnership in tenancy'. This was a direct equivalent to the custom of male primogeniture in the area. The general principle was that the holding belonged to one person, and could only be transferred to one person; it was not owned by a group of brothers, for example, and partitioned between them as in peasant societies. As I have argued in the article already cited, the presence of primogeniture and impartible inheritance, and the consequent disinheritance from the main holding of the other children, which many observers have noted to be more extreme in England than anywhere else in the world, is inconceivable in a 'peasant' society. In a peasant society, the estate is held jointly by the children; it may be temporarily partitioned according to their needs, in which case all the males have equal rights. In most of England, the main estate could not be divided or partitioned, though extra pieces which had been accumulated could be given to other children. Thus it could be argued that merely finding impartible inheritance, as we do in the tenant-right area, is a sure index of the absence of a true peasantry.

Unfortunately it is not possible to deal here with the considerable areas of partible inheritance in England, particularly in the upland areas. One of the best documented of these was in Dentdale, which lay alongside Kirkby Lonsdale. The contrast between the two parishes is very instructive and has been illuminated in a general way by Dr Thirsk.[30] It would be very useful to obtain an account of the relations between family and economy in such a region, testing out the hypotheses concerning a peasant social structure. It would also be useful to know more concerning women's property rights. In peasant societies, land is not owned individually, and therefore when a woman marries out of a village or family she may not take land with her, though she may own moveable objects and possess livestock. But in both Lupton and Killington, as elsewhere in England, women's property rights were extensive. A number of the wills for these two townships mention women holding landed property, and it has already been mentioned that a widow would succeed to her

---

[29] Ewbank, *Antiquary on Horseback*, p. 3.
[30] Thirsk, 'Industries in the Countryside'.

husband's estate, followed by one daughter when a son had not survived. Men could thus hold land 'in the right of their wife'.

If further proof of individualistic property rights is needed, it may be found in the numerous proceedings in cases which came from the parish of Kirkby Lonsdale to be heard in Chancery. The court dealt with numerous disputes where one individual sought to obtain rights over a specific piece of land or other property. Reading through the roughly 70 000 words of information in sixteenth- and seventeenth-century cases from this parish has not once given any hint or suspicion that there was a strong link between a family group and a holding in the sense that some group larger than the individual owned the property.[31] The head of the household or registered landowner clearly owned the property in the full sense, and was not merely the organizer of a joint labour group. There is no trace of the family as the basic unit of ownership and production.

It might be objected that the wife and children did, in this area, have inalienable rights in the family property. It could be pointed out that by tenant-right the widow inherited the whole of her husband's estate during her 'pure' widowhood, that is as long as she did not remarry or have sexual intercourse. Furthermore, Kirkby Lonsdale was within the archdiocese of York, where there was a custom until 1692 that a wife and children each had a right to one-third of their husband's/father's moveable goods at his death.[32] If we look more closely at both Common Law as it applied to freehold lands and manorial customs, it is clear that this was not a joint estate. The wife only had rights as long as she was a widow, and the children had no inalienable rights in their parent's land or other real estate. Even with moveable goods, a man could give them all away in his life-time, just as he could sell or give away all his land. In Kirkby Lonsdale, as in the rest of England, the principle that 'a living man has no heirs', that children had no inalienable rights in a family estate, appears to have been present.[33] Thus a father could totally disinherit a son if he so wished; primogeniture merely meant that an eldest male heir would inherit if no will or transfer before death had been made to the

---

[31] Most of the Kirkby Lonsdale proceedings have been found among the papers of the Six Clerks, in classes C.5–C.10 in the Public Record Office, Chancery Lane. A standard description of this much under-used source is W. J. Jones, *The Elizabethan Court of Chancery* (Oxford, 1967).

[32] H. Swinburne, *A Treatise of Testaments and Last Wills*, 5th edition (London, 1728), pp. 204–5.

[33] Maitland stated that this principle was grasped in the thirteenth century: Sir F. Pollock and F. W. Maitland, *The History of English Law Before the Time of Edward I*, 2nd edition (Cambridge, 1968), Vol. II, p. 308.

contrary. It did not mean that a son would automatically inherit.
Thus, for example, in Lupton we find in the will of John Wooddes in
1682 that, because the eldest son Roland 'would never doe my
counsell nor be ordered by me neyther is a fyth man to serve the
quenes majestie nor the lords for these causes and consyderation',
the whole estate was given to the younger son, who was merely to
pay his elder brother £6 13s 4d.[34] In Killington, a man could do what
he liked with his real estate, with the exception that a widow had
one-third as a dower for life. In Lupton, he could do what he liked
before his death, or after the death of his wife, on condition that the
inherited estate was not divided.

One consequence of the highly developed private property rights
in the area was the enormous amount of litigation in the central
courts of equity, primarily Chancery. Another result was the making
of a very large number of wills dealing with chattels and real estate. It
has been pointed out that in peasant societies, for example in Russia
before 1930,[35] wills were either unknown, or regarded with great
dislike. Since the dying father is not the private owner of the
property, he cannot devise it to a specific individual. The sons are
co-owners with the father, just as they are co-workers. But in Kirkby
Lonsdale numerous wills were made which embody the principle of
devisability of land, thus extending the father's power after his death.
For example, the township of Lupton, with a total population of
about 150 persons at the end of the seventeenth century, produced
115 wills during the period 1550–1720. Many of these were concerned
with allocating cash portions to younger males and to girls who
would not normally benefit directly from the land holding, but they
also frequently confirmed the disposition of real estate.

Another feature we associate with traditional peasantry is geographical immobility; both families and individuals tend to remain for
their lives in one village or group of villages. This does not seem to
have been the case in Kirkby Lonsdale. To start with the crude index
of the survival of family names, we may look to see how many of the
28 surnames of those who held land in the township of Lupton in
1642 according to a tenant list were still present two generations later
in a list for 1710.[36] The answer is twelve; thus less than half were still
present. Of course we have to allow for change of name at marriage,
or the chance that unrelated individuals with identical surnames had

---

[34] The will is among those for the Deanery of Lonsdale in the Lancashire Record Office
at Preston.
[35] T. Shanin, *The Awkward Class* (Oxford, 1972), p. 223.
[36] The lists are among the Lonsdale papers (D/Lons) at the Record Office, Carlisle.

come into the parish. Further research will establish how many of the holdings were in the same family throughout this period. What is certain is that the rate of change of ownership increased in the middle of the eighteenth century so that there was hardly a farm owned by the same family throughout the period 1642–1800. It is also clear from preliminary work that, even before the introduction of turnpike roads and other pressures which are believed to have destroyed the old patterns, there was very considerable mobility of farm holdings. There is no evidence whatsoever, from the figures, from the wording of wills or from the contents of legal cases, that families and farms were closely attached by sentiment. It is symbolic that the farms were hardly ever called after families, but after natural features: Foulstone, Greenside, Fellhouses. Contemporaries only seem to have talked occasionally of the 'Burrows of Foulstone' to differentiate them from other persons of the same surname in the parish. The situation was a long way from the imaginary world of Cold Comfort Farm; 'there have always been Starkadders at Cold Comfort . . .'. But even more striking than the movement of whole families is the degree of individual mobility.

Although there is some out-migration, and daughters often move to a nearby village at marriage, one of the central features of peasant societies is their low rate of geographical mobility. Except in times of crisis, a man born in a village is likely to remain there all his life, working on the jointly held estate and receiving his rightful share when married. Girls would stay to work for the communal labour pool until marriage. Farm labour is family labour, the unit of production swelling and contracting over the life-cycle. The unit of production is based on the biological family, with adopted and in-marrying additions. It is now known that nothing like this occurred in Kirkby Lonsdale in the seventeenth century. Preliminary figures published some years ago showed that a very considerable proportion of the children left home in their early or middle teens.[37] Using a combination of parish register and a listing of inhabitants, it is possible to estimate the frequency with which those baptized in the parish remained there. In Lupton, for example, of twenty males baptized in the period 1660–9 who were not recorded as buried before 1695, only six were present in the listing of that year. Fourteen had disappeared from the township. Women were even more mobile. Of 23 girls baptized in the same period whose burial is not recorded, not a single one was present in the listing of 1695. A search for both boys

---

[37] A. Macfarlane, *The Family Life of Ralph Josselin* (Cambridge, 1970), pp. 209–10.

and girls for the decades after this also suggests that very few of the children stayed in Lupton after the first few years of their lives, even though their parents remained. Far from settling down on a family farm, younger sons and all daughters moved away. Even the eldest son often went away for a number of years before returning to take over a holding. The central feature of the situation seems again to have been the opposite of the 'peasant' situation. Rather than the holding absorbing the children's labour, the parental home shed the children just as they began to be net producers. If extra labour was needed, it was hired in the form of labourers or servants. This was related to a particular and peculiar household structure.

It is characteristic of peasant societies that in operation and some-times in residence as well the basic unit is the 'extended family'. Married sons and their wives and parents work together and con-sume together, pooling labour and sharing proceeds. This is often reflected in residential arrangements or household structure. Thus households are often large and contain more than one currently married couple – as, for example, in a 'stem' family, with a married couple, their married son and wife and their grandchildren. It is clear that in Kirkby Lonsdale, as elsewhere in England at this time, such complex and extended households were absent. The listing for Lupton in 1695 does not show a single instance of a married child living with his or her parents, not even with a widowed parent. The Killington listing mentions two cases only among 222 names; a widow living with a married son, and a widower with a married daughter. The idea that two married couples should live or work together is never expressed in any of the documents. Nor are there any cases of anything equivalent to the Indian joint family, where brothers and their wives live together or work a communal estate together. Throughout Kirkby Lonsdale, the listings for the nine townships show, with very few exceptions indeed, only nuclear families, parents and unmarried children. It is true that wills fairly frequently mention that children are married, but in such cases the married child seems to have lived elsewhere.

It is obvious that analysis of residential or household structure is not by itself enough to disprove the absence of 'extended' or 'joint' families. Co-residence is only one of the indexes. Although the Kirkby Lonsdale families did not live in complex households and do not seem to have been 'eating from the same pot' as they would have done in pre-revolutionary Russia, they could still have been acting as joint families in terms of ownership, production and consumption. It is well known that the joint residential unit, for instance in India, is often more an ideal than an actuality, and that most people, most of the time, live in nuclear households, even in peasant societies.[38] Even if it is clear from comparing the Kirkby Lonsdale listing and parish register that the situation was far removed from that described by Berkner for parts of Austria, where most people spend a part of their lives living in an extended household,[39] it might be that operationally there was some form of co-operation. We might find a group of married couples, parents, brothers and wives and children living in the same village and working a communal plot.

Literary evidence makes us suspect that even joint families defined in terms of operation rather than residence did not exist. It was not just a matter, as Arthur Young put it when attacking the settlement laws,[40] of the young 'abhorring' the thought of living with their fathers or mothers after marriage; it was a question of discipline, self-government, independence. A description of norms which would astound an 'ideal-type' peasant is given in 1624 by William Whately when counselling young people.[41]

When thou art married, if it may be, live of thy selfe with thy wife, in a family of thine owne, and not with another, in one family, as it were, betwixt you both . . . The mixing of governours in an household, or subordinating or uniting of two Masters, or two Dames, under one roofe, doth fall out most times, to be a matter of much unquietnes to all parties: to make the young folks so wholly resigne themselves unto the elder, as not to be discontented with their proceedings; or to make the elder so much to deny themselves, as to condescend unto the wills of the younger . . . in the common sort of people [is] altogether impossible. Whereof, as the young Bees do seek unto themselves another Hive, so let the young couple another house . . .

This advocates not merely a physical separation, but a social one also, the setting up of an economically and jurally independent unit. We find that local records support this idea of separate units.

Wills, inventories, deeds and manorial records, as well as the listings, make it clear that families did not operate as communal units in production and consumption. Despite earlier quoted remarks about the concentration of family names, the listings do not reveal heavy concentrations of people with the same surname, possibly kin, living near to each other. In Killington, for example, the majority of

[38] W. J. Goode, *World Revolution and Family Patterns* (New York, 1963), p. 17; figures for India are summarized on p. 242.

[39] L. K. Berkner, 'The Stem Family and the Developmental Cycle of the Peasant Household . . .', *American Historical Review* 77 (1972), pp. 398–418.

[40] Quoted in W. E. Tate, *The Parish Chest* (Cambridge, 1960), p. 214.

[41] W. Whately, *A Bride-Bush: or, a Direction for Married Persons* (London, 1619), sig. A6^{r-v}.

the surnames of heads of household only occur once in the listing. In only nine cases did surnames occur in more than two households. The most common surname in the parish was Barker, fifteen of the 222 persons in the parish being called by that name; eleven were called Atkinson. If we concentrate on these two names, we find that, although each of them was to be found in eight separate households, this was by no means a situation of a group of 'kindred' farming a set of neighbouring estates or one large farm. In the case of the Barkers, there were three households with three Barkers in each, one with two people of that name, and five households merely containing one person of that name, usually as a servant. The Atkinsons were even more spread out, with one set of three, one of two, and the rest single individuals. Since both these names were common in the region, it is quite likely that a number of the individuals were not related, except very distantly. If we turn to the wills, there is nowhere in the nearly two thousand for the parish a suggestion that brothers were farming jointly. The probate inventories show where people's livestock was at the time of their death and to whom they owed debts; in neither case is there any hint of communal farming. The unit of production was the husband and wife and hired labour (not children). This helps to explain, and is given support by, the incidence of servanthood in the area.

It appears from studies of India, Russia and other peasant societies that farm servants and domestic servants are relatively rare and unimportant in traditional peasantries. Farm labour is family labour. In Kirkby Lonsdale, a search of the listings shows that the absent child labour was replaced by hired labour. In Killington, of an adult male population of approximately eighty, ten were stated to be servants and nine were day labourers; thus approximately one-quarter were hired labour. Another quarter were stated to be 'pensioners' in receipt of parish poor relief. Thus one half of the population was supporting or paying for the labour of the other half. There were also thirteen women stated to be servants. It seems to have been the case that movement into an unrelated household, either as apprentice, servant or day labourer, was a central feature of the area. In other words, instead of the unit of labour being determined by the demographic expansion and contraction of the family as sons were born and grew and parents died (as in the classic Chayanovian model), people regulated the amount of labour by hiring labour. As their holding expanded, they could bring in more labour. Half the parish hired the other half. In this situation, economics were not dependent on demography. Furthermore, with a free labour supply, two important consequences followed. First, there was no great incentive to marry young and to have many children; young adults could be hired without the inconvenience of having to be fed and clothed in their young and unproductive years. Secondly, there was an incentive to saving and accumulation, since such saving could be used to purchase more land and more labour. Expansion was not limited by the inelasticity of labour. A consequence of this was that the pattern of social mobility in the area was very different from that experienced in peasant societies.

It has been suggested that the typical pattern, at least of the pre-revolutionary Russian peasantry, is one of 'cyclical mobility', by which families move as a whole, and in which over time a family will accumulate property, have more children, partition the estate and become poorer again. Thus there are no long-term divisions into permanent 'classes'.[42] The pattern in Kirkby Lonsdale was totally different. Families did not move as a whole; daughters and younger sons often moved downwards while the eldest son would move upwards. We have to trace individual mobility, rather than family mobility, for the pressure of impartibility and private as opposed to family estates was dominant. Furthermore, there are traces of a growing separation between the rich and the poor, which turned into a permanent class barrier, even in this supposedly egalitarian region. In Killington at the time of the 1695 listing, approximately one-third of the population were in receipt of poor relief or were 'pensioners'. In the main township of Kirkby Lonsdale, in the year of the listing some 52 persons were listed in the poor overseer's accounts as receiving alms. If we assume that they had roughly the same number of dependants as the poor in Killington, this would again constitute one-third of the population. We are witnessing the formation in this rural area of a permanent and large category of landless and largely propertyless labouring families. The townships were already divided into certain individuals who owned the farms and shops and others who worked for them.

If we combine the various features described above, we may present an over-simplified, yet basically correct, general model which depicts this parish as populated by a set of highly individualistic, highly mobile (in both the geographical and the social sense) and capitalistic farmers and craftsmen. This is further confirmed if we look at the extensive web of debts and credit to non-kin revealed in the probate inventories. It is also both supported and integrated into

---

[42] Shanin, *The Awkward Class*, part II.

one ideal-type life portrait in a description of what life was like in one
of these northern valleys. The account was written in the nineteenth
century, looking back to the early eighteenth, but, judging by the
accounts we have looked at, it would appear to hold true of the
second half of the seventeenth century also. Bearing in mind the
stability and 'family property' complex of an Indian or east European
peasant, it is worth quoting the description in full.[43]

The farm labourer of the dales, then (and he is more often than not the son of
a small farmer or yeoman), is nothing akin to his southern brother . . . he is
early sent to school, but at fourteen leaves home to earn his own living. He
has been well schooled, in a way, and looks forward to 'service'. At the
half-yearly hiring – Whitsuntide or Martinmas – after he has attained his 'first
majority', he goes to the nearest country town and stands in the market-
place. He is attired in a brand new suit, with a capacious necktie of green and
red. These articles he has donned upon the memorable morning, and as a gift
from his parents they constitute his start in life . . . As an outward and visible
sign of his intention, the lad sticks a straw in his mouth and awaits the issue
. . . After waiting a greater part of the morning and seeing many of his
fellow-men and maid-servants hired, he is accosted by a stalwart yeoman,
who inquires if he wants a 'spot' – a place, a situation. The lad replies that he
does; that he is willing to do anything; and that he will engage for £4 the
half-year – 'if it pleases' . . . At sixteen or seventeen he is stalwart enough to
hire as a man, and now his wages are doubled; he asks and obtains £12 for the
year, or even £14 if entering upon the summer half. The farm servants of the
dales 'live in', and have all found . . . In proportion, the girls are much better
off in the matter of wages than the men. There is probably less competition
among them, owing to the fact that there is a great temptation for country
girls to migrate and enter service in provincial towns . . . Many of the men,
when about thirty years of age, are able to take small farms of their own.
Nearly all the statesmen's sons do this, and probably without any outside
help; for, as a class, these labourers are not only industrious but thrifty. I
knew a man who had saved £120, which sum he had divided and deposited
in three banks . . . From the fact of 'living in', as nearly all the valley servants
do, it need hardly be said that early marriages are rare. All the better men
look forward to the time when they can have a farm of their own; and when
they obtain a holding, they then look out for a wife.

Here we see all the features: the absence of ties between sons and
their father's holding; geographical mobility; hired labour; saving and
thrift; late age at marriage; the movement of girls away from the area.
In every respect it is a contrast with peasantry.

It would be foolish to over-stress the absence of a peasant social
structure in England in the sixteenth and seventeenth centuries.
Although it cannot be found in the lowlands or in Kirkby Lonsdale, it

---

[43] *The Annals of a Quiet Valley* by a Country Parson, edited by John Watson (London,
1894), pp. 94–100.

is possible that there may be areas, for example northern Cumbria, Redesdale, Cornwall, in which farm and family were more closely identified. Yet it does not seem possible to sustain the belief that England as a whole was a 'peasant' society before the Industrial Revolution. To what extent this placed it apart from continental Europe, Scotland and Ireland, needs to be investigated. We shall also need to examine when this alternative pattern emerged and what its consequences were. Here we have merely sought to establish that direct analogies between the supposedly 'peasant' nation of England in the fifteenth to eighteenth century and peasantries in other nations in the past and present should be treated with considerable caution.

11

Poverty, poor relief and the life-cycle: some evidence from seventeenth-century Norfolk*

TIM WALES

In October 1602 Widow Dixe of Kelling petitioned Sir Nathaniel Bacon, JP, for relief. Her plea is that she has three children at her charge, that she 'hath no meanes for living but hir hand labor: is sett on worke by a comber onely of whom shee is sometyme not wrought by a weeks space: That shee had no relief of the overseers since Christmas, except iis vid for her rent at Midsomer',[1] that her landlord has turned her out and that the overseer is refusing to help. In January 1662 George Cock of Holt was granted an annual pension of 40s out of county funds in response to a petition subscribed by 'most of the Chiefe inhabitants of the same towne' and sworn to by 'severall persons of Creditt'. In it he claimed that about thirty years earlier he had been pressed and wounded in Charles I's overseas wars; 'but he beinge then younge & somewt able to gett a poore livelyhood by mendinge of shoes would not put the country to any charge for his maintenance, but he being now very old & very lame by reason of his sayd wounds is not able to worke any longer for his liveinge'.[2]

Neither of these pleas for relief is particularly remarkable in itself, but both are valuable for focusing on the way in which institutional relief fitted into the livelihood of the poor. Widow Dixe, attempting to maintain herself and her three children by her hand labour on wool irregularly put out to her to spin, turned to parish relief to supply what she could not earn. George Cock put together a living from

---

* I am very grateful for advice and comments on this paper to Susan Amussen, Ruth Gladden, John Morrill, David Souden, Lawrence Stone and John Walter. I am especially grateful to Richard Smith for his editorial patience and encouragement.
[1] Bacon Memorandum Book 1602–6; Bradfer Lawrence X.d., p. 11. All references to manuscript sources are to documents in Norfolk Record Office (hereafter NRO), unless otherwise stated.
[2] C/S2/2: Fakenham Sessions, January 1662.

shoemaking so long as he was physically able, and then fell back on institutional aid.

It is perhaps an obvious point that poor relief needs to be seen in the wider context of the economy of the poor. However, with rare exceptions, studies of the Poor Laws have concentrated on the minutiae of administration, to the exclusion of any real social context. The poor themselves have tended to get left out, and such important topics as the attitudes of parish officers and rate payers, social relationships, and the structures of poverty and employment have only recently begun to receive attention.[3]

Above all, parish relief cannot be seen in isolation from the variety of means whereby the poor put together a living. One does not find parish paupers on one side, and the rest of the poor on the other. Many paupers were clearly partial wage earners. All the poor depended, in degrees varying according to the nature of the local economy and society, on a whole series of sources of income to support themselves – day labour, by-employments and casual jobs, common rights, charitable doles, neighbourly and/or kin support, loans and begging. Above all, this was an economy which rested upon the family as the unit of earning. In a society where, in the late seventeenth century, up to one-third of the population was under fifteen,[4] and where under-employment was the norm, all household

[3] Important examples of such studies are E. M. Leonard, *The Early History of English Poor Relief* (Cambridge, 1900), and E. M. Hampson, *The Treatment of Poverty in Cambridgeshire 1601–1834* (Cambridge, 1934). Valuable exceptions to this trend are A. Clark, *The Working Life of Women in the Seventeenth Century* (London, 1919), Chapters 3 and 4; P. A. Slack, 'Poverty and Politics in Salisbury, 1598–1664', in P. A. Slack and P. A. Clark, editors, *Crisis and Order in English Towns 1500–1700* (London, 1972); P. A. Slack, 'Vagrants and Vagrancy in England, 1598–1664', *Economic History Review* 2nd series 27 (1974), pp. 360–79; A. L. Beier, 'The Social Problems of an Elizabethan County Town: Warwick, 1580–1590', in P. A. Clark, editor, *County Towns in Pre-Industrial England* (Leicester, 1981); and W. Newman Brown, 'The Receipt of Poor Relief and Family Situation: Aldenham, Hertfordshire, 1630–90', in this volume. For a more general perspective on the labour and livelihoods of the poor in early modern England, see D. C. Coleman, 'Labour in the English Economy of the Seventeenth Century', in E. M. Carus Wilson, editor, *Essays in Economic History, Vol. II* (London, 1962); A. M. Everitt, 'Farm Labourers', in J. Thirsk, editor, *Agrarian History of England and Wales, Vol. IV* (Cambridge, 1967); K. Wrightson and D. C. Levine, *Poverty and Piety in an English Village: Terling* (London, 1979), especially Chapters 2 and 7; P. A. Slack, *Social Problems and Social Policies*, Open University Course A322, English Urban History 1500–1780 (Milton Keynes, 1977); R. W. Malcolmson, *Life and Labour in England 1700–1780* (London, 1981), Chapter 2; R. M. Smith, 'Fertility, Economy and Household Formation in England over Three Centuries', *Population and Development Review* 7 (1981), pp. 595–622; and R. M. Smith, 'Introduction' to this volume, pp. 68–85. I am currently preparing a general paper discussing the relationships between poverty, poor relief and society in early modern England.

[4] E. A. Wrigley and R. S. Schofield, *The Population History of England 1541–1871: A Reconstruction* (London, 1981), Appendix 3.1, pp. 528–9.

members rather than the head alone were of necessity earners, whether as a proto-industrial unit of production or through the pooling of earnings from different sources. The welfare of the poor household rested on the employment of as many of its members as possible.

Those on poor relief were, to a great extent, the victims of the breakdown of the household economy – widows left alone in old age and unable to get enough to support themselves, widows left with young children to bring up; occasionally families where the husband was alive but which were over-burdened with children to bring up and continuously needed parish relief, but more often families which were victims when short-term crises (illnesses, dearth, trade depression) pushed the precariously balanced economy over the edge. To understand the workings of parish relief one needs to relate it to the life-cycle nature of poverty, to understand in what circumstances any general bias towards the aged and the impotent was modified, and indeed to study the degree to which the aged were dependent on wage labour.

The aim of this paper is to explore the critical points in the life-cycle where parish relief was likely to become necessary for the poor, and to place such formal relief in the context of 'the economy of makeshifts' of the poor (to borrow Olwen Hufton's evocative phrase[5]). Poor relief was not a neutral supplement to other sources of income, but was mediated through social attitudes and relations in the village – attitudes to charity or to behaviour fitting in the poor. The Coton (Cambs.) parish officers, protesting against a 2s a week pension granted to an (allegedly) 114-year-old man, revealingly combined moral, regulative and economic motives when they complained that he abused the officers, that he never came to church and that he spent any money he had in the alehouse, and did not need the money anyway as he had a cow and a calf.[6] But the links between parish relief and the needs of the poor were close, and I intend to discuss them using Norfolk as a case study.[7]

The survival of overseers' accounts for Norfolk before the eighteenth century is very patchy indeed, yet it seems simply wrong to

---

[5] O. Hufton, *The Poor of Eighteenth Century France* (Oxford, 1974), Chapter 3.

[6] W. M. Palmer, 'The Reformation of the Cambridge Corporation, July 1662', *Proceedings of the Cambridge Antiquarian Society* new series II (1913), p. 92. I am grateful to Patrick Higgins for this reference.

[7] The following generalizations are based on a survey of Norfolk parish accounts and Quarter Sessions records for the period 1580–1700. Fuller documentation must await my forthcoming Cambridge Ph.D. thesis, 'The Parish and the Poor: Poverty and Administration in Seventeenth Century Norfolk'.

assume that because so few survive now the Poor Laws were not particularly important in the early seventeenth century.[8] Such accounts as survive are widely scattered in place and type of settlement – including small villages as well as larger parishes – and their content and form point to well-established routine and practice. Supplemented by the evidence of the Quarter Sessions Rolls, they show a system of poor relief into which the parish was fully integrated.

However, as the century progressed the parish relief became increasingly important in terms of numbers relieved and amounts given out, though this expansion appears to have been rather more by jumps in certain short phases than by a continuous process of development, and the process can only partly be explained away by the inflation of the early seventeenth century. Parish relief became increasingly important in the maintenance of individual paupers, although in the late seventeenth century most paupers at any one time would still have been only partially dependent on it.

One needs to be cautious in drawing trends from a small number of parishes scattered over a county of over six hundred parishes. Throughout the period parish officers were providing rent, clothes, fuel and sickness payments for the poor, but it is impossible to see any discernible difference either in degree or in the category of person in receipt of this type of aid between the early and latter parts of the period. It is not likely that changes in such payments would distort our picture of those trends in the relief of weekly or monthly pensioners (or, to use a seventeenth-century word, collectioners) that provided the core of parish relief.

In the first half of the century this regular relief was generally low, with 6d a week as the normal maximum. For most of the second half of the century, 1s a week was the usual maximum. When somebody was paid more, the recipient was either a child or peculiarly disabled. For example, in 1653/4 the overseers of Great Melton paid out £7 16s 8d for the boarding out of Robert Goodred, 'a poore blinde man'.[9] In some but not all parishes a further rise is to be seen at the very end of the century and the beginning of the next.

The doubling of the maximum would appear to pivot on the years of political, religious and economic crisis 1647–50.[10] It was in those

[8] For this view, see, in particular, W. K. Jordan, *Philanthropy in England 1480–1660* (1959), Chapter 5, especially pp. 139–41.

[9] EVL, 645, 463x9.

[10] See, for instance, the overseers' accounts for Wighton (1642–1712), Foulsham (1640–85) and North Walsham (1621–48, 1648–79), kept in the parish and at NRO (AYL 453: PD 5/31; PD 50/43; PD 209/187).

years that 1s a week became a standard payment for the poorest of the paupers, where before it had been relatively uncommon, and, along with the evidence of notably higher levels of payments and collectioners between the late sixteenth and the early seventeenth centuries, shows the parish taking a larger share of the relief of the poor and, to a certain extent, replacing other means of support. Thus at Bunwell in 1598 there were 25 individuals on poor relief, but of these 23 were orphans (suggesting some exceptional circumstances) and only two were aged poor, each receiving 3d a week.[11] All the fourteen collectioners in 1635 had been described five years earlier as aged and impotent, and twelve received between 4d and 6d.[12] By 1697 only one pauper out of ten was receiving as little as 6d, the rest were receiving 1s or more.[13] The figures for North Walsham, a large market town in the north-east of the country, illustrate the changing role of parish relief.[14]

In 1586 there were ten collectioners given about 8s a month, a very small number in a town of about 900 inhabitants. For most of the early part of the seventeenth century about 25 to 30 pensioners were receiving around £2 10s per month. In the Interregnum about 35 to 50 collectioners were paid in all between £7 10s and £8 per month – levels which lasted through to the 1680s. Monthly disbursements rose from £8 10s to £10 per month in the 1690s and 1700s for about the same number of recipients.

Table 11.1 illustrates these changes at the level of individual collectioners. The 1636 figure is distorted by the presence of several expensive children and 'the Innocent'. Even so, in 1609 twenty out of 24 collectioners were paid 6d a week or less; in 1636 thirteen out of 22. In 1656 nineteen out of 37 (i.e. just over half) were still being paid 6d or less, but six were being paid 1s a week, and five more up to 2s. In 1706 none were paid less than 6d a week, ten were being paid that much and eleven were given 1s a week.

Changes in poor relief can be only partially explained away by

[11] Bunwell overseers' account 1598 – original in parish, xeroxes in NRO and Cambridge Group for the History of Population and Social Structure.
[12] Frere MSS: Depwade Hundred, 12 K A (Bunwell Bundle).
[13] Bunwell overseers' accounts, kept in the parish.
[14] North Walsham overseers' accounts (5 volumes: I, 1563–73, 1578–88; II, 1608–15; III, 1621–48; IV, 1648–79; V, 1679–1721). This very important archive is still kept in the parish chest. The rise in the number of collectioners between the early and the late seventeenth century (though not between the Elizabethan and the former period) is probably not disproportionate to overall population increase in the town – by the 1670s it had perhaps 1,600 inhabitants. I am grateful for this point to Richard Smith. Population estimates for 1603 and the 1670 are taken from J. Patten, *English Towns 1500–1700* (Folkestone, 1978), p. 251.

Table 11.1. *North Walsham parish paupers: sample months*

	1609	1636	1656	1706
1d–5d	12	7	15	
6d	8	8	9	10
7d–11d	1	2	2	3
1s	1	2	6	11
1s 1d–1s 5d	2	1	1	2
1s 6d		2	2	7
1s 7d–1s 11d				2
2s			2	2
2s 1d–3s				3
Total	24	22	37	40

Source: Overseers' account books (1608–15, 1621–48, 1648–79, 1679–1721) retained in parish.

inflation. Between 1590 and 1650 day labourers' money wages in the south of England rose by 36.5 per cent and stabilized thereafter;[15] maximum levels of relief doubled at the very end of this phase. Given that paupers may well have had a lower margin for survival, their relief may have risen more in reaction to inflation. But the timing, coming so late and maintained after the catastrophic harvests of the late 1640s, suggests at best a lagging relationship between poor relief and price trends. Moreover, it seems unlikely that a pauper could survive solely on 6d a week in the early seventeenth century. In the late seventeenth century, it is at least highly likely that an individual living alone could survive on 1s a week.

The sum compares interestingly with Gregory King's estimate that the cottager or pauper household had an income of £6 10s per annum, while the *per capita* income was £2 per annum (i.e. 9¼d per week).[16] Allowing that rent, clothing and firewood would often be paid on top of the weekly allowance, the figure is suggestive. If it is accurate, then it is arguable that in the second half of the century parish relief became the sole, or at least by far the most important, source of income for the parish pauper, but that this was much less the case before. One could cite other contemporary estimates which suggest

[15] D. C. Coleman, *The Economy of England, 1450–1750* (Oxford, 1977), p. 23.
[16] J. Thirsk and J. P. Cooper, *Seventeenth Century Economic Documents* (Oxford, 1972), pp. 780–1. As early as 1594 Clement Paston was leaving a bequest of 1s a week to 6 almshouse inmates, and for the pre-1660 period this sum has been estimated as the standard amount left to Norfolk almsmen: W. K. Jordan, *The Charities of Rural England* (London, 1959), p. 129.

that 1s is too low – in the 1680s one writer estimated the cost of a man's diet as 5d a day and a woman's at 1s 6d; another that it cost 2s 'to keep a poor man or woman (with good husbandry) one whole week'.[17] Writing from a condition rather removed from that of those scraping a living, such commentators are obviously somewhat unreliable guides. Moreover, given the significance of family employments and forms of income other than wage labour, it is highly artificial to draw up a notional budget for the poor.

More work needs to be done on the problem, but given the low price of barley in the late seventeenth century, the frequent provision of rent, fuel and clothing by parish officers, and support from some contemporary writers and the one modern attempt to estimate a budget for the poor,[18] it does seem likely that 1s a week was a sum the poor could survive on. It is even possible that the standard of living of the parish pauper and that of the day labourer with a family were comparable, a situation that David Thomson has found to hold for rural England in the 1840s.[19]

One has, therefore, the parish taking upon itself an increasingly large part in the maintenance of the aged poor; the importance of this in the lives of the poor is reflected in the increasing tendency for paupers' goods to be regarded as the property of the parish at their death. The development may, by implication, confirm Dudley North's comment on the decline of informal charity: 'I am certain that now, care being taken by overseers publicly chosen in every parish, a great many that have compassionate hearts do not so much in that kind as they would do otherwise; for what is more natural than to think such care needless . . . Many people not only think it needless but foolish to do that which is parish business.'[20]

Given the nature of the sources it is impossible to say whether before the late 1640s parish relief was drifting upwards, as increasing parish relief interacted with or replaced decreasing formal relief; the crisis of 1647–50 appears to have been far more significant in increasing the share of formal than of informal relief.

It is suggestive of a circular tendency of this sort that in the north-east of the county paupers formed a much higher proportion of the poor exempt from the Hearth Tax of 1674 in the market towns

---

[17] A. Clark, *The Working Life of Women in the Seventeenth Century*, pp. 73 and 79.

[18] Wrightson and Levine, *Poverty and Piety*, p. 40.

[19] D. Thomson, 'Provision for the Elderly in England, 1830–1908', unpublished University of Cambridge Ph.D. thesis, 1980, especially Chapter 2, 'The Value of Relief Payments', pp. 45–86.

[20] Quoted in K. V. Thomas, *Religion and the Decline of Magic* (Harmondsworth, 1973), p. 695. North was writing in the 1690s.

than in the smaller villages. In Felbrigg there was one pauper, and at Hanworth there were two (out of, respectively, seventeen and fifteen poor). In Foulsham there were eighteen collectioners to seventy exempt, and in North Walsham 45 to 185 exempt (i.e. 25.7 per cent and 24.3 per cent).[21] It may well be that in the smaller villages with a higher proportion of poverty of the 'structural' kind, but less extreme forms of social stratification, the claims of neighbourhood may have been less worn away. The contrast between Felbrigg and Foulsham is especially striking. The former was a village of 33 households in 1674 (hence some 51.5 per cent were exempt); the latter was a market town of 130 households (53.8 per cent exempt). In the former there was only one collectioner for most of the 1670s, and from one to three in the 1680s and 1690s; none between 1671 and 1693 received more than 6d a week. Against this, in Foulsham the situation in 1673 was as shown in Table 11.2.

It must nevertheless be emphasized that the sorts of people on poor relief – the aged, the widowed and the orphaned – predominated amongst collectioners in the towns as in the villages. What, then, were the forms of charitable aid? There were small bequests and funeral doles paid several times a year at the most. These clearly had their place in the economy of the poor. At Alburgh in 1674 it was noted of the exempt poor that they were 'such as we conceive are not fitt or lyable to be charged with that duty of harth money by Rason they are such as take Almes of the Towne and not charged with anything for church or poore'.[22] At North Walsham, as against twenty

---

[21] The numbers of collectioners are drawn from overseers' accounts for Foulsham and North Walsham still in the parish; at Norfolk Record Office the references are AYL 453 (Hanworth) and WKE 180, 464x (Felbrigg). The exempt are taken from certificates in PRO E 179/336 and E 179/337, Tunstead, North Erpingham and Eynsford bundles, and tax payers from E 179/154/697. A third village in the north-east, Guestwick, proved too small for valid comparison. In 1674 there were about 21 households in the village, of whom 7 were exempt and of the latter 2 were in receipt of parish relief in 1672–3 and 1673–4. It is very possible that the lower proportion of exempt poor in Guestwick resulted from its being a closed village. The smallness of the number of rate-payers (14) was matched by unusually unequal divisions of wealth between them. The local gentry family, the Bulwers, not only held the manor but also were paying over half the poor rate contributed by residents. The yeoman presence appears to have been much weaker than in Hanworth and Felbrigg, while the 7 exempt poor (of whom 5 were men and 3 explicitly noted as day labourers in a certificate of 1671) can hardly have provided a sufficient workforce for intensive sheep–corn husbandry. Sufficient labour may have come from a greater reliance on servants-in-husbandry, or, indeed, from drawing on a pool of labourers in adjacent Foulsham: PD 5/31 (PRO E 179/337); F. Blomefield and C. Parkin, *An Essay Towards a Topographical History of the County of Norfolk* (London, 1808), Vol. VII, p. 218. I intend to deal more fully with the relationship between settlement size, land holding, poverty and pauperism in my thesis.

[22] PRO, E 179/337. Earsham bundle.

Table 11.2. *Payments to Foulsham collectioners, Easter 1673–Easter 1674*

Payments to collectioners per month	No. of collectioners
4s	6
3s 6d	1
3s	4
2s	5
	18 (+ two children to be kept at 10s 8d per month)

collectioners, there were 78 people receiving between 2d and 7d from the annual rent from Pigg's farm.[23] Such typical charities were usually small-scale and of relatively slight importance.

Rather more important were varying types of informal relief, of whose decline the rise in overseers' disbursements provides the obverse. Gentry largesse formed one element, and voluntary contributions lower down the social scale another. In Hanworth in 1645 and 1646 (apparently) and in 1647 (definitely) no poor rates were raised. In the latter year £1 19s 6d was disbursed by the overseers, who noted: 'Beside itt beinge held fitter by our Minister to provide for the Pore rather by voluntary contributions than by rates and collections there have been divers several sumes of moneye contributed and distributed amongst these and other Poore persons within the said Parish.'[24]

The clearest expression of the interrelationship between formal and informal relief is to be found in a Hertfordshire petition from 1638 against the royal proclamation against maltsters – farmers and maltsters had refused to set the poor on work, alleging the restraint in maltmaking. 'And when we raised them in theyr taxes to the maintenance of those labourers, they withdrew theyr Charitie to the impotent poore who dayly repaire to theyr howses for reliefe.'[25]

The passage is interesting because it describes a situation where the very individuals who were the main focus of the 1601 Act were still being relieved by informal means over 35 years later. There are overtones of the provision in the 1597 (but not the 1601) Act, where begging licensed by the parish officers was allowed – surely an attempt to regularize customary practice. In 1601 the overseers of Holkham reported: 'There be dyverse pore allsoe within the said

[23] North Walsham Overseers' Accounts, 1621–48; the figures are drawn from 1621.
[24] AYL 453.   [25] PRO, SP 16/342, no. 93.

parishe wch have noe Contribucon of money: by reason they have by order dayly relieffe at the houses of the inhabitantes.'[26] In the preceding year there were twelve who 'by order have dayly relief at the houses of the inhabitantes', five of whom were among the seven collectioners. Faced with dearth in 1631, the JPs of South Erpingham and Eynsford in the north-east found localized begging acceptable.

And albeit this yere have inforced manie pooer people to begge & seeke abroade for releife, yet we have not found in the check watches . . . that any considerable number of strange beggers or suspitious persons have bene apprehended, no dangerous rogues such as use to travell this Countrie . . ., wch makes us suppose that if anie doe begge they are but neare dwellers.[27]

Yet one needs to press beyond questions of overseers' payments, charity and informal relief. The differences between individual villages' proportions of paupers in 1674 had more to do with variations in local economic structures than with different degrees of neighbourly charity. Overseers' accounts – as at North Walsham and Hedenham (Table 11.1 and Figure 11.1) – reveal wide variations between individual levels of payments. These variations, especially after 1650, reflect the inadequacies of other earnings. Only a minority of paupers at any one time would have been on 1s a week, and, as at Hedenham, many would never have attained that much before their death.

One needs to break down the poor and the paupers in more detail, and to place pauperism in the life-cycle and circumstances of individual families. This is, at the least, necessary to justify the assumption that generally a pauper on relief had only himself (or more often, herself) to maintain on the parish weekly pay; though obviously there were important exceptions to the prevailing trend.

This assumption is made on two general grounds. First, there was the very high proportion of widows on relief, suggesting up to a point the elderly (see Table 11.3), though of course younger women widowed with several children to bring up often appear on relief – a point to which I shall return. This general trend is suggested even more by the simple fact that, once on relief, the only way off it for most was by death. Again one needs a proviso that by the time a widow's children had left the household (given a late female marriage age) she might be on relief because of old age. However, in these circumstances, as children became less of a burden as they grew older, one might expect payments over the years to follow a course that was not continuously upward. With most collectioners in the late

---

[26] Norfolk overseers' accounts. Bradfer-Lawrence VII a.(1).
[27] PRO, SP 16/197, no. 13.

Table 11.3. Collectioners in selected Norfolk settlements by sex, marital status and age

Village or town	Holkham*	Great Walsingham	Wighton	Bunwell	Carlton Rode	North Walsham				Foulsham		Cawston		Hedenham††
Date	1600/1	1614/15	1614/15	1630/1	1635/6	1621/2	1636/7	1706/7	1640/1	1660/1	1673/4	1601§	1699**	1662–1709 / 1662/3–1708/9
1. Widows	8	14	7	12	5	12	8	23	4	12	12	9	8	17
2. Women[a]	1	3	2	—	1	4	9	4	4	1	3	3	1	5
3. Men	3	8	1	7†	4	4	6	12	11	5	—	7	10	15
4. Children[b]	—					2	5‡	2	1	2	4	5	—	1
5. ?[c]	—					3		3				—	—	1
Total	12	25	10	19	10	25	29	44	20	20	19	24	19	39
Widows as % of total	66.6	56	70	63.2	50	48	27.6	52.3	20	60	63.2	37.5	42	44.7
All women as % of total	75	68	90	63.2	60	64	58.6	61.8	40	64	78.9	50	47.5	57.9

[a] This line includes all women described as 'wife' or 'goody' in text and (rather more common) all those whose marital status is unspecified.

[b] In this table, total numbers of children dependent on the weekly collection have been given where possible. Where the children are linked in an entry with a surviving parent, they have been included in the column relevant to the parent.

[c] This line is made up of individuals where the details in the account are insufficient as a guide to the sex or age of the pauper (for instance, where the surname could belong to either sex, or where an individual may be a child, though not described as such in the text).

* This figure includes both collectioners and those receiving relief at parishioners' houses.

† These seven male pauper households are made up of four where the wife was alive and three where the man was living alone.

‡ This is a minimum number – there were children from three families noted, but only one family for which the singular rather than the plural was given in the overseers' accounts.

§ Differences between these figures and those in Tables 11.4–11.7 arise from including all paupers here, rather than just pauper households.

** The source for this column, an inventory of pauper goods, includes only householders.

†† For the conventions used to reach these figures, see Appendix 2.

Sources: Holkham, Great Walsingham and Wighton: Overseers' Accounts Bradfer-Lawrence VII a(i)
Bunwell and Carlton Rode, Frere MSS: Depwade Hundred, 12 K A
Cawston 1601: NRS, 2604, 12 B 2
Cawston 1699: PD 193/3
Hedenham: PD 302/41
North Walsham and Foulsham: Parish Chest

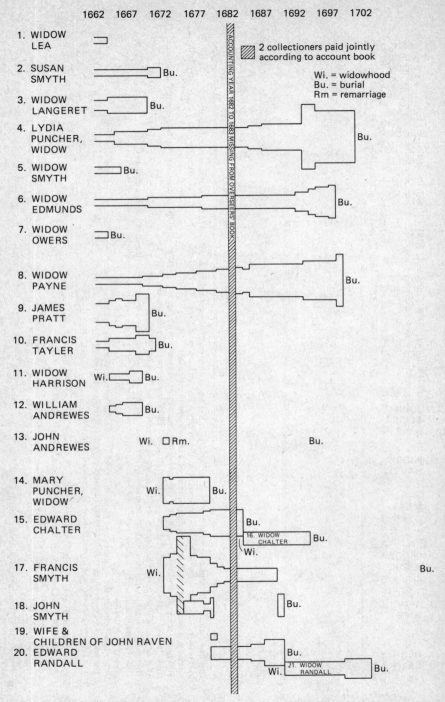

Figure 11.1 Monthly payments to collectors, Hedenham: Easter 1662 to Easter 1709 (collated with parish registers)*

* For the accompanying family histories, see Appendix 2.

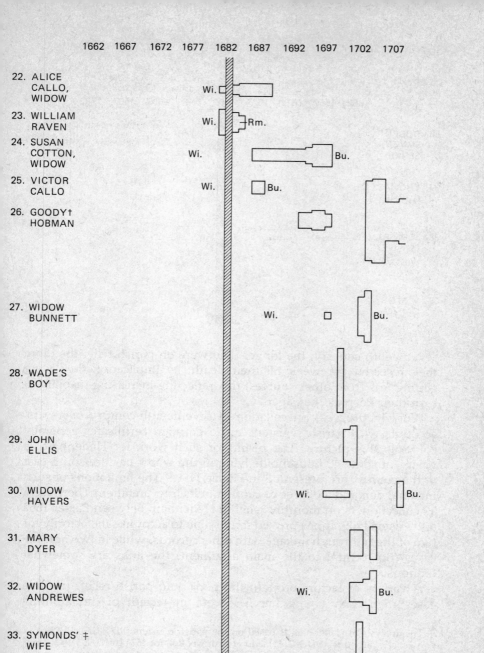

	1662	1667	1672	1677	1682	1687	1692	1697	1702	1707

22. ALICE CALLO, WIDOW   Wi.

23. WILLIAM RAVEN   Wi.   Rm.

24. SUSAN COTTON, WIDOW   Wi.   Bu.

25. VICTOR CALLO   Wi.   Bu.

26. GOODY† HOBMAN

27. WIDOW BUNNETT   Wi.   Bu.

28. WADE'S BOY

29. JOHN ELLIS

30. WIDOW HAVERS   Wi.   Bu.

31. MARY DYER

32. WIDOW ANDREWES   Wi.   Bu.

33. SYMONDS' ‡ WIFE

34. HENRY REYNOLDS   Bu.   35. WIDOW REYNOLDS   Wi. ➡

† From 1703 Widow Hobman was keeping Symonds' children, a girl and boy (the latter bound out in 1706).

‡ Symonds' wife was paid for maintaining her children 1s 6d a week for the first 10 weeks of 1703/4; thereafter Widow Hobman maintained them.

Sources: PD 302/41; PD 302/1

Figure 11.1 (Cont.)

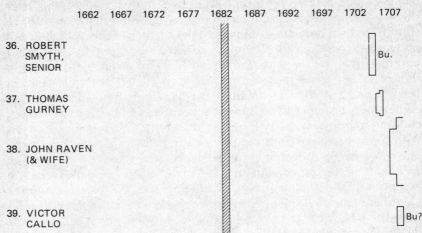

seventeenth century, the longer they were on parish relief the more they received per week till their death; by implication they were getting less from other sources, this reflecting increasing inability to earn their keep as they aged.

Work in progress on collation of seventeenth-century overseers' accounts with parish registers and exemption certificates generally confirms this picture. The results of such work for Hedenham, a village of some 40 households lying in the wood–pasture south-east of the county, are presented in Figure 11.1.[28] The limitations of such material demand a degree of caution in its interpretation. There were 39 collectioners on monthly relief in Hedenham between Easter 1662 and Easter 1709. It has proved impossible to account satisfactorily for two of them through linkage with other records, while in two or three cases (not central to the main argument) the links are somewhat tenuous.[29]

A variety of factors brought the poor onto parish relief. In three cases men with young families were in receipt of the monthly

---

[28] The analysis of Hedenham is based on the parish registers (PD 302/1, PD 302/2), overseers' accounts (PD 302/41); and Hearth Tax Roll for 1674 (PRO, E 179) 154/697 and exemption certificates (PRO E 179/336). Reasons of time and distance prevented me from utilizing other sources – notably church court depositions and wills – but it is extremely doubtful whether either would alter the picture drawn from the records used.

[29] A full picture of the limitations of the sources is to be found in the notes to Table 11.3.

collection for one to four years; sickness was certainly the cause for one man, and is plausible for the other two, though for both the latter there is a hint that the financial strains of widowhood may have contributed.[30] There are examples of the financial burden of children on women or more directly on the parish in six cases. In 1702–3 and part of 1703–4, for instance, Symonds' wife was receiving 6s a month; thereafter she disappeared from the account but her two children were kept by Widow Hobman at the parish charge. The latter had earlier been on relief herself for five years when she had two young children to bring up. Mary Puncher, widow, was a young woman left with four young children ranging in age from infancy to ten years. She was a parish collectioner for ten years, after which her remarriage took her off the rates. But in Hedenham such paupers were the exceptions, and for most paupers ageing was the most significant identifier. Out of the 36 paupers on whom we have some information, the parish ceased paying 23 (possibly 24) of them only at their death. Five were collectioners in the last year or two of their lives, but in four cases these poor were almost certainly elderly, while two (and possibly three) other collectioners not linkable in this way were old. Of the 36 poor 24 were on relief for four or more years. In five cases the financial burden of young children figures most prominently; in one of these the level of relief stayed the same as long as it was paid, in two it rose and fell over the years, and in the other two cases it fell over the year. The course of relief payments to Francis Smyth, strikingly different from other patterns in Hedenham, can be explained in terms of the changing costs of keeping children. In 1672 his wife died leaving him with at least three young children, aged twelve, eight and six, and a two-month-old baby daughter. There were early peaks in the amounts paid him, followed by a steady dropping over the years as the children got older. Payments stabilized when his second-youngest daughter was fifteen and ceased when his youngest reached seventeen. Smyth's difficulties were compounded by his own sickness in 1672 and the partial upkeep of an aged father, but the parish was paying heavily towards the latter's support until the burden of children eased.

These families reflect one pattern of family life-cycle pauperism. Where children were the main cause of pauperism, the financial burden demanded of the parish would, if anything, lessen over the years as they grew to earning capacity; in the other nineteen cases

---

[30] John Andrewes was a collectioner for the year preceding his remarriage only. William Raven was on relief in the years before his remarriage, his relief ceased the year after his remarriage.

pauperism can be ascribed to ageing. All but one pauper died while in receipt of poor relief.[31] Excluding that one and Smyth's father (because of the complications of kin support) from the following calculations, in eleven out of seventeen cases it is possible to link the accounts not only with a burial but also with either a marriage or a first recorded child baptized in the parish. The mean number of years between either of the latter and appearance in the parish accounts was 30.8 years (a figure distorted upwards as five of the eleven were on relief in 1662–3 and we do not know how long before they had been on relief; excluding them the mean drops to 29.0 years). The mean number of years between first register entry and burial was 46.1, a figure pushed upwards by three for whom the intervals were of over 60 years; without them the mean would have been 38.3 years. The number of years between first register entry and first appearance in the surviving accounts varied from about 23 to 36 years; between the former and burial entry from (excluding the extreme cases) about 30 to 45 years. If one assumes that the mean age of marriage or of first child recorded was in the late twenties, it seems likely that most paupers went onto the parish in their fifties or sixties and died between about 60 and 75. Three of the paupers – Widows Edmunds, Payne and Puncher – were on relief for over 30 years, but for most five to twelve years appears to have been more normal (the mean number of years as a collectioner among the seventeen was 13.8 including these three widows but only 8.7 without them), and there is no evidence that, where age was the main cause of pauperism, women went on relief earlier than men. However, there were more female collectioners than male – they made up at least 22 of the 38, while of the 23 paupers on the parish for at least four years three of the five with young children and twelve of the nineteen who were aged were women (eleven of the latter explicitly being listed as widows). It may be too neat in individual cases to draw too sharp a distinction between ageing and overburdened families as causes of pauperism. Lydia Puncher, widow, had been married 29 years before she appeared in the overseers' account, so she was at least in her fifties. The parish registers are defective for the 1650s, but it is possible that she had at least two or three children in their early teens partially dependent on her in 1662–3. However, if this was so, it was more her declining earning ability that made her financially vulner-

---

[31] The exception is Alice Callo, widow, for whom see below, p. 363. She appeared on relief 18 years after her first entry in the register, the baptism of a child. The family had been removed from Carlton Rode while she was pregnant with this child on grounds of potential chargeability: C3S2/2, Norwich Sessions, October 1663.

able, and the steady mounting of payments to her in the ensuing years can only be ascribed to ageing, for within a few years the children would have been fully able to earn their own keep or would have left home.[32] Figure 11.1 bears ample witness to the way in which, for the elderly poor, ageing was accompanied by increasing levels of relief from the parish authorities. For two of these seventeen longer-term paupers buried in the parish levels of relief stayed the same, but for the other fifteen they grew as individuals declined into economic dependency.

The accounts, then, show individuals appearing on relief as they gradually ceased to be economically self-supporting, and as their ability to earn declined they received more from the parish. This point needs emphasizing in as much as the problem of ageing in early modern England has been a relatively neglected topic. The statutory distinctions as embodied in the 1601 Poor Law between the able-bodied poor and 'the lame ympotente olde blynde and such other amonge them beinge poore and not able to worke' suggests a twentieth-century distinction between the able-bodied, part of the economic life of the community, and the aged and disabled with little or no economic role except dependency. But one must avoid anachronism. Ageing in seventeenth-century society was a process of gradual withdrawal from economic productivity and self-support. The urban censuses of the poor for the period are full of such individuals as Mother Ingram of Ipswich who in 1597 was receiving poor relief to supplement her income from carding and spinning – she was eighty years old. One may usefully cite four households from the census of the poor taken in Norwich in 1570:

Margaret Baxter, wedowe of 70 yeres, that spin hir owne work in woollen & worketh not, & Agnes, hir daughter, the wyf of Richard Caly, Husbandman, who have bene from hyr this 8 yere, & she is 36 yere of age, & spin white warpe, & have dwelt here ever. [This family received 2d a week from the authorities.]

Elizabeth Mason, wedow, Semans mother of 80 yere, a lame woman of one hand, & spin & wynd with one hande, & hath dwelt here 40 yere.

Margaret Fen, wedow, of 60 yeris, a lame woman & worketh not but go about, & is an unruly woman, & dwelt here ever. [To go to the hospital:] 2d. a weke. Veri pore.

Margaret Lamas of 56 yeris, a wedow, a lame woman & worketh not but stylleth aqua vitae, & now lyv upon hyr fryndes, & hath dwelt here 16 yeris.[33]

---

[32] Other probable examples of the phenomenon, the former interesting because the householder was a married man, were Edward Chalter and Alice Callo.

[33] J. Webb, editor, *Poor Relief in Elizabethan Ipswich*, Suffolk Record Society (Ipswich,

These women clearly had their counterparts in the countryside of seventeenth-century Norfolk. By-employments were also important in the rural areas of the country, and as ageing was a gradual process, then these activities would have figured prominently in the household economies of the elderly poor. The evidence for this is partly inferential, contained in the overseers' accounts themselves, and direct only insofar as one can glean incidental references from court records. Thus in 1631 Alice Fendick had a fatal stroke on being accused of witchcraft, and the matter came before Quarter Sessions. Fendick had apparently been receiving charitable help. She had also had hemp put out to her to work by a labourer in the same village, and the fatal accusation came in the course of the labourer's accusing her of keeping back hemp for herself.[34] In the same year Quarter Sessions received a petition from various inhabitants of Terrington St John's against their overseer, John Waters; among the charges was one

That the said Jo: Waters hath given by waye of Colleccon (as by his accounte maye further appeare) fortye or fiftye shillings or there abouts to the said Widdow Addeson in money & coles, & hath payd and allowed to him self for her house rent xs., yett he knew that John Rawlinge senior & Robt. Borthesby did offer the said Widdowe her dwellinge & dyett with them for her worke & that shee should not bee chargeable to the towne, yf shee would leave her sonn in lawe (John Game) who lived idle & refused to labour although able of body.[35]

The order of the JPs of East Norfolk in 1623 is equally revealing; they envisaged stocks *not* to set the able-bodied poor on work but rather

That for such as are so oulde & weake as they are not able or fitt for any other worke, there be provided a stock of hemp in the pillinge whereof they may be imployed, & for that purppose every man who is an occupier of land shall sowe hempe accordinge to the statute.

Parish officers' presentments from Cawston in 1606 show the same understanding of setting the poor on work.[36] Henry Arthington in his 'Provision for the Poor' (1597) referred to an important intermediate category between 'the impotent poore' and 'such as may earn their whole maintenance'.

The poore not able to live by their labour, and yett fitte and willing to take paines, are of three sorts also,

---

1966), p. 135; J. F. Pound editor, *The Norwich Census of the Poor 1570*, Norfolk Record Society (Norwich, 1971), pp. 28–9.   [34] C/S3/28.

[35] C/S3/28A, 'Remonstrances of the Misdemeanours and noteable abuses comytted & done by John Waters, yeoman', December 1630.

[36] Bodleian, MS Tanner 73(2), f. 390; Cawston Parish Presentment 1606.

1. Orphaned children above seven yeares olde.
2. Such as be overcharged with children, having nothing to maintaine them but their hand labour.
3. Such as fall to decay in their workes, by reson of theyr yeares, weaknesse or infirmities.

All which ought to be relieved in part, as their necessitie shal require.[37]

This category needs to be heavily emphasized, because it is here that one may see most clearly the interaction between the family economy of the poor and the relief provided by the parish. One sees here the decline into increasing economic dependence and the danger of the family being unable to support itself fully financially – and this was all the more the case when the family economy was disrupted by the death of the father. Thus some widows on poor relief were younger women with families to maintain. In the Lancashire parish of Kirkham in 1636, there were amongst the paupers three widows receiving 8d a week, but whereas Widow Swartbreke was 'aged' and Widow Yates 'poor, impotent', Widow Thistleton had two young children. A fourth woman, Widow Hodgson, with her two young children who were not old enough to be put out, had a house provided by the parish '& maintaineth herselfe by her worke without any weekly allowance'.[38]

The Hedenham parish records have shown similar examples of widows with young families. Analysis of the relationship between pauperism and family structure can be pushed further by studying the one detailed listing which survives for a Norfolk parish in the seventeenth century – that of Cawston, a market town of about 600–700 inhabitants.[39] The town lay in the sheep–corn north-east of the county, a region which was also closely tied into the production of New Draperies and the consequent by-employments. Cawston also possessed extensive commons, whose turf and undergrowth provided fuel that had an important place in the economy of the poor. In December 1601 a deponent in an Exchequer suit declared (in words that bring out well the blending of use-rights, by-employments and informal relief in the livelihoods of the town's poor) that

---

[37] H. Arthington, *Provision for the Poor* (1597), unpaginated.
[38] PRO, SP 16/330, no. 64.
[39] Unless otherwise stated, this discussion is based on the documents cited in the text, all of which are in NRS, 2604, C 2 B 2, except one of the June listings, in the possession of Mrs Janet Hammond, with a copy in the SSRC Cambridge Group library. A fuller social analysis of seventeenth-century Cawston is to be found in S. D. Amussen, 'Governors and Governed: Class and Gender Relations in English Villages, 1590–1725', unpublished Brown University Ph.D. thesis, 1982, Chapter 2, pp. 43–81. Dr Amussen and I are preparing an edition of the Cawston parish archive (1595–1620) for publication by the Norfolk Record Society.

for the space of twelve or sixteen yeres or thereaboutes diverse pore people inhabitants of Cawston have yerelie used to gett the most part of ther lyvinges by graving of Flagges and Cutting of lyng for dyverse other inhabitantes from and after the Annunciacon of or Ladie untill the first day of August in everie yere upon the Commons of Cawston and he saith that he doth think that the pore people aforesaid have ther Cheipest lyving and mayntenances by graving of flages and Cutting of lynges for wthout that he thinketh that some of them might begg ther bread[40]

In 1601 there were 78 ratepayers to 97 too poor to contribute; the latter made up some 58.8 per cent of households in the town, a high figure but comparable to that for several market towns in Norfolk, and for that for the area as a whole, in the 1670s.[41] In 1601, however, the New Draperies probably provided a less firm base of by-employments than later in the century. This, combined with a probably higher familial burden of children than in later, and easier, demographic conditions, provides partial explanation of the different profile of pauperism from that in late seventeenth-century Hedenham. The other side of the issue lies in differences of size and type of settlement. In Cawston the burden of children in 1601 put more widowed households on the rates than old age by itself. The listing is important for showing the relationship between poverty and the life-cycle, and can be collated with overseers' accounts for that year. The brief analysis that follows is static, concentrating on 1601, the year of the listing, though more information can be gleaned from correlation with accounts for other years, a very deficient parish register and manorial records. The sources for the analysis are as follows.

1. The Poor Account for the year Easter 1601 to Easter 1602.
2. A list of all those too poor to pay the poor rates, divided partly by age and partly by degree of poverty. This list includes parish paupers, and notes whether the poor had a cow or a cottage.
3. Two lists of all those too poor to pay the poor rate but not receiving regular relief, divided up by whether the poor had a cow or a cottage, or not, both dated 2 June 1601.

The four sources have been combined in Appendix 1. They correlate very closely, with only occasional disparities in the size of household, while the age/poverty listing has just one name that occurs only there, while no other names appear on the other listings. All calculations are based on the former listing, except where there is a disparity between it and the poor account. The latter was drawn up

---

[40] PRO, E 134/43 and 44 Eliz. Mich. no. 7, deposition of Henry Yonges, cited in Amussen, 'Governors and Governed', p. 49.

[41] For a full discussion of the regional structure of poverty in Norfolk in the 1670s, the reader is referred to my forthcoming thesis.

several months later and is a more accurate guide to the forces leading to pauperism. The key listing divides the poor into four groups:

A 'The names of the pore above the age of three score years and the number in ech famylie'.

B 'The names of the pore abought fortye & upwards & the numb^r of their famyles'.

C 'Certayn other not so p[oor]'.

D 'more not able to geve eny thyng'.

The categories are broadly drawn, and, while household size is given except for some families on weekly relief, one cannot be certain that the households are made up of parents and children alone. The basis of the listing on two separate criteria, age and poverty, particularly obscures the degree to which differences in mean household size simply reflect different stages in the cycle of individual families. On the other hand, that dual basis is extremely valuable – there is no doubt that the groups based on age were regarded as poorer than the other two. One is able to draw distinctions and gradations otherwise impossible.[42]

Groups A and C are broadly comparable in terms of mean household size (1.81 and 1.78 respectively) and in the predominance of women household heads. In A, all but four householders were women, and fifteen out of that seventeen were identified as widows, whereas all the householders in C were women. But, whereas eight of the 21 poor in A were weekly collectioners and a further two received small sums from the parish, seven out of the nine in C had a cow or a cottage. In short, nearly two-fifths of the poor in A were paupers (i.e. weekly collectioners), while most in C had some property which contributed towards their living.

The same distinction may be drawn between groups B and D – nearly one-third in the former were paupers, while a rather higher proportion in the latter had either a cow or a cottage. The differences in mean household size (MHS) between the two groups is suggestive,

---

[42] The age categories, while doubtless generally reliable, appear to have been broadly drawn and imprecise. The ages given with depositions in the 1601 Exchequer suit, PRO, E 134/43 and 44 Eliz. Mich. no. 7, confirm that Reynold Bishope and Johane, wife of Nicholas Brooke, are in the age groups in which they are listed. The former is given as aged 40 in his deposition, and appears in group B, the latter as aged 78 when she deposed and appears in group A. On the other hand, Thomas Jerbridge appears in group B, despite deposing his age as 64. The lack of precision may presumably be ascribed to the estimates made by parish officers and probably also to the frequent vagueness about age in the period (for instance, every deponent's age when given has the qualification 'or thereabouts'). For evidence on the latter point, see K. Thomas, *Age and Authority in Early Modern England*, Raleigh Lecture on History 1976, *Proceedings of the British Academy* 62 (1976), pp. 3–5.

Table 11.4. *Mean household size, groups B and D; Cawston 1601*

	Households	Persons	MHS
B. Paupers	11	55	5.00
Non-paupers	24	96	4.00
All	35	151	4.31
D. Without cow or cottage	18	53	2.94
With cow or cottage	14	55	3.93
All	32	108	3.38

Source: NRS, 2604, 12 B 2.

even allowing for the small numbers involved (see Table 11.4). The poorer of the two groups had a MHS that was about a quarter the size again than that of the better off – a difference of 0.93.

The difference in MHS between families with a cow or cottage in D, and non-paupers in B is negligible – it is, after all, hardly surprising that those with a cow or cottage should be better off than those with the same size of family who did not have them. Those without property in D are better off than those in B because they have substantially smaller families. They had a MHS of 2.94 as against 4.0 for non-paupers, and 5.0 for paupers in B – that is, the groups in B had mean household sizes about one-third and two-thirds as large again as those of the propertyless in D. To be better off in Cawston, one either had to have a cow or a cottage or fewer children. 'Better off' in this context is, of course, a relative term – in 1601 the inhabitants of Cawston were appealing for rate-in-aid from other parishes on the grounds of the poverty of its rate payers, many of whom were labourers, and this lay behind the drawing up of at least one of the listings.

Calculation of MHS is an insensitive method of linking poverty and the life-cycle, though a valuable preliminary; one must further break down the listings by the sex of the householder and the number of other members of the household, as has been done in Table 11.5. I have assumed that where the householder is a man he will be married (with one obvious exception, where there is only one person in the household) and calculated household members other than the married couple. This probably involves slight error, just as does the assumption that all of the other members were children – some would almost certainly have been inmates and adult offspring. This, one suspects, is the case in the two largest households in A – Widow

Table 11.5. *Cawston 1601: breakdown of families by sex of householder and other members*

	No. of households containing	Paupers
A. *Women*		
Alone	10	3
+1*	6	3
+2		
+3	1	
+4	1	
Married couples		
Alone	2	1
Man		
Alone	1	1 (6 weeks)
	—	—
	21	8

		Poor with cow or cottage
C. *Women*		
Alone	4	3
+1	3	1
+2	2	2
	—	—
	9	6

		Paupers
B. *Women*		
Alone	5	1†
+1	—	
+2	3	2
+3	—	
+4	4	3
	—	—
	12	6
Married couples		
Alone	—	—
+1	7	—
+2	2	—
+3	6	2
+4	2	1
+5	3	—
+6	2	1
+7	1	1
	—	—
	23	5

(Cont.)

Table 11.5 (*cont.*)

	No. of households containing	Paupers
Summary		
Women		
Alone	5	1
With children (all 2–4)	7	4
	12	5
Married couples		
Only		
2 children or less	9	—
2 children +	14	5
	23	5

		Poor with cow or cottage
D. *Women*		
Alone	3	2
+1	1	—
Married couples		
Alone	6	2
+1	9	3
+2	6	4
+3	2	—
+4	3	3
+5	2	2
	32	16

* Including the Wolvye and Dearne households
† Johan Hamerton had a bastard being partially supported on the rates in 1601
Source: NRS, 2604, 12 B 2

Clarke with three, and Widow Fassel with four others (neither of those widows were paupers) – and may well be the case in other families.

The more detailed analysis reinforced the evidence of the MHSs – generally speaking, as the family size increased, so did the family's impoverishment. Of course family size by itself was not the only factor, even among the propertyless. Nine couples in group B as against eight of those without cow or cottage in D had one or two children. Neverthless, family size was an important factor. Eighteen out of 35 households in B (40 per cent) had three or more children, and just over one-third of those were paupers; the paupers were weighted towards the higher family sizes. Only two households in D had as many as three children and did not also have a cow or cottage. None were any larger. At the other end of the spectrum of family development all six childless couples were in D. The very distinctions employed by those who drew up the listing suggest family life-cycle poverty. Group B was 'the pore abought fortye & upwards', which makes a weighting towards larger family size and the absence of childless couples unsurprising. Thomas Jerbridge, with his wife and one other in the household, in an exchequer deposition in the same year was noted as aged 64,[43] a reminder that small family size could presumably reflect children's having left home as the parents aged.

Group D was made up, therefore, of the poor with cow or cottage, often with larger families, and the unpropertied with smaller families. The very naming of group B suggests how much, for those without a little property, increase in family size meant greater poverty. The more children one had, the worse off one became – and this despite the presence of spinning and stocking knitting as employment for poor children in the town.

Such evidence hardly supports the attitude which sees children as economic assets – a view explicit in, for instance, David Levine's argument that the Shepshed stocking knitters' family formation was influenced by a desire to have child labour within the family.[44] Undoubtedly children played a key part in the family economy, but their net contributions were ambiguous. The report of the Justices of South Erpingham and Eynsford hundreds in the crisis of 1631 is especially significant. On the one hand, one sees the crucial import-ance of family labour: 'Soe as we hope that the yeere growinge on with expectacon of a prosperous harvest our poore may be Con-teyned in some reasonable order, if the decaye of Stuffe trade, do not give color to the Weavers and Coomers too muche to beate downe the Wages of poore Woomen & Children spinsters, beinge the greatest

---

[43] PRO, E 134/43 and 44 Eliz. Mich. no. 7. (Thomas Jerbridge's appearance in group B, though he gives his age as 64, suggests that the age categories, whilst generally reliable, were broadly drawn, with imprecision arising from the estimates of parish officers or contemporary vagueness about precise ages). Thomas Bulman's house-hold appears to have been at a similar stage in its cycle to Jerbridge's. In the listings he appears in group D with a household size of three and without either cow or cottage; in the same Exchanger case he described himself as a linen weaver, aged 56. His skill may explain why he appears in D when Jerbridge, who styled himself as a labourer, appears in B.

[44] D. C. Levine, *Family Formation in an Age of Nascent Capitalism* (London, 1977), p. 80.

imployment of our poore.'[45] On the other hand, those relieved by rates were 'the impotent poore and the meanest sorte of labourers overburthened with Children, Sickness or the extreame prizes of Corne and wante of worke', while the JPs bound out as apprentices 'Soe manie pooer Children, as we canne finde Masters fitt to be charged wth such'. Pauper apprenticeship should be seen as a means of transferring children from families which could not support them to families which could. The poor couple, in seventeenth-century England as in eighteenth-century France at marriage 'probably possessed more than they would ever again possess'.[46] The coming of children would further impoverish the poor family, but it is unlikely that a child would be a net producer until his late teens, when he would probably have left home, and even those children who could partly earn their keep would have been offset by their younger siblings.[47]

The listings reveal the plight of widows and women householders, whether with or without children, even more strikingly. Eight out of 21 householders in A were collectioners in 1601, but these included six out of the eighteen women householders in that group. It is perhaps surprising that only one-third of the women in A, the poorest of the aged women, were on regular relief, with two receiving small doles. Some were later to become collectioners; two others in A were collectioners by 1608. Nevertheless seven out of ten women living alone in A, and three out of six with one other in the household, were not regular collectioners. They were able, presumably, to piece together a living from informal aid, spinning and stocking knitting, common rights and casual jobs. None of the women in A had either a cow or a cottage, of course. In the other three groups there were fifteen such propertyless women, but it is a further sign of the greater degree of poverty of the women householders that all but three of these were in group B. Group C was certainly made up of just women, but even though seven of them were

---

[45] PRO, sp 16/193, no. 40.

[46] O. Hufton, *Poor of Eighteenth Century France*, p. 37. The phrase has a bleak echo in a petition that the inhabitants of Hempton presented to Quarter Sessions in May 1630, seeking to be indemnified against any possible charges arising from the settlement of a young family. They complained that 'on Francis Randoll in our said towne, hath given enterteynment into a Chamber of his in Hempton aforesaid on Fauxe, as it seemeth to us a very poore man havinge a wyfe and on child alredye, and beinge bothe yonge people are lyke to increase or Charge, having noe calling or profession as appearethe to gitt ther lyvinges': C/S3/28A.

[47] See, for instance, the listing of poor children set on work in Cawston, in January 1604 (original in possession of Mrs Hammond, copy held by Cambridge Group), and J. Webb, editor, *Poor Relief in Elizabethan Ipswich*, pp. 122–40.

noted as having either a cow or a cottage, the way the listing is phrased ('Certayn other not so p[oor]', followed by the others simply noted as not able to give anything) and the format (with group D tagged on as an afterthought) suggests that C was regarded as intermediate in poverty between A and B on the one hand and D on the other. That group may have contained mainly elderly widows – the ages are not given, and there were four widows on their own, three with one other member in the household and two with two others. But the main criterion in drawing up the group was the lesser poverty, and for such widows property rather than age appears to have been the determining factor.

For women in group B, however, family size was the determinant of whether they would be on poor relief. In that group only one out of the five women on their own was on the parish, and that woman, Johan Hamerton, on relief for 29 weeks and having borne a child in that year or shortly before, is an ambiguous case. But five out of seven women with children were on relief – all those with three or four children and two of the three with only two children. Two of the women were wives left on their own with four children; indeed, Edward Patterson had left not only his wife and children as a charge on the parish but a bastard who was being kept by William Dack, another parish pauper with three children of his own. The differences in levels of relief between male- and female-headed households further illustrate the worse plight of the latter. None of the couples with two children were in receipt of regular relief. Five of the fourteen couples with more children received weekly relief; the three male paupers with three and four children all received low totals (3s 2d, 4s 2d and 7s 6d), and two were collectioners for less than half the year, each receiving 2d a week. Against that the three women with four children were on relief the whole year and received:

Edmund Patterson's wife:	17 weeks @ 4d	
	31 weeks @ 2d	
	1 week @ 3d	
	half-year's rent 5s	
	flags 4s	Total 20s
Widow Sterky:	51 weeks @ 4d	
	sickness 11d	Total 17s 11d
Widow Torre:	10 weeks @ 6d	
	41 weeks @ 4d	
	sickness 4s	Total 23s 6d

Only the larger families headed by men – for instance, John Allins

and Nicholas Wodehouse (with seven children each) receiving 34s 8d
and 35s 8d respectively – exceed the female paupers in group B in the
amounts that were given to them. In group A four of the paupers
were on a rate as high as, or higher than, that of the widows with
families, one receiving 37s 4d but the other three the more comparable sums of 16s 9d, 17s and 20s.

The Cawston listing shows graphically the relationship between
family life-cycle and poverty. The more children a family had, the
poorer it became, and by-employments for wife and children do not
appear to have adequately made up for the increased economic
burden the children placed upon their parents. The relative situation
of widows and women alone, deprived of the male income and
unable to earn as high a wage, was much worse even though a small
number of widows who lived alone and did not receive weekly relief
can be detected in the listing. Even with a cow or cottage, a woman
was liable to be worse off than men with largish families who also had
such property. And· if she had no such property, but did have
children, she was more than likely to be not merely poorer but
actually in receipt of parish relief. In Cawston the number of women
on relief who were over sixty, or under sixty but with children was
the same – six. In group B six out of seven women with families were
on relief; in group A there were six out of seventeen women over
sixty. The results of differentiating the households by sex may be seen
in Tables 11.6 and 11.7. Thus women householders formed just over
40 per cent of the poor in Cawston, and over 60 per cent of the
paupers, and as we have seen there were significant differences
between male and female paupers, at least until the males reached
old age.

The figures provide valuable comparisons with other overseers'
accounts for later periods. Work in progress on the collation of
exemption certificates suggests that Cawston had relatively more
widows on relief because they had children to support than because
of old age *per se* than in Shelton, Hedenham and Caistor St Edmund
in the late seventeenth century. But this may arise more from
differences in type and size of settlement than from shifts in patterns
over time. My impression from looking at certificates of several
hundreds suggests that those parishes with the highest proportions
of women among the poor were generally the largest.[48]

Thus the proportion of poor women householders in the market
towns in 1674 was nearer the 1601 Cawston figure than the average

[48] I intend to deal with this important point more fully in my thesis.

Table 11.6. *Householders by sex: Cawston 1601*

	A*	B	C	D	All
Female	18	12	9	3	42
Male	3	23		29	55
All	21	35	9	32	97

*Categories are as in Table 11.5.
Source: NRS 2604, 12 B 2

Table 11.7. *Numbers (and percentages) of paupers in Cawston divided by sex of householders 1601*

	All poor		Paupers		Poor with cow or cottage	
	No.	%	No.	%	No.	%
Female	42	43.3	12	63.3	9	42.9
Male	55	56.7	7	36.7	12	57.1
All	97		19		21	

Source: NRS 2604, 12 B 2

figures for the hundreds, and it is possible that the proportions of women paupers (and the relative importance of children or ageing in pushing them onto relief) would reflect a similar picture. For poor women the 1601 listing and the 1674 certificates are comparable: the definition of poverty in Cawston derived from an inability to pay parish rates, and the same criterion was generally used for exemption from payment of the Hearth Tax.[49] To prove conclusively that this was the case a great deal of work correlating Hearth Tax and Poor Law records with parish registers, such as I am doing for the smaller parishes would be needed; if it were proved, it would again suggest the greater difficulties of employment for *household* labour, and not simply for individual paupers, in the towns' less flexible economies.

[49] At Hedenham and Felbrigg no exempt householder paid parish rates. However, at Shelton 3 out of the 21 exempt were contributing towards the poor rate (PD 358/41, PRO E 179/335, Part 3). While there was a frequent correlation between exemption from HT and not having to pay parish rates, it was not universal due to the overlapping grounds upon which the former was granted – i.e. not inhabiting houses of greater value than 20s per annum upon the full improved rent; not occupying lands worth more than 20s per annum; not having lands or goods worth more than £10; not living in houses with more than two chimneys; and not being liable to pay parish rates.

As such it would explain the higher ratios of paupers in the urban settlements. However, it is clear that women householders generally formed a much higher proportion of the poor than they did of tax payers; and they generally formed an even higher proportion of regular weekly collectioners. They formed in the various hundreds in 1674 over 25 per cent of the exempt poor. Sample years taken from different parishes (Table 11.3) suggest that women frequently formed up to, or over, 60 per cent of parish paupers. In Foulsham in 1674 they made up 34 per cent of the poor and 63 per cent of collectioners. They appear to have formed much lower proportions of rate payers and tax payers. In 1604 in Cawston they formed only 12 per cent of rate payers (nine out of 75).[50] In an undated Hearth Tax return for Hockwold-cum-Wilton there were three women out of 67 tax payers; against that there were twelve women among the 49 exempt.[51]

The high percentages of widows exempt from payment of the Hearth Tax in a sample of seven hundreds in the early 1670s is illustrated below (Table 11.8). Due to sloppy labelling, it is not always clear whether a woman is a widow or not, so while Table 11.8 gives only the percentages of males and widows, the percentage of all widows lies somewhere between the figure for those so designated in the certificates and the male percentage subtracted from 100 per cent. One should allow that the sex of 2–3 per cent of the poor is unknown; usually they have the name Frances/is, which, given the vagaries of seventeenth-century spelling, could be either male or female.

In short, over a quarter of the exempt poor in Norfolk were women, overwhelmingly widows. Old age is obviously an important determinant of their poverty; also, of course, the break-up of their vulnerable household economies. The proportion of women among the poor is higher than among Hearth Tax payers, which may partially reflect downward mobility with age, as smallholders' widows were driven into landlessness with the husband's employment gone. It probably reflects even more the difficulties of remarriage for propertyless widows. Within these groups the factors which pushed women onto parish pay in Cawston obtained elsewhere throughout the period. Impressment of the husband for service in the Civil War could throw a woman onto relief. At Stockton, John Bird was sent to the wars, and died shortly after his return from wounds he received at Naseby; during his absence and after his death his wife, left with a child, was a parish pauper.[52] Impressing large numbers of men for the fleet of 1666

---

[50] NRS, 2604, B 2.   [51] Frere MSS: Grimshoe Hundred, K 12 (A).
[52] NRO, microfilm reel 33/1, references to John and Widow Bird in Stockton Town Book in the late 1640s and 1650s, especially 1645/6.

Table 11.8. *Proportions of widows among exempt poor: selected Norfolk hundreds 1671–4*

	Male	Widows	Other	Total no.
Eynsford (1674)	72.5	20.6	6.9	710
N. Erpingham (1673)	66.5	19	14.5	651
Clacklose (1671)	71.3	23.1	5.6	450
Diss (Feb. 1673)	73.5	22.0	4.7	431
N. Greenhoe (Dec. 1673–July 1674)	70.6	24.2	5.2	786
Depwade (1674)	70.3	20.8	8.9	612
Freebridge Marshland (1674)	73.6	22	4.4	387

Sources: PRO E179/336 and 337.

caused a serious crisis in poor relief at Wells through the large number of women and children left at the parish charge.[53]

The woman left on her own, whether with or without children, had to piece together her living as best she could. Many widows were clearly able to keep off the rates, though the Cawston material suggests the circumstances in which that would become impossible. Widow Sharlow of Shelton lost her husband in 1665, and had been married for 26 years; she was possibly about fifty. In 1673/4 and 1674/5 she was in receipt of parish relief, so she was a widow for eight years before she went onto the parish. She may have been helped in maintaining herself without recourse to parish pay because her children were both adults in the mid-1660s (assuming they were still alive; their only appearance in the register is at their birth). The widow herself was not buried in the parish; she may have been resettled by the parish, as suggested by an ambiguous reference in the overseers' accounts, or she may have gone to live with her children (other possibilities are remarriage – improbable at that age – or going into service).[54]

In the case of Rachell Mercy of Fakenham there is direct evidence of her having a family to maintain, and of how she maintained it. In 1643 the local notables rallied to her defence against a charge of sedition:

Rachell Mercye the wyfe of Hughe Mercye ys an honest poore woman and one that taketh great paynes & Labor for to maynteyne herselfe & child wythout the releife or helpe of any her husband haveinge left her many yeres

[53] C3S2/2 Fakenham Sessions, Midsummer 1666.
[54] PD 358/1 and PD 358/41. I am grateful to David Souden for pointing out the possibility of returning into service as an option for widows.

since . . . [her accuser, Stanton], owed he[r] evill wyll, by reason that the wyfe of the said Stanton ys a keeper of weomen in child bed, and the said Rachell doeth likewyse keepe weomen in childbed doeth as he conceive hinder his wyfe.[55]

Midwifery was a useful by-employment for women.[56] But besides the work provided by local agriculture and industry there was a whole network of odd jobs, casual labour, and the like. It is arguable that the work provided by a gentleman's house did more for the economy of the poor through demands for household help than did gentry largesse – at Blickling in the 1680s children were employed in casual labour in the fields and widows in such chores as laundering by the Hobarts.[57]

One important question has so far been avoided in this paper, an important one but one to which it is impossible to give a definite answer. What was the likelihood of a poor individual ending up on the parish in old age? Most of those exempted from paying the Hearth Tax could be pushed over into temporary dependence on the parish. The ranks of the aged paupers might well be swelled by smallholders losing their land in old age – such was the experience of John Murriell of Caistor St Edmund, who in ten years sank from overseer with a little land to a landless pauper.[58] The Cawston listing brings out well the variations in poverty and the protection a little property could provide against pauperism. Most of the poor who outlived their physical capacities – which, beyond their meagre household goods, was probably all many of them had – would end up dependent on others. But, for instance, we know very little of kin support among the poor – for formal relief there are fairly systematic records, for kin support inference and occasional references in the Quarter Sessions records. My work on the poor in several Norfolk villages is incomplete, and it is impossible here to state more than general impressions except in the case of Hedenham. In both Shelton and Hedenham one can find aged parish paupers who probably had adult children alive, though probably living outside the parish. In fact, one can also point to exempt poor in 1674, who probably had adult children living away from the parish, and who were not later buried in the parish. Remarriage elsewhere, return to service or some

[55] C/S3/34.
[56] See also, for example, TES/8, 1693, Petition of Rector and parish officers of ACLE on behalf of Elizabeth Barber, a poor woman presented for practising midwifery without a licence. The petition is quoted in Amussen, 'Governors and Governed', p. 330.
[57] NRS, 21415, 39 C, e.g. pp. 5, 6, 22, 36, 66, 115.
[58] PD 8/21.

form of removal by the parish authorities[59] are all possibilities. But an obvious possibility is that some were living with or near their children.

This is mere inference, but surviving material from Quarter Sessions and other JPs' material suggests that the pressures on families and aged individuals among the poor were varied and complex. A view of the family life of the poor which concentrated on the undoubted predominance of the nuclear family to the exclusion of these complexities deriving from the pressures on, and experience of, the poor would give an inadequate impression of the degree and nature of family support. Many poor, of course, would not have been financially able to aid their parents. The small number of Quarter Sessions orders where close kin are made to fulfil the statutory obligation to contribute towards the relief of paupers all suggest strongly that parish officers only tried to enforce it when they thought children could well afford it.[60] But kin did support, and co-operate with, each other on other occasions. Grandparents are to be found bringing up grandchildren often. Necessity could force family help in certain circumstances where in others it made it impossible. In the 1630s Robert Greene of Sprowston 'tooke in his sister with 3 or 4 Children as an Inmate in case of necessity who being displaced were enforced to lye in the church porch but sithence ther have beene some provision for hir elsewhere'.[61] At Acle John Webster had several inmates – John Woodes, 'a poore man with wife & Children', who paid rent of £1 6s 8d per annum, and Thomas Block 'a Poore man with wife & Children that must have Colleccon from the towne but that the Widdow Goate his mother live with him in the same reome that pay one pound sixteene shillinges'.[62] With family support, it is impossible to press beyond impressionism at these levels of society. But a view of poor relief which ignores, for instance, the poor inmates of the 1630s, or Mary Wright and her child, who in want stayed with 'kinred' and friends while her husband was in Ireland, is narrow.[63] Just as it is

[59] More work needs to be done on the operation of the Settlement Laws and of more informal controls. Strictly speaking, before the 1690s the former dealt only with the settlement of newcomers, but parish authorities could often also manipulate legal and extra-legal mechanisms. For instance, the Myddle overseers obtained a Quarter Session order for Andrew Weston's son-in-law to pay them 2s a week for his support and used this and the threat of a lawsuit to lever him out of the parish and into the home of the latter: R. Gough, *The History of Myddle*, edited by D. Hey (Harmondsworth, 1981), pp. 253–5.

[60] For example, D. E. H. James, editor, *Norfolk Sessions Order Book 1650–1657*, Norfolk Record Society (Norwich, 1955), pp. 38 and 52.

[61] PRO, SP 16/272, no. 44.   [62] PRO, SP 16/310, no. 104.

[63] James, editor, *Order Book*, p. 31.

difficult to discern family aid, so the mutual support of neighbours is but rarely glimpsed – for instance, Henry Wright of Haynsford, who in the 1630s was a cottager and had two very poor widows living with him in his cottage '& both the said Wright & the said Inmates have no place of abode if they be turned away'.[64]

It is important to emphasize the presence or possibility of kin support, just because it is easy to neglect and impossible to quantify. Nevertheless, it is probable that the parish was of greater importance as a source of support. At Hedenham there is far more evidence of aged poor who, despite probably having adult children alive, were yet collectioners and were buried on parish relief. There were (in all) 25 exempt households in the parish in 1672 and 1674, and their family histories were traced to assess the relative significance of parish and family.[65] The numbers involved are very small and will have to be tested against other parishes, but they are nonetheless suggestive. In two cases families apparently moved away within a few years (one after the loss of the male head); three appear only briefly in the records, while the family of a sixth proved unreconstitutable. Of the remaining nineteen, the husbands or widows from five, despite having completed their families in Hedenham, were not buried there. The evidence of a failure to be buried in the parish is ambiguous, of course, but it does also suggest a conscious geographical move which may be linked with the search for some sort of economic maintenance at an age when other parishes would have been unwilling to allow settlement for fear of imminent chargeability. The two younger individuals are known to have remained. For two of the others there is a probability that adult children were alive outside the parish, and the same may be true of the third. For instance, when she went on relief she had at least four children, aged eighteen, sixteen, fourteen and twelve. She was on relief eight years, then disappears from the accounts; there is no burial entry for her in the register. There is, then, some evidence of movement away from the parish before death, which might be linked to kin support.

The heads and widows from the remaining fourteen households were all buried in the parish (in three cases the household heads in the 1670s were widows anyway). Two male householders had not gone on parish relief before the accounts finish – one died in 1710 and one in 1712. A third, John Callow, died in 1673; that his wife never went on parish relief in the fifteen years she lived in Hedenham up to

---

[64] PRO, SP 16/272, no. 44.
[65] For the evidence on which these comments are based, see above, note 28, and Appendix 2.

her death can probably be ascribed to childlessness and relative youth.

Of the remaining households nine certainly (and two very possibly) produced paupers who died whilst on parish relief. There were nine widowed and two (perhaps four) male collectioners from these eleven households. Ten of these households probably had adult children alive, but for only one is it certain that one was settled in the parish during the time the parent was on poor relief (though if the two male householders who may have been on relief actually were one could add two more examples).

In Hedenham, the parish was more important than children in supporting the aged poor. Collectioners came from eleven of the nineteen households from the 1670s completed in the village. Given the constraints of distance (in a highly mobile society) and even more of poverty among adult children with families of their own to bring up and with few enough reserves against prolonged sickness or misfortune, the greater prominence of the parish is hardly surprising. Yet there undoubtedly was some kin support in Hedenham.

In 1671, on top of the monthly collection to Lydia Puncher, widow, was an extra payment to 'Will. Puncher & his mother', suggesting expectation of some family support, but this must have been fairly unsystematic as the upward course of relief to the mother as she aged preceded the son's death. Only among poor smallholders is there a probability that support by children was much more significant. The retirement of a father and his support by children may well explain why Thomas Baldry had not gone on the parish by 1709, and such a course seems highly likely for John Smyth (d. 1690) and Victor Callo (d. 1688). Nevertheless, such smallholders were in a minority in Hedenham; both men needed parish relief in the last year or two of their lives; and the evidence of father supporting son is so strong for the Smyths just because the son's own family difficulties made them heavily dependent on the parish for many years.

The parish must be at the centre of any study of the economy of the poor because it alone provides a systematic way into the problem. Its centrality is further indicated in that the parish authorities did not assume a passive role. They could enforce kin support, or pay poor neighbours to look after paupers;[66] they could regulate settlement;

---

[66] It was a very common practice for parish officers to pay neighbours (themselves frequently poor) for keeping orphaned, disabled or aged paupers, or helping them out when sick. For instance, in Great Malton in 1639–40 the overseers paid Arthur Lightwyn 2s a week to keep Barbara Baker, 'a lame wench', while Goodwife Lury was paid 1s 6d for keeping a poor wife in her sickness: EVL 645, 463x9.

allow or prevent keeping of inmates;[67] regulate alehouses as a by-employment of the poor or as a suspected drain on the incomes of poor householders;[68] and use informal means to prevent the marriage of couples too poor to maintain a household.[69] The complexity where active parish decisions blurred together with neighbourly and kin support may be seen in the petition of Henry Gill of Tottenhill, labourer, to Quarter Sessions in 1643, he

being a poore man and dwelling in part of A house belonging to the Towne and doeth maynetayne itt in Repayre and have Contynewed in itt with his mother, ffirst being a poore widow and had ffower small Children he the said Henry Gill being the eldest of them and did worke for his mother and the other Three Children Twelve or Thirteene yeares and did helpe to Repayre sum part of those houses and hence I was marrid I did helpe to maynetayne my mother according as I was able she being of Three scoore and tenne yeares of age before she died and I did maynetayne her Aleaven weakes in her sicknes when she was not able to helpe her selfe, the Towne then did allow her but sixe pence the weake, and after I was marrid I hired A house for my selfe and my wife, my mother Contynewing in that house with another widow, tell part of the house fell down they not being able to Repayre itt and about Two yeares ago Thomas Marison being one of the Church wardens of the said Towne did wish me to Repayre itt agayne, and dwell in itt with my mother and so I did.[70]

It is worth emphasizing that the 1601 Poor Law was very much designed to relieve life-cycle poverty of the sort that we have been studying. The provision of work for the able-bodied never seems to have been particularly effective – in Norfolk there is a little evidence for it in some parishes in the 1630s;[71] but only Swaffham and Jacobean Cawston provide evidence of any moderately systematic attempt to enforce it outside the orders of JPs and Assize Judges. At Cawston and elsewhere such poor as were provided with work were less the fully able-bodied than the marginal poor, verging on pauperism. One

[67] For instance, of three inmates of Thomas Waters of Acle it was noted that they 'are all poore laborers & have wifes & severall children & if they be put out cannot be provided in this towne & by reason of ther charge and poverty are not likely to be interteyned elsewhere': PRO, SP 16/304, no. 104. By allowing these inmates to stay where they were for the reasons given, the JPs were almost certainly merely reflecting the thinking of the parish officers.

[68] K. E. Wrightson, 'Ale-Houses, Order and Reformation in Rural England, 1590–1660', in E. Yeo and S. Yeo, editors, Peoples, Cultures and Class Conflict 1500–1914 (Brighton, 1981), pp. 1–27.

[69] Wrightson and Levine, Poverty and Piety, pp. 80 and 133; F. G. Emmison, editor, Early Essex Town Meetings (Chelmsford, 1970), p. 117. In 1638 the parish officers of Ashton-under-Lyme (Lancs.) presented 2 clergymen for marrying couples thought likely to become chargeable to the parish: PRO, SP 16/404, no. 96.

[70] C/S3/33.

[71] PD 52/72; NRO, microfilm reel 33/1; Banham town book (1621–1721), (the last is kept in the parish chest).

implication of this – and one that would go far beyond the immediate scope of this paper – is that fully to appreciate the relationship of poverty and parish relief in early modern England one must look at the structure of the local economy and the degree to which it could adequately provide livelihoods for the bulk of the poor. This would require far more attention paid to the interrelationship of population and economic structure; yet, as has been shown, ageing itself was a slow economic withdrawal from employment. Spinning and knitting by women and children had their place in the earnings of the ageing widow as much as in those of the young day labourer's family, while the higher levels of pauperism in the market towns than in the smaller villages of the north-east attests greater problems of employment and livelihood for the same categories of poor in the former than in the latter. It should be noted that the market towns of Norfolk seem generally to have had above average levels of exempt poor, and of women householders among the exempt poor.

Such problems emphasize that the history of poor relief is important not simply for itself but as a way into the history of poverty and local society and economy generally. Parish relief had an important place in the economy of the poor in seventeenth-century Norfolk. It was important as sickness benefit or for providing fuel for many poor families. It was especially important for those at certain stages in the life-cycle, notably the orphan and the widow and the aged generally, and (much more rarely except in times of distress) for the poor but 'complete' household economically over-burdened with children. These former groups were provided with weekly relief by the parish, which expanded over the century, with the middle of the century being pivotal in the change. After mid-century parish relief stabilized in terms of numbers on relief and of amounts given out. It also stabilized as crisis relief (as needed in 1631 and 1647) became far less important in the face of demographic stabilization, agricultural improvement and the expansion of the Norfolk wool industry. The stabilization of poor relief in the late seventeenth century seems to have involved a decline in informal relief: it may also have produced a greater gulf between the aged parish pauper and the rest of the poor, as the former became a more distinct group – though, given the gradual nature of ageing, this can at most have been a relative process. More certainly, by the second half of the seventeenth century the relationship between the declining or inadequate earning capacity of the pauper and parish relief was much simpler than in the late sixteenth or early seventeenth centuries, when people in similar life-cycle circumstances relied more heavily on informal aid.

In conclusion, the place of parish relief in the budget of the pauper is strikingly caught in the petitition Edward Messenger of Ashwicken presented to Quarter Sessions at Walsingham in the hard winter of 1647/8 (in what was arguably a period when parish relief was becoming increasingly important for its recipients). In Messenger's petition is seen the combination of sources which provided his livelihood.

yor said poore petitioner being aged fourescore years, almost blinde, and very lame of his ancles, by wch infirmityes he is made unable by labour to sustaine himselfe any longer or to travell abroad to gather releife from charitable people, and is allowed but six pence by the weeke from the towne wherein he inhabiteth, which in these hard times of dearth and scarcitye will not buy any considerable or competent maintenance for his reliefe; also the house wherein he dwelleth for lack of repaire (wch he is utterly unable to bestow upon it) will not shelter and defend him from wind and raine.

But the petition serves to emphasize even more the centrality of relief by parish authorities when all else failed, and the expectation of the poor who depended upon it.

soe that he perceiveth such distresse comeinge upon him in his decrepete old age that he is likely to perish by hunger and cold, and sees noe meanes left to him whereby to escape that imminent misery which otherwise will inevitably come upon him, but onely by makeing knowne this his pitifull distressed condition to yor Wor^{P}s. the Justices at this present Session, hopeing that you will not turne away yor eyes and eares from the cry of the poore, but rather cause them to whom it belongs to allow some more competent reliefe and provision for supply of these his great wants made knowne unto you.[72]

The variety of sources which made up the incomes of the parish pauper and the increased prominence of parish relief lie at the heart of the relationship between the workings of the Poor Law and the life-cycle in seventeenth-century Norfolk.

[72] C/S3/38. The justices ordered the parish to pay Messenger 12d a week. I am indebted to Susan Amussen for this reference.

Appendix 1 Correlation of Cawston listings and Overseer's Accounts, 1601

The listings on which this correlation is based are described more fully in the text. The main listing to which the other sources have been correlated is listing 1, breaking down the poor partly by age and partly by degree of poverty. There is some evidence that this listing was drawn up slightly earlier than those dated 2 June. A widow appears on it who is crossed off the rougher of the latter listings and does not appear at all on the fairer copy, while the names of two men were written on it who both died in May.

Columns 1 to 4 contain information from that listing alone:
1. Name of householder as given on the listing
2. Status of householder. 'P' here means pauper (on the original a small circle was used).

    'h' and 'c' are used as they were on the original; they clearly refer to those with cow or cottage, but one does not know whether 'h' means house or heifer, or 'c' cow or cottage.

    'x' has been used for those households which do not fall into the above categories. They are the families which appear as having neither cow nor cottage on the 2 June listings.
3. Household size.
4. Household size minus the head of the household and (where relevant) his wife.

Columns 5 and 6 include material derived from the other sources. It should be noted that only one collectioner appears on the 2 June listings, and she probably went on regular relief some time after the list was drawn up. A few other individuals appear on the 2 June listings and the overseers' accounts, but these were people who received extraordinary payments rather than the weekly collection. On the listings family size is given; in the accounts one often has more detail of the family, and family size has been given in square brackets. These details are not given for all collectioners' families, however.

5. Status of householder –

      'P' equals pauper.

      'E' equals recipient of extraordinary relief.

      'x' equals a householder with neither cow nor cottage.

      'y' equals a householder with either a cow or a cottage.

6. Household size.

In conclusion it should be noted that the lettering given to the different categories on the age/poverty listing has been imposed by me. Moreover, there is some material in the overseers' accounts which has not been included here, insofar as it relates not to householders but to the five fatherless children noted on the listings.

I am very grateful to the Norfolk Record Office for permission to reproduce the Cawston listings in this correlated form.

(1) Name of householder	(2)	(3)	(4)	(5)	(6)
[A.] 'The names of the pore above the age of three score years and the number in ech famylie.'					
Martyne Wolvye & his wife[73]	P	3	1	P 17w. @ 6d 1w. @ 8d 33w. @ 4d ——— 20s 2d	[3] Widow Wolvye, her late husband and one child
Nicholas Broke & his wife	P	2	—	P 2w. @ 6d 43w. @ 8d 6w. @ 10d ——— 37s 4d	[2] Himself and his wife
The Widd Bulman	P	1	—	P 43w. @ 6d 6w. @ 4d 2w. @ 8d ——— 24s 10d	1
The Widd Paterson	x	1	—	x	1
The Widd Vale	x	1	—	Ex 8d	1
The Widd Springall	x	1	—	x	1
The Widd Walker	P	2	1	P 49w. @ 4d 1w. @ 2d 1w. @ 3d ——— 16s 9d	[2] Herself and her daughter

[73] The name has 'ded' written beside it and 'the wedow' written above it. Martin Wolvye was buried on 8.5.1601.

(1) Name of householder	(2)	(3)	(4)	(5)	(6)
The Widd Fassell	*x*	5	4	*x*	5
The Widd Graye	P	1	—	P	1
				51w. @ 4d	
				17s	
The Widd Acres	*x*	2	1	*x*	2
The Widd Clarke	*x*	2	1	*x*	2
The Widd Warde	*x*	4	3	*x*	4
The Widd Marsham	*x*	1	—	*x*	1
The Widd Harman	*x*	2	1	*x*	2
The Widd Payne	*x*	1	—	*x*	1
The Widd Avets	*x*	1	—	Ex	1
				14d	
				'at dyverse tymes'	
Agnes Grex	*x*	1	—	*x*	1
John Megoe & his wife	*x*	2	—	*x*	2
William Dearne & his wife[74]	P	3	1	P	Relief paid to
				5w. @ 6d	Widow Dearne –
				3w. @ 4d	no family size
				3s 6d	given on a/c
Edmund Elwarde	P	1	—	P	
				6w. @ 2d	
				12d	
Agnes Bakon	P	1	—	P	
				48w. @ 2d	
				8s	

[B]. 'The names of the pore abought fortye & upwards & the numb^r of their familyes'

Richard Jhonson & his wife	*x*	4	2	*x*	4
William Bayfield & his wife	*x*	6	4	*x*	6
Edmund Paterson & his wife[75]	P	6	4	P	[5]
				17w. @ 4d	Edmund Paterson's
				31w. @ 2d	wife and four
				1w. @ 3d	children
				+ 5s half-year's	
				house-farm	
				+ load of flags 4s	
				20s 1d	
Robert Raynie & his wife[76]	P	6	4	P	[6]
				25w. @ 2d	'for the Relefe
				4s 2d	of his wife iiii
					chylderne'
John Elison's wife	*x*	5	4	Ex	5
				14d towards burying	
				Elison's wife; 10d	
				to John Elison	

[74] 'The wedowe' has been inserted over the name. William Dearne was buried on 20.5.1601.

[75] Edmund Paterson also had a base child being supported by the parish; 8s 1d was paid for clothing it, while William Dack was paid 12s 1d for keeping it.

[76] On an assessment of 1604 Raynie appears as a rate payer, albeit one whose land was valued at a yearly value of only 70s.

(1) Name of householder	(2)	(3)	(4)	(5)	(6)
Nicholas Wodehouse & his wife	P	8	6	P 51w. @ 6d 1w. @ 8d ——— 35s 8d	[8] him, his wife and six children
Thomas Brother & his wife	x	5	3	x	5
William Coke & his wife	x	7	5	x	7
John Nicols & his wife	x	3	1	x	3
John Lyghtfoote & his wife	x	3	1	x	3
John Poule & his wife	x	8	6	x	8
Richard Tompson & his wife	x	5	3	x	5
Thomas Mallet & his wife	x	3	1	x	3
John Baker & his wife[77]	x	3	1	x	3
John Broke & his wife	x	7	5	x	7
Thomas Jerbridg & his wife	x	3	1	x	3
Thomas Bonde & his wife	x	3	1	x	3
William Dack & his wife[78]	P	5	3	P 19w. @ 2d ——— 3s 2d	
Raynold Byshope & his wife	x	4	2	x	5
John Allins & his wife	P	8	6	P 2w. @ 6d 43w. @ 8d 6w. @ 10d ——— 34s 8d	[9] him, his wife and seven children.
George Metton & his wife	x	7	5	x	7
William Baker & his wife	x	5	3	x	5
William Broke & his wife	x	3	1	x	3
Wedow Brestow	x	1	—	x	1
Syslye Juby	x	1	—	Ex 'at dyverse tyms in her sicknes' 4s 2d	1
William Bullman & his wife	P	5	3	P 1w. @ 12d 1w. @ 4d 43w. @ 2d ——— 7s 6d	
Robt. Lest & his wife	x	5	3	x	5
The Widd Wells	x	1	—	Ex 4d	2
The Widd Howes[79]	x	3	2	Px 20w. @ 2d ——— 3s 4d	3
The Widd Hewe Bartlet	x	3	2	x	3
The Widd Starkyne	P	5	4	P 51w. @ 4d 'at dyverse tyms in her sicknes' 11d ——— 17s 11d	[5] her and four children

[77] Above his name on the listing (1) has been crossed out 'John Barker & his wif 3' with the mark for a collectioner written by it.   [78] See Appendix 1 note 3.

[79] The Widow Howes is the only regular collectioner who is not marked as such on the age/poverty listing and appears on 2 June listing – presumably her twenty weeks in collection were after they had been drawn up.

(1) Name of householder	(2)	(3)	(4)	(5)	(6)
The Widd Torr	P	5	4	P 10w. @ 6d 41w. @ 4d sickness 4 —————— 23s 6d	[5] her and four children
Th Widd Jubbye	P	3	2	P 6w. @ 2d 45w. @ 3d —————— 12s 3d	[3] her and two children
Ales Wright	*x*	1	—	*x*	1
Jhone Hamerton[80]	P	1	—	P 27w. @ 2d 3w. @ 3d —————— 5s	

[C]. 'Certayn other not so p[oor]'

The Widd Halle	h	2	1	*y*	2
Margaret Bartlet Widd	h	1	—	*y*	1
The Widd Brome	*x*	1	—	*x*	1
The Widd Temple	*x*	2	1	*x*	1
The Widd Harman	c	1	—	*y*	1
The Widd Monye	h	1	—	*y*	1
The Widd Balden	h	3	2	*y*	3
The Widd Whithed	c	3	2	*y*	3
The Widd Sampole[81]	h	2	1	*y*	2

[D]. 'mor not able to gev eny thyng'.

Thomas Blome	h	4	2	*y*	4
Thomas Bullman	*x*	3	1	*y*	3
Thomas Gray	*x*	4	2	*x*	4
Thomas Sporle	*x*	3	1	*x*	3
William Grene	*x*	3	1	*x*	3
Peter Johnson	*x*	4	2	*x*	4
Symond Salmon	*x*	4	—	*x*	2
John Blome	*x*	5	3	*x*	5
Thomas Newland	*x*	3	1	*x*	3
Symond Blome	h	3	1	*y*	3
Roger Grey	*x*	4	2	*x*	4
Barnard Steward	*x*	5	3	*x*	5
The Wedow Baxter	*x*	2	1	*x*	2
Richard Sweten	h	4	2	*y*	4
Johan Sweting	*x*	1	—	*x*	1
Robt. Jexson[82]	*x*	3	1	*x*	3
John Selworth [?][83]	h	4	2	—	—
John Pryor	h	2	—	*y*	2
Valentyn Bund	*x*	2	—	*y*	2

[80] 9d was paid towards keeping her base child.
[81] Widow Sampole only appears on one of the listings dated 2 June (apparently the rougher copy of the two), and the name is crossed out there. Widow Sampole does not appear in the burial entries in the Cawston parish register in 1600-2.
[82] Jexson's name only appears on the rougher of the listings of 2 June.
[83] Selworth's name is heavily erased in the text, and appears neither in the account nor on the other listings; he is excluded for all calculations.

(1) Name of householder	(2)	(3)	(4)	(5)	(6)
Robt. Betts	x	2	—	x	2
Raphe Bund	x	2	—	x	2
'a pore man in Jerbrege Wod'	x	2	—	—	—
Wedow Esby	h	1	—	y	1
Roger Sterky	h	3	1	y	3
Margret Lytfote	h	1	—	y	1
Edward Durrant	c	6	4	y	6
John Wighton	c	6	4	y	6
Raphe Gouldsmith	c	3	1	y	3
William Balls	c	2	—	y	2
John Acres	h	7	5	y	7
Nicholas Denys	c	6	4	y	6
Richard Porritt[84]	c	7	5	y	7
Robt. Grant	x	3	1	x	3

'fatherless cheldern mayntayned by the towne
alece & Temperance Bastes
Durythe Smeth
Salmans ii'

Both 2 June listings refer to five fatherless children kept by the town; a Richard Sallom had clothing provided for by the parish and was apprenticed out, as was Thomas Wodhowse, presumably the son of Nicholas Wodehouse (group B). Other references in the accounts – to John Smeth, Elizabeth Smeth's base child, to one Margret Rose and to Agnis Barker – seem not to fit in with the names of householders or fatherless children.

[84] Richard Porritt's name has been erased from group B and inserted at the end.

Appendix 2

The aim in Figure 11.1 is to present in compact form the results of collating parish registers with overseers' accounts for one village. A glance at the family histories in the accompanying notes will show how limited linkage within and between such sources often is, and the material presented here should be seen as a rough and imprecise guide to the relationship between pauperism and the life-cycle. For most individuals, one has the record of their marriage or of the first child baptized in the parish – very rarely that of their own baptism. The sex and age of children in the year their parent became a collectioner have been noted, and where there is evidence of these children appearing in the parish registers (apart from their own baptisms), this has been given. For instance, Lydia Puncher had two female children and four male, ranging from a woman of 28 to a boy of twelve, in the year that we first see her as a collectioner. This material enables one to see that she had children in her family at least partially dependent on her, and that she had adult children, at least one of whom settled in the parish. This sort of material is a good, if rough-and-ready guide to life-cycle poverty and the potential for kin support. But its imprecision must be accepted. One does not know if the first child baptized in the parish was also the first-born of the family, thus leading one to under-estimate family size. One does not know when children left home, and one does not know how many had died outside the parish, this working in the opposite direction, to inflate the number of children who were alive and away from home. The assumption in my analysis, that a child whose only appearance in the register is at baptism will settle away from the parish, is one supported by the considerable evidence of mobility in early modern England, but it is an assumption that would miss a child who, for instance, did not marry and left the village after the death of the

395

parent. The family histories in the following notes are, then, incomplete, and this incompleteness is compounded by defective registration in the late 1640s and 1650s (especially for burials and marriages). One has presumably lost some deaths of children, as well as the baptisms of others, so that the information on families whose child-bearing period spanned that period must be especially problematic. Enough collectioners' children would have survived the most dangerous years of infancy before the registers become defective in the 1640s to make one fairly confident that one is not wildly overestimating surviving adult children by insufficiently allowing for infant and child mortality, while a due allowance that, among younger children, one is dealing with minima, is adequate precaution for the limited uses to which this material is put in the text.

The poor described in Figure 11.1 do not represent all those dependent at various times on some form of parish relief, but only the monthly collectioners who, at various phases in their life, needed continuous parish aid. There are some references in the overseers' accounts to sickness payment and to wood bought for the poor, but almost certainly many extraordinary payments to the poor would have appeared in the churchwardens' accounts, which no longer survive, so it would be misleading to include those few which appear in the former record. I have included in the table, somewhat arbitrarily, three payments which are more comparable with the monthly collection – the money paid to John Smith in the year before he became a regular monthly collectioner, £1 paid to John Raven's wife and children, and the very heavy sickness payments to John Ellis. The format for the vast majority of these entries was to record either the amount received per month or the total for the year, with the number of months in the accounting year given in the account. There were, in the early eighteenth century, some calculations of weeky payments, which have been rounded to give an approximation for monthly payments in the table. In the case of Francis Smith, a similar policy has been adopted. The amount paid to him in his first year on relief, and the 40s monthly collection plus 40s towards nursing his child have both been rendered by dividing the total by the number of months in those accounting years, to make the figures consistent with the standard format of the monthly collection (which was used for all later payments to him).

In the following notes on collectioners' families, when 'ba.' is given as a first entry in the register it refers to the baptism of a child of that individual, and not to his or her own baptism. An asterisk by a name means that the individual had adult children settled in the parish during the time that he or she was on parish relief. At Hedenham, as elsewhere, the accounting year ran from Easter to Easter. The date given in brackets refers to the first calendar year in which the accounting began.

(a) to (h) are those householders exempt from the Hearth Tax in 1672 and 1674 who never appeared as parish collectioners in Hedenham. Here the year of baptism of children is given, while an asterisk denotes that adult children were settled in the parish during the last years of the householder's life.

---

1. *Widow Lea* (1662–3).
   No entry in parish registers.
2. *Susan Smyth* (1662–71).
   Bu. 17.8.1671.
   No prior entry in register.
3. *Widow Langeret* (1662–70).
   Bu. 22.3.1670, Mary Langround, widow.
   Impossible to link from register. She may be the widow of Arthur Langrod, bu. 1644, but there is insufficient evidence to say for sure. It is possible that during her period on parish relief she had a kinsman alive in the parish (Joseph Langerwood, ba. 1625, bu. 1682), but the exact nature of the relationship cannot be established. The date when she was widowed likewise cannot be ascertained.
*4. *Lydia Puncher, Widow* (1662–1701).
   Bu. 12.6.1701.   HT1672 and 1674.
   First entry: William Puncher m. Lydia Tower, 20.1.1633.
   Children: F28, M25, F20, M18, M16, M13, M12.

   > M25: William Puncher (see below, no. 14).
   > F20: Lydia, m. William Hartley 1669.
   > F12: Elizabeth, bu. 1665.

   William stayed in the parish until his death and may have helped his mother out (as noted in the text, p. 385). Lydia m. in the parish, but there is no other entry relating to her in the registers, and the Hartley family do not appear in the Hearth Tax records of the early 1670s. Two of William's children appear to have settled in the parish, so in the closing years of her life Lydia would have had adult grandchildren living in the parish. Date of widowhood unknown: post-1650.
5. *Widow Smyth* (1662–5).
   Bu. 16.5.1655, Margaret Smyth, widow.
   First entry: ba. 12.1.1623.
   Children: M39, F38, bu. 1641?
   Widowed: 1639 (23 years) or 1648 (14 years).
   Due to there being several families surnamed Smyth in the village, the establishment of fuller kin links is impracticable.

6. *Widow Edmunds* (1662–98).   HT1672 and 1674
    Bu. 23.4.1698, Martha Edmunds, widow.
    First entry: Arthur Edmunds m. Martha London, 28.10.1629.
    Children: F30, F27, F23, M19, F16.
    Widowed: 1659 (3 years).

7. *Widow Owers* (1662–3).
    Bu. 14.5.1663, Prudence Owers, widow.
    First entry: James Ewers m. Prudence Saccar, 13.5.1642.
    Children: M20.
    Date of widowhood unknown: post-1642.

8. *Widow Payne* (1662–99).   HT1672 and 1674
    Bu. 22.1.1699, Abigail Payne, widow.
    First entry: ba. 18.1.1635.
    Children: F26, M23, F21, M16, F14, M11.
           F21: Mary, bu. 1663.
    Date of widowhood unknown: post-1651.

9. *James Pratt* (1662–9).
    Bu. 7.10.1669.
    First entry: ba. 18.4.1625.
    Children: M35, M33, M29, F24.
    First wife bu. 1638; second wife bu. 8.8.1664.

10. *Francis Tayler* (1662–70).
    Bu. 17.1.1671.
    Unlinkable – given the Christian name, one cannot even be
    sure of Tayler's sex.

11. *Widow Harrison* (1664–70).
    Bu. 22.10.1668, Susan Harrison, widow.
    First entry: ba. 30.4.1628.
    Children: F36, M30, M23.
    Widowed: 19.5.1663.

12. *William Andrewes* (1664–8).
    Bu. 31.7.1668 or 25.8.1668.
    Unlinkable – there are two William Andrewes buried within a
    month of each other. The only preceding references in the
    register to individuals of that name are to bas. in 1600 and
    1667.

13. *John Andrewes* (1672).   HT1672
    Bu. 12.8.1694.
    First entry: ba. 22.5.1653.
    Children: M14, M12, F9.
    Widowed: 13.8.1670.
    Remarriage: John Andrewes m. Mary Smyth, 18.10.1672 (see
    infra, no. 32 for his widow).

14. *Mary Puncher, Widow* (1672–8).   HT1672 and 1674
    No record of burial in parish.
    First entry: ba. 7.12.1662.
    Children: M10, M8, M7, F0.
    Remarriage: Thomas Whiteing m. Mary Punchard, widow,
    21.10.1678. There is one entry to the Whiteings in the parish

register, a child ba. 1679. Then no further entry. Two children apparently settled in the parish.

   M10: John, m. 1686, bas. 1687, 1693, 1694, 1700, 1706, 1708.
   M8: William, bas. 1686, 1687, 1689, 1690, 1692, 1695.
Widowed: 14.4.1672.

There is some confusion on the 1672 exemption certificate, with William Puncher given as alive though the certificate is dated several months after his death, while the only Widow Puncher named is Mary rather than Lydia. Given consistency between parish registers, Overseers' Accounts and other Hearth Tax records, I have assumed that this is merely a clerk's error.

15.   *Edward Chalter* 1672–82).   HT1672 and 1674
Bu. 9.11.1682.
First entry: ba. 2.7.1647.
Children: M23, M15, F13, F8.

16.   *Widow Chalter* (1682–92).   Husband HT1672 and 1674
Bu. 11.10.1692, Frances Chalter, widow.
First entry: ba. 15.2.1657.
Children: M33 (stepson), M25, F23, F18.
Widowed: 1682.
Date of wedding not recorded: between 1652 (death of previous wife) and 1657.

*(?)17.   *Francis Smyth* (1672–88).   HT1672 and 1674
Bu. 31.3.1710, Francis Smyth, widower.
First entry: his own ba. 14.10.1632; then ba. 26.12.1660.
Children: F12(?), F8, M6, F3, F0.
Widowed: 17.8.1671.
No evidence of remarriage.
Francis was a rate payer in 1671 and 1679–94. A John Smyth appears rated from 1695 until 1699 – it might be M6, born 1666, but there is no other evidence outside the rating lists to support this inference. There is a John Smyth with bas. F1697, M1702, M&F1710. F3 may be Frances Smyth m. Richard Wiley, 1692, ba. 28.5.1693 (Robt). No reference thereafter to parents, but a Robert was bu. 1720.

*18.   *John Smyth* (1672–9, 1689).
Bu. 19.3.1690.
First certain entry: ba. 20.3.1625.
Children: M47, F44, M42, M40
M40: Francis Smyth (see above).
Widowed: possibly 1662.
Rate payer 1662–7 jointly with a Robert Smyth

36.   *Robert Smyth* senior (1704).   HT1672 and 1674
Bu. 5.12.1704.
Children untraceable.
Wife untraceable.

   a. Richard Smyth   HT1672 and 1674
Unlinkable. Bu. either 1680, 1687 (less likely) or outside parish.
If 1687 his wife may have died seven months earlier.

There was a plethora of Smyths in Hedenham throughout the seventeenth century, making reconstitution often impossible. In the early 1670s there were five households of that name:

Richard (assessed for HT on 5 hearths)
Robert (assessed for HT on 2 hearths)
Richard (exempt)
Francis (exempt)
Robert (not recorded in HT; a low rate payer in years around those for which the former source survives; styled in assessments either 'senior' or 'tailor' to distinguish him from the yeoman). Kin linkage for the exempt Richard and Robert senior is impossible.

19. *Wife and children of John Raven* (1679).
                                                Husband HT1672 and 1674

*(?)38. *John Raven* (& wife) (1707–8).
HT and parish records combined suggest only one family of John Raven in Hedenham in 1672 and 1674. However, by 1679 one has either one with a remarriage or two separate households.

(19) Bu. 28.11.1710 or 21.12.1713.
First entry: possibly his own ba. 28.8.1636; thereafter ba. 19.6.59 by wife Susan F20, M18, F15, M12, F5. Susan bu. 10.7.1675. No remarriage in village, but ba. 24.12.1676, John and Mary; so M3 and M ba. (and bu.) January 1680; F1681, F1684. An Elizabeth Raven, daughter of John (no ba. recorded) bu. 5.4.1689.

(38) is also ambiguous. It could be the elder John, as above, dying in either 1710 or 1713, of John Raven who m. Mary Baker 1.10.1703, with, in 1707, M3 (with another son born in the accounting year 1708, M 25.3.1709, who is not buried before 1730 in the parish). This John may be the son of the elder, ba. 10.3.1661.

20. *Edward Randall* (1679–89).   HT1672 and 1674
Bu. 28.10.1689.
First entry: Edward Randall m. Elizabeth Levicke, 1642.
Children: F36, M34, M32, M19.
                M32: Edward, m. 1666, ba. 1667. No longer in
                village by early 1670s.
First wife probably died 1666; second marriage not recorded, but he is succeeded on relief by

21. *Widow Randall* (1689–1701).   Husband HT1672 and 1674
Bu. 22.8.1702.
Stepchildren by Randall
Widowed: 28.10.1689.

22. *Alice Callo, Widow* (1681–9).   Husband HT1672
No burial or remarriage entry.
Children: M18, F16, ?14, M12.
First entry: ba. 30.8.1663 (reference to removal from Carlton Rode, C/S2/2, Norwich Sessions October 1663).
Widowed: 4.10.1681.

Husband may have been born 1636, son to Richard and Martha Callo.

23. *William Raven* (1683–4).   HT1672 and 1674
No bu. entry.
Firsty entry: William Raven m. Sarah Bunnett, 4.10.1666.
Children: F15, M12, M8, M5.
First wife bu. 1679.
Remarriage: William Raven, widower m. Catherine Edmonds, widow, 1.4.1684.

24. *Susan Cotten, Widow* (1686–98).   Husband HT1672 and 1674
Bu. 12.4.1698.
Widowed: 29.5.1678.
Another Susan Cotton bu. 18.5.1692.

*25. *Victor Callo* (1686–7).

*(?)39. *Victor Callo* (1708)   HT1672
Adequate kin links from the register and accounts are slightly problematic, as the name was a common one in Hedenham, but the two Victors were either father and son or father and grandson. Victor Callo had a son, ba. 5.2.1643, who is the first child and only son recorded in the register. The inferential evidence of VC (25) reitiring in favour of his son derives from collating overseers; payments and rate assessments with HT records, taking into account that the Roll and assessment for 1674 suggest that those paying the one would also pay the other. There was always a VC paying the poor rate from 1662 to 1689, but whereas the other man of that name was explicitly named as 'Victor Callo jnr' in an exemption certificate of February 1672 (E179/335, Part 4), the pauper of 1688 was noted in the account as 'old Vic Callo'. Given that there were no other VCs in the village, this suggests very strongly a transfer from father to son. The change cannot be dated. It may have been at the father's widowhood in 1680 or possibly earlier. There is no VC recorded on the February 1674 exemption certificate, though there had been in February 1672 and December 1674, leaving only one VC household recorded in the village that paid the poor rate and HT. Perhaps the father's household had ceased to exist as an independent unit; if so it would have occurred at a time when he was possibly 56 and at about the time of the first of the son's children to be baptized in the village. However, exemption certificates were too carelessly drawn to bear much weight for individual households, and the date of the transfer is much less certain than the fact of its occurring. There is no evidence of such a transfer occurring between VC junior and his son after 1689, when he is last recorded in the rates. It is not clear whether the pauper of 1708 is the son or the grandson of the first. The grandson has two children by Frances Callo, and a widow of that name remarried 12.2.1710. The pauper may be the son, either because he was dying or his own son was, or the grandson.

Certainly there is no record of Callos in that branch in the village after 1709.

(25) Bu. 10.6.1688.

First entry: very possibly his own ba. 19.7.1618; thereafter ba. 5.2.1643.

Children: M43, F40, F39.

        M43: see below.

        F39 may be Mary C. James Skelton, 23.6.1679.

(38) Bu. 6.3.1709.

Either son (F43) above:

First entry: ba. 5.2.1643.

Children: M36, M34, M33, F30, F27.

Widowed: 7.1.1696

or else:

his son (M36): F5, F2.

26. *Goody Hobman* (1693–7). (1703–8 – keeping Symonds children)

No bu. entry.

First reference: Robt Hobman m. Sarah Swigate, widow.

Children: M5, F2.

In 1693–7 she is referred to as 'Goody' in the accounts, in 1703–8 as 'widow', but no evidence of a husband dying until (possibly) bu. of Robert Hobman, bu. 22.12.1710.

27. *Widow Bunnett* (1697, 1702, 1703).   Husband HT1672 and 1674

Bu. 22.3.1704, Audry Bunnett, widow.

First entry: ba. 1649.

Children: F48, F38

        F38: Elizabeth m. 21.1.1686, ba. 12.12.1689

Widowed: 22.3.1689.

28. *Wade's Boy* (1699)

Unlinkable. Two bus. referring to male Wades, 1718 and 1727. Note: only a collectioner in 1699/1700; but in the year after £7 11s 7d was spent on his clothing and other expenses.

29. *John Ellis* (1700–1)

Bu. 13.9.1750 (aged about 86 according to register).

First entry: John Ellis m. Elizabeth Sewell, 12.11.1690.

Children: F9, F6, F0, and three children to follow.

30. *Widow Havers* (1697–1700, 1708).   Husband HT1674

Bu. 5.6.1709.

First entry: ba. 13.7.1680.

Children: M17, M15, M12.

Widowed: 30.4.1692.

31. *Mary Dyer* (1701, 1702, 1704)

No reference in register.

32. *Widow Andrewes* (1701–4).   Husband HT1672 and 1674

Bu. 3.1.1705.

First entry: John Andrewes m. Mary Smyth, 18.10.1672.

Stepchildren: M34, M41, F38.

Widowed: 12.8.1694 (see above, no. 13 for husband).

33. *Symonds' wife and children* (1702–8).

Inadequate linkage – neither m. nor bus. of parents recorded,

unless father is the same John Symonds bu. 1.12.1715.
Two bas.: 24.3.1696–F (parents John and Anne)
                18.9.1700–F (parents John and Susan)
But the overseers' accounts refer explicitly to a girl (bound out
in 1706) and a boy.

34. *Henry Reynolds* (1701–7).
     Bu. 23.8.1707.
     Child: F24.

35. *Widow Reynolds* (1707–8).
     Bu. 6.8.1720, Margaret Reynolds, widow.
     Child: F30.
     Widowed: 23.8.1707.

36. *Robert Smyth senior* (1704)
     See above.

37. *Thomas Gurney* (1705 – 10 months only)   HT1674
     Not bu. in parish.
     First entry: ba. 24.11.1661.
     Children: F35(2), F32, F30.

38. See above.
39. See above.

  a. *Richard Smyth:* see above.   HT1672 and 1674
  b. *John Callo*   HT1672 and 1674
      First entry: John Callo m. An Hayward, 5.10.1669.
      Bu. 6.12.1673.
      Widow bu. 10.6.1688, An Callo, widow.
      There appears to be a clerk's error in the exemption
      certificate, dated February 1674.
  c. *Benjamin Randall*   HT1672 and 1674
      Only entry: bu. 30.4.1681.
  d. *Samuel Gurney*   HT1674
      Only entry: m. 11.5.1673.
  e. *Widow Wigg*   HT1672 and 1674
      Not bu. in parish.
      Three children born to John and Sarah Wigg 1626, 1632
      and 1640, all of whom apparently die in infancy.
      Was another child born before 1626 elsewhere, or one
      during period of defective registration?
      Date of widowhood unknown.
  f. *Daniel Sewell*   HT1672 and 1674
      Bu. 11.11.1676.
      First entry: bu. of wife, 1663.
      Remarriage: 1664.
      Children ba. F1665, F1669, F1673.
      An Elizabeth Sewell, possibly Daniel's eldest daughter,
      m. John Ellis, 12.11.1690.
  g. *John Whytlofs*   HT1672
      No entries for a John, but there are for William (clerk's
      error?).
      First entry: William Whiteloaf m. 29.10.1666.

Children: F1667, M1670, F1673, M1678, F1678 (last died 1680).

Thereafter no record of family – parents presumably moved.

*(?)h. *Thomas Baldry*   HT1672 and 1674
Bu. 23.1.1712.
First entry: ba. 3.1.1664.
Children: M1664.
Widowed: 1692.

The records here are inadequate for full linkage. There is record of one child ba. in the parish (John) not dying there, but a Thomas may have been born elsewhere. It is possible that Thomas senior transferred land to sons John and Thomas. Thus among the small rate payers one has

1687–8   One Thomas Baldry
1689–1700   Thomas Baldry junior and Thomas Baldry
            senior
1701–4   Thomas Baldry junior
1705–8   Thomas Baldry junior and John Baldry (a
tithe book shows Thomas to have been a carpenter and John a gardener) (microfilm reel 36/2).

But are the Thomas and Mary who have a child ba. 1672 the same with bas. F1689, M1690 (d. 1691) with the wife apparently dying in 1700? He may remarry (but more likely a different generation), as a TB has children by Elizabeth F1703, F1706 and M1711. John m. 1691 and has children M1696, F1698, M1703 and F1713. The long baptism interval for Thomas and Mary, ending in 1689 when TB junior first appears, may suggest that he had been away and returned to the parish, reappearing in the register in the first year he appears on rating lists; but evidence is lacking to make this more than speculation.

12

The receipt of poor relief and family situation: Aldenham, Hertfordshire 1630–90

W. NEWMAN BROWN

Since Louis Henry pioneered the technique of family reconstitution over twenty years ago and E. A. Wrigley adapted it to fit English parish registers, our knowledge of the functioning of the family as a reproductive unit has advanced considerably. Much less progress has been made in linking information on the reconstituted families with other parochial sources, which will give us a fuller impression of past family life than could be derived from one source taken in isolation.

The reconstitution of families in the Aldenham parish registers dating from 1560 can, like every other reconstitution, be illuminated by the integration of other material such as records of estate transactions, the sale and purchase of property, subsidies, taxes of various kinds and the listing of inhabitants of the parish in whole or in part according to the requirements of legislation devised for a variety of purposes. For the most part these records refer either to a specific event of relatively transitory significance to the reconstitution (such as an election) or endure for relatively short periods (e.g. Hearth and Poll Taxes, or Militia Rolls).

One enactment, however, of universal application survived the passage of over two centuries and remains the basis of local finance to the present time. The Poor Law Act of 1598, re-enacted in 1601, required of the parish that, through its churchwardens,

four substantial householders there who shall be nominated yearly in Easter week, under the hand and seal of two or more Justices of the Peace in the same county, whereof one to be of the Quorum, dwelling in or near the same parish, shall be called Overseers of the Poor of the same parish; and they or the greater part of them shall take order from time to time by and with the consent of two or more such Justices of the Peace for setting to work of the children of all such whose parents shall not by the said persons be thought able to keep and maintain their children. And also such persons married or unmarried as having no means to maintain them use no ordinary and daily

405

trade of life to get their living by; and also to raise weekly or otherwise (by taxation of every inhabitant and every occupier of lands in the said parish in such competent sum and sums of money as they shall think fit) a convenient stock of flax, hemp, wool, thread, iron, and other necessary ware and stuff to set the poor on work, and also competent sums of money for and towards the necessary relief of the lame, impotent, old, blind, and such other among them being poor and not able to work, and also for the putting out of such children to be apprentices, to be gathered out of the same parish according to the ability of the said parish; and to do and execute all other things, as well for disposing of the said stock as otherwise concerning the premises, as to them shall seem convenient . . .[1]

The work fell on the overseers almost totally, and because they were answerable to the parish, and to the Justices as the supervising agents of government, records of the rates raised and the disbursements made had to be kept for inspection annually. For Aldenham these records survive, commencing with a volume containing the accounts for 1628–53 and the assessments for 1637–53.[2]

Much has in fact been written about the earliest years of this system of local administration, yet we know relatively little concerning the manner in which the communally financed fund impinged upon the lives either of those who were regular or of those who were occasional recipients from it. One might suppose, given the stipulation in the 1601 Poor Act that 'the children of every poor, old, blind, lame and impotent person . . . shall at their *own* charges relieve and maintain every such poor person',[3] that the beneficiaries of the fund would constitute a small minority of the population – those unable to subsist in the absence of kin or those whose privations in the face of poverty not even the tenacious bonds of kinship could remedy.

However, these expectations might be excessive given what is increasingly known about kinship in early modern England. Unfortunately, we know little about the co-residential patterning of kin groups in seventeenth-century Aldenham, as no listing of inhabitants survives. Others, including contributors to this volume of essays, have asserted that the English system of kinship is categorically bi-lateral and highly ego-centred.[4] Furthermore, certain implications of the discovery of the nuclear family system in pre-industrial England are suggested by Peter Laslett's phrase 'nuclear family

---

[1] For a discussion of these acts and of differences between them, see E. M. Leonard, *The Early History of English Poor Relief* (Cambridge, 1900), pp. 132–8.

[2] Hertfordshire County Record Office, Aldenham Poor Accounts 1628–53, 1654–84 and 1698–1708; Assessment Books 1637–53, 1654–84 and 1698–1708 (not paginated).

[3] 43 Eliz. c.2. The liability of parents to support their children, imposed in 1597, was in 1601 extended to grandparents: see Leonard, *Early History of English Poor Relief*, p. 134.   [4] See above, Chapter 9.

hardship'.[5] The term supposes that, since the nuclear family household predominated in early modern England, certain hardships such
as the death of the husband, death of the wife, unemployment or
sickness would have made it difficult for many of these households to
provide for themselves.

What did happen to those households struck by hardship? There is
relatively little evidence to suggest that they starved either in
Aldenham or in England as a whole in the seventeenth century. We
cannot in the absence of an informative listing establish whether they
moved in with their kin to establish extended households. Nor can
we readily discover whether they received aid while they lived
physically apart from their kin. We can, though, begin to investigate
the extent to which parish relief was used to deal with victims of
'nuclear family hardship' because of our ability to link evidence in
parish registers with that in the assessment and account books of
Aldenham's overseers of the poor.

This short paper has the modest aim of identifying the approximate
proportion of the population in receipt of casual and regular relief,
the proportions contributing on a regular and irregular basis to
Aldenham's welfare fund and the family circumstances of those
known to have been in receipt of relief in the final two-thirds of the
seventeenth century.

Aldenham lies on the southern boundary of Hertfordshire some
fifteen miles north of the city of London. Its position, situated just off
Watling Street, within the migration pathways leading into London,
greatly influenced the character of its population. Its economic
structure through the period of this study suggests it to have been a
parish of arable farmers and labourers, never dominated by one
single land owner. Furthermore, it was a parish characterized by a
small number of 'life-time stayers' (i.e. persons who were known
from the parish registers to have been baptized, married and buried
in Aldenham).[6]

Lists of names of persons in receipt of relief in an overseers of the
poor account book are only of limited value to the social historian
unless he can place this information into some context. One fundamental first step would be to gain some estimate of the proportion

---

[5] P. Laslett, 'Family and Collectivity', *Sociology and Social Research* 63 (1979), pp. 432–42;
and Smith above, pp. 72–5.

[6] For a detailed consideration of these patterns, relating the evidence in Aldenham to a
large number of other English parishes, see D. C. Souden, 'Pre-Industrial English
Local Migration Fields', unpublished University of Cambridge Ph.D. thesis, 1981,
Chapter 3.

of the local population both contributing to the communal welfare fund and receiving relief from it. This is no easy task. Nonetheless, in the absence of a listing – or, more specifically, a series of listings – the Family Reconstitution Forms (FRFs) contain information relating to the constitution, life and termination of the family and can be used to gauge a very approximate estimate of the population total at a specific point in time. Certain rules and conventions are required to perform this task: a date is chosen (in the case of Aldenham, 30 June for each decade commencing 30 June 1561) and decisions are made as to whether or not there are reasonable grounds for supposing an individual on the FRF was or was not in residence in the parish at that date. Thus, if a baptism occurs prior to the selected date and another baptism of the same family is registered afterwards, and if there is no qualifying description which indicates that the parents are from another parish, then it is reasonable to infer that both the parents and the first child baptized were alive and resident in the parish on the selected date, unless some other event intervened. This can occur, for instance, with the burial of the first child or either of the parents.

The most important assumption to be observed is for certain children whose baptism may be recorded but for whom no marriage or burial event is known. The assumption adopted in this study is that in such cases children remained in the parish to the age of 21 years, after which they left. Families for whom there are only a limited number of events such as baptisms or baptisms and burials of children within a short space of time can usually be regarded as transient and are not included in more than one estimate after the last recorded event.

A count of population using these conventions is best kept in two parts: (a) of those for whom there is a recorded event both before and after the 'census' date; and (b) of those for whom there is a single event, usually prior to the census date but sometimes (usually in the case of a child burial) after the census date, but which it is reasonable to assume should be included.

From the population total derived in this way another count was made of those supposed to have been household heads. This count included those who, while single or widowed, might be considered as forming a household unit even if this household was located in lodgings. In this task the information from the FRFs could occasionally be supplemented by the overseers' accounts in which other household heads could be identified. Elderly bachelors or spinsters (who would not appear on FRFs) to whom regular relief payments were made are the most obvious cases. The accounts also include entries of regular relief payments to individuals, nearly always widows for whom identification is not possible in the parish registers. These are likely to have been survivors of common law marriages or those who had returned late in life to their native parish. Of course, other individuals generally considered to have been highly transient (such as servants, vagrants, short-stay families unlikely to impinge upon the Poor Law administration) are lost in this type of analysis. For that reason, it must be stressed that this attempt to construct a population count constitutes a rough estimate that can be used as a context within which to situate our discussion of relief and family circumstances.

What is clear from this exercise is that at no point in the seventeenth century is a majority of the local households assessed, and that among those assessed a clear minority was responsible for providing the bulk of the income with which the overseers undertook their work. This view is confirmed by the evidence from a revaluation in 1739, when an exceptional list of those assessed was made. Table 12.1

Table 12.1. *Aldenham rate payers in 1739*

Rateable value	Less than £2	£2–£5	£5–£10	£10–50	Over £50
No.	47	100	28	22	32
Category	I	II	III	IV	V

breaks down the 1739 list into groups based upon rateable values. In that year 229 assessments were made; this can be compared with Table 12.2, in which the number of those assessed is shown at decennial intervals. Almost immediately after 1739 a large number of those in groups I and II in Table 12.2 were dropped from the assessment lists. Furthermore, since the number of assessments in the seventeenth century varied annually between a minimum of 101 and a maximum of 119, it is clear that the bulk of the households in groups I and II during this earlier period escaped the overseer's net. Rarely were more than 45 per cent of the households believed to have been resident in Aldenham contributing to the communal welfare fund in the seventeenth century. Furthermore, close to one-third of the household heads neither received relief from, nor contributed to, the fund (see column 8 in Table 12.2).

Given that the assessments do not commence until February 1637, it is somewhat difficult to gain an accurate measure of the trend in the level of relief. From the amount of money disbursed, and from the

Table 12.2

Year	Population count (a)	count (b)	counts (a)+(b)	Household heads	Heads assessed No.	%	Heads relieved No.	%	Heads neither assessed nor relieved No.	%	Married males No.	%	Widowers No.	%	Bachelors No.	%	Widows No.	%	Spinsters No.	%
1601	606	366	972	237							205	82.0	16	6.4	3	1.2	26	10.4	2	0.0
1611	700	369	1,069	250							204	75.5	20	7.4	–	–	44	16.3	1	0.4
1621	613	391	1,004	270							209	74.9	18	6.4	6	2.2	45	16.1	5	1.7
1631	653	417	1,070	279							228	76.3	18	6.0	7	2.3	41	13.7	5	1.7
1641	747	413	1,160	299	101	33.8	84	28.1	114	39.1	220	75.3	20	6.9	2	0.7	45	15.4	3	1.2
1651	703	374	1,077	292	115	39.4	82	28.1	95	32.5	195	76.8	15	5.9	1	0.4	40	15.7	7	3.1
1661	614	338	952	251	119	47.1	55	21.9	77	31.0	152	68.2	23	10.3	3	1.4	38	17.0	5	2.1
1671	533	248	781	223	104	46.6	74	33.2	45	21.2	176	72.4	22	9.1	3	1.2	37	15.2	2	0.8
1681	554	248	802	243	113	46.7	88	36.4	42	16.9	180	74.4	14	5.8	2	0.8	44	18.2	3	1.2
1691	581	338	919	242	115	47.5	40*	16.5	87	36.0	178	73.9	25	10.4	2	0.8	33	13.7		
1701	600	360	960	241	105	43.6	60*	24.1	76	32.3										

*This figure is derived from only part of the decade.

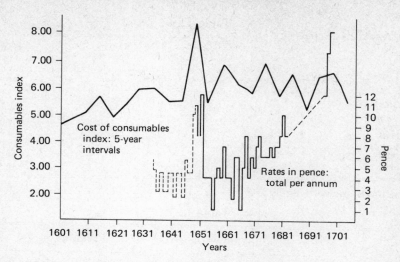

Figure 12.1. Poor rate assessments (pence in £): relation to cost of living, Aldenham 1601–1701

evidence of the level of rate assessment, we see some indications that towards the end of the century a large increase in the burden of relief had occurred (see Figure 12.1).

The bulk of the relief through the fifty-year period of this study concerned that aid called 'the monthly collection' which involved assistance on a regular basis, often continuing with adjustments over a period of several years. These cases were concentrated upon (a) the aged – whether as married couples, widows, widowers, bachelors or spinsters; (b) those families in need of relief because of imbalances between parental (family) income and the size of the biological family; and (c) orphaned children fostered into households of others. Sickness was not usually a cause for regular relief unless it was a permanent disability such as madness or an incapacity of some kind that seriously afflicted younger members of the community. Sickness was relieved, but usually by *ad hoc* payments sometimes given in addition to other relief. Some relief was also dispensed on occasions of widespread community distress such as occurred in periods of high mortality accompanying epidemics.

Those most obvious victims of 'nuclear hardship' in the categories mentioned above accounted for the major part of the relief disbursed in Aldenham, although the exact proportions varied considerably over time. A very high figure of £121 4s 6d in 1651 was in part due to

Table 12.3

Date	Widows	Widowers	Bachelors	Spinsters	couples	Family relief	Children kept	Annual cost of regular relief
								£ s d
1631	15*	3	1	–	3	2	3	50 16 2
1641	7	4*	–	3	1	7	3	51 7 0
1651	16	2	1	3	4	8	10	121 4 6
1661	12*	1	–	1	–	1	4	59 3 0
1671	15	3	–	–	4	2	6	74 1 6
1681	16	3	–	1	–	1	9	78 2 2

*Includes one with family.

Table 12.4

	Widows			Widowers		
	Total resident	Relieved		Total resident	Relieved	
		No.	%		No.	%
1631	–	15	–	–	3	–
1641	41	7	17.1	18	4*	22.2
1651	45	16	35.5	20	2	10.0
1661	40	12*	30.0	15	1	6.7
1671	38	15	39.5	23	3	13.1
1681	37	16	43.2	22	3	13.6

*Includes one with family.

the maintenance of a large number of children who had lost both or one of their parents in the high mortality of the preceding decade.

By far the largest category of regular recipients were the widows and widowers who constituted a little over 20 per cent of household heads (see Table 12.2). Yet these individuals accounted for almost 60 per cent of the regular adult collectioners and received an even higher percentage of the relief disbursed (see Table 12.3). Furthermore, it is clear that widows were far more likely to have been in receipt of regular relief than widowers (see Table 12.4).[7] In 1671 there were 38 widows and 23 widowers in our reconstituted population, and it is

---

[7] For similar findings, see Wales, above, pp. 360–88. For discussions of remarriage differences between widows and widowers, see R. Schofield and E. A. Wrigley, 'Remarriage Intervals and the Effect of Marriage Order on Fertility', in J. Dupâquier, et al., editors, *Marriage and Remarriage in Populations of the Past* (London, 1981), pp. 211–28; Holderness, below, pp. 430–1.

possible to calculate the length of bereavement of 57 of them – 26 of the widows and 21 of the widowers. Of those identifiable in 1671 only four, one widow and three widowers, remarried. These latter individuals were all men left with children – a factor which may have helped to precipitate their remarriage. But too much should not be made of this, for in 22 cases there were children under the age of 21 in the family of the widowed, but in only four instances did these families receive relief.

One of these four, Widow Fox (alias Oxden) was aged 54 in 1671 and was almost certainly living alone although she had two daughters, aged 21 and eighteen, and a fourteen-year-old son. There are no further references to the daughters, suggesting that they may have left the parish. The son, Humphrey, in 1681 at the age of 23 began his own family. From 1671 to 1681 Widow Fox had received 2s per week, which ceased in the year of her son's marriage.[8] We hear nothing more of her until her burial in 1695 as an 'alms woman'. It is likely, therefore, that she had been living in the almshouse from 1681, although the connection between her son's marriage and her departure for the almshouse is not at all clear. Her entry into the almshouse may have vacated her house for her son's possession at his marriage. This case suggests that Humphrey did not take in his elderly mother in his newly created household; nor is it likely that his income before marriage was used to support his widowed mother, whether he had been resident in Aldenham or away in service.

In another case, that of Joan Hilyard, who was widowed in her late thirties, it is possible to see that the departure of children from the household was accompanied by a reduction in the amounts of relief received by the shrunken family. When her husband died Joan received 6s relief per month. This was reduced to 4s after four months of widowhood, when her eldest child John was sent off to work at the age of thirteen years and three months. Thomas, the second child, was 'putt out' at Easter 1676 when aged sixteen years. Whether income received from the out-migrating children or reduced household expenditure because of their departure was responsible for a reduction in Joan's monthly relief to 3s is impossible to establish from the evidence at our disposal. Her situation did, however, deteriorate,

---

[8] All calculations of ages derives from a family reconstitution study of the parish of Aldenham, the results of which are available from the SSRC Cambridge Group for the History of Population and Social Structure. This study is based upon registers deposited in the Hertfordshire County Record Office (DP 3/1/1–3). Miss Fiona Newall of Clare College, Cambridge is currently completing a detailed study of this parish, its demography and the family economies of its individuals, as part of her research for a Cambridge Ph.D. thesis.

for in 1678 her relief went up to 3s 6d a month and remained at that
level until the gap begins in the source materials. We know too, that
the monthly collection was insufficient to meet her expenses, as her
annual rent of 14s was paid in the year 1680–1.[9]

Clearly, a majority of the widowers and widows were without
children at home, although not necessarily without children married
and living in the parish. Furthermore, the majority consisted of the
aged receiving more as the parish became their principal, and in
many cases their sole means of support. For example, Widow Jane
Cooksey had been supported by the parish in varying degrees for
almost twelve years prior to her death in 1661. Throughout this
period her monthly collection was 4s, 3s, then 4s again, and finally 5s
from 1657 to 1661. In addition, her rent was paid on eight occasions
between 1653 and 1661. Her income was further supplemented by
supplies of wood on seven occasions from a substantial rate payer, a
yeoman farmer Henry Frances. The need for wood points to her
having her own hearth, this suggesting a residential independence
that is further supported in the evidence by the rent subsidies. In her
later years the increase in relief would have been necessary as she
became less and less able to provide for herself in gathering fuel and
cultivating a garden. At that point in her life-cycle (1657–61) her
annual income from the parish amounted to £4 15s (£3 5s from her
collection, 16s for her rent and 14s for fuel).

Parish relief co-existed with support for the poor from privately
endowed almshouses. On 18 January 1600, Richard Platt, citizen and
brewer of London, announced the creation of a 'Grammere School
and certain almshouses in Aldenham'. The almsmen and women
were provided with a livelihood, a roof, an income of £2 per annum
and a gown worth 12s. As with recipients of parish relief it is possible
to reconstruct the family circumstances of certain almsmen and
women. For example, in 1603 it was certified by the vicar of
Aldenham and others that Agnes Hall (Hayle) was 'the poorest,
neediest and most fitt to be admitted and is ordered to be admitted
accordingly'.[10] She was a widow who had married in 1570 and who
had had eight children baptized between 1570 and 1586. It appears
that Agnes had six children alive on her husband's death. In 1603 she

---

[9] This and all subsequent references to expenditures by the overseers of the poor
derive from the account books noted above, note 2.
[10] References to the activities of Richard Platt and to the finance and inmates of the
almshouses are taken from the Court Books of the Worshipful Company of Brewers
deposited in the Guildhall Library: MS 5445, in 37 volumes, for the period 1531–1870;
vols, 10–24 cover the period relevant to the current study.

was over sixty and her eldest son, Thomas, was living in the parish at Roundbush with his own family of six children.

In discussing the age of widows or widowers we have been considering an easily identifiable, 'structurally dependent' group within Aldenham's seventeenth-century population. In absolute terms a larger group was made up of those in the 'middling ground' between those on the margins of assessment on the one hand and those undoubtedly in need on the other. To deal with family economic difficulties among those in the upper levels of the middling group the overseers gave abatements of rates. The difficulties associated with the presence of a growing but youthful family on fixed household resources is well indicated in the case of Edward Harris, who in 1651 was aged 46 with a wife and five children aged seventeen, fifteen, thirteen, seven and five. Between 1650 and 1654 he was given back sums equivalent to rates paid on his assessment, and between 1654 and 1658 he was not assessed at all. After 1658, when his youngest and oldest children were twelve and 24 respectively, he returned to the assessment roll. The improvement in family consumption–production ratios that occurred as children matured might be expected to have been lost when the children left home.[11]

Ageing couples left with the task of running a farm or a small business for which their declining strength was insufficient to provide them with an adequate income would have been vulnerable to economic difficulties. For example, Edward Duncombe was in 1638 assessed for £8 which fell to £7 from 1640 to 1649. He was then assessed 'nil' twice at the beginning of 1650, and nine of the next eleven assessments were either 'abated', 'allowed' or 'given back' on account of his poverty. Over these years, while Edward was in his middle or late sixties, the only child likely to have been living at home was his daughter Mary, and it is striking to discover that after her marriage to William Kemp the abatements to her father cease to be recorded. It is possible, therefore, that William Kemp took over the property as Edward's son-in-law and that it once more became economically viable.

There was, furthermore, another category of individuals receiving relief on a very casual basis. They constituted a group of the 'marginal' poor. For example, in the first six months of 1631 there occurred each month a list of 'poor labouring men' who were

[11] See Smith, *supra*, pp. 68–72, and R. M. Smith, 'Fertility, Economy and Household Formation in England over Three Centuries', *Population and Development Review* 7 (1981), pp. 606–11.

relieved; 43 names appeared on these monthly lists at least once over the six months. Fifteen of the named individuals were listed each month and thirteen only once. Of the 43, forty can be identified through the family reconstitution study and of those fourteen received no other reliefs. In only two cases was relief being given before 1631. But of the 43 appearing on the lists in 1631 there were ten who became impoverished in later life (i.e. becoming part of the 'structurally dependent' poor) who appeared first as recipients of casual relief and then became more permanently present among the monthly collectioners. In each of these ten cases the labourer's widow was placed on monthly collection that lasted for very many years.

It is useful to consider in some detail the case of John Platt (1598–1669), whose own and whose family's receipts in various forms from the parish rates are highly informative as to the ways in which community welfare buttressed the family economy of the 'marginal' poor at critical points along its developmental cycle. There are two clues to John Platt's occupation; in 1657 he was paid 4d for mending a pair of shoes and later in 1658 he was given 'by consent' 12s to buy leather. His first marriage, which lasted for approximately eighteen months, ended childless. However, his remarriage to Anne Altey produced nine children, only four of whom survived to adulthood. In its early years the Platt family economy was supported indirectly by means of payments to John himself, his wife and his children for attending to other inhabitants of Aldenham who were evidently casualties of 'nuclear family hardship'. Throughout 1628 (just two years after her marriage) John Platt's second wife, Anne, was in receipt of weekly payments of 6d to 1s for the care of an aged bachelor, Thomas Wheeler. When Thomas Wheeler died in April 1629 the account books record a final payment to 'Goodwife Platt for watching with him the night he did depart and bread and beere as she had others that weare with her'. John's second child, Alice, is first mentioned at the age of 32 in September 1665 in receipt of payments for 'looking to visited people'. John himself first appears in the record soon after the birth of his child in 1631, when he was paid 6s per month from April to September for 'keeping Eltheridge's boy'. At this time he was among those on the list of 'poor labouring men', being one of those relieved each month from January to June. From the accounting year 1636–7 to 1647–8 he was relieved in each year on at least one occasion, sometimes, though, for months at a time. In 1648 the overseers paid 1s 6d for the burial of his son Thomas and in 1650–1 they paid 20s 'for redeeming Platt's house from Timson', then paid his rent of 15s, following this with a gift of 3s 6d. There seems to have been only a limited connection between the payment of relief and the size and age of John Platt's family, as relief in some form or another was received throughout the 1650s, when it was likely that all of his children, with the possible exception of the last born, had left home. Nonetheless, the late 1650s do appear to suggest a lessening in the degree of parish support for John and his wife. But this phase of relative self-sufficiency was short-lived for in the accounting year 1667–8, when John was aged 68, his health deteriorated and payments were made for his medical treatment. His monthly collection rose to 5s in the months prior to his death in August 1669. On this death the burial expenses were paid from parish rates and his widow, Anne, continued to receive monthly collection for the next 24 years until her death in 1693. Very few years, or indeed months, passed without the Platt household obtaining assistance in some form from the communal fund, whether as a straight supplement to John's income as a cobbler, as indirect payments for his wife's or daughter's work for other impotent paupers, as a foster-parent for orphans or in the form of monthly pensions as his and his widow's sole source of income in old age.[12]

In the early years of an individual's life-cycle parish support could be quite considerable. This assistance tended to take two different forms: the maintenance of orphans, generally under the age of fourteen, and the setting forth to work of adolescents as apprentices. Between 1649–50 and 1705–6 the overseers of Aldenham assisted in at least forty cases (24 boys and sixteen girls) of setting children to work as apprentices. The premiums paid for 32 of these individuals can be established from the accounts, varying in amounts from the highest total of £10 to a minimum sum of 10s. Other cases can be distinguished by the payment for bonds and indentures or sometimes merely by the expenses incurred by the parish on the occasion of the 'putting forth' of the individual concerned.

These charges on the keeping and apprenticising of orphans and of the children of one-parent families could be quite considerable; the Williams family presents an interesting example. For instance, in early October 1688 a Quarter Sessions' removal order sent Elizabeth Williams, recently widowed in nearby Watford, with her children

---

[12] For a wider review of the 'structural dependency' of the elderly in pre-industrial English communities, see more generally R. M. Smith, 'The Family or the State? Some Figures on Kinship Support Through the Ages', *Cambridge Medicine* (Autumn, 1982), pp. 10–11, and (in more detail) *idem.* 'The Structured Dependency of the Elderly: A Twentieth Century Creation?', *Ageing and Society* (forthcoming).

back to Aldenham, where she obviously had a settlement.[13] She apparently became a regular collectioner, being in receipt of 8s per month. Two of her children, John and George, had been baptized in Aldenham in 1685 and 1671; John, at the age of thirteen (a little over a year before his mother's death), appears in the accounts as being kept at the rate of 6s 8d per four weeks until he was apprenticed in January 1699. When John entered his apprenticeship the overseers spent £1 13s 0½d on 'making him a shift', on buying 'cloth and thread', 'a frock', '5½ yards of cloath, buttons, thread, stay tape and a pocket skin' and 'a pair of breeches', 'mending shoes' and 'nayls' for them. Finally, they spent £2 4s 6d at his binding as an apprentice. But no sooner was John apprenticed than the overseers were faced with three of his siblings, who came to Aldenham with a settlement in March 1699. These children were kept at the standard monthly rate of 6s 8d each from then until April 1703, when the monthly payment dropped to 13s 4d when another child was put out to work. The monthly payment fell again in May 1706 when a daughter was bonded as an apprentice for a premium of £5. Throughout this period, in addition to regular monthly payments the overseers had been paying for a number of miscellaneous expenses incurred by the children – shoe repairs, new shoes, gowns, petticoats, bodices and so on.

While apprenticing was a direct involvement by the overseers in helping children to a livelihood, there are very many entries which suggest that the overseers aided parents in the payment of premiums and the provision of clothing for their children before they left for employment away from home: Edward Ray was given £2 'for putting his son forth' in 1649–50, and in 1662 the following entry appears in the accounts: 'layd out on clothing Bateman's son now apprenticed to Henry Francis £2 3s 10d.'

It would be wrong, however, to view the overseers as entirely passive agents in this process, for it appears that they were not prepared for children to be kept at home when they could be expected to go out to work. For instance, in 1701 the vestry ordered that if Widow Dickenson 'doth not forthwith put her daughter to service . . . she shall be stricken out of the monthly collection and be wholly excluded from any further relief'. Her child was then aged thirteen. Taking all the children who are known in the records of apprenticeship between 1649 and 1706, the average age of departure from home was thirteen years and eleven months for the boys and

---

[13] See *Hertfordshire Quarter Session Records*, published by Hertfordshire County Council, Vol. 5, s.a. 1688.

thirteen years and seven months for the girls. It is worth noting that in both their sex ratios and their ages these children conformed to the patterns proposed for the late seventeenth century by Keith Snell in his recent study of pauper apprenticeship.[14] The effect of this convention, given that the setting forth of an apprentice was 'a once and for all payment', was that relatively little relief was dispensed to individuals in the age range 15–30 years, i.e. after the age of leaving home and before the age at which marriage would bring an accumulation of costly, non-productive children into the household.

It has been emphasized by another contributor to this volume that the 1601 Poor Law was very much designed to relieve life-cycle poverty of the sort we have considered in seventeenth-century Aldenham.[15] It was especially important for those at certain stages in the life-cycle, notably the orphan, the widow and the aged generally, and for the poor but 'complete' household economically overburdened with children. This bringing together of the available records indicates that in Aldenham the cycle of family life had the benefit in times of crisis of a system of support operated over a very wide range of needs by a local authority sensitive to the circumstances of those requiring it. This authority was exercised moreover in a face-to-face situation in which the reactions of the overseers can be discerned in their dictation of the details of their disbursements to the usher of the school as he wrote up their accounts: the note of anger when 'Fernando Lucas left ye parish immediately after ye assessment was made' and they could not distrain for his rates of 8s; the self-interest in 'my own charges for two days and ye losse of my worke' when William Barber collapsed at work and died suddenly; their sense of accountability in the detailed expenses given in unusual circumstances, as when taking Richard Williams to 'Bethlehem'; their compassion over the disabled, 'sick, aged and bedrid' (Widow Grubb) or 'aged and almost blind' (Richard Done).

Some of the overseers would have been sensible of the fact that, given some misfortune, they too would be likely to have need of assistance from the parish. The parish interest is stressed throughout the period, and the system's implementation involved a large proportion of Aldenham's residents. The need for parish officers meant that large numbers of rate payers could expect to serve at some stage in

[14] See K. Snell, 'The Standard of Living, Social Relations, the Family and Labour Mobility in South-Eastern and Western Counties 1700–1860', unpublished University of Cambridge Ph.D. thesis, 1980, especially pp. 130–44. This matter is discussed in greater detail in Snell's *Essay on Social Change and Agrarian England 1660–1900* (forthcoming), Chapter 7.

[15] Wales, above, pp. 368–9.

the office of overseer. This involvement is apparent from the information that the family reconstitution has given us concerning the 39 individuals who acted as overseers in the parish from 1674 to 1684 and that is presented in the Appendix. The majority of the overseers were under forty years of age when responsibilities fell upon them. Some, indeed, were in their twenties. Furthermore, in nine out of these ten years there was an overseer who can be shown to have had non-farming interests, even if assessed for a few acres. Philip Cogdell probably kept an alehouse; Thomas Perriman came from a family with craft interests; Thomas Pollin, William Kemp, John Downer and James Hodesden probably kept alehouses for extra income from their land or craft; Andrew Mores was a shoemaker.

Because of their age and their representativeness of the varying strata of the local economy the parochial administration on the one hand ensured a face-to-face connection of administrators with the parish population; on the other hand, with their generous terms of relief, the humble officers facilitated agreements and mutual respect between the 'ranks' and 'orders' of parish society. In the everyday interchange of social attitudes the 'old Poor Law' was an ever-present mediator. The Aldenham records, like those from many other places of the seventeenth and eighteenth centuries, indicate very wide terms of relief and show the way it intruded into so many aspects of parish life and work – in a manner which, for all the welfare developments of the twentieth century, has probably never been replicated on a comparable scale.[16] If the treatment of the elderly in seventeenth-century Aldenham is taken as a guide to the humanity of relief policy in general, the old Poor Law in its first century of formal existence seems to have been largely benevolent and sympathetic in operation.

---

[16] An argument made with great effect by D. Thomson, 'Provision for the Elderly in England 1830–1908', unpublished University of Cambridge Ph.D. thesis, 1980.

Appendix: Overseers serving in Aldenham 1674–84

	Rateable value		Rateable value		Rateable value		Rateable value
John Axtell (29) Delrow	£15			Richard Backer (25) S. Aldenham wood	£21	Phil Cogdell (–) Elstree	£4 10s
Thomas Hampton (–) first annt 1658 Tilehouse farm Theobald Street	£120	John Hatch (43) 'Edmonds' Batlers green	£36	Thomas Perriman (ba. 1677) craftsman? bricklayer or weaver Elstree check	Nil	Robert Edwards (W44) Bright Street farm	£30
Robert Francis (?41) m. Anne Hatch dau. of John Inventory £231 6s 4d probably working for father	(£40)	John Ewer (42) or (68) LB – 1683 Gills hill (E)	£10 to 1673	William Smith (41) Wingfield farm Aldenham common	£68	Ralph Weedon (21) or (12) Slades farm Aldenham wood	£84
Thomas Woodward (c. 25?) m. An Warner sister of John probably working for father	(£114)	John Warner (28) or (57) Patchetts Green (West) farm	£11	John Finch (c. 32?) Slyes' farm	£45	Edward Porter (bt. 77) (W24) Kidder Caldecote hill	£3
Fardinando Lucas (–) (Anabaptist) Medbarn (5) farm Watling Street	£86	John Harvie (ba. 1678) ?Organhall farm Theobald Street	probably about £100	Thomas Pollin The Hollybush Elstree	£6	Andrew Mores (ba. 1664) shoemaker Caldecote hill	£10

(Cont.)

Appendix (Cont.)

	Rateable value		Rateable value		Rateable value		Rateable value
Michael Nicholl (33) Pondinyarde Batlers Green	£32	Edmund Dell (24) ?Darnells farm Radlett	£42	Robert Grover (–) Caldecote hill	£3	Sylas Palmer (ba. 1674) ?wheelwright Elstree	£8
Philip Aldwin Higgler Letchmore heath	£14	Miles Clarke (bt 1676) Huetts Letchmore heath	£22	Francis Sansome (67) ?farm Caldecote hill	£44	Robert Taylor (24) ?Bowyers Caldecote hill	£8
Edward Grover (33) m. Martha Backer sister of Richard Cobdenhill farm Watling Street		Thomas Grover (27) Brooklands farm Theobald Street	£100	William Kemp (W54) The Wrestlers Aldenham wood	£21	Richard Kirton (–) probably Elstree	£8
John Downer (31) The Compasses Hedgegrove	£4	James Hodesden (36) The Red Lion Radlett		Richard Grubb (25) ?farm Caldecote hill	£8	Thomas Readwood (30) Cobden hill farm Watling Street (F)	£42
Thomas Wafford (45) High Grove	£4 5s	John Leper (–) Wold farm Theobald Street	£20 15s	Dan Danser (–) ?Coach and Horses Caldecote hill		Joseph West (–) baker Elstree	£6

Key

Figures in parentheses indicate age at first appointment.

annt = announcement

ba. = baptised

422

13

Widows in pre-industrial society: an essay upon their economic functions

B. A. HOLDERNESS

i

Widowhood has always borne overtones of comedy or satire in Europe. Apart from the bitter embroilments of the witch craze or the sombre portraits of crow-like widows and old maids in Balzac's *Comédie humaine*, the common image of the widow has been formed not out of respectful deference, still less out of pious solemnity. The Wife of Bath represents a stereotype, timeless and international, frequently employed in popular entertainments or in the drama and prose literature of the reading public of each generation from the fourteenth to the nineteenth century. Her kind has added immeasurably to the gaiety of European man and to his folklore of irreverence. But this literary view of widowhood not only exaggerates the traits and features of the institution but also makes it appear more brittle and insubstantial than the historical record reveals the role and function of such women to have been in pre-industrial societies. In an age which has yet again begun to reappraise the history of women in our past, the current alliance between economic history and social anthropology provides a method particularly appropriate for the investigation of status and social organization before the nineteenth century. This chapter pretends only to be a cursory attempt at exegesis of the place and function of widows, chiefly in seventeenth-century England, by an economic historian whose interests lie essentially in the economic and pecuniary relationships between the various social groups which composed village and small-town society before 1750. The theme perhaps deserves more extended and more profound treatment, but the nature of the source material is such that several intriguing and possibly important questions relating to widows in the fabric of social behaviour or to their enjoyment of titles to property cannot yet, and may never be, answered satisfactorily.

Our view of the pre-industrial past is still filtered through the prism of nineteenth-century history, by which time widowhood had become almost invisible. Beyond their ceremonial function in periods of mourning widows played no clearly defined part in Victorian society. Women in general underwent a phase in eclipse after about 1780–1830 except in the field of polite literature, not because women no longer performed any useful task save procreation but because the social ideal of the times enhanced the patriarchal authority of men and effaced the public countenance, if not the self-respect, of women. Widows, being outside the conventional orbit of male despotism, fell virtually into a status-less void. This opinion runs counter to that most commonly expressed by modern social historians of the Industrial Revolution and after, but it can be justified by looking backwards over a longer span of the pre-industrial past than nineteenth-century specialists usually do; however, both cases rest precariously upon assertion rather than proof. Early and mid-nineteenth-century changes in the laws of property tended also to discriminate against women, especially against widows' customary rights, and not all the legion of Victorian blue stockings made much countervailing impact before the 1880s, in face of the 'middle-class' exaltation of the *pater familias*. The queen's avowal of Prince Albert's familial, as distinct from her monarchial, authority in the royal household, was itself symbolic of bourgeois attitudes in her life-time. Industrialization, *pace* Harold Perkin, also assisted in the process of female subordination. The trend towards mass organization of labour in factories or large capital plants, the lowly status of women's work and the growing sense of class, in which the normative influence was decidedly male, can be over-stated as causes of change in the structure of the family, but there is little doubt that the external or public role of women shrank, with the decline of domestic manufacturing, with the decay of customary traditions, and perhaps also with the development of greater specialization within the sector of self-employment. Looking back beyond the nineteenth century the perspectives are rather different. Much indeed of that peasant-centred past remained in the nineteenth century, but as residual, not formative, elements in the evolution of Victorian society.[1]

If industrialization and the *embourgeoisement* of British society

---

[1] The classic statement is in Harold Perkin, *The Origins of Modern English Society* (London, 1969), pp. 149ff. I hold to the view that Perkin is presenting not so much an actual as a potential or prospective view of nineteenth-century female emancipation. Most of what he says about working-class women applied, with greater force, to the earlier period, and middle-class feminist voices before about 1880 were no more effective than had been Mary Astell's around 1700.

reduced the status and weakened the economic position of women, we cannot in fairness state that the decline was precipitate. Women in pre-industrial England were subordinate to the authority of their husbands and fathers to the extent that they were generally allowed little discretion or outward responsibility. On the other hand, they did enjoy certain advantages rarely provided in Victorian Britain, and, as far as historical records are concerned, the presence of women in several different contexts is notably more evident in the seventeenth century than in the nineteenth century. The co-operation of husband and wife in work, especially in domestic industry, is a familiar feature of economic life in pre-industrial Europe, although in this the wife stood beside her husband as his adjutant, not normally as his equal. Nevertheless many wives were also active as partners in business and agriculture, often at every level of activity, from sharing hard physical labour to the casting of accounts. Goody has suggested that pre-industrial societies in western Europe, especially peasant societies, made no sharp distinction between the social and economic functions of men and women comparable to the precisely formulated sexual divisions of labour and responsibilities which he found in West Africa. Men and women could, up to a point, exchange roles.[2] Even so, the status of women in Europe did change in the course of time from the tenth to the eighteenth century. The tightening bonds of paternal domination over family life which affected continental societies from the later middle ages apparently constricted English womanhood to a lesser extent. Visitors from across the Channel, from Plattner to Taine, for example, commented with amusement or astonishment upon the comparative independence of English women. As Jacob Rathgeb observed in 1592, 'The females have great liberty and are almost like masters'; and several visitors believed that English children among the gentry and nobility suffered from the lack of a warm family environment, as a result of comparative parental detachment.[3] This self-reliance of women reached its apogee in the seventeenth-century Independent sects which stressed the equality of men and women both before God and in material affairs. Female autonomy withered after the Restoration, although Quaker women continued to prove to all who cared to learn that they were capable of taking up the responsibilities of husbands or fathers. Sarah Fell,

[2] J. Goody, 'Inheritance, Property and Women', in J. R. Goody, J. Thirsk and E. Thompson, editors, *Family and Inheritance: Rural Society in Western Europe, 1200–1800* (Cambridge, 1976), pp. 12 and 13.
[3] See P. Aries, *L'Enfant et la vie familiale sous l'ancien régime* (Paris, 1960), *passim*; J. Thirsk, 'The Family', *Past and Present* 27 (1964) pp. 116–22; W. B. Rye, *England as Seen by Foreigners* (London, 1865), especially p. 14.

managing the affairs of her father Judge Fell at Swarthmore in Furness, is a well-known example, but there were many others who found, by default, that family life and business survival depended upon them. When John Banks was imprisoned in Carlisle in 1684 he wrote of his longing to see his wife but admitted that she could not come to him, 'considering thy concerns in this Season of the Year, being Harvest time and the Journey so long'. James Taylor, another Quaker, mourned a wife who had been so busy about his affairs during pregnancy that she had died of the exertions.[4]

The financial acumen of many women, from peeresses to peasants, was often acknowledged in the trust placed in them by husbands or fathers. Ralph Josselin once dealt with the daughter of a prospective tenant for the hire of his farm at Mallories in Essex, and Adam Eyre, the Yorkshire diarist, relied much upon his wife in business.[5] Even gentlewomen were not exempt from this apparent reversal of roles. Christopher Mitford, a Northumbrian coal owner of good lineage, appointed his sister Jane Legard as executrix of his estates and business ventures in 1623, and Elizabeth Mansell, widow of a great entrepreneur, Sir Hugh Mansell, acquired some notoriety for her sharpness in business after her husband's death. Lady Mary Hevingham of Ketteringham, Norfolk, was similarly responsible for amending her ancestral estates in the mid-seventeenth century.[6] When such formidable ladies as Elizabeth I, the great and much feared Countess of Shrewsbury, Lady Anne Clifford or Sarah, Duchess of Marlborough, stood at the head of English society in the period 1550–1720, the enterprise and achievement of other less exalted women is not at all surprising. Women in responsible positions were not necessarily capable of success. For the few outstanding examples there must have been dozens reluctant, bemused or overthrown by the duties foisted upon them. We should place Joan Dant, Dorothy Petty, Elizabeth Parkin and Ruperta Howe beside Aphra Behn, Jane Baker,

---

[4] N. Penny, editor, *The Household Accounts Books of Sarah Fell* (Cambridge, 1920); J. Banks, *A Journal of the Life of John Banks* (London, 1712), p. 129; Mary Batt, *Testimony of the Life and Death of Mary Batt* (London, 1683), pp. 5–7. Cf. K. V. Thomas, 'Women and the Civil War sects', *Past and Present* 13 (1958), pp. 42–62.

[5] A. Macfarlane, editor, *The Diary of Ralph Josselin 1616–1683*, British Academy, Records of Social and Economic History, new series iii (London, 1976), p. 86; H. J. Moorehouse, editor, 'The Diurnell of Adam Eyre', in *Yorkshire Diaries*, Surtees Society lxv (London, 1875), pp. 16, 36. Cf. P. Heylin, *Historical and Miscellaneous Tracts* (London, 1681), pp. 18–19; R. Parkinson, editor, *The Life of Adam Martindale, Written by Himself*, Chetham Society, old series iv (Manchester, 1845), p. 172.

[6] R. Welford, *A History of Newcastle and Gateshead* (London, 1885), Vol. III, p. 252; State Papers Domestic (hereafter SPD), CXLVIII, 52 (1623); J. Hunter, *History and Topography of Ketteringham* (Norwich, 1851), p. 46.

Elizabeth Elstob and Lady Mary Wortley Montagu in any illustration of what women could achieve in the economic as well as the literary and intellectual spheres of life in the seventeenth and eighteenth centuries; but the list of genuinely accomplished and successful women in the early modern period is brief beside that of their male contemporaries. It is, however, interesting that English writers repeatedly emphasized the superior situation of Dutchwomen in business and social life, sometimes merely in scorn, as in Wycherley, but most frequently with real admiration.[7] Alice Clark, in a little classic of concentrated research, produced numerous examples of less celebrated women active in commerce, manufacturing, agriculture and finance, which indicate that England was not barren ground for women as executives or partners with their husbands or fathers in many ventures.[8]

The acceptance of women, in contemporary opinion, in the stead of men in most occupations outside the higher professions evidently affected their status and function within the society in which men and women co-existed and co-operated. At bottom women enjoyed status because of the bridewealth or dower which were attached to their marriage contracts. They had rights in property enshrined in custom and protected at law, which patriarchal authority could void only by due process or testamentary provision that often ran against the grain of local opinion. This protection did not apply to women among the propertyless poor, of course, but in that large, amorphous section of society the woman's role as joint breadwinner frequently produced the same result in the equilibrium of the sexes. In propertied families, however, the rights possessed by women usually constituted a reversionary interest in an estate, not a freedom to dispose of their own during the life-time of husbands or fathers. Rather against modern ideas of marriage and conjugal status, therefore, women in pre-industrial Europe reached the height of their social influence and enjoyed their greatest rights out of coverture, as the common law expressed it, especially in widowhood.[9] The widow of property, whether in dower or in absolute possession, performed a number of economic functions which pre-industrial societies assigned to her,

---

[7] See, for example, 'England's Way to Win Wealth and to Employ Ships and Mariners . . .' *Harleian Miscellany*, Vol. III, p. 383; Sir J. Child, *A New Discourse of Trade* (London, 1964), pp. 4–5; James Howell, *Familiar Letters* (London, 1754), p. 103; W. Wycherley, *The Gentleman Dancing Master*, in *Plays* (London, 1735), p. 21.

[8] A. C. Clark, *Working Life of Women in the 17th Century* (London, 1919; reprinted 1968).

[9] Coverture was not necessarily a barrier to a wife's enjoyment of some property rights. For examples, see E. P. Thompson, 'The Grid of Inheritance: A Comment', in Goody *et al.*, editors, *Family and Inheritance*, p. 355 note.

from an established and identifiable position. Custom, it is need-less to say was not the only element in the definition of her role; economic necessity and particularly the evolving monetization of rural societies were no less insistent. The marriageable widow, even more the widow as money lender, fufilled two wants, by offering a channel for relieving the material appetites of ambitious young men, and by supplying part at least of the credit which peasant and small-town societies needed so extensively in seventeenth-century England.

Not all widows were well endowed or were eligible for remarriage. The sad case of Jan Finch of Chelmsford, who was both penurious and friendless when she died in 1597 with her cloak in pawn, resembled many others during the period.[10] Destitute or insolvent widows and old maids almost certainly outnumbered those who had property to live upon or savings to invest. Thus the frequency with which widows' names appear on lists of houses excused from the Hearth Tax in the 1670s, and the provisions made in statutes or local ordinances concerning poor relief for the care of impotent widows, suggest how extensive the problem of impoverished single women was. Neglect of their plight in this essay is not intended to imply that it was insignificant: the poor widow, however, is less important as a historical phenomenon than her wealthier contemporaries.

ii

The first weapon in the armoury of the widow was remarriage. Well-endowed widows, young and old, were in great demand at all levels of north-west European society by suitors anxious to combine companionship with material advantage. Much of the fun in the literary portrayal of widows was elicited from the ploys of the everlasting fishing match between hopeful angler and artful 'catch'. In describing medieval conditions Professor Postan has proposed another metaphor, of a marriage 'fugue', to characterize the com-plicated scheme of marital connections in many rural manors.[11] Marriageability was always central to the predicament of widow-hood. Pair bonding, for a complex of biological, social and economic reasons, has always been assumed to be the natural expression of the relationship of the sexes in European societies, and accidental vacan-

---

[10] F. G. Emmison, *Elizabethan Life: Home, Work and Land* (Chelmsford, 1976), p. 93.
[11] Quoted in J. Z. Titow, 'Some Differences Between Manors and Their Effects on the Condition of the Peasant in the Thirteenth Century', *Agricultural History Review* 10 (1962), pp. 7.

cies brought about by death of one partner have in consequence been supplied by new unions. Given the high risk of mortality among adults and the comparatively small number of households headed by single individuals, remarriage must, therefore, have been a common experience of both widows and widowers before the twentieth century added its quota of divorcees to the stock of eligible spouses.[12] The rate of remarriage, considered as an aspect of changes in vital statistics, is, however, far from easy to compute except by way of family reconstitution. The picture, however, must be seen complete within its socio-legal frame. It is evident that the frequency of second or subsequent marriages was inhibited by customs and attitudes affecting the transmission of property, despite the real needs for remarriage that were manifest in the overt experience of rural or small-town society in early modern times.

According to the available evidence of French and English demographic studies covering different periods frm the seventeenth to the nineteenth century, about one marriage in every ten was a second marriage.[13] Unfortunately many of the more detailed analyses of population movements are silent on the question of remarriage. Some historical demographers apparently did not collect the required information in their regional or local studies; others found it impossible to disentangle the data of first and subsequent marriages in the nuptial registers. Michael Drake, however, suggested that the rate of re-marriage in his West Riding district might at times have exceeded 15 per cent, while in Sogner's study of Coalbrookedale, from 1711 to 1760, known cases of widows and widowers remarrying made up fewer than 3 per cent of all recorded marriages. This discrepancy is essentially unreal. Drake's 15 per cent was very much an upper limit, and Sogner referred only to cases in which partners were marked as widowed in the registers.[14] The question of remarriage is so important, however, that more evidence must be found to permit navigators in this still unfamiliar sea to fix their positions and chart a safe course homewards.

Family reconstitution, as we have said, apparently offers the best

[12] P. Laslett, however, believes that pre-industrial England had an unusually high proportion of households headed by single adults: P. Laslett and R. Wall, editors, 'Mean Household Size in England since the Sixteenth Century', in *Household and Family in Past Time* (Cambridge, 1972), p. 147.

[13] See D. V. Glass and D. E. C. Eversley, editors, *Population in History* (London, 1965), p. 42.

[14] K. M. Drake, 'An Elementary Exercise in Parish Register Demography', *Economic History Review*. 2nd series 14 (1962), p. 443; S. Sogner, 'Aspects of the Demographic Situation in Seventeen Parishes in Shropshire, 1711–60', *Population Studies* 17 (1963), p. 132 footnote 13.

opportunity of a secure and reliable guide to the frequency, number and type of second marriages in pre-industrial England. In the hands of a practitioner more skilled in the methods of family reconstitution, and less impatient for results, the method of reconstitution will certainly provide just such an accurate measure. My attempt to achieve results by employing the method while short-circuiting the laborious process of accumulation of data, cross-checking and extensive indexing is frankly unsatisfactory, but the figures which have emerged from the experiment are consistent and logically sound enough to suggest that they are not merely specious.

The survey was confined to certain quite large, chiefly rural, parishes of Yorkshire, Lincolnshire and Norfolk: viz. Addingham in Wharfedale, Braithwell, Swillington, Kildwick in Craven, Riccall, all in Yorkshire; Spilsby and Wrangle, and Burgh le Marsh in Lincolnshire; and Acle, Garboldisham, Lopham and South Walsham in Norfolk.[15] Marriage data only were considered, except in a few cases of cross-checking, and only for a period beginning in about 1665–70 and ending in 1715–30. At best the findings are tentative, but an aggregate rate of remarriage of 11.2 per cent is at least well within the probable order of magnitude. Variations between parishes were not significant, allowing for the quality of the source material. Thus the range extended between 6 per cent and 13 per cent. On the basis of an even more cursory view of many other parish registers in the three counties, a norm of remarriage in the seventeenth century may well have been 10 per cent, as Bourgeois-Pichat intimated for eighteenth-century France.[16] Returns of notably less than 10 per cent were often affected by *lacunae* in the marriage registers which could not be supplied from other sources. On the other hand the numbers of second marriages fluctuated from one period to another within the span of time under investigation. Whether such variations were statistically significant remains to be seen. However, during a phase of relatively high death rates, in 1678–82 for example, the volume of remarriages apparently rose to about 15 per cent of total marriages. The increase was quite general and widespread in the eastern

---

[15] The study of parish registers was based on published data in Yorkshire Records Series, Parish Register Section (various dates to 1970) of places named; Lincolnshire registers still in possession of parishes when the data were gathered in 1961–2; Norfolk registers at Norfolk and Norwich Record Office, Acle PD 164/15; Garboldisham PD 197/1; Lopham PD 120/2; South Walsham (both parishes) PR 252/17. Several Norfolk marriage registers have been edited and published by Phillimore in 11 volumes issued from 1899 to 1926.

[16] J. Bourgeois-Pichat, 'The General Development of the Population of France since the Eighteenth Century' in D. Glass and D. E. C. Eversley, editors, *Population in History*, p. 484.

counties. On this aspect of the problem more work is needed, but it is likely that similar, or even opposing, patterns of remarriage in relation to intervals of exceptionally high or low mortality developed throughout the early modern period in Europe.

Analysis by sex suggests further intriguing possibilities. Widowers were much more likely to seek new partners than widows. This is obvious given the circumstances of domestic life and the rather larger freedom of men in remarrying. Taking Laslett's evidence of household size and type in pre-industrial England as our guide, it appears that not much more than 5 per cent of families were headed by widowers and about 13 per cent by widows.[17] Some from both groups may subsequently have married again, although the majority probably reflected the residue of elderly or ineligible single householders for whom remarriage was out of the question. In our sample the proportion of marriages involving widowers was about 13 per cent, and involving widows only 8.7 per cent. There is room for error in this calculation, particularly because several individuals, most commonly men, undertook more than two marriages, but only one case is securely established of a person who embarked upon four marriages in his life-time. By contrast, only eighteen cases of widows marrying for a third time can be found in the twelve parishes in the period around 1700.

It has not been possible to produce evidence of the ages at which widows most commonly sought to remarry. Men seem to have taken new wives soon after bereavement at all ages. The remarriage of widowers was especially frequent in early manhood or early middle age because of the comparative high rate of puerperal mortality among women, and although young widows certainly did marry again the constraints upon their freedom of choice were often much greater than any social sanctions applied to the men. The widow frequently offered the best prospect to a suitor when she was not encumbered with a young family by her former marriage or bound by legal or customary obligations to her late husband's kin. The surviving, and in the seventeenth century often still vigorous, custom in copyhold manors, especially in southern and western England, of the widow's free bench gave a woman standing and influence in rural society; but, because the bench constituted a particular portion of a family estate or holding which was transmitted patrilineally, the widow's entitlement was necessarily temporary, determinable at death or when her dependence upon the family into which she married ceased, and her enjoyment of this portion often caused

[17] Laslett, 'Mean Household Size', p. 147.

difficulty and resentment to the legal heirs of the patrimony. In English there is a good deal of terminological confusion between dowry and dower. *Dower*, or free bench, was not a right conveyed to women in widowhood by reason of the *dowry* which they brought at marriage. Bridewealth may have influenced the size of the widow's dower or portion, but as a rule the custom of the manor was similar whether the dowry was great or small. The most frequently encountered arrangement was apparently for the widow to enjoy one-third of her husband's estate as long as she did not remarry. In some copyhold manors the widow's portion amounted to one-half, and in a few to the whole of the estate as a conditional life-interest. This was apparently the custom at Preston, Petworth and Sutton in Sussex, and at Mardon and Crawley in Hampshire, where Borough English prevailed. Ultimogeniture probably encouraged men to associate or confuse widow's rights with the duties of guardianship in proprietory as well as in personal terms.[18]

Land held in dower could pose a threat to the integrity of patrimonial estates. The widow's remarriage was therefore usually marked by confiscation of her life-interest in the dower estate. This, however, was not the rule everywhere. In several manors remarriage did not affect the free bench of widows, and second husbands were often registered as such in the court rolls, although it was usually necessary for the new men to pay entry fines to enjoy widows' lifeholds. Eric Kerridge believes that this custom was subject to abuse, for scheming young women were alleged to marry elderly men for the sake of a life-interest in their copyhold or freehold estates. In such circumstances the widow was certainly freer to choose a more attractive or amenable husband the second time around. The problem was serious enough for the court baron of Berkeley in Gloucestershire to disallow widows' lifeholds in marriage contracted *in extremis*.[19] Evidence of the use of serial marriages as a means of transmitting property, especially tenements, from one family to another in some medieval manors like Witney, Oxfordshire – Professor Postan's marriage fugue – cannot certainly be found in

[18] Charles Watkins, *A Treatise on Copyholds* (London, 1851), especially Vol. II; *The Court Rolls of the Manor of Preston*, Sussex Record Society xxvii (Lewes, 1921); Lord Leconfield, *The Manor of Petworth in the 17th Century* (Oxford, 1954), pp. 13–15, and *Sutton and Dunston Manors* (Oxford, 1956), p. 3; M. Imber, *Abstract of the Custom of the Manor of Mardon in Hursley (Hants)* (London, 1707); N. S. B. and E. C. Gras, *Economic and Social History of an English Village* (Cambridge, Mass., 1930), pp. 156 and 528ff.; C. Torr, *Wreyland Documents* (London, 1910), pp. xxvii–xxviii and lxii; cf. R. B. Fisher, *A Practical Treatise of Copyhold Tenure* (London, 1794), *passim*.

[19] E. Kerridge, *Agrarian Problems in the Sixteenth Century and After* (London, 1965), p. 83; Watkins, *Treatise on Copyholds*, Vol. II, p. 479.

post-medieval records. According to Postan and Titow, widows in manors where assart land was very scarce frequently acted in the thirteenth century as agents of social mobility by transferring their rights in customary tenures *via* second husbands to new families.[20] The use of special formulas or rough music to punish the misdemeanours of errant widows in public ridicule was in itself often an admission that second husbands could not be denied access to their dower.[21] As a rule, however, changes in the incidence and distribution of ancient tenures, the decay of copyholds for lives and the much smaller proportion of the peasantry with rights of inheritance in English land by 1700 altered the social and legal functions of particular, readily identifiable groups such as widows to a marked degree. Practical men like Edward Laurence looked forward to the day when the custom of free bench, confined vestigially to benighted communities in the west, as he alleged, would have departed entirely from England.[22] Even where it survived, adherence to the custom of the particular manor was probably firmer in 1650 than had been the case in 1300, not least because the discretionary powers of the lord were more circumscribed, and aberrations from due form were frowned upon by tenants and lawyers alike. To break inheritance customs, either to favour or to slight a widow, was possible by entail, by will or by conditional surrender to secure a mortgage, all of which could override custom; but the abiding impression from a study of hundreds of seventeenth-century wills is that most countrymen were content not to upset the traditional relationship of widows and children in the inheritance of their property rights. Wills frequently contain clauses in which bequests were made conditional upon dutiful or decent behaviour, but most testators attempted to be fair to all rightful claimants upon their estates, using wills to modify or supplement customs of inheritance. Conditional surrenders to secure mortgages, however, may have been more widely used as a means of favouring widows or, indeed, any members of the family who were to be singled out for preferential treatment. Borrowing on security of land to provide a sum of money was widely employed during the

---

[20] J. Z. Titow, 'Some Differences', pp. 6–11; R. J. Faith, 'Peasant Families and Inheritance Customs in Medieval England', in *Agricultural History Review* 14 (1966), p. 91. Cf. R. H. Hilton, *The English Peasantry in the Later Middle Ages* (Oxford, 1975), pp. 98–101; G. C. Homans, *English Villagers of the Thirteenth Century* (Cambridge, Mass., 1941), *passim*.

[21] See, especially, Thomas Blount, *Fragmenta Antiquitatis . . .*, edited by Joseph Beckwith (York, 1784), pp. 265–6; C. Watkins, *Treatise on Copyholds* Vol. II, p. 559.

[22] Edward Laurence, *The Duty of a Steward to his Lord* (London, 1727), p. 60. Watkins' evidence suggests that the north and east were districts in which dower customers were weak by 1700: Watkins, *Treatise on Copyholds*, Vol. II, pp. 477–576.

seventeenth century, although the use to which the loans were put is not often recorded. Directions in wills occasionally intimate that rights in property were, or were intended to be, mortgaged to supply legacies, including special provision for widows. Whether or, indeed, how often, such arrangements transgressed customary precedents is uncertain, but it is sufficient to know that instruments existed for modifying the descent of copyhold tenures. That this flexibility could be manipulated either to the disadvantage or to the particular benefit of widows subtracts nothing from the premise that the inhibitions imposed by custom upon the widow's autonomy were not insuperable obstacles.

Outside the narrowing circle of copyhold tenures the widow's position was less clearly defined, despite the common law precept that she was entitled to one-third of a husband's estate. Widows so often continued to manage their late husband's business concerns that this in itself was a powerful weapon in their hands. Examples are legion. In at least one cradlehold manor, Mardon in Hursley (Hants.), eleven out of 52 copyholders were women, mostly occupying the land in guardianship; and one of the most troublesome and sharpest tenants of St John's College, Cambridge, in about 1700 was a woman who had outlived two husbands and had repudiated the debts of both. Even when leases or tenancies at will predominated in agriculture widows can be found in estate records carrying on their husband's farming. Some indeed transferred, with the landlord's approval or at his behest, responsibility for their farms to second husbands. In the period after 1670, when good farm tenants were at a premium, estate administrators were often pleased to accept whomsoever they could find. A sturdy man able to manage the capital accumulated by a dead tenant was preferable in many instances to a new and possibly unknown applicant. In the towns many gilds allowed widows to continue in their husband's occupations, and the number of examples discovered by Alice Clark many years ago is impressive. An especially instructive example, though, one hopes, not fully representative of the experience of remarriage among craftsmen's widows, came before the Council in 1639, when Sarah, late wife of John Davys, feltmaker, who had left her well provided, complained about her second husband, Davys' former journeyman, Robert Westwood, who had consumed her livelihood and abused her person.[23] In their access to circulating capital, except in the profes-

[23] See, *inter alia*, Imber, *Abstract of the Custom*; E. P. Thompson, 'The Grid of Inheritance', in Goody, *et al.*, editors, *Family and Inheritance*, p. 346; Clark, *Working Life of Women*, pp. 160ff., 11, 30–4, 167–73 and *passim*; SPD, ccccxxxv, 42 (6.12.1639).

sions, widows were often in an especially favourable position for exploiting their standing as relicts or guardians. Legend instilled the notion in men's minds that the master's widow, even if less desirable than his daughter, was the surest way to success for a servant or poor suitor. Business capital, more often no doubt than real property, might thus be transmitted collaterally, although in no case was this ever simply a matter of course after remarriage, because so many external influences came into play in determining its disposal *post-mortem*. But apart from the issues of business capital or property, widows rich in money, furniture or moveable treasure were no less attractive to fortune hunters than their dowered sisters.

In most cases the widow's marriageability was hedged about with qualifications determined by tensions, overt or latent, between her interests and those of due heirs to patrilineal estates or family wealth. Inheritance through widows by outsiders, i.e. by men who were not members of the husband's family, was resented, and may have been actively resisted, by claimants whose title was by blood, even when no law had been broken. There were, however, marriages which were childless, in some of which the surviving widows enjoyed, by will if not in custom, an absolute title to the conjoint estate. Even if only a fraction of the childless marriages, probably between 10 and 20 per cent of all marriages, resulted in the widow's absolute possession of an inheritance, a degree of social mobility favouring new families ensued in the manner of the medieval transactions described by Titow.

Within the transmission system devised to regulate the material well-being of pre-industrial societies in England and Europe, remarriage was a shift of some complexity. The implications of the widow's marriageability remain elusive, with proof forever constrained by inadequate or contradictory evidence. The provisions which societies, peasant and *petit bourgeois* as much as aristocratic or capitalist, made to account for the various contingencies of widowhood suggest an interpretation in which widows played an important economic role in maintaining the social balance of pre-industrial communities. In this respect remarriage was a current within the main stream of their contribution. As an agency of social mobility it was a secondary, not a primary, influence, but it is an influence which historians have often unjustifiably ignored.

iii

The most prominent economic function of the widow in English rural society between 1500 and 1900 was money lending. The constraints upon her disposal of property did not apply, as a rule, to the use of moveable or liquid assets inherited or accumulated by saving and investment. Every collection of wills and inventories, published or unpublished, contains examples of widows, and spinsters, in possession of sheaves of promissory notes or bonds of debt owing to them at death.[24] Few were *grandes usurières*; indeed, the 'professional' element in money lending in English rural society was lacking, to a large extent, in both medieval and post-medieval times.[25] For the majority of widows or old maids the problem, which was at least partly solved by letting out money at interest, was simply to make the best use for their own well-being of a legacy or of the proceeds which accrued from a dispersal sale, without trenching too deeply into the capital value of their assets. The danger of eating the seed corn was a metaphor universally understood in societies which retained their connections with agriculture. Surprisingly perhaps, the propensity for hoarding was not strongly marked in the mentality of English countrymen in the early modern period. For those men and women who were able to save or who enjoyed the fruits of inheritance or profit-making enterprise – for the 'kulaks', so to speak, of peasant communities – the low ratio of cash in hand to other moveable assets, especially to 'credits', is surely significant. The sock filled with coins or treasures and stuffed in the mattress of the master's bed, alleged by many modern writers to be a characteristic of peasant societies, apparently played little or no part in the enjoyment of wealth in the era which we are here investigating.

Money lending was a heterogeneous activity in societies where the distribution of personal wealth was not heavily concentrated in the hands of very few individuals. Credit was a stem with many branches, and the dividends upon the creditor's willingness to give loans arose from several different instruments or media of lending. For widows from comparatively well-to-do and socially exalted families, aristocratic, mercantile or professional, the investment of dower monies, bequests or other increments to secure a prosperous and trouble-free retirement had long been customary in the arrangement of their financial affairs before the era of government Consolidated Funds and Bank Stock offered a much broader perspective to the

---

[24] See, for example, F. Steer, *Farm and Cottage Inventories of Mid-Essex 1635–1747* (Chelmsford, 1950); M. A. Havinden, *Household and Farm Inventories in Oxfordshire 1550–90*, Oxford Record Society xliv (Oxford, 1965); J. S. Moore, *The Goods and Chattels of our Forefathers* (Chichester, 1976); D. C. Vaisey, *Probate Inventories of Lichfield and District 1568–1680*, Staffordshire Record Society iv/5 (Stafford, 1969).

[25] Cf. M. M. Postan, 'Medieval Agrarian Society in its Prime: England', in M. M. Postan, editor, *Cambridge Economic History of Europe, Vol. I* (Cambridge, 1966), p. 627.

material tranquility of widowhood. By the later eighteenth century, *bourgeoises rentières*, among the most important beneficiaries of the Financial Revolution which transformed British commercial life after about 1680, were numerous, living in genteel retirement in London, in one of the fashionable resorts or even in country towns and villages. The comfortable and secure interest on public stocks was so generally acknowledged in the upper echelons of society that it was not at all uncommon for husbands or their trustees to make provision for widows or other legatees by making the necessary purchase on their behalf, thus taking away from their widows the right or obligation of choosing their own investments. The widowed fund holder, however, was at the apex of the pyramid of female money lenders.

Before the development of an industrial capital market centred in London, widows and the retired rich had to rely upon other species of long-term investment. The social division which is to be observed in the development and diffusion of the institutions of credit is evident in the use to which annuities and a good deal of English mortgage lending were applied in securing periodic incomes. The annuity, which remained popular as a means of supplying retirement income, was mostly confined to the gentry or bourgeois families, which also made use of the funds for similar purposes. As a life-interest, purchased or bequeathed, in the proceeds of a rentier estate or, less often, in the profits of a business or profession, the annuity superficially resembled the institution of the free bench. During the seventeenth century, when annuities were in widespread use, the evolution of a formal market in such life-rents not only predated and influenced the growth of the capital market in the Funds but became a principal means of acquiring loan capital by landowners or entrepreneurs, especially for long-term projects of investment.[26] The transfer of investible funds from widows, spinsters or the retired into productive employment was one of the chief advantages of the system of credit as it developed, at all levels from the provision of annuities to the emission of promissory notes. Similar conditions applied to the use and incidence of mortgage lending. So long as land was held to be the safest of investments, the mortgage, like the annuity, offered the best outlet for funds, short of purchasing the fee simple of property. By the later seventeenth century mortgage lending as much as mortgage borrowing possessed many advantages for both parties to the contract. It could, and

[26] See, for example B. A. Holderness, 'Elizabeth Parkin and her Investments 1733–66 . . .', *Trans. of the Hunter Archaeological Society* (1972), pp. 81–7.

according to Bruce Anderson probably did, form the basis of an institutional capital market through the medium of brokers such as country attorneys, who acted as agents in pecuniary transactions in the same way as they served as conveyancers of legal consultants.[27] The case papers of seventeenth- and eighteenth-century lawyers like David Arkinson of Louth, or Benjamin Smith of Horbling (Lincs.) contain a good deal of general information about activities on behalf of widows concerning trusteeships, mortgage dealing and the nego- tiation of annuities, bonds of debt and other casual investments.[28] Few if any of their clients could be described as peasant women, but the essential character of lending with or without security of land differed little across the social spectrum.

Peasant widows as mortgagees were not uncommon by the seven- teenth century. Because so few mortgage deeds still survive we must rely upon impressions, but from the evidence of wills and inventor- ies, proceedings *re* debts in various courts and an assortment of personal or casual documents, some idea of the variety of lending by village women does emerge quite clearly. According to the evidence as to money lending by 620 widows who lived and died in the seventeenth century, and most of whom lived in East Anglia and Lincolnshire, between 10 and 15 per cent of specific contracts of debt were mortgages. More significantly, the proportion of the principal which was lent upon mortgage amounted to at least one-third, and probably to about two-fifths, by value of the total sum.[29] These findings must be regarded as provisional, and further research, especially in the archives of Chancery and related courts, will doubtless modify the figures, but the pattern, if not the details, cannot be much awry.[30] It recurs too often in the fabric of particular personal estates to be seriously inaccurate.

Especially interesting is the way in which the majority of women money lenders – and be it said, of male ones also – divided the assets which they put out on loan into several distinct categories. As a service to the variety of would-be borrowers, whose particular needs

---

[27] B. L. Anderson, 'Money and the Structure of Credit in the Eighteenth Century', *Business History* 12:2 (1970), pp. 85–101.

[28] Lincolnshire Archives Office: Emeris MSS, Papers of David Arkinson of Louth; *idem*, Smith of Horbling MSS, *passim*; Thos Powell, *The Mistery and Misery of Lending and Borrowing*, Somers Tract, Vol. VII.

[29] Inventories of widows, 1630–1710, in Dioceses of Lincoln (Archdeaconries of Lincoln and Leicester) and Norwich (Archdeaconries of Norwich, Norfolk, Sudbury and Suffolk) at Lincoln, Leicester, Norfolk and Norwich, Ipswich and Bury Record Offices respectively.

[30] For a list of possible sources, see Moore, *Goods and Chattels*, pp. 6–8; A. Conyers, editor, *Wiltshire Extents for Debts*, Wiltshire Record Society xxviii (Devizes, 1973).

often differed considerably, this behaviour could be rationally justified, but the impulse behind the preference for diversity is more
likely to have been the desire to spread risks. We know from the
activities of such acute businesswomen as Lady Mary Heveningham
and Elizabeth Parkin of Sheffield that the 'mixed portfolio' of investments, mortgages, unsecured loans, stocks and shares, among other
species of capital, was commonplace in the larger world of commerce
and landownership.[31] At the village level the different degree of risk,
and perhaps the different returns, which were associated with
mortgages, bonds and bills, pawns or sales credit in itself rather
encouraged diversification by percipient creditors. Unfortunately it
has not been possible to distinguish loans by type except in the case
of mortgages. Pawnbroking perhaps accounted for no more than 5
per cent of widows' money lending, except when it was organized as
a professional venture. The female pawnbroker has left little mark on
history, but she existed, especially in the county towns which
possessed a diverse occupational structure.[32] It was certainty regarded as an avocation, if not as a full-time business, open to, and fit
for, single women with cash in hand to use for stock in trade. Bills
and bonds, promissory notes, notes of hand, 'sales' credit (including
deferred payment for a service rendered) were seldom treated separately except in debt ledgers or in the probate papers of merchants,
shopkeepers and the like, because the chief interest at the time lay in
the standing, not the type, of the debts, that is to say, whether they
were good or bad, 'sperate or desperate'.

There is no clearly marked distinction either in the composition of
their lending or in the general willingness to give credit between men
and women or between peasant and non-peasant communities and
social groups. In the supply of local credit widows were not unique,
nor did they offer a service different from that provided by others
with money to lend. The widespread distribution and social diffusion
of credit in pre-industrial England have been discussed elsewhere. As
part of a larger pattern of social behaviour, moreover, the contribution made by widows has frequently been recognized. In effect, a
proportion, but almost certainly a minority, of widows in rural society
placed a substantial share of their wealth, which was usually larger
than that supplied by any other social group, at the disposal of their
relatives, friends and neighbours. According to the data from 170

[31] See above, p. 424, note 1; J. Hunter, *History and Topography of Ketteringham* (Norwich, 1851), pp. 46–9.
[32] See, for example, R. Brathwaite, *The English Gentleman and English Gentlewoman* (London, 1641), p. 300.

probate inventories concerning widows who died with debts owing to them, 43.5 per cent of their personal estates were comprised debts owed to them.[33] Moreover, 68 per cent (116) left 30 per cent or more of their moveable wealth in the form of credits, and eighteen had over 90 per cent of sometimes considerable valuations as loans or book debts. It should be pointed out that at least as many widows in the same period died without credits to their names, and that they were notably poorer on average than the money lending widows. These findings are confirmed by comparison with data obtained from published collections of probate inventories for different regions of England.[34]

Two problems stand in the way of a simple interpretation of the significance of the widow's function as money lender: first, the question of the destination of loans in village society; secondly, the equally vital question whether widows charged interest upon their bonds, vills and notes; for if they were unable or unwilling to take interest the argument about their use of money lending as a means of earning a livelihood necessarily falls to the ground. Who were the borrowers? The most likely candidates were kinsmen and neighbours, not least because lending beyond the horizon of acquaintance incurred risks which may have been too great for the nerve of comparatively poor folk. Kin certainly expected to be given priority, for the ties of blood, even in districts of nuclear households, were especially potent in the disposition of property. In anthropological terms, indeed, it is possible to describe money lending by widows and single people as an adjunct of family relationships. Within the network of the family, cousins probably rated higher than neighbours in the granting of loans, but whether preferential treatment went beyond the exercise of this choice was a decision not necessarily determined by the priority of blood.

Inventories seldom provide lists of debtors' names, but it is possible from the study of wills to gain an impression of the recipients of widows' largess. Wills confirm that at least one-third of the debtors mentioned by name were acknowledged as kin. Sons and daughters, brothers and sisters easily outnumbered all other categories of affinity, although remoter kin, who were generally indicated by their degree of relationship, did feature as borrowers or debtors. But the

[33] For reference, see above, p. 424, note 1.
[34] Moore, *Goods and Chattels*, p. 23; L. A. Clarkson, *The Pre-Industrial Economy in England 1500–1750* (London, 1971), p. 148 and note 1. M. A. Havinden and Margaret Spufford have found the same phenomenon in their own researches (private communication).

form in which most wills were cast gives little indication of the whole register of an individual's debtors. Indeed, most named debtors appearing in wills were recorded because their debts were forgiven by the testators. They were thus not a typical sample. From a small cluster of administration accounts for intestate estates in mid-seventeenth-century Lincolnshire – 42 in all, and *not* confined to widows – which give the names of debtors, we have found that about 40 per cent could be identified as relatives by blood or marriage. On the other hand, 10–20 per cent do not seem to have lived in the immediate vicinity, although it is improbable, on the face of it, that many of them were settled outside a ten-mile radius of the dead person's residence.[35] Without much more information it is not possible to offer a more complete picture of the flow and direction of rural credit in the pre-industrial period. The most we can claim is that funds available for investment in particular villages were not appropriated exclusively, or indeed predominantly, by kinsmen. There is perhaps a parallel in the economic behaviour of Dissenters both inside and outside their own denominations. Their preference for helping co-religionists was more or less equal in its incidence to the pecuniary demands of kinship upon widows' resources. Quakers and Baptists, for example, lent money and offered sales credit as promiscuously and extensively as conformists among the countrymen who acted as money lenders.

The extensive nature of rural credit and the important part played therein by widows are not in doubt. But what the returns upon loan capital or deferred payment may have been to the lenders in the village community is a question which cannot yet be answered with any certainty. The slow assimilation of the notion of interest among peasants resulted in many expressions of antipathy against 'usury' during the sixteenth and seventeenth centuries, and remained for long an obstacle to the realization of the full opportunities contingent upon money lending, especially when relatives and close friends were involved. Within the circle of family borrowing the demand for interest as a return upon a loan would not have been accepted as normal or just, largely because kin groups retained a general, if not particular, sense of the 'commonness' of property inside the 'family', at least in the face of exogenous claims. In the case of widows or similar vulnerable individuals, the use of loans to accommodate kinsmen or acquaintances in return for a promise, or the expectation,

[35] Lincolnshire Archives Office, Admon. A/cs. 1620–50, collected by the writer several years ago in connection with a different enquiry, the results of which are unpublished.

of a future favour – that is to say, to accumulate good will – is not
uncommon in some non-European peasant societies, and on an *ad hoc*
basis it occurs even now in the patterns of social behaviour observable
in some neighbourhood or family universes. However, there is no
proof that this arrangement was any more customary in seventeenth-
century England than the taking of interest. Harrison observed a new
attitude to interest taking by the 1570s, and the frequent complaints
against usurers in various law courts before 1660 were evidently
addressed to the receipt of *excessive* interest, which from 1560 to 1660
seems to have meant anything over about 10 per cent.[36] Considering
the diversity of social types arraigned for usury it is fair to assume
that the taking of interest at an equitable rate had become well
established, and may indeed have been normal by 1630–50 within
English rural society. Many widows, from gentlewomen downwards,
did rely upon income from money lending to augment their livelihood. It is, indeed, hard to conceive of so well-developed and
sophisticated a system of rural credit without provision being made
for interest of 'use' in its evolution. The rates of interest, except where
they were deemed to be usurious, cannot be discovered in most
cases, but it is unlikely that they were inflexible. Variations between
interest-free and interest-bearing loans, and equally between loans at
rates which were fixed according to the dictates of personal preference, consanguinity or risk are the most probable concomitants of a
system of borrowing and lending which owed little to metropolitan
influences or to the legal constraints of statute, except in their breach.
Peasant lending was a well-tuned instrument by 1650–1700. It was, so
far as we can judge, appropriate to the diversity and volume of needs
and resources of rural liquid assets. As such the contribution of
widows, which remained vital to the health of the system of local
lending throughout the seventeenth and eighteenth centuries, differed in kind not at all from that of the other social or occupational
groups engaged in this considerable traffic in money.

[36] See William Harrison, *Description of England* (London, 1577), pp. 202–3; T. Wilson,
Discourse upon Usury, edited by R. H. Tawney, Classics of Social and Political Science
(London, 1925), Introduction. Usury was an offence dealt with in Quarter Sessions,
in ecclesiastical courts and in certain of the prerogative courts of the Crown before
1640: see, for example J. C. Atkinson, editor, *North Riding Quarter Sessions Records*,
Vol. I, p. 46; F. G. Emmison, editor, *Elizabethan Life: Morals and Church Courts*
(Chelmsford, 1973), pp. 72–4; N. J. Williams, *Early Stuart Tradesmen*, Wiltshire
Archaeological Society xv (Devizes, 1962) *passim*; Clark, *Working Life of Women*, p. 29.

14

Real property, marriage and children: the
evidence from four pre-industrial
communities*

RICHARD WALL

Introduction

If land is to yield a profit or even a livelihood to its possessors[1] it has
to be worked. Whether the labour comes from the family or is hired
depends on the size of the enterprise, the nature of the agricultural
activity (some demanding more labour than others), and the ease
with which non-family labour may be purchased. It would seem to
follow, therefore, that land must influence the composition of the
possessor's household. More precisely it could be said that this
should contain (though not, of course, at all stages of its development) either offspring of working age, or farm servants who live in or
even kin in need of employment or shelter, or one or more of these in
various combinations. If land were the only economic influence on
household forms we might risk a further prediction that possessors of
land would have larger, more complex households with more servants and adult offspring than those without, always assuming of
course that such economic influences are not overridden by cultural
or social-status ones.

However, if we are thinking in terms of English villages, the
influence of non-farming occupation has also to be considered and
has indeed already been observed to have an important bearing on

* I am grateful to Roger Schofield, Tony Wrigley, Peter Laslett and Richard Smith of
the SSRC Cambridge Group for their comments on an earlier version of this chapter.
Keith Snell of King's College, Cambridge, offered valuable advice on the influence of
the administration of the Poor Law on aspects of familial behaviour such as the age
at which children left the parental home. I should also like to thank Margaret Escott
who, as research assistant to the SSRC Cambridge Group, helped prepare the
analysis of land holding patterns in the parish of Binfield.
[1] The word 'possessors' embraces both the owner and the occupier of land, although
in this chapter the focus will be on the latter, whether or not they were the actual
owners (i.e. possessing the freehold).

household structure. Peter Laslett, for example, has demonstrated for pre-industrial England that gentry households more often contained kin and servants than did yeoman households and that the proportion of yeoman households with kin and servants exceeded in turn those of the husbandmen as those of the husbandmen did the tradesmen and craftsmen and so on down the status hierarchy until one reached paupers with the smallest households, fewest servants and fewest kin.[2] Only in the case of resident children was this hierarchical pattern broken. Interestingly, in the light of what was predicted above about the influence of land on the household, labourers, virtually landless, had almost as many resident offspring as the landed yeomen, while tradesmen and craftsmen had rather more. There is a problem, however, in that occupation is closely bound up with the possession of land, particularly of course in the case of yeomen, but affecting in varying degrees other groups as well. In this study, therefore, an attempt will be made to separate the two: to distinguish those tradesmen, craftsmen and labourers who possessed land from those who did not; and, instead of looking simply at the household in general, attention will be focused on those aspects of domestic group structure which land seems most likely to have influenced, namely kin and servants. It is important also to look closely for the presence of offspring of working age, to see if the break in the status hierarchy will be confirmed in the four communities that have been selected for investigation. It is also possible, using a technique not available when the general outline of the pre-industrial English household was drawn in 1972,[3] to consider resident children not in isolation from their family's past history but as a proportion of all surviving offspring. In this way it is possible to counter any differences resulting from any of the groups having fewer resident offspring because fewer had been born as a result of their parents having postponed marriage. The purpose of this particular enquiry is to establish whether labour is shed when not needed and differentially so by the poorer people.

Delayed marriage is an issue that cannot be ignored completely, though, since the possession of land may well have been partly responsible for this most characteristic feature of English pre-industrial demography.[4] Consider for a moment the situation that arises

---

[2] Peter Laslett and Richard Wall, editors, *Household and Family in Past Time* (Cambridge, 1972), p. 154.

[3] The technique is described in detail in R. Wall, 'Age at Leaving Home', *Journal of Family History* 3:2 (1978), pp. 181–202.

[4] Colyton, one of the parishes that has been selected for further analysis here, of course shares this feature: see E. A. Wrigley, 'Family Limitation in Pre-Industrial

when landed wealth has to be transferred between generations. The ideal is that the son should come to maturity at the moment when the father is willing to retire or dies. There may, of course, be no son or too many (and some will eventually have to leave), or they may all be too young. However, it is the situation in which they are too old that is relevant here. If the enterprise could support a retired couple a complex household might result for a time in the form of two co-residing family units. On the other hand the owner might retire from the property. The possibilities of this strategy have not been measured, and it would scarcely be practical on the available evidence to attempt such measurement. But, since the strategy would involve for the older generation the risk of a sudden deterioration in life-style, it would seem more likely that father and son would farm together, the latter without much choice, doing increasingly more of the work and postponing his own marriage until such time as he achieved full economic and personal independence.[5]

Whether this latter strategy was applied in practice we shall try to determine below by examining the marriage data for nineteenth-century Colyton according to the degree of access to land. Since the focus will be on marriage age differences at a point in time, it is not possible to offer direct comment on the Levine–Wrigley debate on the relative importance of economic as opposed to demographic determinants of the pattern of delayed marriage – that is, between de-industrialization and the instinctive prudence of a population reacting to the experience of the mortality crisis of 1645–6.[6] However, since it is also our intention to examine the economic influences on age at marriage (in the form of both landed and occupational differences) it is relevant to set out in what respects the present approach differs from that of Levine. The latter's argument is complex but in essence says that marriage age for women varies with economic circumstances, falling, for example, in response to the development of by-employments in textiles, while marriage age for men is stable (or

England', *Economic History Review* 19 (1966), pp. 82–109. David Levine, in *Family Formation in an Age of Nascent Capitalism* (London, 1977), provides a conflicting interpretation of Colyton's marriage patterns.
[5] This should not be viewed as an inevitable consequence of father and son farming together but could be considered as likely if one of the following circumstances applied:
  1. The father's control of the property gave him the right to disinherit the son.
  2. There was insufficient land to support a further adult and little prospect of obtaining non-agricultural employment.
  3. Marriage with a man still dependent on his father was against the cultural norm.
[6] This is the debate as expressed in Levine's own terms (Levine, *Family Formation*, p. 104) and does not necessarily indicate approval of his argument.

varies less) because the primary influence on male age at marriage is the number of vacant slots in the economic structure of the community.[7] Any economic crisis, so the argument goes, since it increases mortality, provides employment opportunities and permits the marriages of those males who would, other things being equal, have postponed marriage. The implication here is that both land and employment are relatively inflexible in the face of population pressure; that there are only a limited number of land holdings and a limited number of employment opportunities for those who are to remain in the community; and that it is for this reason that control over fertility is alternately tightened and slackened through variations in female marriage age. According to Levine the variation has to be expressed through female age at marriage because men come into their holdings 'early' when mortality is high and the local economy (he assumes) in difficulty but 'late' when mortality is low and there is less need for population restraint.[8]

In the absence of direct evidence on the influence of land and employment on age at marriage, however, these influences are assumed rather than proven. The first objective, therefore, is to establish more clearly than has yet been possible whether a man's occupation or what property he held did in fact influence both his own age at marriage and that of his spouse; this is what is attempted below. Nevertheless, as proof of Levine's argument it falls somewhat short of what is required. Indeed, drawing attention to the differences in male marriage age according to occupation, and to the effect of male occupation on the age at marriage of the bride, underlines the point that any argument which tries to tie marriage age to the number of available slots in the local economy has also to take into consideration any changes in the occupational mix of the community; for these there is some evidence in the case of Colyton.[9]

The questions for this chapter, then, include the influence of occupation as well as land on marriage, household and family; the focus will be on Colyton in the early nineteenth century. At the same time appropriate comparisons will be drawn with other settlements in southern England at varying points in time: Swindon (Wilts.) in the 1690s, Cardington (Beds.) in the 1780s and Binfield (Berks.) in the last

---

[7] Women do not form part of this system, as their economic activity is part-time and conditioned by the vagaries of a national rather than local market for the produce of their industry.

[8] Levine, *Family Formation*, p. 110.

[9] E. A. Wrigley, 'The Changing Occupational Structure of Colyton over Two Centuries', *Local Population Studies* 18 (1977), pp. 9–21.

years of the eighteenth and opening years of the nineteenth century.[10] The sources are the parish registers, lists of inhabitants (enumerators' schedules for the 1841 census in the case of Colyton) and assessments in connection with the land tax and poor rate. These raise a number of problems of definition, particularly as to what should be taken to constitute a land holding, that must now be considered.

i. Land: some definitions

The nature of the impact of the possession of land on the form and structure of the families which own it will depend partly on the quality, type and quantity of that land and partly on the strength of the possessor's rights. In most previous studies the emphasis has been on the ownership of land, yet between the owner and his property may intervene a number of other individuals (lessees, tenants) so that the land itself (as opposed to the profits derived from ownership) becomes scarcely relevant to the immediate circumstances of the family. In addition there is the problem that ownership spans parishes while most sources are parish based. If, on the other hand, one can identify the family which actually works or lives on the land in question,[11] then it is self-evident that the relationship between land and family must be fairly close. This does not mean, of course, that it is a relationship which is constant in form, since the possessor can, in theory, balance land against labour either by releasing or acquiring land so that the amount at his disposal is adjusted to the familial labour supply, or alternatively by hiring such extra labour as is required, in the form of servants or kin. In other words the holder of land may either adjust his family to the land or the land to his family. For both theoretical and practical reasons, therefore, the focus in this chapter is on the occupation of land, and on land holders rather than land owners. Admittedly this does pose some problems when it comes to studying the transmission of land. An individual's own property can be passed to his own descendant, but there can be no guarantee that an individual's rights to the occupation of another man's property will not cease on the death of the current possessor.[12]

---

[10] The extent to which these settlements differed in terms of mobility and occupational structure are set out in Wall, 'Age at Leaving Home', pp. 187–9.

[11] The relationship will, of course, be different according to whether land provides a mere residence or is worked. In the former case the occupation of land implies a certain style of living and might still be associated with a particular family type.

[12] Leases could be for a term of years or for lives, while tenants at will could be turned from their holdings at short notice and claim from the law no more than the safe

The expectation of holding land may still, of course, be passed on. Yet, even if sufficient profit has accrued to permit the heir to take on a similar land holding elsewhere, there would be less motive for parents and children to co-reside and no distinctive household grouping associated with land holding to be observed.

Some account must also be taken of the value and amount of land occupied. Here again the sources create difficulties in that only in the case of Binfield are land holdings described in acres. For the rest, the only information is the amount of land tax paid[13] (land tax and poor rate in the case of Colyton),[14] which bears an uncertain and perhaps even variable relationship both to the amount and to the value of land held. For the most part, therefore, the analysis will be framed around the simple divide of tax payers and non-tax payers. Despite its crudity, this measure, it can be argued, makes good sense in the context of English villagers between the seventeenth and the nineteenth century. Land holding is an inaccurate marker in the societies that concern us here, since it highlights the yeomen but leaves the rest of the village population an undifferentiated mass. What is needed is a measure which distinguishes those who display-ed, if they did not always succeed in passing to the next generation, respectable status, one that was on the right side of the Poor Law.[15] For this, payment or no-payment of tax is probably a good proxy.

It is impossible, however, to ignore entirely the question of how much land is represented by the payment of a given amount of tax. If a man paid ½d under a 1d rate in the poor assessment of Colyton in 1835, or was assessed at 6s in the land tax of Cardington in 1782, it is possible that no land was at issue other than that on which his house stood. To refer to all payers of the poor rate and land tax as landholders could therefore be misleading.[16] For these payers as a

---

harvesting of the crops they had put in the ground: see E. Kerridge, *Agrarian Problems in the Sixteenth Century and After* (London, 1969) p. 87.

[13] For Swindon it is possible to judge the importance of land in the local taxation system as there survives a separate list of the payers of tax on personal estate. In fact only 2 persons paid personal estate tax without having contributed to the land tax, whereas 80 paid land tax and not personal estate (19% of all land tax payers). Middle rank land tax payers (£1–£4) were most likely to pay on personal estate as well (30% did so).

[14] It would considerably have extended the scope of this study to have included information from the Tithe Award for the parish of Colyton, but it is hoped to incorporate this at a later stage.

[15] See E. P. Thompson, 'The Grid of Inheritance: A Comment', in J. R. Goody, J. Thirsk and E. P. Thompson, editors, *Family and Inheritance: Rural Society in Western Europe, 1200–1800* (Cambridge, 1976), p. 359.

[16] It is well known that even those assessed for the land tax included some who were tradesmen and craftsmen and not farmers: see W. B. Stephens, *Sources for English*

Table 14.1. *Number and proportion of families having access to real property*

	Year	Total families	Real property holders	
			No.	%
Settlement				
Swindon	1693	89	41	46
Cardington	1782	175	67	38
Binfield	1790	45	28	62
Colyton	1832*	225	53	24
Colyton	1835†	263	152	58

* Families not resident in Colyton in 1841 or not baptizing their children in Colyton before 1832 are excluded, together with those families whose holding of real property could not be definitely established, i.e. when information on surname, Christian name (when given) and residence in 1832 proved insufficient to identify the same family in the census of 1841.
† The exclusions are on the same lines as those for 1832 (see above), except that families baptizing children after 1832 but before 1835 and still resident in 1841 are included.

group, 'real property holders' seems a more appropriate term, and it is as such that they will be described in the rest of this study. As a definition of those with access to land it no doubt errs on the side of generosity. Even so, as Table 14.1 makes clear, in two of the four parishes chosen for analysis the proportion of families holding real property does not exceed 50 per cent, and even in the case of the other two parishes a substantial minority would appear to have been landless.[17] These percentages should be treated with a certain

Local History (Manchester, 1973), p. 121. As an assessment of the value of land the land tax by 1782 was long out of date, as the original assessment was made in 1692 (see D. B. Grigg, 'The Land Tax Returns', *Agricultural History Review* 11 (1963), pp. 82–94) and included some buildings (Stephens, *Sources*, p. 121). As to the proportion of the population who paid this, it can be derived empirically for the communities surveyed in this study (see Table 14.1). The correlation between the amount paid to the poor rate, and the householder's occupation and status is explored in Table 14.3.

[17] There are two sets of figures for Colyton, showing the effect of moving the basis of property assessment from the land tax to the poor rate. The former does not specify as many properties and on occasion leaves it ambiguous whether or not a property is owner-occupied. However, even the poor rate assessment is not truly comprehensive since a number of smaller properties are described as in the occupation of one man 'and others'. There are also two further points to be borne in mind. First, since the register of entries and the census of 1841 provided the control on the families under observation in 1832 and 1835 (the years of the land tax and poor rate assessments), it is necessary to restrict the analysis to those families who baptized some of their children in Colyton before these dates. The proportion of unmarried persons or persons who had completed their family building before arrival in Colyton and who held real property cannot therefore be determined. Secondly,

amount of caution. What is being measured is the frequency with which families were or were not recorded in taxation registers and it is possible that returns from some parishes may have been less than comprehensive. Rather than the holding of real property, it is the holding of real property subject to tax and so recorded that is being measured. A further qualification arises from the fact that both the Cardington and Binfield lists exclude the most substantial members of the community,[18] the gentry. Nevertheless, there seems no reason to doubt that the degree of real property holding was close to that depicted in Table 14.1.

Table 14.2 adds an occupational dimension to the previous set of figures.[19] As might be expected, real property holding is closely tied to status. Widows apart, labourers are least likely and yeomen most likely to hold land, though precisely how many in each category does seem to have varied considerably from parish to parish. In Swindon, for example, a particularly large gulf existed between the labourers and the tradesmen and craftsmen in the matter of real property holding. Nor were widows always in the same position. In Cardington they were the group least likely to hold real property, whereas in Colyton they held property more frequently than labourers, although not as frequently as tradesmen and craftsmen. The different background of the Colyton widows provides the most likely explanation (the trade–craft element being the most important in the population), but it would require a larger group of widows and some information on the occupations of their former spouses to establish this for certain.

Another seeming puzzle is that not all of the yeomen held land.[20] However, it must be remembered that land holding is only identified

some holders of real property appearing as owner–occupiers could not be found in either the parish registers or the census and may never have resided in Colyton.

18 Lack of detail on certain families and particularly, in Cardington, on farming families means that the more detailed observations rest on a narrower base. The exclusions are specified below as they become relevant to the discussion.

19 Information on occupation is taken from the enumerators' schedules of the 1841 census, supplemented by parish register entries in the case of those few individuals no longer gainfully employed in 1841.

20 The use of the term 'yeomen' in relation to nineteenth-century evidence requires some justification. 16 of the family heads known to have baptized children in Colyton prior to the census were recorded as yeomen by the census enumerator, against 20 who were described as farmers. The difference was one not just of wealth but of 'position' in the parish. 13 of the 16 yeomen had married in Colyton; only 9 of the 20 farmers had done so. Yeomen also paid less in tax than farmers (median assessment 2s 7d against 7s 0¾d, No. = 7,11). However, the two groups were too small to be analysed separately. Keith Snell, in a personal communication, has drawn my attention to the fact that there is considerable variation between one area

Table 14.2. *Number and proportion of families with access to real property by occupation and status**

	Cardington			Swindon			Colyton		
	Real property holders			Real property holders			Real property holders		
	No.		%	No.		%	No.		%
Occupation or status									
Yeoman and farmers	20	16	80	5	3	—	27	21	74
Tradesmen and craftsmen	23	13	56	37	23	62	104	73	70
Labourers	99	27	27	33	5	15	68	26	38
Widows	24	5	21		—		47	22	47

* Excludes unclassifiable occupations.

at one point in time and occupation at another.[21] Although care has been taken to include all those families who were probably resident in the parish at the time of the assessment, there is always the possibility that some may have changed occupations in the intervening period or had worked land without being its formal occupier. The existence of such an element in the life-cycle of the yeoman family is deserving of special attention. Presence in the parish was defined by marriage or the baptism of children in the parish prior to assessment day and no evidence of outward mobility. It follows, therefore, that as many as 20 per cent of yeomen had established families before they were registered as parish land holders. It has to be borne in mind that it cannot be claimed that these yeomen had no connection with property at the time of the assessments, since they may have occupied land outside the parish or worked the lands of others within it. Nevertheless, whichever of these two possibilities is closer to the truth the implication is that marriage for those who were or ultimately became yeomen was certainly not always conditioned by the necessity of waiting for a particular holding to fall vacant.

In Table 14.2, owing to a small number of cases, it is only possible to consider occupations within a few very broad categories. Using the

and another in the meaning to be attached to the term 'yeoman'. In some cases it might be used of a man with no real property and no recent history of renting land or even applied simultaneously with 'labourer' to the same man.

[21] 1835 against 1841 (but see above, note 20). There is also the possibility of evasion, although certainly nothing on the scale of the cases cited by Grigg, 'Land Tax Returns', p. 63.

Table 14.3. *Colyton: level of poor rate assessment* by occupation and status of family head*

	No payment	Under 1	1–2	2–4	5–11	12+	Total	% no payment
Occupation or status								
Yeomen and farmers	6	0	0	0	1	20	27	22
Dealing	3	1	2	9	2	3	20	15
Industry	20	12	7	4	2	4	49	41
Building	8	15	4	5	1	2	35	23
Labourers	42	19	5	2	0	0	68	62
Widows	25	9	5	5	0	3	47	53
Miscellaneous	7	2	2	3	0	3	17	41
Total	111	58	25	28	6	35	263	42
With servants	7	5	5	6	2	23	48	
%	6	9	20	21	33	66	18	

* Expressed in terms of the number of pennies payable for a rate of one penny in the pound.

occupational groupings adopted by Wrigley,[22] a finer occupational break-down can be attempted for the larger Colyton population (Table 14.3) as a partial check on the earlier analysis. One result is the identification of another group in the population (those with industrial occupations) with a relatively large number of individuals not holding real property. Most interest, however, centres on the distribution of payments within occupational groups.[23] Both yeomen and labourers emerge as distinct groups, whereas those involved in dealing, industry and building (the trade–craft group of Table 14.2) are more heterogeneous, including a number of major real property holders and, in the case of dealers, an absence of many making small payments. To group all tradesmen and craftsmen together as in Table 14.2 does, therefore, result in a certain amount of 'error'. Yet it has to be tolerated, given that any more refined grouping of occupations simply results in categories containing only a handful of cases.

The opportunity has also been taken of measuring the proportion of households with servants (a popular measure of social status when no other information is available) against the amount of the assess-

---

[22] For the logic behind these groups and for a list of all occupations in Colyton in 1851 by group, see E. A. Wrigley, 'Age at Marriage in Early Modern England', paper presented to XIIIth International Congress of Genealogical and Heraldic Science, 1976.

[23] Sums payable on properties in the occupation of more than one person have been arbitrarily divided by the number of payers.

ment. The final row of figures in Table 14.3 proves that the proportion of households with servants does indeed rise with the level of the assessment, although the rise is uneven, with two major steps in the distribution – first for those who paid 1d as opposed to $\frac{1}{2}$d and secondly for those who paid over 1s.[24] In detail the effect is to emphasize again the labourer and yeoman groups at the opposite ends of the economic spectrum, but the important general point is the confirmation of the relevance of tax payment to an investigation of differences in social structure.

ii. Property and parenthood

Elsewhere I have attempted to establish the processes governing the separation of children from their parents in these and some present-day English[25] settlements. Factors which influenced the timing of departure included the marital status and occupation of the parent, the sex of the child and even his or her place in the birth order. Separation of parent and child was deemed to have come late with relatively few leaving the parental home before the age of fifteen. Many stayed beyond puberty, rendering unlikely those explanations which have argued that a fear of sexual attraction caused parents to place their children in the households of others. The additional information now available on real property holding facilitates the discussion of other issues. One object will be to see whether there is any tendency for those with real property to keep at least one child over fifteen at home.[26] This might be construed as an attempt to identify a resident heir or heiress, but there could be another aspect to this. Since the heir has to be resident (for the purpose of this study, that is) it might follow that the property is capable of supporting an additional adult and that any difference between the holders of real property and others in the retention of the services of one child could

[24] The use of steps as markers rather than to distinguish between those who paid and those who did not deserves some consideration. Their use was considered impractical for this population because of the small number of cases that would be separated out.

[25] Wall, 'Age at Leaving Home'.

[26] 15 is admittedly an arbitrary cut-off point and for the purposes in hand a somewhat higher age, one set at the point at which children would be expected to marry, had certain attractions. In setting it as low as 15 regard has been paid to 3 considerations. First, 15 is well below the age at which maximum earning potential was usually achieved (below, note 47). Secondly, setting the age at 15 captured any tendency to delay outward movement from the parental home as well as permanent residence. Thirdly, there would again be only a small number of cases (because more parents would have died) if choice fell on a higher age.

therefore be taken as a measure of the support the family derived from the occupation of property.[27]

Yet in fact it cannot be known that a child continued to reside because the family had access to property. There might be some other factor, parental occupation for example, which gave the family both real property and a motive for delaying the separation of parent and child. Therefore, wherever possible, the presence of children in the homes of the holders and non-holders of real property has to be examined in the light of the father's occupations. However, there may indeed be other factors that cannot be controlled, and all that can be established is whether there is an association between children staying at home and the possession of real property. The question of cause has to come later.

A glance at Tables 14.4 and 14.5, though, is sufficient to show that real property has virtually no impact on the residential patterns of children. Such differences as there are in favour of more of the propertied keeping a child at home are completely overshadowed by differences in patterns between parishes. The latter are so great that it is probably impossible to make any generalizations about the pattern of movement. In Cardington, for example, the majority of families let all sons over fifteen leave home, though most, though not all, retained the services of a daughter. On the other hand, the pattern in Binfield was almost the reverse, two-thirds of the families losing all daughters and considerably fewer losing all sons. The explanation clearly does not lie with real property or its absence. Rather it would seem that the explanation will be found in the nature of the local employment situation,[28] in Cardington a lack of employment opportunities for males coupled with domestic industry for females in lace making and linen and jersey spinning, and in Binfield perhaps service opportunities for girls in the households of farmers and gentry.

It might also be argued that the figures indicate the extent to which children established an independent existence prior to their parents' death. Such a claim, however, could only be made subject to two qualifications. The first is that only those children over fifteen are considered; some of the families without resident offspring over fifteen may have had younger offspring still at home. Secondly, it has been demonstrated to date only that children were away from home, not that they had achieved full economic independence. If marriage is

[27] See above, note 12.
[28] Wall, 'Age at Leaving Home', p. 195. The building of a workhouse as early as 1757 is also suggestive of considerable male unemployment, according to Keith Snell.

Table 14.4. *Residence patterns of sons 15+ by access to real property*

	Holding real property			No real property		
	At least 1 son 15+	At least 1 son 15+ resident		At least 1 son 15+	At least 1 son 15+ resident	
		No.	%		No.	%
Settlement						
Cardington	18	3	17	28	6	21
Binfield	24	13	54	14	6	43
Colyton	100	52	52	53	26	49

Table 14.5. *Residence patterns of daughters 15+ by access to real property*

	Holding real property			No real property		
	At least 1 dau. 15+	At least 1 dau. 15+ resident		At least 1 dau. 15+	At least 1 dau. 15+ resident	
		No.	%		No.	%
Settlement						
Cardington	23	16	70	39	24	62
Binfield	26	9	35	13	4	31
Colyton	86	52	60	55	27	49

taken to represent such independence,[29] then at Cardington (the only parish for which there is information available on the marital status of all offspring) in 1782 this had been achieved by 40 per cent of all sons then over fifteen and by 30 per cent of daughters, and by 80 per cent of sons and 66 per cent of daughters then over the age of 25.[30] It is particularly interesting that more sons than daughters married during

[29] It is only being claimed here that marriage represents one measure of such independence, not the sole one. As representing for most a permanent commitment to a new family and household, marriage clearly has some status as an indicator, but it may be noted that there were some married children living with their parents (3% of all married sons and 12% of all married daughters). Consideration might also be given to the issue of whether independence from parents was achieved when a child left home and worked as a labourer. The problem is to know where this is different from leaving home to live as a farm servant in the household of a stranger, a position from which many children are known to have returned home at periodic intervals.

[30] Calculated from R. S. Schofield, 'Age Specific Mobility in an Eighteenth Century Rural English Parish', *Annales de démographie historique* (1970), p. 265. These percentages should not be confused with those in Table 14.12, which yield equivalent percentages of marriages traced for all sons and daughters listed in 1782 (33%).

their parents' life-time, and it will be necessary to return to this issue when considering the question of differences in age at first marriage in Cardington.

One other objection can be made to the figures in Tables 14.4 and 14.5, and that is the absence of any reference to occupation. Unfortunately the Binfield and Cardington populations are too small and not sufficiently diverse to permit such a detailed analysis, and Tables 14.6 and 14.7 have to be restricted to Colyton. The following conclusions seem in order. First it can be said again that in Colyton the possession of real property – subject to a couple of exceptions which will be considered in a moment – makes almost no difference as to whether the services of a son or daughter are retained. The crucial influence governing the separation of children from the parental home is parental occupation,[31] with yeomen most likely to hold onto a child and labourers least. The sex of child was also important, though less so than in the parishes of Cardington and Binfield. Tradesmen and craftsmen seem to have been more inclined to retain a daughter than a son and it would be difficult to single out any occupational group as expressing a clear preference for a son over a daughter.[32] Real property as a factor influencing this process, cannot be dismissed entirely – first because yeomen, with the distinctive pattern of keeping at least one child at home, were the major real property holders (see Table 14.3), and secondly because of a surprising finding that fewer labourers with property retained a son than labourers without real property. This latter result contradicts the initial hypothesis that the possession of real property, if it has any influence at all on the retention of children at home, would be in the direction of more rather than fewer children staying on in the parental household.[33] One possibility is that these labourers with real property

[31] Though the interrelationship between the possession of real property and the status of yeomen has to be noted, and a less direct relationship might operate in the case of other occupational groups – for example if the possession of real property led to the development of cottage industry. This suggestion was put to me by Keith Snell, although the holding of real property would seem here to be more of a liability than an asset.

[32] If the numbers at issue had permitted an examination of the process of leaving home for individual occupations, it is possible that the preferential retention of the services of a child of a particular sex might have been determined: for example, blacksmiths or carpenters keeping sons at home.

[33] It could be argued that these parents had to send their children away as they of all groups were most in need of the income. Note that, if this meant that children left home earlier than they would otherwise have done, property holding is again a liability (cf. above, note 32). However, it is open to doubt whether a family would in all circumstances be better off if their children lived elsewhere. Admittedly the parents would not in such circumstances have to bear the cost of maintenance, but if

Table 14.6. *Colyton: residence patterns of sons 15+ by access to real property and occupation or status of parent*

	Holding real property			No real property		
	At least 1 son 15+	At least 1 son 15+ resident		At least 1 son 15+	At least 1 son 15+ resident	
		No.	%		No.	%
Occupation or status						
Yeomen and farmers	18	15	83	—	—	—
Tradesmen and craftsmen	45	22	49	11	6	54
Labourers	17	5	29	20	9	45
Widows	14	7	50	17	8	47

were the keenest to push their sons into service positions with yeomen or others. The principal fact to note, however, is the low *N* values in Table 14.6, and it would be rash to speculate too much on what might be no more than a quirk in the figures produced by a small number of cases.

Attention so far has been focused on the retention of the services of one child after the age of fifteen. It may be argued, however, that the virtue of possessing real property was that it gave a livelihood (and conceivably employment) to those age groups who would otherwise be forced into positions of domestic and farm servants in the household of others. This possibility is considered in Table 14.8 from which it emerges yet again that real property has only a minimal impact on the pattern of familial behaviour. It may be noted that focusing on all children between ten and nineteen, rather than on families with at least one child over fifteen, reverses the relationship (discussed at length above) between real property and residence patterns for labourers, since those without real property are the least likely to have had sons of this age at home. Perhaps the most surprising result, though, is that yeomen should themselves have lost almost as many children as other occupational groups just at an age at which one would anticipate their offspring becoming valued

the child was in lodgings rather than service then the costs still had to be met. It would also be necessary for the absent child to remit to the parents sufficient earnings to balance what he would have contributed over and above the costs of his maintenance had he remained at home and worked on or off the property.

Table 14.7. *Colyton: residence patterns of daughters 15+ by access to real property and occupation or status of parent*

	Holding real property			No real property		
	At least 1 dau. 15+	At least 1 dau. 15+ resident		At least 1 dau. 15+	At least 1 dau. 15+ resident	
		No.	%		No.	%
Occupation or status						
Yeomen and farmers	16	12	75			
Tradesmen and craftsmen	38	24	63	13	9	69
Labourers	16	9	56	18	8	44
Widows	13	6	46	18	7	39

Table 14.8. *Colyton: residence patterns of children 10–19 by occupation of father and access to real property**

	Sons						Daughters					
	Holding real property			No real property			Holding real property			No real property		
	No.	Resident		No.	Resident		No.	Resident		No.	Resident	
		No.	%		No.	%		No.	%		No.	%
Father's occupation												
Tradesmen–craftsmen	47	36	76	12	9	75	45	33	73	26	23	88
Labourers	14	10	71	24	12	50	24	15	62	17	11	65
Yeomen and farmers	19	15	79	—	—	—	25	16	64	—	—	—

* Table 14.8 differs from Tables 14.4–14.7 in considering all children in the relevant category as opposed to families with one or more children.

auxiliaries on the farm. Almost all of this group would have been unmarried and may be presumed (unless in residential schools, which seems unlikely) to be in subordinate positions in the households of others, either as servants or as kin. It is impossible to be more precise about this because absence from the parental home, particularly for service, often meant leaving the parish. It is not possible, therefore, to undertake a detailed discussion of how farmers balanced their labour force. Nevertheless the familial context to this movement is clear enough. The yeoman–farmer allowed offspring to go because he had other children to call upon and could always recoup his 'losses' by employing living-in farm servants.[34]

iii. Household structure

Property, therefore, is of limited importance for the timing of the departure of children from the parental home. Its importance in relation to household structure (the co-resident domestic group as opposed to the 'biological' family) is at least in one sense clearer, since it has already been demonstrated that the occupation of real property was positively associated with the keeping of servants, domestic or otherwise. The intention now is to investigate whether it equally determines the presence in the household of kin, sometimes taken to be substitutes for servants. First, however, it is necessary to set out the structure of the household according to the occupation of the head (Table 14.9), since only a handful of studies have to date investigated household structure in the nineteenth century in relation to social and occupational status.[35] The categories used to define structures are a simplified version of those recommended in Laslett and Wall (1972, p. 31). The basic unit is that of the co-resident familial unit, be it married couple alone or married couple, widower or widow with children. These, when accompanied by a relative outside the nuclear base, form extended or even multiple households (the latter if two or more of these basic units co-reside). The remaining categories, solitaries and non-family, allow for persons living on their own or as members of a group not constituting a familial group. A word of caution, however, is needed about this table and the succeeding one. In order to comprehend structures, evidence is needed on relationship to the head of the household, and since the 1841 census, as is well known, does not give this information, relationships have to be inferred from links between surname groups established through comparing households in the census with families in the reconstitution. Caution is recommended not so much because errors may have

[34] One suggestion put to me by Keith Snell is that a yeoman had to balance the advantages of employing young single children (his own) against the risk of leaving unemployed married labourers who would raise the poor rates he was paying. This hypothesis is particularly difficult to test as even from the enumerators' schedules for the 1851 census it is only possible to discover how many resident and non-resident labourers were employed by particular farmers, and not who these farmers employed. Personally I would doubt whether the movement from the parental home of farmers' children was principally dictated by considerations about the level of poor rates. A much more likely factor in my opinion is the need for these children to experience work on other types of farm.

[35] See M. Anderson, *Family Structure in Nineteenth Century Lancashire* (Cambridge, 1971); A. Armstrong, *Stability and Change in an English County Town: A Social Study of York, 1801–1851* (Cambridge, 1974).

Table 14.9. *Colyton: household structure in 1841 by occupation or status of family head**

Category	Yeoman	Dealing	Industry	Building	Labourer	Misc.†
1. Solitaries	1	1	2	1	2	8
2. No family	2	0	3	0	1	2
3a. Married couple	3	2	8	3	5	9
b. Married couple+child(ren)	22	11	35	24	44	4
c. Widower+child(ren)	0	0	1	1	3	0
d. Widow+child(ren)	0	3	3	1	5	4
All simple family households (type 3)	25	16	47	29	57	17
4. Extended	6	2	7	3	14	4
5. Multiple	1	1	3	0	3	0
6. Unidentifiable	0	0	0	0	1	1
Total	35	20	62	34	78	32
Households complex (types 4–5) (%)	20	15	16	12	23	16

* As in 1841 except for those no longer gainfully employed (see note 20); the widows who are classed wherever possible according to the occupation of their late husband.
† Includes, besides households whose heads' occupations could not be classified, female-headed households where the occupation of late husband could not be traced in the registers. Excludes all families not married in Colyton.

been made with the linkages, although doubtless some relatives have escaped detection, but because it was necessary to restrict analysis to the more stable elements in the community – those who had married in Colyton.[36] It is therefore at some risk that figures on household structure are compared with those derived for other, complete populations.

For a study of inter-occupational differences in household structure they are more acceptable, although, representing those known to have been married, they cannot fully indicate the extent to which people with particular occupations lived on their own. Most reliance, therefore, should rest on the proportion of households described as complex (extended and multiple combined). These, as Table 14.9 makes abundantly clear, are in fact to be found in all occupational groups, and there is no more than a slight indication that labourers and yeomen might have more complex households than other groups.

[36] Marriage was insisted upon because of the need to identify resident kin of the wife. These households represented 55% of the 472 households resident in Colyton in 1841. Households where the head had married elsewhere constituted 28%, and the remainder (17%) could not be matched with any family reconstitution form in 1841. This last category includes not only the transients and the never-married but those, married or unmarried, who could only be located on the Family Reconstitution Form of their parents (i.e. they had been baptized in the parish), or who had been married or had baptized children in Colyton only after 1841.

The proportion of households that are complex is by no means negligible, bearing in mind that we are looking at a cross-section of households over the life-cycle and that some could be at a stage where the presence of kin is unlikely. The presence of kin in nineteenth-century communities, however, has been discussed before. What has not received sufficient attention is the extent to which complex households occur throughout the social spectrum. In this English community, at any rate, occupation had little influence on household composition, by contrast to its role in the nuclear family, where it helped to determine the timing of the separation of parent and child. Obligations to kin were obviously of a different kind and would be met regardless of occupation. This is not to say that obligations to kin would be met regardless of the economics of the situation, since the taking in of kin might still have been prompted by either the needs of the kin or those of the host household. Only the latter hypothesis, if true, would mean that occupation, as it has been defined in this study, was not an effective measure of financial circumstance.

The matter can be pursued further within a broader occupational framework through a consideration of whether the possession of real property influences the proportion of complex households. The results (Table 14.10) are inconclusive, although this may be because of the very small number of cases in some of the categories, particularly for labourers holding real property. Among tradesmen and craftsmen, those without real property were more likely than those holding real property to take in kin. Labourers, on the other hand, were in a very different situation. Those labourers who had real property emerge as the group most likely to have lived in complex households. Very much a minority, it must be emphasized, in the population of nineteenth-century Colyton, they come closest to the concept of a peasant group which, if relevant at all in English villages of this date, would be best applied to those who worked for others but still had access to land. It is interesting, therefore, that they of all the occupational categories should emerge as most closely associated with more complex forms of the household, with proportions of a similar order to that identified for some peasant populations in mainland Europe.[37]

[37] For the households of European 'peasants', see, for example, Berkner on Heidenreichsten (L. K. Berkner, 'The Stem Family and the Development Cycle of the Peasant Household: An Eighteenth Century Austrian Example', *American Historical Review* 77 (1972), pp. 398–418; see especially Table 3, which shows a rise in the percentage of extended households according to the value of the farm). See also E. Todd, 'Seven Peasant Communities in Pre-Industrial Europe: A Comparative Study

Table 14.10. *Colyton: household structure in 1841 by occupation or status of family head and access to real property in 1835*

	Yeoman	Tradesmen and craftsmen		Labourers		Total
		Holding real property	No real property	Holding real property	No real property	
Category						
1. Solitaries	1	3	0	0	1	5
2. No family	2	1	0	0	0	3
3a. Married couple	1	6	1	1	2	11
b. Married couple +child(ren)	18	31	21	10	18	98
c. Widower +child(ren)	1	1	0	1	1	4
d. Widow +child(ren)	0	3	3	0	5	11
All simple family households (type 3)	20	41	25	12	26	124
4. Extended	4	6	3	6	4	23
5. Multiple	1	2	0	1	1	5
6. Unidentifiable	0	0	0	0	0	0
Total*	28	53	28	19	32	160
Households complex (types 4–5) (%)	18	6	11	37	16	18

* Totals differ from those in Table 14.9 because they exclude families formed after 1835 and whose property holding could not be definitely established.

iv. Marriage and property in Colyton and Cardington

It would be impossible to conclude this investigation of the relationship between property and familial and household structures without giving some consideration to the question of the influence of

of French, Italian and Swedish Rural Parishes in the Eighteenth and Early Nineteenth Centuries', unpublished University of Cambridge Ph.D. thesis, 1976, pp. 42–4 and 60–74. The comparison between Colyton labourers with real property and European 'peasants' must not be pushed too far because of differences in the size and type of land held and possible differences in familial patterns. For example, as far as the latter is concerned, labourers in Colyton who held real property were clearly no more inclined to keep sons at home than were labourers without real property (see above, Table 14.4). It might be noted also that it is not entirely clear what constitutes an extended household in Berkner's terminology.

the possession of property on the age at marriage of both men and women. The timing of marriage governs the pace of household formation in all societies, where marriage entails for most a new household and determines, together with service patterns (if we discount differences in infant and child mortality), the number of children who remain with their parents into their twenties. Marriage, however, is not an easy topic to investigate because a large proportion of marriages take place in a parish other than that of birth. Searching other registers for these marriages is a rather fruitless exercise, since without reconstitutions of all the parishes in the area so many couples cannot be successfully identified. Of necessity, therefore, attention has to be focused on those couples who married in the same parish as their residence at the time of the census. This is to risk the introduction of all sorts of biases in the direction of more stable elements in the community. It can be plausibly argued, for example, that, if the possession of real property is of any significance at all, and particularly if it is the dominant ideology, it should tie people to the land and give them less reason for moving from parish to parish and less chance of finding a marriage partner there. Certain occupations, on the other hand, might encourage mobility, since, by their very nature, they brought people into contact with outsiders. Table 14.11 (on Colyton) has to be examined, then, first for any occupational bias that might arise from our reliance on those who married in the parish, and secondly for any sign that the propertied element within each occupational group was less mobile than the non-propertied. In fact, neither factor appears likely to have had a significant impact on results derived from the analysis of ages at marriage within a single parish.[38] The only group to show any above-average tendency to have married in another parish are dealers; nor is there any firm evidence that those who had married elsewhere were in any sense richer (as measured by the possession of property) than those who had married in Colyton.[39]

The problems of analysing age at marriage in Cardington are a little

---

[38] A different test led Tony Wrigley to a similar conclusion. For 10 parishes whose registers had been reconstituted he was able to show that there was no significant difference in the marriage age of the bride between when the groom was foreign to the parish and when he was not. Wrigley, 'Age at Marriage', Table 4, p. 12.

[39] There might conceivably be something to be made of the fact that slightly more from the industrial and building groups who married locally were not propertied, whereas of the labourers and widows it was those who had married elsewhere who were inclined to be without property. However, the number of cases of which these results are based is very small and it would be unwise to presume too much upon them. See also above, note 21, for differences between yeomen and farmers.

Table 14.11. *Colyton: access to real property by marital endogamy,*
*occupation and status**

	No.	Married in Colyton (%)	Married in Colyton and no real property (%)	Not married in Colyton and no real property (%)
Occupation or status				
Yeomen and farmers	31	61	22	22
Dealing	22	54	10	20
Industry	57	68	42	38
Building	39	64	24	20
Labourers	80	65	58	66
Widows	50	72	48	64
Miscellaneous	18	39	28	50
Total	297	64	40	46

* Excludes families formed after 1836, families not traced to a family reconstitution form, and, in the case of the last two columns, families whose holding of real property could not be definitely established. The population in observation for the purposes of the latter calculations is the same as in Tables 14.1–14.3, rather than offspring of such families (as in Table 14.12). Families not traced to a reconstitution form have to be excluded because there is no direct evidence on marital status in the 1841 enumerators' schedules.

different, first because David Baker has successfully traced many of the marriages of Cardington inhabitants in the registers of surrounding parishes, and secondly because it is intended to study the marriages of offspring as well as of parents. Even for the latter the analysis of marriage can be more comprehensive than in the case of Colyton. According to figures in Baker's study,[40] 88 per cent of the marriages of labourers could be traced, 63 per cent of those involving tradesmen and craftsmen and 36 per cent of those of farmers. The failure to locate so many of the marriages of farmers reflects the lack of detail in the list on farming families; they have therefore been excluded from the analysis of marriage age. Baker also searched other registers for the marriages of children born before 1782. Considerably fewer of these were traced, possibly because the search was less thorough,[41] but principally, one suspects, because offspring may in

[40] D. Baker, 'The Inhabitants of Cardington in 1782', *Bedfordshire Historical Record Society* 52 (1973), p. 19.

[41] *Ibid.*, p. 18. The method is not described, but the fact that place of birth was given for both parents considerably eased the path towards identifying the place of marriage.

Table 14.12. *Cardington: number and percentage of offspring whose marriages could be traced by sex, by occupation of father and by access to real property*

	Married sons				Married daughters			
	Holding real property		No real property		Holding real property		No real property	
	No.	%	No.	%	No.	%	No.	%
Occupation of father								
Farmers	48	23	—	—	31	19	—	—
Tradesmen + Craftsmen	16	31	24	21	22	36	25	28
Labourers	51	41	95	28	44	27	93	34

general have been more mobile than their parents as the surplus of each rural generation found its way to the towns.

It might be anticipated, therefore, that the marriage patterns of the two generations would differ in significant respects – as, indeed, they might do if the marriages of all offspring could be traced. However, as Table 14.12 makes clear, only a minority of marriages in the offspring generation were located. The comparison, then – and for the present purpose it is a fitting one – is between locally married offspring and their parents. In Table 14.12 the opportunity has also been taken to see whether the possession of real property made any difference as to whether marriage was celebrated locally. Here, in contrast with what was observed in Colyton for the parental generation, there is some evidence to suggest that parental real property was associated with local marriage for offspring, daughters of labourers excepted.[42] One final point to note from the table is the low proportion of daughters' marriages that were traced – low, that is, when it is considered that many, unlikely their brothers, were working at home and might have been expected to marry locally.[43] This, however, is a point best

For children, place of residence was given in the list for those married before 1782, but no such clue, of course, was available for those still unmarried at the time of the list.

[42] And assuming also that further information on farmers, or a more thorough search would have led to the identification of more marriages.

[43] The percentages in Table 14.12 differ little from those derived for all children over 15 married by 1782 (see above). This similarity is purely coincidental. The latter show how many were married over a set age in a particular year, while the former are the outcome of an attempt to trace the marriages of all offspring over a much longer time span.

considered once we have looked more closely at the ages at which sons and daughters married.

v. Age at first marriage

Real property for a number of reasons should be important in determining age at marriage. Marriage involved not only a commitment to a new biological unit (the family) but in most cases a new residential unit (the household), and the expense had to be met from past savings and future prospects. Real property, it could be argued, gave an individual an additional reserve and a greater security. In this way it facilitated savings and may be thought to have permitted early marriage. However, it was not infinitely divisible. In larger families and on smaller properties some, if not all, of the offspring were in a situation akin to that of the landless. Nevertheless, even in these circumstances parental real property may have encouraged expectations of a life-style which offspring would wish to emulate both for its own sake and to avoid losing status in relation to parents and siblings. Some of the offspring of propertied parents might therefore have to postpone marriage in order to accumulate sufficient wherewithal to establish their own family at a level on a par with that to which they were accustomed. Since to these it would also be necessary to add the immediate inheritors of real property (landed or otherwise) who could not establish an independent economic existence until their parents either formally retired and resigned their prime interest in the property or died, it is clear that a sizeable section of the propertied might have to delay marriage.

It must also be anticipated, of course, that the degree of delay would vary with individual circumstances (according to birth order for example) and the amount and type of parental property involved. The overall impact of real property on age at first marriage is therefore not likely to be uniform, yet unfortunately the small size of village populations will not permit the detailed break-down of marriages by age, occupation, time period[44] and family circumstances that theory requires. Indeed, only a simple distinction can be drawn between the ages at marriage of the propertied and the propertyless. Before we turn to the data, two further points need to be made. Up to the present the argument has been couched mainly in terms of the effect of real property on male marriage age. What happened to female

---

[44] A preliminary analysis was made of the patterns as they affected labourers and tradesmen and craftsmen in Colyton. It suggested that there could have been a trend towards earlier marriage for women between 1800 and 1835.

marriage age would depend not only on the financial contribution women (or their families) were expected to make towards the establishment of the new household but also on the extent to which men compensated for their own late marriage by choosing women somewhat younger than themselves. Secondly, there is the position of those without real property to consider. It would be naive to think of the absence of the prudential restraint of real property as leading naturally and inevitably to a universal early age at marriage. Any slackening in the demand for labour or difficulties over accommodation for new households reduces the number of marriages that are contracted. This effect is usually only temporary. In 'good times' the marriage rate picks up again and may peak as many of the delayed marriages are celebrated. The point, however, is this: in times of hardship labourers, in common with most other elements in village society, may have postponed marriage.[45] Nevertheless the fact that they achieved maximum earning power at an early age provided a good general incentive to early marriage.[46]

We are able, therefore, to approach with an open mind the marriage data that have been assembled for the two villages of Cardington and Colyton. There might be good reason for those with property to marry relatively late and those without to marry relatively early. For those without real property there might be a peak period of marriage following the achievement of maximum earnings; the only certainty would seem to be a widely spread distribution of individual ages at marriage, especially on the part of the propertied, this reflecting the variety of individual circumstances. Attention has also already been drawn to the differing patterns that can be expected

---

[45] Even Malthus, for example, argued that labourers would postpone marriage if not corrupted by the poor law (T. R. Malthus, *An Essay on the Principle of Population* (1798), edited by A. Flew (London, 1970), pp. 91–7). The latter point was picked up in post-1834 reports on the poor, which emphasized that one effect of the poor law was to encourage the marriage of bachelors as married men received priority in employment.

[46] Labourers seem to have reached their maximum earning power by the age of 20. This at least is the model age of maximum adult earning power in the wage rates of farm servants set by Quarter Sessions between 1503 and 1724 (see A. Kussmaul, *Servants in Husbandry in Early Modern England*, unpublished Toronto Ph.D. thesis, 1978, p. 286). Analysis of the figures on the probable weekly earnings of labourers in the Dorset parish of Corfe Castle in 1790 also suggests that 20 is the age at which adult wages were generally received. (Information from manuscript analysis in the Library of the SSRC Cambridge Group.) Receipt of these wages does not automatically mean of course that they were able to establish a home of their own: for that a period of saving would be necessary. It does not follow, however, that because labourers earned less than tradesmen and craftsmen it would necessarily take them longer to establish new homes, as their expectations about these homes might be such that they could be obtained at less cost.

from looking at the marriages of parents and offspring respectively. When working on the marriage age of parents it has to be recognized that here the direction of the initial hypotheses about property is reversed, for these parents were married before they were assessed for the poor rate in 1835. In other words we could be looking at the effect of marriage age on real property and not the reverse. The word 'could' is used advisedly. Although it is not possible to tell how much real property the parents had and how it governed the marriage choices of the parental generation, it can be determined whether couples who married early differed from those who married late in the matter of whether there was any real property in their possession after marriage. The hypothesis that can be tested is close, but not exactly equivalent, to that set out above. We are looking here for an association between real property and marriage age, in the expectation that those without real property will have married relatively early, having achieved maximum earning potential at a young age,[47] and that the propertied will have married relatively late because of the need to accumulate savings or possibly because of having to await transfers of wealth from other members of the family.

An appropriate place to begin analysis is with the differences between the marriage patterns of the three principal occupational groups within Colyton's population (Figures 14.1–14.4);[48] for it is impossible, as became clear from the pattern of children leaving the parental home, to consider real property in isolation from occupation. Each of the figures below is laid out in the same way to show the per centage of each group who had married by a particular age. For example, taking Figure 14.1, it emerges that at the age of 24 only 35 per cent of yeomen were married, a much lower percentage than the 56 per cent of labourers and the 60 per cent plus of the tradesmen and craftsmen. It is important, however, since the number of cases is small, not to place too great a reliance on the percentages for individual ages. Instead it is the general differences between the various sections of the population that are worth emphasizing: for example, and using Figure 14.1 again, that yeomen generally married later than other families with real property.

Continuing the same line of argument, the following set of conclusions can be drawn from this first set of results. First, it is clear that

[47] For the evidence on this point, see above, note 46.
[48] Establishing age, occupation and property necessitates the following restrictions: married before 1835 and not widowed by 1835, presence in 1841, occupation in census or register, first marriage for both partners, no uncertainty about possession of land, information on age either from the 1851 census or calculated by links between marriage and baptism registers.

differences between occupational groups are greater for men (Figures 14.1 and 14.3) than for their spouses (Figures 14.2 and 14.4) and in the case of women are greater for those with property than for those without. Secondly, it emerges that tradesmen and craftsmen on the whole marry at an earlier age than labourers, who in turn marry earlier than yeomen. The difference between labourers and tradesmen and craftsmen holds regardless of whether the groups were propertied, although the shape of the graphs is by no means the same. The group of labourers with real property contained a number of late marriers, who push the distribution in the direction of the yeoman group and away from that of the tradesmen and craftsmen that it had formerly paralleled.

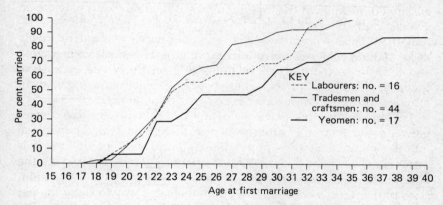

Figure 14.1. Colyton. Age at first marriage: tradesmen, craftsmen, labourers and yeomen with real property

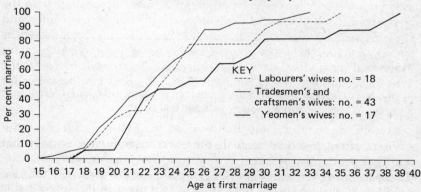

Figure 14.2. Colyton. Age at first marriage: wives of tradesmen, craftsmen, labourers and yeomen with real property

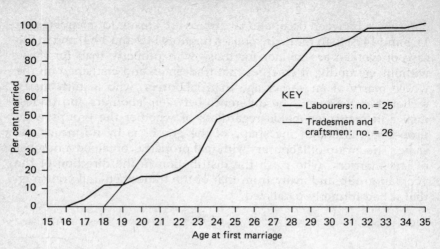

Figure 14.3. Colyton. Age at first marriage: tradesmen and labourers without real property

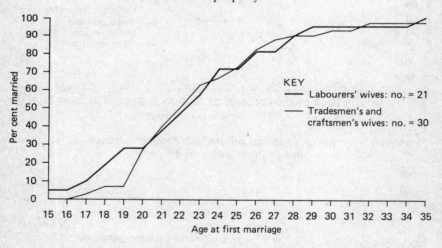

Figure 14.4. Colyton. Age at first marriage: wives of tradesmen, craftsmen and labourers without real property

Occupation, it would appear, did exert an influence on marriage age independently of whether real property was or was not held. There is, however, the important qualification to be made that the amount of real property held by the various groups differed (the yeomen, it will be remembered, held most), and that it is impossible given the number of cases to determine the separate influences of

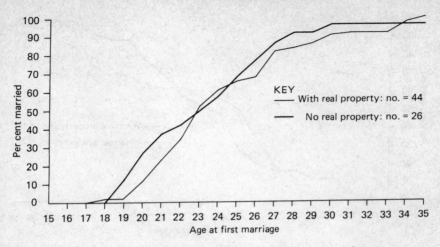

Figure 14.5. Colyton. Age at first marriage: tradesmen and craftsmen

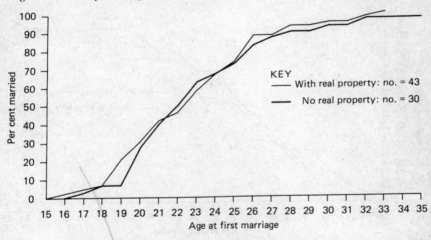

Figure 14.6. Colyton. Age at first marriage: wives of tradesmen and craftsmen

property and occupation. An alternative approach, minimizing this problem, is to look for differences between holders and non-holders of real property within the broad occupational groups that have been defined. Figures 14.5 and 14.6 do this for tradesmen and craftsmen, and Figures 14.7 and 14.8 cover labourers. From these figures it can be said at once that the influence of real property on age at first marriage was not great. Tradesmen and craftsmen with real property might have married slightly later on average than those without

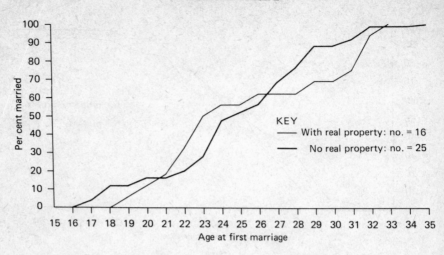

Figure 14.7. Colyton. Age at first marriage: labourers

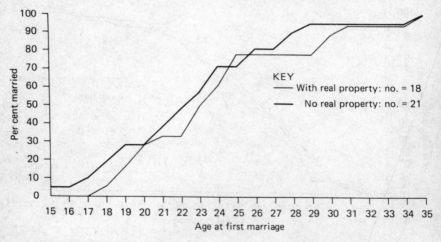

Figure 14.8. Colyton. Age at first marriage: wives of labourers

(Figure 14.5), so too might the wives of labourers with real property (Figure 14.8) but the differences are slight and effectively it can be said that real property (as defined in the present study) has no measurable impact on the age at marriage of the couples concerned.

Given this situation in Colyton it is time to consider the other parish, Cardington. In this instance the analysis is restricted to labourers, since the trade and craft group is too small to be split on a property/no property basis, and farmers' marriages have to be

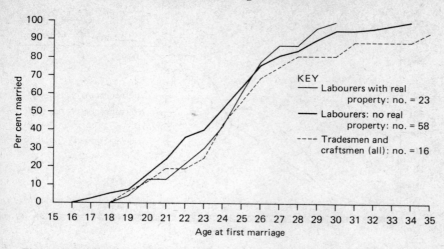

Figure 14.9. Cardington. Age at first marriage: labourers (with and without real property), tradesmen and craftsmen

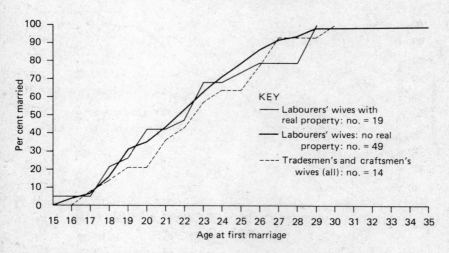

Figure 14.10. Cardington. Age at first marriage: wives of labourers (with and without real property), tradesmen and craftsmen

excluded, as mentioned above, because of insufficient detail on their families in the list. However, it is clear that for labourers access to real property made as little difference to the age at marriage as it did in the case of Colyton (Figures 14.9–10). In Cardington, however, it is possible to proceed a stage further and examine the influence of real

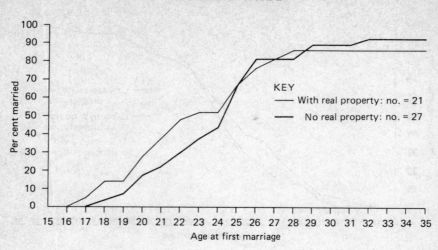

Figure 14.11 Cardington. Age at first marriage: sons of labourers

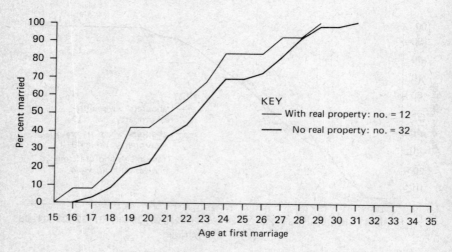

Figure 14.12. Cardington. Age at first marriage: daughters of labourers

property on the marriage ages of the offspring (Figures 14.11–14.12). This produces a somewhat different result in that sons and even more clearly daughters (although on the basis of very small numbers) whose parents were holders of real property did in fact marry at an earlier age than sons and daughters of non-property holders.

In a final set of results (Figures 14.13–14.16) the marriage ages of the

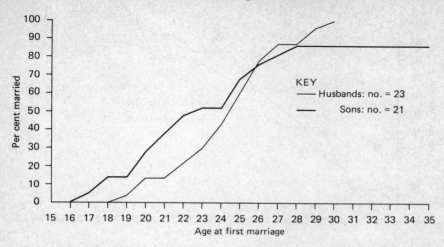

Figure 14.13. Cardington. Age at first marriage: labourers with real property (fathers and sons)

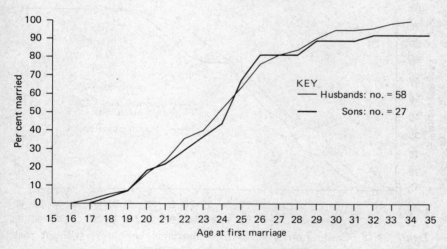

Figure 14.14. Cardington. Age at first marriage: labourers without real property (fathers and sons)

offspring generation have been plotted against those of the parental generation, first for the holders of real property and then for the others. In certain respects this led to some surprising results. It is known from reconstitutions of various English parish registers that age at first marriage was lower for both sexes in the late eighteenth

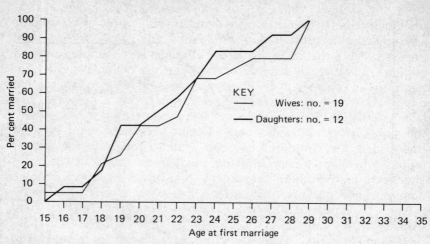

Figure 14.15. Cardington. Age at first marriage: labourers with real property (wives and daughters)

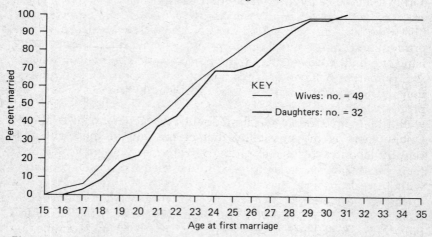

Figure 14.16. Cardington. Age at first marriage: Labourers without real property (wives and daughters)

century than in earlier periods.[49] Cardington is not one of these reconstituted parishes, but elements of the same pattern are detectable, since in two of the four cases children were marrying at an earlier age than their parents. However, there were exceptions. Sons whose parents were propertied were likely to marry at an earlier age

[49] Wrigley, 'Age at Marriage'.

than their fathers,[50] yet there was almost no difference in the marriage age patterns of those fathers and sons who were without real property. The situation in regard to daughters is even more confused because of the small number of marriages involving daughters of parents with property. Nevertheless, there is evidence to suggest that daughters whose parents lacked real property were marrying at a later age than their mothers (Figure 14.16). We are left therefore with the somewhat puzzling situation of having to explain why the sons of the propertyless continued to marry at much the same age as their fathers when apparently similarly situated daughters married at a later age than their mothers, and why the shift to an earlier marriage among sons was confined to those whose parents were propertied.

Given the nature of the evidence no firm conclusions can be drawn. Consider, for example, an earlier set of results (Figures 14.11–14.12) which demonstrated that the offspring of the propertied married at an earlier age than the offspring of the propertyless, when real property had made little difference to the marriage ages of the parents. There are at least three explanations that are plausible. It could be argued first that we are witnessing in Cardington the collapse of the prudential restraint of real property on age at marriage. On the other hand the differences might simply be occasioned by the fact that we are comparing behaviour in relation to real property of two generations. The parents married late to assemble the necessary real property, while their offspring married early on the proceeds. This would be 'conventional wisdom' about inter-generational relations. Finally there is the possibility that at the end of the eighteenth century labourers with real property were marrying earlier because their circumstances had improved rather than worsened. Labourers without real property married no earlier because their situation was unchanged or deteriorating. The suggestion of such a long-term crisis would be odd for many parishes at the end of the eighteenth century, but Cardington is not a typical parish. There is, for example, no baptism surplus as in most parish registers of this period (although the presence of a community of Baptists may have undermined the registration system if they used the parish church for burial but not for baptism), and the poverty of the area was notorious. The latter perhaps makes more explicable the late marriage age of daughters in relation to their mothers. Osamu Saito, in his interesting paper, has drawn attention to the extremely high level of female employment in

---

[50] The terms and 'mother–daughter', below, are used loosely as synonyms for the parental and offspring generations. No attempt is made here to measure ages at marriage of offspring in relation to the ages at marriage of their own parents.

Cardington and the corresponding lack of employment opportunities for males; this could have created a situation in which parents were so dependent on the labour of daughters that it acted as a restraint on their daughters' marrying early.[51] For Cardington, therefore, it is possible to put forward a contrary argument to that of Levine:[52] that opportunities in textiles led to delayed marriage for girls. It is also worth bearing in mind in this connection the figures discussed earlier which showed that at the time of the 1782 list fewer daughters had actually married than sons. Some girls, it would seem, were spinsters for the life-time of their parents.[53]

However, parts of this argument do push the evidence further than is really justified. Although quite a lot is known about Cardington in 1782 – its poverty, its lack of employment for unmarried males and the prevalence of by-employments for females – it is impossible to know how these factors may have varied over time or between the groups in question. Rightly the overall emphasis has to be on the individuality of marriage-age experiences. Real property explains few, and occupation only some, of the variations that are in evidence.

Conclusion

This paper began with a discussion of the role of land as an influence on the structure of family and household. Redefined as 'real property' it emerged as a useful marker in village society. A divider, if an unequal one, of most occupational groups, real property was yet without major impact either on the shape of the co-resident domestic group or on the processes of family formation. Admittedly its influence was not always negligible – one could point to its import-ance for this or that sub-group of the population, for example to its effect on the marriage ages of labourers' daughters in Cardington or on residential patterns among sons of labourers between the ages of ten and nineteen in Colyton. The behaviour of yeomen in regard to marriage age and the keeping of children at home was usually distinctive,[54] and it is yeomen who best represent the influence of

---

[51] Co-residence of married offspring and parents was rare in Cardington, as it was elsewhere in England at this time, but when co-residence did occur it is worth noting that it involved daughters rather than sons (Schofield, 'Age Specific Mobility').

[52] Cf. Levine, *Family Formation*, p. 111.

[53] On the other hand, only half the unmarried girls over 30 in 1782 were at home; the rest were in service (Schofield, 'Age Specific Mobility', p. 267).

[54] Though not in connection with the percentage of sons at home between the ages of 10 and 19, where there was little difference between yeomen and either tradesmen–craftsmen or labourers.

land in its more traditional definition. There could therefore be a threshold beyond which 'land' did start to exercise a certain influence on the form of the family.

However, even with yeomen farmers the shape of the household seems scarcely notable. Real property or occupation, whatever they might do to family forms, seem scarcely to have touched the structure of the household, servants excepted. This dichotomy between household and family seems surprising in view of the fact that simulation experiments have suggested that household forms are particularly sensitive to changes in age at marriage. That these results are not borne out on the ground (though admittedly for just one community) suggests that there may have been compensating factors at work. Families may have been trying to avoid having to live together in complex households. Two things however must be made clear. First, more communities need to be investigated than it was possible to include here, and secondly, the family and particularly the parent–child group is equally deserving of attention as the currently more popular pursuit of wider kin. After all, in Colyton it was the family rather than the household that was the more closely bound up with people's livelihoods.

None of these differences, however, should be allowed to obscure the more general findings on the residential patterns of children. More than seven out of ten children aged between ten and nineteen whose parents were alive lived with them. Children left home late, far later than has customarily been believed. Yet at the same time many families eventually parted from their children, a substantial proportion of whom married while their parents were still alive. The existence of the stem family, defined even weakly as the co-residence of a married or unmarried son of working age (Table 14.6) looks even more problematical for these English villagers. The fact that at the same time there existed a substantial minority of complex households (Table 14.10) provides further evidence that the role of kinship within the household reflected in the English experience the influence of factors other than transmission of property, business or even a household from father to son.

15

The nineteenth-century peasantry of Melbourn, Cambridgeshire*

DENNIS R. MILLS

This essay attempts to answer the question as to the extent to which a peasantry survived in nineteenth-century Melbourn and the factors involved in its survival. The evidence used relates to the occupations of the families concerned, as well as to land, kinship and inheritance. Occupations are important because the definition of 'peasantry' used in this chapter embraces many kinds of rural entrepreneurs, who usually also had some kind of interest in the land. A peasant is regarded as any self-employed man below the rank of the large tenant farmers and the yeomen (i.e. the large owner–occupier farmers). Unlike the labourer, he did not rely entirely on wages and, unlike the higher groups, he did not rely mainly on directing the work of others. His living was obtained by virtue of a combination of a modest amount of capital with family labour and, in some instances, hired help. The typical Melbourn peasant was a dual-occupationist, and this also helped to distinguish him from the full-time farmers, whether they were tenants or yeomen, and from the very few professional men who lived in the village.

i. Melbourn in 1839–41

Melbourn is situated on the lower parts of the chalk plain about ten miles south of Cambridge where corn farming had been traditional

* The research on which this chapter is based was carried out with the help of grants from the Open University and the Social Science Research Council. I am particularly grateful to the SSRC for the opportunity of a year-long sabbatical 1976–7. I should also like to acknowledge the help of the Open University Library, the libraries of Nottingham and Leicester Universities, the Cambridgeshire Libraries and Record Office, Cambridge University Library and the Ely Diocesan Record Office and the Lambeth Palace Library. I have been afforded much encouragement and constructive criticism by Mr A. J. Palmer of Melbourn and members of the SSRC Cambridge Group.

for several centuries.[1] By local standards it was both a large parish and a large village. It was not enclosed until 1839, the same year as the tithe survey. The tithe survey and the enclosure award, combined with the 1841 enumeration, are the basis of much of what follows.[2] The tithe commissioners recorded a total of about 4,600 acres, of which about 300 lay in old enclosures and about 800 constituted the commonable 'wastes' of moor and heath. The remaining 3,500 acres were in common field, indicating the predominance of arable farming, and the survey of 1836[3] leaves no doubt that half-acre and one-acre strips were still the typical unit of cultivation (Figure 15).

A number of factors appear to have been responsible for the lateness of enclosure and the absence of piecemeal consolidation of strips. As the area was suited to barley and wheat farming in conjunction with sheep, common-field agriculture could be tolerated more easily than in an area where pasture was the 'natural' basis of farming. The existence of several manorial lords, none of them resident, and a total of no less than 163 proprietors, including several institutions, must have inhibited the growth of a strong lobby for enclosure in earlier years. In 1834 Alfred Power reported that Melbourn was one of several Cambridgeshire parishes in which enclosure was held up by parliamentary and other expenses and by the difficulty of arranging tithes to everyone's satisfaction. The chief land owner, John Hitch, who was also lord of the combined manor of Argentine and Trayles, took refuge first in France and later in Belgium between 1832 and 1847, to avoid facing his creditors; he was therefore unavailable to lead the village towards enclosure. The aggressive Dissenting tradition of the village probably made tithes an especially difficult problem. However, in 1836 the vestry took the initiative by voting a rate of 2s 6d in the pound to cover the costs of the survey, which would have amounted to about £400. The significance of this decision can be seen by comparison with the poor rate, running at about 4–5s at this time and considered far too high. No

---

[1] M. Spufford, *Contrasting Communities: English Villages in the Sixteenth and Seventeenth Centuries* (London, 1974), pp. 33 and 36; S. Jonas, 'On the Farming of Cambridgeshire', *Journal of the Royal Agricultural Society of England* 7 (1847), pp. 38 and 40.

[2] The tithe apportionment is in the Ely Diocesan Records at Cambridge University Library; one copy of the enclosure award is in the Cambridgeshire Record Office (hereafter CRO) (Q.RDc 63, R 60/24/1/12); the Public Record Office (hereafter PRC) reference for the enumeration is HO 107/63. This essay is part of a larger study of Melbourn; see my 1977 report to the SSRC entitled *An Economic, Tenurial, Social and Demographic Study of an English Peasant Village* (P 3932), which, *inter alia*, describes the techniques of community reconstitution used.

[3] Terrier and valuation of the parish of Melbourn, 1836, deposited by Mr A. J. Palmer at CRO (R 61/14/1).

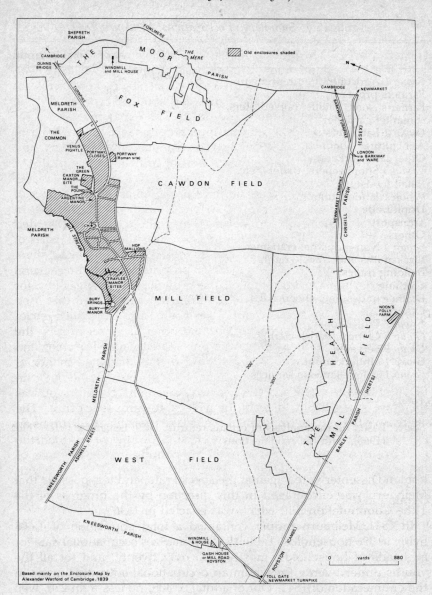

Figure 15.1. Melbourn, Cambs.: pre-enclosure landscape

Table 15.1. *Summary of occupations; Melbourn 1841*

	No.	Total in group
Group 1 Agricultural entrepreneurs		34
Farmers proper	28	
Farmers' sons, bailiffs, horsedealers, market gardener	6	
Group 2 Labourers		186
Agricultural labourers	182	
Other landworkers	4	
Group 3 Shopkeepers, traders, etc.		38
Retail foodstuffs	14	
Wholesale foodstuffs	9	
Drink trade	6	
Transport	6	
Others	3	
Group 4 Non-industrial craftsmen		76
Blacksmiths and wheelwrights	14	
Building trades	26	
Clothing	14	
Leather trades, inc. shoemakers	17	
Others	5	
Group 7 Professional		12
Group 8 Clerical (Parish clerk)		1
Group 9 Servants		32
Group 10 Independent		23
Group 11 Miscellaneous services		3
Total		405

Source: Based on the analysis of census returns, DC9, issued by Peter Tillot (1966), with my modifications.

known Dissenter voted against the special rate, and it is possible that Melbourn was encouraged in this direction by the progress of the Tithe Commutation Bill, which was enacted in 1836.[4]

In 1841 Melbourn proper contained a total population of 1,608 living in 326 households. Table 15.1 summarizes occupational data for all heads of households, mostly men over twenty, and for all the youths under twenty for whom an occupational entry was made in the enumeration of 1841. Out of a total of 405, no less than 220, well

[4] *Report from the Poor Law Commissioners* (London, 1834), Vol. xxviii (IUP edition Vol. viii, p. 245A), Appendix A (1); Lambeth Palace Library (hereafter LPL) *Ranson and Knott* v. *Campkin*, Court of Arches 7523, H 755/1–23 and CRO, Copy of deposition in the same case, pp. 97–107; Spufford, *Contrasting Communities*, pp. 269–96; Melbourn Town Book, Vol. ii, p. 15 (by courtesy of Melbourn Parish Council).

over one-half, were classed as engaged in agriculture, but 186 of these were labourers. The bulk of the peasantry were listed in groups 3 and 4, which comprised 114 craftsmen and traders. This formal division between the agricultural and non-agricultural populations will, however, be shown as an artificial division which hides the duality of occupations so prevalent at this time.

In this period of rapidly rising population, the piecemeal expansion of non-agricultural activities of many kinds, but not including any industry,[5] appears to have provided increased employment at a time when demand from agriculture was stagnant. Despite the presence of Royston, a market town three miles to the south, Melbourn became a significant service centre for its own large population and for that of villages for several miles around. The more specialized services included those of surgeon, exciseman, millwright, bird stuffer, watchmaker, corn factor, fish man, chemist, several horse dealers and two plumbers and glaziers. Although brewing may have survived in beerhouses, the terrier of 1836 and the rate book of 1839[6] list only one malting, and the census includes no maltster.

ii. The distribution of land ownership in 1839

The average size of land holding (27.5 acres) at Melbourn in 1839 was low compared with the general experience of English rural land ownership in this period. For example, out of over 300 Leicestershire townships only 28 were more fragmented than Melbourn. However, according to the 1870 Domesday of Owners, Cambridgeshire had more small estates than Leicestershire, the latter county being not far above the national average. A brief study of the land tax assessments for the villages lying between Cambridge and Melbourn confirms that, while there were more small owners in Melbourn than elsewhere, most south Cambridgeshire villages were of the same general type. In parishes with numerous small owners a large proportion of the acreage was often in the hands of a few large proprietors. A discussion of the size distribution of owners is, therefore, the next step in our analysis, and in order to see the Melbourn data in a less parochial context comparable information is given for two other parishes. One is Ardington, an estate village on the Berkshire Downs;

[5] Industry is defined here as enterprises producing mainly for export out of the district, such as the lace makers in nearby Bedfordshire. The craftsmen in Melbourn appear to have supplied only their own locality, and apart from a good representation of occupations associated with traffic on the Cambridge–London turnpike the village contained no specialized activity.
[6] LPL, Court of Arches 7523, Ff.58.

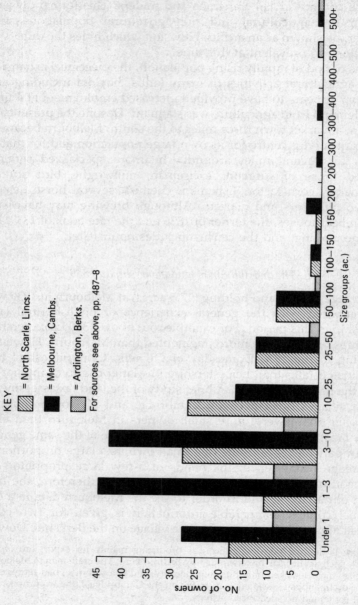

Figure 15.2. Numbers of owners by size groups in three English parishes in the early nineteenth century

the other is North Scarle, a highly fragmented township in the Trent Valley, about ten miles south-west of Lincoln.[7]

The Berkshire parish later became part of the very large and intensively developed Wantage estate, and by 1811 82.4 per cent of it was already in the hands of two large owners, respectively of 452 and 1,035 acres. Over one-half of the thirty owners were in the two smallest categories, but their estates represented only 1.3 per cent of the total area. The Lincolnshire parish provides a sharp contrast in both total number of owners and the distribution of land between them, despite a very similar total acreage. The largest estate covered only 175 acres, and the two most numerous groups of owners controlled one-third of the parish in parcels of 3–10 or 10–25 acres. The mean acreage per owner was only sixteen, compared with 60 at Ardington and 27.5 at Melbourn.

The distribution of land between Melbourn owners – there was about two-and-a-half times as much – contained elements of both profiles (Figure 15.2). As at Ardington, there were two large owners, Wortham Hitch with 469 acres, and his brother John with 1,030. These acreages are almost identical to those of Clarke and Bastard at Ardington, but they represent only one-third of the total Melbourn area. The Hitches were settled in the village in the sixteenth century and bought the manor of Argentine and Trayles, which also control-led property in Meldreth, in 1703. In 1841 John Hitch, a lawyer, was away from home on census night, but both the census and the directories show that his family was normally resident, not at either of the manorial sites, but at an early nineteenth-century house known as The Lodge, while his brother was a lawyer in Gray's Inn but came home for the baptism of one of his children in 1831. Although the Hitches were known as gentlemen, they belonged to the upper professional echelons rather than to the lower ranks of country gentry, a conclusion confirmed by both field and documentary work,

---

[7] D. R. Mills, 'The Peasant Tradition', *Local Historian* 11 (1974), pp. 200–6; *idem*, 'Landownership and Rural Population with Special Reference to Leicestershire in the Mid-Nineteenth Century', unpublished University of Leicester Ph.D. thesis, 1963, Appendix 4. F. M. L. Thompson, *English Landed Society in the Nineteenth Century* (London, 1963), p. 117, states that 38.5% of England was in estates of 1–1,000 acres, 45 per cent of Leicestershire and 51% of Cambridgeshire, only Middlesex and Cumberland having higher figures. For Ardington, See M. A. Havinden, *Estate Villages* (London, 1966), pp. 53 and 205–6; by 1870 all but a few acres were in the hands of Lord Wantage. The information on North Scarle is from the tithe survey, LRO, F/129. The size categories used in Table 15.2 are those adopted by V. M. Lavrovsky, 'Parliamentary Enclosures in Suffolk 1797–1814', *Economic History Review* 7 (1937), p. 191.

for they made practically no attempt to develop the landscape of a country estate.[8]

At the opposite end of the scale there were many small owners, smaller than at North Scarle, for the modal group was the one- to three-acre category at Melbourn and the three- to ten-acre category at North Scarle. The ranks of small owners were swollen by the interest of Royston tradesmen in Melbourn land adjoining the town, where the street name Graden Walk still testifies to one reason for this interest. Estates of the middle sizes, 25–150 acres, were correspondingly less numerous in Melbourn, accounting for only 30 per cent of the land, compared with almost 60 per cent in North Scarle. We may suspect, therefore, that yeoman farming was weaker in Melbourn than in the somewhat exceptional Lincolnshire parish, but still stronger than at Ardington. In brief, owners were well spread out across the size categories in the large parish of Melbourn.

Is it reasonable to assume that Melbourn was also traditionally a village of many small owners? As fragmentation of property was frequently associated with a multiplicity of manors, reference to manorial history can provide useful evidence in partial answer to this question. At the time of Domesday Book there were five manorial lords with property in Melbourn, which was already a substantial village of 52 families. During the medieval period there is both documentary and archaeological evidence for the existence of several manors and manor houses in the village. The sites are generally known today by the following names (see Figure 15.1):

1. the Bury manor, at the south end of the village, given by King Edgar to the Abbot of Ely and bought by the Fordhams from the Dean and Chapter in the second half of the nineteenth century.
2. the Trayles manor, marked by the Old Manor House in the High Street opposite Greenbanks and by moats in the meadows behind it.
3. the Argentine manor, at Lordship Farm at the north end of the High Street, which belonged to the Hitches in 1839 and had absorbed the Trayles property.
4. the Caxton manor, marked by numerous moats in 1839, one still surviving near Moats House, at the far north end of the village.

At the time of enclosure John Hitch and the Dean and Chapter of Ely were able to claim manorial rights successfully, along with the

---

[8] CRO, R 51/22/5; Pigot and Company's *Directories of Bedfordshire, Cambridgeshire,* (London, 1830, 1839); *Kelly's Post Office Directory of Nine Counties* (London, 1846); R. Gardner, *Directory of Cambridgeshire* (Peterborough, 1851); and Melbourn Parish Registers.

Table 15.2. *Summary of land owners by size in North Scarle, Lincs.,*
*Melbourn, Cambs. and Ardington, Berks.**

	North Scarle 1839		Melbourn 1839		Ardington 1811	
	No.	% of land owned	No.	% of land owned	No.	% of land owned
Size (ac.)						
Under 1	18	0.2	28	0.2	9	0.2
1–3	11	1.0	45	1.8	8	1.1
3–10	28	9.4	43	5.4	7	1.6
10–25	27	20.7	16	5.5	0	—
25–50	13	21.4	13	10.6	2	4.3
50–100	9	26.3	9	13.5	1	3.6
100–150	2	11.8	2	5.3	1	6.7
150–200	1	9.0	3	12.6	0	—
200–300	0	—	1	5.3	0	—
300–400	0	—	1	6.8	0	—
400–500	0	—	1	10.2	1	25.0
Over 500	0	—	1	22.6	1	57.4
Total	109	1,753 ac.	163	4,565 ac.	30	1,803 ac.

* See above, note 8, for references.

owners of four manors mainly situated in Meldreth, the next village
to the west, with which Melbourn has shared much of its history.[9]

A second relevant area of evidence concerns the fact that the
Puritan tradition was very strong in Melbourn, and that Noncon-
formity in both the seventeenth and the nineteenth century was
frequently associated with a widespread social distribution of land
ownership. Melbourn distinguished itself by ousting the Sheriff's
men when they came to collect arrears of Ship Money in 1640. This
event did not come out of the blue, as Bishop Wren's visitation in
1638 had unearthed a good deal of unorthodox religious behaviour.
In the mid-seventeenth century the registers are indicative of an
Anabaptist following, which leads on to the firm establishment of
both Baptist and Independent congregations of considerable vigour.[10]

[9] L. F. Salzman, editor, *Victoria County History of Cambridgeshire*, Vol. II (London,
1948), especially pp. 35–6; W. Farrer, *Feudal Cambridgeshire* (Cambridge, 1920), pp.
27–8; W. M. Palmer, 'Argentine's Manor, Melbourn, 1317–8', *Cambridgeshire Antiqua-*
rian Society 28 (1927), pp. 16–79; W. M. Palmer and H. H. McNeice, *Melbourn,*
Cambridgeshire: Notes on Cambridgeshire Villages No. 1 (Cambridge, 1925), especially
pp. 3–7; Melbourn enclosure award, CRO Q.RDc.63, R 60/24/1/12; and D. and S.
Lysons, *Magna Britannia, Cambridgeshire*, Vol. II, Part I (London, 1808), p. 234.

[10] Spufford, *Contrasting Communities*, pp. 234, 268–97 and 349; W. M. Palmer and H. W.

Table 15.3. *Distribution of hearths between tax payers; Melbourn 1674*

No. of persons	No. of hearths per person	Total owned
1	12	12
1	8	8
1	6	6
3	5	15
5	4	20
14	3	42
28	2	56
73*	1	73
Total 126		232

*Including 31 exempt from payment
Source: PRO, E 179/244/23

These facts are consistent with the absence of a strong, centralized manorial system and a powerful resident lord, and suggest that the peasantry had a modest socio-economic independence to match their independence in religious affairs.

Finally, some statistical evidence can be quoted suggesting that Melbourn was traditionally a community in which the peasantry had flourished. The Subsidy Roll of 1327, the Poll Tax of 1377, the Bishop's Returns of 1563 and the Hearth Taxes all indicate that Melbourn was consistently one of the largest villages in south Cambridgshire.[11] The analysis of the 1674 Hearth Tax seen in Table 15.3 shows that there was a considerable village of 126 households, including 47 in the medium range of prosperity corresponding to taxation on two to four hearths. While there are signs of a burgeoning proletariat in the 73 houses with one hearth, there is no great house with over twenty hearths. Mr John Payne, who paid on twelve hearths, and John North, who paid on eight, were probably lessees of the Bury Manor and Lordship Farm (Argentine Manor).

The first line of freeholders is that of 1722 recorded in connection with the election of knights of the shire. The substantial number of 31

Saunders, *Documents Relating to Cambridgeshire Villages*, (Cambridge, 1926–7) Vol. III, pp. 67–8; W. M. Palmer, *The Puritan in Melbourn, Cambs.–Gleanings from History Concerning a County Parish 1640–88* (Royston, 1895); G. P. Chapple, *Congregationalism at Melbourn 1694–1894* (London, 1895).

[11] W. M. Palmer and H. W. Saunders, *Documents Relating to Cambridgeshire Villages*, Vol. VI, Part 2 (Cambridgeshire, 1926–7).

men voted on the franchise of Melbourn property, all but five actually living there; this compares interestingly with the figure of 39 for the market town of March and of seventeen for the Cambridgeshire part of Royston. In addition the Argentine court books and the enclosure award show that there must have been a significant number of copyholders. The 1722 figure is also very nearly the same as that of voters in the elections of 1780 and 1802.[12] Manorial history, the history of dissent, and data relating to population, taxation and freeholders all suggest that it is reasonable to speak in terms of a *survival* of a peasantry into the nineteenth century – in other words, of a continuity rather than a new development.

iii. The occupation of property

While the last section will have demonstrated some of the difficulties of farm and estate engrossment, as well as hindrances to enclosure, which strengthened the position of the owner–occupier peasantry, here we are concerned with the actual uses to which property was put and with evaluating the extent to which these help to explain the survival of the Melbourn peasantry. Before focusing on the peasantry, the principal farms will be described (see Table 15.4). The separation of the principal farmers from the peasantry is an arbitrary distinction based on the occupation of a hundred acres or more after enclosure, or the right of sheepwalk before enclosure (or both). (George Gilby, who occupied just over a hundred acres, was excluded on the grounds that census and directories describe him as the village's leading innkeeper and carrier, with the implication that oat growing and grazing for horses impinged on normal farming activities.)

Table 15.4 indicates that rather more than three-quarters of the parish was farmed in the eighteen principal units, with a mean area of 190 acres each and a range from 78 to 459 acres. These figures are based on the post-enclosure position, when common rights and rights of sheepwalk had been eliminated, but much the same story is told by the 1836 terrier. All but four of these principal farmers were engaged full-time on their farms. Joseph Stockbridge combined horse dealing with farming; William Crole Carver was still responsible for

---

[12] E. Carter, *History of the County of Cambridge* (Cambridge, 1819), pp. 238 and 241. (N.B. This is a re-issue of an earlier work of 1753.) The writer's copy contains MS notes which show that an earlier owner compared the lists of 1722 with MSS in the Bodleian Library to ascertain their date of compilation. See also 'Polls for the Election of two MPs for Cambridgeshire, 1780–1835' (Cambridge University Library, MS CAM c.291.4.1).

Table 15.4. *Melbourn 1839: principal farmers**

Farmer	Acreage 1839 after enclosure	Ownership	Mean no. sheep before enclosure (i.e. right of sheepwalk on common fields)
William Baker	234	% of 20 acs.,† rest Wm Hitch	12 score
Valentine Beldam	267	% of 200 acs., rest of Lord Dacre	Farmed from Royston, Probably had intercommon
James Bullen	212	Tenant of Wm Hitch	12 score
Wm Crole Carver	265	All but 40 owner-occupied	8 score
Robert Dean	144	Tenant of J. Hitch	$4\frac{1}{2}$ score
Joseph Dickason snr	160	All owner-occupied	4 score
Joseph Ellis	190	Tenant of Peterhouse	6 score
John E. Fordham	232	All but 30 leased from Dean & Chapter of Ely (Bury Manor)	17 score
Nathaniel Holmes	459	J. Hitch's Lordship Farm	12 score
James Jarman	83	Almost all %	4 score
Thomas Jarman jnr	88	All owner-occupied	2 score

492

William Long	424	J. Hitch's High St Farm	12 score
William Phypers	129	Ann and Sarah Wortham	Noon's Folly Farm was early enclosed and had no right of sheep walk
Ellis Smith	125	All owner-occupied	2 score
George Stanford	111	Almost all leased from Dean and Chapter	2 score
Joseph Stockbridge snr and jnr	78	57 rented from St John's College	2 score
Mynott Titchmarsh	109	81 acs. rented from his son, remainder from Elizabeth Leader	Nil
Thomas Wood	119	Owner-occupied	2 score belonging to Edward Freshwater
Total	3,428 acres.		2,030 sheep

* Criteria for inclusion in the table: over 100 ac. or the right of sheepwalk. Median size of farm = 152 acres. Several farmers, especially Carver and the Stockbridges, also farmed in Meldreth (land tax assessments 1839).
† % = owner-occupied

Source: Tithe apportionment (Ely Diocesan RO), 1836 Terrier and Enclosure Award (CRO, R 61/14/1 and R 60/24/1/12) and 1839 rate book (Lambeth Palace Library, Court of Arches 7523, fo. 58).

the small Nonconformist boys' boarding school which his minister father had started, and was also listed as a miller in 1846. However, in 1841 his household contained another farmer, William Crole, probably a cousin who managed some of his affairs. The house repopulation also suggests that Valentine Beldam and J. E. Fordham farmed through bailiffs, a point that emphasizes, rather than detracts from, the professionalism involved.

About one-half of the principal farmers could be described as belonging to the large-scale tenant–farmer type for which the Victorian corn growing estates were so well known. Among the others, characteristics of yeoman farming were to be found, notably the owner–occupier status of modest proportions possessed by W. C. Carver, Joseph Dickason, the Jarmans, Ellis Smith and cousins Titchmarsh and Wood. These men probably had much in common with the peasantry, usually being members of well-established Melbourn families, rather than newcomers (see comments on Figure 15.5).

While it would be foolish to deny the contrast between these eighteen large farms and their medieval forerunners of one or two yardlands (or, for that matter, to ignore the large number of labourers employer per farm – over six at ten of them in 1851), it is equally important to recognize the very large number of small owners and occupiers living in Melbourn around 1840. These are the people we are justified in calling a peasantry, despite the difference between their relative economic and social position and that of, say, the medieval villein. Individually they counted for little, but collectively they were a political, as well as a socio-economic, force to be reckoned with. Commenting on his analysis of capital at death in Cambridgeshire in the period 1848–57, J. R. Vincent has pointed out that, apart from the large farmers, 'those who carried on the normal economic life of Cambridgeshire needed singularly little of its capital to do so', and has argued that 'Victorian society achieved very great inequality at the top without affecting the fraternity, liberty and equality of the town population – the craftsmen, retailers, publicans and skilled employees and small masters'.[13] Table 15.1 shows that, although Melbourn was not a town, it contained considerable 'urban'

[13] J. R. Vincent, *Pollbooks: How Victorians Voted* (London, 1967), pp. 41–2; P. Horn, *Labouring Life in the Victorian Countryside* (Dublin, 1976), p. 93. In Melbourn, political expression was at its clearest in the dispute over the 1848 church rate, in which the parson, John Hitch and their big farmer allies were ranged against the Congregationalist minister, Joseph Campkin, and a majority of those who voted, but not against a majority of *votes*, because of block votes based on property: see my forthcoming article in *Local History Bulletin: East Midlands Region*.

elements as defined by Vincent; but, because so many of these retained direct interests in the land, it can be argued that they were peasants. They belonged to a social stratum below the landed classes, the large tenant farmers and the clergy of the Established Church; but they showed a marked reluctance to inter-marry with the labourers, thus underlining their relatively superior status. The family reconstitution forms show that 80 per cent of the marriages for which full occupational data are available took place *within* the two main social groups, defined as labourers and non-labourers (No. = 84).

Table 15.5 gathers together the most important information available on the peasantry. Out of the 163 owners of property in Melbourn in 1839, 82 have been traced as normally resident in the village in 1841. Out of the 82, no fewer than 57 can be recognized as peasant owners, if the large land owning farmers, a few professional people and a number of agricultural labourers who owned one or two tenements apiece and very occasionally an acre or two of land are excluded. In addition to the 57, there were a further dozen peasants who owned none of the land they occupied, but otherwise got their living in a similar way. The total of 69 entries in the table, however, represents only 60 families, because of joint ownership and the residence of some single owners in households occupying other property. For example, Mary Ellis owned two acres and a tenement, but she let these out and lived with Sarah Cole, another aged woman without family.

This tabulation is based on a combination of sources. Property details are taken from the tithe survey of 1839, representing the position immediately after enclosure. Common rights have been abstracted from the 1836 terrier, with the result that changes in ownership between 1836 and 1839 may account for a few of the blanks in that column. A single common right was compensated by an acre or two of land at enclosure, depending on location; as a common right was often attached to a single messuage, or tenement and garden, this explains why there were so many small properties of an acre or two, like that belonging to John Webb, the butcher. The remaining information is derived variously from the 1841 enumeration, the family reconstitution, the 1836 terrier, the 1839 rating before enclosure, the 1846 directory and the first two Town Books.[14]

Ten of the 69 persons listed in Table 15.5 were actually described as farmers in the 1841 census. They occupied a mean area of nearly 23 acres each, rather more than the average of thirteen acres for the

---

[14] See above, notes 3, 4, 7 and 9. The first Town Book is in CRO, P117/8/1; the second volume, which starts at 1835, is in the possession of the Parish Council.

Table 15.5. Profile of the Melbourn peasantry 1839–41*

Names	post-enclosure property owned	Occupied	Rented	Let out common	1836 rights	Occupations and other comments, c. 1841
BAKER, James	—	3½ ac. + T	3½ ac. + T	—	—	Baker [sic]; has three landlords; overseer 1836
BAKER, William	5 ac. + H	5 ac. + H	—	—	1	Plumber and glazier; assistant overseer 1834, constable 1842
BULLEN, Edward	2 ac. + H	31 ac. + T	31 ac. + T	—	—	Farmer; had three landlords
BULLEN, George		2 ac. + H		—	1	Independent (= retired?)
CAMPKIN, David	9 ac.	9 ac.		—	1	Farmer; widower in John Campkin's household
CAMPKIN, John	3½ ac. + H	3 ac. + H	H	H	1	Grocer; lived in a house belonging to Joseph Campkin, to whom he let out a house and shop; assistant overseer 1842
CAMPKIN, John & Caroline	H + shop			H + shop	—	Let this house and shop to Peter Campkin.
CAMPKIN, Joseph	53 ac. + H + 22 Ts	53 ac. + H	H	H + 22 Ts	1	Grocer and draper, uncle of Peter q.v.; assistant overseer 1826–7, chairman of vestry 1838, 1841; overseer 1843
CAMPKIN, Peter		H + shop	H + shop		—	Tailor and licensee Tailors' Arms; assistant overseer 1848–9; surveyor 1851
CAMPKIN, Stephen	1¼ ac. + 3Ts	1¼ ac. + T		2Ts	1	Shoemaker; two sons shoemakers
CAMPKIN, Stoughton	28 ac. + PH	28 ac. + PH		Portion of H	1	Farmer and licensee of Spotted Dog; constable 1828
CHAPPELL, Henry	3Ts	T			—	Tailor; rated to carpenter's shop 1839
COILE, James	2 ac. + PH	22 ac. + PH	20 ac.	2Ts	1	Publican and beerhouse keeper; had 3 landlords; moved to new PH (Black Horse) 1846
COLE, Sarah	2 ac. + H	H	2 ac.		1	Independent: aged 65 1841; widow of James Cole, farmer
DEARMAN, Susan	4 ac.	2½ ac. + PH	2½ ac. + PH		—	Publican at Red Lion
DEARMAN, William		4 ac.			—	Agricultural labourer who lived with widowed mother in home of her father, William Taylor q.v.
DELLAR, William	5 ac. + PH	10¼ ac. + PH	5½ ac.		1	Shoemaker and beerhouse keeper; new PH (Royal Oak) 1844
DICKASON, Joseph jnr		12 ac. + H	12 ac. + H		—	Farmer
DISBURY, John, snr	T + garden	9 ac. + T	9 ac. + 6T	Sublet 5T	—	Poulterer
DISBURY, John, jnr	T + garden	T + garden			1	Pig dealer; the Disburys lived on the edge of the Moor
ELLIS, David	8 ac. + H	8 ac. + H	—	—	1	Farmer

496

Name				No.	Notes
ELLIS, Mary	2 ac. + T	—	2 ac. + T	1	Lived as independent (retired?) in household of Sarah Cole, q.v.
ELLIS, Samuel	3 ac.	11 ac. + H	8 ac. + H	1	Blacksmith; had three landlords
FLANDERS, Zachariah	2½ ac. + 2T	T	—	1	Carpenter
FRENCH, George	2 ac. + 11Ts	2 ac. + T	2½ ac. + T; 10Ts	1	Bricklayer; 1 son bricklayer; rated on druggist's shop 1836
FRENCH, William	15 ac. + H + 10Ts	15 ac. + H	—	2	Builder; lime and timber merchant; 3 sons bricklayers; overseer 1839, 1848
FRESHWATER, Edward	35 ac. + 2Hs	35 ac. + H	H	2	Harness maker employing 2 men 1851; let out sheepwalk to Thomas Wood
GILBY, George	8 ac.	103 ac. + PH	95 ac. + PH	—	Innkeeper (Rose = principal inn); ran carrier's service twice weekly to London; had 3 landlords
GOULDTHORPE, John	—	½ac. T + blacksmith's shop	—	1	Blacksmith
HAGGAR, Joseph	2 ac. + H	2 ac. + H	—	1	Harness maker, also his son; overseer 1832; constable 1828
HARRIS, Thomas	5 ac. + H	5 ac. + H	—	1	Farmer (aged 70); probably licensee of the White Horse
HAWES, Charles	2 ac., 4Ts	60 ac. + PH	2 ac., 4Ts	—	Publican at Dolphin, second inn of village, alias bricklayer
HUGGINS, William	Blacksmith shop; 4 ac + 2Ts	T	Blacksmith's shop; 2Ts	1	Agricultural labourer; son a shoemaker occupying one of his tenements
JARMAN, Joseph	2 ac. + H	4 ac.	2 ac.	—	Bricklayer; also rated on limekiln 1839; two sons bricklayers
JARMAN, Thos, snr	13 ac. + H	22 ac. + H	10 ac.	1	Farmer
JOHNSTON, Samuel	T + Orchard	T + Orchard	—	1	Bricklayer
KING, Elizabeth	7 ac. + T	7 ac. + H	—	—	Baker
KING, Joel	½ac. + T	½ac. + 3Ts	2Ts; Sublet 2Ts	—	Carrier
MUMFORD, John	8 ac.	8 ac. (+ T?)	2Ts; Sublet 1T	—	Not in 1841 census, but listed in 1846 as grocer and draper
NEGUS, Henry	10-perch garden	7 ac. + gdn + T	7 ac. + T	—	Jobber
NEGUS, John	1 ac. + 2Ts	1 ac. + T	1T	1	Cordwainer; let second tenement to his father, agricultural labourer
NEGUS, Samuel	1 ac.	—	1 ac.	—	Aged 19 1841; castrator, living in household of Stephen Negus q.v.
NEGUS, Stephen	10 ac. + mill	46 ac.	37 ac.	1	Farmer and pig jobber
NEWLING, William	T	—	Mill; T	—	Farmer, living with his father-in-law Joseph Dickason (see Table 15.4)
NORMAN, John	T + shop	T + shop	—	—	Shopkeeper, alias labourer and tailor
OLIVER, Silvester	4 ac. + T	6 ac. + T	2 ac.	1	Butcher; passed for constable 1842
PLUCK, Benjamin	3 ac. + T	3 ac. + 5T	3 ac. + 5T; sublet 4Ts	—	Publican, probably of the Red Cow
PRYOR, Alfred	2 ac.	—	2 ac.	—	Butcher's apprentice living in household of James Pryor q.v.

(Cont.)

Table 15.5 (Cont.)

	post-enclosure property owned	Occupied	Rented	Let out common	1836 rights	Occupations and other comments, c. 1841
PRYOR, James	7ac. + 3Ts	14ac. + T	7ac. + T	3Ts	1	Carpenter; had 3 landlords, including his wife and Alfred Pryor; surveyor 1836
PRYOR, Joseph	11ac. + 6Ts + T + brewhouse	15ac. + T + brewhouse	4ac.	6Ts	—	Carpenter and licensee of Carriers PH
RANSOM, James	45ac. + H	45ac. + H	—		1	Farmer, son of Army captain; son-in-law of Nathaniel Holmes (see Table 15.4), overseer 1844; churchwarden 1848
SAVAGE, Ann	53ac. + H + 7Ts	53ac. + H	—	7Ts	1	Farmer, recently widowed; sold out soon afterwards
SCRUBY, William	—	2ac. + H	2ac. + H	—	—	Butcher; also rated on beershop 1839
SMITH, Edward	2ac. + 2Ts	2ac. + T	T	—	—	Son of farmer, Ellis Smith, (see Table 14.4)
STANFORD, Rhoda	2ac. + T	—	2ac. + T	—	1	Lived in household of brother, George Stanford (see Table 14.4)
STOCKBRIDGE, Charlotte	75ac. + H + 7Ts	½ac.	—	75ac., H, 7Ts	4	This property had belonged to first husband, Thomas Dickason; in 1841 lived with second husband, Thomas Stockbridge q.v.
STOCKBRIDGE, Jonathan	4ac. + mill + 2Ts	6ac. + mill + 2Ts + 2ac.		1/2Ts	1	Possibly living in Fowlmere 1841; watermill was on boundary stream
STOCKBRIDGE, Rebecca Ann	2ac. + 4Ts	2ac. + T	—	3Ts	1	Independent (widowed), son a baker; brother W.C. Carver (see Table 14.4)
STOCKBRIDGE, Thomas	9ac. + H	9ac. + H	—	—	1	Horsedealer; rated on malting 1836; see Charlotte his wife
TAYLOR, William	14ac. + H	14ac. + H	—	—	1	Farmer, rated on wheelwright's shop 1836; aged 70 1841; see above for William Dearman, his grandson who lived in his household
THOMPSON, John snr	9ac. + H + 3Ts	9ac. + H	—	3Ts	2	Cooper; also his son John jnr, who lives in part of house and lets out his 2Ts
THURLEY, Thomas	2ac. + 4Ts	2ac. + T	—	3Ts	1	Jobber; aged 76 1841; Mary was his wife
WARD, George	2ac. + T	2ac. + T	—	—	1	Glazier and plumber; established 1819; constable 1830
WEBB, John	2ac. + H	2ac. + T	—	—	1	Butcher
WEDD, Ebenezer	2ac. + 2Ts	2ac. + T	—	T	1	Wheelwright; son apprentice wheelwright
WEDD, Peter	5ac. + 7Ts	5ac. + PH	PH	7Ts	1	Harness maker; licensee Hoops PH, third-ranking inn, with lodgers; also rated to butcher's shop 1839
WING, Dan	4ac. + 4Ts	4ac. + T	—	3Ts	1	Butcher 1829; journeyman-carpenter 1841
WOOD, William & George	2ac. + 2Ts	2ac. + T(Wm)	—	T	1	George probably his son; William pig jobber 1820–9; agricultural labourer 1841
WOOTTON, William	—	Orchard + T	Orchard + 4Ts	Sublet 3Ts	—	Tailor; sublet 2Ts to relatives, one also a tailor; also rated on tailor's shop 1839; passed for constable 1842, 1845, 1846

* For sources and further explanation, see above, p. 495.

† H = house; T = tenement; ac. = approx. area; PH = public house

whole list of occupiers, of whom there were 63. Several of the non-farmers occupied substantial acreages – George Gilby with 103, the special case already noted; Joseph Campkin, grocer, with 53; James Coile, publican, with 22; Edward Freshwater, harness maker, with 35; Charles Hawes, publican, with 60; and so on (see Figures 15.3 and 15.4 for Gilby and Campkin). The typical holding, however, was not enough to support a family. In most cases the duality of occupation is evident, but it is left to our imagination as to how David Ellis subsisted on eight acres or David Campkin on his nine acres (see Figure 15.4 for Campkin). If the traditions of both Lincolnshire and Wales in the earlier years of the present century are any guide, such men were probably labourers on other men's holding for most of their time, and this is probably the meaning of of the term 'jobber', which Thomas Thurley and Henry Negus used when asked for their occupations at the census.[15]

However, the typical entry in Table 15.5 indicates a combination of a craft, a trade or a public house with a smallholding, this emphasizing the importance of the expansion in these secondary rural occupations for the survival of the Melbourn peasantry until the middle of the nineteenth century. Whether successful craftsmen added smallholdings to their enterprises, or whether the subdivision of larger holdings pushed heirs into non-agricultural pursuits, we may never know, but it is safe to guess that both developments occurred to some extent. What we *can* consider seriously is why these dual enterprises were viable.

Both the keeping of animals and the growing of crops were important. Horse-drawn transport was sometimes essential for business purposes, as in the case of George Ward, plumber and glazier, whose accounts show that he travelled to many of the villages within an eight-mile radius of Melbourn, especially northwards and westwards.[16] Up to 1839, about forty common rights belonged to the peasantry; they were intended primarily for cow keeping, but might also have afforded some grazing for horses. By contrast, the many labourers had only a handful of common rights, about half of which belonged to the principal farmers and their landlords. The tithe survey shows that some of these common rights were converted to grass allotments, no doubt because their owners considered that their grassland resources in the village were insufficient.

---

[15] For Lincolnshire, I am relying on family information; for Wales, see D. Jenkins, *The Agricultural Community in South West Wales at the Turn of the Twentieth Century* (Cardiff, 1971), especially pp. 13 and 43ff. Other examples would not be difficult to find.   [16] CRO, 358B 1–2.

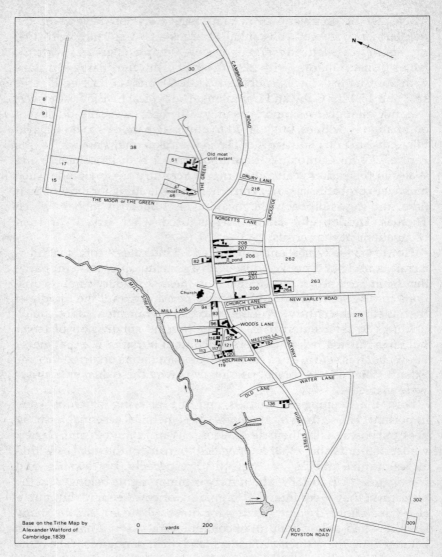

Figure 15.3. Melbourn, Cambs.: detail of Wood and Campkin 'empires'. (See pp. 502–504 for key.)

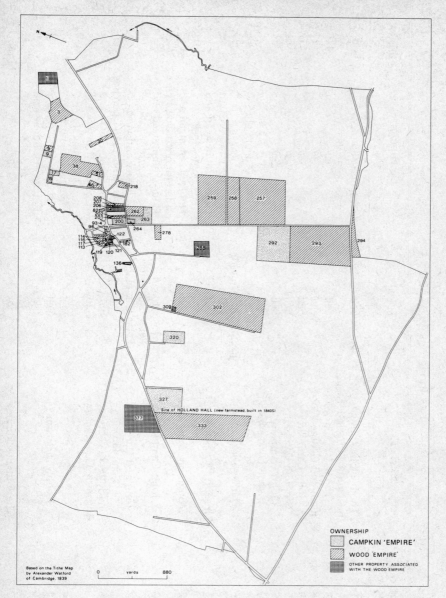

Figure 15.4. Melbourn, Cambs.: the Wood and Campkin 'empires'. (See pp. 502–504 for key.)

Key to Figures 15.3 and 15.4

Tithe parcel no.	Owner	Occupier	Description	Approx. acreage
1	Thomas Stockbridge (husband of Charlotte)	Self	Grass allotment	8
3	Thomas Wood	Self	*do.*	11½
8	William and George Wood	Selves	*do.*	1¾
9	John Campkin	Self	*do.*	1¾
15	Stephen Campkin	Self	*do.*	1½
17	John Campkin	Self	*do.*	1½
30	Joseph Dickason	Self	Portway Close	3¼
38	*do.*	*do.*	Grass allotment	20½
46	James Dickason	Joseph Dickason jnr	*do.*	1¾
47	*do.*	*do.*	Homstead and orchard	¾
51	Joseph Dickason snr	self	House, homestead and home close	1½
82	Stoughton Campkin	Self	House, homestead and garden (Spotted Dog PH)	¾
93	John Campkin	Joseph and Peter Campkin	House, homestead and garden	½
94	John and Caroline Campkin	Peter Campkin	House and yard (Tailors Arms PH)11 perches	
96	Charlotte Stockbridge (formerly C. Dickason)	Self and Geo, Gilby	House, homestead and garden (Docwra's messuage)	¾
113	*do.*	Self	Gray's Close (grass)	½
114	Joseph Dickason	Self	Nelson's Close (grass)	1½
116	*do.*	Various	Tenements, homestead and close	1¼
117	Charlotte Stockbridge	*do.*	Tenements	13 perches

No.	Name	Occupier	Description	23 perches
119	Stephen Campkin	Self and others	Tenements and gardens	$\frac{1}{4}$
120	Joseph Campkin	do.	do.	$\frac{1}{4}$
121	John Phillips	Various	Home close	$\frac{1}{2}$
122	do.	George Gilby	Homestead and garden (Rose Inn)	$3\frac{3}{4}$
136	Thomas Stockbridge	Self	House, homestead and orchard	$3\frac{3}{4}$
182	Charlotte Stockbridge	Various	Tenements, garden and grass close	$\frac{1}{2}$
200	Joseph Campkin	Self and others	Tenements and Church Lane Close (arable)	$2\frac{3}{4}$
201	Thomas Dickason Titchmarsh	Mynott Titchmarsh (his father)	House, homestead and orchard	$1\frac{1}{4}$
202	William and George Wood	William Wood and others	Tenements and orchard	$\frac{1}{2}$
206	Wortham Hitch	Thomas Wood	House, homestead and grass close	$2\frac{3}{4}$
207	do.	do.	Grass close	1
208	Thomas Wood	Self	House, homestead and garden	$1\frac{1}{4}$
218	do.	do.	Chappel's Close (grass)	$1\frac{1}{2}$
257	Charlotte Stockbridge	George Gilby	Arable allotment	74
258	Joseph Dickason snr	do.	do.	20
259	do.	Self	do.	52
262	Thomas Dickason Titchmarsh	Mynott Titchmarsh	do.	6
263	Joseph Campkin	Self	do.	9
264	do.	John Campkin and others	Tenements, homestead and gardens	1
278	James Dickason	Joseph Dickason jnr	Arable allotment	3
288	George Gilby	Self	do.	8

(Cont.)

503

Key to Figures 15.3 & 15.4 (Cont.)

292	Joseph Campkin	Self	40
293	Joseph Dickason snr	Self	81
294	do.	Joseph Dickason jnr	6
302	Thomas Wood	Self	$101\tfrac{3}{4}$
309	Susannah Pocklington	Thomas Wood	9
320	David Campkin	Self	27
327	Stoughton Campkin	Self	75
333	Thomas Dickason Titchmarsh	Mynott Titchmarsh	28
377	Mrs Elizabeth Leader	do.	

Notes

1. Members of the Campkin 'empire' are all identifiable by the surname, but relationships between the Campkins are unclear, except that Peter is known to have been the nephew of Joseph.

2. The remaining names are mostly those of the members of the Wood 'empire' (Figure 15.5): Thomas Wood, William and George Wood, Joseph Dickason snr and jnr, Charlotte Stockbridge, Thomas Dickason Titchmarsh. Other owners and occupiers have been included to complete the picture. Note that Charlotte Dickason became Charlotte, wife of Thomas Stockbridge, both of whom owned property. George Gilby married Elizabeth King, sister of Charlotte Stockbridge and probably daughter of a former tenant of the Rose, the principal inn of the village.

3. *Re* tithe parcels 47 and 122, which are described as homesteads: evidence independent of the tithe survey shows that these parcels included houses as well as farm buildings.

504

It is necessary to make guesses as to the use of arable land after 1839, though before enclosure there is no evidence of open-field strips being used for anything except wheat and barley. A few acres of barley would make a considerable difference if a peasant family kept a pig or two, which seems very likely in view of the presence in the village of several pig jobbers (men who dealt in pigs and/or killed them for their owners). When crop returns started in 1867 there were 600 pigs in Melbourn; indeed, Cambridgeshire has remained well-known for its pig keeping down to the present day. Home brewing is likely to have died out, except at the beer shops and the still independent public houses. Wheat and potatoes could also help with family subsistence; and the orchards at the rear end of messuages hint at the future development of fruit farming, which belongs chiefly to the railway age but had already some commercial possibilities in the 1840s, when plums went to London by road wagon.[17] Family land, family labour and direct subsistence – these are the hallmarks of peasantry in many lands and many times.

The previous 60 years in Melbourn had, however, been a period of exceptional population growth; the extra families had been accommodated partly by splitting up old homesteads but mainly by building rows of tenement cottages, described in the 1836 terrier and 1839 ratebook by the formula 'Cottage in three tenements', 'Two cottages in five tenements', and so on. The peasantry owned about a hundred tenements, let out to agricultural labourers, retired folk and journeymen–craftsmen. About one-quarter of the peasants had direct interests in the building trade, being described in 1841 as bricklayer, carpenter, plumber, etc. The brothers French with some of their sons were in a relatively big way of trade and could be described as builders. By owning a limekiln they controlled some of their raw materials, and their end product sometimes remained in their own hands. In fact, twenty tenements were built on land attached to their houses. The peasantry were, therefore, what we would now call small-scale developers and property speculators.

As Melbourn was situated on the main turnpike road from London to Cambridge, skills associated with travel were well represented among the harness makers, horsedealers, wheelwrights, blacksmiths and carriers. The drink trade too was well developed, twenty named licensed premises having been recorded for the period 1840–60. This large number is to be explained partly in terms of the passing traffic, partly by the miserable home conditions of the labourer in this period

[17] J. F. Ward, *West Cambridgeshire Fruit Growing Area: A Survey of Soils and Fruit 1925–7*, Ministry of Agriculture and Fisheries Bulletin lxi (London, 1933), p. 31.

and partly by relative laxity in licensing practice.[18] Even the three principal inns, however, were not regarded as full-time occupations. George Gilby has already been described, Charles Hawes at the Dolphin farmed on a substantial scale and let out his blacksmith's premises and several tenements, and Peter Wedd at the Hoops was a harness maker among other things. Serving the public and taking in lodgers and casual guests no doubt gave women and children chances of gainful employment, which were otherwise scarce in this non-industrial corn growing parish.

We have seen, then, that the peasantry put their small pieces of land and property to multifarious uses, and that there was a general lack of specialized functions in the village. Despite the growth of monopoly capitalism in rural England generally, there were still niches, like Melbourn, in which peasant independence survived and even flourished.[19] At the bottom end of the social hierarchy, the peasantry were hardly distinguishable from the labourers. A jobber with two acres and a tenement was unlikely to lead a life any different in essentials from an agricultural labourer who had managed to obtain a similar property. Both were probably heirs to subdivisions of inheritances too small for the maintenance of a family, but there was the question of pride, social standing and a sense of independence, in a period when a surplus of agricultural labour created a pauperized proletariat.[20]

At the top end of the scale, the peasantry included some very substantial entrepreneurs, such as Joseph Campkin, George Gilby, William French and Thomas and Charlotte Stockbridge (see Figures 15.3 and 15.4 for all but French). The Town Books show that their social standing was also recognized in the political system of the village. The offices of churchwarden and overseer were generally occupied by minor gentry, in effect professional men, such as the Fordhams and the Hitches, or by the big farmers, both yeomen and tenants. The importance of social standing, relative to length of residence, is demonstrated in a number of instances, the best-documented of which are that of William Baker, farmer, who came to

---

[18] For neighbouring areas in this period housing conditions are described in *Morning Chronicle*, 8 May 1850 (letter xxxvi) and 27 September 1850 (letter xxxvii) and other letters published in P. E. Razzell and R. W. Wainwright, *The Victorian Working Class* (London, 1973). On the licensing problem, see B. Harrison, *Drink and the Victorians: The Temperance Question in England, 1815–72* (London, 1971), especially pp. 45–8.

[19] For a summary of the geography of this subject, see my article 'The Peasant Tradition', cited in note 8.

[20] I have explored this aspect of the subject in an article entitled 'Bread and Potatoes, Clay Bat and Clunch: Evidence from Melbourn, Cambridgeshire, Relating to the Quality of Life in the Early Victorian Period'.

Wortham Hitch's White House Farm in 1830 and was churchwarden 1835–45 and 1848, and Nathaniel Holmes, who took John Hitch's Lordship Farm in 1836 and served as churchwarden 1844–8.[21] Nevertheless, William French, James Baker, Joseph Campkin and Joseph Hagger all rose to the rank of overseer, and Joseph Campkin actually took the chair at the vestry meeting on two occasions. James Ranson, who served as both overseer and churchwarden, was a special case, having married Nathaniel Holmes' daughter. Many of the peasantry, notably William Fench and Joseph Campkin, were in practice, though not in theory, debarred from the office of churchwarden by being Dissenters.[22] However, Table 15.5. indicates that more typically the peasantry served in the lower-ranking offices of surveyor, constable or paid assistant overseer. The governing oligarchy were pleased to have the hard work done for them, provided too much power and status was not acquired and the office holders could be relied upon to keep the labourers in their place. It would be difficult to demonstrate more aptly the in-between position of the peasantry.

v. The importance of house property

Reference has already been made to the role of developer played by some of the Melbourn peasants, and Table 15.5 contains details of substantial numbers of house properties owned, let and sublet by the peasantry. In view of the importance of family connections already suggested, it is desirable to ask the question to what extent house property was let to kin. Unfortunately a crystal clear answer cannot be obtained, but cross-reference between the tithe survey, the 1841 enumeration and Family Reconstitution Forms (FRFs) has not been without profit and the tenurial connections between kin displayed in Table 15.6 represent a *minimum*. The 48 persons represented in the table were the total number of those who either owned house property surplus to their own requirements, or were principal tenants in a position to sublet. Five large farmers are included and ten high-status agricultural labourers, but the majority, 35 out of the 48, were peasants.

Of the 48 persons concerned, FRFs are not available for ten, while for a further twenty the forms do not reveal any married kin living in

---

[21] CRO, uncalendared deposit, *Ranson and Knott* v. *Campkin*, Copy of deposition, Court of Arches, pp. 31, 126, 137.

[22] Dissenting churchwardens are recorded, for example, at Leeds in the 1830s by D. Fraser, *Urban Politics in Victorian England: The Structure of Politics in Victorian Cities* (Leicester, 1976), p. 33.

Table 15.6. *Summary of tenurial and kinship links with reference to house property in Melbourn 1839–41*

	Without apparent connections	With apparent kin–tenurial connections
Persons able to let house property		
No FRFs	10	4	6
FRFs, but no married kin	20	14	6
FRFs indicate married kin in Melbourn	18	9	9
Total	48	27	21

Melbourn in 1841. This is because the known kin are often parents who had already died, or can be presumed dead (the burial registers for Melbourn are especially disappointing, as they seldom identify adults in anyway other than by age). Even where there were known kinship links between households, there is the problem that the whole kinship network may not be in view. This prevents us from weighing accurately the balance of advantage in having propertied relatives; it is also one of the reasons why the known instances of coincidence between kinship and tenurial connections must be regarded as a minimum.

Half of the owners with traceable kin had let some of their dwelling space to kin. Several of them let to more than one related household head – William Huggins, agricultural labourer, for example, who rented one of his two tenements to his son (William Huggins, shoemaker) and the other to his son-in-law, William Flanders, the fish man. Similarly, William Wotton, master tailor, who rented a row of four tenement cottages and a workshop, sublet one to his father (also a tailor) and one to his brother, a journeyman carpenter.

Among the other half of the owners with traceable kin as household heads, there were several instances of both sets of kin having independent access to house property. For example, John Disbury senior had about five sub-tenants on his property, but these did not include his son, who owned a cottage of his own. Joseph Dickason senior had no need to let his second farmstead to his son, because the latter rented a farm from James Dickason, probably a relative. The data suggest, but no more, that letting or subletting of house properties may have been more important in the labouring and impoverished peasant families than among the more substantial peasantry. As inter-marriage between labourers and others was comparatively infrequent, the spread of families across social groups was probably much less than at earlier periods of Cambridgeshire history.[23] This would also limit the possibilities of letting dwellings to relations in less fortunate circumstances.

Where no kin can be traced there is still the reasonable possibility of inferring a coincidence of kinship and tenurial connection. Among the estimated twelve possibilities we can again mention William French, the builder, for in one of his tenements there lived another William French, bricklayer. While the younger man occurs neither on the older William's FRF, nor on George French's FRF, in view of the patchy record of baptisms in Melbourn it is entirely reasonable to infer that he was related to one of them, probably to William. Despite a lack of good FRFs, the Campkin 'family', which, like the French family, consisted of Dissenters, provides some most interesting inter-connections. Joseph Campkin, grocer, aged 56, owned no less than 22 dwellings, yet he could be located in none of them. Instead he was living in a house belonging to John Campkin, aged 30, also a grocer, while the said John, along with his widowed 'brother' David, a small farmer, lived in a house belonging to Joseph. John was also joint-owner with Caroline of a house next to where Joseph kept his grocer's shop. This was occupied by Peter Campkin, aged 25, tailor, where soon afterwards the Tailors' Arms was kept; also living here in 1841 was Caroline, aged nineteen, presumably single, and working as a straw-bonnet maker. It is difficult not to conclude that Peter, David, Caroline and John were siblings or cousins and that Joseph was their uncle or father, since his household in 1841 also contained five younger daughters all unbaptized. (See Figures 15.3 and 15.4; since this was written papers relating to the church rate case, in which Joseph Campkin was the defendant, have revealed that Peter was his nephew.)[24]

The Campkin 'family' illustrates both the diversity of occupational interests mentioned above and the possibility of young people starting out in business long before the death or senility of their father. Twenty-six wills, all those surviving for the period 1800–50 have been analysed to test the hypothesis that (a) a wide range of kin benefited from a will and (b) this facilitated the entrepreneurship of relatively young people (Table 15.7).

Whether these wills were entirely representative would be difficult to say, but there is some evidence that they reflected the attitudes of

[23] Spufford, *Contrasting Communities*, pp. 108–11, gives a particularly good example from seventeenth-century Orwell, a village within a few miles of Melbourn.
[24] CRO (see above, note 21), p. 59.

Table 15.7. Abstract of 26 Melbourn wills 1800–51

Will maker & date	No. of beneficiaries	Residue left to	Arrangements for land	Legacies To children	Legacies To others	Annuities or money to be invested	Date proved	Goods valued under £x
BAKER, Benjamin, weaver, 1806	3	Younger son Benjamin	Messuage to Benjamin with joint use to wife		Choice of furniture to wife if she lives separate from Benjamin	£2 p.a. to older son David after death of wife	1811	£20
HUGGINS, Thomas 'yeoman', † 1802	1		Messuage and goods to nephew John Smith Huggins,* only son of his sister Mary Huggins by John Smith				1811	£10
JARMAN, John,* farmer, 1801	1		All messuages, real and personal estate to his wife				1806	£100
SCRUBY, Thomas,* 'yeoman', 1800	4	Son Thomas,* includes real	Double messuage to wife for life, thence to Thomas	Married dau. £20; unmarried dau. £260	Furniture and £10 to wife	£20 p.a. to wife	1807	£800
WEDD, Peter, farmer, 1813	3+	After wife's death to son Peter* (Table 15.5)	All messuages to wife subject to mortgage	£30 apiece to other children after wife's death			1813	£200
COLE, Robert,* carpenter, 1821	5+	Son Joseph*	All messuages etc. to wife, thence new messuage to unmarried dau.	£10 each to 2 married daus. after wife's death			1825	£20
SMITH, Edward, farmer, 1817	5+	All messuages and residue to only son Ellis* (Table 15.4)		3 married daus., £30, £100; 1 of £100 revoked later	£20 each to children of deceased dau.		1819	?
STANFORD, John, farmer, 1822	8	All 7 daus. to share equally or as they wish	All messuages leased from Dean and Chapter to son George* (Table 15.4)	Married daus., £30, £60; unmarried daus. £50, £50, £55 + bedroom furniture (Rhoda in Table 15.5)			1824	£600
ELLIS, Jonathan, farmer, 1827	12	Residue of effects to 2 daus., 1 dau.-in-law	All land to grandson Edward Walbey*		Money to 6 grandchildren and 1 nephew (Amounts £2–£20)	£10 p.a. to wife	1827	£450
PRIME, John, labourer, 1820	1		All messuages and goods to friend John Negus,* father of John Negus (Table 15.5)				1826	£100
COLE, James,* farmer, 1834	1		All real and moveable property to wife Sarah* (Table 15.5)				1836	£200

510

(Cont.)

511

Name	No.	Main heir	Property disposition	Daughters / other	Other bequests	Annuity / trust	Year	Value
DICKASON, Thomas,* 1835 (also died 1835)	4		Wife Charlotte Stockbridge,* bro.-in-law William Newling,* and George Gilby, wife's bro.-in-law (all Table 15.5). Division uncertain, but bulk to Charlotte	Childless	19 guineas to George Gilby, neighbour	£10 p.a. to Susan Wood, step-grand-mother (see under T. Wood)	1839	£800
FLANDERS, David,* farmer, 1839	4		Arable to pay off mortgage. Messuage etc. to wife, thence equally to 3 sons, including Zachariah* (Table 15.5)				1839	£200
JARMAN, Thomas,* 1828	10	Probably son Thomas* and grandson	All land and stock to son Thomas* (Table 15.5)	4 married daus. £200 each; also furniture to 1	3 grandchildren £40 each at 21; children of dead son £50 each for 2 girls; furniture and book debts (investments) to grandson Thomas Jarman	£120 for first 3 grandchildren invested – interest for education and clothes	1836	£2,000
OLIVER, Henry,* butcher, 1831	4	Dau. Sarah	One messuage, shop etc. to son Sylvester.* New messuage to unmarried dau. Sarah*	Married dau. £10; son £5 and furniture			1834	£20
STOCKBRIDGE, Thomas, 'yeoman', 1831	5	Wife	Freehold arable to wife; 3 copyhold messuages to dau. Eliz. Wing* wife of Dan Wing (Table 15.5); thence to be shared by 3 Wing grandsons*				1837	£50
WOOD, Thomas,* 'yeoman', 1827	31+	Grandson Thomas Dickason* (see above)	Land shared by Grandson Thomas Wood* (Table 15.4), Thomas Dickason,* great grandson Thomas Tichmarsh* (son of Mynott T., Table 15.4) and nephew William Wood* (Table 15.5), with George,* grand nephew, to inherit subsequently. (See Figure 15.5 for identifications.)	£20 and household goods to married dau.	£200 and household goods to second wife Susan,* £50 to brother; 19 guineas to sister; £5 to £10 each to 16 nephews and nieces; £200 to grandson Thomas Dickason; £200 to granddau. Hannah Dickason* (= Mrs Wm Newling, Table 15.5); £50 each to 6 grandchildren; 19 guineas to 1 later grandchild added in codicil 1829	Wife £10 p.a. £200 on trust interest to married daughter	1834	£1,500

Table 15.7 (Cont.)

	No. of beneficiaries	Residue left to	Arrangements for land	Legacies		Annuities or money to be invested	Date proved	Goods valued under £x
				To children	To others			
BAKER, Elizabeth, widow, 1839	7	Son William		£60 each to 3 daus., 1 single, 1 married, 1 widowed; £20 each to 2 daus., 1 married	One grandson £20		1844	£200
CHARTER, Charles,* (see text), labourer, 1847	4+	Son Joseph	All to son Joseph,* provided he allows mother and brother Charles* to live in second tenement		Joseph to pay Charles' children £30 on marriage or coming of age		1847	£100
COOPER, William,* 'yeoman' (ag. lab. 1841), 1840	7		All to be sold and proceeds shared equally between wife and 6 children (3 sons, 3 daus., one unmarried)				1842	£200
GOULDTHORP, John,* the Elder, blacksmith, 1844	5		All to be sold and shared equally between wife and 2 sons, 1 married dau. and her daus.				1845	£200
SEYMOUR, Margaret,* late of Chatteris, widow, 1835 (probably widow of vicar of Melbourn)	1	Hannah Ashley	All to H. Ashley, a governess aged 25 in 1841, living with Mrs Seymour in rented tenement				1847	£600
THURLEY, Thomas,* (Table 15.5), 1844	3+	All household effects and 10 guineas to White Lion Club, Royston	All to dau. Mary Fordham,* thence to grandson John*		£40 to granddau. on death of her mother		1847	£50
ELLIS, Mary, spinster (Table 15.5), 1849	2	Uncle Ellis Baker*	All real and personal estate		£5 to cousin		1850	£10
GILBY, George* (Table 15.5), innkeeper, 1847	5+	Wife	All to wife, while she is a widow; thence to be sold and shared equally between all children and grandchildren living – at age 21 for boys and at age 21 or marriage for girls.				1849	£1,500
TAYLOR, William,* 'yeoman' (Table 15.5), 1851	2		All real and personal estate to be sold and shared equally between 2 married granddaughters				1854	£20

* Identified in registers and/or 1841 enumeration.
† The occupations are as stated in the wills, with the effect that the term 'yeoman' does not here correspond to its use in the text.
Source: Cambridge University Library: Archdeaconry of Ely Probate Records.

512

the middling peasantry of traditional Melbourn stock. Few wills were made by labourers, but in most cases valuation revealed personal estate worth less than £200, which is comparable with Vincent's figures for a much larger number of craftsmen, yeomen, publicans and shopkeepers.[25] Many of the will makers are identifiable in the FRFs, and all except one had a surname common in Melbourn. Taken in conjunction with an absence of men identifiable as large tenant farmers, these facts suggest that the wills are representative of Melbourn tradition, even in the case of Thomas Wood, a yeoman farmer and owner–occupier of considerable standing.

Equal splitting of estates is mentioned only in four wills late in the series, but three other common types of division occur. One pattern was to divide real estate between sons and make cash payments to daughters, another pattern being a variation in which younger sons were treated in similar fashion to the daughters. It was not unusual for married daughters to receive much less than unmarried, this implying that dowries were given. Where a wife was alive, the third pattern of wills often accommodated her by making her the responsibility of the eldest son, or leaving her a small house of her own. Only in a few wills is it possible to read of wives inheriting all the estate, without mention of subsequent division between the children.

These examples do not suggest that there was a consensus in Melbourn as to how property should be transmitted, except on one vital point. There seem to have been few inhibitions about the splitting up of property, and certainly no elaborate precautions designed to keep estates in one block. The Melbourn peasant inheritance practices were, therefore, in strong contrast with the exercise of primogeniture on large estates in the same period, not to mention the entailed estates (though occasionally there are directions as to how a piece of property is to be split subsequently between grandchildren).

In twelve wills, or nearly one-half, provision is made for persons other than the deceased's spouse and children; a wide range of persons benefited, including distant kin and even friends, though the bulk of the wealth always passed to direct kin where we know them to have been alive. Omitting the exceptional circumstances surrounding the Wood estate, a mean of over four persons was mentioned in each will. This is a minimum figure because it is impossible to guess at the real numbers implied by such phrases as 'the surviving children of my daughter Sarah'. It was not uncommon for children and young persons to inherit money and even real estate – as in the

---

[25] Vincent, *Pollbooks*, p. 37.

case of Edward Walbey who inherited a farm at age 25 from Jonathan Ellis because his father had died, and likewise Thomas Jarman at age eighteen (Table 15.7). Other examples can be found in the tithe survey (Table 15.5), where young persons under age were the owners of modest pieces of property which enhanced their life chances. One is Caroline Campkin, aged nineteen, a straw-bonnet maker, living with Peter Campkin, possibly her brother. The property she shared with John Campkin in the middle of 1839 can be identified in the spring rate book as that belonging to Ephraim Campkin, possibly their father. Susannah Pocklington was one of the grandchildren of Jonathan Ellis and inherited cash, which she appears to have invested in the three roods of land she owned in 1839. William Dearman, agricultural labourer, aged twenty, lived in his grandfather's household with his widowed mother. He was owner–occupier of four acres of arable, which he probably cultivated with his grandfather's farm tackle. Samuel Negus, aged nineteen, described as a castrator in the 1841 census, let his acre of arable to his father, Stephen, a farmer and pig jobber. As Stephen appears to have remarried, it is possible that this acre came to Samuel on his mother's death. Alfred Pryor, fifteen, butcher's apprentice, rented his two-acre arable allotment to James Pryor, carpenter, with whom the boy lived, although they were not father and son. Significantly, in later years all three boys appear as self-employed tradesmen.

Good examples of the subdivision of small amounts of real estate are to be found in the wills of David Flanders, Henry Oliver and Thomas Stockbridge (Table 15.7). However, the clearest example of widespread division of property and the willing of it to grandchildren and even great-grandchildren is to be found in the exceptional will of Thomas Wood, yeoman, who died in 1834 at the age of 90 or 94. (See Figure 15.5 for his family tree.) His estate was valued at not above £1,500, a considerable sum but not enough perhaps to make the old man break with the Melbourn traditions which he had observed during his long life. No less than thirty people were mentioned in his will – his second wife, one brother and sister (the other four presumably dead), one of his three children, fifteen nephews and nieces, four grandchildren and seven great-grandchildren. The majority received sums of money ranging from £5 to £200, and his wife and widowed daughter got an annuity each and shared the household goods.

The real estate was divided between four male relatives, the two principal farms going to grandson Thomas Wood and great-grandson Thomas Dickason Titchmarsh, a boy of sixteen. The latter seems to

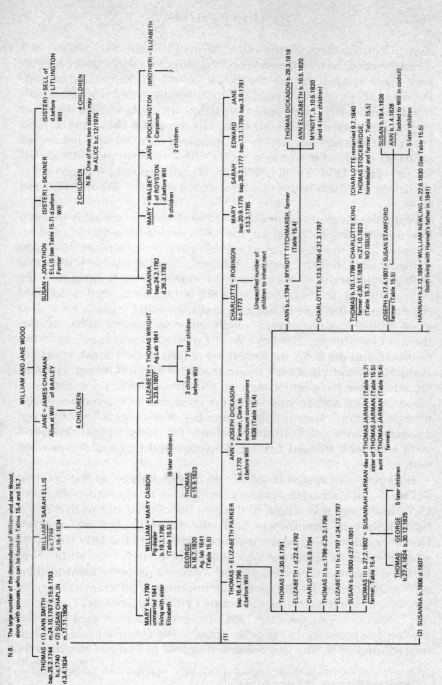

Sources: Parish registers and Wills
Names underlined = beneficiaries in will of Feb 2 1827

N.B. The large number of the descendants of William and Jane Wood,
along with spouses, who can be found in Tables 15.4 and 15.7

WILLIAM AND JANE WOOD

THOMAS = (1) ANN SMITH
bap.25.2.1744   m.24.10.1767 d.15.9.1793
b.c.1740   (2) SUSAN CHAPLIN
d.3.4.1834   m.17.11.1806

JANE = JAMES CHAPMAN
Alive at Will   of BARLEY

4 CHILDREN

WILLIAM = SARAH ELLIS
b.c.1749
d.16.4.1834

SUSAN = JONATHON
        ELLIS (see Table 15.7)
        Farmer

2 CHILDREN

(SISTER) = SKINNER
          (see Table 15.7) d.before
          Will

(SISTER) = SELL =
           d.before
           Will

LITLINGTON

4 CHILDREN

N.B. One of these two sisters may
be ALICE b.c.12/1975

MARY b.c.1790
unmarried 1841
living with sister
Elizabeth

WILLIAM = MARY CASBON
Pig dealer
b.19.1.1795
(Table 15.5)

ELIZABETH = THOMAS WRIGHT
b.23.6.1807   Ag. Lab 1841

3 children
before Will

7 later children

MARY = WALBEY
       of ROYSTON
       d.before Will

9 children

SUSANNA
bap.24.2.1782
d.26.3.1783

JANE = POCKLINGTON
       Carpenter

2 children

(BROTHER) = ELIZABETH
?

GEORGE
b.16.7.1820
Ag. lab 1841
(Table 15.5)

THOMAS
b.15.9.1823

(6 later children)

THOMAS = ELIZABETH PARKER
bap.16.4.1796
d.before Will

(1)

THOMAS I d.30.8.1791

ELIZABETH I d.22.4.1792

CHARLOTTE b.5.9.1794

THOMAS II b.c.1796 d.25.2.1796

ELIZABETH II b.c.1797 d.24.12.1797

SUSAN b.c.1800 d.27.6.1801

THOMAS III b.27.2.1802 = SUSANNAH JARMAN (Table 15.7) dau of THOMAS JARMAN (Table 15.5)
farmer, Table 15.4   sister of THOMAS JARMAN (Table 15.5)
                                                      aunt of THOMAS JARMAN (Table 15.4)

THOMAS   GEORGE   5 later children
b.27.4.1824   b.30.12.1825

ANN = JOSEPH DICKASON
b.c.1770   Farmer, Clerk to
d.before Will   enclosure commissioners
                1839 (Table 15.4)

CHARLOTTE = ROBINSON
b.c.1773

Unspecified number of
children to inherit next

ANN b.c.1794 = MYNOTT TITCHMARSH, farmer
               (Table 15.4)

CHARLOTTE b.13.5.1796 d.31.3.1797

THOMAS b.10.1.1799 = CHARLOTTE KING
farmer d.30.11.1835   m.21.10.1823
(Table 15.7)   NO ISSUE

JOSEPH b.17.4.1801 = SUSAN STAMFORD
farmer (Table 15.5)

HANNAH b.2.12.1804 = WILLIAM NEWLING m.22.6.1830 (See Table 15.5)
                     (both living with Hannah's father in 1841)

MARY   SARAH   EDWARD   JANE
bap.20.9.1775 bap.28.2.1777 bap.13.1.1780 bap.3.9.1781
d.13.3.1785

THOMAS DICKASON b.29.3.1818

ANN ELIZABETH b.10.5.1820

MYNOTT, b.10.5.1820
(and 4 later children)

[CHARLOTTE remarried 9.7.1840
THOMAS STOCKBRIDGE,
horsedealer and farmer, Table 15.5]

SUSAN b.19.4.1826

ANN b.1.4.1828
(added to Will in codicil)

5 later children

(2) SUSANNA b.1806 d.1807

Figure 15.5. Simplified family tree of Thomas Wood the elder

have inherited through the claim of his dead mother, who was a direct descendant of Thomas Wood the elder, while his father Mynott was made tenant during the boy's minority. Another grandson, Thomas Dickason, was given Docwra's messuage and workshop with thirteen-and-a-half acres of open field, which he added to other pieces of property (mostly his own, but some of it belonging to John Hitch and absentee owner Mary Chandler), to make up a holding of about 90 acres, four common rights, three workshops and a dozen tenements in 1836. Finally, William Wood, nephew, was given the messuage in which he was living with the old man (Figures 15.3 and 15.4).

While the break-up of an estate of 250 acres or so probably meant a lost opportunity to create at the 1839 enclosure a viable modern farming unit, the dispersal of wealth gave opportunities of a very different kind to many people. Vincent's point about the low capital outlay necessary to start an enterprise in this period is again relevant in considering the significance of £5 gifts. Given hard work and enterprise on the part of the recipient they could mean a great deal more than the piglet conventionally given to farmers' sons, to start them off in farming. The boys were expected to scavenge round the farmyard and the fields for something to feed to the animal, which on slaughter brought in a cash return ready for the next round. Here, in miniature, we have an example of the peasant-style combination of labour, capital and an interest in the economic independence of the next generation. The significant number of females inheriting from Thomas Wood's will is further evidence for believing that dowries – or at least well stocked bottom drawers – were part of the peasant system.

The process of fission could not go on indefinitely, as the example of David and Zachariah Flanders shows very nicely (Tables 15.5 and 15.7), and there was a limit to the number of occupations that could be followed in conjunction with the farming of a bit of land. However, fusion also sometimes occurred and in the 1839 survey 23 women's names appear among the list of owners, not all of them widows; this excludes cases where women's property went in their husbands' names.[26] The potential importance of transmission of property in the female line is illustrated by the succession of events at the Docwra messuage after 1834. Thomas Dickason died in 1835, leaving his property to his wife, though the confused will was not proved until 1839. She was remarried in 1840 to Thomas Stockbridge,

[26] Married women with husbands still alive have been excluded from Table 15.5 in the interests of economy and simplicity.

a horsedealer; they were one of the few couples, perhaps significantly, to get married by special licence. Charlotte's choice of second
husband allowed a relatively young couple, aged about forty, to bring
together diverse pieces of property into a peasant enterprise where
farming, horsedealing and the letting of a 73-acre farm, a workshop
and tenements provided a widely based income (Figures 15.3 and
15.4).

Conclusion

At the outset this essay raised the question as to the extent to which a
peasantry had survived in Melbourn to 1839 and the factors which
could explain this survival. We have seen that the community
consisted of three major groupings of families – the landless proletariat and the large farmers at the bottom and the top of the social
hierarchy, with the peasantry holding the middle ground. So Melbourn was by no means an entirely peasant village in 1839. Moreover,
those who have been described as peasants were generally not
wholly dependent on the land for their living.

This brings us to one of the main factors in the survival of the
peasantry. Although their holdings were no longer viable units of
agricultural production, they provided an excellent basis for many
rural secondary occupations, where land for house building, the
pasturing of horses or traditional subsistence could be integrated with
a non-agricultural enterprise. Examples of rural dual occupationists
are not difficult to find elsewhere. What made Melbourn outstanding
was its development as a service centre which sustained both these
businesses and a very rapid population growth in the first half of the
century.

The supply of small properties would almost certainly not have
been so great if the long-established resident land owners had not
been willing to subdivide their property on transmission to the next
generation. The yeoman families, unlike the tenant farmers, were at
the core of the community. The considerable subdivision in the Wood
will is reflected also in the wills of Thomas Scruby, Edward Smith,
John Stanford, Jonathan Ellis and Thomas Jarman, where by chance
one male heir is balanced by several female heirs who inherit
substantial cash sums. This subdivision was one of the processes
which provided the basis of so many peasant enterprises. It is also
one of the reasons why it is not possible to understand how the
peasantry fared without looking at the behaviour of the yeomanry.
Indeed, the fluctuating fortunes of individual families, influenced

partly by demographic luck, is probably at least a partial explanation of the inconsistent use of the term 'yeoman', which Vincent also noted.[27] Old men like William Cooper and Thomas Stockbridge, who left very little to their heirs, may have been inclined to call themselves yeomen because their fathers had been much more substantial men and had passed on part of their yeoman status and property.

The final major reason for the peasantry's survival arises from the behaviour of the manorial lords and the main institutional owners. They do not appear to have entered the land market in any substantial way to enlarge their estates. In this respect they were quite different from Lord Wantage and his predecessors at Ardington. In John Hitch's case lack of cash would have held him back, but the very large number of small owners must have acted as a deterrent to large owners who considered buying Melbourn land for investment purposes only. While each English village lived through its own unique experience, there was probably a threshold level as to the numbers of owners, which once crossed made it unlikely that a village would become the scene of major engrossing activities on the part of a landed family.

[27] Vincent, *Pollbooks*, pp. 37–8.

Consolidated Bibliography

Anderson, B. L., 'Money and the Structure of Credit in the Eighteenth Century', *Business History* 12:2 (1970), pp. 85–101

Anderson, M., *Approaches to the History of the Western Family 1500–1914* (London, 1980)

Family Structure in Nineteenth Century Lancashire (Cambridge, 1971)

'The Impact on the Family Relationships of the Elderly of Changes since Victorian Times in Governmental Income-Maintenance Provision' in E. Shanas and M. Sussman, editors, *Family, Bureaucracy and the Elderly*, pp. 36–69

Appleby, A. B., 'Disease or Famine? Mortality in Cumberland and Westmorland, 1580–1640', *Economic History Review* 2nd series 26 (1973), pp. 403–32

Ariès, P., *L'Enfant et la vie familiale sous l'ancien régime* (Paris, 1960)

Armstrong, A., *Stability and Change in an English County Town: A Social Study of York, 1801–1851* (Cambridge, 1974)

Arthington, H., *Provision for the Poore* (London, 1597)

Aston, T. H., *et al.*, editors, *Social Relations and Ideas* (Cambridge, 1983)

Atkinson, J. C. editor, *North Riding Quarter Sessions Records*, Vol. I (London, 1884)

Ault, W. O., *Open-Field Farming in Medieval England* (London, 1972).

Bagot, A., 'Mr Gilpin and Manorial Customs', *Transactions of the Cumberland and Westmorland Antiquarian and Archaeological Society* new series 62 (1961), pp. 224–45

Baker, A. R. H., 'Field Systems in South-East England', in A. R. H. Baker and R. A. Butlin, editors, *Studies of Field Systems in the British Isles*, pp. 377–425

'Open Fields and Partible Inheritance on a Kent Manor', *Economic History Review* 2nd series 17 (1964–5), pp. 1–22

'Some Fields and Farms in Medieval Kent', *Archaeologia Cantiana*, 80 (1965), pp. 152–74

and R. A. Butlin, editors, *Studies of Field Systems in the British Isles* (Cambridge, 1973)

Baker, D., 'The Inhabitants of Cardington in 1782', *Bedfordshire Historical Record Society* 52 (1973)

Banks, J., *A Journal of the Life of John Banks* (London, 1712)

Batt, M., *Testimony of the Life and Death of Mary Batt* (London, 1683)

Bean, J. M. W., 'Plague, Population and Economic Decline in England in the

Later Middle Ages', *Economic History Review* 2nd series 15 (1962–3), pp. 423–37

Beckerman, J. S., 'Customary Law in Manorial Courts in the Thirteenth Century', unpublished University of London Ph.D. thesis, 1972

Beier, A. L., 'The Social Problems of an Elizabethan Country Town: Warwick, 1580–90', in P. Clark, editor, *Country Towns in Pre-Industrial England* (Leicester, 1981), pp. 46–85

Bennett, J. M., 'Gender, Family and Community: A Comparative Study of the English Peasantry', unpublished Toronto Ph.D. thesis, 1981

Beresford, M. W., 'A Review of Historical Research', in M. W. Beresford and J. G. Beresford, editors, *Deserted Medieval Villages*, pp. 3–144

and J. G. Beresford, editors, *Deserted Medieval Villages* (London, 1971)

and H. P. R. Finberg, *Medieval English Boroughs* (Newton Abbott, 1973)

Berkner, L. K., 'Inheritance, Land Tenure and Peasant Family Structure: A German Regional Comparison', in J. Goody *et al.*, editors, *Family and Inheritance*, pp. 71–95

'The Stem Family and Development Cycle of the Peasant Household: An Eighteenth-Century Austrian Example', *American Historical Review* 77 (1972), pp. 398–418

and J. W. Shaffer, 'The Joint Family in the Nivernais', *Journal of Family History* 3 (1978), pp. 150–62

Birdsall, N., 'Fertility and Economic Change in Eighteenth and Nineteenth Century Europe: An Extension of Smith's Analysis', *Population and Development Review* 9 (1983), pp. 111–23

Blanchard, I., 'Derbyshire Lead Production, 1195–1505', *Derbyshire Archaeological Journal* 91 (1971), pp. 119–40

The Duchy of Lancaster's Estates in Derbyshire, 1485–1540, Derbyshire Archaeological Society Record Series iii (Derby, 1967)

'Economic Change in Derbyshire in the Late Middle Ages, 1272–1540', unpublished University of London Ph.D. thesis, 1967

'Labour Productivity and Work Psychology in the English Mining Industry 1400–1600', *Economic History Review* 2nd series 31 (1978), pp. 1–24

'The Miner and the Agricultural Community in Late Medieval England', *Agricultural History Review* 20:2 (1972), pp. 93–106

'Population Change, Enclosure and the Early Tudor Economy', *Economic History Review* 23 (1970), pp. 427–45

'Stannator Fabulosus', *Agricultural History Review* 22:1 (1974), pp. 62–74

Blomefield, F., and C. Parkin, *An Essay Towards a Topographical History of the County of Norfolk*, Vol. vii (London, 1808)

Blount, T., *Fragmenta Antiquitatis; or, Antient Tenures of Land, and Jocular Customs of Some Manors*, with explanatory notes by J. Beckwith (York, 1784)

Bolton, J. L., *The Medieval English Economy 1150–1500* (London, 1980)

Bonfield, L., 'Marriage Settlements and the "Rise of Great Estates": the Demographic Aspect', *Economic History Review* 32 (1979), pp. 483–93

Bouch, C. M. L., and G. P. Jones, *A Short Economic and Social History of the Lake Counties 1500–1830* (Manchester, 1961)

Brathwaite, R., *The English Gentleman and English Gentlewoman* (London, 1641)

Brenner, R., 'Agrarian Class Structure and Economic Development in Pre-Industrial Europe', *Past and Present* 70 (1976), pp. 30–75

'The Agrarian Roots of European Capitalism', *Past and Present* 97 (1982), pp. 16–113

Bridbury, A. R., 'The Black Death', *Economic History Review* 2nd series 26 (1973), pp. 577–92

Britnell, R. H., 'Production for the Market on a Small Fourteenth-Century Estate', *Economic History Review* 2nd series 19 (1966), pp. 380–7

Britton, E., *The Community of the Vill: A Study in the History of the Family and Village Life in Fourteenth Century England* (Toronto, 1977)

'The Peasant Family in Fourteenth Century England', *Peasant Studies* 5 (1976), pp. 2–7

Butler, W., 'The Customs and Tenant Right Tenures of the Northern Counties with Particulars of Those in the District of Furness in the County of Lancashire', *Transactions of the Cumberland and Westmorland Antiquarian and Archaeological Society* new series 26 (1926), pp. 318–36

Cain, M., 'Perspectives on Family and Fertility in Developing Countries', *Population Studies* 36 (1982), pp. 159–76

'Risk and Fertility in India and Bangladesh', *Population and Development Review* 7 (1981), pp. 435–74

S. Rokeya Khanam, and S. Nahar, 'Class, Patriarchy and Women's Work in Bangladesh', *Population and Development Review* 5 (1979), pp. 305–438

Campbell, B. M. S., 'Agricultural Progress in Medieval England: Some Evidence from Eastern Norfolk', *Economic History Review* 2nd series 36 (1983), pp. 26–46

'Arable Productivity in Medieval England: Some Evidence from Norfolk', *Journal of Economic History*, 43 (1983), pp. 379–404

'The Extent and Layout of Commonfields in Eastern Norfolk', *Norfolk Archaeology* 38 (1981), pp. 18–20

'Field Systems in Eastern Norfolk during the Middle Ages: A Study with Particular Reference to the Demographic and Agrarian Changes of the Fourteenth Century', unpublished University of Cambridge Ph.D. thesis, 1975

'Population Change and the Genesis of Commonfields on a Norfolk Manor', *Economic History Review* 2nd series 33 (1980), pp. 174–92

'The Regional Uniqueness of English Field Systems? Some Evidence from Eastern Norfolk', *Agricultural History Review* 29 (1981), pp. 16–28

Campbell, J. K., *Honour, Family and Patronage: A Study of Institutions and Moral Values in a Greek Mountain Community* (Oxford, 1964)

Carter, E., *History of the County of Cambridge* (Cambridge, 1819)

Carus Wilson, E. M., editor, *Essays in Economic History, Vol. II* (London, 1962)

Chambers, J. D., *Population, Economy, and Society in Pre-Industrial England* (Oxford, 1972)

Chapple, G. P., *Congregationalism at Melbourn 1694–1894* (London, 1895)

Chayanov, A. V., *Organizatsiya Krest' yanskogo khozyaistia*, translated by R. E. F. Smith in D. B. Thorner *et al.*, editors, *A. V. Chayanov on the Theory of Peasant Economy*, pp. 53–69

Chaytor, M., 'Household and Kinship: Ryton in the Late Sixteenth and Early Seventeenth Centuries', *History Workshop Journal* 10 (1980), pp. 25–60

Child, Sir Josiah, *A New Discourse of Trade* (London, 1694)

Clark, A. C., *The Working Life of Women in the Seventeenth Century* (London, 1919; repr. 1968)

Clark, E., 'Some Aspects of Social Security in Medieval England', *Journal of Family History* 7 (1982), pp. 307–20

Clark, P., 'The Alehouse and the Alternative Society', in D. Pennington and K. Thomas, editors, *Puritans and Revolutionaries: Essays in Seventeenth Century History presented to Christopher Hill*, pp. 47–72

editor, *Country Towns in Pre-Industrial England* (Leicester, 1981)

and J. G. Clark, 'The Social Economy of the Canterbury Suburbs: The Evidence of the Census of 1563', in A. Detsicas and N. Yates, editors, *Studies in Modern Kentish History*, pp. 65–86

Clarkson, L A., *The Pre-Industrial Economy in England 1500–1750* (London, 1971)

Cliffe, J. T., *The Yorkshire Gentry from the Reformation to the Civil War* (London, 1969)

Coleman, D. C., *The Economy of England, 1450–1750* (Oxford, 1977)

'Labour in the English Economy of the Seventeenth Century' in E. M. Carus Wilson, editor, *Essays in Economic History*, Vol. II, pp. 291–308

Connell, K. H., 'Peasant Marriage in Ireland: Its Structure and Development since the Famine', *Economic History Review*, 2nd series 24 (1961–2), pp. 502–23.

Conyers, A., editor, *Wiltshire Extents for Debts*, Wiltshire Record Society xxviii (Devizes, 1973)

Conze, W., *Sozialgeschichte du Families in der Neuzeit Europas* (Stuttgart, 1976)

The Court Rolls of the Manor of Preston, Sussex Record Society (Lewes, 1921)

Cowper, H. S., *Hawkshead* (London, 1899)

Creighton, C., 'Family, Property and Relations of Production in Western Europe', *Economy and Society* 9 (1980), pp. 129–67

Czap, P., 'The Perennial Multiple Family Household, Mishino, Russia, 1782–1858', *Journal of Family History* 7 (1982), pp. 5–26

Dalton, G., 'Peasantries in Anthropology and History', *Current Anthropology* 13 (1972) pp. 385–415

Darby, H. C., *The Domesday Geography of Eastern England* (Cambridge, 1952)

editor, *A New Historical Geography of England* (Cambridge, 1973)

Davenport, F. J., *The Economic Development of a Norfolk Manor* (Cambridge, 1906)

Detsicas, A., and N. Yates, editor, *Studies in Modern Kentish History* (Maidstone, 1983)

Dewey, H., 'Lead, Silver Lead and Zinc Ores of Cornwall, Devon and Somerset', *Memoirs of the Geological Survey of England and Wales* (1921)

Dewindt, E. B., *Land and People in Holywell-cum-Needingworth: Structures of Tenure and Patterns of Social Organization in an East Midlands Village 1252–1457* (Toronto, 1972)

Dobson, R. B., *The Peasants' Revolt of 1381* (London, 1970)

Dodgshon, R. A., 'The Interpretation of Sub-Divided Fields: A Study in Private or Common Interests', in T. Rowley, editor, *The Origins of Open Field Agriculture*, pp. 130–144

The Origin of the British Field Systems: An Interpretation (London, 1980)

Dodwell, B., 'The Free Peasantry of East Anglia in Domesday', *Norfolk Archaeology* 27 (1939), pp. 145–57

'Holdings and Inheritance in Medieval East Anglia', *Economic History Review* 2nd series 20 (1967), pp. 53–66

Douglas, D. C., *The Social Structure of Medieval East Anglia*, Oxford Studies in Social and Legal History lx (Oxford, 1927)

Drake, K. M., 'An Elementary Exercise in Parish Register Demography', *Economic History Review* 2nd series 14 (1962), pp. 427–45

Du Boulay, F. R. H., *The Lordship of Canterbury* (London, 1966)

Dunning, R. W., 'The Administration of the Diocese of Bath and Wells 1401–1491', unpublished University of Bristol Ph.D. thesis, 1963

Dyer, A. D., *The City of Worcester in the Sixteenth Century* (Leicester, 1973)

Dyer, C., 'Deserted Medieval Villages in the West Midlands', *Economic History Review* 2nd series 35 (1982), pp. 19–34

'The Estates of the Bishopric of Worcester, 680–1540', unpublished University of Birmingham Ph.D. thesis, 1977

Lords and Peasants in a Changing Society: The Estates of the Bishopric of Worcester, 680–1540 (Cambridge, 1980)

'A Redistribution of Incomes in Fifteenth Century?', *Past and Present* 39 (1968), pp. 11–33

Warwickshire Farming, 1349–c.1520: Preparations for Agricultural Revolution, Dugdale Society Occasional Papers xxvii (London, 1981)

Emmison, F. G., *Elizabethan Life: Home, Work and Land* (Chelmsford, 1976)

Early Essex Town Meetings (Chelmsford, 1970)

Elizabethan Life: Morals and Church Courts (Chelmsford, 1973)

Everitt, A. M., *Change in the Provinces: the Seventeenth Century*, Occasional Papers of the Department of Local History, series ii: 1 (Leicester, 1970)

Everitt, A. M., 'Farm Labourers', in J. Thirsk, editor, *The Agrarian History of England and Wales*, Vol. IV, pp. 396–465

Ewbank, J. M., editor, *Antiquary on Horseback* (Kendal, 1963)

Faith, R. J., 'Peasant Families and Inheritance Customs in Medieval England', *Agricultural History Review* 14 (1966), pp. 77–95

'The Peasant Land Market in Berkshire during the Later Middle Ages', unpublished University of Leicester Ph.D. thesis, 1962

Farmer, D. L., 'Some Grain Price Movements in Thirteenth Century England', *Economic History Review* 2nd series 10 (1957), pp. 207–20

Farrer, W., *Feudal Cambridgeshire* (Cambridge, 1920)

and J. F. Curwen, *Records Relating to the Barony of Kendale, Vol. II* (Kendal, 1924)

Fisher, F. J., *Essays in the Economic and Social History of Tudor and Stuart England* (Cambridge, 1961)

Fisher, R. B., *A Practical Treatise of Copyhold Tenure* (London, 1794)

Ford, J. R., 'The Customary Tenant-right of the Manors of Yealand', *Transactions of the Cumberland and Westmorland Antiquarian and Archaeological Society* new series 9 (1909), pp. 147–60

Fraser, D., *Urban Politics in Victorian England: The Structure of Politics in Victorian Cities* (Leicester, 1976)

Freedman, M., editor, *Family and Kinship in Chinese Society* (Stanford, Cal., 1970)

Freedman, R., Ming-Cheng Chang, and Te-Hsiung Sun, 'Household Composition, Extended Kinship and Reproduction in Taiwan, 1973–1980', *Population Studies* 35 (1982), pp. 395–412

Gattrell, P., 'Historians and Peasants: Studies of Medieval English Society in a Russian Context', *Past and Present* 96 (1982), pp. 22–50

Glass, D. V., and D. E. C. Eversley, editors, *Population in History* (London, 1965)

Gluckman, M., *Custom and Conflict in Africa* (Oxford, 1955)

Goode, W. J., *World Revolution and Family Patterns* (New York, 1963)

Goodman, L. A., N. Keyfitz, and T. W. Pullum, 'Family Formation and the Frequency of Various Kinship Relations', *Theoretical Population Biology* 5 (1974), pp. 1–22

Goody, J. R., *Death, Property and the Ancestors* (London, 1962)
  The Development of the Family and Marriage in Europe (Cambridge, 1983)
  'The Evolution of the Family', in P. Laslett and R. Wall, editors, *Household and Family in Past Time*, pp. 103–24
  'Inheritance, Property and Women: Some Comparative Considerations', in J. R. Goody *et al.*, editors *Family and Inheritance*, pp. 10–36
  Production and Reproduction: A Comparative Study of the Domestic Domain (Cambridge, 1970)
  and G. A. Harrison, 'Strategies of Heirship', *Comparative Studies in Society and History* 15 (1973), pp. 3–21; reprinted as Chapter 7 in J. Goody, *Production and Reproduction* (Cambridge, 1976)
  J. Thirsk, and E. P. Thompson, editors, *Family and Inheritance: Rural Society in Western Europe, 1200–1800* (Cambridge, 1976)

Gough, J., *Manners and Customs of Westmorland* (Kendal, 1847)

Gough, J. W., *The Mines of Mendip* (Oxford, 1930)

Gough, R., *The History of Myddle* (Harmondsworth, 1979)

Gras, N. S. B., and E. C. Gras, *Economic and Social History of an English Village* (Cambridge, Mass., 1930)

Gray, H. L., *English Field Systems* (Cambridge, Mass., 1915)

Green, D., C. Haselgrove, and M. Spriggs, editors, *Social Organization and Settlement* (Oxford, 1978)

Greven, P. J., *Four Generations: Population, Land and Family in Colonial Andover, Massachusetts* (Ithaca, NY, 1970)

Grigg, D. B., 'The Land Tax Returns', *Agricultural History Review* II (1963), pp. 82–94

Hajnal, J., 'Two Kinds of Household Formation Systems', *Population and Development Review* 8 (1982), pp. 449–94

Hallam, H. E., 'The Postan Thesis', *Historical Studies* 15 (1972), pp. 203–22
  Rural England 1066–1384 (Glasgow, 1981)
  'Some Thirteenth Century Censuses', *Economic History Review* 2nd series 10 (1958), pp. 349–55

Hammel, E. A., 'Household Structure in Fourteenth Century Macedonia', *Journal of Family History* 5 (1980), pp. 242–73

Hampson, E. M., *The Treatment of Poverty in Cambridgeshire 1601–1834* (Cambridge, 1934)

Hanssen, B., 'Hushållens Sammansältning', *Rig* (1976), pp. 33–61

Harrison, B., *Drink and the Victorians: The Temperance Question in England, 1815–72* (London, 1971)

Harrison, M., 'Chayanov and the Economics of the Russian Peasantry', *Journal of Peasant Studies* 2 (1975), pp. 389–417
  'Resource Allocation and Agrarian Class Formation: The Problem of Social Mobility among Russian Peasant Households, 1880–1930', *Journal of Peasant Studies* 4 (1978), pp. 298–322

Harrison, W., *Description of England* (London, 1577)

Harvey, B., 'The Population Trend in England between 1300 and 1348', *Transactions of the Royal Historical Society* 5th series 16 (1966), pp. 23–42
Westminster Abbey and its Estates in the Middle Ages (Oxford, 1977)

Hatcher, J., 'English Serfdom and Villeinage: Towards a Reassessment', 2*Past and Present* 90 (1981), pp. 3–39
Plague, Population and the English Economy 1348–1530 (London, 1977)

Havinden, M. A., *Estate Villages* (London, 1966)
Household and Farm Inventories in Oxfordshire 1550–90, Oxford Record Society xliv (Oxford, 1965)

Helleiner, K., 'The Population of Europe from the Black Death to the Eve of the Vital Revolution', in E. E. Rich and C. H. Wilson, editors, *The Cambridge Economic History of Europe*, Vol. IV, pp. 1–95.

Hembry, P. M., *The Bishops of Bath and Wells 1540–1640: Social and Economic Problems*, University of London Historical Studies xx (London, 1967)

Herbst, S., editor, *Spoleczenstwo, gospordarke, kultura; studia ofiaowane M. Malowistowi u czterdzcestolencia pracy nankowej* (Warsaw, 1974)

Hey, D. G., *An English Rural Community: Myddle under the Tudors and Stuarts* (Leicester, 1974)

Heylin, P., *Historical and Miscellaneous Tracts* (London, 1681)

Hill, C., *Society and Puritanism in Pre-Revolutionary England* (London, 1964)

Hilton, R. H., *Bond Men Made Free: Medieval Peasant Movements and the English Rising of 1381* (London, 1973)
'A Crisis of Feudalism', *Past and Present* 80 (1978), pp. 3–19
The Economic Development of Some Leicestershire Estates in the Fourteenth and Fifteenth Centuries (Oxford, 1947)
The English Peasantry in the Later Middle Ages (Oxford, 1975)
'Freedom and Villeinage in England', in R. H. Hilton, editor, *Peasants, Knights and Heretics: Studies in Medieval English Social History*, pp. 174–91
'Individualism and the English Peasantry', *New Left Review* 120 (1980), pp. 109–11
'Lords, Burgesses and Hucksters', *Past and Present* 97 (1982), pp. 3–15
A Medieval Society, 2nd edition (Cambridge, 1983)
editor, *Peasants, Knights and Heretics: Studies in Medieval English Social History* (Cambridge, 1976)
'Reasons for Inequality among Medieval Peasants', *Journal of Peasant Studies* 5 (1978), pp. 271–84
'Some Social and Economic Evidence in the Late Medieval English Tax Returns', in S. Herbst, editor, *Spoleczenstwo, gospordarke, kultura; studia ofiaowane M. Malowistowi u czterdzcestolencia pracy nankowej*, pp. 111–28
editor, *The Stoneleigh Leger Book*, Dugdale Society xxiv (London, 1960)

Hollings, M., editor, *Red Book of Worcester*, Worcestershire Historical Society (Worcester, 1934–50)

Holderness, B. A., 'Elizabeth Parkin and her Investments 1733–66: Aspects of the Sheffield Money Market in the Eighteenth Century', *Transactions of the Hunter Archaeological Society* (1972), pp. 81–7

Homans, G. C., *English Villagers of the Thirteenth Century* (Cambridge, Mass., 1941; reprinted New York, 1960
'The Explanation of English Regional Differences', *Past and Present* 42 (1969), pp. 18–34

'The Rural Sociology of Medieval England', *Past and Present* 4 (1953), pp. 32–43

Horn, P., *Labouring Life in the Victorian Countryside* (Dublin, 1976)

Hoskins, W. G., *The Midland Peasant: The Economic and Social History of a Leicestershire Village* (London, 1957)

Houston, R., and R. M. Smith, 'A New Approach to Family History?', *History Workshop* 14 (1982), pp. 120–31

Howell, C., *Land, Family and Inheritance in Transition: Kibworth Harcourt* (Cambridge, 1983)
'Peasant Inheritance Customs in the Midlands, 1280–1700', in J. R. Goody et al., editors, *Family and Inheritance*, pp. 112–55
'Stability and Change 1300–1700: The Socio-Economic Context of the Self Perpetuating Family Farm in England', *Journal of Peasant Studies* 2 (1975), pp. 468–82

Howell, J., *Familiar Letters* (London, 1754)

Hudson, W., 'Manorial Life', *History Teachers Miscellany* 1 (1921)
'The Prior of Norwich's Manor of Hindolveston: Its Early Organisation and Rights of the Customary Tenants to Alienate their Strips of Land', *Norfolk Archaeology* 20 (1921), pp. 179–214
'Three Manorial Extents in the Thirteenth Century', *Norfolk Archaeology* 14 (1901), pp. 1–56

Hufton, O., *The Poor of Eighteenth Century France* (Oxford, 1974)

Hunter, J., *History and Topography of Ketteringham* (Norwich, 1851)

Hyams, P. R., *King, Lords and Peasants in Medieval England: The Common Law of Villeinage in the Twelfth and Thirteenth Centuries* (Oxford, 1980)
'The Origins of a Peasant Land Market in England', *Economic History Review* 2nd series 23 (1970), pp. 18–31

Imber, M., *Abstract of the Custom of the Manor of Mardon in Hursley (Hants.)* (London, 1707)

James, D. E. H., editor, *Norfolk Sessions Order Book 1650–1657*, Norfolk Record Society (Norwich, 1955)

James, M. E., *Family, Lineage and Civil Society: A Study of Society, Politics and Mentality in the Durham Region, 1500–1640* (Oxford, 1974)

Jenkins, D., *The Agricultural Community in South West Wales at the Turn of the Twentieth Century* (Cardiff, 1971)

Johnston, J. A., 'The Probate Inventories and Wills of a Worcestershire Parish, 1676–1775', *Midland History* 1 (1971), pp. 20–33

Jonas, S., 'On the Farming of Cambridgeshire', *Journal of the Royal Agricultural Society of England*, 7 (1974), pp. 35–71

Jones, A. C., 'The Customary Land Market in Fifteenth Century Bedfordshire', unpublished University of Southampton Ph.D. thesis, 1975
'Land and People at Leighton Buzzard in the Later Fifteenth Century', *Economic History Review* 2nd series 25 (1972), pp. 18–27

Jones, W. J., *The Elizabethan Court of Chancery* (Oxford, 1967)

Jordan, W. K., *The Charities of Rural England, 1480–1660: The Aspirations and the Achievements of the Rural Society* (London, 1961)
Philanthropy in England 1480–1660 (London, 1959)

Kemp, T., editor, *The Book of John Fisher, 1580–1588* (n.p., n.d.)

Kerridge, E., *Agrarian Problems in the Sixteenth Century and After* (London, 1969)

Kershaw, I., 'The Great Famine and Agrarian Crisis in England, 1315–1322', *Past and Present* 59 (1973), pp. 3–50

King, E., *Peterborough Abbey 1086–1310: A Study in the Land Market* (Cambridge, 1973)

Kosminsky, E. A., *Studies in the Agrarian History of England in the Thirteenth Century*, edited by R. H. Hilton (Oxford, 1956)

Krauss, R., 'Chaucerian Problems: Especially the Petherton Forestership and the Question of Thomas Chaucer', in *Three Chaucer Studies* (New York, 1932), pp. 60–9

Kussmaul, A. S., 'The Ambiguous Mobility of Farm Servants', *Economic History Review* 24 (1981), pp. 229–34

'Servants in Husbandry in Early Modern England', unpublished Toronto Ph.D. thesis, 1978

Servants in Husbandry in Early England (Cambridge, 1981)

'Time and Space, Hoofs and Grain: The Seasonality of Marriage in England', *Journal of Interdisciplinary History* (forthcoming)

Ladurie, E. le Roy, 'Family Structures and Inheritance Customs in Sixteenth Century France', in J. R. Goody *et al.*, editors, *Family and Inheritance*, pp. 37–70

Lambert, J. M., *et al.*, *The Making of the Broads: A Reconsideration of Their Origin in the Light of New Evidence*, Royal Geographical Society Research Series iii (London, 1960)

Larking, L. D. editor, *The Knights Hospitallers in England*, Camden Society (London, 1857)

Laslett, P., 'Family and Collectivity', *Sociology and Social Research* 63 (1979), pp. 432–42

Family Life and Illicit Love in Earlier Generations (Cambridge, 1977)

'Mean Household Size in England Since the Sixteenth Century', in P. Laslett and R. Wall, editors, *Household and Family in Past Time*, pp. 125–58

and R. Wall, editors, *Household and Family in Past Time* (Cambridge, 1972)

Laurence, E., *The Duty of a Steward to his Lord* (London, 1727)

Lavrovosky, V. M., 'Parliamentary Enclosures in Suffolk 1797–1814', *Economic History Review* 7 (1937), pp. 186–208

Leadam, I. S., editor, *The Domesday of Inclosures*, Royal Historical Society (London, 1897)

Le Bras, H., 'Evolution des liens de famille au cours de l'existence; une comparaison entre la France actuelle et la France du XVIIIᵉ siècle', in 2Les *Ages de la vie*, Actes du Colloque, VIIᵉ Colloque National de Demographie Strasbourg 5–7 mai 1982, pp. 27–45

Leconfield, Lord, *The Manor of Petworth in the Seventeenth Century* (Oxford, 1954)

Sutton and Dunston Manors (Oxford, 1956)

Lenin, V. I., *The Development of Capitalism in Russia*, in *Collected Works*, Vol. III (Moscow, 1964)

Leonard, E. M., *The Early History of English Poor Relief* (Cambridge, 1900)

Lesthaeghe, R., 'On the Social Control of Human Reproduction', *Population and Development Review* 6 (1980), pp. 527–48

Levine, D. C., *Family Formation in an Age of Nascent Capitalism* (London, 1977)

'"For Their Own Reasons": Individual Marriage Decisions and Family Life', *Journal of Family History* 7 (1982), pp. 255–64

Lloyd, T. H., *The Movement of Wool Prices in Medieval England*, Economic History Review Supplement vi (London, 1973)

Löfgren, O., 'Family and Household among Scandinavian Peasants: An Explanatory Essay', *Ethnologia Scandinavica* 74 (1974), pp. 17–52

Lomas, T., 'Land and People in South-East Durham in the Later Middle Ages', unpublished CNAA Ph.D. thesis, 1976

Lucas, H. S., 'The Great European Famine of 1315, 1316, and 1317', *Speculum* 5 (1930), pp. 343–77

Lysons, D., and S. Lysons, *Magna Britannia: Cambridgeshire, II, Part I* (London, 1808)

MacDermott, E. T., *History of the Forest of Exmoor* (Taunton, 1911)

Macfarlane, A., *The Family Life of Ralph Josselin, A Seventeenth Century Clergyman: An Essay in Historical Anthropology* (Cambridge, 1970)

The Origins of English Individualism: The Family, Property and Social Transition (Oxford, 1978)

'The Peasantry in England before the Industrial Revolution: A Mythical Model?', in D. Green *et al.*, editors, *Social Organization and Settlement*, pp. 323–41

Reconstructing Historical Communities (Cambridge, 1977)

Witchcraft in Tudor and Stuart England: A Regional and Comparative Study (London, 1970)

editor, *The Diary of Ralph Josselin 1616–1683*, British Academy Records of Social and Economic History, new series iii (London, 1976)

McIntosh, M. J., 'Land Tenure and Population in the Royal Manor of Havering, Essex, 1251–1352/3', *Economic History Review* 33 (1980), pp. 17–31

Maddicott, J. R., 'The English Peasantry and the Demands of the Crown, 1294–1341', *Past and Present* supplement i (1975), pp. 45–67

Maitland, F. W., editor, *Bracton's Note Book* (London, 1887)

Malcolmson, R. W., *Life and Labour in England, 1700–1780* (London, 1981)

Malthus, T. R., *An Essay on the Principle of Population* (London, 1798); reprinted for the Royal Economic Society (London, 1926)

Principles of Political Economy, 2nd edition (London, 1836)

Mate, M., 'High Prices in Early Fourteenth Century England', *Economic History Review* 2nd series 28 (1975), pp. 1–16

May, A. N., 'An Index of Thirteenth-Century Peasant Impoverishment? Manor Court Fines', *Economic History Review* 2nd series 26 (1973), pp. 389–402

Medick, H., 'The Proto-Industrial Family Economy: The Structural Function of the Household During the Transition from Peasant Society to Industrial Capitalism', *Social History* 3 (1976)

and D. Sabean, editors, *Interest and Emotion: Essays in the Study of Family and Kinship* (Cambridge, 1984)

Mendels, F., 'La composition du ménage paysan en France au XIXe siècle: une analyse économique du mode production domestique', *Annales Économies Sociétés Civilisations* (1978), pp. 780–802

Miller, E., and M. J. Hatcher, *Medieval England: Rural Society and Economic Change 1086–1348* (London, 1978)

Mills, D. R., 'Landownership and Rural Population with Special Reference to Leicestershire in the Mid-Nineteenth Century', unpublished University of Leicester Ph.D. thesis, 1963

'The Peasant Tradition', *Local Historian* II (1974), pp. 200–6

Moore, J., *The Goods and Chattels of our Forefathers* (Chichester, 1976)

Moorehouse, H. J., editor, 'The Diurnall of Adam Eyre', in *Three Yorkshire Diaries*, Surtees Society lxv (1875), pp. 1–118

Mueller, E., 'The Economic Value of Children in Peasant Agriculture', in R. G. Ridker, editor, *Population and Development* (Baltimore, Md, 1976), pp. 98–153

Munby, L. M., editor, *Life and Death in King's Langley: Wills and Inventories 1498–1659* (King's Langley, 1981)

Nakajuma, C., 'Subsistence and Commercial Family Farms: Some Theoretical Models of Subjective Equilibrium', in W. R. Charton, Jr, editor, *Subsistence Agriculture and Economic Development* (Chicago, Ill. 1969), pp. 165–84

Netting, R. M., *Balancing on an Alp: Ecological Change and Continuity in a Swiss Mountain Community* (Cambridge, 1981)

Nicholson, J., and R. Burn, *The History and Antiquities of the Counties of Westmorland and Cumberland*, Vol. II (London, 1777)

Ohlin, G., 'Mortality, Marriage and Growth in Pre-Industrial Populations', *Population Studies* 14 (1961), pp. 190–7

Oman, C. W. C., *The Great Revolt of 1381* (Oxford, 1906)

Page, F. M., *The Estates of Crowland Abbey: A Study in Manorial Organisation* (Cambridge, 1934)

Palliser, D. M., 'Tawney's Century: Brave New World or Malthusian Trap?', *Economic History Review* 2nd series 35 (1982), pp. 339–53

Palmer, W. M., 'Argentine's Manor, Melbourn, 1317-8', *Cambridgeshire Antiquarian Society* 28 (1927), pp. 16–79

The Puritan in Melbourn, Cambs. – Gleanings from History Concerning a Country Parish 1640–88 (Royston, Herts., 1895)

'The Reformation of the Cambridge Corporation, July 1662', *Proceedings of the Cambridge Antiquarian Society* new series 11 (1913), pp. 75–136

and H. H. McNeill, *Melbourn, Cambridgeshire: Notes on Cambridgeshire Villages, No. 1* (Cambridge, 1925)

and H. W. Saunders, *Documents Relating to Cambridgeshire Villages, No. 1* (Cambridge, 1926–7)

Parkinson, R., editor, *The Life of Adam Martindale, Written by Himself*, Chetham Society, old series iv (Manchester, 1845)

Patten, J., *English Towns (1500–1700)* (Folkestone, 1978)

Pennington, D., and K. Thomas, editors, *Puritans and Revolutionaries: Essays in Seventeenth Century History Presented to Christopher Hill* (Oxford, 1978)

Penny, N., editor, *The Household Account Books of Sarah Fell* (Cambridge, 1920)

Perkin, H., *The Origins of Modern English Society* (London, 1969)

Phelps Brown, E. H., and S. V. Hopkins, 'Seven Centuries of the Prices of Consumables Compared with Builders' Wage-Rates', in E. M. Carus Wilson, editor, *Essays in Economic History, II*, pp. 179–96

Phythian-Adams, C., and P. Slack, editors, *The Traditional Community under Stress* (Milton Keynes, 1977)

Pollock, Sir Fredrick, and F. W. Maitland, *The History of English Law Before the Time of Edward I*, Vol. II (Cambridge, 1968)

Poos, L. R., 'Population and Mortality in Two Fourteenth-Century Essex Communities', unpublished research fellowship dissertation, 1980

'The Social Context of Statute of Labourers Enforcement', *Law and History Review* 1 (1983), pp. 27–52

and R. M. Smith, 'Late Medieval English Tax Sources and English Nuptiality Patterns' (forthcoming)

Postan, M. M., 'The Charters of the Villeins', in C. N. L. Brooke and M. M. Postan editors, *Carte Navitorum: A Peterborough Abbey Cartulary of the Fourteenth Century*; reprinted in M. M. Postan, *Essays on Medieval Agriculture and General Problems of the Medieval Economy*, as Chapter 7

Essays on Medieval Agriculture and General Problems of the Medieval Economy (Cambridge, 1973)

The Medieval Economy and Society: An Economic History of Britain in the Middle Ages (London, 1972)

'Some Economic Evidence of Declining Population in the Later Middle Ages', *Economic History Review* 2nd series, 2 (1950), pp. 221–46

editor, *Cambridge Economic History of Europe, Vol. I: The Agrarian Life of the Middle Ages*, 2nd edition (Cambridge, 1966)

'Medieval Agrarian Society in its Prime: England', in *The Cambridge Economic History of Europe*, Vol. I, pp. 549–632

and J. Z. Titow, 'Heriots and Prices on Winchester Manors', *Economic History Review* 2nd series 11 (1959), pp. 392–411

and C. N. L. Brooke, editors, *Carte Nativorum: A Peterborough Abbey Cartulary of the Fourteenth Century*, Northamptonshire Record Society xx (Oxford, 1960)

Pound, J. F., editor, *The Norwich Census of the Poor 1570*, Norfolk Record Society (Norwich, 1971)

Prestwich, M., 'Edward I's Monetary Policies and their Consequences', *Economic History Review* 2nd series 22 (1969), pp. 406–16

Raftis, J. A., 'Changes in an English Village after the Black Death', *Mediaeval Studies* 29 (1967), pp. 158–77

'Social Structures in Five East Midland Villages', *Economic History Review* 2nd series 18 (1965), pp. 83–99

Raftis, J. A., *Tenure and Mobility: Studies in the Social History of the Mediaeval English Village* (Toronto, 1964)

Warboys: Two Hundred Years in the Life of an English Medieval Village (Toronto, 1974)

Rainbird Clarke, R. R., *East Anglia* (London, 1960)

Ravensdale, J. R., *Liable to Floods* (Cambridge, 1974)

Razi, Z., 'Family, Land and the Village Community in Later Medieval England', *Past and Present* 93 (1981), pp. 3–36

Life, Marriage and Death in a Medieval Parish: Economy, Society and Demography in Halesowen (1270–1400) (Cambridge, 1980)

'The Struggles between the Abbots of Halesowen and their Tenants in the Thirteenth and Fourteenth Centuries', in T. H. Aston, *et al.*, editors, *Social Relations and Ideas*, pp. 151–67

Razzell, P. E., and R. W. Wainwright, *The Victorian Working Class* (London, 1973)

Redfield, R., *Peasant Society and Culture* (Chicago, Ill., 1960)

Rich, E. E., and C. H. Wilson, editors, *The Cambridge Economic History of*

Europe, Vol. IV: The Economy of Expanding Europe in the Sixteenth and Seventeenth Centuries (Cambridge, 1967)

Ridker, R. G., editor, *Population and Development* (Baltimore, Md, 1976)

Ritchie, N., 'Labour Conditions in Essex in the Reign of Richard II', *Economic History Review* 4 (1934)

Rowley, T., editor, *The Origins of Open Field Agriculture* (London, 1981)

Russell, J. C., 'The Preplague Population of England', *Journal of British Studies* 5:2 (1966), pp. 1–21

Rye, W. B., *England as Seen by Foreigners* (London, 1865)

Sabean, D., 'Aspects of Kinship Behaviour and Property in Rural Western Europe before 1800', in J. R. Goody *et al.*, editor, *Family and Inheritance*, pp. 96–111

'Young Bees in an Empty Hive: Relations between Brothers-in-Law in a Swabian Village', in H. Medick and D. Sabian, editors, *Interest and Emotion: Essays in the Study of Family and Kinship* (Cambridge, 1984), pp. 171–86

Saito, O., 'Labour Supply Behaviour of the Poor in the English Industrial Revolution', *The Journal of European Economic History* 10 (1981), pp. 633–51

Saltmarsh, J., 'Plague and Economic Decline in England in the Later Middle Ages', *Cambridge Historical Journal* 7 (1941–3), pp. 23–41

Salzman, L. F., editor, *Victoria County History of Cambridgeshire*, Vol. II (London, 1948)

Samuel, R., editor, *People's History and Socialist Theory* (London, 1981)

Saul, A., 'Great Yarmouth in the Fourteenth Century: A Study in Trade, Politics and Society', unpublished University of Oxford D.Phil. thesis, 1975

Saunders, H. W., *Documents Relating to Cambridgeshire Villages, No. 1*, Part III (Cambridge, 1926–7)

An Introduction to the Obedientiary and Manor Rolls of Norwich Cathedral Priory (Norwich, 1930)

Schofield, R. S., 'Age Specific Mobility in an Eighteenth Century Rural English Parish', *Annales de Démographie Historique* (1970), pp. 261–74

'The Relationship between Demographic Structure and Environment in Pre-Industrial Western Europe', in W. Conze, *Sozialgeschichte du Families in der Neuzeit Europas* (Stuttgart, 1976), pp. 147–60

and E. A. Wrigley, 'Remarriage Intervals and the Effects of Marriage Order on Fertility', in J. Dupâquier, *et al.*, editors, *Marriage and Remarriage in Populations of the Past* (London, 1981), pp. 211–28

Scott, S. H., *A Westmorland Village* (London, 1904)

Searle, E., 'Seigneurial Control of Women's Marriage: The Antecedents and Function of Merchet in England', *Past and Present* 82 (1979), pp. 3–43

Shaffer, J. W., *Family and Farm: Agrarian Change and Household Organisation in the Loire Valley, 1500–1900* (Albany, NY, 1982)

Shanas, E., and M. Sussman, editors, *Family, Bureaucracy and the Elderly* (Durham, NC, 1977)

Shanin, T., *The Awkward Class: Political Sociology of Peasantry in a Developing Society, Russia 1910–1925* (Oxford, 1972)

editor, *Peasants and Peasant Societies* (Harmondsworth, 1971)

Shrewsbury, J. F. D., *A History of Bubonic Plague in the British Isles* (Cambridge, 1970)

Slack, P. A., 'Poverty and Politics in Salisbury, 1598–1666', in P. A. Slack and
    P. Clark, editors, *Crisis and Order in English Towns 1500–1700*, pp. 164–203
    'Social Policies and Social Problems', in C. Phythian-Adams and P. Slack,
    editors, *The Traditional Community under Stress* (Milton Keynes, 1977)
    'Vagrants and Vagrancy in England, 1598–1664', *Economic History Review*
    2nd series 27 (1974), pp. 360–79
    editor, *Poverty in Early Stuart Salisbury*, Wiltshire Record Society xxxi
    (Devizes, 1975)
    and P. Clark, editors, *Crisis and Order in English Towns 1500–1700* (London,
    1972)
Smith, R. M., 'Brewing, the Family Economy and Life-Cycle Stage' (forth-
    coming)
    *English Peasant Life-Cycles and Socio-Economic Networks – A Quantitative
    Geographical Case Study*, unpublished University of Cambridge Ph.D.
    thesis, 1974
    'The Family or the State? Some Figures on Kinship Support through the
    Ages', *Cambridge Medicine* (Autumn 1982), pp. 10–11
    'Fertility, Economy and Household Formation in England over Three
    Centuries', *Population and Development Review* 7 (1981), pp. 595–622
    'Hypothèses sur la nuptialité en Angleterre aux XIIIᵉ–XIVᵉ siècles', *Annales
    Économies, Sociétés, Civilisations* (1983), pp. 107–36
    'Kin and Neighbours in a Thirteenth Century Suffolk Community', *Journal
    of Family History* 4 (1979), pp. 219–56
    'On Some Problems of Putting the Child before the Marriage: A Response
    to Nancy Birdsall', *Population and Development Review* 9 (1983), pp. 34–52
    [Review of] Z. Razi, *Life, Marriage and Death in a Medieval Parish*, in *Journal of
    Historical Geography* 8 (1982), pp. 305–6
    'Some Thoughts on "Hereditary" and "Proprietary" Rights in Land under
    Customary Law in Thirteenth and Early Fourteenth Century England',
    Law and History Review 1 (1983), pp. 95–128
    'The Structured Dependency of the Elderly in the Middle Ages and
    Thereafter', *Ageing and Society* (forthcoming)
Snell, K. D., 'Agricultural Seasonal Unemployment, the Standard of Living
    and Women's Work in the South and East: 1690–1860', *Economic History
    Review* 2nd series 34 (1981), pp. 407–37
    Essays on Social Change in Agrarian England 1660–1900 (Cambridge, forth-
    coming)
    'The Standard of Living, Social Relations, the Family and Labour Mobility
    in South-Eastern and Western Counties 1700–1860', unpublished Uni-
    versity of Cambridge Ph.D. thesis, 1980
Sogner, S., 'Aspects of the Demographic Situation in Seventeen Parishes in
    Shropshire, 1711–60', *Population Studies* 17 (1963)
Souden, D. C., 'Pre-Industrial English Local Migration Fields', unpublished
    University of Cambridge Ph.D. thesis, 1981
Spufford, M., *Contrasting Communities: English Villagers in the Sixteenth and
    Seventeenth Centuries* (Cambridge, 1974)
    'Peasant Inheritance Customs and Land Distribution in Cambridgeshire
    from the Sixteenth to the Eighteenth Centuries' in J. R. Goody, *et al.*,
    editors, *Family and Inheritance*, pp. 156–76
Statutes of the Realm (London, 1810)

Steer, F., *Farm and Cottage Inventories of Mid-Essex 1635–1747* (Chelmsford, 1950)

Stephens, W. B., *Sources for English Local History* (Manchester, 1973)

Stone, L., *The Crisis of the Aristocracy, 1558–1641*, abridged edition (Oxford, 1965)

The Family, Sex and Marriage in England, 1500–1800 (London, 1977)

'The Rise of the Nuclear Family in Early Modern England', in C. Rosenberg, editor, *The Family in History* (Philadelphia, Pa, 1975), pp. 13–57

Swinburne, H., *A Treatise of Testaments and Last Wills* (London, 1728)

Tate, W. E., *The Parish Chest* (Cambridge, 1960)

Tawney, R. H., *The Agrarian Problem in the Sixteenth Century* (London, 1912)

Thirsk, J., 'The Common Fields', *Past and Present* 29 (1964), pp. 3–25

English Peasant Farming (London, 1957)

'The Family', *Past and Present*, 27 (1964), pp. 116–122

editor, *The Agrarian History of England and Wales*, Vol. IV (Cambridge, 1967)

and J. P. Cooper, *Seventeenth Century Economic Documents* (Oxford, 1972)

Thomas, K. V., *Religion and the Decline of Magic* (Harmondsworth, 1973)

'Women and the Civil War Sects', *Past and Present* 13 (1958), pp. 42–62

Thompson, E. P., 'The Grid of Inheritance: A Comment', in J. R. Goody *et al.*, editors, *Family and Inheritance*, pp. 328–60

Thompson, F. M. L., *English Landed Society in the Nineteenth Century* (London, 1963)

Thomson, D., 'Historians and the Welfare State' (forthcoming)

'Provision for the Elderly in England, 1830–1908', unpublished University of Cambridge Ph.D. thesis, 1980

Thomson, R. M., editor, *The Archives of Bury St Edmunds Abbey*, Suffolk Record Society xx (Woodbridge, 1980)

Thorner, D., B. Kerblay, and R. E. F. Smith, editors, *A. V. Chayanov on the Theory of Peasant Economy* (Homewood, Ill., 1966)

Thrupp, S. L., 'The Problem of Replacement Rates in Late Medieval English Population', *Economic History Review* 2nd series 18 (1965), pp. 101–19

Tierney, B., 'The Decretists and the "Deserving Poor"', *Comparative Studies in Society and History* 1 (1959), pp. 360–76

Tilly, C., editor, *Historical Studies of Changing Fertility* (Princeton, NJ, 1978)

Titow, J. Z., *English Rural Society 1200–1350* (London, 1969)

'Some Differences between Manors and their Effects on the Conditions of the Peasantry in the Thirteenth Century', *Agricultural History Review* 10 (1962), pp. 1–13

'Some Evidence of the Thirteenth-Century Population Increase', *Economic History Review* 2nd series 14 (1961), pp. 218–53

Todd, E., 'Seven Peasant Communities in Pre-Industrial Europe: A Comparative Study of French, Italian and Swedish Rural Parishes in the Eighteenth and Early Nineteenth Centuries', unpublished University of Cambridge Ph.D. thesis, 1976

Toms, E., editor, *Chertsey Abbey Court Roll Abstracts*, Surrey Record Society xxxviii (Guildford, 1937) and xlviii (Guildford, 1954)

Torr, C., *Wreyland Documents* (London, 1910)

Townsend, P., 'The Structured Dependency of the Elderly: A Creation of Social Policy in the Twentieth Century', *Ageing and Society* 1 (1981), pp. 5–28

Vaisey, D. C., *Probate Inventories of Lichfield and District 1568–1680*, Staffordshire Record Society iv: 5 (Stafford, 1969)

Vann, R., 'Wills and the Family in an English Town: Banbury, 1550–1800', *Journal of Family History* 4 (1979), pp. 346–67

Vincent, J. R., *Pollbooks: How Victorians Voted* (London, 1967)

Vinogradoff, P., *Villeinage in England* (Oxford, 1892)

Wachter, K. W., and P. Laslett, 'Measuring Patriline Extinction for Modelling Social Mobility in the Past', in K. W. Wachter, with E. A. Hammel and P. Laslett, editors, *Statistical Studies of Historical Social Structure*, pp. 113–36

Wachter, K. W., with E. A. Hammel and P. Laslett, *Statistical Studies of Historical Social Structure* (London, 1979)

Wales, T. C., 'The Parish and the Poor: Poverty and Administration in Seventeenth Century Norfolk', University of Cambridge Ph.D. thesis, forthcoming

Wall, R., 'Age at Leaving Home', *Journal of Family History* 3 (1978), pp. 181–202

'The Household: Demographic and Economic Change in England, 1650–1970', in R. Wall, editor, *Family Forms in Historic Europe* (Cambridge, 1983), pp. 493–512

'Mean Household Size in England from Printed Sources', in R. Laslett and R. Wall, editors, *Household and Family in Past Time*, pp. 159–204

'Regional and Temporal Variations in English Household Structure from 1650', in J. Hobcraft and P. Rees, editors, *Regional Demographic Development* (London, 1979), pp. 89–113

J. Robin, and P. Laslett (eds), *Family Forms in Historic Europe* (Cambridge, 1983)

Ward, J. F., *West Cambridgeshire Fruit Growing Areas: A Survey of Soils and Fruit 1925–7*, Ministry of Agriculture and Fisheries Bulletin lxi (London, 1933)

Watford, C., *Gilds: Their Origin, Constitution, Objects and Later History* (London, 1879)

Watkins, C., *A Treatise on Copyholds* (London, 1851)

Watson, J., editor, *The Annals of a Quiet Valley by a Country Parson* (London, 1894)

Watts, D. G., 'A Model for the Early Fourteenth Century', *Economic History Review* 2nd series 20 (1967), pp. 543–7

Webb, J., editor, *Poor Relief in Elizabethan Ipswich*, Suffolk Record Society (Ipswich, 1966)

Welford, R., *A History of Newcastle and Gateshead*, Vol. III (London, 1885)

West, J., 'The Administration and Economy of the Forest of Feckenham during the Early Middle Ages', unpublished University of Birmingham M.A. thesis, 1964

Westlake, H. F., *The Parish Gilds of Medieval England* (London, 1919)

Wharton, W. R., Jr, editor, *Subsistence Agriculture and Economic Development* (Chicago, Ill., 1969)

Whatley, W., *A Bride-Bush: or, A Direction for Married Persons* (London, 1916)

Williams, K., *From Pauperism to Poverty* (London, 1981)

Williams, N. J., *Tradesmen in Early-Stuart Wiltshire*, Wiltshire Archaeological Society xv (Devizes, 1960)

Williams, W. M., *The Sociology of an English Village: Gosforth* (London, 1956)

A West Country Village: Ashworthy. Family, Kinship and Land (London, 1963)

Williamson, J., 'Peasant Holdings in Medieval Norfolk: A Detailed Investigation of the Holdings of the Peasantry in Three Norfolk Villages in the Thirteenth Century', unpublished University of Reading Ph.D. thesis, 1976

Wilson, T., *A Discourse upon Usury by Way of a Dialogue,* with an historical introduction by R. H. Tawney, Classics of Social and Political Science (London, 1925)

Wolf, E. R., *Peasants* (Englewood Cliffs, NJ, 1966)

Worsley, P., 'Village Economies', in R. Samuel, editor, *People's History and Socialist Theory* (London, 1981), pp. 80–5

Wrightson, K., 'Ale-Houses, Order and Reformation in Rural England, 1590–1660', in E. Yeo and S. Yeo, editors, *Popular Culture and Class Conflict 1590–1914,* pp. 1–27

English Society 1580–1680 (London, 1982)

'Household and Kinship in Sixteenth Century England', *History Workshop Journal* 12 (1982), pp. 1–33

'The Puritan Reformation of Manners', unpublished University of Cambridge Ph.D. thesis, 1974

and D. C. Levine, *Poverty and Piety in an English Village – Terling 1525–1700* (London, 1979)

Wrigley, E. A., 'Age at Marriage in Early Modern England', paper presented to XIIIth International Congress of Genealogical and Heraldic Science, 1976

'The Changing Occupational Structure of Colyton over Two Centuries', *Local Population Studies* 18 (1977), pp. 9–21

'Family Limitation in Pre-Industrial England', *Economic History Review* 2nd series, 19 (1966), pp. 82–109

'Fertility Strategy for the Individual and the Group', in C. Tilly, editor, *Historical Studies in Changing Fertility,* pp. 135–54

'Mortality in Pre-Industrial England: The Example of Colyton, Devon, over Three Centuries', *Daedalus* 97 (1968), pp. 546–80

Population and History (London, 1969)

and R. S. Schofield, *The Population History of England, 1541–1871: A Reconstruction* (London, 1981)

Wycherley, W., 'The Gentleman Dancing Master', in *Plays* (London, 1735)

Index